THE HISTORY OF GREENLAND
III

THE HISTORY OF GREENLAND

III

1782 - 1808

by

FINN GAD

McGILL-QUEEN'S UNIVERSITY PRESS
KINGSTON AND MONTREAL

This is a translation from the Danish edition
Grønlands Historie III, 1782-1808, 1975,
published by Nyt Nordisk Forlag Arnold Busck, Copenhagen.
Translated by Charles Jones

ISBN 87-17-05005-7

Typesetting carvi-sats, Copenhagen
and printed by Villadsen og Christensen, Copenhagen
Printed in Denmark 1982

Contents

Preface

As the title shows, this continuation of the History of Greenland covers a shorter period than the previous volumes, much shorter than originally planned. As it was being written it became clear that a detailed and documented account of the development according to the original plan would require more than one volume of normal size could contain. A limitation was necessary, and it seemed best to cut down the period covered. The discontinuance of the normal sailings between Denmark-Norway and West Greenland 1807-14/15, caused by the expansion of the European war, brought development in West Greenland to a standstill. In 1808 news of the war reached Greenland. Therefore that year became the terminus of this account.

Several reasons underlie the fact that the account of the period 1782-1808 takes up so many pages. Two are paramount. First, this period has never been subjected to scholarly investigation, neither in its context nor to the extent and depth that the sources permit. This has now been done.

Along with the systematic study of the sources, it secondly appeared that it was possible to compose a sort of "status-report" covering the state of Greenlandic affairs up to 1808. Simultaneously several aspects of development could be traced. The latter caused special studies of which several are printed, in Danish, in periodicals or (four) in a separate book. Moreover, some fundamental problems are discussed in this volume, and the development of certain situations related in detail. This has been done mostly because the subject is discussed or related for the first time, at least in such detail and seen as part of a greater whole.

It cannot be denied that a multitude of details characterizes this account, perhaps straining the general outlook. But one cannot eat one's cake and have it. It must be said that these volumes are not intended to provide a survey of the history of Greenland.

Nowadays, the idea of what history is or ought to be demands much of the historian. His sphere has widened. History is no more confined to the field of politics, or the description of the progress of events - more or less subjectively selected as the most important – and the elucidation of probable causal relations. Whether the historian wants to describe a special facet of a society, or the growth of the whole of it, he must go into details to illustrate what constitutes his interpretation of the progress in question. He must embrace as many as possible of the activities which are characteristic of his subject. This means a call for exemplification and thus details. The historiographer's object and the research-worker's studies become fused. The historiographer cannot form his narrative without simultaneous scholarly research. This will come to evidence in his narrative if he does not want to be superficial. The problem of subjectivity versus objectivity is quite another question which is not to be discussed now. It may be enough to say here that the documentation of every statement again is a call for details.

The multitude of these was characteristic of volume II, observed by several reviewers of it. They stressed that the information offered an important basis of comparison for ethnogeographers, ethnologists, ethnographers and historians, in short everyone who studies or is concerned with situations of culture contact. That was exactly my aim. In this volume as well it has been one of my points to offer the same diverse standards of comparison. That is another reason why this account involves as many *representative* details as possible, and representative only: I assure the reader that considerably more exist.

There is still more to be said about details. In the context of the history of Greenland what seems to be petty detail is not really so. Circumstances, events and actions which in description of a larger society would seem unimportant, assume quite different dimensions when one is describing a narrow society. What an individual or a small group intend to do or actually do, plays a much more important role in the drama as a whole, and likewise what they shrink from doing or do not do. The importance of the single details is in fact in inverse proportion to the number of individuals in the society in question. In the period 1782-1808 the West Greenlandic society numbered 5-6000 Greenlanders and some 200 Europeans. Furthermore the population was scattered along the coast in many smaller societies. The activity (in all aspects) of the individual in his own situation was predetermined to play an important role. In describing such a small society it is possible for the narrator to embrace the whole spectre of details handed down. In this our account comes as close as possible to "reliving the real life of the past". That is the second purpose of this history of Greenland.

Writing about the details I may furthermore point out, that I have tried to show the reactions of the Greenlanders as much as I could and the sources permitted. In most cases I have attempted to show the Greenlandic way of thinking (and feeling). Sometimes that is difficult to explain, and to a European to accept. But it is the only way to take a look beneath the surface. These attempts are of course based upon what I have learned from other people's published observations and my own studies or experience. But I am myself totally responsible for the different interpretations, and acknowledge them, strange as they may look.

One question, however, remains: does the reader have the chance to obtain a general view? I regret to write that this must be the reader's problem. I have done my best to help the reader as much as possible, especially by repeating or referring to what has been told previously, in this volume or in volume II. But I cannot promise easy reading. It must also be remembered – as I have stressed before – that this work is meant as a handbook on Greenlandic affairs.

The translator, Mr. *Charles Jones,* B.A., an ethnologist himself, has produced an excellent result in my view, for which I wish to express my gratitude. My Danish text is "transformed" rather than translated into English by an American with a deep and wide knowledge of the modern Scandinavian languages, and of the scholarly terms. After reviewing the "transforming" myself in collaboration with Mr. Jones I can say that he, for me to read, has been completely loyal to the Danish original. He has been able to transcribe Danish idioms and proverbial locutions into quite corresponding English. His translations of letters, quoted in the text, may be strange to the reader. Mr. Jones has kept his presentation very close to the Danish wording and syntax. He thought that it would cause a vague feeling af distance or remoteness to the reader, and preferred that to any form of linguistic pastiche of 18th century English. And I have agreed to that.

The translation manuscript has been slightly revised by Mrs. Bente Gammeltoft, who also read the proofs of this edition, and myself. The translation has been printed unabridged according to my obligations, mentioned below. I therefore feel bound to point out that the translation of volume II does not follow the same principle. One of the reviewers of vol. II has revealed one distorting cut, which alarmed me as responsible for the content of the account. The conclusive paragraph page 429 of the English edition goes: *The integration of Greenland with Denmark was about to take place.* No more, no less, but anyhow far from the Danish original. I never concipated such nonsense. Partly verbatim, partly interpreted (and as the reviewer fully understood) I wrote: *Thus the development in the first 60 years of colonization also meant that Danish society, in a modest scale to be sure, began to feel its obligation towards the society of Greenland, which so to speak had an increasing effect on Danish consciousness.* This may or may not be proper English, but it expresses my view. The distorted passage was not submitted to me before printing. There may be others for which I refuse to have any responsibility as well, but I do not have sufficient time to spare examing vol. II for eventual other severe mistakes.

Statens humanistiske Forskningsråd (Danish Research Council for the Humanities) has met the entire cost of the translation for which I render my deepest thanks. The grant has been given to cover the payment for the translation of the *unabridged and unchanged* Danish text, precisely to achieve the aim mentioned above: to offer material for comparison by international scholars studying situations of culture contact and their development. Responsibility for the contents of the detailed account remains entirely mine.

In this preface to the English edition of volume III I will also repeat my thanks to the said Council for its financial help to me up to the present time. This has carried me over the many extra expenses associated with my work. In addition to that the Council has recommended me to a yearly personal grant which has been offered me on the Danish State's budget, to secure my position as lektor in the career, and thus my personal living, with permanent leave for concentrating my capacity of work on these historical studies. This English edition has also benefited from it. At the same time I would like to repeat my thanks to the *University of Copenhagen* which for years has kept me under its protective wing, and to my colleagues at the same university's *Institute of Eskimology.* I also want to thank the publishers, *Nyt Nordisk Forlag Arnold Busck A/S* of Copenhagen, who has been the patient publisher of most of what I have got printed, and of this English edition of volume III. In this connection I want to make some remarks, to explain why it has taken so long before this English edition has been published. The Danish volume III appeared in 1976, and in September 1977 the English translation was ready for the publisher. During the following years of disastrous inflation it became obvious to the English publisher of volume I and II that he was unable to publish volume III. We had to face that in July 1979. Then it was up to me to secure financial help for the publishing, because the translator got his fee, when he delivered the manuscript of the translation. In the following years until March 1981 I had to pass round the hat to different funds, and this turned out well. Finally the publishing of the translated manuscript could have a start.

I therefore want to render my deepest thanks to the following funds: *H. M. Dronning Margrethes og H. K. H. Prins Henriks Fond, Augustinus Fonden, Sparekassen "Bikuben"s Jubilæums Fond, Velux-Fondet, Knud Højgaards Fond, Konsul Georg Jorck's og Hustru Emma Jorck's Fond,* and *Fondet til Fædrelandets Vel.* All of them Danish, and all of them have given their grants to the unabridged Danish text translated.

I may confess that I have one sore point in this volume: the illustrations. As with volume II it has been difficult to find suitable ones, either contemporary or reasonably informative, and simultaneously avoiding too many tiresome repetitions of what is already well known. The hunt for illustrations has been lengthy and not very fruitful; for example it appeared to be impossible to find a contemporary picture of a Greenlander. This period is a pictorial vacuum compared with those before and those still to come. I apologize for the meagre bag I have obtained from my hunting. All have appeared in the Danish edition. I therefore here repeat my thanks to *Carlsberg Bryggeriernes Fond til Minde om Brygger J. C. Jacobsen,* which gave me a grant to meet the cost of the colour plates. It has been impossible to provide this volume (both in the Danish and English editions) with sufficient maps. The Danish publishers, Nyt Nordisk Forlag Arnold Busck, have in 1978 published an Atlas of Greenland with about 4000 geographical names, including all those referred to in the three volumes so far of this History of Greenland. The reader is referred to this atlas.

Finally it remains to mention some practical items. The notes are made specially for the English edition, bringing some supplementary remarks, some references to literature in other languages than Danish, and some cross-references to volume II. As in volume II there is an appendix on the source material with a very short list of literature, except that in Danish. Here, too, a glossary follows as an appendix. Special names, titles and terms are explained in this glossary, some are explained in the notes and some (e.g. equivalents of measures) in brackets in the text.

As a conclusion of this rather protracted preface, I feel obliged to state that further studies have been progressing since 1976, often restrained by other business. The exact publication date for the next volume in Danish cannot yet be predicted. As far as English translations of the volumes to come are concerned I want to be reticent, considering what trouble and delay the former have caused.

Gentofte in April 1981,

FINN GAD

I. 1782

A New Era

It has become a tradition to set 1782 as the beginning of a new era in the history of Greenland. This tradition has developed for practical reasons and in order to facilitate a general survey, and it can only be maintained for the same reasons. The new era applies, however, only to the development of the West Greenlandic society, and even here is limited to that part of the West Coast where the population has come into permanent contact with Europeans, mainly Danes and Norwegians. In geographic terms, this means the coastal rim from the southern tip of the great island up to and including Upernavik and the regions immediately north of it; at its northernmost, the area around Tasiussaq.

The remaining inhabited areas: Cape York with its Polar Eskimos and the populations of East Greenland, were still isolated from contact with Europeans; essentially because on the East Coast it was almost insurmountably difficult to traverse the Storis, and on the Northwest Coast to reach Cape York, while it was possible for the sailing ships of the time to navigate in these waters. Even somewhat into the nineteenth century, the stretches of coast north of Kaiser Franz Joseph Fjord in East Greenland were still inhabited, although probably quite sparsely and certainly only sporadically. Everywhere here, populations developed and maintained their special characteristics on the basis of the conditions for human existence afforded at each place. Of the life of these people throughout the nineteenth century, we have only whatever knowledge is given by archaeology, as well as the glimpses afforded by traditions, sagas, and the reports of expeditions. The history of these outlying areas can not be told in detail; it fades into impervious obscurity, in which even the memory of the people themselves fades.

With the watershed of development thus limited to West Greenland to the extent detailed above, we must at the same time realize that the West Greenlander himself did not perceive 1782 as an epoch-making year, if he at all thought in terms of years or calculated much with them. Not until much later, through historical perception, did a minority recognize this watershed, and by then it had long since lost any direct significance for the great majority.

We must limit the importance of our watershed even further: it applied in reality, and most perceptibly, only to be development of trade, and only indirectly to that of the mission. Its most conspicuous indication was thus, that the two inspectors royally appointed the previous year, assumed their functions in 1782. Most likely a Greenlander of the time only noticed the arrival of a new nâlagaq at Godthåb and Godhavn, different from the missionary, more like a kind of trader or trading chief, but still in a special position over all traders, assistants and the colony crew. He was apparently to be obeyed by all of these: a new nâlagaq: "one to be obeyed". West Greenland got a demonstration of the autocratic hierarchy of offices, and the West Greenlanders thus received a supplement to their vague notions of this system; but as remarked previously, they probably only noticed it. Their experiences with the new nâlagaq belonged to the future. Their approval of him would depend on how each one functioned in society. They had gradually become accustomed to civil servants coming, staying for six to eight years and then drifting out of the horizon, leaving larger, or - as was usually the case - smaller, traces in the memory of the people. Relatively few spent the rest of their lives in Greenland. Only few of those who returned home continued to influence Greenland.

Very remarkable traces in the memory of West Greenlanders were left, and the most lasting influence on conditions in West Greenland was exercised by the Egedes. Thus perhaps the only real watershed in 1782 for Greenlanders was the fact that this year more or less concluded what one might call "the period of the Egedes". For in just that year Niels Egede concluded his long period of work in Greenland and returned home, to die shortly after his arrival in Denmark. Subsequently, of the direct descendants of Hans Egede and Giertrud Rasch, there remained in Greenland only Niels Egede's son Jørgen, who continued as a trader at Holsteinsborg, but was discharged in 1786 due to certain disagreements with the board of directors of the Royal Greenland Trade. He had been systematically persecuted by an inspector of little esteem, Bendt Olrik, who encompassed in his curious hate anyone who in any way was connected with the Egedes. Poul Egede passed the watershed in Copenhagen as a member of the Missionskollegium and advisor in Greenlandic affairs, as he had been since 1741. He died in 1788. More distant relatives of the Egedes had left Greenland previous to 1782; none of them seems to have participated actively in further developments in Greenland.

The third epoch-making aspect of the year 1782 was something which

Greenlanders could form no immediate idea of, with good reason, since none of them had the slightest inkling of what it was all about. Only with the passage of time did it acquire importance for them, and then only indirectly. On 19 April 1782 the so-called Trade and Whaling Order was issued: an attempt by the secular administration to create the basis of order and uniformity in the Trade and in its relations with Greenlanders.

In the fourth place, the establishment of the offices of inspector made the division between North and South Greenland effective; this division lasted for the next 168 years.

In addition to these factors there were others, which partially arose from previous conditions, gradually beginning in the period of the Royal Chartered General Trading Company, which lasted until 1774, or after the establishment of the Royal Greenland Trade in 1774–76. For example, the activity of the Trade as a producer in Greenland itself, alongside Greenlandic fangers. This entailed a growing infiltration of the Royal Greenland Trade into the Greenlandic economic pattern, born of whaling and the semi-individual fanger activity of the colony crew, which extended to other prey in addition to whales.

The Division of West Greenland

Whaling remained, however, the main interest of the Royal Greenland Trade as a producer. It took place mainly in the Northern Inspectorate, while in the Southern Inspectorate it was conducted efficiently only at Holsteinsborg, and elsewhere in the south only sporadically. As a consequence, most importance was attached to the Northern Inspectorate, as sealing, a secondary pursuit, was conducted with more or less equal intensity along the entire coast. Gradually the purchasing posts in the Northern Inspectorate came to provide the most blubber. The center of gravity of West Greenland moved from the south up to Disko Bay. From 1782, and for decades thereafter, Godhavn was more important than Godthåb.

This appears likewise in the stationing of the two inspectors appointed on 5 September 1781 by royal decree. Johan Fr. Schwabe, who had proved to be the most efficient of the two supervisors stationed in 1780, was put over the Northern Inspectorate; Bendt Olrik was assigned to the south, and probably felt it as a personal defeat.

When West Greenland was divided into the two inspectorates, Holsteinsborg was peculiarly assigned to the Southern Inspectorate. Perhaps it would have been more reasonable if this place, where whaling from land actually began, had been connected with the growing whaling centre, Disko Bay. That this would have been natural appears also from the lively correspondence which was carried on between Godhavn and Holsteinsborg during the following years. Holsteinsborg shared more problems in common with the administration of Disko Bay than with the Southern Inspectorate. Sometimes the Southern Inspector at Godthåb must have felt slighted, when the above-mentioned correspondence did not pass through him. Perhaps Holsteinsborg was assigned to the Southern Inspectorate in order to give the south at least a semblance of organized whaling.

At the same time, one gets the impression that the division was made on the basis of purely quantitative criteria. Each inspectorate was assigned more or less the same number of districts. The Northern Inspectorate included Upernavik, Umánaq, Ritenbenk, Jakobshavn, Christianshåb, Godhavn and Egedesminde, totalling seven districts. The Southern Inspectorate was assigned Holsteinsborg, Sukkertoppen, Godthåb, Fiskenæsset, Frederikshåb and Julianehåb: six districts, of which Godthåb was the smallest but exercised a kind of management of Fiskenæsset.

Characteristic of the Southern Inspectorate was that at most places the sea did not freeze up, or rather did so only for short periods, and that the colonies were situated at great distances apart over more than 1000 kilometres of coastal rim. Frederikshåb and Julianehåb were during part of the spring and summer blocked by the storis, which to a great extent restricted navigation, but on the other hand provided a wealth of game animals. The settlement of the Northern Inspectorate were more concentrated, on a stretch of coast measuring 700 kilometres as the crow flies.

The deliberations which must have taken place before the division have not been committed to writing, so there is a free field for speculation. It is, however, quite improbable that political motives were involved in this division into two provinces, as they were later called. On the other hand, economic and administrative considerations were obviously involved.

Administratively, this quantitative division resulted in more or less the same number of Trade employees under each inspector. It was easier for the inspector at Godthåb to travel most of the year. On the other hand, the inspector at Godhavn could get around in his inspectorate more quickly and more often, when Disko Bay was frozen up – except for Upernavik, which constantly suffered from being relatively far and difficult of navigation from Godhavn.

Communication between Holsteinsborg and Godhavn could only be established during the summer, and these conditions prevailed within the remainder of the Southern Inspectorate. This made it natural for the administration of Holsteinsborg to lie to the south, with which communications could be established earlier than with the north.

There was presumably an attempt to create a sort of economic balance between the two inspectorates. There could be no question of an equal distribution of the population as long as the exact size of the population was not even approximately known. The areas south of Lichtenau in Julianehåb District (founded in 1774), were not yet well known. The same was true of Upernavik District. But the population of the two inspectorates was probably estimated as being more or less equal, perhaps with a preponderance in the south.

Without knowing what the future might bring, the economic yield of the two areas was probably also estimated as more or less the same, quantitatively speaking. Here too there were no reliable figures to depend on. Whaling had not turned out to be the profitable adventure predicted before the great project of 1776. Sealing was at this time in general rather equally distributed along the coast. Individual districts in each inspectorate specialized in other game animals.

Although a balance thus seems to have been attempted in the division, the Northern Inspectorate came to be the more important. This was due to whaling, on which great hopes were still based, in spite of previous disappointments. Perhaps the government did not want the great project which it had initiated to fail completely. The situation gives one the impression that they tried to save what could be saved. Furthermore, the Order of 1782 is unmistakably based on conditions in Disko Bay, this being one of the criteria for its having been written by Johan Fr. Schwabe. Several of the conditions which it mentions and regulates, furthermore and reasonable enough, point to factors reported and criticized by Schwabe. Thus in the Order, priority was given in advance to conditions in Disko Bay, further emphasizing the preponderant importance ascribed to the Northern Inspectorate. This immediately caused difficulties for the Southern Inspectorate.

The Inspector's Authority Extended

Even before the inspectors had begun to function, their authority was extended by the Royal Ordinance of 17 April 1782, according to which they were empowered, "... each in the province assigned to him, sine exceptione fori, when required to call witnesses and receive their sworn statements in all cases in which they find it necessary, and these sworn examinations and proceedings thus conducted by them shall thereafter in all courts of law be presumed to have the same validity as other evidence." Thus the two inspectors were equipped, each in his inspectorate, with some, but far from all of the powers of a judge.

Here there was no question of setting up special courts of law in Greenland, or consequently, real judgeships. This would also have been inappropriate, partly because the administrative duties of the inspectors would thus have been coupled with a judicial authority, and partly because this would have constituted an encroachment on the rights of the Royal Greenland Trade. Schwabe himself later characterized the offices of inspector by saying that they encompassed "as well as the ordinary functions of a prefect, some of those of a judge, etc." Here he is referring to the authority granted by the Ordinance of 17 April 1782.

These late powers were embodied in the Order of 1782, specifically in the 12th Article, §5, which deals with the right of examination possessed by the inspector in criminal cases and cases of minor violations which because of their extent could not be decided then and there, as well as in cases demanding trial; and finally the right to dictate the fines and penalties connected with such examinations.

This paragraph gives the impression of having been strangely tacked on to the remaining text of the Order, of being an addition to a finished whole. It is conspicuous that it does not refer to the Ordinance of 17 April 1782. The text of the Ordinance is not used; the provisions of the paragraph are justified in indefinite terms: "... according to permission and command most graciously granted by His Majesty the King." This indicated that the paragraph was written before the Royal Ordinance; this entire formulation sounds more like the justifications in a representation to the king previous to a decree and the drawing up of an ordinance. This extra authority was probably known of previously and incorporated into the Order in its final version, before it was formally issued.

II. The Order of 1782

The Origin of the Order

This fundamental document has already been mentioned several times and characterized quite briefly. The main role of a 33-year-old lawyer, Johan Fr. Schwabe, in its formulation, has been hinted at, and it is probably not possible to expound more on this than in terms of probability. Its formulation was most likely not undertaken by him alone. A strange circumstance connected with the approval of the draft can perhaps shed some light on this aspect of the origin of the Order.

On 13 April, the executive manager of the Royal Greenland Trade, Hartvig Marcus Frisch, circulated the draft to members of the General Board of Directors. The Order was dated and signed on the 19th of the same month, less than a week after its circularization. Previous to the 19th, the draft must have been returned with few corrections and additions. These were incorporated into the text, which was then sent to the printers. This was reported at a meeting of the General Board of Directors on 20 April, on which date it was formally sanctioned - the day after it had been signed! The time for critical perusal of this comprehensive "draft" is thus further limited to but a few days.

The "draft" must have been more than just what the name indicates. It must have been fully drawn up, allowing for the rapid incorporation of more or less essential corrections and additions. The short time available for study of the "draft" indicates that the members of the General Board of Directors must have gotten acquainted with it before it was circulated to them, or at various times while it was being drawn up. In the minutes of the meeting of the General Board of Directors, nothing is said about work on the Order, either its beginning or its progress, and no sketches of the Order exist in the various archives.

The most prominent members of this General Board of Directors were the Secretary of the Royal Council, Ove Høegh-Guldberg, and the Minister of Finance, C.L. Stemann. Neither of these could be left out of consideration, so the only remaining possibility is that at least one of them had more to do with this matter than the source material reveals. Since it is known that Høegh-Guldberg especially around this time drew more and more matters under his jurisdiction and felt authorized to participate personally in big as well as small affairs, it might not be going too far to ascribe to him a more active participation in this matter concerning Greenland. In this case, the other members of the Board of Directors would have realized this and kept their fingers off a matter appropriated by the key figures in the government.

Considering the lively correspondence between Schwabe and Høegh-Guldberg, as well as the similarity between the content of these letters and the provisions of the Order, we might well imagine that work on the Order was undertaken upon request from Høegh-Guldberg to Schwabe, and with some collaboration between them, perhaps with C.L. Stemann as a third figure.[1] Then the two remaining members of the four-man General Board of Directors would only have been able to exercise a modest influence on its formulation. The same would probably also apply to the Board of Managers, Guldberg and Stemann would certainly be completely familiar with the "draft" so that the executive manager could act with a haste which at first glance seems inappropriate.

This would put the Ordinance of 17 April 1782 concerning the Inspector's right of examination in a somewhat different light. From the start, the authorities wanted to avoid setting up judgeships in Greenland and thus further involving the state in the affairs of the island; but while the draft order was being drawn up, the necessity was seen of creating some contact with the Danish judicial authorities, since Danish law applied and must apply to Europeans stationed in Greenland. Guldberg, therefore probably saw to the drawing up of the Royal Ordinance, actually a compromise between necessity and political principle.

As a further indication of Høegh-Guldberg's participation, it can be emphasized that the Order of 1782 differs essentially from other Orders from similar Companies by also including a political programme. This also justifies putting the Order on such a high level.

The Order of 1782

Although during the administration of Høegh-Guldberg much became law by Order in Council, drawn up at his request, without going through the central administration; and although the Order of 1782 apparently originated close to the highest level of government, there is still no reason for calling this Order, as it has been called, "the first law of Greenland". This is, and will continue to be, a fundamental misunderstanding. The

Order was – and at the time could only be – what its name clearly indicates.

The Order is totally without the signature of the King. Only the names of the members of the General Board of Directors and the Board of Managers are printed under the long text of the Order. To have issued this Order with royal confirmation would not have followed the Danish policy on Greenland which can be called almost traditional for that time: directly to involve the state as little as possible in these matters. That it became more and more difficult to enforce this traditional policy is another matter, which was not topical at that time.

There are other reasons why the title "the Law of Greenland" is out of place in connection with the Order of 1782. The most important of these is that it only applied to the personnel of the Royal Greenland Trade: a limited segment of the population of the island; indeed, an element many of which only stayed in Greenland for a relatively short time. The limited applicability of the Order appears in no uncertain terms in its full title.[2] As far as the actual Greenlandic population was concerned, the Order provided only rules for relations with them on the part of stationed employees of the Trade, not vice versa, except in cases in which Greenlanders themselves were employed by the Trade.

Nor was the Order directly applicable to those working in the missions, either the Royal Mission or that of the Moravian Brethren. Apparently the administration at first did not even give the latter a thought; the Brethren were not even sworn in. Shortly after the issuance of the Order and the Ordinance on the Inspector's right of examination, the Missionskollegium was informed of the Ordinance and, strange as it seems, of only an extract from the Order. The Missionskollegium was asked to see to it that the missionaries were told to observe the provisions of the Order. In return, the Missionskollegium asked the Board of Managers to instruct the Inspectors to "render assistance to the missionaries when they are required to appeal to them in distress." This the Trade agreed to, but only "in so far as it may appear to serve the best interests of the Trade, or to maintain order." This clause reveals something of the intentions of the Royal Greenland Trade with the Order, and what at that time it still considered its most important objective.

This correspondence, and the title of the Order itself, situate it in its proper place: A set of house rules and regulations, corresponding to those possessed by all the chartered trading companies of the time. Judicially, such regulations depended on the extensive autonomy with which such trading companies were equipped. Especially for overseas companies, communications with proper domestic courts were difficult.

As mentioned previously, it was almost certainly out of respect for such judicial autonomy that the inspectors in Greenland were not granted the authority of judges of the first instance. They were royal civil servants, later nominated for appointment by the Board of Managers of the Royal Greenland Trade, and their duties were to supervise the employees of the trade, in the future on the basis of the Order of 1782. In this way they were both independent of and dependent on the Trade. The office demanded a sense of balance, which was not possessed by all those who subsequently filled it.

The Order has a certain vagueness, in that the authority of the inspectors is only to a certain extent included in its provisions; their authority is, on the other hand, seemingly situated outside of or parallel to that of other officials in and outside Greenland. Here, consideration for the especially difficult state of communications in Greenland may also have asserted itself. Consideration of these conditions was taken extensively in all the provisions of the Order - as far as was possible. This is one of the peculiarities which characterize this Order, and to which it perhaps owed its long life.

Another peculiarity of the Order of 1782 is that, unlike other company regulations of the time, it not only regulates existing conditions, but also states a programme of action, and thus the lines of future development in almost all respects.

Principles of the Order of 1782

From beginning to end, the Order declares the main objective of all in the service of the Trade and whaling to be "to seek the best interest and advantage of the Royal Trade and Fishing with diligence and zeal - at all times and in all conditions.". It can hardly be stated more directly or more openly. This can be interpreted as a clear command to press trade and fishing to the utmost, and it is not impossible that certain persons took their duties in such a simple and uncomplicated way. On the other hand, one could hardly expect a trading company's regulations for its employees, in its preamble, to specify the very opposite. One must also remember that this declaration is immediately followed by the next general demand on the activities of traders and assistants.

The production of animal produce is to be encouraged and supported in all respects; this is also in the best interest of the Trade, but also a prerequesite for the following, which is quite versatile for an introduction:

"He should deal with Greenlanders in a reasonable and careful manner" in every way attempt to promote and support their economic activity, act didactically in private economic matters, develop cooperation between Trade and whaling employees and Greenlanders with the help of equitable contracts, and "take care of their interests when and where conditions demand. With untiring diligence and zeal, and without insulting the inhabitants or depriving them of necessities, he (the trader and his assistant) should seasonably purchase" their produce and send it back to Denmark.

Here economy and industry were laid down, coupled with didactics and the protection of the Greenlanders as the second main objective of the Trade. These lines, and the manner in which they permeate all the other provisions of the Order, have formed the basis of calling the Royal Greenland Trade monopoly a "tutelary" or protecting one. Humanitarianism is a conspicuous characteristic of rationalism, but utility should be the first consideration of reason. Of course, making the Greenlanders more productive was also to the advantage of the Trade, at the same time as the increased production was also for their own good. This furthermore emphasizes the common interest. In general this is a tune which could be heard from the Trade previously, but only faintly. It is undoubtedly due to Schwabe that it now sounds considerably louder and has become the leitmotif of the Order. Behind him, according to the above interpretation, was most certainly the hand of Høegh-Guldberg, who at least externally was quite influenced by the rationalistic concepts of morality, duty, thrift and diligence.

In this manner, the principles of the Order are a strange mixture of mercantilistic tradition and physiocratic innovation, perhaps quite characteristic for the age of rationalism. The physiocratic concept is discernible in its assertion of Greenland's natural economy and the exploitation of its natural production opportunities. The mercantilism is evident first and foremost in the fact that it is a monopoly applying these principles; then in the manner in which all enterprise, even including the life of the individual, is thus standardized and subordinated to the principles laid down. Just as in the old European society occupation of the individual could be said to have been determined, partly by a patriarchal organization; here the individual in Greenland was, as far as possible, to be directed to fangst and related occupations. The provisions of the Order relating to occupation and population policies are clearly characterized by such traditional mercantilism - incidentally quite in the spirit of Guldberg.

The moral concept of rationalism was rooted in religion, "a true and pure worship of God," as the Order expresses it: i.e., the organized faith of the Evangelical Lutheran state church. Morality was to be manifested in exterior actions. Therefore the Order turns quickly from general considerations to a number of detailed provisions which all emphasize the proper active morality. They can be condensed by saying that the Europeans stationed in Greenland was to act, behave and live as it behoved a Christian from an enlightened society, for the honour of God and the King, as a model for others, and in the best interests of his country - and the Trade.

One other principle forms the basis of the Order. It is never directly mentioned, but is implied throughout. This is the continually repeated principle of autocracy: uniformity. This demand was continuously maintained, to the relief of the central administration, and in order to obtain the greatest possible amount of justice in decision making. Now the picture of Greenland, if not kaleidoscopic, at least far too un-uniform, was to be changed for the Trade, just as it had been attempted to change it in the missions - in spite of the Moravian Brethren.

The Provisions of the Order

It was a duty to go to church and assist at the services, morning and evening worship which were to be conducted by the missionary, or, in the absence of a missionary, by the catechist or the trader or his assistant, in order to strengthen the morals of the individual so that "nothing at all should be done which can arouse the wrath of God or give offence to or outrage the Greenlanders." Even in the first provision of the Order, duty towards the local inhabitants made its appearance.

That outrageous and offensive conduct took place was a matter of experience. Therefore a number of prohibitions were issued, including one on free intercourse between Europeans and Greenlanders. This might look suspiciously like discrimination of the Greenlanders, but it must be strongly emphasized that these provisions were committed to the Order exclusively in order to protect them, as this "too great and free intercourse - has been the cause of laziness, neglect of the fangst, luxury, debauchery, and much disorder .... any suspicious intercourse with the female sex" was especially prohibited. Rigorous rules were issued regulating the age of Greenlandic women a European could employ as his housekeeper or as rowers in an umiak or take along on expeditions. It was not allowed to get Greenlanders drunk, even less to give them distilled spirits;

and they were not to be spoiled with coffee, tea and other European things "as such things only ruin their health, pervert their style of life and make them want to loiter in the houses of Europeans."

If, in spite of everything, improper intercourse with the Greenlandic female sex resulted in an illegitimate child, fixed rules were provided about support payments for the child. At the same time the raising of such children, especially boys, was regulated.

Individuals were only allowed to marry with permission. Here a sharp division was made between executives of the Trade on one hand, and artisans, labourers and whaling sailors on the other. Only the former were allowed to marry Europeans. Marriage to full-blooded Greenlandic women was totally forbidden to them, but they could be permitted to marry daughters of mixed descent. Their subordinates, if they wished to marry in Greenland or stay as married, were only allowed to marry Greenlandic women of mixed blood, naturally only with permission. In all cases contributions to the widows' fund were to be assured as soon as possible.

This clause reveals the real reason for such provisions. The Trade had first and foremost to think of its economy. Mortality was great at that time, and if marriages were not controlled, the Trade could for an incalculable period of time be responsible for an incalculable number of widows. A European father could also die leaving minor children; so that rules were drawn up regulating the raising of children of mixed marriages.

These rules were an element in the active population policy of the Trade, which reveals it as a child of the mercantilistic ideology of autocracy. "Mixtures" or "half-breeds", as the children of "mixed marriages" were called, were juridically still considered Greenlanders. They could marry freely, but if they married "real Greenlandic women", i.e., full-blooded Greenlanders, they were obliged to stay in Greenland. If they were employed by the Trade with a salary of 50 rigsdalers per year, they were to contribute to the widow's fund.

This was but one side of the duties of Europeans stationed in Greenland. Regulations were provided for the purchase of Greenlanders' produce as well as for production carried on by employees of the Trade; in the first place, for the supplying to each colony of necessities which could be acquired locally. Foxes were to be hunted and seals to be netted. All trade was to be carried on by the trader, including the purchase of necessary Greenlandic products, such as hides for trousers and kamik boots, blubber for lamps, etc. The goods over which a monopoly was exercised were listed; the list is not long, and except for one category of goods, it is carried over from the previous trading enterprises. It shows that the Trade had appropriated almost all production of value. The monopoly commodities were blubber; whale oil; baleen; bear, reindeer, seal and fox hides; narwhal and walrus tusks; and a relatively new item: eiderdown.

Here the protection of the Greenlandic population is again mentioned. No trapping, hunting or collection of down, eggs, etc., was to be carried on by hired Greenlandic labour, e.g., by giving a Greenlander a gun and ammunition, and then taking the profits of his fangst.

The only one of the chapters of the Order which according to its title deals with Greenlanders is Chapter Four. All its paragraphs deal with what the trader should do to promote production and to give Greenlanders the best opportunities for their occupation and its development. Only the first paragraph lays down, in very cautious and vague terms, what is to happen when Greenlanders commit offences. Only if the offence or crime is especially great should they be "punished for it according to the circumstances and the nature of the crime."

According to the wording of this paragraph and subsequent practice, it appears that it was only a question of offences and crimes against the Trade. It is not thus an ordinary penal code, and there can be no question of calling it the first penal code in Greenland. It was never applied to what one might call ordinary offences and crimes, and absolutely never to conflicts between Greenlanders. Where it was possible, such relationships with the Trade were concluded amicably - at least during the first decades after the issuance of the Order. Here the word "Greenlander" usually means "real Greenlander", i.e., full-blooded Greenlander; in some cases "mixtures", or half-breeds, are considered juridically as Greenlanders, in others the provisions of the Order, applicable to Europeans stationed in Greenland, are also applied to them.

Chapter Four continued with provisions for the promotion of various kinds of fangst, including the netting of seals and belugas, fox trapping and whaling, the latter in cooperation with European whalers stationed in Greenland. The trader is also to get the population to carry on usual fishing for cod, black halibut and halibut, and to teach the Greenlanders how to prepare and dry fish.

The trader is to deal with the demographic problem; i.e., see to it that the population does not concentrate in the settlements, but spreads out over the most favourable fangst sites. The implementation of this policy was one of the measures designed to promote productivity; it had been done for quite some time. It was a consequence of the attempt at all costs to keep the Greenlandic fangers in their occupation, on which not only the Trade, but also the Mission, and not least, the Greenlanders themselves, depended.

Therefore the Greenlanders must not be "spoiled", i.e., be lured away from the fundamental occupation by getting dependent on the colonies for their necessities. They were not to be allotted imported provisions except in bad game periods and famines, or when ill. The trader was to see to it that especially the boys were raised up as fangers. No competent fanger was to be employed by the Trade. Greenlanders who were bad providers were to set to work by the trader in production which they could manage, and which was useful in Greenland. Otherwise, the trader, with the permission of the Inspector, would be allowed to employ a bad kayak rower in the service of the Trade or at whaling. This was especially applied to the sons of mixed marriages.

Chapters Five to Eight of the Order deal with the economy and administration of the colonies, the purchase of Greenlandic produce, shipping, and finally with the undesirable illicit trading in monopoly commodities not conducted through the Royal Greenland Trade. Here there is no need to go into detail; it suffices to state that reading the provisions gives a quite good and nuanced picture of everyday life at a colony or whaling station. There was more than enough work for all. And the local crew had to be kept on their toes, also for reasons of health and morality.

In Chapter Six, dealing with the purchase of Greenlandic produce, consideration for the Greenlanders is predominant. Trade "should be conducted intelligently and cautiously;" the trader must not deprive the Greenlanders of what they needed for their upkeep and that of their occupation but "honestly barter for the surplus." Tubs of verified standards were to be used in purchasing, to compensate for shrinkage and leakage measuring one and a third barrel for a barrel. Thawed blubber was to be measured level, but frozen blubber heaping. "If anyone acts to the contrary or measures blubber with tubs which are either not verified or whose bottoms are missing, he shall be punished as a falsifier." This provision must be the result of Schwabe's experience. Such techniques must have been quite extensive, however, at least in Disko Bay, since others had observed them previous to 1782.

The watchdogs of morality were naturally to repudiate as violently as possible obviously dishonest trading methods; but one wonders whether the traders did not trade according to the customs of the time. In the past, trade often moved near the boundary of what was morally permissible; in addition the traders in Greenland had to protect themselves because of the extended credit they were in fact compelled by circumstances to grant the Greenlanders. They suffered severe losses, and knew from experience that trading in Greenland was no lucrative private business. They were responsible and accountable, in all their innocence of bookkeeping, for the finances of each colony. The Order attempted, therefore, to limit credit, and at the same time introduces, in Chapter Eleven, a more modern and efficient accounting procedure for control over each district.

This also served the cause of uniformity, which of course was to apply to purchase as well as selling prices. The Order established prices for the monopoly commodities, whereas sales prices were established by the annual general schedule, of which we shall hear more later on. Uniformity could also promote efficiency, and for this reason uniform rules for the handling of ships at the colonies were included in the Order.

All this was also to serve the implementation of control measures. All trading in monopoly commodities outside the Royal Greenland Trade was still prohibited, but it was realized that prohibitions could still be circumvented subsequent to the issuance of the Order, just as they had been previously. Rigorous provisions dealing with forbidden trade were laid down; foreign ships were especially focussed on.

With respect to visits by foreign whalers, especially in the districts of the Northern Inspectorate, the Order was dealing with a delicate subject. It is most likely for this reason that it has such vague provisions against forbidden trade by such foreigners that the inspector was actually powerless to stop it, as would later turn out to be the case.

Notable is Chapter Nine, which contains but two short paragraphs. Its title is "The Conservation of the Eider", and it is neither more nor less than the first preservation regulation ever issued for any animal in the world. Of course it is not made to the benefit of this animal itself, but to prevent this valuable bird from being extinct through the ruthless collection of down. It was forbidden to take its eggs with young birds in them or to kill the young birds in breeding time. It is also notable that the collection of eider down was reserved for the Greenlandic inhabitants. No European was allowed to collect down, "as it should be reserved for the Greenlanders, as a livelihood belonging to the country."

The semi-patriarchal nature of the entire Trade organisation was reflected in regulations concerning the estates of deceased persons and the auctions arranged in connection with them, especially inventories, when an accountable officer of the Trade died. It is not directly spelled out that the claims of the Trade have priority on such estates, but this is implied in the wording of the provisions.

All the provisions of the Order, or at least most of them, included rules for punishment in case of violation. Chapter Twelve contained more detailed regulations for the imposing of these penalties, and measures in connection with general disciplinary offences. The trader was given limited authority to impose disciplinary penalties on the basis of the Order. Interrogations were always to be conducted. Fines over ten rigsdalers or sentences of "more than ten blows on the back" could be appealed by the "convict" to the Inspector or the Board of Managers. This shows in no uncertain terms that the Order was and remained a set of house rules.

Thus Chapter Twelve concluded with a paragraph on "Offences and crimes which are of such a nature that they cannot be settled by fine or other punishment, as well as all matters of importance which should be prosecuted here in a proper trial". "Here"means in Denmark. Mention is here made of the powers of the inspectors, specified in the Ordinance of 17 April 1782. Detailed rules of conduct are given for the chief trader, including cases in which it should prove impossible to get in touch with the Inspector.

This entire paragraph deals only with employees of the Trade, strictly according to its wording only the crew. This article could thus not be applied to Greenlanders, and it was a question of interpretation whether it could be applied to "mixtures": if so, only if they too were employees of the Trade. The paragraph, then, is kept within the boundaries of the Order as a whole, and it did not authorize the local trading officials or the Inspector to interfere in relations or conflicts between Greenlanders.

There is a jump to the next Chapter, which contains a general encouragement to keep one's eyes open for mineralogical singularities, especially of the kind which could prove economically profitable if exploited.

As a conclusion to the ordinary provisions of the Order, especially those dealing with the Trade, we have Chapter Fourteen, which again enjoins obedience to the provisions of the Order and in the general fulfillment of the duties it imposes on traders and assistants. If they prove themselves loyal and efficient in accordance with the Order, they can participate in the annual surplus of the post, with 10% going to the trader and 5% to an assistant. Whaling chiefs and assistants had, however, a special arrangement.

Whaling is, then, the subject of the Fifteenth and final Chapter of the Order of 1782.[3] In addition to rules regulating the conduct of the whaling commanders and crews out whaling, it contained a number of rules for the functions of traders and whaling assistants in whaling, especially in collaboration with the stationed whalers. Several of these rules repeat what is said elsewhere in the Order, especially about relations with the local Greenlanders. In this connection, certain provisions are laid down dealing with the economic side of whaling conducted jointly between Danes and Greenlanders. Such partnership gave rise to a good deal of squabbling, of which we shall hear more later.

The content of the Order of 1782 is of course not exhausted by this survey, not to mention its influence on developments. The principles embodied in it, its economic and social programme, formulated in detail, and finally, the order and uniformity which were its objectives, made the Order an important factor in the life of West Greenland after 1782, especially in relations between Greenlanders and Europeans stationed there.

The Order and the Population Groups of West Greenland

Characteristic of the demographic situation in West Greenland at the time is that the Order, without ever directly saying so, operates generally with five population groups. This is partly due to the fact that it directly applies only to Trade and whaling employees - as a set of house rules - and partly because, due to the functions of the Trade and whaling in West Greenland, it had to deal with groups outside these narrow confines. The five groups are thus 1. Trade and whaling employees, 2. Mission employees, 3. The West Greenlandic population of Eskimo origin, 4. the "mixtures" or half-breeds, and finally, 5. foreigners: i.e., all those from outside Greenland except for those stationed there, such as whalers, of whatever nationality they might be. The fifth group can really not be considered as part of the population, since they only spent a short time, usually around two or three months, in or around Greenland. But as a factor in the life of Greenland, this group played a not insignificant role, especially in and to the north of the Disko Bugt area.

The fourth group was the subject of special rules in the Order.[4] Problems with this group had developed since the 1750's. Those the Order considered as "mixtures", however, were not the same as those who seem to have previously borne this title. As indicated above, the Order considered as "mixtures" children with Danish fathers and Greenlandic mothers, who might either be "real Greenlandic women" (i.e., pure Eskimos or descendants of the population existent in 1721) or themselves born in mixed marriages. The Order did not consider as "mixtures" children born in or out of marriage whose descent clearly led back to an unknown European man. Nor did it consider as "mixtures" - contrary to previous practice - illegitimate children whose putative father was European. According to the Order, then, this is a juridically defined social group, rather than a biological one.

This group had gradually become relatively numerous, so numerous in any case, that it entailed social problems which the administration considered that it must deal with, just as it had attempted to do in 1777.[5] The rather inflexible directions then given had apparently not been followed. The Order therefore repeated these rules, modified on certain points and more firmly detailed on others.

Such problems asserted themselves all along the coast, so that the Order had to set up rules for the measures to be taken by the local authorities, partly to channel this supplement to the population into the existing society, and partly to make them socially useful from a mercantilistic and rationalistic point of view.

Distributed among the various articles of the Order are regulations dealing with these "mixtures", mostly in Chapter Two: Marriage. This was an attempt to create an opportunity to limit mixed marriages, so that "real Greenlandic women" were so to speak reserved for the ordinary Greenlanders. This was due not to any idea of racial protection, but simply to the social experience that children of mixed marriages were usually not raised as ordinary Greenlanders: i.e., for the boys to be fanger, and for the girls to be the wives of fangers. In addition, it was considered indesirable in their way of life for them to be "spoiled" with respect to diet, because the European way of life was considered unsuitable for fanger families. It created demands for a standard of living which the occupation of fanger could not supply.

Mixed marriages could not be avoided, as experience had shown and would continue to show. This was anticipated by the Order,which attempted to limit their number with the marriage provisions mentioned above. The sons of mixed marriages, in consideration of the fact that juridically they were Greenlanders, had, as mentioned above, the right to marry whom they wished, but only in accordance with the rules.

"So that children of mixed marriages may not be a burden on the country and themselves, they should in general be taught Greenlandic trades and sustained with domestic supplies," says the Order and elaborates with the modified provisions of 1777. If boys cannot be taught to be good fangers ("good Greenlanders"), they must be taught a trade useful in Greenland, "taken into the service of the Trade, or transferred to whaling or other fishing." Strangely enough, the service of the Mission is here unnamed. There were reasons for this, presumably that the Mission was known not to have many employment opportunities for native catechists, but mostly that the Order applied to whaling and the Trade, not to the Mission.

The Order apparently hesitated to list special rules for those half-breeds who were employed in the service of the Trade. Their juridical situation was later interpreted by Inspector Johan Fr. Schwabe as being that of Europeans. They did not, however, receive the same salary in money as the stationed Europeans, but did get a diet allowance and were allowed to purchase blubber for their lamps at the Trade's purchase price. The provisions of the Order concerning employees of the Trade seem, however, not to have distinguished between half-breeds and stationed Europeans. Half-breeds seem, too, to have been subject to the arbitrary penal provisions applied to all the employees of the Trade and in whaling, but this must have been due to an interpretation, since juridically "mixtures" were considered Greenlanders, and the penal provisions were only applicable to those who were employed by the Trade or in whaling. It cannot be determined whether this omission of half-breeds is due to neglect, or whether special provisions were deliberately avoided; nor whether this took place for the sake of the desired degree of uniformity.

The General Schedule

When the Order was issued, a new schedule was published of the prices of all the goods to be sold in Greenland to the Greenlandic population, according to their needs (Chapter Six, prgrph. 4 of the Order). At the same time, the Order specified the prices, in rigsdalers and skillings, to be paid by traders for Greenlanders' commodities.

Under the title "General Schedule", the price list was submitted to the General Board of Directors a few days after the signing of the Order. It contains a curious "didactic" division of merchandise into "Necessary, Useful and Luxurious". The last means not strictly necessary. Later a fourth category appeared: "Curiosities", which at least as far as provisions are concerned corresponded to the "groceries", such as spices, wine and spirits, coffee, tea and other groceries which formerly had been shipped to trading employees in definite quantities for delivery on credit up to a sum of 50 rigsdalers annually. Such goods were in general not to be sold to Greenlanders – in order to protect them from being "spoiled" with imported foods and stimulants, and also in order to prevent possible illicit trade.

The division into the three first-mentioned categories formed the basis of the Trade's calculations regarding profit, covering costs and shrinkage:

quite legal and natural measures in ordinary trade. In presenting the Schedule, the Executive Manager Hartvig Marcus Frisch commented that there was an average surcharge of approximately 25% on all goods; with 20% being added to the purchase price of "necessary" goods, 30% to "useful" goods, and 45% to "luxurious" ones. By far the greatest quantity of goods shipped to Greenland belonged to the first category, including all the categories of merchandise which were ordinarily used in everyday life in Greenland, and which were of decisive significance for the carrying on of Greenlandic occupations.

On merchandise solely destined for Europeans stationed in Greenland, there was a surcharge of 25%; still the prices of such merchandise would be under those prevailing in Copenhagen because export to Greenland and warehousing for shipping were free of public duties, customs and port charges. This would mean that these goods would be sold in Greenland at quite attractive prices, and that they would not have to be paid for if they were damaged on arrival.

In general, the prices in the new General Schedule had been changed quite substantially, relative to previously published schedules. This was because Frisch thought that for many years selling prices had not been adjusted according to cost-prices, and that now a "general change", as he expressed it, was to be made. His idea was that sales prices should be determined by purchase prices, and thus be adjusted every year to agree with them. Thus the General Schedule was formulated as a list of goods with a blank space for the prices, set with each shipment. Since there was only one shipment per year, prices prevailed for a year at a time. Frisch thought, however, that changes should only be made when purchase prices changed considerably.

Frisch wanted to change the procedure so that every employee could order "groceries" up to 50 rigsdalers on credit, or for more if he had other means, and would thus only be sent what he himself desired and would not receive other merchandise.

The General Board of Directors approved the Schedule submitted by Frisch, but decided on changes in the profit rates, with a surcharge of 12% on "necessary" goods, 30% on "useful" merchandise, and 46% on "luxurious" things. Rifles, which were considered necessary, were set up only 8%; and gunpowder, lead, and sabre and sword blades, as well as arrow iron, were to be sold to the Greenlandic consumer at purchase prices.

This determined the price policy which prevailed until 1950. The monopoly, by isolating the West Greenlandic society, created an economic enclave with the most tenuous possible connections with other economic units, and these only indirectly – via the Royal Greenland Trade. The principle was that no profit was to be made on merchandise which was deemed essential for the maintenance of Greenlandic occupations and thereby of the standard of living in Greenland. Profits were taken on categories of merchandise which were judged more or less dispensable. With the slight surcharge of 12% over purchase price on "necessary" goods, the costs of purchase, transportation and shrinkage could not be covered; this loss was made up by higher profits on "luxurious" merchandise.

The Greenlandic Schedule

Along with the General Schedule, Director Frisch submitted what he called "the draft of a Greenland schedule." Its purpose was to show the value of Greenlandic produce, converted into money, in relation to the merchandise sold at the settlements by traders. It was to be translated into Greenlandic and given to the Greenlanders so they could all see what they could get for the commodities they sold.

Frisch fully realized that such a "Greenland Schedule" would entail great difficulties. Even if the translation difficulties could be overcome, it would be hard for the Greenlanders to understand, "since the Greenlanders have no knowledge of either money, measures or weights, and even less of reckoning", as he said when submitting the draft on 27 April 1782. His intention was that this schedule would make it impossible for the traders to "injure" the inhabitants. Perhaps the journal enjoined by the Order would be sufficient to prevent such misconduct, along with the General Schedule; he also realized the difficulties changes in the General Schedule would make for the Greenland Schedule; all the barter values would have to be changed every time there was a change in the sales price of a single article of merchandise.

The General Board of Directors decided therefore to submit the Greenland Schedule to the inspectors for their comment and possible translation. The idea was attractive – also as an instrument of control in the hands of the inhabitants, but because of the difficulties it entailed, it became the object of a long discussion across the Atlantic and in Greenland. This discussion ran parallel to criticism of the provisions of the Order and the General Schedule as a whole.

Criticism of the New Rules

Naturally the new provisions of the Order and the new prices in the General Schedule gave rise to a rain of critical remarks in the south as well as in the north. The very fact that criticism was aired immediately is noteworthy: so little repressed were the traders and assistants in Greenland by the autocratic and patriarchal principle. The missionaries were probably more reserved, most likely because neither document affected them in all its points. But where these two innovations did affect their well-earned rights, they gradually lifted their voices no less loudly in protest.

Criticism in the Northern Inspectorate was summarized by Inspector Schwabe in a long memorandum to the Board of Managers of the Royal Greenland Trade as early as 16 September 1782. The various protests were thus not slow to arise. The innovations had apparently been an even greater shock then the stationing of the two young controllers in 1779 who had now returned as Royal Inspectors: from the point of view of Europeans stationed in Greenland, as permanent snoopers.

In this memorandum Inspector Schwabe found it appropriate, in order, as it were, to throw the criticism into what to him was proper relief, to cite certain facts from former trading practices - conditions he himself had experienced. At Godhavn, for example, the tubs seal blubber had previously been measured in when purchased were 23 pots larger than the 1⅓ barrels (160 pots) which the new blubber measurements, according to the Order, were to contain. They were thus 14% larger, or over 1½ barrels for a barrel. Likewise, the measures used for purchasing whale blubber contained 29% more than the 160 pots per barrel provided by the Order. The reason for this difference in measures between seal blubber and whale blubber was said to be that whale blubber was usually purchased frozen and shrank more than seal blubber.

Because merchandise sold was also converted into tubs, as Schwabe expressed it, prices varied greatly. Merchandise which according to the General Schedule was supposed to be necessary and therefore cheaper, had thus become more expensive; goods now to be considered as "luxurious", on the contrary, had become cheaper. The value of a tub of blubber in barter thus varied from under 24 skillings to over one rigsdaler.

A comparison of the previously communicated samples of sales prices[6] and the prices from previous schedules listed by Inspector Schwabe in his memorandum shows that prices had risen and that there was a conspicuous lack of uniformity in pricing. Prices seem also to have previously depended on whether the fangst had been good or bad. "When the fangst has been good, the Greenlander has been reasonable, delivering more Greenlandic products and paying more for European goods," says Schwabe. Rather than being reasonable, the Greenlander in such cases probably did not reflect on what he was getting for his blubber, as long as he got the merchandise he wanted in return. Greenlandic price consciousness was of a specific nature: rather a merchandise consciousness than a critical attitude toward the prices of things.

Price fluctuations could in other respects be even greater than indicated above by the value of blubber. A good rifle could at one time and place cost 20 pieces of baleen over one metre, or about 12½ rigsdalers; and at another time and place 25, or even up to 40 pieces of the same sort of baleen. Barter was thus revealed in its worst light, especially in the different treatment Greenlanders could receive at the very same place.

Another unfortunate aspect of this barter system, as it had gradually developed, was that traders could let Greenlanders unsuspectingly pay the unpaid debts of other Greenlanders who had died or moved away by having them put more in the measures than they were otherwise accustomed to do, not to speak of obvious cheating with bottomless blubber measures. Besides, proper accounts were not kept on how much European merchandise each trader or assistant sold at each place, on each trip, and to whom; often only the amounts purchased were summarized. The final accounts were therefore not true, but depended on what inventories of imported goods the trader had at the end of the fiscal year. The difference between on the one hand last year's stock and what had been imported, and on the other hand this year's stock, was the figure sold.

In other words, trading was one big mess, which the new Order was to try to clean up. Inspector Schwabe would far from deny that there were many honest traders in Greenland, but the old system had given too free a rein to the dishonest ones.

Taking all this into account, it was quite natural that the traders' criticism of the new provisions was mostly directed to the verified blubber measures, calculated according to the Order at 1⅓ barrel per barrel. The traders asserted that they could not break even with only a third of a barrel's overmeasure (40 pots) for shrinkage and leakage. They gave various reasons: large shrinkage during summer transport, shrinkage when the blubber had to wait before being barrelled, frozen blubber shrinking more than thawed. When the blubber was to be shipped, the barrels had to be filled up, and these barrels were not adjusted, but could contain more or less than standard. In one way or another the traders had to cover their losses in giving credit to Greenlanders.

Now that the Greenlanders were to get full price for their blubber when selling it, converted to money values, the trader would not be able to manage with the 40 pots overmeasure: it would not even cover shrinkage and leakage. Besides, it would not be possible to manipulate between the various products and their different relations to the merchandise sold. In addition, not one single trader had become wealthy by trading in Greenland. Resistance to the new provisions was also justified by contending that Greenlanders would never agree to the new blubber measures, not to mention the much higher prices of the General Schedule. It was also impossible to keep exact accounts of what was purchased and sold on expeditions, mostly because small quantities were bartered to and from each person. The weather was not propitious for keeping accounts on trading expeditions, with numb and greasy fingers, often out of doors, and in the greatest haste in order to take advantage of good travelling conditions.

Criticism by employees of the Trade thus concentrated on three factors: the blubber measures, the evaluation of Greenlandic produce in money values when purchasing it, and finally, bookkeeping. Inspector Schwabe had to admit that blubber did undergo a great amount of shrinkage on trading expeditions and in storage, especially when failed and it had to be stored from one year to the other. He would attempt to make shipping barrels uniform, corresponding to the blubber measures without the 40 pots overmeasure. Incidentally, this was of no importance for whaling chiefs, who settled accounts in whale oil, not in measures of blubber.

Inspector Schwabe also had to agree with the traders that they could not cover both shrinkage, leakage and accounts unsettled with the overmeasure on the blubber measures, while keeping to a price of one rigsdaler per barrel (with 40 pots overmeasure). When the prices of the General Schedule in rigsdalers were weighed against the conversion values in the same monetary unit for Greenlandic produce, the traders, especially with "necessary" goods so cheap, would not be able to make sufficient incomes, calculated in rigsdalers. Schwabe was therefore afraid of the risk of embezzlement.

Schwabe could not see that the problem of more accurate accounts was an insuperable one. "And what revenue officer in the realms and lands of the King is exempt from rendering an account of receipts and expenses?" he asked and continued: "Greenlanders pay no regular tax, but instead they are bound to deliver their goods for a tolerable price; and it is the trader who receives them." Here Schwabe indirectly asserted, at least in part, the reason why only one rigsdaler was paid for a barrel of blubber.

The profit made by the Royal Greenland Trade on rendered and auctioned whale oil was, in addition to shipping and other expenses, also to cover public expenses in Greenland. In this sense it was proper to compare traders with other "revenue officers", while the traders themselves thought of themselves as businessmen and not tax collectors, not even public servants: the Trade was still considered as a chartered business enterprice. This mixture of state and private activity made it difficult for the employees of the Trade to understand their role in society.

Inspector Schwabe was, then, forced partly to acknowledge the traders' criticism of two very essential points: the blubber measures, and the impossibility of covering credit risks, shrinkage and leakage with a more accurate conversion into monetary units. He therefore concluded with three proposals to remedy the situation, of which he himself preferred one: to raise the capacity of blubber measures from 1⅓ to 1½ barrels per barrel. In this connection he recalled that both traders and assistants according to the Order earned percentages of the surplus at each post. Finally, he proposed certain alleviations in bookkeeping.

Later in the year, the Board of Managers approved most of Schwabe's proposed changes, of which the most important was that the blubber measure was raised to 1½ barrel. Alleviations in bookkeeping were also approved. But on one point the Board stuck to its established principle.

Schwabe had suggested the possibility of fixing the prices in the General Schedule, at least for several years at a time. He was afraid of irregular accounts and dissatisfaction, also among Greenlanders, with annual price changes, since remaining stocks would thereafter be sold at new prices, in contradistinction to previous practice, in which price changes only applied to new shipments. The Board maintained the accepted principle of the General Schedule, according to which the prices were blank. However, not many changes were predicted; they would apply to only twenty to twenty-five of the varieties of merchandise on sale.

Reactions in the Southern Inspectorate

The traders of the Southern Inspectorate also voiced criticism of the new system, especially concerning the use of blubber measures and price changes in the General Schedule. Traders from Frederikshåb, Fiskenæsset and Julianehåb stated in more or less the same terms that they could not always use the blubber measures sent them – for several reasons. In the first place, Greenlanders in the south were not used to having their blubber purchased according to the barrel, but rather according to the number of seals it came from. For example, the blubber of one harp seal sold at 16 skillings, which in the new blubber measure, including an over-measure of one-third, would amount to one-sixth of the measure.

Since as a rule not even the blubber of whole seals was purchased, but only parts of a seal, it would be quite impossible to measure exactly in whole or half blubber measures. One trader asserted that the Greenlanders, unfamiliar with the new method of measurement, had clearly "expressed doubt both in words and gestures" about what the trader had told them of the new system, and thought he intended to cheat them. If Greenlanders avoided selling the blubber of such parts of seals, the Trade would lose large quantities, with all the small pieces put together. This, of course, the Board had to repudiate. It had never been their intention not to purchase small quantities.

Inspector Olrik, to whom the same complaints had been reported, did the only reasonable thing under the circumstances, and had measure tubs of one-eigth and one-sixteenth of a blubber measure made. With these even one-thirty-second of a blubber measure could be measured more or less accurately. This apparently put an end to the problem, as the traders were permitted to use the traditional system alongside the blubber measures, naturally in close agreement with the new price schedule.

The southern Greenland traders also pleaded for fixed prices on merchandise in the General Schedule, at least no price raise on certain goods without a substantial reduction on others "since the Greenlanders in their simplicity conclude that for blubber of the same quality and quantity they should always get merchandise of the same quality and quantity." This opinion had been heard before, and had been supported by the vehement reactions of Greenlanders when prices were changed in the 1770's.[7] Just as when the same criticism was voiced in North Greenland, the Board failed to approve repeated South Greenland appeals for price stability.

In connection with the above mentioned mistrust manifested by Greenlanders toward their local trader, he had the General Schedule completely translated into Greenlandic, so that the inhabitants could see with their own eyes that he neither had cheated them nor intended to do so. This was a prudent move; subsequently no complaints were heard from this place. On the whole, attitudes toward the Order as well as toward the General Schedule apparently developed more calmly in the Southern Inspectorate than in the Northern.

The So-called Greenlandic Schedule

At one place the trader had done the obvious thing and had had the General Schedule translated into Greenlandic to prevent the local Greenlanders from getting incorrect ideas of what it contained. The Board of Managers praised him for his initiative, which it itself apparently either had recoiled from undertaking or had even considered. There is no indication that the Executive Manager ever considered this when he submitted the General Schedule to the General Board of Directors.

On the other hand, when he submitted the General Schedule on 27 April 1782, he mentioned the Greenlandic Schedule, which at a later meeting on 31 July was referred to closer discussion with the Inspectors. The purpose of this schedule was, as mentioned above, to give Greenlanders in tralslated form some contact with what the traders and assistants were doing when purchasing and selling. This was the same objective as that of the single South Greenland trader mentioned above, who went in the opposite direction by having the General Schedule itself, i.e., the list of selling prices, translated.

The Board of Directors thought this was useless, as neither weights, measures, nor the value of money was supposed to be commonly known among the Greenlanders. The South Greenlandic trader must have been of another opinion.

Inspector Schwabe was not sure of the usefulness of such a Greenlandic Schedule. In addition, even few small changes in the prices of the General Schedule would create huge changes in the reciprocal values of Greenlandic products. He preferred to await the result of the General Schedule and the new bookkeeping system before committing himself to the implementation of this project. He never gave a thought to the opportunities for a Greenlander to control purchase and selling, only to the control the Inspector could exercise in going through the ledger of each settlement. In addition he thought that such a Greenlandic schedule would be so complicated that Greenlanders in general would not be able to understand it. His criticism led the Board of Managers to put the project on ice.

Inspector Olrik in the Southern Inspectorate had a quite different opinion about the usefulness of the Greenland Schedule. He went to a lot of trouble to get it translated, and in 1783 adjusted it to the new General Schedule prices. Along with the new, smaller blubber measures he had had made, it was tested in Sukkertoppen District; both at Napassoq and Umánaq, a trading post slightly north of Napassoq, Greenlanders had been very satisfied with both. "They vied with each other in bringing in blubber, and they gave us to understand that they were very glad to buy, now that they were being treated so honestly." Unless this report is due to a certain amount of bragging, which one might suspect, taking in account Olrik's general situation, it bears witness to a positive attitude toward the new system. There are few cases where Greenlandic attitudes are expressed; perhaps we can accept this statement of Olrik's at face value.

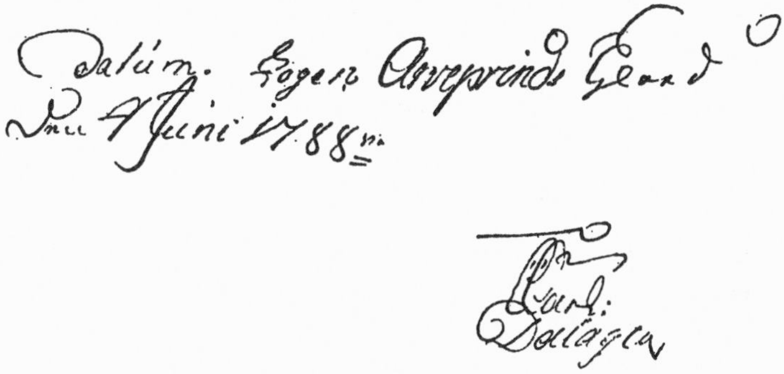

A reduced copy of the signature of C.C. Dalager.

But nothing more developed from this initiative. It appears that the not very positive attitude toward it, represented by the doubts of Inspector Schwabe as to the usefulness of the Greenlandic Schedule, predominated. Apparently Schwabe's opinion was more important than what Olrik liked. This can be considered one more small weight on the side of North Greenland predominance. The Executive Manager's intention in presenting this project can, furthermore, be seen as a part of the general tendency towards better information, and thus in step with the times. But it got no further than good intentions.

Criticism of the new system began to wane surprisingly soon; by a year after its introduction it had ceased. Conditions straightened themselves out, and the Order became a commonplace, probably because as a whole it was sober and reasonable. It was good for everyone to have something concrete to refer to.

The relation of the Moravian Brethren to the Order and the General Schedule was settled by a number of conferences in the General Board of Directors, so that the Brethren were granted free transportation for persons and personal effects, but were otherwise required to procure their provisions through the local trading chief, who was also to purchase produce from the Greenlandic members of the Brethren. The European

Brethren in Greenland were not allowed to purchase Greenlandic products themselves.

Those traders who had spent quite some time in Greenland, some of them employed before the establishment of the Royal Greenland Trade, never felt entirely satisfied, however. Some resigned; others continued, and were suspected of continuing along the old lines. In 1785, annoyances about auditors' comments on his old accounts and a suspicion, in his opinion unjustified, of dishonesty in whaling at Klokkerhuk, brought C.C. Dalager, a trader of long standing, to remark: "I must therefore deplore my present fate, which seems to resemble that of the carpenters who built Noah's ark, for they themselves did not get in!!!"

III.
The Royal Greenland Trade and Whaling

Transitional Difficulties

Besides being of epoch-making importance in Greenland, the Order of 1782 was also an expression of what was expected from the administration of the Royal Greenland Trade according to the new system of 1781. The transition itself to the new system and the new administration naturally resulted in immediate difficulties.

These difficulties were concentrated in taking over from the former administration (1774/76–1781). For the Royal Greenland Trade as well as for the other branches of trade under the jurisdiction of the General Board of Directors of the Royal Greenland, Iceland, Finmark and Faroese Trade, it was actually a question of a kind of transfer transactions. As far as the Royal Greenland Trade was concerned, these continued well into 1782, and were essentially concerned with the evaluation of stocks and inventories, including buildings and ships in Denmark (Copenhagen) as well as Greenland. The bookkeeping confusion was never quite untangled so that a true evaluation could not be reached.

According to the regulation of 2 July 1781, §6, the new administration of the Royal Greenland Trade, in return for its part of the fund that was intended to be set up, was to have transferred whatever had belonged to the Royal Greenland Trade under its previous administration. From the total fund, shares were to be issued with a face value of 100 rigsdalers each. This capital was partially to be secured by properties taken over at their estimated book values. "But if these properties together, according to their previously mentioned estimate, cannot make the fixed capital of two million, We will most graciously contribute the remainder from Our treasury." I.e., it was a question of getting as large a contribution as possible to draw on for operating the various trading branches, and reciprocally, of taking over the dormant capital of the "properties together" at as low an evaluation as possible.

It was hard work completing various accounts. The year 1781 expired before this could be accomplished. In January 1782, the Overskattedirektion pressed for the delivery of the shares. The various branches of trade under the General Board of Directors were already functioning, and payments were made, financed by Kurantbanken, of course with the state as guarantor. As late as April 1782 the share holdings had not yet been delivered to the tax office.

An important reason why at least the Management of the Royal Greenland Trade had not delivered the share certificates for its part in the fund seems to be that it had had trouble getting the final accounts from the former administration for auditing and approval of the property evaluations. The Management was unable to approve the annual balance which the Overskattedirektion had sent it until the accounts mentioned above had been audited with respect to the ledgers.

The amounts at which colonies, lodges, ships and other vessels in Greenland and Copenhagen in 1781 had been evaluated, were, according to the Management, totally out of touch with reality. It demonstrated that no account had ever been taken of depreciation. "The Settlements in Greenland are listed at 168,263 rigsdalers. That this sum is so huge and really exaggerated arises from the fact that this account has continually been debited for the total costs of the colonies without depreciation ever being deducted." The Management wanted a proper statement of capital, and had no intention of paying for previous operational deficits.

Accounting methods were still the same hopelessly complicated ones that so far had been used in the trading companies. The eleven colonies were thus entered at 168,263 rigsdalers, or approximately 15,300 rigsdalers apiece. The lodges and whaling stations, of which there were seven, were booked at 56,642 rigsdalers, or 8,072 rigsdalers each. The book value of such figures alone was thus estimated at around a quarter of a million rigsdalers. This means that the Royal Greenland Trade would hereafter have to pay for the dormant capital in establishments and installations alone over one-fourth of its share of the two million rigsdalers, which was 950,000 rigsdalers. To this would be added the value of the installations in Copenhagen, and all the ships and other vessels. This would make far too great a dent in its share of the fund and put the new management in an unfavourable position during the reorganisation. It would take some time before it began to function, so that as much liquidity as possible was needed.

To make a long story short, the administration succeeded in getting the final evaluation reduced considerably. Thus the evaluation of the colonies alone was cut to under half: 71,500 rigsdalers. Likewise, all the other capital items were reduced, so that the total evaluation was 505,500 rigsdalers. Thus there remained 444,500 rigsdalers of the Royal Greenland

Trade's share of the fund which the administration could draw on for operations. In addition, §6 of the regulation opened the possibility of the administration taking out a loan in Kurantbanken - with the state as guarantor - up to one million rigsdalers.

This entire picture of take-over difficulties serves to illustrate the distance which the state formally put between itself and the various trading enterprises. It is true that important members of the cabinet were in the General Board of Directors over all the enterprises, but the Managements of the various "companies" took full responsibility for operations. This must have put the Managements on a tightrope. The take-over transactions, as sketched here, show, however, that at least the Management of the Royal Greenland Trade did not automatically approve the summary decisions of the central administration. They really had a certain degree of freedom to criticise them, and could negotiate a more favourable solution to problems. Autocracy was not identical with a continual and universal demand for blind submission and literal obedience.

But when the activity of the Management of the Trade assumed a political character or might have political consequences, especially outwardly, its freedom of action was curtailed. This was a matter of course. The responsibility for actions undertaken under such curtailed freedom remained, however, with the Management. Naturally this had a general tendency to hamper the free development of the Management, just as dependence on the state treasury as the contributor of capital had a moderating influence. Finally, one must remember that according to the regulation of 2 July 1781, the system was to last only thirty years. During this period the government could interfere in the administration of the Trade; at least there was no provision that it could not.

The take-over commotion also shows the desire for a clean start. The new system is thus in itself epoch-making. It developed gradually - a development which was naturally linked with subsequent events in both Greenland and Denmark, and which probably did not quite turn out as Guldberg had imagined.

The Whaling Project

The take-over from the previous administration of the Royal Greenland Trade included the grandiose whaling project, which had apparently failed (cf. Vol. II, p. 385 sq.). Since the autumn of 1780 it had not been quite abandoned, but the plans were considerably reduced. In 1781 the new administration had to attempt to carry out the winter plan for whaling, as the normal provisioning of the respective colonies took place by means of the whaling ships which were stationed in Greenland throughout the winter. The following year, it took unusually long for the five ships which were stationed to return, so that the Management had only three ships which could be used for winter whaling and transport to Holsteinsborg, Jakobshavn (including Claushavn) and Godhavn in 1789.

The reduction in the number of ships used for whaling was considerable:[1]

1777/78	19	ships	
1778/79	12	-	
1779/80	6	-	
1780/81	14	-	
1781/82	5	-	(cf. above)
1782/83	7	-	(4 in addition to the 3 mentioned above presumably in the Davis Stræde)
1783/84	8	-	

At the same time, the crews were reduced, at least on some of the ships. In 1781 it was thus decided that only two of the five ships which were to be sent out in September should sail with a full crew; the remaining three were to sail with half a crew. The intention was that the reduced crews of these three ships would conduct whaling from the coast in partnership with the Greenlandic whalers at the places where the ships would be stationed for the winter. These were the ships destined for Holsteinsborg, Jakobshavn and Christianshåb.

Niels Egede's old idea, which had already been implemented to a certain extent at Holsteinsborg and Fortune Bay/Godhavn, was to be extended and serve as an efficiency measure. This practice was now to be more controlled.

At first the Management wanted partnerships between Greenlanders and stationed whalers to be contracted in advance according to a set of fixed rules. It would be locally decided whether Greenlanders and Europeans would each man their own sloops separately, or whether the crews would be mixed. Here the Management would not insist on Greenlanders not using the umiak, "but in general they should use Danish sloops and Danish Whaling equipment." This is not an expression of tolerance, nor of a conscious desire to teach Greenlanders European whaling. If Greenlanders participated in whaling in their own umiaks, there would be little basis for the whale-sharing contracts the Management wanted to see used.

There had previously been strife and disagreement between Greenlanders and whaling chiefs about the nature of contracts (cf. Vol. II, p. 408 seq.). It looked in 1781 as though the Management would get its way. In directions to Holsteinsborg, Christianshåb and Jakobshavn (Claushavn) it was laid down that Greenlanders who participated in whaling were to get one half of each captured whale, excluding the baleen. This must mean that the number of Greenlanders participating was to be the same as that of the stationed whalers, and that it was half of the blubber which they were to get. The other half of the blubber was to go to the whaling ship, i.e., the Royal Greenland Trade. The meat is not mentioned, but we can assume that in any case it would be appropriated by the native inhabitants, at least those Greenlanders participating in the whaling.

According to the above direction, the Greenlanders' share of the blubber was to be delivered to them on board the whaling ship after flensing. The Greenlandic partners were to participate in flensing, so that the Trade's share was to be flensed first, then the Greenlanders'. The stationed whalers were also to take part in the flensing of the Greenlanders' share, "if the Greenlanders themselves have no objections," said the Management. The Greenlanders' share was to be measured on board ship. For each tub, i.e. for each barrel with overmeasure (1⅓ or 1½ barrel per barrel), the Greenlanders were to be credited one rigsdaler. Compared with the contract entered into in Godhavn in 1779, this is a higher price; then the Greenlanders got one rigsdaler for two barrels (with variable overmeasure) of blubber. The payment was to be divided only among those Greenlanders who had entered into a fixed contract or participated actively in the whaling in question; it was to be given in merchandise. If the Greenlanders were not willing to give up their share of the blubber on the ship, "of course they cannot be forced to do so; your actions must be guided by the circumstances." Previous disagreements had made the administration realize that they had to act with caution. The system was to be voluntary.

It is a question of temperament whether one wishes to interpret this as a matter of principle. It was written before the Order of 1782, which contained no provisions of coercion for Greenlanders. In 1781, when this directive was issued, it is possible that Schwabe's opinions were already exercising an influence. In any case this principle of voluntary cooperation coincides with the general attitude of the Order toward the Greenlandic population and with the concept of them as a free people: i.e., a people completely free of coercive laws, which persisted throughout the century.

With respect to contracts, the directive contained certain other interesting provisions, all expressions of a desire to determine conditions on the basis of experience, and to strive for uniformity. It must be due to the experience of Godhavn that it was decided that Greenlanders should be allowed to purchase baleen at the price paid by the Trade, if a local need should suddenly arise. Likewise, in times of need blubber was to be delivered to the Greenlanders; first from the trader's stock, and if he had none, the whaling commander was to deliver it in return for equal compensation from the shares of the Greenlanders in future whales. The trader was, on the contrary, apparently to deliver it to them on ordinary credit.

Greenlanders who had made fixed contracts were to take part in the periodical whale watching: a watch along the coast, from outlying islands, or in sloops, for whales to turn up. It is not mentioned whether such Greenlanders on watching had meals provided. But it is believed that this had been done at Godhavn. At this point the Order of 1782 had not yet come into force.

The Order of 1782 and Whaling

If this special directive of 1781 contained no provisions for the meals of Greenlanders on whale watch, one would think that the Order of 1782 would have dealt with it. But there are no such provisions, either in Chapter Fifteen, which especially deals with whaling, or in other articles. In §§4 and 5 of Chapter Four it is specifically mentioned that Danish, that is to say, European, provisions must not be delivered to Greenlanders unless there is a situation of absolute need. §6 of this Chapter states, however, that an "incompetent provider" may be hired as a whaler. If employed by the Trade, he was to be paid 10 or 20 rigsdalers per annum and full or half board, respectively. This is a condition of steady employment. There is no mention of meals for contracted Greenlanders watching for whales. It must then have depended on local decisions or customs, as those which had developed at Godhavn, for example.

The provisions of the Order on whaling in general, contained in its Chapter Fifteen, dealt mainly with the conditions of the whalers, commanders and assistants. Only §4 deals with the participation of Greenlanders. Its provisions are rather vague, and open up the possibility of several types of cooperation. Greenlanders taking part in whaling can be paid according to the ordinary "award list", with a fixed payment for each whale caught per man. If they do not agree to this, the whaling assistant may, or rather must, agree with those who want to take part on a contract in advance for a share of the catch. These Greenlanders are then to get a certain sum's worth of merchandise for each one's part in the captured whale, determined according to the number of manned vessels they participate with.

As a general prerequisite, however, it is stipulated that the contracting Greenlanders should use the Trade's sloops and whaling equipment, "for which they at least, when they whaled alone, had to pay half of the baleen." This was to be taken into consideration when contracting. The Order insists then, that at least the greater part of the baleen from a captured whale was to go to the Trade, and stipulates that this is rent for use of the Trade's boats and whaling equipment. In addition, the same provisions are made for the re-sale of baleen and blubber in times of distress as in the directive of 1781, mentioned above.

The Order of 1782 thus differentiates between Greenlanders employed by the Royal Greenland Trade as whalers, and those who take part sporadically or on contract. The general provisions were, as we have seen, rather vague; they were perhaps intentionally not made too strict or too numerous. So much depended on local conditions that it would have been unfortunate to bind chiefs too strictly to rigorous regulations, so that much had to rest on the judgment of the individual, on the basis of certain comprehensive provisions of principle. The forming of customary rules was left to the future.

The Question of Payment

The vagueness of the Order of 1782 on partnership and the payment of participating Greenlanders is partly due to the fact that different traditions had developed at different stations. In this connection Sandgreen, the trader at Godhavn, directed an inquiry to the Management in 1782, before the arrival of Schwabe, the new Inspector. Sandgreen referred to the practice which apparently had prevailed at Godhavn so far, that Greenlandic whalers had borrowed both sloops and whaling equipment without paying rent to the trade. The Greenlanders at Godhavn had been warned by others of the practice which the Management wanted to introduce elsewhere. Sandgreen was informed by the Management that for the loan of sloops and whaling equipment Greenlanders should pay half of the captured whale, asserting that this practice had been put through at Kronprinsens Ejland. It would be better "in less fortunate times to be able to treat them more leniently," while in this case of a good whaling season at Godhavn the regulations should be followed which the Management wished to prevail everywhere. In addition the Management referred Sandgreen to the newly appointed Inspector, whom he was to obey.[2]

After his arrival, Schwabe, because of the divergent practices which had developed, was compelled to emphasize local leniency, while insisting that the provisions and general policy of the Order in this connection should form the basis of the local decisions. He also dealt with flensing, for which the Order also had certain regulations: one could not and ought not, he said, to force Greenlanders who by themselves had captured whales with sloops and whaling equipment borrowed from the Trade to flense in the European manner. Only that part of the whale they were to pay to the Trade should be flensed under supervision. The Greenlanders' share should be left to themselves, if they could not be convinced to flense properly. "When all Greenlanders are present, both those who have taken part in fishing and those who have not, flense all at once, according to the old custom of the country, so that each one keeps what he cuts off, and delivers to the Trade what he wishes to, much is lost during flensing as well as later; and it is up to the trader, before the illicit ones, to purchase what the Greenlanders themselves do not need." Here again is a clear expression of the principle of not depriving Greenlanders of the necessities of life.

It appears that the Management had abandoned the system which the directive of 1781 attempted to introduce. It became more and more common that half of the baleen as well as the blubber went to the Greenlanders, at least when they whaled alone, and that the other half of the whale went to the Trade. The meat was always ignored. But it took a long time to acquire uniformity.

At Holsteinsborg, Inspector Olrik had attempted to introduce a special practice different from what had prevailed in whaling there, and also different from what was attempted in the Northern Inspectorate. Exaggerated rumours of the advantages enjoyed by Greenlandic whalers in the North induced the Greenlanders at Holsteinsborg to practice obstruction. "This winter I have suffered much annoyance and even victimization from the Greenlanders at Holsteinsborg," wrote Olrik to Schwabe, asking for information on payment practices in Schwabe's Inspectorate.

The following year Olrik received the information he had requested, but it was still not possible for him to introduce at Holsteinsborg a system corresponding to that of the Northern Inspectorate. "They will by no means listen to my representations; they will sell me no fish whole, nor give half a fish for the use of sloops and whaling equipment; they will only deign to give for the use of the previously mentioned things of the Trade, the baleen of one side of each fish, no more. Objections on my part would have no other result than to put me in the grave before my time. The stubbornness of the Greenlanders of Holsteinsborg is undescribable, and the reasons for their conduct against me, or rather against the regulations, which here are quite trodden under foot, are even partly incomprehensible to me." This administrative deadlock, however, most likely only applied to Holsteinsborg itself. At the whaling station of Qerrortussoq, not far away, the Greenlandic whalers seem to have accepted the Management's conditions: "but of course it will not be long before, encouraged by their neighbours' unbridled conduct, they soon will dare the same, and elude whatever according to their confused concepts entails a sort of coercion or in the least restricts their wilfulness, waste and other dubious practices with what they acquire, to their own great harm and loss as well as that of the Trade."

This quotation reveals immediately the lack of understanding of Inspector Olrik, quite inflexible and short-sighted as he was, of the situation, as well as of the reaction of the Greenlanders. The danger that the whalers of Qerrortussoq would make common cause with those of Holsteinsborg was a product of Olrik's European imagination. An entirely different tradition had prevailed here from that of Holsteinsborg, and, as it turned out later, there was a clear antagonism between the two places. Olrik had no feeling for local bonds to a whaling ground and its traditions.

The insistence of the Holsteinsborg whalers was not the expression of "stubbornness", not to speak of disrespect for the regulations. One wonders whether they even had any knowledge of these. The whaling Greenlanders of Holsteinsborg were bound to the traditions set in the time of Niels Egede and continued by his son Jørgen Egede. They could have no confidence in Olrik, the newly arrived nâlagaq; nor was he one who by his conduct could create confidence.

There are clear indications that these bounds of tradition were connected with the person of Jørgen Egede, and thereby indirectly to Niels Egede. The administration directly blamed Jørgen Egede for a good deal of the intractability of the Holsteinsborgers. After his departure, they seem to have yielded; at least there were no further skirmishes in this affair in the years immediately following.

Whaling at Sukkertoppen

In 1785 Inspector Olrik proposed, as a possible counter to the "stubbornness" of the Holsteinsborgers, to abandon whaling at Sukkertoppen with Greenlandic whalers, and move the stationed whalers to Holsteinsborg.

The whaling attempt at Sukkertoppen had been proposed by trader Smith in the general eagerness to set up whaling from the various colonies and lodges of the coast. Trader Smith's proposal and its approval by the Management were an essential motivating force in the decision to move the colony south from Kangamiut in 1781. A whaling ship was sent out with commander, speck sioneers (blubber cutters) and a whaling crew.

Neither the first winter nor any of the immediately succeeding ones was the whaling successful, however. According to all the reports this was partly due to the fact that the waters were too narrow and full of skerries, which hampered pursuing the harpooned whales; and partly that the assistance of the Greenlandic inhabitants was needed both for towing and flensing, but the Greenlandic fangers were disinclined to perform these tasks because it interfered with their sealing, by means of which they got their sustenance.

It was therefore decided - most likely by Inspector Olrik - to move the whaling to Holsteinsborg; this must have begun by 1786. Thus the recommendation of the Management had not been followed that this pressure should only be applied to the Holsteinsborgers if they persisted in their inflexibility. Moving the whalers from Sukkertoppen was presumably decided because they could be more efficiently employed at Holsteinsborg, so that it was not an element of pressure against the Holsteinsborgers, although the whalers who were stationed there can have been instrumental in the transition to the new conditions of payment. Only part of the Sukkertoppen crew was moved to Holsteinsborg. With a certain perseverance it was still attempted to derive some profit from whaling at Sukkertoppen. And finally in 1787 the first whale was caught! The administration was still worried about the great cost of this attempt, the final results of which were doubtful. In the winter of 1789/90 two large whales were caught; at the same time we are told of the great difficulties for the whale watch caused by the ice.

Subsequently, luck does not seem to have been with whaling at Sukkertoppen, so in 1795 it was finally decided to discontinue the attempt. All the equipment and sloops which were usable were to be delivered to Holsteinsborg or Qerrortussoq upon requisition. This ended the role of the Sukkertoppen trader as a whaling chief. Nor was the Inspector of South Greenland especially glad to see the attempt stopped. Whaling was the most important factor to both the Management and the inspectors, so that the Inspector of South Greenland saw himself being outdistanced in this field by his northern colleague.

Whaling was also attempted at other places along the coast of the Southern Inspectorate. At Frederikshåb it was repeatedly attempted to get qiporqaq (humpback) whales; but even when one was wounded it was not often that it could be landed. At times whalers succeeded in landing carcasses. Besides Holsteinsborg, organised, systematic whaling was not carried on in the Southern Inspectorate. Sealing was relied on, both for blubber and skin. But even here the North outdistanced the South.

It must be assumed from scattered comments in the source material that the South Greenlandic fangers' dependence on and persistance in traditional sealing - and the entire traditional fangst cycle - was the most important reason why efficient whaling in the south failed. There whaling could only take place sporadically. It was, as has been mentioned, also characteristic for the Northern Inspectorate that organised whaling in cooperation with Greenlandic whalers only made real progress where sealing was bad or at least less profitable. In connection with the issuance of the Order of 1782, the Management toyed with the idea that less proficient or actually incompetent Greenlandic "providers", as they were called, "unable to provide for themselves in the Greenlandic manner," could be convinced to move to the Northern Inspectorate and find employment in whaling. Several transfers did take place in subsequent years, but they seem to have been voluntary, i.e., due more to general wanderlust than to persuasion on the part of the authorities.

The Reorganisation of Whaling

The Management repeated this request to Inspector Olrik in 1783, in connection with a plan to revise whaling completely both at Holsteinsborg and in the Northern Inspectorate. This reorganisation was already in the cradle, so to speak, in 1781. Now in 1783 this losing proposition was to be completely cleaned up; winter whaling was to be reorganised.

In the spring of 1783 the Management had decided not to send whaling ships to winter stations in the Northern Inspectorate, but instead to station one at Holsteinsborg. At the same time both inspectors, Schwabe and Olrik, were asked for their opinions and proposals for the coming reorganisation, the plan of which was sketched in more or less the same language to both: "We believe that if each station had 4 or 5 Europeans, principally officers, in addition to a competent commander or foreman, these along with the Greenlanders and the so-called incompetent providers, whom one would have to make an effort to attract to the stations, could conduct whaling in the most economical manner from land, without the necessity of sending a ship over."

In the midst of his conflicts with the Holsteinsborg whalers, and on the basis of the previously unsuccessful whaling at Sukkertoppen, Inspector Olrik was especially positive towards this idea of the Management. Inspector Schwabe, on the other hand, discussed in his opinion how whaling from the stations could be organised in the future. In his opinion this could be done in two ways: either with Europeans and a few Greenlanders; or in the European way, but with Greenlanders and only a few Europeans. In his argumentation he made some interesting evaluations of Greenlandic and European efficiency.

Inspector Schwabe thought the first way could be presumed to give the greatest profit. The Greenlanders were "wilful", and would only go on whale watching when they saw fit. Their "rambling" meant that one could not always be sure of having a sufficient crew, so that many good fishing days would go lost. Here Schwabe was referring to the fact that in the Northern Inspectorate, just as in the Southern, Greenlanders preferred to attend to the traditional fangst cycle. He asserted that they were only interested in capturing whales, not in landing and flensing them in the way which was most advantageous for the Trade: i.e., the European way.

But European crews were expensive to maintain and difficult to keep occupied outside of the whaling period. Greenlanders were good and lucky whalers and good harpooners, better than Europeans, even if the latter went on frequent whale watches, "so that none of the winter crews has so far had the good catches the Greenlanders have made on their own." The second of Schwabe's proposals ought therefore to be attempted, "since this way is much less harmful to the manners of the Greenlanders than whaling with Europeans alone." But benefits must of course be assured to the Trade. Schwabe thus presented two reasons for preferring the latter way: that it was cheaper and that it was best for the inhabitants. This latter consideration is typical of his didactic-moral manner of thinking. There is no doubt that he regarded it as the consideration which carried the most weight.

Schwabe could not, however, ignore the instability of the Greenlanders. They were worse flensers, from the point of view of the Trade. Only good blubber cutters and sailors and competent whaling assistants, who had a mastery of the Greenlandic language, could get the Greenlanders to flense properly. In addition, he thought that Greenlanders should be paid as whalers on their own, if they preferred. They should get half of each whale caught, while the other half should go to the Trade as rent for sloops and whaling equipment. It is thus the form of payment mentioned above that he wishes to have laid down.

If whaling was in the future to be carried on mainly by Greenlanders, each station would need only one competent European officer or harpooner, "as the Greenlanders are very good harpooners," as well as some good blubber cutters, who could perhaps be found among the sailors, who would have to be stationed in sufficient numbers to man a sloop. Then he dealt with the exact number of personnel to be stationed, including those already at the stations and desiring to remain.

Schwabe sent his opinion at the same time as his discussion with Olrik on the manner of payment was going on. Incidentally, he linked the payment of Greenlandic partners with the assistance fund for the Northern Inspectorate which he attempted to get established in 1783.

The Management's proposal, submitted for the inspectors' further consideration, was in itself a continuation of the directive of 1781 to the traders at Holsteinsborg, Christianshåb and Jakobshavn. The Management consequently preferred the form of organisation preferred by Schwabe, and for which he had argued at greatest length. It thus became standard for whaling from stations in the following decades.

In this period whaling was carried on from the stations at Godhavn Næs (1782-1802); from three stations on Arveprinsens Ejland: Ritenbenk, Igdlutsiaq (1783-1804), and Klokkerhuk (most often called by the name of the island, Arveprinsens Ejland) (1784-1805); from Isefjord Station (at Claushavn) (1780-1826); from Kronprinsens Ejland; in Egedesminde district: from Hunde Ejland (1787 seq.), and later also from Vester Ejland. In the southern district of Egedesminde, it was attempted to profit from whale carcasses which washed ashore, for which reasons the station at Rifcol, near Agto, among others, was established. At Fortune Bay, west of Godhavn, set up in 1778, there was a special system. The ship "Taasinge Slot" was stationed here from 1782 to 1786, partly manned by European crew and with a Frisian whaling commander.[3] The crew was supplemented with hired Greenlandic whalers. The most important aspect of Fortune Bay was the experience which had been gained throughout the years of whaling from land and of mixed whaling crews.

Besides these stations in Disko Bugt, some whaling was attempted off Umanaq Fjord, but it was never reasonably profitable. In addition, there was continuous whaling, as mentioned above, from Holsteinsborg and Qerrortussoq in the Southern Inspectorate. It is difficult to relate anything as to the utility of this reorganisation of whaling. The Royal Greenland Trade's rendering of whale oil in Copenhagen, from 1777 to 1784 averaged 2600 barrels per year. In 1778 and 1781 production was considerably over this average, whereas the other six years it was a few hundred barrels under, being as low as 1725 barrels in 1779. The years from 1780 to 1784 show a relative stability in whale oil production at around 2400 barrels, except for the record year of 1781, with 3459 barrels.[4]

Individual Whaling Stations

The rise and fall of whale oil production, however, reveals nothing of the fortunes and misfortunes of whaling in general or at the individual stations. These fluctuations cannot be followed. It can only be observed that whaling in Greenland, especially in Disko Bay, was slowly expanded according to the approved standards in the years following 1782/83.

As early as 1767, the administration at that time of the General Trading Company ordered C.C. Dalager to attempt whaling at Klokkerhuk at the south-west point of Arveprinsens Ejland.[5] It does not appear that this order was followed. C.C. Dalager was transferred to Jakobshavn in 1771. Perhaps he did carry on some whaling at Arveprinsens Ejland from Jakobshavn with Greenlanders from Jakobshavn. In any case the sons of trader Dalager must have got a comprehensive training in harpooning techniques, for it was with the skill of two of them that he carried on whaling at Klokkerhuk.

Late in the summer of 1782, Schwabe spoke to C.C. Dalager at Christianshåb, where systematic whaling at Klokkerhuk was agreed on. Dalager promised to "attract" the necessary number of Greenlanders to this site and to have his son Jens supervise the whaling. This attempt did not really get underway until the then 58-year-old Dalager had the necessary buildings built and moved to the lodge called Arveprinsens Ejland in 1784. With shifting fortunes, whaling was here carried out in subsequent years. But the same factor made its presence felt in the long run as at many of the other whaling stations: it was a bad site for any other kind of fangst.

On the other hand whaling which had been initiated at Claushavn (in Christianshåb district), had not been blessed with sufficient fortune, so that the Management decided to recall the European whalers. It had turned out that the Greenlandic fangers at Claushavn were eager to engage in whaling at the so-called Isefjord Station by themselves and in the European manner. The trader at Christianshåb, whose jurisdiction extended to Claushavn and the whaling station, promised fluctuating, but in general good profits both for the Trade and the Greenlandic inhabitants. In 1785, therefore, only a carpenter, a cooper and two "sailors" were employed there, exclusively in order that the blubber and baleen could be purchased according to regulations and barrelled, that the baleen could be sorted and packed, and that boats and buildings could be maintained by a competent artisan.

About 15 kilometres farther north on the west coast of the island Arveprinsens Ejland, the whaling station Igdlutsiaq was established in 1783. It too turned out to be a bad site for any other kind of fangst than whaling, and even that was in the long run not sufficiently profitable. The first whaling assistant there was Carl Dorf, son of Johannes Pedersen Dorf, former trader and catechist at Egedesminde, and a Greenlandic woman. The sons of C.C. Dalager, also good whalers, were likewise products of a mixed marriage. In general, the sons of various mixed marriages in Disko Bugt attracted favourable notice as harpooners and leaders in the new organisation of whaling, European style. This confirmed the correctness and reasonableness of the provisions of the Order on the raising and employment of sons of mixed marriages, when they could not be raised up to be "good Greenlanders".

Igdlutsiaq and Klokkerhuk were actually too close to each other, which gave rise to much dissension about harpooned whales which had got away but were later washed ashore, or found by "rivals". This closeness can also have had an unfavourable effect on the catch. Furthermore, these whaling stations were only 11 kilometres south of Zwarte Vogel Bay, to which Ritenbenk had been moved in 1781. In the long run it was not efficient to maintain three stations in this vicinity.

Even before the reorganisation, cooperation with Greenlanders had been tried in whaling at Kronprinsens Ejland. The lodge was set up in 1781 under the leadership of Adam Thorning, and whaling was carried on with stationed crews and ships in the winter. But from 1781 on it seems that this form of whaling was to be abandoned. At least no ships were sent out to carry on winter whaling from the lodge. Assistant Thorning therefore reported in 1782 that he had had a good deal of difficulty keeping the whaling going, because he only had one man to help him; and the local Greenlanders had never caught whales in the European way before, and did not even understand how to put a sloop in proper whaling condition. The two of them had to do all the work, he wrote. It seems, however, that the Greenlandic fangers took part in the whaling proper and gradually also in the preparatory work. They seem to have learned quickly, for later in the year, "thanks be to God they have come so far that every harpooner can now make his equipment ready himself." In partnership they also succeeded in catching as many as four whales! Under various whaling assistants, whaling at Kronprinsens Ejland developed favourably.

The prevalent whaling fever caught on farther south. On several occasions the chief traders at Egedesminde had made efforts to begin whaling operations, especially since Egedesminde, as a colony district, otherwise yielded relatively modest profits, both to the Trade and to its Greenlandic inhabitants. For three years in a row, from 1782 to 1784, the Greenlanders living on Vester Ejland had asked for one or two sloops and some whaling equipment, but in vain. A local epidemic depopulated the island. Therefore whaling plans had to be shelved for some time, as no local experience could be gained.

In 1787 attempts were made at Hunde Ejland north of Egedesminde. They promised well, and from 1788 on whaling was continuously carried on from there. However, the trader at Egedesminde sensed competition from whaling on Kronprinsens Ejland. There were rumours that the whaling assistant there, M.N. Myhlenphort, wanted to set up a kind of partnership between the Greenlanders of Kronprinsens Ejland and those of Hunde Ejland, which would affect the quantity purchased in Egedesminde district. An interesting aspect of this little affair is that at the same time, the trader at Egedesminde was being pressured by the fangers of the colony, who threatened to move to Hunde Ejland unless they, like the Greenlanders there, could rent sloops and whaling equipment, for whaling between the colony and Manîtsoq Island (Bonke Ejland), west of Egedesminde. The trader warned against the move, which would overpopulate Hunde Ejland in relation to its resources. On the other hand, there had been periods of famine at the colony, so that whaling at Manîtsoq ought to be attempted. He mentioned that previously the Dutch had done some very good whaling in those waters, and named as an essential factor that Greenlanders, "where whaling is fully operational, have shown and still show that they far surpass foreign whalers." This agree with other testimonials to the skill of Greenlanders in harpooning whales.

Whaling at Manîtsoq was started the following year under the supervision of the catechist Mathias Aronsen, originally from Holsteinsborg, the son of a stationed carpenter and a Greenlandic woman. He was not the best supervisor one could imagine, and whaling never really got off the ground. Up to 1791, when this attempt was discontinued, only one whale was caught. The year before the catechist had been transferred to Egedesminde colony.

Whaling from the stations on Disko Island yielded a fluctuating profit. It gradually turned out that whaling from Fortune Bay with the ship "Taasinge Slot" was not functioning according to plan. In 1785-1786 both the ship and its crew had to spend the winter at Godhavn. A better base for this form of whaling, a last relic of the past, was therefore considered, but was not found, or rather it was abandoned in 1788, and the station was closed for whaling in 1791. The same situation prevailed here as on Arveprinsens Ejland: whaling stations were too close together and competed for whales; whaling had been carried on from Godhavns Næs since 1782, and from Godhavn itself as well.

Other Aspects of the Reorganisation of Whaling

The competition between the three stations on the south coast of Disko Island deteriorated into dissension between Greenlanders and Danish whalers. This "unfairness, strife, envy and enmity" was perhaps one of the reasons why the whaling catch went down. The only remedy could be found in partnerships between Greenlanders and stationed whalers "for their common interest under the supervision of a just and competent leader." Such a partnership was thus entered into the winter of 1788-1789 between the crew of the "Taasinge Slot" and Greenlandic whalers from Godhavn, under the leadership of the wellknown whaling commander Riewert Boysen.

At Godhavn, the Greenlanders were especially interested in whaling because, as we have seen, the conditions for other kinds of fangst were bad. When luck came their way in the shape of a whale, the threat of hard times was immediately alleviated - at least for some time. Frequent times of need and doubtful fangst opportunities besides whaling made it necessary to distribute European rations to the Greenlandic inhabitants at various times and places. If the whaling failed, hard times came knocking at everyone's door. If food was not distributed, the Greenlanders could not be counted on to go whale watching.

This quite naturally developed into a situation where, for example, Greenlanders who took part in flensing received a sort of payment in kind. For example, at Holsteinsborg in 1787 and 1788 barley groats, field peas and bread were distributed for flensing, preparing sloops and equipment, and whale watching; as a matter of custom, of course. But imported provisions were not only used in such cases. The assistant at Qerrortussoq had, for example, requisitioned some merchandise from Holsteinsborg. It was brought over by three Greenlandic women, who as payment received half a pound of tobacco and one pound of bread each. The consequences of such payment for services rendered, based on custom, will be dealt with later.[6]

Such distribution of provisions was in itself not contrary to the provisions of the Order of 1782, which in Chapter Four, §5, states explicitly that "Danish provisions" may only be distributed to Greenlanders "in times of hunger or disease, or when they are steadily employed by the Trade or are whaling in partnership with Europeans, at a time when they themselves are in need." This clause was intended to limit such distribution, so that the Greenlanders, as stated elsewhere, "should not be spoiled" from their national diet. This was an illusion, however, because Greenlanders employed in whaling could not then carry on other kinds of fangst, even if such fangst were otherwise possible. They and their families were therefore more or less dependent on rations alloted to them. Previous to the Order of 1782, it was customary to distribute provisions at Holsteinsborg as well as at Godhavn (Fortune Bay); one can here characterize the provisions of the Order as an attempt to turn the clock back, which was impossible.

Hard times and the need for provisions could be so compelling that the local inhabitants took matters into their own hands. Sometimes theft and burglary took place in the stores. As we have seen, the various whaling stations afforded little opportunity for ordinary fangst. The need of help was pointed out in 1788 by the trader at Ritenbenk, where a situation of permanent need seems to have developed. In the previous fiscal year (1787-1788), he had expended more than 100 rigsdalers of his own funds for "bread, field peas, barley groats and butter to keep these poor people alive."

In connection with the distribution of provisions as a kind of payment for whaling and during the more or less permanent times of need, we must also discuss the problem of credit. It was necessary to grant Greenlandic whalers a good deal of credit, or the local whaling leader could risk seeing his Greenlanders move away - naturally to places which they knew were better for fangst in general. At times, such credit entailed quite considerable personal losses for the leaders.

The provisions distributed were not always of unexceptionable quality. There were, for example, complaints from Greenlandic whalers that peas "tasted somewhat mouldy". Not that they did not have something to wash them down with. "The harpooners and steerers received distilled spirits and beer as well as bread; but the rowers only got peas, beer and bread," we hear from Holsteinsborg in January 1788.

This was another traditional custom which was continued. Diaries written in Holsteinsborg in 1787–1788 mention frequently, and as a matter of custom, that Greenlanders working at whaling at both Holsteinsborg and Qerrortussoq received distilled spirits and beer. "In the afternoon of 12 December 7 barrels 1⅓ skæppe (997 litres) of malt and 21 pounds of hops were turned over for brewing. Of this malt and hops, 3 barrels of beer are marked for Greenlanders on whale watching."

This beer was not very strong, but the situation with distilled spirits was not so good. It seems that at certain places these were a kind of privilege for harpooners and other skilled persons, but at other places they were given to other mortals. Even the Inspector at Godhavn had to approve the necessity of giving distilled spirits to Greenlanders. Everyone must realize "how hard it is in the spring to get Greenlanders to land the fish which have been caught, and that schnapps is unfortunately the only means of encouraging these people, when the fish has to be landed after a successful catch." Two years later, in 1788, the same inspector felt called upon to thunder against drunkenness at Godhavn, this time in direct connection with the public brewing of beer. This weak beer had, then, as later became well-known, an intoxicating effect.

Whaling and especially the long whale watches were hard work, and demanded a considerable number of calories. It was also dangerous work. In letters and diaries of the period can be found many examples of the almost daily risk one was exposed to. An especially sad story comes from Godhavn in 1786. The catechist Jonas, who besides being a good catechist was also a skilful harpooner, was in 1783 for his double skill recommended for receiving each year half of the provisions needed by an ordinary man. Finally in 1786 this was granted, but he never enjoyed the provisions. The same year, at Godhavn Næs, during an attempt to land the sloops of the station in a storm, he "was hurled into the sea by violent breakers over the cliffs, along with 4 sloops, and there perished."

Whaling assistant Carl Dorf tells of a frightful whale watch on 22 April 1783. It is most clear in his own words: "It is my humble duty to report to the exalted Management what happened to us on 22 April of the past winter, when our luck was very bad, for when I went out on a whale watching with 4 sloops the weather was very good, but around 4 o'clock a horrible storm came from the south-west, with snow flurries and much ice, so that you could not see the least bit, so all hope of saving our lives was gone. A Dane by the name of Techel Jonsen was thrown out of a sloop by the sea and pressed down by a big icefloe so he had to remain there. Two Greenlanders were crushed between the sloops and the ice by the frightfully turbulent sea; one could not move but had to despair of his life, we covered him as best we could and had to leave him. The other got away somewhat but was so wet and exhausted by frost and cold that he died. A Greenlander by the name of Paul lost two fingers of his right hand between the sloops and the ice edges. The sloops we were in were crushed so quickly we were all in the sea and swam. I was the last one left and floated among the crushed sloops until with great difficulty a rope was thrown to me and I was pulled up."

This tale seems to have certain defects in its inner logic, but if even some of it is true, it presents a horrible enough picture. The very fact that it is officially reported shows that such events were relatively infrequent. But still it gives one an impression of the dangers inherent in whaling. The dangers of the life of a fanger were not unknown to Greenlanders; traditional umiak whaling was also dangerous.

During the period up to 1788, alongside the "new" whaling method, whaling was still carried on in umiaks, although opportunities for building and maintaining them were poor because of the bad sealing at the whaling stations: they were covered with sealskin. For several reasons, the Management of the Royal Greenland Trade was not interested in supporting this method. It was difficult to maintain due to the lack of hides. Umiak whaling was considered unprofitable both for the Greenlanders and for the Trade. Umiaks had one advantage in that they were silent; on the other hand they were quite fragile. It was difficult to pursue a harpooned whale in them because they were sensitive to wind, weather, and ice. Too much of the catch, including harpooned whales, were lost. Nor from the point of view of profit was it fortunate that in umiak whaling the Greenlandic inhabitants disposed over the entire catch. In this case far too much was wasted to no earthly use, either for the Greenlanders or for the Trade. Besides, illicit trading was an old nightmare for the Trade. If the catch were under no control, it could be traded with foreigners, or even with the crews of stationed ships, so that the administration preferred whaling to be carried on with rented sloops and whaling equipment rather than in umiaks. The development among the Greenlanders themselves was also pointing in that direction, mostly because they understood the greater risk to life and to limb of umiak whaling as well as the lesser certainty of profit involved in it. Umiak whaling was quietly ousted in the competition with the European method. Umiak whaling was also exempted from the (small) bounties for whales caught.

Skilful umiak whalers took employment in European whaling. An allotment list of the whalers at Godhavn, for example, mentions "Korisinna an Angekok, is good at old-fashioned Greenlandic whaling by means of superstition." It is possible that this unconverted Greenlander, of which there were many at both Godhavn and Fortune Bay stations, was not an umiak whaler, but took part in European whaling, and used his talents as a shaman before and during the hunt. Around 1788 the new method was in full blossom at all the whaling stations.

It therefore seems a bit out of date that the 77-year-old Poul Egede in 1785 proposed that the Management of the Royal Greenland Trade carry on whaling "with the natives of the country, without the help of Europeans." Development in that direction was already in progress, but European leadership could not be dispensed with. That he at the same time requested the removal of Inspector Olrik is due to the systematic persecution by this potentate of the Egede family. The previous year the old man had sent in six harpoons which he had had made, and which he thought were better than those which had been used so far. Most likely they were made on the model of Niels Egede's so-called double harpoon. They were shipped out for testing, but nothing was later heard of the results of the test. Plenty of complaints were heard later, however, about the shipping of poorly forged harpoons. C.C. Dalager, the trader at Arveprinsens Ejland, constructed another kind of double harpoon, in the form of two harpoons on a fork-shaped shaft, but it was hard to get them into the whales. The ordinary harpoons which were shipped to Greenland had a tendency to break when jabbed into the whale. It must have been possible to get better harpoons; foreign whalers off Greenland had far better ones than those from the Royal Greenland Trade and the harpoonsmith in Copenhagen. He advised improving the quality of harpoons, because it would be difficult to get the Greenlandic whalers really interested in whaling if they constantly lost their whales due to poor equipment. This is but one further proof of the "quality consciousness" of the Greenlanders towards the merchandise they were shipped.

The reorganisation of whaling went its laborious way. The picture presented by Inspector Schwabe in the report he delivered when he was recalled in 1787 was probably too optimistic and too summary: "Instead of insecure umiak whaling, and instead of whaling with wintering ships, the Greenlanders now conduct whaling in the European manner with the help of a few Europeans who mainly serve to land the catch and inspect the whaling equipment. They have acquired such skill that they throw their harpoons better than our whalers, and as well as the best Englishman. This is one of the most important aspects of whaling, as the fish often leaves before one can get close enough to put the harpoon in."

Johan Fr. Schwabe did not understand - and could hardly be expected to have a keen eye for - the fact that by reorganising whaling, the Royal Greenland Trade had exercised the greatest direct interference so far in the economy of Northwest Greenland, especially in Disko Bugt. During the same period other interferences were also made, some of which developed rather slowly. To a much greater extent than previously, The Trade had now entered into production in Greenland itself. This also manifested itself in other fields.

From 1782 to 1788, other noteworthy events, innovations and changes of development took place in other areas. These will be dealt with in context, for the entire period of 1782 to 1808. The change of government in Denmark in 1784, however, threw the problems of Greenland into a new phase.

The "Norway-Monument" in the park of Fredensborg Palace, North Sealand, Denmark. It was formed in 1765-66 by the Danish artist *Johannes Wiedewelt*. The female figure in the centre holds an escutcheon bearing the Norwegian lion. The four medallions on plints show from the left: the bearing of the Scandinavian Union (the three crowns), Iceland's stockfish, Greenland's polar bear and the Faroes' ram.

(Photo F. Gad, April 1976)

The Greenland medallion in the "Norway-Monument" supported by crossed bundles of harpoons with lines on, and the mouth of a swivel gun.

(Photo F. Gad, April 1976)

PLATE II

Johan Friederich Schwabe. Copy of oil painting, signed "Painted in August in the year 1795 by Fr. Petersen".

(After H. Ostermann *Nordmænd på Grønland* II, plate 53)

"The Inspector's residence at Godthaab after its original arrangement." Survey drawn about 1850.

(Library of the Royal Academy of Fine Arts, Copenhagen, Collection of Architectural Drawings, A8515, o; scale much reduced)

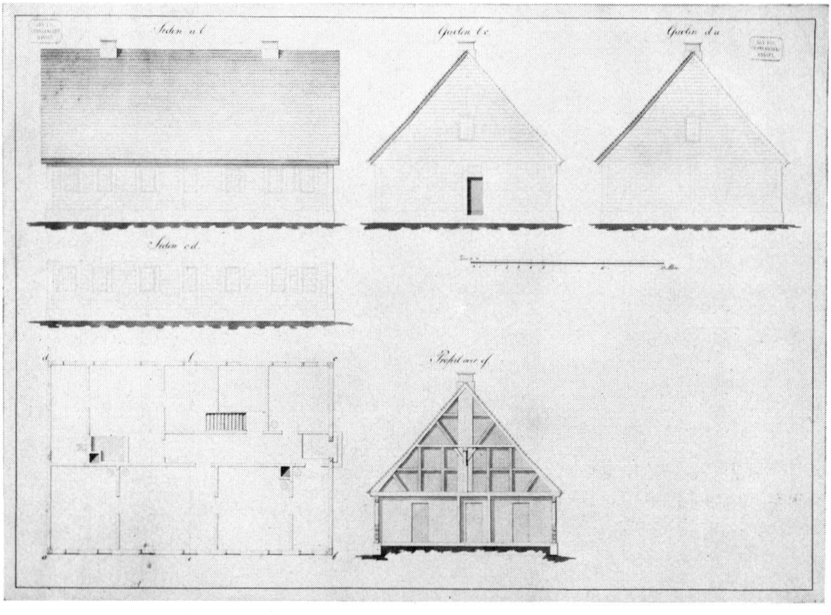

IV. The Commission of 1788

The Change of Government and the Royal Greenland Trade

On 14 April 1784, the so-called court revolution took place at Christiansborg Palace in Copenhagen. Guldberg's semi-cabinet administration was eliminated by a veritable coup. New, reform-oriented men, with Crown Prince Frederik as the top figure, became the helmsmen of the ship of state. Their policy for the twin realms signified a fundamental change from the past. The Konseil regained its central importance. The new government seemingly put its hand at once to a new reform programme. The lesser reforms came first; more important ones had to await the necessary preparations and consultations.

Guldberg's semi-cabinet administration had gradually grown up since 1772. In spite of certain reforms, it was enormously reactionary, especially in the context of the political and economic ideas of the time, which had manifested themselves in Western Europe for twenty years and across the Atlantic had found expression in the Declaration of Independence of the United States of America. Liberalism, humanism, respect for man and the fundamental rights of man, freedom from unjust coercion for both the individual and for economic life: these are well-known watchwords which together express this political ideology. Manifested outside France and the United States, however, this ideology did not bring about a democratization, but seems to have been incorporated into the autocratic system, so that it eased its way over into what was called "enlightened despotism". Properly speaking, it was this form of autocracy Struensee (1770–72) introduced into Denmark-Norway, but in a not very fortunate manner.

In the field of economy, the new government intended to terminate the previous policy of mercantilism. That Guldberg's regime had here been infected with corruption was one thing. The old-fashioned economic rules had far too extensively been followed in principle. One company after the other had been set up, and new projects had been completed, all with more or less open state support. The state had finally had to take over several enterprises. Some trade enterprises had been doomed from the start and had only been able to flourish hectically and lead an inflated existence on the basis of the war markets, which were favourable for neutral countries. Others were somewhat better consolidated or had a special position within the realms. Among the latter was the Royal Greenland Trade.

From a liberalistic point of view, the new government would have to oppose the maintenance of Guldberg's mercantilistic enterprises, and seek to disengage the state from them, so they would have to stand on their own feet or fall.

It is an established fact that for many reasons, the new leaders did not take harsh measures. On the other hand, they considered it their task to clean up the economic attic which Danish-Norwegian production and trade had become. It is characteristic of the new government that in the very year in which they acceeded to power they delivered a blow to the whaling monopoly of the Royal Greenland Trade. In October 1784 a royal notice was issued which actually demonopolized whaling and sealing in the Davis Stræde, at Svalbard and Jan Mayen. At the same time they showed moderation in not suddenly abolishing the privileges and subsidies of the monopoly, but rather extending them to anyone who wanted to conduct whaling or sealing. In other words, they watered down the monopoly so that free competition could be decisive. So much was retained of previous economic practice; the state did not immediately abandon all support of business.

This rather softened encouragement of private whaling actually entailed a slight advantage for the Royal Greenland Trade. For a reasonable payment private whalers could according to the notice, purchase items from the Trade's stocks of barrels and whaling equipment, deposited after the winding up in 1781 of the great whaling project. It was not possible for the newly-established local whaling operations in Greenland to use up this surplus materiel, so that it was a good idea to get rid of the stocks.

Although this materiel could be paid for in future deliveries of whale oil or blubber, it was apparently not sufficiently alluring – nor were the other privileges of various kinds proffered by the royal notice. Apparently no private whaling was started, at least not in Greenlandic waters. In the period subsequent to 1784, the market was not exactly favourable to new trading enterprises. The Executive Manager of the Iceland Trade, Carl Pontoppidan, attempted, however, to advocate them.[1] In a little book published in 1785 he encouraged the formation of private whaling companies, mentioning the prize-paper responses of Andreas Henrik Stibolt, a Navy civil servant, to the Agricultural Society in 1773 and 1774 concerning the formation of such capital partnerships. Pontoppidan thus tried to revive the times before the Guldberg administration had revealed its true reactionary nature – approximately as far back as Crown Prince Frederik had done that 14 April 1784 at Christiansborg.[2] Presumably Pontoppidan did this consciously; it is somehow symptomatic of the spirit of the times: a parenthesis was to be placed around the Guldberg administration.

Between 1774 and 1784 the state's great whaling project had knocked the private entrepreneurs quite off their feet. The prize papers of the Agricultural Society had had a liberalistic intention, which was smothered. The so far rather stable "Greenland Sealing Company", of Korsør (Denmark), gave up in advance in December 1775, faced with the state project. In February of the following year it sold its ship to the state. Now ten years later private initiative was to be if not quite enthroned, at least revived. This could not be accomplished at one blow, at least not in Danish-Norwegian whaling. In 1787 Hartvig Marcus Frisch, the Executive Manager of the Royal Greenland Trade and one Donner, a representative of the Herring Company at Altona, could observe that "experience had shown private shipowners in Denmark and Norway would not enter into this trade, in spite of the considerable bounty offered in 1784," directly referring to the royal notice and the step taken by the government towards liberalism which it signified.

The Commission of 1788 Is Established

Frisch and Donner brought this "experience" to the attention of the government to support a proposal that the Herring Company at Altona and the Royal Greenland Trade be merged into one enterprise. The real reason for their suggestion was, however, "that whaling, which is of extreme importance, will be better encouraged by such an institution."

This recommendation was submitted to the Finanskollegium, which hesitated to follow its suggestions. The Finanskollegium thought that the desired capital subvention was too great, and that the profits would not sufficiently cover depreciation and interest. "In conclusion, it cannot be presumed that the main objective of this trade and fishery, namely, increasing the national product, can be attained as easily with such an institution as if the same business were conducted by private traders, who can make use of all their local and personal advantages." This argument could well have been taken from Adam Smith's economic masterpiece *The Wealth of Nations,* 1776.

During discussions of the Royal Greenland Trade's freedom from customs duties for imported goods, The Royal West Indian and Guinean Finance and General Customs Administration had in 1782 proposed the abolition of the Royal Greenland Trade. This was already implied in the formulation of the directive of 2 July 1781, in which the duration of the entire system was set down as 30 years, but in which the state was obliged to take over all the properties of the merged "Trades" at their appraised value when they went out of business. The said Finance and Customs Administration was apparently thinking in more "modern" terms by 1782, when the mercantilistic administration of Guldberg still existed; so that in theoretical discussions there can be observed a slight schism between the government and at least a part of the financial administration of the realms.

Liberalistic policies prevailed in other areas of the northern trade, but were carried out leniently. In late August of 1786 a royal notice was issued demonopolizing the Iceland Trade, and in early September of the following year the same took place for the Finmark Trade. Of the four "Trades" which were merged in 1781, it now, six years after their merger, appeared that only two, the Greenland Trade and the Faroese Trade, would continue. And what fate was intended for them? This question must have occupied their respective managers from 1786–1787 on, and given them a feeling of insecurity. The thirty-year "concession" of the directive of 1781 could apparently be abolished by the stroke of a pen. Frisch and Donner's proposal of 1787 should also be seen in this context.

The Finanskollegium was obviously prepared to promote free competition. In 1787 four Danish shipowners proposed to take over all whaling off Greenland in partnership, but the Finanskollegium would not agree, because they wanted more and smaller shipping firms, and wanted the offer to purchase the ships of the Royal Greenland Trade to be extended so "that the offer of these ships to all the subjects of His Majesty everywhere shall be an encouragement to whaling in Norway, which in many aspects is more convenient therefore than any other country." This was the immediate background for the representation to the King of 8 January 1788, in which the Finanskollegium proposed the appointment of a committee to collect all necessary information and calculations dealing with the present state of the Royal Greenland Trade, and thereafter submit a report on whether it would be liquidated and the Greenland trade demonopolized and if not, submit a plan according to which the Greenland trade would be continued by the state. This representation was of course inspired by the new men at the head of the Finanskollegium, first and foremost Christian D. Reventlow.

The King, i.e., the Crown Prince and the Konseil, agreed the following day to appoint the commission immediately. It was to be composed of the managers of the Royal Greenland Trade, the members of the Iceland Trade Liquidation Commission of 1787, Inspector Johan Fr. Schwabe, as well as certain top figures. The members of the commission were thus, in addition to Schwabe, Christian D. Reventlow (Finanskollegium and Rentekammer), H.E. Schimmelmann (Finanskollegium and Økonomi- og Kommercekollegium) member of the Konseil, and later Finance Minister), The former prefect of Iceland L.A. Thodal (member of the Iceland Trade Liquidation Commission, and head of the Iceland, Greenland and Faroese office in the Rentekammer), Jacob Edvard Colbiørnsen (professor of law and a deputy in the Rentekammer), Fr. Martini (since 1782 executive co-manager of the Royal Greenland Trade), Hartvig Marcus Frisch (executive manager of the Royal Greenland Trade), Carl Pontoppidan (member of the Iceland Trade Liquidation Commission, and finally Christian U.D. von Eggers (an economist, professor of law, and inter alia a member of the Iceland Trade Liquidation Commission).

Of these persons, Christian D. Reventlow was well-known as one of the men behind the change of government and probably the greatest prime mover in the great Agriculture Commission of 1786, a humanist zealous for reforms, and a landowner who fought for the liberation of the peasants and various other liberalistic reforms. Jacob Edv. Colbiørnsen was likewise a reform-minded member of the Agriculture Committee, of which his brother, the brilliant lawyer Christian Colbiørnsen, was the very active secretary. H.E. Schimmelmann, also known to be one of the personalities involved in the change of government, excelled in financial matters. He has been characterized as a man "permeated with the humanism of the times," and was moderately reform-oriented in a liberal direction. Christian U.D. von Eggers was not only a brilliant scholar of constitutional law, but also in practice a splendid organiser and economist. Before he became co-manager of the Royal Greenland Trade, Fr. Martini had held certain court offices of a financial nature. His membership, as a manager in the Trade, was, as was that of H.M. Frisch, determined in advance by the mandate of the commission. Likewise, the participation of Carl Pontoppidan and Prefect Thodal, as members of the Iceland Trade Liquidation Commission, was also laid down by the mandate.[3]

The qualifications of these members of the commission are themselves an expression of the commissions's actual objective. It was apparently implicit that it would reach a liberalistic result. Among its members, only Schwabe, Frisch and Martini could defend the previous policy in Greenland and thus the monopoly and the state's continuation of the Trade. It was therefore so much the stranger that the commission concluded by coming to the opposite result of what had implicitly been desired.

One thing was the personal claim of the members to participation in the commission - their theoretical economic and political background. Something else again was the knowledge they possessed of Greenland and conditions there. Here we can observe that actually only one of the members, Inspector Schwabe, was personally familiar with conditions in Greenland. The Executive Manager H.M. Frisch had never set foot on the rocky soil of Greenland, but he did have some experience from his office. The same, but to a somewhat lesser degree, must have applied to Fr. Martini. None of the others had any profound knowledge of these conditions.

It is further characteristic of the bureaucratic autocracy that no one serving in Greenland was appointed to the commission. Inspector Schwabe had actually resigned. Nor was a thought given to various persons who had worked for the Trade in Greenland but who in 1788 were employed by it in Copenhagen. Of course the government did not even consider any employees of the Mission; the Trade exclusively was to be investigated. There was no question of taking a look at activities in Greenland as a whole.

The First Year of the Commission

It might seem like an admission of lack of knowledge that in the representation by the Finanskollegium to the King, as well as in the royal decree establishing the commission, the first task of the commission was to "make a detailed investigation into the state of the Trade." This survey was to be submitted to the Rentekammer, but was probably just as much intended as a collection of necessary information for the use of the committee members, without which they would be unable to form their opinions on the problems involved.

In early February 1788 the committee convened and began its work. It was of course the task of the Royal Greenland Trade to collect the necessary information. Schwabe presented a relatively detailed report which he had actually written in September 1787.

The most curious aspect of Inspector Schwabe's report in its first form is that it concludes with a short defense of continuing the Trade under state control. He had formulated his report as a short description and evaluation of conditions before 1782, in sharp contrast to those prevailing thereafter. In it he briefly denigrated the trade enterprises previous to the issuance of the Order of 1782, including the first years of the Royal Greenland Trade, but emphasized on the other hand how contrastingly efficient and promising the last five years under the Trade (and especially under the inspectors) had been. He listed all the positive aspects of the activity of this relatively short period, and concluded: "These and many other important advantages would be lost if this trade were either completely demonopolized (in which case considerable difficulties would appear) or the colonies were leased out to private traders. The good state of the country at present would cease along with the new arrangements, and the Greenlanders would flock to those places where for the products of their country they could receive payment in European provisions: coffee, tea, distilled spirits and items of luxury. Lavishness, poverty, and a striking decline of population, leading to ruin, would then be the consequences of entrusting the simple and ignorant Greenlanders to the selfish treatment of independent businessmen; and in time, the King, moved by the miserable condition of his Greenlandic subjects, would take back the trade in a deplorable state."

Schwabe continued: "If these arrangements thus continue (to exist: i.e., the Order of 1782, the offices of inspector, the various whaling stations and colony posts, as well as the Royal Greenland Trade, under the supervision of the state), if the properties of the Trade are reduced in the accounts to their true value, if the ships are used for their actual purpose, and everything here is done in the most thrifty manner, I am not only certain that the Royal Greenland Trade will be able to balance its books, which it has actually done in recent years, since its deficit is solely due to previous speculative trade, but I have good reason to hope that it will earn a quite considerable profit."

This report has been quoted in such detail because the activity of the commission was thus decisively shifted right in the beginning. Even before the commission was planned, Schwabe must have had an inkling of what was in the wind, and thus formulated his report, later submitted to the committee, as a defence of the "arrangements" he himself had helped to create. There is no doubt that this emotional plea, especially with its warm defence of the protective function of the monopoly towards the "simple and ignorant" Greenlanders, had its effect on the other members of the committee. If Schwabe's words were not so common in the prose of

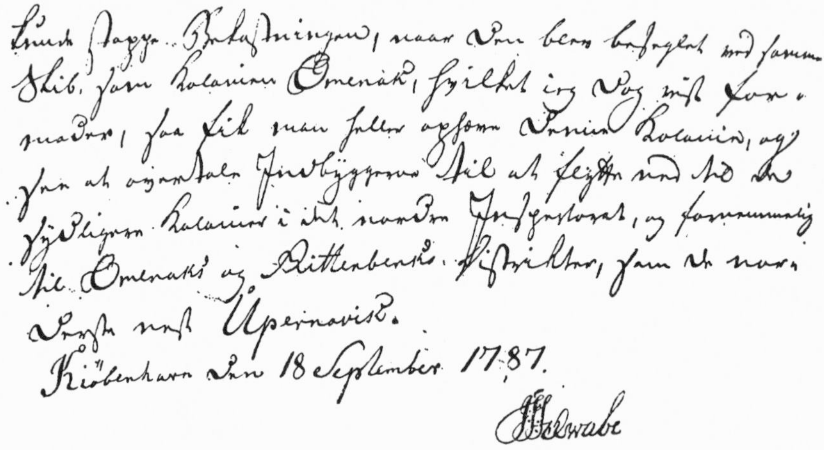

("If, however, Upernavik, the northernmost of the Greenlandic colonies, cannot) cover its expenses when visited by the same ship as the colony of Omenak, which I however presume, then it would be better to discontinue this colony, and attempt to convince its inhabitants to move down to the more southern colonies of the Northern Inspectorate, especially to the districts of Omenak and Rittenbenk, which are the most northern ones after Upernavik.

Copenhagen, 18 September 1787
J.F. Schwabe"

The last page of Schwabe's report of 18 September 1787 (reduced size).

the day, one might be tempted to compare them with the formulations used by Hans Egede; they are in any case expressions of the same sympathetic frame of mind.

Schwabe's report and emotional words did not make the commission tack and change course at once, but it was considered so important that it was immediately circulated among the members for further study. Behind the dry resolution to circulate it we can faintly perceive Reventlow and Schimmelmann's surprise at this unexpected and, for the economic leitmotif of the government, disturbing report, which in addition, was formulated in precisely the same direct and clear style that Reventlow himself cast his reports and letters in, and was just as emotional.

It was, however, resolved "that Professor Eggers, as soon as the calculations are submitted, is to draft a plan for turning the trade over to private entrepreneurs in such a manner that the misgivings expressed by the Kammerraad (Schwabe) can as far as possible be precluded."

The same resolution ventilated the idea of demonopolizing whaling and sealing, but keeping the Royal Greenland Trade and its monopoly for the colonies. This not only suggests a certain uneasiness about the expediency of the actual objective of the commission, but must also have seemed quite impossible to the managers of the Trade. Whaling was integrated into the activity of the colonies: completely in the Northern Inspectorate, partly in the Southern. In connection with this idea in the resolution, the possibilities of selling the whaling ships were to be investigated.

This appears from Inspector Schwabe's next contribution, which to judge by its introduction was directly instigated by the final clause of the above resolution. Schwabe thought that whaling around Svalbard (probably including Jan Mayen) must be considered a different institution from whaling in Davis Stræde. The former could without difficulty be split off and demonopolized. Perhaps it would also be possible to split off whaling in Davis Strait from the Trade, but on this point he had greater misgivings. At least he doubted whether the 12 whaling ships owned by the Trade could be sold so easily, and all at once. One of his misgivings about such a sudden sale was the unemployment, during a bad market for shipping, which would be forced on the 500 employees on these ships.

The operation of these ships, said Schwabe, was woven into the expenses of the colonies, which would cost a lot more without them. They were to a great extent used to supply the colonies and to ship their products back to Denmark. From this point of view, he must have thought that whaling should be expanded.

Consequently, it is uncertain whether Schwabe meant that whaling from the stations in Greenland should be included in whaling in Davis Stræde, especially as he explicitly mentioned the function of the whaling ships in supplying the colonies.

Furthermore, Schwabe did not believe that the whaling ships could be easily and quickly sold during the prevalent bad economic conditions for shipping. Shipowners had apparently preferred to lay their ships up rather than take their chances in whaling, even after the royal notice of 1784. For that reason Schwabe made four proposals: "1. The ships should not be sold until it could be certain they could be used in whaling; 2. their value ought to be written down; 3. trade and whaling (and here he obviously means whaling on the open sea) should he split off; and 4. the future system (probably meaning for the trade) had to be laid down." In conclusion he expressed his fear that the Royal Greenland Trade would have to keep the worst of the ships as unsaleable.

The commission seems henceforth to have put the sale of the whaling ships on ice for the time being. On the other hand, their possible sale must be prepared. Schwabe's misgivings and the clear desire of the majority of the commission to liquidate the whaling fleet must have led to discussions about greater powers for the commission. The royal decree of 2 April 1788 thus ordered the commission to deal with the current affairs of the Royal Greenland Trade. The Management of the Trade was thus instructed to submit every dealing of whatever size to the commission, which assumed the role of the former General Board of Directors, perhaps to an even greater extent.

During the course of 1788 some of the ships were thus offered for sale. The commission thus functioned as a kind of "liquidation commission" like that appointed for the Iceland and Finmark trade. In late October, two ships were sold; but Schwabe's express desire that they should be reserved for whaling was not fulfilled. One of them was to be used for sailing to Iceland, the other to certain Norwegian ports.

Meanwhile the administration of the Royal Greenland Trade was collecting the necessary material for a survey of the state of the Trade, as prescribed in the committee's mandate. As the basis of further discussion and evaluation of the situation, more certain knowledge of the number of inhabitants in the known part of Greenland was necessary. In 1787, a more or less reliable census had just been taken in Denmark, but not in other parts of the realms. The Greenland census of 1776 had been ordered, but had petered out.[4] There were no figures available.

Orders were now sent to all traders and chief assistants to collect "an exact knowledge of the inhabitants, baptized as well as unbaptized" in each district. The administration wanted lists with total figures distributed as to sex, age, and residence. It fully realized that a meticulously accurate counting and distribution could not be expected. If, for example, the traders could not get exact figures from places distant from the centres of the districts, they would have to be content with the most reasonable guesses." Without daring to give instructions to the missionaries in this connection, the Management expressed its hope that they would cooperate. The final results of the census were not expected until 1789.

Carl Pontoppidan's Report and Schwabe's Critique

Meanwhile, the reports of the various members of the commission began to come in. The first was that of Carl Pontoppidan, dated 10 July 1788. It was based on each of the three main themes of the commissions's mandate.

1. *The demonopolization of the Greenland trade.* This he most definitely advised against at the present time. It would be disadvantageous to the Greenlandic inhabitants as well as to the "treasury of the King or the state". The Greenlanders were too uncivilized. They were not settled, and there were neither law nor authorities in the country. There were, of course, the inspectors, but "the combination of these offices under the present arrangement of the monopolistic trade can never exercise a good influence on the character and mentality of this people." By "the combination of these offices" he apparently meant that the inspectors were at one and the same time royal civil servants and subject to the Royal Greenland Trade. Pontoppidan further pointed out that the use of money and currency was unknown in Greenland.

For these and several other reasons it was "impossible to entrust such a far away stretch of land to complete free trade without a preparation of at least 6 or perhaps 10 years." During this period the deficiencies he mentioned could be remedied. A "more natural arrangement of trade than the monopolistic" and the remedying of the above-mentioned deficiencies should develop the Greenlanders towards a money economy, saving, the acquisition of movable and immovable property, and not least settled residence.

2. *Turning the Greenland trade over to private traders.* This he also advised against. Too hasty a transition from "coercion of monopoly trade" to free trade would "be very damaging and dangerous for the basic state of the country." If, however, this change were to be decided, then trade and navigation should take place from cities in Norway. Whaling would be able to pay its own way since it had "an actual internal surplus," which he unconvincingly attempted to demonstrate.

3. If it should be decided to continue the Greenland trade as a royal enterprise, a heavy capital subvention would be needed. Expenses would have to be reduced. The number of "Danish workers and consumers" would have to be limited. "The natives of the country itself" should get intensive training instead, not only in whaling but also in appropriate crafts. This training could take place in Greenland, or, for example, in Norway as well.

These are the essentials of Pontoppidan's not very comprehensive report. What remains is not especially innovative or enlightening; some of it will appear in Schwabe's critique, which will be summarized later. On balance, Pontoppidan's recommendations bear witness to a rather superficial knowledge of the conditions and opportunities of Greenland. Here one must immediately come to his defence by wondering how he could have got a deeper knowledge. His views were of necessity theoretical, since he could not draw on his experiences from Iceland.

Schwabe of course set on the obvious weaknesses of Pontoppidan's recommendation. He quite disagreed with him that the Greenlanders should be settled, that a legal code and a secular authority not linked to the monopoly trade were necessary, that money should be introduced, that Greenlanders were being "corrupted" by the present system, or that they should learn agriculture. This last suggestion had actually been seriously made by Pontoppidan, at the same time as he ventilated the old idea of settling Icelandic and Norwegian families in Greenland as fishers and farmers (cattle raisers). This was also opposed by Schwabe. He furthermore disparaged Pontoppidan's calculations on the economy of the Trade, and most purgently countered the idea that "the employees of the Trade oppressed the Greenlanders by infringement of their rights when trading." He found it unproven that the state derived any advantage from the Greenland trade, and did not consider it beneficial "to train the natives of the country to be workers at the colonies;" that would be taking them away from their most important occupations: hunting and fangst. He denied, finally, that the condition of the Greenlanders was worse than that of other peoples.

Only on one point did Schwabe agree with Pontoppidan. They both pleaded for a continuation of the Mission; but Schwabe went even further: he wanted it to be more solidly organised, for Danish catechists to be stationed, and desired better one-year training in Greenland itself of the missionaries as curates. Finally, he wished something previously unheard of from the Trade: for the so-called "national" catechists: i.e., catechists of Greenlandic descent to "obtain such conditions that they can live without want and work with pleasure."

By far the most points, Schwabe was negative toward Pontoppidan's views. Compared with Schwabe's own report presented at the first meeting of the commission in February, his critique in some places gives the impression that he is arguing against his own better judgment. His critical remarks exist only in a short account in the minutes, but in that form his statements leave the impression of a sharp almost indignant defence of the monopoly and the policies carried out so far in Greenland, at least after 1782, Schwabe was apparently playing the role of the devil's advocate. Did his previous connection with the fallen potentate Ove Høegh-Guldberg influence him, so that he in some way felt obliged to defend the system which he himself, in agreement with Guldberg, had created? This is a question which cannot be answered, but which one can not help asking.

In conclusion Schwabe dealt directly with the system of 1782. The account in the minutes summarizes his view concisely: "From what the Kammerraad (Schwabe) has said here and what he presented in his recommendation of 11 February 1788, he draws these conclusions:
1. that a proper free trade can by no means exist in Greenland.
2. that leasing the country to unfamiliar or private interests will contribute to the decline of the population and finally bring about their ruin;
3. that the arrangement of the present Trade, as introduced in 1782, is the most perfect and best."

The former inspector took a clearly conservative position. It is only strange - judging from the account - that he did not to a much greater extent agree with and support Pontoppidan's arguments against demonopolization.

Reactions in Greenland

"In letters from my friends I have this year got news of a rumour which makes me tremble. A storm is brewing over Greenland," wrote Schwabe's successor as the Inspector of North Greenland, J.C. Wille. In his typical pathetic style, he painted for the Management a picture of the most distressful future for Greenland, in the event of demonopolization. "Good God, can it be true! Then luxury and lechery will quite ruin the country and annihilate all industry." Free trade or the leasing of the colonies would entail the empoverishment of the Greenlanders in few years, and when there was no more to acquire, the free traders or leasers would leave the country, abandoning it to its fate. "The poor Greenlanders must then, as incompetent and lecherous people, roam without help or solace and freeze and starve to death." Actually, these were arguments which Schwabe himself had used, couched in a far more sober style. Wille gave free rein to his quill pen and exclaimed: "Oh, my dear country, is this to be my fate? Nay, thou hast men to whom thy King has entrusted rule over thee, and they will free thee from the threat of misfortune." This was a rather direct invitation to the Management to hamper the commission in its work.

It is again doubtful whether the Management was enthusiastic about such support. Although Wille, in his fear of what could take place, painted the same picture of the future as that called forth by Schwabe, it is hardly likely that the Management could make use of such passages, deprived as they were of factual arguments.

As such, Wille's reaction was characteristic. The Management of the Trade had not bothered to send any notice to Greenland of the appointment of the commission. It was not uncommon that in Greenland one only found out about one or another important innovation in Denmark through the inscrutable paths of rumour. In some way it is also understandable that Wille did not dare to present any real arguments, for he did not really know what he was arguing against. So he resorted to rhetoric.

It appears obvious from the lack of comment from Greenland on the appointment of the commission that knowledgeable persons there were biding their time. A personality such as C.C. Dalager at Arveprinsens Ejland sensed the faint gleam of dawn; he spied the possibility of returning to the freedom of former times for traders in the colonies. The majority prudently refrained from commenting on the event.

Wille's fear, coupled with the general silence, may have been an expression of the same feeling of insecurity which prevailed in Greenland from 1779 to 1881, when the two young controllers were travelling around in Disko Bugt.[5] Was a new change in the offing, now that the system of 1782 had gradually begun to function, and developments were proceeding excellently?

Further Developments in the Commission

Both Copenhagen and Greenland would gradually learn of the influence of the commission. In 1788, it was as yet obvious only in a few matters of principle. A single affair which extended to more than Greenland was inherited by the commission from the now deceased General Board of Directors.

This affair involved the foreign policy of the realms of the Danish King, and dealt with relations to foreign, especially English whalers off the coasts of Greenland. The arrival of their ships with their motley crews had sparked off a number of unpleasant incidents. The visits of these ships to Greenlandic ports, intercourse between their crews and Greenlanders (which could entail unfortunate consequences including undisguised trading), and especially the depletion made by the whalers in the whale and seal catches as well as in the collection of eiderdown – all of these factors were violations of the monopoly and fell under the concept of illicit trading. Both Schwabe in his time, and from 1786 on especially Inspector

Wille, had pointed out the many unfortunate aspects and the powerlessness of the inspectors to prevent or counter them.

This matter was, however, but part of a long development both before and after 1788, which will be dealt with later in context. It is only mentioned here to relate it to the work of the commission in its first year.

The Foreign Office - and thus the Foreign Minister A.P. Bernstorff - was involved in this matter in 1787, but had partly dismissed it and left it to the Management of the Royal Greenland Trade to take measures to defend the rights of the crown in Greenland. This the Management did not dare to do, but handed over the matter to the General Board of Directors, and thus eventually to the committee. It was then decided to supply the colonies and whaling stations in Disko Bugt with light arms which could be used for defence.

Schwabe had misgivings about this measure; he thought that "caution and wisdom are the surest weapons in Greenland," also when dealing with foreigners. He certainly must have realized that the inspector as well as the individual colony employees, who might be exposed to a situation of acute conflict with foreigners, and the Management of the Royal Greenland Trade, would not get much support from the Foreign Office if a conflict was ever brought up to so high a level. And at that time there was some danger that it could be. The commission thus urged caution in this delicate matter of principle, which naturally was reflected in the directives of the Trade to the inspector.

Enough here of this matter, which is a clear example of how the commission, after the mandate extension of 1 April 1788, functioned as a General Board of Directors: here in proper collaboration with the Foreign Office. In such a case the authority of the commission entailed an alleviation of the responsibility of the Trade, because the commission at this time was in a better position to communicate with the Foreign Office and its powerful head.

The question of selling the whaling ships, which presumably was the actual reason for extending the commission's powers, took in August 1788 a turn which further intensified the activity of the commission as a General Board of Directors. Professor Eggers presented a number of proposals concerning the ships and their equipment.

Eggers suggested first to direct the Royal Greenland Trade expressly to stop the equipping of ships for winter whaling in 1788-1789. Secondly, the chartering of supply ships should be done through public bidding, not by private treaties. Thirdly, the Management of the Trade should be required to get the approval of the commission for the equipment of the ships, which should also preferably be acquired through public bidding. His fourth proposal was less an administrative recommendation than an energetic reprimand to the Management: the commission should realize that "the books of the Trade will be seriously audited."

The commission approved all of Professor Eggers' suggestions and sent them on as orders to the Management, which further limited its freedom of action. The reprimand was, however, formulated as a kind of reminder which had the same effect. The commission demanded "from the auditors detailed information as to how far they had progressed." Taking into account how peculiar and complicated the bookkeeping of the Trade was, even for the times, the commission apparently thought it would have to be content for the time being with a report on the progress of the auditing, which had been going on for almost six months.

The Second Year of the Commission

The auditing difficulties appear in various ways in a representation, or rather a provisional recommendation, from the commission to the King, dated 2 March 1789. The commission here advanced as a kind of excuse for not having completed its work long ago, that the review of the books had turned out to be a job which "was so complicated that it was not possible to present our most humble report at the recommended time, namely before the ships sailed last year." The auditing had also been slowed down by dealing with current matters. Therefore the commission decided to split off the colony trade and wait with its recommendation about that until a later occasion. Instead, a recommendation was now submitted on the equipment of ships for whaling and sealing. This agreed with the commission's view of the possibility of splitting off whaling and sealing in general and treating them independently of the remaining activities of the Royal Greenland Trade. The implementation of this idea, however, caused a good deal of trouble.

This appears in no uncertain terms in the recommendation, which is rather comprehensive and provided with several supplements. In principle, the calculations were to the effect that the ships and their equipment represented something less than half of the 950,000 rigsdalers which the capital fund had consisted of in 1781, or more exactly: 420,834 rigsdalers. In consideration of their equipment and so forth, the commission set the actual value of the ships according to the expenses of 1781 to 188 rigsdalers per kommerce læst. The 12 ships then represented a total of 1160.5 kommerce læst for a value of 218,174 rigsdalers. This was con-

Hartvig Marcus Frisch, executive manager of the Royal Greenland Trade. Copy of oil painting by *C.A. Lorentzen.*

(National Historic Museum at Frederiksborg, Hillerød, Denmark, Collection of Pictures, A2029; scale much reduced)

Architectural drawing of the twelve houses for the crew, (whaling project of 1777) some of which were built at different places in Disko Bugt.

(Library of the Royal Academy of Fine Arts, Copenhagen, Collection of architectural Drawings, A8515 d; scale much reduced)

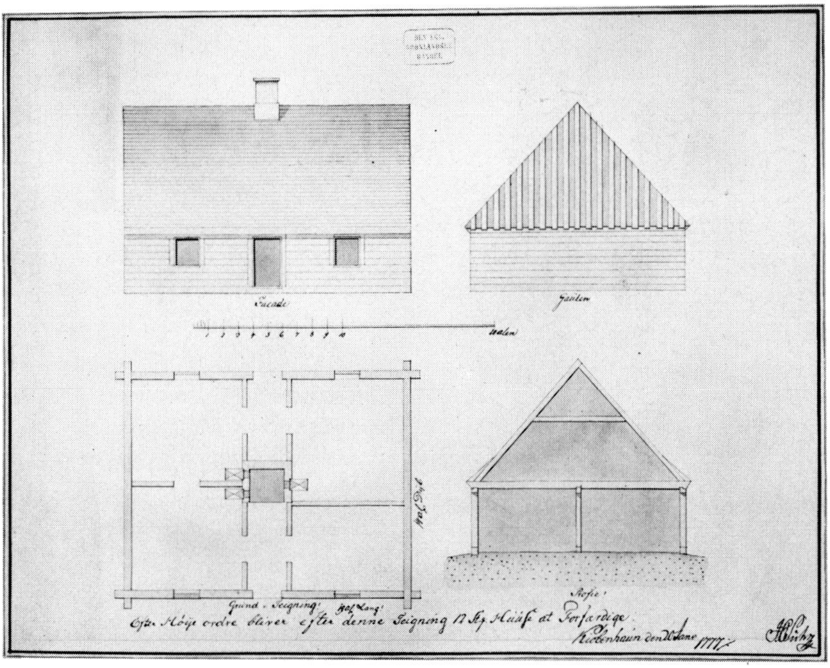

Chr. D. Reventlow

H.E. Schimmelmann

Jacob Edv. Colbiørnsen

Chr. U.D. von Eggers

Members of the Commission of 1788.
No portraits of *Carl Pontoppidan* and of *L.A. Thodal* exist.
(All from The Royal Library, Copenhagen, collection of Maps and Pictures)

sidered a not unreasonable sum according to the market in 1781. It is typical of the bookkeeping that it was not possible to ascertain the amount actually paid for each ship; a calculation had to be resorted to.

In annual depreciation on these ships, which had not been carried out in the books, the commission calculated 6 rigsdalers per kommerce læst for a total of 6963 rigsdalers annually. This is a modest depreciation: from 3.19% the first year, rising in subsequent years to almost 4%. To this was added 4% interest on the capital: a declining expense for the Royal Greenland Trade throughout the years.

Meanwhile, 3 of the original number of ships had wrecked, representing a total loss of 67,384 rigsdalers. They had been replaced by three new ships costing 68,256 rigsdalers. Of these, one had wrecked, and another one of the ships had left the fleet. The Royal Greenland Trade had lent several of the ships for sailing to the West Indies, and thereby suffered a loss of 40,000 rigsdalers. Due to bookkeeping omissions and other reasons it was not possible to keep this loss out of the accounts, mostly because the Trade had not received any insurance for the wrecks or payment for the ships lent (to another state enterprise, now liquidated).[6] Calculations were made of the equipment of 73 ships in whaling and sealing; it was observed that none of these ships had produced a catch which had brought in more money than its equipment had cost. The loss involved in the loan to the West Indies was therefore more or less the same as the amount the Royal Greenland Trade would have lost if the same ships had been used for whaling and sealing.

By calculating the expenses of equipping ships, a share of the Royal Greenland Trade's administrative expenses, the rendering of the produce taken, etc., the commission determined that the expenses of whaling and sealing from 1781 to 1787 had amounted to 544,022 rigsdalers, against receipts of 436,897 rigsdalers: a total loss of 107,125 rigsdalers, or 15,303 rigsdalers annually. Further auditing and calculations could only reduce this loss to a total of 93,125 rigsdalers. In comparison, private shipowners had, it was claimed, in the same period carried on whaling and sealing, which they would not have done at such a loss as that accrued by the state.

The commission thought that the reason for the loss was that the enterprise was too large and comprehensive. They therefore recommended to the King that the Royal Greenland Trade cease fitting ships for whaling and sealing and that these ships be sold to private enterprise.

It is worth while to stop at this point and evaluate this recommendation to some extent. The commissions's arguments here seem remarkably weak. There is no concrete basis for comparison in the form of, for

6.

example, accounts or even summary statements from private shipowners. The commission apparently took no trouble to get the most necessary information for making a comparison. One wonders whether it would have been at all possible to acquire such a basis for comparison. One could hardly say that the Atlantic, not to speak of Davis Stræde, was overrun with whalers and sealers from the realms of the King in that decade. Another thing is whether the commission at all desired to procure such material. The real objective of the commission was to get whaling and sealing demonopolized and get the state out of it. Any other than purely verbal comparison was in the proper sense of the word undesirable, because it could possibly weaken the now prevailing argument for abolishing state participation. This interpretation cannot be documented; it is purely an impression.

The recommendation as a whole, and especially this argumentation, give rise to two suspicions. One is that the leading figures in the commission may have begun to understand that a liberalization of navigation and trade with Greenland would be impossible, that the colonies would have to be maintained under the monopoly and thus under the Royal Greenland Trade. Greenland would thus be entirely left out of the total reform programme which especially Christian D. Reventlow represented. The second suspicion is that the same leading figures therefore insisted that liberalization be implemented in the remainder of this North Atlantic state enterprise. This was to take place as soon as possible – out of consideration for the state treasury and finances – and it would be done in that area which caused the state the greatest loss and which therefore could hardly be necessary for the maintenance of the remainder of the Royal Greenland Trade and its monopoly. Reform politics needed positive results at that time.

The recommendation therefore rose to verbal heights, almost developing a manifesto of political economy. It is too typical to remain hidden in the archives: The ships should be sold to private persons who could equip them "to the greater advantage of the country. For the Greenland traffic procures for the state so many and important advantages that (it) will certainly be one of the branches of trade which deserve the greatest encouragement. It is an excellent school, from which the most diligent seamen, hardened by all the dangers and the severity of the elements, can be taken for Your Majesty's Navy; the products which are hereby exploited from the sea form a not inconsiderable increment of the wealth of the nation, and many of Your Majesty's subjects on the sea coast gain through this traffic an opportunity to earn their livelihood, which they otherwise would have to seek abroad, to the loss of the population of the nation and the lessening of internal movement and circulation. The English have sufficiently shown that they regard the advantages to be accrued from this traffic as very important, as they always encouraged the same, especially in recent years, since their colonies in North America became independent of the parent State."

This final clause contains perhaps the most important argument for the demonopolization of whaling and sealing. English whaling was exclusively in the hands of private shipowners. But at the same time one can find an expression of Schwabe's concern for unemployment among seamen in case the ships were sold. This is expressed even more cogently later on in the recommendation.

At first the commission described how they thought the ships could be sold. Here experience with the Iceland and Finmark Liquidation Commission made its contribution. The fishing hookers of the Iceland Trade had been quite easy to sell. The commission thought that the ships of the Royal Greenland Trade, now totalling 1072.5 kommerce læster, could be sold at a maximum price of 105 rigsdalers per kommerce læst, which would yield 113,245 rigsdalers - that is, if the shipowners were allowed to let the purchase price remain as a mortgage on the ships at 2% interest, which was quite cheap, as the prevailing interest rate on loans was 4 to 5%; 2. if they were granted the fitting premium of 15 rigsdalers per kommerce læst according to the decree of 1784; and 3. if these premiums would follow the individual ship as long as it was in traffic. The mortgage arrangement was a bow to the still prevailing lack of capital in the realms and countries of the King. In addition, the sale of the ships should be postponed until autumn.

This postponement was motivated by Schwabe's fear of unemployment among the seamen, and that they would immediately move abroad. The commission proposed to fit out the ships as usual for 1789, but if prospective buyers turned up, it would be better to take advantage of the opportunity. This had already happened in the case of one ship.

The decision was taken on this representation a week after it was submitted, giving permission for the sale of the whaling ships, not to be announced until September. However, one ship was sold on 4 March, and later 12 more were sold. They yielded a total of 121,905 rigsdalers, most of it in mortgage deeds, to be sure. Only two of the ships were partly paid for in cash. The total sum amounts to less than 101 rigsdalers per kommerce læst, less than the stipulated average of 105 rigsdalers per kommerce læst. The ships were, incidentally, easier to sell than Schwabe had anticipated.

Fear among those stationed in Greenland of what the commission might bring about was further aroused. The Management of the Royal Greenland Trade gave all those stationed in Greenland a shock by sending a directive to the inspectors that they must be prepared to pay a surtax, ½ % of each estate or 5% of wages, according to the decree of 11 March 1789, which stated explicitly that its provisions should be in force "everywhere within or outside of Our realms and lands with colonies appurtaining thereto." It thus seemingly applied in Greenland, but a whole year was given to get prepared for the unavoidable.

The Management succeeded, however, presumably with the help of the commission, in avoiding the unavoidable in 1790, so that all could breath a sigh of relief. This affair would have sunk into obscurity, were it not for the fact that this decision itself set a precedence for exemption from personal taxation for personnel in Greenland. This had not been officially determined so far. That the monopoly trade itself had enjoyed certain customs and taxation exemptions since 1723 did not imply that its employees were exempted from personal taxes in Greenland; this had, however, been the accepted practice, which was now officially confirmed by this exemption from the surtax.

Eggers' Recommendation

In late August of 1789 the most important and decisive report on the conditions and future of the Royal Greenland Trade was submitted: Professor Eggers' detailed exposition filling around 100 closely written folio pages.

A good deal of this report consists of an introduction: a comprehensive account of the development of whaling and sealing up to 1787, as well as the activity of the commission up to the recommendation of 2 March 1789. He also dealt with the entire situation of the Royal Greenland Trade. He established that the Finanskollegium, in its representation to the King of 8 January 1788 requesting the appointment of the commission, had assumed "that it was incontestable that this trade in general had been unfavourable to His Majesty's treasury." – "The commission had, then, according to the previously mentioned circumstances, sufficient reason to desire the size of the institution of the Greenland Trade limited rather than extended." Probably without consciously realizing it, he thus revealed that in reality the commission had decided in advance the matter which it had been appointed to investigate.

Further on in his recommendation, Eggers contested the various evaluations by Executive Manager Hartvig Marcus Frisch of the state of affairs of the Royal Greenland Trade. He established that this enterprise had had an annual loss of 51,000 rigsdalers for six years, in addition to annual working deficits. It was his opinion that at the end of 1787 the Royal Greenland Trade was actually well on its way towards "a splendid bankruptcy", as its original capital was almost exhausted and credit was beginning to fail, thereby raising the spectre of liquidity problems. It was therefore in 1789 high time, and logical, that the committee had recommended, and got approved, that that part of the Trade's activity which involved the greatest losses, namely whaling and sealing, be abandoned as soon as possible.

On the last 23 pages of his recommendation, Eggers investigated the colony trade itself. The losses of six years, including the depreciation on inventory and interest on its capital value, he estimated at 144,922 rigsdalers, or approximately 24,000 rigsdalers annually. "But this very loss, which is larger than I myself had imagined, would make it very precarious, in my opinion to turn the colony trade over to private interests at the present time." This conclusion, which apparently was just as surprising to him as the entire course of the discussions had been to the commission's members, he justified with a comprehensive description of Greenlandic society, as he understood its structure: the trade, the economy and the mission. He correctly appreciated the fangst cycle and the lack of settled residence, and thought it desirable that under these economic circumstances the inhabitants should not be concentrated more than absolutely necessary. He recognized that the fluctuations in the economy of the individual districts were due to factors which could not be controlled. But what one colony lost one year was made up for by what another colony earned the same year. The organisation of the Trade in Greenland was a whole, which also included social and purely public functions. These were difficult to separate.

Eggers explicitly mentioned here the functions of the inspectors, especially what Schwabe had created during his period of office. If the trade was to be demonopolized and entrusted to private entrepreneurs, these would have to agree to let the newly created institutions remain under the supervision of the inspectors, "even though this in some cases might contradict their temporary interests."

The Mission, he thought, ought to "deserve all encouragement from the side of the Trade," because it "should always be considered a suitable means of civilizing the Greenlanders." Here he took up the ideas of both Pontoppidan and Schwabe: "It is even to be desired that facilities for education be somewhat available among the Greenlanders." The conditions of the "national" catechists ought to be improved, and Danish catechists should be stationed in Greenland. He desired tightening and extension of the organisation of the Mission similar to Schwabe's proposal (with assistant rural deans and curates), and like Schwabe he insisted that Missionaries should have a mastery of the Greenlandic language.

"And what could move a tradesman to undertake a trade limited in so many points and conducted under a difficult control?" he asked. Such a trade would have to yield an exceptionally large profit in proportion to the capital invested. He had previously believed that this could be done, but a closer study of the operations of the Trade and conditions in general had changed his opinion.

Eggers tried to imagine the consequence if several private entrepreneurs undertook this trade under the conditions which would have to be demanded of them. Eternal quarrels and strife, and consequent court cases would be the result, especially in consideration of the unsettled way of life of the Greenlanders. One would thus have to see to it that one enterprise extended over the entire country, or at least a whole inspectorate. This would demand such a considerable capital investment that the risk would be too great. Even if a private person were to undertake this trade, one would "hear nothing but unpleasant complaints about the ruin of the trade and constant cries for adjustments of the agreed conditions" if there was but one bad year. "The recommended control would without a doubt be blamed." The state would then be forced to one alleviation after the other, until the King would finally have to take over the Greenland trade in a much worse shape than the losses which it was now proposed to avoid.

This was a distinct echo of Schwabe's report of 1787–1788. But Eggers' conclusion contained other factors. The Greenland trade was "certainly not an unimportant object in relation to the balance of trade of the realms," it created new production, occupied many persons and created circulation in production and trade in Copenhagen. This was worth while maintaining, even if the state would have to sacrifice a few thousand rigsdalers a year to keep the Greenland trade going. These were far from liberalistic tones. This was an opinion clearly based on political economy.

Eggers' final conclusion was then "In these circumstances and for the above-mentioned reasons, I for one consider it dangerous, the Greenlanders being in their present state, to propose an essential change or the leasing of the trade to private persons." On the contrary, he advised obtaining the report of Schwabe and the Royal Greenland Trade, and formulating a new plan for the Trade for the next ten years.

Thus the report of Christian U.D. von Eggers gave the coup de grace to the idea of demonopolizing the Greenland trade. It only remained for the commission to formulate its final report or representation to the King.

Eggers in his report advised procuring further reports from Schwabe and the Management of the Trade. These were possibly submitted in mid-December 1789, but their text is unknown.

The Royal Decree of 26 May 1790

It appears that just at the end of its second year of existence, the commission agreed on a final decision as to the future of the Royal Greenland Trade, and abandoned a liberalistic reform of conditions in Greenland. The final decision was then made to submit a representation to the King showing first the losses suffered by the Trade as a whole from 1781 to 1787, and then the losses from 1782 to 1787 of the colony trade alone. All the reasons were collected which supported a continuation of the colony trade under royal administration; the main reason was explicitly "the present state of the Greenlanders," in the words of Eggers. The commission would later present a new set of rules, to apply provisionally for the next ten years. The basic capital of the colony trade was to be reduced to 250,000 rigsdalers, on which the commission thought it could promise a return of 4% per year, if the King undertook to pay the salaries of the inspectors, as well as current expenses for pensions and temporary unemployment compensation. These latter were intended to be deducted from the annual payment of interest.

It was decided at the same time that Schwabe, as arranged with the executive managers of the Royal Greenland Trade, was, with them, to consider and submit proposals for a new set of regulations for the Royal Greenland Trade.

It is characteristic of this resolution, as of the entire work of the commission, that the only reason directly mentioned is consideration for "the present state of the Greenlanders". In all its brevity this formulation expresses the humane attitude inspiring the members of the commission, and even a majority of the politicians and civil servants in the Konseil of the King after 1784. Schwabe was also under the sway of such attitude, so that in all his serious modesty he came to be the central figure of the commission, just as he was the first to submit his report defending the monopoly, and the last to be mentioned by name in the decree of 1790. He was entrusted with a decisive role in the continuation of the monopoly, although he had actually left its service. His opinions were those which carried the most weight.

In late May of 1790 the commission finally submitted, through the Rentekammer, its representation to the King and on 26 May a royal decree was issued. As usual it was a concentrated extract of the representation, omitting various details. In all its brevity it stated the following:

The Greenland colony trade was to continue as a royal enterprise, but under a new set of rules enjoining the most strict order and economy. A new evaluation of the combined properties of the Trade was to be made at the end of 1789. Every year the commission was to present a report on the outcome of the trade. When the decree explicitly states that the "previously decreed administration of this trade" was abolished, this must refer to the General Board of Directors of the Greenland, Iceland, Finmark and Faroese Trade, since the commission was to take its place.

The decree appointed the previous secretary of the Iceland and Finmark Liquidation Commission, Hans Leganger Wexelsen, as a manager, to function alongside Hartvig Marcus Frisch and Fr. Martini. Somewhat later the same year, Carl Pontoppidan was appointed to the Management, but he resigned his office the next year.

The stage was now set for a new decade in the development of the Trade.

V. Demography

The new order manifested itself in Greenland only indirectly. In the daily life of the colonies, the standard was still set for the Trade by the Order of 1782, with its subsequent supplements and amendments. In this sense no change could be observed – for either the better or the worse. The fact that the committee still existed was noted in Greenland, but it was mostly the inspectors who would notice it. Its presence was felt in the background, so to speak; the fear of what it might do faded away, and life continued more or less as usual.

The Census of 1789

Among the material collected for the Commission of 1788* was a census of the population of West Greenland, excluding stationed Europeans. The results of this census were available before the Commission submitted its report, but they did not play any role in the proceedings of the Commission, even less were they mentioned in either the report or the representation to the King submitted in 1790.

The census took place, as had been expected, under great difficulties. Permission had been given to make estimates in special cases. An example of such estimates occurred in Julianehåb District. Here the baptized Greenlanders could be counted more or less accurately; but only a superficial estimate was available of how many unbaptized Greenlanders there were. There was, however, a figure for unbaptized fangers: 155. On this basis an unbaptized population of 930 was estimated, allowing for an average of five other persons, women and children, in the family of each fanger. This questionable calculation is probably the most flagrant case of estimation in this census, but among the other figures are hidden several estimates of lesser importance, which together make this census unreliable.[1]

---

*) Henceforth: the Commission.

Growth and Movement in the Population of Greenland from 1789 to 1808

With all due reservation, the census of 1789, compared with later censuses, nevertheless does give certain indications as to the growth and distribution of the population. Although one must treat the figures themselves with caution, some tendencies in the development can be read from relationships between them. For the period from 1789 to 1808 there are total figures for at least 4 years:

1789: 5122
1789: 6141
1802: 5865
1805: 5888[2]

Two factors make these figures unreliable as absolute quantities in relation to each other. In the first place the previously mentioned estimate for Julianehåb District is included in the figures for 1789, and even in 1802 and 1805 the count was uncertain in this district. Secondly, Upernavik District is included in the figures for 1799, 1802 and 1805, but not for 1789. A direct comparison can therefore not even give an approximately credible picture of growth or decline in the Greenlandic population.

By subtracting the figures for both Julianehåb and Upernavik Districts from all the census totals for the various years, one can get a comparison between them of some reasonable value. This comparison thus applies to 7 districts of the Northern Inspectorate and 5 of the Southern, as illustrated in Table 1, page 89.

The total figures at the bottom show an unmistakable growth of the population between 1789 to 1799, then a decline between 1799 and 1802, and finally a very modest gain between 1802 and 1805. But the total figures from either inspectorate show that the development was not identical in the two provinces, so that the general pattern of growth and decline does not apply to them, or to the individual districts.

The Northern Inspectorate shows a considerable growth between 1789 to 1799, then an unmistakable decline between 1799 and 1802 which is almost compensated for by growth from 1802 to 1805. The growth from 1789 to 1799 must, however, be regarded critically, among other reasons because the figures for Upernavik District are omitted. The most important part of this growth took place in Umánaq District: from 173 to 397.

Table 1.

	1789	1799			1802			1805		
	Pop.	Pop.	+/-	+/-%	Pop.	+/-	+/-%	Pop.	+/-	+/-%
Northern Inspectorate										
Umánaq	173	397	+224	+129	403	+6	+2	392	-11	-3
Ritenbenk and Arveprinsens Ejland	407	336	-71	-17	433	+97	+29	408	-25	-6
Godhavn	139	201	+62	+45	215	+14	+7	182	-33	-15
Jakobshavn	233	247	+14	+6	173	-74	-30	270	+97	+56
Christianshåb ..	280	315	+35	+13	317	+2	+1	282	-35	-11
Egedesminde* ..	298	291	-7	-2	186	-105	-36	218	+32	+17
Kronprinsens Ejland*	47	160	+113	+240	142	-18	-11	172	+30	+21
TOTAL	1577	1947	+370	+23	1869	-78	-4	1924	+55	+3
Southern Inspectorate										
Holsteinsborg ..	357	300	-57	-16	81	-219	-73	129	+48	+59
Sukkertoppen ..	249	317	+68	+27	330	+13	+4	277	-53	-16
Godthåb	465	437	-28	-6	411	-26	-6	409	-2	-0.5
Fiskenæsset	342	357	+15	+4	320	-37	-10	303	-17	-5
Frederikshåb ...	693	547	-146	-21	555**	+8	+1	579	+24	+4
TOTAL	2106	1958	-148	-7	1697	-261	-13	1697	0	0
Northern Insp. .	1577	1947			1869			1924		
Southern Insp. ..	2106	1958			1697			1697		
TOTAL	3683	3905	+222	+6	3566	-339	-9	3621	+55	+2

* Hunde Ejland, which in 1789 belonged to Egedesminde District, was in 1796 transferred to Kronprinsens Ejland District.
** By 1803 the 1802 figures for Frederikshåb had not yet arrived, so the 1800 figures were used instead.

This violent increase in these ten years does not correspond to the much calmer development later. The growth of Umánaq District appears more reasonable in Table 2, tabulated and partly calculated on the basis of the civil registry lists.

Some movement of population is known to have taken place from Umánaq to Upernavik District previous to 1789, perhaps due to fear of the epidemic in Disko Bugt from 1785 to 1787. In Umánaq District itself "serious disease" is reported in 1785, from which the inhabitants may have fled. When Upernavik was temporarily closed as an independent trading post in 1791, it is known that a goodly number of Greenlanders moved from

Table 2.

	Total	Immigrated	Emigrated				
1789	173	-	28				
(1791	402?	229?		=	+229	=	+132%?)
1792	355	-	42	=	-47	=	-12%
1793	404	-	-	=	+49	=	+13%
1794	303	18	110	=	-101	=	-25%
1795	388	46	8	=	+85	=	+28%
1796	448	-	3	=	+60	=	+15%
1797	442	-	58	=	-6	=	-1%
1798	345	1	23	=	-97	=	-21%
1799	397	33	7	=	+52	=	+15%

The figures of the civil registry lists for deaths and births are *not* included in this table, but have been included in the calculations for 1791, made on the basis of the figures for 1792. Otherwise, these figures do not agree with the differences between the totals for the various years, but neither are the figures for immigrants and emigrants certain. Figures for baptized families seem to have been more reliable. The numbers and movements of unbaptized families were rather indefinite. (-) indicates no figure available. (?) indicates that the figures are calculated.

here to Umánaq. That is why that year is included in the table; its figures have been arrived at by calculation. In subsequent years some of these families moved back again, as appears opposite 1792 and 1794 in the table.

If one continues the table past 1799 to 1816, which has not been done here, approximately the same movements appear, if one ignores 1791, the year of great immigration. Large dips in the population appear for 1794, 1798, 1804 and 1813. It looks very much as if these movements up and down correspond to a kind of nomadic cycle. They may be pure coincidence; but there seems to be a tendency to some kind of stability in the population during the two dangerous periods. These were the period from 1800 to 1803 with the Mid-Greenland smallpox epidemic and a threat of war; and the war years themselves after 1807, during which there was a fear of foreigners in Greenland, and people preferred to remain where they sensed a certain degree of security. So that special conditions lie hidden in the figures for Umánaq.

The figures for Ritenbenk and Arveprinsens Ejland have been merged in Table 1 because the latter place was closed in 1801 and thereafter counted under Ritenbenk; some of the population moved to other places, however, including Jakobshavn.[3] The table shows a decline for Godhavn between 1802 and 1805. For unknown reasons there was a steady emigration not compensated for by immigration. The same applies to Christianshåb, which was in steady decline after 1800 as a fangst site. Jakobshavn experienced a bit of the smallpox epidemic, giving rise to a drastic decline in 1802, which was compensated for by 1805.

The smallpox epidemic of 1800–1801 hit Egedesminde District hard, as appears from a loss of 105, or 36%, between 1799 and 1802. In the epidemic year itself the population of this district was reduced by 42%. It is possible that its gain after 1802 took place at the expense of Christianshåb and Godhavn Districts, but the material reveals nothing of this matter.

The populations of Egedesminde District in 1789 and in 1799 are not comparable, because in 1799, Egedesminde District was deprived of the inhabitants of Hunde Ejland, which in 1796 had been joined to Kronprinsens Ejland. Some of the growth of Kronprinsens Ejland thus "belongs" to Egedesminde District. By calculating the population of Hunde Ejland in 1789, the decline of Egedesminde District can be changed to a reasonable growth. On the basis of the civil registry lists, Table 3 can be calculated.

Table 3.

	1789	1791	1793	1794	1795	1796	1797	1798	1799	1800	1801
+ Kronprinsens Ejland	47	56	--	--	42	43	139	148	160	153	152
Hunde Ejland .	55 ?	70?	106	--	--	--	90?	--	--	--	--
TOTAL	102 ?	126?					139	148	160	153	152
– Egedesminde .	298	--	--	418	465	--	363	--	291	335	179
TOTAL	240 +			320 +			363		291	335	179

-- = unknown
\+ = approximately

The actual figures for the population of Hunde Ejland in 1789 are not known; but in 1791, 79 persons are listed by name in the civil registry list – 9 of these cannot be considered juridically as Greenlanders. In 1793 calculations show a population of 106, of whom presumably 10, according to the same criteria, cannot be considered Greenlanders. In 1797 the population of Hunde Ejland can be calculated at approximately 90. Whaling from Hunde Ejland did not really get off the ground until 1789, so previous immigration cannot have been very great. The figures listed are from a cautious calculation. According to this, the population of Egedesminde in 1789 can be estimated at about 240. Thus we arrive at the movements for Egedesminde indicated in Table 4.

Table 4.

1789	240?			
1794	320?	+80	+33%	
1797	363	+43	+13%	
1799	291	−72	−20%	
1800	335	+44	+15%	
1801	179	−156	−47%	(42% dead, 5% emigrated)
1802	189	+7	+4%	
1803	193	+4	+2%	
1804	181	−12	−6%	
1805	218	+37	+20%	
1806	250	+32	+15%	
1807	266	+16	+6%	
1808	275	+9	+3%	

These movements seem more reasonable. The great decline from 1800 to 1801 has been explained above. The decline from 1797 to 1799 has, however, no elucidation in other source material. This district is very extensive: it covers a large area with an indented coast, long fjords and long distances between the shore and the icecap. Long voyages apparently took place frequently. The seemingly certain figures of the civil registry lists are perhaps not so reliable, after all. They often represented estimated quantities, without this being indicated. Such indications were never made, even when discrepancies were conspicuous. It is typical that the figures are lacking here for several years which are represented in other lists. Fluctuating reliability in counting, coupled with quite uncontrollable "wandering" may have been the reason for otherwise inexplicable growth or decline within a district, or at a particular locality.

The figures of Table 4 are also more reasonable for Kronprinsens Ejland, although reliable figures are lacking for several years for the Greenlandic population both of this place and of Hunde Ejland. If the total figure for both places in 1791, 126, is approximately correct, these two places together had a total growth of 13 or more than 10% by 1799, which seems quite unreasonable. Letters from Kronprinsens Ejland sometimes mention the unreliability of Greenlandic participation in whaling because of immigration and emigration, mostly on fangst journeys. This seems in some degree to be reflected in the figures of Table 4.

The total population of the Southern Inspectorate (Table 1) shows a constant decline. The totals for 1802 show a decline in both inspectorates, clearly due to the smallpox epidemic of 1800–1801. This loss is proportionately larger in the Southern Inspectorate, because Holsteinsborg lost

89% of its population in 1801. Its subsequent growth, which began between 1801 and 1802 and continued thereafter, is especially due to immigration from Sukkertoppen. This immigration, as well as a lesser immigration to Frederikshåb corresponds to a decline in the other districts. This seems to indicate that these movements took place within the Inspectorate. Between 1802 and 1805, Julianehåb District had a slight decline of 13 persons, or 0.72%. This district has been omitted in the table and calculations here, but if it had been included, it would not have changed the pattern by more than a growth of 0.36%, which is so negligable that it can well be omitted, especially as the figures are uncertain.

The decline of the population of the Southern Inspectorate between 1789 and 1799 is distributed among 3 districts: Holsteinsborg, Frederikshåb and Godthåb; the figures from the last case will be discussed in greater detail later. The decline of these districts must essentially be due to emigration, which is, however, not compensated for by growth of Sukkertoppen and Fiskenæsset. The deficit of 148 persons must partially be explained by immigration to the Northern Inspectorate; it would amount to 40% of the growth of the Northern Inspectorate between 1789 and 1799. Whaling attracted immigrants, so much that the Northern Inspectorate has a population which in 1802 was over 10%, and in 1805 over 13% greater than the Southern Inspectorate - still ignoring Upernavik and Julianehåb Districts.

That the five districts of the Southern Inspectorate listed in Table 1 had in 1789 a population 34% greater than the seven districts listed from the Northern Inspectorate, while ten years later these populations were almost equal, with the Northern Inspectorate overtaking the Southern considerably in subsequent years, is a good illustration of the greater economic importance of the Northern Inspectorate in this period due to whaling.

The decline of the population of Godthåb, the oldest colony of Western Greenland, becomes quite conspicuous when compared with previous figures, supplemented with information from various civil registry lists and summaries.[4] Table 5 shows a decline in 34 years of 428 or 78% for the Royal Mission, and 238 or 45% for the Moravian Brethren. The total decline from 1075 to 409 is 666 or 62%. The most fatal period was from February 1782 to the end of June 1783, when 297 persons died in a typhoid epidemic. During this winter only two children were born in Godthåb parish. The epidemic apparently spread north along the entire coast and caused many mortalities, but nowhere did it rage as violently as at Godthåb. Incidentally, it was not until the 1930's that this district again reached its 1791 population. The explanation of this fact, as well as of the continual decline from

Table 5.

	Royal Mission	Moravian Brethren	TOTAL
1771	546	529	1075
1772	495	535	1030
1777	462	493	955[5]
1782	296	268	564
1783	192	275	467
1787	192	274	466
1788	187	266	453
1789	191	274	465
1792	192	286	478
1794	145	295	440
1799	158	279	437
1802	?	?	411
1805	118	291	409

1789 to 1805, is to be found in large individual waves of emigration, not least due to the fact that Godthåb area was not particularly attractive for those who had to make their living from fangst. The central built-up area of the district was, and continued to be, artificial.

The growth and movement of population of these districts can thus be illustrated for the period under consideration. The main tendencies seem to be clear. The relationship between births and deaths is more difficult to illustrate with the quite unreliable figures and information available. Random samples from civil registry lists have generally verified the figures given in Table 6, and a comparison with the period from 1901 to 1930 supports the picture.

Table 6.

	Total Pop.	Births	0/00	Deaths	0/00	Surplus 0/00
1789 N.I.*	1577	51	32	41	26	6
- S.I.**	2106	80	38	57	27	11
1799 S.I.	1958	71	36	52	27	9
- N.I.***	1160	53	46	50	43	3
1808 N.I.	2433	75	31	65	27	4
1901-30 { N.G.§			39.6		27.8	11.8
1901-30 { S.G.§§			40.8		27.6	13.2

* Northern Inspectorate
** Southern Inspectorate
*** Northern Inspectorate, but only 4 districts: Godhavn, Christianshåb, Jakobshavn and Umánaq
§ North Greenland
§§ South Greenland

The pattern we get is one of a greater surplus of births over deaths in the Southern Inspectorate than in the Northern. This further supports the contention that the growth of the North Greenland population seen in Table 1 must have been due to immigration from the south. Both Julianehåb and Upernavik had their own life, so to speak, and regarded from this point of view it is also reasonable to keep these two districts out of our considerations.

Distribution of Population

Although these figures from the childhood of statistics must be treated with caution, we can learn something of the distribution of population in Greenland from them. Table 1 shows that the preponderance of population in 1789 of five of the districts of the Southern Inspectorate over seven of the districts of the Northern was equalized by 1799 and reversed by 1802. But if the figures for Julianehåb and Upernavik Districts are included, the picture is changed, making the Southern Inspectorate the most populous throughout the period dealt with here: in 1802 and 1805 around one and a half times more than the north. Although the figures from these districts are unreliable, the total difference is so great that little doubt can remain as to this preponderance.

It is more difficult to calculate the distribution of the population along the coast; one can only arrive at approximate figures, including the

Table 7.

	Kilometres of coast	Population	Per km. of coast
1789 N.I. (7)	950	1577	1.66
S.I. (5)	750	2106	2.81
Julianehåb	185	1443	7.88
1799 N.I. (7)	950	1947	2.05
S.I. (5)	750	1958	2.61
Julianehåb	185	1809	9.78
1802 N.I. (7)	950	1869	1.97
S.I. (5)	750	1697	2.26
Julianehåb	185	1805	9.76
1805 N.I. (7)	950	1924	2.03
S.I. (5)	750	1697	2.26
Julianehåb	185	1818	9.83

N.I. (7) = the seven districts of the Northern Inspectorate listed in Table 1.
S.I. (5) = the five districts of the Southern Inspectorate listed in Table 1.

length as the crow flies of the coasts themselves. If we estimate the length of the coasts for the seven northern districts and five southern districts, as in Table 7, we see a certain relationship between the geographic distribution of the two inspectorates. The figures for Julianehåb district have been added to illustrate the special conditions prevailing here.

This table shows that the population was on the average denser in the Southern Inspectorate than in the Northern. Also in this respect, Julianehåb differs considerably from the other districts.

If we take only the districts in Disko Bugt and estimate the coast around the bay as 500 kilometres as the crow flies, we get the following population densities: 1789:2.81 inhabitants per kilometre; 1799:3.10; 1802:2.93; and 1805:3.06. The density of these 6 northern districts is thus greater than that of the five southern districts listed. If we continue to ignore Julianehåb with its special conditions, these figures illustrate the moderate concentration which took place in Disko Bugt from 1789 to 1805. A comparison with the census of 1901 shows that this condition has more or less maintained itself, which further substantiates the older figures. In 1901 Disko Bugt had 3039 inhabitants, or 6.07 inhabitants per kilometre. The five southern districts had 3335 inhabitants, or 4.45 inhabitants per kilometre of coast. In 1805 Disko Bugt was thus 35% more densely populated per kilometre of coast than the five southern districts, and in 1901 36%. In 1901 Julianehåb, with 240 kilometres of coast, had a density of 10.07 inhabitants per kilometre, which compares quite well with 9.83 in 1805.

The same confirmation of the first censuses by comparison with a later calculation can be achieved by comparing distribution according to sex in the same seven and five districts from our four early censuses with that of 1901. This has been done in Table 8.

According to this table, women have over a long period of time constituted over half of the West Greenlandic population. This does not agree with the current opinion of the time, when equality was incorrectly assumed. As early as 1792, Inspector Børge J. Schultz pointed out that "a greater number of the female sex is curiously present everywhere here" in the Northern Inspectorate. But the difference was not as great as he obviously thought.

Quite early the problem of widows had been a difficult one.[6] It can therefore be worth while to investigate the proportion of widows and widowers in the Greenlandic population. Table 9 shows that the proportion of widowers remained more or less constant, fluctuating around 1%, with lower values at the beginning of the period under consideration. There is some degree of uniformity between the two inspectorates. This

Table 8.

	M	F	TOTAL	% F
1789 N.I. (7)	708	869	1577	55
S.I. (5)	865	1241	2106	59
1799 N.I. (7)	872	1075	1947	55
S.I. (5)	817	1141	1958	58
1802 N.I. (7)	842	1027	1869	55
S.I. (5)	692	1005	1697	59
1805 N.I. (7)	854	1070	1924	56
S.I.	748	949	1697	56
1901 N.G.	2428	2739	5167	53
S.G.	2831	3285	6116	54
TOTAL	5259	6024	11283	53

situation is different with respect to widows, the proportion of which changes in the two inspectorates, but in opposite directions. While the proportion of widows in the south declines slightly during the period in

Table 9.

	POP.	WIDOWERS	%	WIDOWS	%
1789 N.I.[a]	1577	4	0.25	29	1.8
S.I.[b]	2106	7	0.33	228	11
TOTAL	3683	11	0.30	257	7
1799 N.I.[a]	1947	10	0.51	88	5
S.I.[c]	1521	16	1	139	9
TOTAL	3468	26	0.75	227	7
1802 N.I.[a]	1869	38	2	109	6
S.I.[d]	822	6	0.73	64	8
TOTAL	2691	44	2	173	6
1805 N.I.[e]	1250	18	1	80	6
S.I.[f]	2807	29	1	240	9
TOTAL	4057	47	1	320	8

N.I. = Northern Inspectorate
S.I. = Southern Inspectorate
a) Excluding Upernavik District
b) Excluding Julianehåb District
c) Excluding Julianehåb and Godthåb Districts
d) Excluding Julianehåb, Frederikshåb and Fiskenæsset Districts
e) Excluding Upernavik, Umánaq and Christianshåb Districts
f) Excluding Frederikshåb and Holsteinsborg Districts

question, it is constantly higher than in the north, where it climbs steeply between 1789 and 1799, when it stabilizes at about 6%. What the two inspectorates have in common is that both the number and proportion of widows is far greater than that of widowers. I.e., this social problem of support was acute throughout the period in question as it has been previously.

The greater proportion of widows may be an indication that women lived longer than men, but this is only an assumption, as we cannot document average longevity for the sexes in this period with figures. On the other hand we can, by comparing the mortality rate for the two groups for selected years, show the probability of a greater longevity for women in Greenland, as was the case elsewhere. This is done in Table 10.

It appears from these figures that mortality fluctuated greatly, and that in some years, certain districts deviated from the average mortality. This is undoubtedly due to the small number we are dealing with. In spite of this factor, the table shows that the mortality of either group is usually different from that of the population as a whole; in four cases male mor-

Table 10.

	MALE			FEMALE			TOTAL			Mortality ‰ in entire Inspect.
	Deaths	Pop.	‰	Deaths	Pop.	‰	Deaths	Pop.	‰	
1789 N.I.[a]	11	462	24	4	584	24	25	1046	24	26
S.I.[b]	8	333	24	3	474	6	11	807	14	27
1800 N.I.[a]	22	913	24	20	1152	17	42	2065	20	
Sukker-toppen	5	148	34	6	175	34	11	323	34	
1804 N.I.[a]	17	743	23	10	884	11	28	1626	17	
Sukker-toppen	2	144	14	3	157	19	5	301	17	
1806 N.I.[c]	32	965	33	29	1126	26	61	2091	29	
1808 N.I.[d]	25	934	27	30	1067	28	55	2001	27	27
Sum	122	4642	26	115	5619	20	237	10261	23	

This table is based on civil registry lists in which deaths are listed by sex.
N.I. = Northern Inspectorate
S.I. = Southern Inspectorate
a) Excluding Upernavik District
b) Only Godthåb and Fiskenæsset Districts
c) Excluding Upernavik and Christianshåb Districts
d) Excluding Umánaq District

tality is considerably higher than total mortality, while female mortality is only higher in two cases, and in two cases the mortality is equal. In four of the selected years, female mortality is lower than total mortality, and far lower than the corresponding male mortality.

Summing the figures shows this relationship more distinctly. Here female mortality is clearly lower than total mortality, while male mortality is higher. The main tendency must therefore have been for lower mortality among women than among men; and for women to have had a greater longevity than men in West Greenland in the period in question.

As a correction to Table 10 it should be noted that the "total mortality" is lower than the mortality for all of West Greenland in this period, while male mortality is close to this latter figure. No special difference can be distinguished in the mortality of the sexes among children. In this area, however, there is every good reason to treat the civil registry lists with caution; it is not known whether their figures cover children deceased shortly after birth, or during their first year. The figures for child mortality before the age of 12 are curiously small.

Children constituted about one-third of the population, as illustrated in Table 11. The impression of many children which even the earliest visitors to Greenland in the modern period had, is thus confirmed for the

Table 11.

	Pop.	Under 12	%
1789 N.I. (7)	1577	500	32
S.I. (5)	2106	665	32
1799 N.I. (6)[a]	1855	657	35
S.I. (3)[b]	1204	405	34
1802 N.I. (7)	1947	670	34
S.I. (3)[c]	822	259	31
1805 N.I. (5)[d]	1250	443	35
S.I. (4)[e]	2807	969	35
1901 N.G.	5107	1725	34
S.G.	6116	1960	32

N.I. = Northern Inspectorate
S.I. = Southern Inspectorate
N.G. = North Greenland
S.G. = South Greenland
a) Excluding Arveprinsens Ejland District
b) Excluding Julianehåb, Godthåb and Sukkertoppen Districts
c) Excluding Frederikshåb and Fiskenæsset Districts
d) Excluding Christianshåb and Umánaq Districts
e) Excluding Frederikshåb and Holsteinsborg Districts, but including Julianehåb Distr.

period under consideration. The comparison with 1901 seems to show that this social pattern continued; the figures from this year likewise confirm those of the former period. The socio-economic structure of the family had its special character. There were many mouths to feed; this was the task of the fangers.

In calculating the number of unbaptized persons in Julianehåb District in 1789, five additional persons were estimated per fanger, i.e., per provider, as we have seen. Fangers were thus estimated to constitute one-sixth of the unbaptized population. In the 1789 tables there was a heading for "providers": fangers. If we list these figures district by district, we get the proportions shown in Table 12.

Table 12.

	Pop.	"Providers"	%
N.I. 1789			
Umánaq	173	36	21
Ritenbenk and Arveprinsens Ejland	407	82	20
Godhavn	139	27	19
Jakobshavn	233	27	12
Christianshåb	280	61	22
Egedesminde	298	61	20
Kronprinsens Ejland	47	2	4
TOTAL	1577	293	19
S.I. 1789			
Holsteinsborg	357	61	17
Sukkertoppen	249	54	22
Godthåb	465	56	12
Fiskenæsset	342	65	19
Frederikshåb	693	76	11
TOTAL	2106	312	15
GRAND TOTAL	3683	605	16

N.I. = Northern Inspectorate
S.I. = Southern Inspectorate

The one-sixth of the population, which were in Julianehåb estimated to be fangers, corresponds quite well to the 16% of Table 10, especially considering the small numbers dealt with. If we assume that the figures for fangers in 1789 were close to the truth, we can calculate the percentage of fangers in 1799, 1802 and 1805 on the basis of the figures for males over 12 years of age. This is done in Table 13.

Table 13.

	Males	Males under 12	Males over 12	Total pop.	% Males over 12	% Fangers
1789 N.I. (7)	708	128	580	1577	37	19
S.I. (5)	865	215	650	2106	31	15
1799 N.I. (6)	817	292	525	1855	28	(14?)
S.I. (3)	505	189	316	1204	26	(13?)
1802 N.I. (7)	842	313	529	1947	27	(14?)
S.I. (3)	361	138	223	822	27	(14?)
1805 N.I. (5)	554	219	335	1250	27	(14?)
S.I. (4)	1204	499	705	2807	25	(13?)

( ) = number of districts, corresponding to Table 11.
(?) = calculated on basis of the other figures in this table.

The many epidemics, especially the smallpox epidemic of 1800–1801, are expressed in these figures; nevertheless, the low 12% for Godthåb and Jakobshavn in Table 12 does seem strange. But it is supported by an accurate account of the fangers at every locality in Julianehåb District, made by the trader Johan Christian Mørch in 1805 and recorded in his journal that year. He counted 208 fangers in a population of 1818, or over 11%.

Between one-seventh and one-ninth of the population was thus "providers" at the close of this period. Seen throughout the period, the development does not seem to have been favourable. The beginning of the period can be illustrated in Table 14 by figures from a single district for six years. These figures are from Godthåb District, which is unfortunately not typical, and in addition apply only to the Royal Mission, not to the Moravian Brethren.

An epidemic such as the one which raged in Godthåb in 1782 reduced the number of fangers to between 13% and 14% of the surviving population, a figure which often appears in Table 13. It is thus probable that the picture presented by these figures corresponds more or less to reality.

Table 14. Godthåb District

Year	Population	Fangers	
		Number	Per cent
1783	192	26	14
1784	188	29	15
1785	183	30	16
1786	182	35	19
1787	192	37	19
1788	186	33	18

Since not all the civil registry lists mention the number of "providers", one must make use of the ones which do in attempting to calculate the percentages, as far as possible, of "providers" in the total population of each district.

Thus in 1787 Sukkertoppen District had a population of 298, of which only 46, or 15%, were fangers. In 1789 the figure was 77 out of 345, or 22%. The whaling stations at Holsteinsborg and Qerrortussoq were special cases: in 1787, Qerrortussoq had 29 providers out of a total population of 121, or 24%; while in 1788, Holsteinsborg had as many as 78 providers, or 39% of the total population of 198.

Farther south in Frederikshåb, a pronounced fanger district, there were in 1789, according to the civil registry lists, 693 inhabitants, of which 113, or 16%, were fangers. Julianehåb District, mentioned specially above, had in 1805 a population of 1818, distributed among 37 localities, including the colony seat. Of these, only 208, or slightly over 11%, were registered as fangers.

Likewise, Umánaq, a pronounced fanger district in the north, had in 1792 only 62 fangers in a population of 355, corresponding to slightly over 17%.

These random selections show how much the percentages fluctuated from district to district and from year to year; but they also show that the previous calculations must present a rather credible picture, which is corrected to some extent when one remembers that no other occupations

Table 15.

	Total Pop.	Half-breeds	Percentage
Godhavn:			
1799	201	25	12
1800	196	24	12
1803	211	20	10
1805	182	62	34
1809	239	92	39
Sukkertoppen:			
1800	323	13	4
1803	282	11	4
1804	301	14	5
Julianehåb:			
1800	1809	35	2
Fiskenæsset:			
1801	333	18	5
1803	337	20	6

than that of fanger are considered. Greenlanders, including "mixtures", who were employed by the Trade or the Mission, were not counted as "providers"; but an ordinary whaling bargeman was. This latter factor is perhaps the reason for the large percentages of fangers in whaling areas. Our conclusion must be that the percentages available are on the whole valid for the entire area.

All statistics on Greenland have always dealt with small absolute numbers, so that small fluctuations give rise to large percentage differences. One factor which to some extent distorts the picture is thus the so-called "mixtures", as well as catechists and Greenlanders employed by the Trade. It is difficult to get any figures as to the numbers of "mixtures" in the population. Some of them, by the way, left Greenland for good as adolescents or adults. In Table 15, we can see the fluctuations in these figures for a few characteristic locations.

Table 16 shows the proportion of half-breeds in six districts of the Northern Inspectorate for two different years; this proportion varied considerably between the various districts. An even greater difference existed in this respect between the two Inspectorates: a good deal more marriages had taken place between Greenlandic women and stationed Europeans in the Northern Inspectorate than in the Southern, due to the greater num-

Table 16.

	Total Pop.	Half-breeds	Percentage
1800:			
Godhavn	196	24	12
Kronprinsens Ejland	153	17	11
Egedesminde	335	22	7
Christianshåb	358	63	18
Jakobshavn	271	17	6
Ritenbenk	311	26	8
TOTAL	1624	169	10
1805:			
Godhavn	182	62	34
Kronprinsens Ejland	172	19	11
Egedesminde	218	32	15
Christianshåb	483	65	13
Jakobshavn	270	18	7
Ritenbenk	408	39	10
TOTAL	1733	235	14

ber of single men stationed for whaling in the north. They were, according to the Order of 1782, allowed to marry Greenlandic women of "mixed" descent, which to some extent explains the rising proportion of half-breeds during the period under consideration.

In this connection, there is a question of the definition of the term "mixture", as mentioned above. Children born outside of marriage with a European father were not ordinarily considered "mixtures" unless their mothers were already mixtures. The term was also not used for children born to a woman married to a Greenlander, even though their father was European. On the other hand, children born in marriages between "mixtures" were also considered such, which further explains the great rise of 66, or 39%, in the numbers of this group from 1800 to 1805, since many such marriages took place during this period and previous to it.

Half-breeds played no negligable role in the life of Western Greenland, a role inversely proportional to their figures. Considering the Order of 1782, we have noted the problems connected with their upbringing. As much as possible, they were to be raised to be "good Greenlanders", but if this could not be achieved, they were to be trained for employment by the Trade or the Mission. Gradually, not a few were actually employed by the

Table 17.

	1775	1780	1785	1790	1795	1800	1805	1810
Julianehåb	0	0	1	2	2	3	3	3
Frederikshåb	0	1	1	2	2	2	2	3
Fiskenæsset	1	1	2	2	3	4	2	4
Godthåb	1	0	0	0	0	1	1	2
Sukkertoppen	1	1	2	2	1	1	0	2
Holsteinsborg	0	0	0	2	1	5	4	7
Southern Inspectorate	3	3	6	10	9	16	12	21
Egedesminde	0	0	1	0	2	2(3)	0	0
Kronprinsens Ejland	0	0	1	1	1	3	4	4
Godhavn	1	1	7	6	10	6	8	7
Christianshåb	0	1	3	3	2	4	5	4
Claushavn	0	0	1	1	2	0	0	0
Jakobshavn	2	3	3	3	4	4(3)	3	2
Arveprinsens Ejland	0	0	3	3	4	4	2	2
Ritenbenk	1	0	3	6	5	6	10	7
Umánaq	0	1	2	2	0	0	1	1
Upernavik	0	1	2	2	0	0	1	1
Northern Inspectorate	4	7	25	26	32	30	34	28
West Greenland	7	10	31	36	41	46	46	49

Trade, and some went to the Mission. On the basis of the "wage-books" of the Trade, we can show the development in this field from 1775 to 1810. This is presented in Table 17, which lists "Greenlanders in the service of the Trade"; most of these "Greenlanders" were actually half-breeds.

Again we are dealing with small absolute numbers, but they do show a considerable growth, especially from 1780 on. The growth in the Southern Inspectorate between 1805 and 1810 is certainly due to war which prevented new workers from coming from Denmark and caused several of those in Greenland to leave. Again we see that the number of Greenlanders (half-breeds) in the service of the Trade was larger in the Northern Inspectorate than in the Southern. The number of half-breeds was also greatest in the Northern Inspectorate: in 1805 it amounted to just under 3% of the male population, while in the south the corresponding figure was under 1% for a total of just under 2% of all male West Greenlanders.

If, however, we compare these figures with the total number of Trade employees, we see that in 1785, when there were 81 positions in the Southern Inspectorate, there were 6 Greenlandic employees, or 7.4%; while there were 124 positions in the Northern Inspectorate, of which Greenlanders represented 25, or over 20%. In West Greenland as a whole there were 31 Greenlanders employed, or over 15% of the 205 employees. At the close of the century, the total number of employees was normally around 210, while the 1800 figure for Greenlanders is 46, or just under 22%. This was a considerable rise, the result of a conscious policy.

Of the 35 catechists known to have been employed by the Mission in 1793, only six were known to be "mixtures". If we assume a figure of 37 native catechists for 1793, when only five missionaries were stationed in Greenland, they constituted over 88% of the Mission employees. This says less about the numerical situation, especially in comparison with the Trade, than about the conditions in which the Mission had to work during most of this period. Just a few years before 1793 there had been 10 stationed missionaries, and the number of catechists was then approximately the same, so that the 1793 figures clearly illustrate to what extent the Mission was dependent on Greenlandic employees, especially in consideration of the dispersal of settlement.

Settlements and Movements

We have just mentioned that in Julianehåb District, the most recently founded colony (1774), the population in 1805 was spread out over 37 locations, including the colony itself. This was, to be sure, a large district, the largest on the coast, unbounded on the south, unofficially rounding Cape Farvel and stretching some distance north along the east coast. In this period, however, the inhabitants of West Greenland seldom ventured this far south or east. As the crow flies, the dimensions of the district were about 120 kilometres northwest from the colony seat and about 160 kilometres south of it to Cape Farvel, for a total of about 300 kilometres. Although this district formed a special unit as it were, its settlement pattern is, nevertheless typical of a pronounced sealing area, especially as tendencies towards concentration had not yet functioned for any great length of time.

All along the coast this common Eskimo pattern of settlement was generally followed, except where colonisation had interrupted it or was interrupting it. Up to 1782 there had been alternating tendencies in the organisation of colony installations and the work of colonisation itself.[7] The Mission had, because of its premises and objectives, strived to concentrate the population; it was partially assisted in this by the presence of the Trade, since help in time of need could be got either at the Mission or from the Trade, and since the Trade afforded the opportunity to purchase whatever one might need. At first the Trade also found that its work would be alleviated by concentration, but soon realized that this was not favourable for maintaining fangst as an occupation; in addition, the inhabitants thus tended to live at the expense of the Danish institutions. Further concentration would decrease productivity, and the Trade therefore desired an emigration from the colonies, which was implemented in the 1770's. This dispersal of the population revealed a decentralizing tendency quite opposed to prevailing mercantilistic principles.

Apparently from the very beginning, the paramount objective of the Management of the Royal Greenland Trade was to increase productivity. This is presumably what underlay the establishment of the great whaling project of 1775-1781(1783), the construction of relatively many whaling stations, the local rationalising of whaling in Greenland, and the encouragement given to organise the netting of seals. In demographic policy, it resulted in the continued desire, emphasized in the Order of 1782, to focus the activities of the population on fangst, whereby the occupation of fanger became sacrosanct, as far as fangst which the Trade considered productive was concerned. To support this productivity the Trade desired as little interference in the traditional pattern of life as possible, and thus counteracted tendencies which obstructed productivity.

This principle explains why the Management of the Royal Greenland

Trade wanted to concentrate the population of one locality, but promoted dispersal in another. To build up and maintain whaling from the local stations in Greenland, a relatively large crew, constantly at disposal, was needed. The whaling stations, as described above, were not always set up at locations affording favourable conditions for other kinds of fangst, so that as a rule no Greenlanders lived there previously. They had to be induced to move there.

This appears clearly from a single example among many others. When Ritenbenk colony was moved to Zwarte Vogel Bay in 1781, this locality was uninhabited, and apparently little visited by Greenlanders; immigration had to be arranged.[8] Two years later, the Management had to remind the chief assistant there that "he should apply all his efforts to attract as many Greenlanders as possible to the lodge, in order, along with the Danes at the lodge and the installation, uniting their efforts, to promote the best conduct of whaling; and also to encourage the Greenlanders, as often as opportunity permits, to attempt the netting of seals, etc." It was, however, an absolute principle, that immigration to such localities must take place voluntarily.

On the whole there was no question of forced migration, which would actually have been expected of the trading enterprise based on such pronounced mercantilistic principles. After 1788, when distinctly liberalistic attitudes became manifest, it was of course completely out of the question. When Greenlanders were desired to move, they were to be "induced". If they refused, the Management had to acquiesce.

It goes without saying that there were difficulties in attaching immigrants to the "new" localities, especially when the liberalistic point of view supported the tradition of migration. Trading posts and settlements could be established only to be totally depopulated a few years later. In 1794 some Greenlanders, who for some time had been on Arveprinsens Ejland (Klokkerhuk), moved up the sound east of this island to another island by the name of Igdluluarssuit. Some Greenlanders from Ritenbenk District also settled here. This gave rise to dissension between traders Lunde at Ritenbenk and C.C. Dalager on Arveprinsens Ejland as to which colony or district Igdluluarssuit was to belong to; but this is another story, of the difficulties the traders had in collecting their debts from ordinary Greenlanders and of the conditions of dependence to which they therefore wished to subject them.

A few years later Igdluluarssuit seems to have been abandoned by the Greenlanders from Arveprinsens Ejland (Klokkerhuk), since in 1799 some of its inhabitants had promised the trader at Ritenbenk to remain at

Igdluluarssuit. Shortly after, however, he found out that they had all moved north, and Igdluluarssuit seems thereafter to have been uninhabited. These Greenlanders moved because a proficient Greenlandic fanger at Torssukâtak had died; the inhabitants of Igdluluarssuit, who were related to him, then moved to be with his widow and children. The trader considered this an advantage for trade at Ritenbenk since it was easier from there to get to Torssukâtak than to Igdluluarssuit; purchases of blubber and hides would thus be greater and competition from the trader on Arveprinsens Ejland would be eliminated.

There are several examples of migration for family reasons. Of course, pure visits also took place, and these could well last some time - a year or two!

The competition between Ritenbenk and Arveprinsens Ejland (Klokkerhuk) was also reflected in other migrations. The settlement at Igdlutsiaq was approximately half-way between the two colonies, and its population often migrated between it and the colonies. In 1799, three families out of a population of about 50 suddenly left Igdlutsiaq and moved to Umânaq. The trader presumed that most of the remaining population would then move south to the whaling station at Arveprinsens Ejland, so that he wanted reinforcements from elsewhere in Disko Bugt. However, the 74-year-old trader C.C. Dalager, the founder of the whaling station on the southwesternmost tip of the island, had passed away, thereby considerably lowering the morale of whaling activities there. His death resulted in a change of personnel, and the new trader at Ritenbenk announced that almost all the families at Klokkerhuk had moved to Jakobshavn, "so that there are only some families which previously mainly lived at Igdlutsiaq," just the ones who had been expected to leave. The new trader and his assistant had even themselves "persuaded (them) to move down from Ritenbenk. I know of no other way to reasonably remedy the shortage of population at Arveprinsens Ejland" than by allowing as many as possible to move there from Ritenbenk and Igdlutsiaq, after the trading expeditions had been completed. As late as 1801 the assistant at Ritenbenk announced that most of the Greenlanders had abandoned the locality. The lack of crew seems to have been permanent; the location was finally closed as a whaling station.

The migration from Igdluluarssuit to Torssukâtak was the result of a death, with relatives moving to the settlement of the deceased. Perhaps the reverse was the case at Arveprinsens Ejland. It is possible that C.C. Dalager exercised an almost supernatural effect on his Greenlandic neighbours: he possessed a tremendous authority. The whaling station had been established on his initiative, and it was his strength which kept it going. It could have been superstitious ideas about such a supernatural force which caused the Greenlanders to move. In 1805 an event took place which similarly caused the inhabitants to flee.

The superstitious fear of settling at a certain place still played its role. In 1798 an assistant at Umânaq reported that he had got a fanger to settle in a fjord near Sâtut. This locality had been inhabited previously and was considered a place where fangst was assured when it was bad everywhere else. The Greenlanders did not dare settle there after a fanger in a kayak had been killed by a furious hooded seal: "they will still not live there, unless a Dane enters the place first and remains in their tent." There are also other examples of fatal accidents or deaths causing the inhabitants to move from or to refuse to settle in previously inhabited localities. One must not forget, however, that such so-called superstitious ideas are an important element in the fangst complex with its relationships between the Greenlanders and their game animals, such as it had traditionally developed with numerous mystical aspects.

The problems connected with the immigration of Greenlanders to the whaling stations were soberly evaluated - in the spirit of the Order of 1782 - by an assistant at Arveprinsens Ejland (Klokkerhuk), with respect to the relationship between the settlement at Igdluluarssuit and the whaling station at Klokkerhuk. He had to admit, he wrote, "that the Greenlanders themselves win nothing by moving from good fangst places to whaling (stations), for at the former every good fanger has all he needs for the necessities of life, while at the latter they can at times be exposed to a lack of everything he needs. This was really the case at this place in 1793, when the Greenlanders moved away due to lack of food. Not to speak of the extent to which whaling accustoms them to Danish provisions and style of life, which increases their needs and withdraws them from their national economy." He was nevertheless convinced that it would be advantageous to man the whaling stations with Greenlanders, but only those who had shown themselves quite incompetent at ordinary fangst methods, but who could be proficient as rowers, harpooners and steerers. For him it was a question of distributing the population rationally according to their skill at one or the other form of fangst. This was strictly speaking also what the Management wanted; it therefore asserted the voluntary principle, so that it was exclusively the possibility of getting employment which would determine immigration to the whaling stations.

The civil registry lists and the "designation" lists of the missionaries listed either under a special heading or elsewhere how many persons had moved away and immigrated to the locality in question during the year dealt with. Certain localities can be followed over a number of years; for others figures are only available for certain years. Godthåb, Umánaq, and Kronprinsens Ejland can be followed over a long period of time: Kronprinsens Ejland for the longest period.

Godthåb can be observed in this respect from 1782–1783 to 1787–1788. After this period, a large number of persons moved away in 1789: the entire population of Pisugfik moved to Napassoq in Sukkertoppen District, by accounts for two reasons. One of these was that for several years the fangst had been poor at Pisugfik, so that there was famine almost every year; besides, several of the inhabitants of Pisugfik had been born and raised at Napassoq. The other reason was that at Pisugfik there were no marriageable girls, but a number of young men who wanted to get married. In general, Godthåb District suffered from the lack of marriageable girls. It is indicative of the sharp separation between the Moravian congregation and the Royal Mission that the Moravians, whose congregation included several marriageable girls, would not permit them to marry young men from the congregation of the Royal Mission unless the young men settled at Ny Herrnhut. The list submitted by the missionary Andreas Ginge in 1788 shows the movements presented in Table 18.

Table 18.

Royal Mission at Godthåb	Emigrated	Immigrated
1782–1783	5	0
1783–1784	10	9
1784–1785	46	37
1785–1786	12	1
1786–1787	6	7
1787–1788	2	6

1788 Pisugfik had a population of 32; all of them moved the following year.

A certain stability: i.e., on the whole, a balance between emigrants and immigrants, is characteristic of Godthåb District in this period. Just previously, a violent epidemic had raged. There was, however, a distinct movement in the population, much more obvious in Umánaq District, a pronounced traditional fanger district, as illustrated in Table 19. In 1793 Umánaq District had a population of 404, which death and emigration reduced to 303, a considerable decline, and one which must have been noticeable to the Trade. In general the movements were quite large. Most of the emigrants moved to the Upernavik area; the immigrants were part-

Table 19.

Umánaq	Emigrated	Immigrated
1792	42	?
1794	110	18
1795	8	46
1796	3	0
1797	58	0
1798	23	1
1799	7	33
1800	80	67
1802	0	0
1803	10	2
1804	1	20
1806	1	37
1807	21	17
1808	0	0

ly people returning from Upernavik, and partly immigrants, mentioned above, from Disko Bugt, especially Ritenbenk.

The whaling station at Kronprinsens Ejland shows a special pattern of migration, which in Table 20 has been compared with the total population. A number of years of relative stability were followed by a period of comparatively heavy migration. The 19 immigrants in 1801, when a smallpox epidemic was raging, may have been due to flight from Egedesminde. Kronprinsens Ejland was not gravely struck by the epidemic.

Table 20.

Kronprinsens Ejland	Emigrated	Immigrated	Population
1791	0	0	56
1796	6	0	43
1797	0	0	139*
1798	0	0	148
1799	0	0	160
1800 } smallpox	0	0	153
1801 } epidemic	0	19	152
1802	17	15	152
1803	3	25	166
1804	0	12	182
1805	35	3	172
1806	10	7	164
1807	26	18	162
1808	0	4	152
1809	20	14	155

* Hunde Ejland incorporated into the district.

A survey of random samples taken does not indicate that certain years were much more characterized by migration than others. The reasons for the various migrations must have been numerous and quite accidental: in some cases bad fangst.

"In the evening 3 umiaks from Naparsok landed here; they intend to continue north to Holsteinsborg. Among them are 8 fangers; other families can be expected, which have left Naparsok.... I summoned the people from Naparsok today and they declared that they intended to stay a year at Holsteinsborg, and that the main purpose of their journey was to get some rifles there for the younger of them, who had none; but if they did not think the trader there was very good, they would return." They were all related and wanted to keep together. The trader at Sukkertoppen, where they had landed on their journey, attempted in vain to persuade them to turn back, but they did promise "to come here again some other time.... They said that some of the northerners also wanted to go there. Moreover they all had great expectations of the provisions there as opposed to here."

This clearly shows what the reasons for longer journeys could be: the abundant income to be had from whaling, so that an expensive rifle could be saved up for; and the extra provisions allotted to whaling employees, which the assistant at Arveprinsens Ejland had objected to in 1798 in his evaluation.

It astounded the local administrators that a not inconsiderable portion of the population of Sukkertoppen District moved to Holsteinsborg only because it was rumoured that the chief catechist Frederik Berthelsen was to be stationed there. The missionary had to give up the idea of stationing Frederik Berthelsen at Holsteinsborg at the insistence of the Sukkertoppen trader, who feared that his district would be more or less depopulated if the chief catechist were moved.

Attachment to a personality or especially to an occupation made half-breeds into a stabilising element of the population. It can be seen directly as well as through their employment, that on the whole they were more settled, and as a rule even stayed at the same place all their lives. As the number of half-breeds gradually grew, along with their influence on the local mores, they began to change the traditional pattern of settlement. A similar influence on the population was exercised by credit and the direct interest of the traders in holding on to their debtors so they knew where they were. The attachment of the population to a specific district, continuously desired by the traders, was slowly taking effect. This was what underlay the desire to counteract the migration from Sukkertoppen in

1805 because of the transfer of Frederik Berthelsen, and the same consideration motivated the trader at Sukkertoppen when he attempted to get the emigrants from Napassoq to return in 1802.

Migrations from southern to northern areas of South Greenland gradually became so numerous that it was felt that there was good reason to restrain them. Here too the debt of Greenlanders to their local trader played its role. In 1806 Inspector Myhlenphort made this relationship the subject of a circular concerning whaling at Holsteinsborg. Migrations to Holsteinsborg entailed, he said, "that the good fangers and providers of other places emigrate to seek their fortune in whaling, whereby the colonies from which such emigrants come and the maintenance of which depends on sealing, are stripped of their best providers." In order to prevent this it was decided that only in cases of extreme urgency would Greenlanders who had moved to Holsteinsborg be employed as harpooners or steerers in whaling.

Immigration to Holsteinsborg almost took on the proportions of an invasion. Astrup, the trader at Frederikshåb, confided to his diary that on 12 June 1806 an umiak from Julianehåb passed with about 20 Greenlanders on board, on their way to Holsteinsborg, where they intended to remain. Two days later six umiaks came from Julianehåb, surely accompanied by men in kayaks. If each of the umiaks represented, as did the first one, twenty persons, then these two travelling parties alone entailed a depletion of 140 persons from Julianehåb District. This sounds quite incredible; the account can by no means be verified, so it must be accepted on faith.

The same year, Astrup and his assistant reported emigration to Holsteinsborg from Frederikshåb itself. In May several umiaks passed with a total of about 110 persons, all from the trading post of Narssalik. They intended to remain at least two years at whaling in Holsteinsborg District. "Such emigration does considerable harm to a colony, especially as among them there are a good deal of proficient fangers. It also is a loss to the chief trader, who in such cases loses all the credit he has given the Greenlanders," Here again the argument involving credit is expressed.

This immigration from the south to Holsteinsborg was originally the work of the Management and the inspector: a desired practice when the population of a district had declined considerably, especially due to epidemics. This was the case, for example, as early as 1783, when Inspector Olrik, after the epidemic which raged at Godthåb, contemplated moving good fangers into the district, and received strong support from the

Management, which even reported that the trader at Julianehåb had said that in the northern part of his colony, there were "numbers of providers who could not earn their livelihood; it is suggested, if they find it advantageous, to bring some of them either to Godthåb or to Sukkertoppen, with regard to the possibilities of whaling there." This was at a time when whaling had not yet been abandoned at Sukkertoppen.

After the smallpox epidemic at Egedesminde and Holsteinsborg in 1800 and 1801, to which 42% and 89% respectively of the population succumbed, it was especially important to build Holsteinsborg up again. In a way it was easier to repopulate Egedesminde. At Holsteinsborg, first and foremost, Qerrortussoq, one of the whaling stations, was closed. In subsequent years the survivors at Holsteinsborg proper were supplemented by immigration from the north and the south, presumably of 44 persons including 16 whalers. It seems, however, that there was some hesitation on the part of the Greenlanders about moving there immediately, perhaps out of fear of the epidemic, perhaps due to the above-mentioned superstitions. From 1803 on, immigration seems to have accelerated, so that the population of Holsteinsborg was tripled in four years, rising to 129 by 1805.

This immigration meant that in 1805 Qerrortussoq could be re-established "by the families which have come from the north and the south." During this and the following year, it seems that immigration from the south accelerated, judging by the previously mentioned emigration from Frederikshåb and Julianehåb. Inspector Myhlenphort expressed his regrets to the trader at Sukkertoppen that good fangers were moving from there to Holsteinsborg in 1805.

Much of the travelling done was not really migration, although as we have seen, journeys could last quite a while. In 1787 Rudolph Heide, the missionary at Holsteinsborg, mentioned that several heathens had come from the south; they would not receive instruction and had set off again – where he could not say, nor from where they had come. In 1803, on a trip from Sukkertoppen to Godhavn, the assistant Olrik met boats full of people from Kronprinsens Ejland, Vester Ejland, Jakobshavn, Godhavn, and Hunde Ejland, on their way to Holsteinsborg to sell the eiderdown they had collected. One can imagine these journeys as combined business and social trips, combining profit with visits to relatives who after the smallpox epidemic had settled at Holsteinsborg. There are no reports as to whether these boats returned to their homes in Disko Bugt; but this may well have been the case.

The same may have taken place at least with some of those who came from the south in 1805 and 1806. Both at Frederikshåb and Julianehåb there had been attempts to persuade them not to emigrate, or at least to promise to return. Inspector Myhlenphort made similar attempts, and some of the Greenlanders assured him that they would return to Julianehåb the following year "when they had supplied themselves with bone and tendon, etc." This looks more like a pretext. It is true they could not acquire whalebone and walrus tusks in Julianehåb. Tendons, probably those of reindeer, could be more easily acquired in Sukkertoppen or Godthåb Districts, but also at Holsteinsborg. Nor are there any reports that these emigrants returned as they had promised.

Inspector Myhlenphort was personally opposed to such emigration from the sealing districts, partly for the same reasons as the traders. Although he had got his "Greenlandic upbringing" at the whaling stations in Disko Bugt, his great interest was seal netting. He worked intensely for the introduction of this fangst method into the Southern Inspectorate, the economy of which mainly depended on sealing. He therefore thought he should protect sealing as much as possible. Whaling at Holsteinsborg was thus a cuckoo in the nest of the Southern Inspectorate; it also entailed a concentration of the population, whereas dispersal was the goal of the rest of the Inspectorate.

Dispersal

A dispersal of the population had long been the goal of the Trade, at least in the sealing districts.[9] That this was the most natural form of settlement for a sealing economy was testified to by Johan Christian Mørch, the trader at Julianehåb, in 1795: "At Lichtenau (the Moravian settlement south of Julianehåb) alone live 34 fangers, but where Greenlanders have kept their free will and only act according to the knowledge conferred by nature and experience, 50 fangers are spread out over 19 different places." On the settlement of fangers at Lichtenau and its consequences for the development of sealing he had reported a month previously: "34 fangers thus live at Lichtenau; their congregation has only 14 others, of which 5 live ½ Mil west, 4 stay ½ Mil south and the other 5 about 2 Mil south. When these 34 fangers, as well as the boys under training, so to speak occupy the fangst grounds, the seals necessarily get shy, the fangst is bad, and the Trade loses." He then compared conditions here with those at the Moravians' northern settlement Lichtenfels, near Fiskenæsset, where the seals had been driven out of the fjord by the presence of far too many fangers, so that sealing had to be carried on at other locations far from Lichtenfels.

Trader Mørch thus drew attention to the concentration of population which the Moravians, since the 1740's, had consciously adhered to. He had experienced it himself, first at Lichtenfels, then at Lichtenau; and he knew that it had long been the practice at Ny Herrnhut near Godthåb. Finally at Frederikshåb he had seen that the colony seat itself had a poor level of production, whereas the productive localities of this district were far from the colony. During his years in Julianehåb, an unspoiled sealing area especially in its southern reaches, he experienced that the dispersal of settlement was favourable to production.

Mørch did not realize - and could hardly have been expected to - that social and economic forces could draw individuals such as widows with their children, and other small groups, to the colony seats. With his locally prejudiced view, he could also not approve of the attracting effect of the whaling stations. The mission centre in each district undoubtedly exercised an attracting influence; we have previously seen how just plans for transferring one person could affect settlement. Under the influence of the Mission, immigration to the colony seats had for some time been attractive also for cultural reasons. We can also sense the attracting force of the administrative centres. But we must remember that in absolute numbers, movements of population were quite small. In addition, the differences between the various localities played a role. Whereas in one district dispersal would be to the advantage of all, in another there was a traditional migratory cycle between the colony seat and the fangst grounds, and in a third there were specially good fangst conditions at the colony seats, which therefore had a relatively large production.

Judging from the source material, pressure to disperse from places where the Greenlandic population had concentrated in the course of time focussed on the settlements of the Moravian Brethren: Ny Herrnhut and the trading post Kangeq in Godthåb District, Lichtenfels in Fiskenæsset District, and Lichtenau in Julianehåb Southern District.

The resistance of the Moravians to the dispersal of their congregation had apparently had as a result, that from the 1770's on they had taken cover; in any case, not much was said about their work. At a time when dispersal was topical at other places, nothing similar was undertaken at Ny Herrnhut, and the attachment of the inhabitants to the other localities of the Brethren was maintained.

It is possible that the Management, because of the great interest of the government from 1776 on in the development of whaling, directed its attention more to the establishment of the whaling stations and the immigration of Greenlanders to them than to the concentration problems of the older colonies. It would also have been difficult to carry out a policy of dispersal in certain areas while at the same time attempting to concentrate the population at other places; this would seem inconsistent.

However that may be, not until the Order of 1782 was the question of dispersal taken up again. "Where the Greenlanders may be found to live too concentrated, he (the trader) is to distribute them to the fangst grounds shown by experience to be the best and most profitable." He was to see "that the inhabitants did not group too much around the establishments," also so that they would not be "spoiled" by European provisions. A differentiated settlement policy was now to be initiated, determined by considerations of production, of course also having regard for the best possible living conditions of the population.

In 1783 the Moravian Brethren directed attention to their existence for an entirely different reason: the question of payment for the transportation to and from Greenland of their personnel, and exemption from freight costs for their supplies. A long discussion developed, exclusively of these economic questions, during which it was stressed, as it had been previously, how much good the Brethren did in Greenland. Inspector B. Olrik must have thought, however, that a good deal of illicit trade took place in these congregations, quite simply because produce was hardly ever purchased from their Greenlanders. Therefore he decided that the Order of 1782 was also to apply to the Brethren, so that their Greenlandic members were to sell their surplus production to the Royal Greenland Trade, and conversely, both they and the European members were to acquire their supplies from the Trade. They were, however, granted free transportation across the Atlantic for persons and personal effects.

In this manner the error of omission whereby the Moravian Brethren had not been "sworn in" when the Order of 1782 was introduced, was remedied; the Royal Mission had been "sworn in". If one of the rules of the Order was to be applied to the Moravians, the consequence must be that its other principles should also apply to them and their Greenlandic congregations, including the principle of dispersal. This was a consequence which the leaders of the Brethren must have ignored when they asked for free transportation.

The dispersal of the Moravian congregations was a long and hardly edifying affair. Inspector B. Olrik started off brusquely by ordering dispersal, but immediately encountered tenacious resistance from the leaders of the congregations. Their argument was that dispersal would hinder the progress of the mission; it was expressed by the legal counsellor of the United Brethren when he attempted to intervene in Copenhagen, proposing a compromise whereby the local elders would choose the Greenlanders who were to settle away from Ny Herrnhut – where the question of dispersal was most topical.

"It is believed here that sufficient experience has shown that these people fulfil their vocation religiously and that they heretofore have been of great use in the education of the Greenlanders, which necessarily must exercise a favourable influence on the interest of the Trade." Thus the Management justified to Inspector B. Olrik its approval of the compromise proposed by the representative of the Brethren. "And unless you are prevented by circumstances unknown to us, we would appreciate it if you hereafter would accommodate yourself to this wish of ours, and see that it is carried out." Thus the policy of leniency and caution towards the Moravian Brethren was maintained which had characterized the managements of the trade on Greenland ever since 1733. Perhaps this attitude of the Management can be better understood when we see that in the same period the Danish mission made a number of justified complaints about Inspector Olrik. His intolerance and grossly provocative conduct hardly promoted the desired smooth, balanced growth of the Greenlandic society.

Nothing seems to have resulted from this compromise. Olrik probably did not understand how to implement it, and the local leaders at Ny Herrnhut must have sabotaged it. "It will presumably take a long time to move the Greenlanders from Ny Herrnhut to other, more favourable fangst grounds, since those who are supposed to assist in this dispersal are attempting, on the contrary, to concentrate the Greenlanders," is the observation of the chief assistant at Godthåb in 1791.

By this time Inspector Olrik had been removed, but his successor Andreas Molbech Lund made just as little headway against the Moravians in the matter of dispersal. He voiced a quite different opinion of the Moravians than that previously entertained by the Management. "That the Moravian Brethren are greatly detrimental to the Trade, mainly by conglomerating their Greenlanders, especially at the places where they themselves are, of which Ny Herrnhut is a very poor fangst ground, is only too true; but what can we do with such people?"

"The Moravian or Evangelical Brethren at Ny Herrnhut last year too gave me solemn declarations that they would do all they could to get the Greenlanders living here dispersed; but as previously, these were but empty promises: they come with the excuse that the Greenlanders who were to be dispersed returned too late from their summer camps in the fjords."

He had been "detained and immobilized" with "promises and excuses, repeated and repeated." "My predecessor and I have, using various means, accomplished the same." It was their ceremonial duties: i.e., daily devotions and religious practices, which necessitated the presence of the Greenlanders at Ny Herrnhut, and "the Greenlanders of the Brethren are so subordinate to them, that I or others outside their congregation, whom I believe they consider profane, can do nothing with them, against the wishes of their superior Brethren."

Neither, then, did Inspector Lund accomplish anything in this respect. In subsequent years, Ny Herrnhut was repeatedly mentioned to the Management as a bad fangst ground, which was proven by purchase figures. By March 1796, the Management had heard enough complaints and went directly to the Rentekammer (i.e., Christian D. Reventlow), bypassing the Commission. Here the opinion of the Moravian Brethren had changed considerably from previously. Not only conditions at Ny Herrnhut, but also those at Lichtenau and Lichtenfels, were mentioned. What the Management stressed in its long written complaint was the conflict between the desire for a settlement form based on Greenlandic tradition and promoting production, and the demands of a rigid cultural influence which was essentially foreign to West Greenlandic social organisation.

Not only the poor standard of living created by concentration was pointed out, but also that the training of youth in fangst methods was being neglected, not to mention the loss continuously suffered by the Trade from the unproductive conglomeration of persons. It is not directly stated, but insinuated, that this had a demoralizing effect on other Greenlanders, not members of the Moravian congregations. The Management referred to the Directive of 2 July 1781, Article 13 of which stated that the Moravians were "in accordance with Our most gracious decrees, either issued or hereafter to be issued, in the best interest of the country and the Trade, to take all care that the Greenlanders belonging to their congregations be kept in all possible order in their houses and be held to diligence and industry in their occupations." As it seemed that these desires could not be achieved voluntarily, perhaps certain coercive measures could be applied to the leaders of the Moravian congregations, such as depriving them of their free transport privileges granted in 1783. The Rentekammer went directly to the Committee, which arranged direct negotiation between the Management and the leaders of the Moravian congregation in Ny Herrnhut.

A long report from the elder avoided the issues: all accusations were rejected but with no real arguments, except for the well-worn one that dispersal would be harmful to the souls of the Greenlanders, in consideration of the fact that they were Christians. According to the elder experience had proven and the Greenlanders themselves had told the Brothers and Sisters that "Their souls are harmed, they even get involved in fornication and live like heathens. Their children grow up hearing little of what is profitable for the salvation of their souls."

The action remained without result. "In order to get the Greenlanders of the Moravian Brethren congregation dispersed from Ny Herrnhut and Kangeq to good fangst grounds, I have applied all possible persuasion to the Brethren as well as to the Greenlanders themselves, but as little has been accomplished this year as previously." Some had indeed moved away, but just as many had moved in. "And as most of the Greenlanders in this congregation in this district are poor and are constantly asking for credit, which must be denied them," he gave those who promised to disperse considerable credit as a means of persuasion. This is what the chief assistant at Godthåb reported in 1798.

By 1802, 1804 and 1805, nothing worthy of mention had taken place with respect to dispersal from Ny Herrnhut. Purchases from Greenlandic members of the Brethren at both Ny Herrnhut and Kangeq were quite small, and their nutritional situation was poor. The period under consideration thus elapsed with no improvement in conditions at Ny Herrnhut: rather the contrary.

At the other Moravian localities the situation developed similarly. In 1793, Inspector A.M. Lund attempted in vain to get the Greenlanders to move from Lichtenfels near Fiskenæsset. In 1795 Mørch, at that time the trader in Julianehåb, described the situation at Lichtenfels previously. By 1808 the assistant at Fiskenæsset was still deploring conditions at Lichtenfels. Until March of that year, storm and ice had kept the Greenlanders of Lichtenfels from their fangst, and he had had to lend them blubber. Meanwhile the fangers living elsewhere in the district had had good fangst results and no nutritional problems. In the four years he had spent at Fiskenæsset, the Greenlanders at Lichtenfels had had such problems every year. Dispersal was still to be desired, but met with resistance from the congregation. According to the report of the trader Johan Christian Mørch in 1795, conditions at Lichtenau in Julianehåb District were just as hopeless.

Otherwise dispersal, or rather the traditional settlement habits of Greenlanders, seems to have been achieved in the Southern Inspectorate. In the Northern Inspectorate, dispersal had not previously been quite so necessary. On the whole, settlement was denser there, especially in Disko

Bugt. The establishment of whaling stations interfered, as we have seen, with the pattern. Nevertheless, dispersed settlement at many localities was also characteristic of the Northern Inspectorate. This created great difficulties for the Mission, which along with other problems had a laborious time of it.

Special Conditions

Special conditions prevailed in Umánaq District. As seen in Table 19, there was a constant migration to and from this district. Within the district a tradition had grown of spending the winter at the colony seat and carrying on various forms of fangst and hunting at various places in the summer.

As the interest of the Trade in seal netting in this district grew, and as the colony itself turned out in the long run to be a poor site for this fangst method, the desire for a dispersal to the best netting sites intensified. The problems connected with such dispersal were interwoven with the other fluid settlement conditions and the traditional migratory cycle. When fangst conditions, or rather the availability of seals, changed, these problems were not easier of solution.

Within the district there was a trading post where the Trade had hoped to be able to conduct some whaling. This was Nûgssuaq, where the colony had originally been founded. Fangst conditions and thus the settlement pattern changed constantly. Finally in 1805 the trader at Umánaq reported to the Inspector that Nûgssuaq had been abandoned by the Greenlanders. Kayak rowers considered it an unsuitable place because the seas always ran so high. Sealing was thus not really profitable, and seal netting was almost impossible.

It was therefore necessary to proceed cautiously in this district, and this meant more or less to let the Greenlandic inhabitants themselves decide where to settle and for how long. To some extent, however, they followed the establishment of new fangst grounds.

A certain traditional cycle seems also to have existed in Upernavik. After the colony was reestablished on an experimental basis in 1796, it appeared that the same settlement pattern would prevail here as previously, and as at Umánaq: that only a few fangers and their families settled at the colony seat for the winter season, left it in the spring, travelled around, and did not return until autumn. At that time it was thought that this moving to the colony seat was dictated by the help which was to be had there in times of poor fangst. There is very little material on this, as well as on conditions at Upernavik in general in this period.

The southernmost part of the Inspectorate, Egedesminde District, also had certain settlement problems. The colony seat itself was at first considered a poor fangst ground. Nevertheless immigrations to it took place, for which the Mission was blamed in 1788. Its presence was said to pull in the Greenlanders to the colony seat, where they each year suffered from lack of subsistance opportunities, so that they resorted to the emergency measures of the Trade.

It was therefore necessary to find good fangst grounds out in the district which could attract the Greenlanders. The whaling stations in the vicinity, including one in the district itself, Vester Ejland, also attracted some of the inhabitants of Egedesminde District. When M.N. Myhlenphort came to Egedesminde as a trader in 1791, he immediately began to promote seal netting and found several good netting grounds. In order to expand the district southwards and create opportunities for the more secure settlement of Greenlanders there, he established in 1791 "the Rifkol experiment," which began successfully, but was reported depopulated as early as 1797. In 1799 he enumerated 15 inhabited localities in the district.

Egedesminde District had the same experience as other colonies, that fangst prospects varied with changes in the migratory habits of the fangst animals. In 1799 Egedesminde was characterized as good for seal netting, whereas but 12 years previously it had been described as a poor fangst ground.

Thus the population situation and settlement pattern makes a variegated impression. Influencing the habits of the inhabitants, partially based on tradition, were the interests of the Trade, which in many cases coincided with Greenlandic tradition. In addition there were the interests of the Mission, which often, and for special reasons, were opposite to those of the Trade; but in this period, the Mission was certainly the weaker factor.

As long as settlement was still not stable, there were no essential changes in the construction of dwellings or the use of certain conveniences. In 1786, Inspector Schwabe expressed the desire that the Greenlanders in the Northern Inspectorate "like a number of those in the South build fireplaces in the entrances to their houses, so that often in the winter, when there was a shortage of blubber for their lamps, they could use heather, peat or driftwood, and thus be able to cook the food which they otherwise must let lie or, at the expense of their health, consume uncooked."

Around 1800 the first peat houses with inside panels were built, for example at Niaqornat in Umánaq District: it was intended for the chief of the local trading post. Perhaps such houses were also built for workers stationed at the colonies, but were probably not yet used by Greenlanders.

From the 1790's on jamb stoves and other iron stoves were sent from Denmark for use in the wooden dwellings of the colonies. This was in keeping with the systematic mining of coal in the north. As an experiment in heating a Greenlandic house, a so-called "Menage Stove", an economical stove, was shipped in 1805. Perhaps it was supposed to help the Greenlanders save on blubber: i.e., sell it to the Trade instead of using it for heating. The experiment was a total failure.

The time had not yet come for changes in construction habits. A description of a house in Frederikshåb in 1805 gives the picture of a house of the customary type: "The house in which the Greenlanders lived was, as usual, built of stone, peat and humus, about 30 alens long by 12 to 14 wide, with a flat roof consisting of collected driftwood which was again covered with heather, peat, stone and humus. It had two big peepholes, or two windows, consisting of well-sewn sealgut. The entrance was quite narrow and long, and so low that I had to creep to get in. In it there were over 50 people, including children and old people. The men on the right and the women on the left, they sat naked along the sides of the house on their benches and beds which were covered with seal-skins, which also served as beds, as especially children were sleeping soundly here and there on these benches. About 18 to 20 lamps provided the lighting. 10 or 12 kulupsiuts (i.e., big cooking pots of soapstone) filled with seal meat were hanging over the lamps and cooking away. The steam from these lamps, the raw and half-cooked meat, as well as the number of people, and the great heat here, made it intolerable for me to stay here longer than the 8 to 10 minutes I needed to satisfy my curiosity. I observed that because of the great heat in the house, 1 Greenlander took a knife and dried off the sweat running down his cheeks and breast."

The West Greenlandic Eskimo way of life was still alive.

VI. Social Conditions

The "thick air" in Greenlandic winter houses of the type just described from Uigordleq south of Frederikshåb was at the time thought to cause, or at least promote, disease. As we have seen, half-hearted attempts were made to remedy this condition. But the possible good will of the Management in this respect encountered at least three kinds of resistance. In the first place, there was a lack of capital, too great to even be able to envision reforms in this connection. Secondly, the hygienic knowledge and experience of the time was too small and uncertain: i.e., it was not really known how to improve and "raise" the housing standard. Finally, it was probably totally impossible to even attempt to suggest changes, because of both the set housing traditions and the economy of the West Greenlandic family.

Epidemics

If almost nothing was known of hygiene, as little knowledge was available of the predominant diseases. But to the extent made possible by limited resources, the little knowledge and experience which was available was applied in Greenland.

We have already seen that at several localities epidemics brought about a decline in the population. In the period from 1782 to 1808, especially extensive epidemics raged twice, and at various times there were smaller, more locally limited diseases of an epidemic character.

The first great epidemic broke out in mid-February of 1782 at Godthåb. It is difficult, on the basis of the available, meagre descriptions, to determine the disease in question. In any case it was of a typhoid nature; it may have been trichinosis. It was a violent epidemic with many deaths. In early July of 1782, 198 deaths among the Greenlanders of the Royal Mission and 165 among those of the Moravian Brethren were reported. Two so-called annex missions, which had been established relatively recently, had to be abandoned. As far as supplies were concerned, society was on the verge of catastrophe, as 71 good fangers died during the epidemic.

The epidemic quickly turned south. At Fiskenæsset 74 deaths were reported in October, and 91 the following year. The epidemic seems to have skipped Frederikshåb District, but in the autumn of 1782 it harried in Julianehåb District, where by September 1783 over 100 fangers and even more women and children had died; the following year 28 more fangers and presumably even more women and children died.

In October 1783 the epidemic broke out in Frederikshåb District. From here and from Julianehåb the disease was brought by travelling Greenlanders to the districts of the Northern Inspectorate: first to Kronprinsens Ejland in the autumn of 1785, and shortly thereafter to Jakobshavn. Many deaths were reported from both districts. A curious aspect of the course of the epidemic in Jakobshavn illustrates the degree of social isolation then prevailing between those baptized and the unconverted. The epidemic started among the baptized Greenlanders; those not baptized, who lived some ways from the colony seat, at Sermermiut were not at first affected. The situation became frightful at Jakobshavn; many of those who died were fangers, so that here, too, the food situation was critical. In 1796 the missionary, Jørgen Sverdrup, wrote: "The few who either have not yet been attacked by the disease or have already had it, have to help me almost every day to take the dead out of other houses and bury them." It must finally have become necessary - and natural - for the unconverted to help; in September of 1786 the epidemic came to them. As late as March 1787 it was still raging at Jakobshavn, where by then there were not many Greenlanders left at the colony seat itself; how many are not mentioned.

By 1785 this epidemic had spread to Christianshåb and Claushavn, and it seems to have come to Egedesminde at the same time, taking many lives at all these places. All the way from Julianehåb South District, to which the epidemic had spread from the North District, deaths were reported that same year, but only a few. After 1787 nothing more was heard of this frightful harrying plague, which seems to have totally ignored Ritenbenk, Arveprinsens Ejland, Godhavn and areas farther north.

Once in July 1800 a Greenlandic fanger at Hunde Ejland went on board an English whaling vessel, where he bartered for some used clothes. Thereupon he left Hunde Ejland with his family and went to Christianshåb. By July 21 it was reported that he and his entire family, with the exception of a little daughter, had died of an undetermined disease. The previous day one or another disease had been observed among some of the inhabitants of Egedesminde; two of them died on 24 July, and Myhlenphort, the local trader, immediately initiated a number of quarantine-like measures. A fortnight later there was no doubt in the community that the disease was smallpox; this was confirmed a few days later by a surgeon, Th. Chr. Eulner, who had come from Godhavn.

The surgeon and the trader, assistants and missionaries, artisans and "sailors" did everything in their power to impede the progress of the pestilence. But in vain. The quarantine measures were thwarted by ignorance at Egedesminde, but they seem to have functioned at all the other localities in Disko Bugt: only Jakobshavn suffered any deaths from the epidemic. In the north, the smallpox epidemic was mainly limited to Egedesminde District, where its course was violent: in the course of 1800 and 1801, 42% of the population of the district died.

On 5 August 1800 post kayaks were sent from Holsteinsborg to Egedesminde; they arrived on the 8th and reported that in Egedesminde South District there had been four deaths from the same disease as at Egedesminde Colony. They had visited them. The post kayaks returned home on 5 September, and by the 21st the crew had become ill and the assistant had observed smallpox blisters on them. On 22 and 23 September the two kayak men died, but by that time the contagion had already spread. In spite of isolation and quarantine measures, the epidemic spread. By the end of October, around 100 persons had died at Holsteinsborg and the whaling station at Qerrortussoq. On 18 May 1801 it was reported to the Inspector of the Southern Inspectorate that between 340 and 350 of the population of Holsteinsborg District had succumbed to smallpox: i.e., around 89% of the population of this district had been hit by this fatal plague. To illustrate the situation, "only 2 adults of the station's (i.e. Qerrortussoq) and 14 of the colony's Greenlanders liable to watchings have been spared their lives, and about 30 other adults and children of both sexes at both places together have likewise remained alive." These 16 survivors along with the European crew of the station succeeded in catching and landing 17 whales. Then the epidemic was over. But for a time, the station at Qerrortussoq had to be abandoned. The other colonies of the Southern Inspectorate were completely spared this smallpox epidemic.

One of the hygienic problems of the epidemic was what to do with the dead bodies. The colony could hardly keep up with the demand for coffins; lesser localities had to make out as best they could. Several suggestions were aired: to burn the corpses or sink them in the sea. But all that was done in this respect was to burn all their belongings which might be contagious. Taking care of all the diseased was a Sisyphean labour. It may be that Eulner, the surgeon, succumbed to exhaustion and bitterness at the course of the epidemic and his own powerlessness to control it: he committed suicide at Godhavn in 1801. He was quite respected, being the first surgeon and physician employed to give direct assistance to the Greenlandic population, and was partly paid by the North Greenland welfare fund.

Between these two extensive epidemics both inspectorates were burdened with lesser pestilences, often limited to one or two districts. Some were of a typhoid nature, or perhaps trichinosis; others resembled influenza. Common to all were several mortalities, both adult and infant, during a short period. Such epidemics had a double effect on the state of health of the inhabitants, since they also interfered with the general food situation. Each time, the refrain was voiced that so and so many fangers were dead and the locality was painfully lacking "providers". At Ritenbenk an epidemic in 1797 left the inhabitants in a tired and weak condition so that "the fangers have been unable to accomplish anything, although there has been an abundance of sea animals."

Other Diseases

Epidemics were not the only diseases which plagued the Greenlanders. Acute cases such as gall-bladder infections, tumours, and strange abcess-like illnesses were reported as unique phenomena. Boils were common, and sometimes fatal. Xerophthalmia and conjunctivitis, well known from the reports of Hans Egede, must have continued to plague the Greenlanders, but this cannot be documented. Scabies was common, often of an epidemic nature, sometimes confined to a small locality. Perhaps dysentery should also be counted among the epidemic diseases which harried at various places.

The most common disease, which occurred almost every year, was called "Sniffles, cough, sharp pains and spitting blood." "Almost all the Greenlanders are ill with their usual autumn illness, the cough," is the report from one place. "Sharp pains" are sometimes mentioned as the cause of death. This many-headed disease of the respiratory tract seems to have been prevalent everywhere. As a rule it is identified as tuberculosis, which throughout the 18th century is repeatedly mentioned as "sharp pains" or "weakness of the chest". It is presumably characteristic that during influenza-like epidemics it often appeared, in a worse form. It is typical that "sharp pains" are of a "dangerous" nature at Nanortalik, an area where Greenlanders had not long associated with Europeans. In 1805 such an influenza-like epidemic started at Godthåb: "a malignant and contagious disease consisting of chest weakness, hard coughing and sometimes fever." It attacked both Europeans and Greenlanders, but as a rule was fatal only to Greenlanders. It has since become known that previously healed tuberculosis can flare up and become fatal during an influenza epidemic.

This time, the influenza spread farther south to Fiskenæsset, Frederikshåb and Julianehåb, bringing the loss of smell and taste, "a violent cough, sniffles, a painful headache and tender weakness of the chest." Many died, and the survivors at Julianehåb were feeble and emaciated; "we look like skeletons," wrote Mørch, the trader.

Some deaths were recorded among the Europeans, most probably due to tuberculosis. But the main causes of death of this group seem to have been accidents and old age, although several suicides are mentioned.

Strangely enough accidents, as for example kayak accidents, do not appear as causes of death as often as one would expect; nor do whaling accidents, although the dangers were great. This is probably more due to faulty records than to reality.

All this, compared with impressions gained from the extant civil registry lists and from the reports in the source material, presents the picture of a population which was incredibly vigorous for the harsh conditions in which it existed, but which was plagued by greater or lesser epidemics which flared up quickly, by the erratic wanderings of the fangst animals, and by periodic famines. A poor, dangerous existence near the starvation level.

Famines

"If they have no other fish, they resort to sea scorpions, and lacking them, to mussels. If these are wanting, there is seaweed, and if it is lacking, the Greenlander will resort to the hide of his boat," wrote Jonas Collin in 1809, to which experience of the past can add old kamik boots and anything else containing fats.[1] Perhaps it was taken from the Order of 1782 (Chapter 4, Paragraph 3), when Collin explained the repeated lack of sufficient food by the failure of foresight, to which he added that this lack was "really a consequence of their great frugality." But not even with this addition can we say that Collin understood the real cause of the famines, or rather their causes, for there were probably several.

It is a fact which has been documented in many ways that famines occurred more often after 1750 than previously. For the period from 1782 to 1808 it is actually possible, on the basis of available source material, to construct a chronicle of periods of indigence and distress, occurring one year here, the next year there, and in some years along the entire West coast of Greenland. It was reported almost every year that lamps were extinguished from a lack of animal oil; that fangst was made impossible by either too much ice, or because the ice was too thin or too thick; that high seas and "stormy weather" kept the fangers idle for weeks, and sometimes for a whole month. In Disko Bugt, for example the winter of 1792–1793 was especially bad. Poor fangst had resulted in a lack of hides, which made it impossible to maintain the fangst vessels, so that the Greenlanders could not get out to their fangst grounds to land angmagssat and black halibut. Sled dogs starved to death, thus removing the most common form of winter transport and further impeding fangst.

The regularity with which famines occurred at the end of the 18th century and at least up to 1808 does not indicate that lack of foresight can have been the reason for them. If this really were the reason, one would have to attempt to find the reason or reasons for this lack of foresight; it is not sufficient to explain a condition with a postulated generalisation.

It appears that in the north of West Greenland the autumn months were, on the whole, the most critical. Time after time it is mentioned that the fangst failed in the period from October to around the end of December. Sometimes it is also mentioned that the reasons were either the failure of the fangst animals to appear, unstable weather and ice conditions, one or another contagious disease, or two or more of these reasons at the same time. Farther south, from Sukkertoppen to Fiskenæsset, and perhaps including Frederikshåb, February and March were the critical months. Here it was seldom ice conditions which prevented fangst, but rather week-long storms and the failure of the fangst animals to turn up at their habitual grounds.

When we add to all this the periodic bouts of disease, there are sufficient factors to explain the consequences: the lack of Greenlandic provisions. If we then add the previously mentioned small number of "providers" in proportion to the population, the fact that diseases took a heavy toll in precisely this part of the population, and that the amount of food a kayak fanger could bring home to the many hungry mouths every day was limited, there are certainly sufficient reasons for the occurrence of low supplies and thus of periodic famines.

Illustrative is a report on the situation at Jakobshavn after a typhoid epidemic in 1796–1797. November 1796 to January 1797 only 189 seals were killed, and these had to feed around 250 persons. This did not amount to one whole seal per person for ten weeks in which there were no other Greenlandic provisions to be had. There was great misery, one of the conditions of a subsistence economy, especially at the limit of survival.

There is no doubt that famines were unavoidable and essentially due to the natural conditions of existence, especially the climate. The period from 1740 to 1780 was a pulsation period with large amounts of ice, developing a change of climate with relatively mild winters and a large amount of precipitation, which in turn affected the conditions essential for the existence of the local fauna, and changed their migratory habits. This mild climate seems to have been repeated a few years later and to have continued perhaps until 1810. In precisely these periods the fangst seems to have failed locally, thus worsening the food situation. Famines occurred because of climatic changes and the resultant unstable weather and changes in the occurrence of the fangst animals. There was no question of lack of providence, but rather of a change in natural conditions. The conditions for human beings in such latitudes changed, and the now more than 60-year-old foreign cultural influence and economic changes may have inhibited the adaptability of the Greenlanders. Finally, these conditions can be imagined as being the reasons for the lively migration which was characteristic of the period and which was an expression of the almost instinctive tendency to move according to fangst opportunities.[2]

In any case, these periods of famine were felt as disasters by the inhabitants; they were a social evil which the Management had to undertake to remedy, further emphasizing the aspect of protection in the Greenland policy of the time, which was manifested, inter alia, in the Order of 1782.

Countermeasures

To counter the scourge of famine, the creator of the Order of 1782, Johan Fr. Schwabe, first and foremost attempted to attack the Greenlanders' postulated lack of "providence": i.e., their failure to "save" some fangst produce from good times for poorer times, which he considered to be the reason for repeated periods of indigence. "If they set aside what is necessary for the conduct of fangst and the maintenance of their economy before trading for less necessary or superficial things, etc., their need would never rise to such heights as it does in many winters," he concludes, after a long explanation of which kind of fangst the Greenlandic fangers should, in his opinion, carry on in preference to others. We can almost hear him sigh when he touches on seal netting, which could yield the Greenlanders a lot of produce, especially in periods when fangst was otherwise poor, if they would resort to this method.

But all this was just a kind of introduction, as a justification for an energetic appeal to traders and assistants to promote by all conceivable means the fangst of animals which were profitable to both the Greenlanders and the Trade. In the best mercantilistic fashion, he thought that the Trade should interfere with production and producers by regulating, promoting and distributing; including interference with settlement and dispersal. The essential aspect of this paragraph must be emphasized: that its provisions were to be implemented for the sake of the welfare of the Greenlanders, not in order to increase purchases and thus the revenue and profit of the Trade. One of the motivations in his introduction was that the Greenlanders purchased from the Trade superficial and useless things before assuring the near future, thus providing their "lack of providence". Traders and assistants were then to exercise restraint in selling such items, which were, nevertheless, profitable for them and the Trade.

It was precisely according to this principle that the classification of sales items in the general schedule was made, including the exclusion of Greenlanders from the purchase of certain "luxury items". At several places the Order impressed on traders and assistants to see to it that the Greenlanders did not "deprive themselves of the true necessities required for carrying on fangst and maintaining their households." On the whole, this provision seems to have been observed, partly because it was in the interest of a trader to observe it because of the debt the Greenlanders in his district could get involved in, and which it was in his interest to have as small as possible.

In other words an attempt was made indirectly to influence the consumption habits of the inhabitants, in order thus to restrain the detrimental affects of famines. But this did not exclude taking other measures to remedy the situation, extensions of means previously used to solve this problem. On this point unwanted debts make their appearance again.

The Order of 1782 actually confirmed previous practice in the allotment of food in times of need. When "the need of the inhabitants really demands relief, permitted types of Europeans provisions, dried fish, coarse hardtack and field peas" could be distributed to the needy in proportion to their need, but with thrift. If the fangst failed generally, leading to a long period of famine so that extra rations were necessary for a long time, the poorest Greenlanders could receive them free, "but the others must pay with Greenlandic products when the fangst is good again." This provision can be compared with later provisions dealing with credit in bad times, so that the inhabitants could immediately get "the necessities required by their fangst and their economy, so that they shall not, lacking these, become idle and, with their families, suffer hardship."

The provision concludes with some "wise advice": "It is good if in good times the Greenlanders establish a credit at the Trade to help them in bad times, if only they are not thus cheated." Aside from the fact that this advice seems to counter giving credit to Greenlanders in general, it could doubtlessly encourage traders to purchase produce from fangers to a greater extent than warranted by the principle of foresight. According to this paragraph, it was better for the trader to owe the Greenlanders than vice versa. We cannot, however, see that this bit of advice was ever followed, and for good reason. In this period Greenlanders were seldom seen to have any credit at the Trade. When it did turn out, for example after a death, that the deceased had some credit outstanding, it was usually a small sum.

The trader himself was responsible for provisions allotted on credit in times of need, just as he was personally responsible for all other credit which he granted; he was in fact responsible for the entire economy of the district. The amount which he dared to give free, i.e., in the name of the Trade, was limited, because it would be debited the colony district and thus influence its final account and thereby the trader's own income.

The types of provisions named: "dried fish, coarse hardtack and field peas" were sent to Greenland specifically for "relief and help in time of hunger," and were to be accounted for accurately. There was always to be sufficient on order and sufficient in stock. But what did "sufficient" mean, when times of hardship were so variable in length and severity? And how were stocks to be kept up all the time, when they were being used? Whatever was needed above the quantity sent was to be ordered, as has been mentioned. This system degenerated into the practice of the trader in specific cases feeling obliged by prevailing hardship to allot provisions at his own personal expense, when stocks were exhausted and he dared not allot any more in the name of the Trade.

The above-mentioned types of provisions were called "Greenlander provisions", although the same type of food also formed a part of the rations of stationed Europeans. It gradually became too difficult to keep these identical types of provisions separate in stocks and accounts. In addition, the inhabitants quite naturally gradually developed the attitude that these provisions were sent specially to them, and that they therefore had a right to them in any case, whether in times of hardship or not. This violated both the letter and the spirit of the rules of the Order and of later circulars. The term "Greenlander provisions" was therefore abolished in

1804, but not the rules for allotting provisions in times of need. On the other hand the liability of the trader was increased, if he were not extremely frugal in allotting them. The principle was that "Greenlanders are surely happiest the more they can, independently of Danish help, provide for themselves with their own industry from the supplies of the country."

Sometimes it happened that a far-sighted chief (a trader or a senior assistant) had been fortunate enough to be able to save up Greenlandic produce. In 1806 the January cold had been quite harsh at Fiskenæsset, where the fjord froze up quite a way into the sea. The cold weather lasted until February and made sealing impossible, with the result that all the Greenlanders at Lichtenfels suffered need and hardship. "Every day now they come to me to borrow blubber for their lamps and to get food relief; it would be inhumane to deny them either, for their need is really great and it is impossible for them under the present conditions to remedy it," wrote Heilmann, the senior assistant, in his diary. He had, however, from the autumn seal netting put aside "a rather large number of seal carcasses," which he now distributed to the needy as provisions, "having saved the Trade the expense of European provisions." By "seal carcasses" he must have meant the meat, since the blubber and hides had been delivered to the Trade.

Such an initiative was a relief measure in principle along the lines of the Order of 1782, but in itself it did not help to promote what the Order considered the most effective remedy against famine: providence. It is questionable, as we have seen, whether lack of providence was ever a factor in famine. From the Southern Inspectorate there were also comments on the periodic lack of opportunity to put aside food supplies from good times for bad times.

The Order had, for example, mentioned angmagssat fangst. Andreas Rosenvold, the missionary at Fiskenæsset, described the angmagssat situation there in 1797-1798: "The Greenlanders themselves are now so accustomed and themselves understand the necessity of herring collecting (angmagssat fangst), that they never let an opportunity go by without, according to their ability, taking advantage of this remedy against need; but if the early summer is humid, all their industry and toil is lost, as the herring, which can only be caught at a certain time, rot quickly either during or after their mediocre drying and can by no means be preserved for winter provisions. If the sealing is not then so much the better, there is every reason to fear the most pitiful conditions." This is a shining example among many others that it was not always possible to "put away fangst produce from good times for bad times." The regular repetition of famines also shows that the Greenlandic population was now partially dependent on supplies of food from abroad.

"The King's Ration"

The repeated demands of the Order of 1782 and later of the Management of the Royal Greenland Trade for frugality in the allotment of provisions to the Greenlandic population was presumably the expression of the general reluctance of the leadership to "spoil" this population away from their natural foodstuffs. This frugality assumed the character of miserliness and approached doctrinarianism when an attempt was also made to abolish an old tradition.

It cannot be determined when the custom arose in Greenland of celebrating the birthday of the reigning king with a little treat; perhaps it dates from Governor Pårs' celebration of the monarch's birthday with a festival. Greenlanders present participated in this celebration in 1729. Throughout the century we hear occasionally of the celebration of this day, in different ways at the various colonies. The discussion of this institution reveals that for quite some time this treat had been held, but not at all the colonies. As Christmas gradually began to be specially celebrated at the colonies, the custom of distributing food was extended to include this holiday.

"As today was the exalted birthday of His Majesty the King, bread, grain and rejected white peas were distributed to the Greenlanders. The harpooners and steerers were also served distilled spirits, after which they were all reminded of the obedience and diligence, especially in whaling, which they owed His Majesty the King and their exalted authorities. In commemoration of the King's birthday, flags were hoisted and several cannon shots fired." This is how the day was celebrated at Holsteinsborg in 1788. In 1804 the celebrations were extended to providing a dancing party for all the residents of the colony house.

In 1793 the Management seems, in view of the general encouragement of frugality, inspired by the acute financial crisis, to have intended to abolish this tradition, both the "king's rations" and Christmas rations. This was apparently advocated warmly by A.M. Lund, the extremely rationalistic inspector of the Southern Inspectorate. But in the event, the Management retreated, thinking that it would not be "advisable to abolish it by a direct prohibition," as this custom had now been introduced at various places, but the inspector could surreptitiously attempt to get the custom to die out of its own accord.[3]

In comparison with the consumption of each colony, the amount of provisions used to "celebrate" these two holidays was infinitesimal. The tradition was not broken; it was kept in force right up to 1950.

Such "treats" played of course no role worth mentioning in the general food situation, nor as a remedy against times of need. Efforts to save were carried to extremes of pettiness. One can hardly understand that the idea of not celebrating the king's birthday could even be entertained in this period of autocracy. Although efforts to save were inspired by the government, such an extreme could risk being *lèse-majesté*. Besides, "the king's ration" helped create the devotion of the Greenlandic population to the head of the realm, and thus its emotional sense of belonging to the realm itself. And as far as irrational considerations are concerned, one must add that the Greenlanders felt it was their right to get these rations twice a year.

These two holidays were then, as to some extent also later, special occasions for general charity, elements of the "social welfare" of the time. And they functioned as such in Greenland, so that the rations have been included in this chapter.

The North Greenland Welfare Fund

Although the lack of providence was maintained as the reason for famine, various countermeasures were instituted: the general intensification of the variety of fangst deemed most profitable, relief measures in times of hardship according to the Order of 1782, and finally the North Greenland Welfare Fund.

This welfare fund, which gradually acquired several parallel objectives, was unique in the European consciousness of the time. The idea seems first to have been conceived by S. Sandgreen, the trader at Godhavn. In 1782 twelve whales had been caught in partnership between stationed Europeans and Greenlandic whalers. The proceeds of the catch were to be distributed the share of the Greenlandic whalers amounted to up to 1000 rigsdalers, most of which was covered by what they had got on credit. The difference was 180 rigsdalers, which the trader wanted to set aside, partly to cover further credit which would be given, and partly "I think this little sum should be put aside to help these Greenlanders when their fangst fails and they need it."

Sandgreen's idea of "self-help" was in line not only with the "providence" principle, but also with other similar relief measures locally instituted in West Greenland in the 1760's and 1770's.[4] It was thus Sandgreen's idea to build up some support for the Greenlandic whalers at Godhavn against times of need when the fangst failed and famine set in.

Inspector Schwabe was not slow in adopting Sandgreen's idea; it suited him perfectly. By 2 January 1783 he had, presumably with the 180 rigsdalers, "laid the groundwork of a welfare fund for needy Greenlanders, which I hope will be of much use in time." At the same time he applied for permission to let the fines which, according to the Order of 1782, were assessed in the Northern Inspectorate, accrue to this welfare fund, and to have its contents listed as credit in the accounts of the Trade. The Inspector was to be empowered to requisition necessary amounts. He presented this idea, however, as a suggestion, and did not present a final plan; this would be sent later. It is, nevertheless, worthy of note that Schwabe had already expanded Sandgreen's idea to apply to the whole of Disko Bugt, and that its objective was not to be relief in times of need, but assistance to widows and fatherless children.

The Management immediately "and with much pleasure" approved his plan and resolved that fines already due and all future fines to be imposed within the inspectorate were to accrue to the fund. Schwabe intended the fund to be effective; without waiting for the approval of the Management, he wrote to the trader C.C. Dalager: "I already have a little fund, and I shall take care of it hereafter, so the children of this country in time will thank me in my grave."

He realized, however, that he had to find out first whether Greenlanders' shares in whaling could bear an annual fee to the fund, and secondly, whether he could win over the leaders of the whaling stations to his idea. Finally, it was not unimportant to have a more or less certain estimate of the sum which could be expected annually from the Greenlanders' shares of whaling proceeds; this sum would of course always depend on whaling results, but he proposed to set aside 100, 200 or 300 rigsdalers annually, depending on these results.

It is evident from the preliminary outline of the welfare fund and from Schwabe's inquiry sent round in 1783 to the chiefs of the whaling stations in Disko Bugt, that the money in the fund was to be set aside as a fund, the *interest* on which would be devoted to assistance to widows and fatherless children. The fund would thus not begin to function until it had accumulated sufficient means, these means had drawn interest, and the interest had constituted a sufficiently large sum to enable assistance to be given. The principle applied was thus not that of assurance, but rather the classical principle of capital accumulation.

The interest was thus not to be used as Sandgreen had originally conceived using the 180 rigsdalers: for relief in times of distress. Both Schwabe's letter to the Management and his inquiries to the whaling chiefs state explicitly that the chiefs, in distributing the proceeds from whaling, should see to it that the Greenlanders did not spend their shares immediately, but that a sum could remain to their credit in the local accounts, precisely to satisfy the principle of providence.

This innovation took place in a remote corner of the world, and therefore remained unnoticed by it, most likely also because it appeared in a small population, disregarded in other respects. It was unique because it was the very first social welfare fund essentially based on funds produced by the labour of those to whom assistance was to be granted, and furthermore their fellow-citizens might benefit from it. The idea was realized in Greenland, on the basis of a Greenlandic occupation; it was thus attached to Greenlandic society, but it was conceived in a mind influenced by the profit-and-duty morale of European rationalism and by the respect for human dignity of the time. In the light of the maxim often quoted to characterize the enlightened despotism: "Everything for the people, nothing by the people", it is typical that the primary source of this fund, part of Greenlanders' whaling shares "was, unknown to them, deducted and set aside for the common good..."

In subsequent years this plan was laid down in greater detail, including procedures connected with it. The Inspector was to make payments from the fund and present accounts of receipts and expenses in Greenland. If a need were to arise for payments not included in the original plan, the inspector would have to get the approval of the Management. If the inspector did not think it proper in such cases to await the approval of the Management, he and the four best reputed traders together constituting a council could decide the matter by a voting majority, subject however to later confirmation by the administration. In 1784 Schwabe requested royal confirmation of the establishment of the welfare fund and a royal assurance that its capital and interest would always, undiminished, belong to the Greenlanders of the Northern Inspectorate, regardless of the future fate of the Royal Greenland Trade.

The Management took note of all Schwabe's proposals. Royal confirmation came through on 6 January 1785. Inspector Schwabe then proposed to the Trade to pay interest on the fund at at least 2 per cent. At first the Management carefully avoided the issue, it would "first of all be difficult." The difficulty was that the Management did not know - or dared not decide - how to invest these funds, now that the affair was being represented to the king. The Management did agree to consider this proposal and meanwhile "on all occasions to show the welfare fund as much favour as possible."

By 1788 this question of interest had not yet been decided, and especially in that year, in which a commission had been appointed to investigate the demonopolization of trade in Greenland, the Management was even less inclined to make a decision. It did, however, hold out a prospect that this matter "will perhaps be the subject of further discussion - later on." Schwabe, as a member of the Commission, was now in a position to take up the matter himself. On 18 February 1789 the Management reported that the capital of the fund on 31 December 1787 was 3361 rigsdalers and 24 skillings, and suggested that this capital be invested in royal bonds. In 1790 the Commission resolved, however, that the Trade was to pay interest on the capital of the welfare fund at the rate of two per cent per annum, and at the same time expanded the objectives of the fund to include giving help under special circumstances. In return for this interest, "in years when special relief is needed at one or another colony or station because of the failure of whaling, ⅓ of the amount given to the Greenlanders is to be debited this fund." Hereby Sandgreen's idea was to some extent reincorporated into the objective of the welfare fund, and in addition a precedence was created for further debiting of its means in special cases, in addition to its original purpose.

In 1793, Inspector Schultz expressed his concern as to the condition of the welfare fund, since for two years in a row it had had to supply considerable sums for assistance in bad whaling periods over the whole of Disko Bugt, sums which as decided in 1790 covered one-third of these expenses. It would not be able to bear such a load in the future, so that the rules would have to be set in a more reasonable proportion to the fund's ability to pay. This was done in 1794, when it was determined that the maximum annual share of the Royal Greenland Trade in provisions assistance for the entire inspectorate in times of bad whaling should amount to 500 rigsdalers. Whatever was given in additional assistance would have to be paid by the welfare fund.[5]

This could entail a direct or indirect expansion of the area covered by the welfare fund to include relief in districts outside the whaling areas of Disko Bugt, such as Umánaq or Upernavik, also in cases in which individual groups temporarily moved from such areas to Disko Bugt. This was an unforeseen attack on the reserves and income of the fund, and strictly speaking not included in its statements of objectives.

In the long run, the charter of the welfare fund could not remain geographically limited to the Disko Bugt area, nor could its relatively narrow objective be maintained. In 1798 Inspector Bendeke reported, in connection with his presentation of accounts to the Management of the Royal Greenland Trade, that as an expense in the account of the welfare fund he had listed 20 rigsdalers as an annual contribution towards the raising of illegitimate children whose fathers could not be found for the stipulated support payment. This expenditure was within the objectives provisions of the welfare fund, or could at least be interpreted as such. But another expenditure, of 40 rigsdalers, was not: this sum was listed as payment for medicine used against diseases among the Greenlanders of the inspectorate. This extension of the field of operations of the welfare fund was justified by the fact that it had also participated in the payment of the first surgeon really appointed, in 1792, to attend to all in the Northern Inspectorate.

In 1799 the administration approved these 40 rigsdalers as an annual contribution to medicinal preparedness, but wanted the support payment to illegitimate children as well as support to a Greenlandic cooper's apprentice transferred to other accounts. As early as this, it was important not to overburden the welfare fund.

In 1797 the welfare fund had to spend approximately 530 rigsdalers, in addition to the 500 rigsdalers spent by the Trade according to the provisions of 1794 for the distribution of provisions in times of bad fangst. It seemed that such expenditure would continue. Whaling was apparently not as profitable as previously, so that the income of the fund declined.

The Management investigated the reasons for this, and thought that too much credit was being given to the whalers, whereby too much of what they received as their shares of the whaling proceeds went to cover their debts. The Management had already thought that these Greenlandic whalers were favoured, partly because they received supplementary ration, free during whaling operations and watchings, and partly because in any case they had larger incomes from whaling than did other Greenlanders. On the whole they were better off than sealers, so that perhaps more and more sealers tried to get jobs as whalers, which again raised the relief expenses of the welfare fund and decreased its income.

The inspector was therefore advised to limit credit as much as possible, but with caution. It was possible that some chiefs gave more credit than they actually thought warranted, because they feared their Greenlanders would move to the district of a more generous chief, if they were too stingy. If this took place, they would be faced with a shortage of crew, lose income and have trouble collecting the credit they had already given. The Management apparently did not have full confidence that its chiefs were pulling together with it. It cannot be proven whether the lack of confidence of the Management was justified.

The attitude of the Management towards the welfare fund seems to have been somewhat erratic. The enthusiasm with which the idea was received was perhaps based on the opportunity seen in the future means of the fund for shouldering some of the relief burdens of the Trade. This enthusiasm cooled down somewhat when the Trade was obliged to pay interest on the capital of the welfare fund, and even more when its means showed signs of overloading. They nevertheless wanted it maintained and continued, as it had become a stabilizing factor among the inhabitants of Disko Bugt. Therefore the Management supported efforts to establish a similar fund in the Southern Inspectorate.

The South Greenland Welfare Fund

It was difficult getting the idea of a welfare fund to catch on in the Southern Inspectorate. In the first place, the imagination of responsible persons there did not reach farther than seeing such a fund as a copy of the one in North Greenland, which meant that it would have to be based on whaling. It would have been impossible to base such a fund on sealing, which was the main occupation in the Southern Inspectorate, because sealing was to too great an extent an individual enterprise, not carried on in partnership, and it never produced so much that there could be anything left over for a fund. In reality only whaling could produce sufficiently.

There was only one district where whaling was carried on in the Southern Inspectorate, and that was Holsteinsborg, so that a welfare fund would have to be limited to that area. Dead whales which occasionally drifted into the other districts, and the sporadic fangst of qiporqaq farther south could not form the basis of any fund.

In connection with an explanation of the North Greenland system of payment for borrowed whaling equipment, which the Management wanted to see introduced at Holsteinsborg, it also suggested the establishment of a welfare fund there. The "payment" of the Greenlanders' share in this fund depended on the full yield of blubber and tusks being delivered to the Trade, and on a distribution of the share accruing to the participating Greenlanders. Inspector Olrik had in vain attempted to introduce such a system at Holsteinsborg, but had met compact resistance from the Greenlandic whalers there. Now in 1789 the newly stationed inspector, A.M. Lund, was asked to see if he could succeed. The establishment of a welfare fund depended on a system of distribution, the introduction of which would create various difficulties, prophesied the Management. Of course it was desirable to establish a welfare fund in the Southern Inspectorate, but it was nevertheless thought "that caution advises against attempting this for the time being."

Caution advised against introducing rules without consulting the Greenlanders involved - at least at Holsteinsborg. There is a distinct difference between the attitude of the Management in 1789 and Schwabe's statement in 1783 about withholding some of the distribution "unknown to the Greenlanders". The Greenlandic whalers at Holsteinsborg had a longer tradition of fangst in partnership, with which not even the Management could interfere arbitrarily. The Holsteinsborgers apparently realized to a greater degree what to retain from tradition in order to get the most out of it. One had to negotiate with them in order to get anywhere. This is a noteworthy feature of an otherwise so authoritarian management.

For ten years the question of a welfare fund in South Greenland rested. A conflict between Holsteinsborgers and the inhabitants of Qerrortussoq over the rights to a drift whale was the pretext for taking the matter up again. Inspector N.R. Bull hoped by his own presence to get the conflicting parties to come to terms on the basis of the proceeds from the drift whale being considered as the first contribution to a welfare fund, said in one letter to be "for needy Greenlanders", in another "for food for them and their descendants, when the usual famine threatens these poor souls with death," i.e., saving up for help in hard times. He did not succeed, and had to award the drift whale to the inhabitants of Qerrortussoq.

Meanwhile, the fangst of 1799-1800 was extraordinarily good at both Holsteinsborg and Qerrortussoq. At the latter place, the Greenlandic whalers offered two whale halves to the welfare fund, although it had not yet been set up. Inspector Bull therefore had to let this offer depend on the decision of the Management.

Meanwhile at Holsteinsborg the trader, E.C. Heiberg, had continued discussions with the Greenlandic whalers there. He had confronted them with the choice between either a distribution system with the withholding of a certain part, depending on the role of the individual in the whaling operations; or the full "payment" of one whale, if four were caught, three if the total catch was eight whales, with all whales over eight caught going in full to the welfare fund. And the catch quite surpasses these expectations.

Now the Greenlanders wanted a determination of what each one could expect each year from the prospective welfare fund. For the time being they wanted to have one whale's worth of merchandise the following year. At the same time, they wanted to be assured of continued free rations on whale watchings. Some expressed the desire to purchase certain "luxury" items, such as flour and butter, "in order to be able to bake cakes in the egg season." "In order to satisfy these" Holsteinsborgers, Heiberg had promised to request the Management to send these items "for pancake use". He also had to promise to seek permission for them to buy coffee, tea and sugar, which were otherwise forbidden merchandise.

From the discussions among the Greenlanders, Heiberg understood that they were not disinclined, in good fangst times, "to save up even quite a bit every year but preferably so they would get it all back paid in provisions and a number of types of merchandise instead of letting the capital remain. They think about like the proverb: What the body earns the body should consume." They could not see any use in saving up for their descendants. The future would have to take care of itself. Nor could they recognize a need to help widows and fatherless children: these received food when everyone had food, and were needy when everyone else was. But they could see the use of saving up for hard times.

In his letter to Inspector N.R. Bull in Godthåb, Heiberg summarized this entire argumentation, also in order to point out certain elements which indicated that it might be better to "plan a savings bank for them". This is noteworthy, as savings banks had not yet seen the light of day in either Denmark or Norway. In other words, Heiberg here ventilated an entirely new idea, which apparently no one picked up.

In his letter, Heiberg drew the conclusion from these discussions that in order to succeed in establishing a welfare fund in the form of locked-up capital one would have to "make a clear and determined plan and explain it to them." Otherwise contributions would be made no more than once, "and you will get trouble if you try to compel them."

The Holsteinsborgers had grasped the idea of saving up for the short term for their own immediate advantage, but could not understand long term saving. Such attitudes have - inter alia - so to speak confirmed the opinion that in general Greenlanders live in the present. The explanation of this lack of understanding of the concept of saving must be that subsistance economy with its limited opportunity for preservation proceeding from the very nature of the natural produce afforded no room for the idea of long-term saving. Things decreased in value perceptibly when set aside. This form of economy, with centuries of tradition in the environment of Greenland, in which Greenlandic thinking was formed, could not encompass the abstraction entailed in transfer to an account of the value of what was saved. The close relationship between taking an animal and immediately exchanging or consuming it was a matter of experience from which it was almost impossible to abstract. Here was the entire economic problem of culture contact in a nutshell. The shell was not broken into the kernel - the problem was not solved - as long as subsistance economy prevailed in Greenlandic society, or rather as long as everyday life mainly depended on it.

The smallpox epidemic of 1800-1801 seems to have changed the situation entirely; outside Holsteinsborg a welfare fund seems to have existed in the Southern Inspectorate. In 1802 Inspector N.R. Bull decided that a carpenter at Sukkertoppen was to pay a fine of two rigsdalers to the "welfare fund for needy Greenlanders", because he had engaged in illicit trade with a Greenlander there.[6] That part of the income of the fund had apparently been organized, and judging by the name of the fund, it had a general objective.

As Holsteinsborg was regenerated after 1801, and whaling gradually reorganized, it must have been possible to introduce a distribution system with a partially new set of whalers. It was possible to practice the North Greenland form of profit sharing - seemingly without at the same time practicing the negotiation and information which Heiberg, the trader, had deemed necessary. What is strange is that Holsteinsborg's welfare fund is explicitly mentioned. Under this special description it was credited in 1805 with an additional payment from an incorrectly calculated distribution of the whaling proceeds the previous year.

In any case, whether the South Greenland welfare fund was divided up among the various districts or only that of Holsteinsborg was kept separate from the others (because of whaling), this or these funds could not enjoy such ample incomes as the North Greenland welfare fund. The Greenlandic inhabitants in the south had therefore to resort to the relief measures which tradition had developed at the Trade or the Mission, or to those for which the Order of 1782 had cleared the way.

Educational Assistance

Among the traditional welfare measures were the support of widows, and kayak assistance to boys who would otherwise be prevented from getting training in the vital art of kayak rowing. The provisions of the Order of 1782, the function of the welfare fund in the Northern Inspectorate, and the hard pressed financial situation of the Mission had apparently made the prescriptive right to such assistance dubious. Johan Chr. Mørch, the trader at Frederikshåb, felt called upon in 1792 to have his right to make such support payments confirmed. It was confirmed, and the Management even recognized the Trade's obligation to pay what it previously had been the duty of the Mission to allot. The expenses were, however, in each individual case to be submitted to the Inspector for his approval.

Mostly in the whaling areas, training in kayak rowing seems to have declined during the 1780's. Inspector Schultz noticed – to be sure, shortly after his arrival at Godhavn in 1790 – that the Greenlanders there were not as proficient at kayak rowing as previously. Inspector Lund in the Southern Inspectorate wrote in 1792: "Most of Holsteinsborg's and Qerrortussoq's Greenlanders cannot catch a seal from a kayak because since their childhood they have considered a seal as insignificant in comparison to what they can earn with less labour as rowers on a sloop, in good whaling." In other words, whaling replaced the less profitable sealing, also because the fangers had no time to keep in training, as they had to go on whale watching.

Explicitly authorized by the general appeal of the Order of 1782 to promote the training in Greenlandic occupations, expecially sealing, of illegitimate boys and "mixtures", Inspector Schultz in the Northern Inspectorate instituted important relief measures in this respect. This was done at the instigation of the very active M.N. Myhlenphort, who was the trader at Egedesminde in 1795. He had told the Management that he had discussed this problem with Inspector Schultz, who had offered to have the welfare fund pay for kayaks for boys who were not in a position to get this coveted vessel themselves. Although he had offered free wood to Greenlandic kayak builders, and they had promised to build the kayaks, he had not succeeded in getting more than three built during the spring of 1795. The reason he himself gives is that the Greenlanders in question did not keep their promises. Myhlenphort had to pay 8 to 10 rigsdalers apiece for these kayaks. This would amount to a large sum, as he had counted 32 boys in the district who were proficient at kayak rowing, but owned no kayak themselves. How they had been able to keep in training, he does not say. Nor does he explain the reasons why the number of boys in need of a kayak was so large. The figure 32 seems almost shocking, especially in a district like Egedesminde, where the population consisted mostly of fangers. On the basis of the census of 1789 this would correspond to almost half of all boys under 12. This must have seemed alarming at the time.

This induced the Management to refer Schultz to the means in the welfare fund in 1795, which he himself had already done with Myhlenphort.

Here again the Management turned out to be attempting to unload its obligations on the welfare fund, just as it had done with relief provisions in times of hardship.

The result was a couple of paragraphs in a general circular sent on 13 December 1796 by Inspector Schultz to the chief traders of the Inspectorate, by which they were given permission to provide all boys who were not in a position to supply themselves with sufficient wood for a kayak. If they could get a fanger to cover the kayak with the necessary hides and train the boy in kayak rowing, the fanger was to receive a reward of two rigsdalers.

The paradoxical aspect of this relief measure was that while it was possible to get a kayak frame built up, it was difficult getting hides to cover it. Considering the price named by Myhlenphort, two rigsdalers would not go far either. On request, Schultz had to relax this payment system and give the green light for a higher price.

At Egedesminde Myhlenphort, the trader, therefore used another measure in 1796; he had two kayaks built and lent them to two boys whose proficiency he was more or less certain of in advance. These kayaks were to be returned if the boys did not engage in sufficiently efficient fangst. During the previous two years he had given boys materials for kayaks on credit, if they had no relatives. He trusted that the debt would be repaid.

Both in the Northern and in the Southern Inspectorate the authorization to distribute kayaks in the provisions of the Order of 1782 was thus made diligent use of; in the north, the inspector attempted to defend the meagre resources of the welfare fund from the attacks of the Management. It is all the more strange that C. Møller, the trader at Christianshåb, pointed out a deficiency in this distribution of kayaks which should have been noticed for some time, but which had apparently been overlooked entirely. In his opinion it was not enough to supply "indigent" boys with kayak wood and perhaps hides to cover it with; it was often quite difficult for them to acquire the necessary fangst equipment. He thought therefore that it was best to give these young men finished and fully equipped kayaks, in which case it would also be easier to get fangers to train them in the art of fangst from a kayak.

The two rigsdalers offered as a reward if the "kayak teacher" furnished the boat frame with a skin covering were quite insufficient, Møller thought. In this connection he reported an aspect of fanger life which had previously been unknown. "Since good fangers seldom or never bother to make their own kayaks, but pay someone else to do it," such good fangers would not be inclined to provide the young men with hides as well as train them for two rigsdalers unless the boys were so trained that the fanger could expect to recuperate his expenses quickly.[7]

The expenses of making the kayaks would hereafter be considerably higher, but Inspector Schultz replied that one should nevertheless attempt to go through with the offer. The need was great, and one would have to try to pull through, including the more expensive manufacture of finished and fully equipped kayaks, for which most likely "resources would be created in time." But Inspector Schultz did not comment on Møller's statement concerning the professional manufacture of kayaks. It remains as a unique testimony, which perhaps must be seen in connection with Inspector Schultz' idea of the decline of the art of the kayak. As far as kayak equipment is concerned, it has always been considered as the prevalent custom that the fanger made it himself. The delivery of finished and fully equipped kayaks should therefore have been a rare occurrence.

The need for assistance in procuring kayaks for boys was great. It is remarkable that this need appeared even in pronounced fanger districts. Where the need and those eligible for it are mentioned, it usually turns out that they are fatherless, or boys with no close relatives, or sons or stepsons of fathers who are incapable of making or acquiring a kayak for their sons. It is not possible to trace any tendency towards the unwarranted exploitation of this relief measure, which might otherwise be expected. Quite another matter is that at many of the whaling localities it was impossible to find a proficient kayak fanger who would undertake to train young men. In this connection we can totally exclude "mixtures", who seldom received and almost never had the opportunity to get the proper training.

In this educational or occupational assistance to young men, the Management of the Royal Greenland Trade was interested not only out of considerations of social or educational welfare; it was also in the direct interest of the Trade that sealing did not stagnate. It is perhaps therefore that these relief measures were especially prevalent in the Northern Inspectorate, where at this time sealing was in danger of being ousted by whaling. This was not in the interest of the Trade, as all productive occupations had to be maintained, if for no other reason, in order to provide a supply of food and hides. They were simply vital, especially sealing. This returns us to political economy which only shows that all the various considerations were woven together in one context.

It was at the same time the immediate interest of the Trade and the expansion of occupational opportunities for the inhabitants, and thereby of the human development of the individual, which dictated assistance for the training of craftsmen in the service of the Trade.

It is perhaps a truism to state that this kind of training was foreign to West Greenlandic Eskimo tradition, but this must be kept in mind in order to evaluate the development properly. When the path was opened for the employment as craftsmen for the Trade of persons born in Greenland, this development entailed a number of clashes between the West Greenland culture complex, in a wider sense, and European attitudes. The course of these conflicts determined in its turn the changing inclination of the Trade to employ Greenlandic labour and to rely on it, which again in its turn to a certain extent determined its attitude to the training as craftsmen of young Greenlanders. The former aspect will be treated later; here we shall deal with the social aspects of this matter; but the two are closely connected.

Previous to 1782 the cases of training for service in the Trade and employment there can be counted on the fingers of one hand. As we have seen, the Order of 1782 had perceived social problems in the education of children of certain categories: illegitimate children and the children of mixed marriages, and stipulated certain general directives. From a rationalistic point of view it had to be seen to that these children could develop as useful members of society, in the best interest of society and themselves. Subjects for craftsman training were also most commonly chosen among "mixture boys", who were those who had the poorest opportunities of receiving a training as fangers in the traditional Eskimo fashion.

This development is to a certain degree reflected in the statistics and comments presented above. Between 1780 and 1785 a considerable increase can be observed in the number of Greenlanders, mostly half-breeds, employed by the Trade. This was linked partly to the growing number of Greenlanders engaged in whaling in the Northern Inspectorate, partly to the educational directives of the Order of 1782, and not least to the growing number of "mixtures", who could become a social and economic deadweight if they were not properly "utilized".

To promote the education of these elements of the population, a payment in the form of a reward was introduced in 1787 for any craftsman who would undertake to train a young person in his trade. The reward was 25 rigsdalers. In addition some Greenlanders in the possession of natural talents as craftsmen were employed by the Trade without having any training; they were of such great and versatile use in the manifold activities of the Trade that it was profitable to give them some wages and rations.

In 1796 the Management received a more immediate impulse to accelerate the training of Greenlandic craftsmen. After the fire in Copenhagen in 1795, several European craftsmen were sent back to help rebuild the capital; the Trade then had trouble getting carpenter and cooper journeymen. The Management therefore encouraged the inspectors to seek among the residents of Greenland substitutes for the professionals they were hindered in stationing there, both by getting craftsmen already stationed there to prolong their period of service and by reminding craftsmen of the 25 rigsdalers reward and thus getting more Greenlanders trained as carpenters and coopers.

The issue was thus a relief and support programme. Inspector Schultz mentioned that the reward of 25 rigsdalers was too small, even if the apprentice was assured employment after his training, and that apprentices had to have rations during their apprenticeship. Here the welfare fund was again drawn into the picture: the Management decided that it was to cover the cost of such rations. Thus continued the financing of this relief measures - for males.

The Protection of Women

Due to the attitudes of the time towards women and their social economic, educational and political situation, no one in this period was equally active in the support of their existence and future. But their economic and social importance, both its useful and its harmful aspects, according to the spirit of the time, was not totally ignored.

To a growing extent the welfare fund had to provide for widows, when their relatives did not undertake to do so. To some extent there were pension rules for Greenlandic women who were widows of Europeans stationed in Greenland, so that these women, whose proportion was rising, had some security.

The Order of 1782 realized the role of women in the private sector of the Greenlandic economy and for the productivity of fangers. What was favourable to these two factors was to be prescribed in its provisions dealing with women. In the previously mentioned paragraphs dealing with education, however, nothing special was mentioned about the raising and education of girl children, who were included in the general provision that in general, Greenlandic children were to be "instructed in Greenlandic occupations and maintained with domestic provisions." It was provided that what was saved from support payments made by fathers of illegitimate girls was to be used to acquire an umiak and a tent as a dowry.

It was thus taken for granted that women were to marry. But before this took place - and even afterwards - there were special rules for their protection, which, along with those dealing with mixed marriages, have been dealt with previously. In spite of all the regulations, the number of mixed marriages rose, and likewise the number of illegitimate pregnancies. The number of children born in mixed marriages also rose, giving rise to the previously mentioned problems of raising and education.

Marriage Politics

The female children of mixed marriages had, ever since this group made its appearance, had difficulties finding a place in Greenlandic society, essentially because they were not taught to take care of a West Greenlandic household. This became one in a complex of problems, for which it was necessary to lay down certain guide lines. This was done primarily in the Order of 1782, but it was one thing to make rules and quite another thing to administer them in practice.

"If it were not to get women born in mixed marriages (whom Greenlanders as a rule reject) married, and to prevent them from becoming whores, Europeans should never be allowed to marry them, for these Greenlandic marriages are almost always harmful; but now we will have to agree to them for some time, but be reticent in giving approval." This was the opinion of Inspector Schwabe in 1784. There is no racial discrimination in his attitude; "harmful" here means harmful to the Trade as well as to the relationship between the individual trade employee and this institution. It was thought to be a matter of experience that especially traders and assistants, but also craftsmen and "sailors", got into bottomless debt to the Trade because of their marriages to Greenlandic women.

We must here remember that at that time, marriage as an institution was considered exclusively from a social point of view, with a pronounced economic aspect, in a rationalistic attitude towards its advantageousness and usefulness, or the reverse. This entailed certain duties in marriage, which the parties were to fulfil for the common good. This was the real reason why society, through the state, exercised a guiding influence in the institution of matrimony.

In 1786 Inspector Schwabe therefore proposed putting a stop to marriages with "real Greenlandic women", as the Order had provided, although such marriages had taken place in subsequent years. On the other hand he suggested giving rewards to "real Greenlanders" who married girls born in mixed marriages. But Schwabe's successor in office was less enthusiastic about this idea.

Inspector Wille thought that these daughters of mixed marriages had been raised "far too sentimentally and comfortably", and as previously were not equipped to be the wives of fangers. And he was opposed to Greenlanders marrying them: "A Greenlander who got such a wife would be thoroughly ruined and when the reward was spent I would not like to be in the shoes of the trader who had encouraged that marriage. The entire general store would not be enough to satisfy that Greenlander as often as he would come to blame the trader for having saddled him with a bad wife." The reward ideas came to naught.

On the other hand, certain coercive measures were attempted to prevent marriage between Greenlandic women of mixed descent and Europeans. The Commission of 1788 decided in 1789 that the half portion of rations, previously sold to a subordinate functionary (i.e., a craftsman or "sailor") for 14 rigsdalers per annum, would in the future not be granted at a price under 30 rigsdalers; but this was not to apply to marriages already entered into. The Commission thought that they thus stopped future marriages of this nature, but they neglected one factor in their calculations: human affections – and human weaknesses.

Requests for "Greenlandic marriages" came mostly from the Northern Inspectorate; this was mainly due to the fact that the number of Europeans was greater here due to whaling. It was also at the whaling stations that it was most difficult to raise the children of these families in the Greenlandic manner and to train them for Greenlandic occupations. So these problems were greater in the Northern Inspectorate.

Inspector B.J. Schultz, who in so many fields was gifted with human understanding, grasped this nettle shortly after his arrival in this inspectorate. Either such marriages should be completely prohibited, he thought, or completely permitted; the latter he thought most correct. His justification for this approach is totally rationalistic. In the first place, he argued, there were more women than men, at least in the Northern Inspectorate, contrary to the common opinion that the numbers of the two sexes were equal. As we have attempted to illustrate above, he was right to some extent, although the difference was not as great as he claimed.

Due to this statistic reason, several women would be predestined to remain unmarried. Moral laxity, which according to him was on the rise, and the increasing number of illegitimate pregnancies, argued for permitting more "Greenlandic marriages" rather than trying to hinder them, which would only promote loose relationships.

This led to a change of attitude in the Management; and in subsequent years more permissions were given for "Greenlandic marriages" than previously. There are quite a few tales, both touching and tragic, about such marriages. But it is a fact that more mixed marriages were entered into during the 1790's, which involved a growing number of children of such marriages. This growth was even so great that in its report of 1798, the Management thought that the ordinary growth of population which was perceived, was traceable to the growing number of children in the increasing number of "Greenlandic marriages". That this entailed further pressure on the question of education is another matter, which will be dealt with later, as will the attitude of the mission to the institution of matrimony.

The attitude of the Management was still characterized by a certain mercantilistic demographic policy coupled with a rationalistic view of society. It was therefore still a question of channelling development, including this aspect, in the desired direction. The reward idea was thus taken up again in 1803; the reward consisted in the wood for an umiak, at an estimated value of six or seven rigsdalers, to be given to women born in mixed marriages who were willing to marry "real Greenlanders", as had been proposed in 1786. The reward was also to be given to daughters of mixed marriages who were willing to marry sons of mixed marriages, if these men would support their families with a Greenlandic occupation or got their "income from the employment in the Trade or Mission." This is noteworthy; the number of "mixtures" had now become so great, and their assimilation in Greenlandic society – at least in the south – had progressed so far, that they could be considered equal to "real Greenlanders", as which they had always been considered juridically, with certain modifications.

Paternity Cases

Inspector Schultz thought he observed a growing moral laxity in relations between the sexes, and an increasing number of paternity cases. His two predecessors in office in North Greenland had expressed the same view of these unfortunate conditions. Of course what they mainly meant was loose relations between Greenlandic women and Europeans stationed in Greenland as well as foreigners, especially whalers, so that it is especially from the Northern Inspectorate that we hear these laments.

In the "protective" provisions of the Order of 1782 concerning women, Johan Fr. Schwabe had already attempted at least to restrain debauchery. These provisions were obviously dictated by the prevailing European moral code and the desire for moral order, in order to protect the undisturbed favourable progress of the Trade as well as the welfare of Greenlandic women, and also because of the economic and social difficulties which followed in the wake of immorality. Not a thought was given to Greenlandic-Eskimo sexual habits and moral norms. Apparently the Europeans either thought that these did not exist; or could not approve the norms, habits and traditions perceived, from the point of view of Christian ethics. At that time morals, in the broadest sense of the word, were considered by the ordinary European as a set of rules created by God, and thus universal. Deviation from "official" sexual morals was therefore, in the eyes of morally responsible Europeans, identical with debauchery. From this point of view the responsible Europeans had to take their position towards the prevailing conditions and act accordingly.

The Order of 1782 therefore forbade the crews to be seen in Greenlandic houses "at suspicious times". When crew members had good reasons to be there, they were to behave decently; this of course also applied to traders and their assistants, for whom general rules of decent conduct had been laid down. No subordinate functionary or member of the crew could freely choose a woman to hire as his "waitress", i.e., to wash and sew for him and take care of his leather clothes. Young Greenlandic women and those taking instruction for baptism were as far as possible "to be spared going on expeditions and long journeys with Europeans, especially with ignorant workingmen, in order not to be exposed to temptation." They could thus not just be hired as rowers in umiaks rented or stationed at the colony for expeditions.

Violations of these provisions were to be punished by fines or by flogging. A stationed European who led "a suspicious or indecent life, and who after being warned does not entirely refrain therefrom, should be sent home with the first ship, whether he has served his full term or not."

Although Inspector Schwabe did not mince his words when he later spoke of "the irresponsible and lewd conduct of the Greenlandic women in this northern part of the country," it is clear from the provisions of the Order, that these were directed towards Europeans, both stationed and foreign (whalers), and laid down in order to protect Greenlandic women. Perhaps this principle was due to the fact that no provisions were intended or could be made for Greenlanders. Legally the Trade had no jurisdiction over them; nor were they explicitly subject to Danish or Norwegian laws. This is a fact in the juridical history of Greenland which later played a more important role.

Therefore paternity provisions also only applied to stationed Europeans. The father of an illegitimate child whose mother was a Greenlander (apparently regardless of whether she was a "real Greenlander" or a "mixture") was to pay 6 rigsdalers per annum for the support of the child until it reached 12 years of age: a total of 72 rigsdalers. Detailed rules were made for the yearly payment of support, dispensations, cancellation and refunding. A full refund was made if the child was stillborn or died shortly after birth; proportional refunds were made for deaths previous to the age of 12.

The principle was thus to create legal protection for children resulting from extra-marital relations. The support payment provisions seem, however, to have had unforeseen consequences: it was reported from both north and south that Greenlandic women who had illegitimate children saw an advantage in alleging that a European was the father. It is another matter that the alleged fathers could seldom deny paternity. According to Inspector Wille, it was not so uncommon for members of the colony crew to have to assume the paternity of children whose real fathers were foreign whalers or seamen. This was, however, a postulate which he never proved, but it entered into the deliberations of the Management.

Especially after 1786 the number of paternity cases seems to have risen. Inspector Wille speaks of an increase in moral laxity, including relations with foreigners: i.e., English whalers. It is a question whether or not this increase was a so-called "statistical phenomenon", in that more relationships were revealed or observed than previously. The increasing number of baptised Greenlanders meant that more children were brought to be baptised; in the church books their fathers had to be named. It was thus necessary for the mother of a child to name a father, and for an unwed mother to get a stationed European named as the father for the support money. From a Greenlandic point of view there was nothing unjust or immoral in this. To the authorities, and this meant the inspectors, the testimony of the woman was decisive, even though this meant that the provisions of the Order could be abused. In addition, paternity cases among Greenlanders began to occur, because the rising number of baptisms introduced monogamy. In the period under consideration, the naming of a Greenlandic father did not yet involve the payment of support money. This was outside all legal rules. A catechist who sinned against the sixth commandment with consequences was suspended for two years from his office, but this was punishment for him, not assistance to the mother of his illegitimate child.

It was, inter alia, in order to cut through such unfortunate conditions, that Inspector Schultz advocated permitting more mixed marriages. Another reason was that he had indications that Europeans, to avoid support payments, got the mothers of their children to abort or give birth clandestinely. Abortions seem to have been common.

When everything seemed to show that the system had unfortunate consequences, the Commission of 1788 decided to lower the support payment to a total of 36 rigsdalers, to be paid in full, however, whether the child was stillborn or lived a short or long life. This payment was to be made to a fund; and in either inspectorate the Inspector was to pay from a special account 4 rigsdalers per annum for each illegitimate child. In this way the Committee thought it could avoid the most unfortunate consequences of the provisions of the Order; this measure of social welfare functioned in this way from 1788 on.

The relations between foreign whalers and Greenlanders in general, and Greenlandic women in particular, was a question with broader perspectives. But on the special question of the illegitimate children of foreign fathers, at the time under consideration the only provision - in itself unsatisfactory - was that the fund could make the annual contribution. It was expected that there would be quite a few stillborn children, or children who would live for only a short time, but for whom the full payment would be made, so that so much money would be accumulated in the fund that it would suffice for making payments for illegitimate children whose fathers could not be ascertained. This is the way in which the Management cut through this problem; it was actually not possible to reach a solution which would be just to all parties.

Clandestine Births

Before the discussions of paternity problems, Johan Fr. Schwabe had remarked in 1780, in one of his letters to Ove Høegh-Guldberg: "It is strange that although the Europeans constantly have illicit intercourse and mixture with Greenlandic women, only very few children come into the world; but it is known that quite a few women were pregnant not long after the departure of the ships, although later nothing was noticed of it." He had his information from the local surgeon and from other, undetermined, informants.[8]

These reports can of course be called in question. Just as was the case with so many other phenomena in previous times, it was not in itself the actual reality which was important for political development, but what was perceived as reality, and the manner in which people reacted. In an issue surrounded by so many taboos and involving so much concealment and so many insinuations as this one is, it is impossible to penetrate behind the barriers. It is an unavoidable reality that the authorities and the Europeans stationed in Greenland in general were of the opinion that abortions at an early stage of pregnancy were quite common and taken for granted by Greenlandic women, wherever and however this opinion was derived.

According to Danish and Norwegian law and prevalent European-Christian ethics, it was punishable to commit abortion or to help another do so. The authorities, i.e., the inspectors and the missionaries, were properly speaking obligated to investigate such cases. But they had no legal jurisdiction over Greenlanders, and it was necessary here as elsewhere for cases of abortion or clandestine birth to be reported to the authorities, if they were to take any action.

In the light of this we can at present observe that after 1782 this condition afforded unarticulated opportunities for a cultural conflict; only indirectly could the Europeans attempt to combat what they considered unethical and criminal. The Greenlandic-Eskimo attitude was presumably that a Greenlandic woman did not consider her embryo, at least in the first months of its existence, as a child to be given birth to. The "functionless" aspect of the embryo at this early stage is in accordance with the Greenlandic term for embryo. That it could and should be removed is also in accordance with Eskimo concepts related to *angiaq,* which means both a stillborn child and a premature embryo. An angiaq was according to tradition something dangerous to be got rid of and rendered harmless. Such a case of an angiaq, which according to traditional ritual had been carved up and put aside, was a stillborn child, of whom a Greenlander was indicated as being the father. This is the only documented case of clandestine birth mentioned in the period from 1782 to 1808. The culture conflict appears in the repentence said to have been shown by the woman after the act, which she apparently knew to be wrong according to Christian ethics, but which she nevertheless had carried out according to the traditional ritual.

The unresolved conflict, present in Greenland as elsewhere, between the approved moral code and daily social practice, could of course not be terminated in Greenland. Prevailing conditions could only be patched up; and in this area society concentrated on assuring as far as possible the existence, in the most real sense of the word, of the innocent child, by means of active social welfare.

Obstetric Aid

Obstetric care - direct obstetric aid - was not an unknown phenomenon in the Eskimo world, and thus in the small societies of West Greenland. A couple of elder experienced women usually rendered assistance both previous to and during birth; and there were some extremely firm methods for assisting the progress of birth itself. Reports from the period dealt with in this volume show that such midwifery was common, but it was not granted much recognition. In the Southern Inspectorate a missionary, referring to the high mortality in Godthåb, expressed the need for both medical and obstetrical assistance: he advocated both.

On the whole it was not uncommon for missionaries to be called upon by the Greenlanders of their congregations during childbirth; they were to take the place of the angákut. The missionary serving at Godthåb acquired meagre training in Copenhagen, while staying there for a year. In other cases the surgeons stationed with whalers at the stations in the Northern Inspectorate acted, by virtue of their education, also as midwives, at least occasionally.

In 1800 a Greenlandic woman at Jakobshavn got the "blue stamp" of the inspector as a midwife; her salary was paid by the welfare fund. In 1803 a Greenlandic woman is mentioned at Umánaq who "is the only one in the whole District of Umánaq who understands the science of midwifery; with the help of her practice for many years, at least 40 years, we have been so fortunate that not one out of a hundred has died during childbirth when she had been called in time."

The previously mentioned approved midwife at Jakobshavn was in her practice subordinate to the surgeon hired by the Northern Inspectorate. The two together came to form the nucleus of an organized public health system in West Greenland.

Medical Assistance

At various times surgeons had stayed in Greenland and performed scanty services there, embracing the Greenlandic inhabitants. Otherwise they were stationed for a ship's crew, and therefore also at individual colonies the crews of which were organised as a ship's crew, with sailors and officers. During the great whaling project of 1776, the office of surgeon became more established, still mostly provided for the crews of ships and whaling stations. Therefore these surgeons were, as a rule, hired as both physicians and whaling assistants.[9] This was also the reason why professional medical assistance existed only in the Northern Inspectorate, while the south had to get along with the efforts of laymen. Here certain missionaries undertook the medical vocation; one of them, as we have seen, even acquired a special education.

On the whole people in Greenland had to resort to good household remedies and folk medicine, just as they did in many places in Denmark and Norway during this period. The many-sided social interests of Johan Fr. Schwabe inspired him to take up the question of assistance in sickness. Since in the nature of things it was laymen who had to render such assistance, he drew the quite natural conclusion that they should be provided with a comprehensible handbook. On the basis of Schwabe's report on the most common diseases in West Greenland, the Collegium Medicum of Copenhagen agreed in 1782 to prepare a description of these diseases and an indication of which medicines to prescribe for them. This handbook was provided with a list of the most necessary medicines which the medicine chests, which heretofore had been common at the colonies, should contain in the future.

The services of real physicians, or even of surgeons, was, however, still lacking. This meant that the authorities had to be all the more on their guard, for example at the approach of epidemics. As inspector, Johan Fr. Schwabe immediately issued a quarantine circular when the epidemic of 1785 broke out at Kronprinsens Ejland. The following year, when the epidemic spread, he renewed the circular, extended its validity to the whole of Disko Bugt, and provided it with a mass of detailed instructions to attempt to prevent further contagion, for helping the afflicted, and finally a number of hygienic instructions on burying the dead and sterilizing their property and dwellings.

For the first time in the history of Greenland, "hospitals" are mentioned, but in an extremely modest form: buildings of stone or peat divided into two rooms, one for those seriously ill and the other for those recovering. Schwabe, or perhaps his advisor, the whaling surgeon at Godhavn clearly realized that these two kinds of patients had to be kept separate by one means or another, and that the ill should be isolated from healthy persons, while those who had had the disease could function as a kind of nurse. Those who took care of the patients were to wear something over their ordinary clothes so as not to spread contagion, and so forth.

As a whole this circular is noteworthy, even in a European context, because its instructions reveal a deep understanding of various problems of contagion and the channels of contagion. There is no corresponding set of instructions available which might have been the model for Schwabe's circular, so that it seems to be original, perhaps composed in cooperation with the local surgeons. The formulation of its rules bears witness to Schwabe's distinct administrative talent.

At the end of his circular, Schwabe mentions the most common diseases and other common medical conditions, and recommends that native catechists be trained in bloodletting and the treatment of boils. The welfare fund could pay the expenses of instruments. Neither he nor the Management seem to have known that for quite a few years the catechists, at least in the south, had exercised this function. During the years subsequent to 1786, several catechists were trained in the art of bloodletting and cutting abscesses, and according to reports functioned splendidly in this branch of surgery. But they could not substitute for real physicians, or even surgeons.

In 1791 Inspector B.J. Schultz of the Northern Inspectorate pleaded against the system uniting in one person the vocation of surgeon and the office of whaling assistant, which had provided neither skilful surgeons nor effective whaling assistants. He applied to have a proficient surgeon stationed in his inspectorate. The Management raised this problem with the Commission and proposed putting West Greenland's colonies under the local medical officer system developed in Denmark during the eighteenth century: this system had already been extended to the Faroese Islands, Iceland and Finmark. The Management thus considered Greenland as a part of the realms, and not as a colony. This is noteworthy in another context.

The Management did not succeed, however, in getting this system transplanted to Greenland, but did approve an alternative, which it had itself suggested: that the Inspector and the employees of the Trade in the Northern Inspectorate should pay five per cent of their shares of the Trade's surplus at each locality, and that the welfare fund would pay a further 50 rigsdalers annually. The Trade would then pay the remainder of the wages of a surgeon, who thus would receive from 300 to 400 rigsdalers per annum plus full rations for an "officer". On these terms Theodor Christian Eulner, the first "full-time-surgeon", was hired, with his residence at Godhavn.

The instructions of the surgeon limited his activities to Disko Bugt, most likely because the welfare fund was limited to this area. But when the trade employees and missionary of Umánaq began to contribute to the surgeon's wage, this district was added to his area of operation. He was to give free medical assistance to all persons, both Greenlanders and stationed Europeans; the medicine which he prescribed was to be given free as well. He was to check the local medicine chests and see to it that they were complete, supplementing them with a set of "instructions for use" and instructions in the diagnosis and treatment of the most common diseases among the Greenlanders. These instructions were to be formulated as simply as possible and be easy to understand and practice, in consideration of the Greenlanders' "food, scarcity, domestic way of life, etc., and the difficulties which will everywhere encounter the necessary supervision, etc. of patients." He was to do research, i.e., study the progress of the various diseases, find remedies and cures for them; and be especially attentive to remedies afforded by nature in Greenland. Therefore he was preferably to carry out both botanical and mineralogical investigations.

As the surgeon was also to serve the ships' crews that landed at the harbours of Disko Bugt, he had more than enough to keep him busy. He was constantly travelling around Disko Bugt and up to Umánaq. And during the smallpox epidemic he apparently wore himself out; certainly deeply disappointed at the little headway made by his efforts against the epidemic, he took his life in March of 1801.

He was succeeded in 1802 by the surgeon Johann Frederich Lerch, who operated in Disko Bugt until he left his position in 1840. His activity is mentioned less favourably. But one thing was certain: the system of a resident physician in the Northern Inspectorate was permanent. As bad as it might be said to be, there was at least some help for patients. And it was now a rule that medical help and medicine was to be free for all. This system functioned as a kind of medical insurance society.

Because of this and the fact that there was no welfare fund in the Southern Inspectorate, it was not possible to hire a surgeon here. Nor would it have been possible for one surgeon to serve the population of the entire long coast of the Inspectorate. The southerners had to be content with medicine chests and the handbooks contained in them. Various lesser instructions for special cases, e.g., "On the Way to Bring Drowned Persons to Life", was translated into Greenlandic and copies made and distributed to the trading posts of the Northern Inspectorate. Such things can likewise be supposed to have been done in the south. Even this was considered at the time as a measure dictated by the spirit of thrift, to be asserted in all areas.

It was thus an unfortunate moment in 1791, when Inspector Schultz took up Schwabe's idea of "hospitals" in order to create more permanent, if modest, institutions of this kind. The Management did not approve his idea of building hospitals of stone and mortar, contending that ordinary Greenlandic houses would be cheaper, suit the local inhabitants better and be easier to heat. It was undoubtedly right, but it was the expense of stone buildings which aroused the most resistance. Hospitals were not built at all, most likely because the Management suspected that they would involve an increase in the number of surgeons and medical workers. There were no financial means to pay for such possible consequences.

Preventive Measures

The fear of epidemics caused Johan Fr. Schwabe to issue his circular in 1786. It contained, in addition to rules for helping patients, a number of measures against the spreading of contagion: preventive measures. Two diseases were the most feared: venereal diseases and smallpox.

Among stationed Europeans as well as foreign whalers, cases of venerial disease were discovered from time to time. Although it was known that the diseased persons had had intercourse with Greenlandic women, no Greenlander ever seems to have been infected; at least the cases mentioned which might resemble venereal disease apparently took an extremely uncharacteristic course. The surgeons of the time had a relatively good knowledge of the symptoms and progress of this group of diseases, so it is not likely that they erred in their diagnosis. This led Schwabe to write "that venereal disease can not infect the natives of the country." However this may be, the source material indicates that venereal diseases were not revealed among the Greenlanders of West Greenland from 1782–1808.

The cases observed among the Danish ships' crews and Europeans stationed in Greenland led the Management to issue a circular in 1806 demanding a medical certificate for hiring ship's crew and colony crew members, so that Greenland could at least to some extent protect itself against contagion.

This circular was an expanded version of a former one issued by the Danske Kancelli in 1787, containing certain rules for seamen and passengers sailing to Iceland, extended in 1803 to Greenland. It was another preventive measure in the attempt to do something effective to prevent contagion being spread by the crews and passengers of ships to the Atlantic islands.

The extension in 1803 of this 1787 circular was an element in the action of Carl Pontoppidan, former co-manager of the Royal Greenland Trade, "to prevent smallpox and measles epidemics in Iceland, Greenland and the Faroese Islands." It was surely under the influence of the North Greenland smallpox epidemic of 1800–1801 that in March 1802 he suggested, inter alia, that a medical certificate should be presented six weeks before travel to these islands, or in lieu of this, a certificate of inoculation or vaccination against smallpox. At this time smallpox vaccination was not yet obligatory in Denmark and Norway, so it was impossible to carry out his suggestion.

Smallpox vaccination or inoculation was relatively new (Jenner's inoculations took place in 1798), so it is surprising that in October 1800, Eulner, the surgeon, performed the first inoculation in Greenland. This was at the height of the smallpox epidemic, and he performed the inoculation as en experiment, having little confidence in it. It did not help those who were inoculated. When a new surgeon was to be stationed in Greenland after the death of Eulner, the Management linked this appointment with the matter of vaccination. The Academy of Surgeons in Copenhagen took up the case. Then followed the initiative of Carl Pontoppidan, who also thought that not only should the surgeon himself perform vaccinations, but also instruct others how to do it, and that missionaries and catechists should be sent the proclamation on smallpox vaccination with an illustrative table.

In the Northern Inspectorate, Lerch, the surgeon, began to vaccinate. In the Southern Inspectorate there was no surgeon, so the administration had two young assistants who were about to be stationed in South Greenland instructed in the art; they carried with them to Greenland "vaccine material", as did Dr. Lerch. The experiment was unsuccessful in the case of the two assistants, because their vaccine was too old. Dr. Lerch succeeded, however, in vaccinating first the catechist Magnus Aronsen and his two sons with a favourable result, after which 82 persons were persuaded to be vaccinated at Godhavn, with the same favourable result. Then he travelled around vaccinating and instructing others how to vaccinate. He inoculated 159 times, but only 36% of his inoculations took.

The vaccination campaign throughout West Greenland took place on a voluntary basis. The inhabitants were under no circumstances to be compelled. When the catechist Magnus Aronsen had been vaccinated at Godhavn and people could see that nothing harmful happened to him, there was no difficulty getting the inhabitants of Disko Bugt to be vaccinated. But at other localities it was difficult to persuade the residents. In subsequent years Lerch's vaccinations were unsuccessful up to 1808: the vaccine sent from Denmark was ineffective.

Results in the Southern Inspectorate were better, except for 1802. It was feared in 1803 that smallpox contagion had spread to Frederikshåb; perhaps this fear accelerated vaccinations. The following year Inspector

Myhlenphort reported that 602 persons had been vaccinated, with good results. But the following year, the vaccine failed.

At Julianehåb the assistant, Schytte, had more luck with his vaccinations. Thereafter it appears that South Greenland began to produce its own vaccine: when inoculations took, the contents of the blisters were collected, put into glass, and used in future inoculations. This meant that Julianehåb was able to deliver vaccine to other places in Greenland, so that the vaccine did not get too old.

The willingness of the Greenlandic inhabitants to be vaccinated was erratic. At some localities they were quite willing one year, but not at all willing the following year, for inexplicable reasons. At some places, the chief trader had to promise rations in return for being vaccinated. In 1807 the assistant at Frederikshåb reported that two Greenlanders had been successfully vaccinated; one of them had taken the liquid from one of his own blisters with a nail and scratched his brother with it, with a favourable result: the vaccine was drawn from the brother's only blister to vaccinate two others, likewise with a good result.

The war years from 1807 to 1814 stopped all further progress in this matter. Greenland could not do without supplies of vaccine from Denmark, which did not always produce successful results. In spite of much bad luck and unsuccessful attempts, the matter was pushed both by the Management and by the local authorities. The surgeon, missionaries, catechists, traders and assistants all made a noteworthy contribution to this measure of prevention; the lay element was of great importance. In this area there was a united, common drive to improve the welfare of West Greenland. And it is remarkable that such an innovation as vaccination was made use of so soon after its discovery.

VII. Occupational Development

The welfare of the Greenlandic population was of course mainly dependent on the occupational opportunities available in Greenland; so that it was not only for its own interests that the Trade, in its various activities, attempted to keep the Greenlandic occupations from dying out, either because young men were not trained as fangers, because they were attracted to another, from the Greenlandic point of view less productive, occupation, or because the population were "spoiled from their national food," as it was so often expressed. Translated into modern language, this third reason means that the private economy of Western Greenland was straying disastrously from the natural resources of the country.

As we have seen, it was only a small proportion of the population that engaged in fangst, which not only was the basis of the private economy of West Greenland, but was also necessary for the import of occupational tools and consumer goods which were becoming increasingly indispensable for continued existence. The Trade had therefore to attempt to promote the various forms of fangst and to increase production to keep up with rising demand - preferably somewhat more rapidly than previously.

Sealing

Sealing was and remained the most important factor of the economy: it was the source of supply which the inhabitants always fell back on. Thus the Management as well as the inspectors constantly concentrated on asserting the essential nature of sealing, often at the expense of other kinds of fangst which, if not fully as important as sealing, were nevertheless important for the full life of a Greenlander, especially as elements of tradition. This was presumably less due to an actual lack of understanding than to rationalism's one-track, duty-bound assertion of what was useful, coupled with the almost hysterical rejection by the society of the times of whatever was less beneficial to the common weal. Hence the contempt for all "sumptuousness": i.e., the least little bit of luxury. Diligence was the most respected virtue and laziness almost the worst of vices, at least the one most harmful to the public good.

Diligence was followed by carefulness, which in turn gave rise to thrift. Nothing must be wasted. The Order of 1782 left no room for doubt that the functionaries and crew of the colonies were both to keep the inhabitants busy at fangst and themselves be ready to collect and purchase the produce which the fangers and their families did not need. All waste must be prevented. "It is all too well known," the Management wrote to the trader at Julianehåb in 1782, "that when the Greenlanders learn that their blubber is not being purchased and paid for in time, they let it lie on the ground without making the least effort to preserve it."

A similar waste was reported 14 years later from Julianehåb South District by trader Johan Chr. Mørch, in connection with his desire to set up a southern trading station. South of Tasermiut Fjord, a good way up the east coast, were settled around 60 fangers, distributed among 19 settlements. Thirty of them had brought around 31 tubs of blubber to the colony during a single year, but this was far from what they were able to sell of their surplus. "The Greenlanders have the custom, when they leave their winter Samps in the Spring, of throwing out their old blubber and seal oil and filling their bags again with the newest. That they cannot even take all the new with them in their small umiaks loaded with tents and baggage, but have to leave it to spoil, is the unanimous assertion of them all, just as it is their unanimous wish to live near someone to whom they can sell blubber when they are able to bring it."

This is almost parallel to what Matthias Fersleff reported from his visit to Disko Bugt in 1728, when the Greenlanders living there said that when hunting on the ice in the winter they were not able to transport all the animals home which they had killed, but had to let some lie on the ice. They, too, had said they would be more than happy to sell this surplus if there was only someone to sell it to who would help them transport it.[1]

As late as 1799 Niels Rosing Bull, the Inspector of South Greenland, wrote of the general waste of blubber which undoubtedly had to take place. He mentioned specially Frederikshåb, which had reported 2106 pieces of seal hide to be sent to Denmark; this number of hides was in no reasonable proportion to the amount of blubber reported for shipment. The reasons for this waste were, he assumed, that "the Greenlanders in the District treat" their collected blubber "as uneconomically as they all do," that they "are undoubtedly led to attach little value to blubber, since we cannot at all times, living so far from the Establishment, trade necessities for it," and that "much blubber is spoiled during the milder seasons of the year, when the great distance away of the sealing grounds does not permit quick collection."

The approximately 30 South Greenlandic fangers mentioned by Mørch had delivered, 546 hides which that year represented one-fourth of the total hides purchases at Julianehåb colony. This number of hides must have corresponded to a much greater number of seals than did the 31 tubs of blubber delivered.

As Inspector Bull was to do later, Mørch calculated from the hides production to a larger blubber production than that shown by the purchase figures. Even taking private consumption into consideration, this unequal relationship meant that a lot of blubber was being wasted. We must here remember that opportunities for preservation were much lower in South Greenland than elsewhere on the island. It is also important that both a trader and an inspector put part of the blame for the waste on the fact that the Trade was unable to collect and purchase surplus blubber in time. Diaries continually complain of difficulties in collecting blubber which otherwise would spoil, because of the weather, the insufficient capacity of boats, or the lack of sufficient barrels to station in the remote areas. This latter practice had formerly been warmly advocated, and sometimes also carried out, every year at some location.

The Northern Inspectorate also reported waste. In 1790 Myhlenphort, then the trader at Jakobshavn, observed that a great amount of the fangst was wasted. "To be sure, the Greenlanders themselves do not neglect their fangst, but when they kill a seal, their women can hardly be bothered to cut it up, much less to prepare the hides. I have been to trading posts in the District where Greenlanders have been hunting harp seals, after they had left, and found many large, splendid hides thrown under rocks and in blubber caches quite rotten and of no use."

Waste also took place in connection with other kinds of fangst. In 1796, when contact with Upernavik was reestablished, it was reported that half of 60 casks of whale blubber had oozed away "since due to lack of casks they had to let it lie unflensed until I arrived with the ship." This locality had, however, the two previous years been provided with store-casks distributed to the Greenlanders, but there were not enough of them. Therefore at several different places, "huge piles of beluga blubber had been lost" from an unknown number of beluga whales.

In this context the previously mentioned shortage of hides, which often occurred in the Northern Inspectorate, seems strange indeed. It is hard to find an explanation for these mutually contradictory situations. That there were an enormous amount of sealskins and that nevertheless there was a shortage of hides for kayaks and umiaks seem incompatible. The explanation could be that there were shortages of certain hides used for boat coverings, but a surplus of others. It is also possible that a narrower family economy was spreading, that to a greater degree than previously the individual Greenlandic family sold as much as possible in order to acquire other consumer goods, and that the demand for these was rising. The traditional subsistence economy can also have played a role. It is well known that a subsistence economy involves an enormous waste of the natural resources on which it depends. Finally, this situation may also have been due to distribution difficulties, which are not improbable, given the poor state of communications between districts and even within an individual district.

As we have seen, famines occurred at definite times of the year and were as a rule due to poor fangst. They usually occurred in those seasons when no trading took place. The fangst produce accumulated during the Spring and Summer could normally not be preserved for any length of time, and Autumn fangst did not as a rule yield much. Since there was usually a great waste, and thus a relatively large surplus, of blubber and hides, famines were not usually the result of the Trade having purchased too much of a sealer's produce. The periodic recurrence of poor fangst is, on the other hand, as we have seen, due to changes in the appearance of the fangst animals at the various grounds: changes in their migratory habits. As we have also seen, the climate underwent certain changes, and thus the conditions determining the existence of these animals.

It was also reported time after time that in order to improve the sealing, new grounds would have to be found, and that sealing grounds which had previously been good had suddenly turned bad. The employees of the Trade participated zealously in the search for new and better fangst grounds; partly as such activity was specified in the Order, partly because the best of them wanted themselves to promote the Greenlandic occupations in their districts, for the good of the Greenlanders, the Trade, and themselves.

Changes in Fangst Methods

At times Trade employees also attempted to change traditional fangst methods, and, in addition to the general measures of assistance, to give the fangers the greatest possible service.

It was not so easy to change the traditional fangst methods. Sometimes changes were short-lived matters, which took place more or less by accident. When whaling commander Jürgen Kettelsen at Godhavn reported in 1798 that some fangers had gone sealing in 5 sloops, this was due to new ice in April, in which kayaks could not be used. Since neither kayaks nor the art of using them was common at Godhavn, this may have been a fangst method which, although not traditional in Greenland, was used more than once by fangers not proficient in kayak rowing. The commander mentions that the Greenlanders there had bagged 57 seals in one week, perhaps using this method. Sealing from sloops is not reported from anywhere else.

More astounding is a report which in 1792 suddenly turned up from Egedesminde. M.N. Myhlenphort, the trader who in so many ways worked for the promotion of sealing, wrote to Inspector Schultz: "I have invented a new method of hunting seals on the ice in March and April, when they lie sunning themselves. The Greenlanders have witnessed this experiment, and they assure me they believe it will be effective. I have already sold "Silesian linen" to three Greenlanders so they can make them for themselves."[2] This report, in all its brevity and incompleteness, seems to indicate that in 1792 Myhlenphort invented the shooting sail, which when placed on a little sled concealed the hunter to a seal sunning itself on the ice, which the hunter was trying to get. By that time Myhlenphort had been so long in Greenland that he must have noticed shooting sail sled, if it had already existed. He was not one to take credit for something he did not deserve. There is thus every indication that this ingenious cover, otherwise considered to have been developed in the Greenlandic fangst tradition, was at least apparently introduced at Egedesminde by the trader, Marcus Nissen Myhlenphort. It must have then become common wherever sealing was done on the ice - so common that it was forgotten who invented it. Perhaps this idea has been copied for use in front of a kayak, where the shooting sail has likewise for a long time been made of white linen or sailcloth.[3]

Continually growing in quantity, imported materials, weapons and implements entered into the life of the Greenlandic fanger. Even for the manufacture and repair of that most Eskimo of all fangst implements, the kayak, imported wood was necessary. The kayak frame was made from a certain number of "Trade boards", as they were called. In the south it is mentioned as something which occurred often that when a fanger's kayak ring (around the manhole) had broken, he had a hard time getting wood for a new one. Thus he must have faced the same difficulty when making the kayak. Inspector Lund suggested shipping a certain amount of large flat barrel hoops for this purpose.

The traditional kayak equipment was, however, made from Greenlandic materials, except for wooden handles, and harpoon and knife blades of iron. Sword blades were still used for bird dartheads. The equipment of a fanger now included firearms.

It gradually became a matter of course to use guns instead of bows and arrows in reindeer hunting. Shotguns were also used, presumably in bird hunting. At least quite a number of shotguns were shipped to Greenland, but it seems that it was difficult to sell them to fangers, so it must have been mostly stationed Europeans that used them.

To a constantly growing extent guns were also used in sealing, called seal shooting. This form of fangst took place from land, on the ice (ûtoq-fangst), in holes in the fast ice, and in stretches of open water between ice floes, at the ice edge and in the tidewater line. In other words, wherever a seal could turn up, except at breathing holes where harpooning was still the most efficient method. When a seal was shot in open water, a kayak was necessary to get it home. Apparently seals were not yet shot from kayaks.

Sealing with guns, or rather rifles, was not as reliable as the traditional harpooning. Myhlenphort mentions that once 11 Greenlandic fangers at a hole in the ice fired 136 shots, but only 15 seals were killed. He blamed the small calibre of the rifles, due to which the seals were usually only wounded and disappeared under the ice. This is also indicative of the stage of development this fangst method was in at the time: the combined use of rifle and harpoon had not yet been practiced.

It was often difficult to get deliveries of the best possible firearms. The changing fortunes of peace and war also created difficulties in procuring gunpowder and lead at reasonably stable prices. As firearms gradually became more and more common, it was necessary to increase the importation of weapons as well as accessories at the same rate. The necessity of repairs created additional difficulties.

It is almost as if the use of firearms in West Greenland in this period was at a kind of experimental stage. The right calibre and length of barrel had not yet been found for sealing. At the beginning of the period, the West Greenlandic fanger had not yet learned how to use his rifle to attain the best possible result. There could of course be no question of training the Greenlanders to shoot, an art of which most of the Europeans stationed in Greenland were also ignorant.

It is quite strange to find an indication that the individual fanger took the same attitude towards his gun as towards his traditional weapons: if the shot missed, and this perhaps happened several times in succession, it was the weapon which was at fault, not the fanger!

The rifles delivered to Greenlandic fangers were often subjected to rather rough treatment. Liedemark, the trader at Jakobshavn, made a detailed report: "It is all too well known how they treat even the best rifles when they have had bad luck for one or several days. At the slightest defect they bend them between large staves, knock them into shape, arch them, file them, cut pieces off them, etc., and by such pernicious repair in a short time make them quite useless for anything other than wasting powder and lead, to the detriment both of the Trade and the Greenlanders, whereas with the opposite treatment they could be used for the lifetime of a man. If all the dilapidated flintlocks to be found here in the Northern Inspectorate were collected at one place, what a quantity would we not then see?" He also thought that a not inconsiderable number of them could be made serviceable again instead of being "thrown around the houses or out on the ground."

To stop this abuse of "flintlocks" and to arrange a cheaper and quicker repair of broken rifles, he suggested sending to Greenland a proficient gunsmith. As one of his reasons, he mentioned that "the Greenlanders would not have to send their flintlocks back to Denmark for repair, after which they have to wait a whole year, or even two years, when their rifles are damaged immediately after the departure of the last ship. During this long time they must then be idle or borrow from the trader and thereby incur serious debt which is too great a burden on even the best fanger, or what is even worse, sell the things which are just as necessary for him, such as his umiak, his kayak, or all his dogs, to buy another rifle which is often just as bad as the one he sent to Denmark." A new rifle ordinarily cost 12 rigsdalers, for which the fanger often, according to Liedemark, "got nothing but a polished flintlock instead of a dirty one, but otherwise in almost the same unserviceable condition as when the Greenlander turned it in."

These were harsh words and accusations against the otherwise meritorious gunsmith in Copenhagen. But there must have been something to Liedemark's assertions, both about Greenlanders' treatment of their rifles, the quality of firearms shipped to Greenland, and the efficiency of repairs. In 1794 at Holsteinsborg, on the orders of the Management, rifles shipped were tested before being sold. Of the 12 shipped, four were quite unserviceable. At Egedesminde the 12 rifles shipped in 1793 were tested; eight were superb, but four had to be discarded. In 1794 four rifles for 12 rigsdalers each were shipped, and they were all good. But of 14 rifles to be sold at 10 rigsdalers apiece, "only a few were in working order." In 1792 Myhlenphort reported from Egedesminde that he had a stock of 26 rifles. He had tested them all, and they were "quite useless and poorly made."

This matter has been dealt with in such detail because it is one of the many small issues which together, repeated year after year, gave rise to irritations in the relations between the inhabitants of Greenland, both native and Europeans, on the one hand, and the Royal Greenland Trade and the central administration in Copenhagen on the other. These continual irritations must be taken into consideration in evaluating relations between the colony districts in Greenland and the Management in Denmark, or indeed the relationship between Denmark and Greenland as a whole.

The Greenlandic fangers gradually evolved a quite definite idea of what a rifle should be like to meet their approval. "The Greenlanders want their rifles eight-sided rather than round, tarnished rather than polished, and short rather than long; and this they have learned from experience. This is why: a round polished rifle shines in the spring when the sun shines, so that when a Greenlander aims at a marine animal he is blinded and misses. A long rifle takes a longer time to aim than a short one; and one with a large barrel shoots better and more reliably than one with a small barrel." This was written by Myhlenphort from Egedesminde.

The rifle problem gave rise to a certain amount of bitterness on both sides of the Atlantic. Myhlenphort, who was otherwise not prone to harsh words, felt called upon to write that it was not for his amusement that a trader sent back good and sound merchandise, much less good rifles, which were some of the most important items a trader in Greenland could sell. But a trader "has to be guided by the Greenlanders' taste and cannot force them to buy merchandise which they do not want or which is of no use to them." He had had the rifles which had been shipped to him tested, including the cheaper ones, which there were more of. In one case, which he described in detail, sloppy work was evident. Immediately thereafter he added: "When a Greenlander is going to buy a rifle in this country, he tests it as accurately as possible; and they are not easy to fool, as they are on the whole good shots." If the rifles shot better when tested in Copenhagen, this was presumably due, he thought, to the quality of the gunpowder used: polished rather than ordinary powder. The previous year he had explicitly pointed out that "The price does not mean much to a Greenlander at Egedesminde, if only the rifle is good."

The Management of the Royal Greenland Trade continued testing rifles immediately when delivered. They had complained to the manufacturer and even warned him that they might cancel their order. Although the rifles had been tested separately and approved, complaints were made about them. "We therefore admit that we know of no other way of supplying the country with better rifles at a lower price," the Management wrote, concluding a long discussion in 1799 with the Inspector of South Greenland, from which complaints had also come throughout the years. Nevertheless one could order a rifle for 20 rigsdalers, which was the price paid by the Trade itself.

"In order to provide the Greenlanders with a rifle, the fangst implement so important to them, of as good a quality as possible, the Establishments are this year being supplied with an even better, but most likely also more expensive, kind of rifle," wrote Inspector P.H. Motzfeldt in a circular in 1806. But in order not to create payment problems for fangers, the possibility was opened of the Inspector lowering the price for a proficient fanger who was in great and immediate need of the best firearm.

This chain of events illustrates several facets of the development of West Greenland. In the first place, the change in fangst methods. Then the quality consciousness revealed by the Greenlandic fangers; the authorities in Greenland were behind them and supported them against the Trade. The Trade, for its part, apparently did what it could to reach a satisfactory result, at the same time maintaining the price policy laid down in 1782. By 1806 the point had been reached where "social indications" could even lower the price of rifles below the price paid by the Trade. The price of gunpowder was subject to the same policy, but in wartime the price of powder rose considerably.

The Production of Seal Oil and Skins

These changes in fangst methods ought to increase production, both of seal blubber and sealskin. The modest growth which can be observed in both these areas is, however, due to other factors. As far as can be seen, the production of the fangers did not increase, presumably because the number of fangers and their proportion to the rest of the population declined during this period, as shown above. The production of the individual fanger was limited by various factors, one of the most essential of which was the fact that all the fangst methods used by fangers took a certain amount of time, so there was a limit on how many seals could be taken in a single hunt. There was also a limit to how much produce could be taken home by kayak or sled. Sealing was as a rule a one-man operation.

Table 21.

Four-year period	Average number of barrels per year	Above or below total average of 2276 barrels
1777–1780	2169	below
1781–1784	1496	below
1788–1791	2368	above
1792–1795	2256	below
1796–1799	2942	above
1800–1803	2933	above
1804–1807	1609	below

It is possible to some extent to illustrate the development of sealing production in figures, and thereby indicate some growth. The production of seal and beluga oil, in four-year periods, is shown in Table 21. With an average population in West Greenland of 5500, the total average oil production corresponds to about one-half barrel per person annually, rendered from two thirds barrel of blubber. The oil production of the Royal Greenland Trade, deriving from its purchases of seal and beluga blubber, does not indicate any exploitation of the West Greenlandic fanger. As a matter of fact, a not inconsiderable part of the seal blubber resulted from seal netting carried on by Europeans stationed in the colonies, of which we shall hear more later.

The same seems to apply to the export of sealskin from the colonies, as tabulated in Table 22. The total average of exported sealskins corresponds to 1½ seal per inhabitant per year, using the same average population of 5500. Here, too, a good deal of the skins derived from seal netting in the colonies.

Table 22.

Four-year period	Average number of sealskins per year	Above or below total average of 8918 skins
1777–1780	8763	below
1781–1784	3766	below
1788–1791	6780	below
1792–1795	9799	above
1796–1799	10636	above
1800–1803	13685	above
1804–1807	9003	above

Graph 1

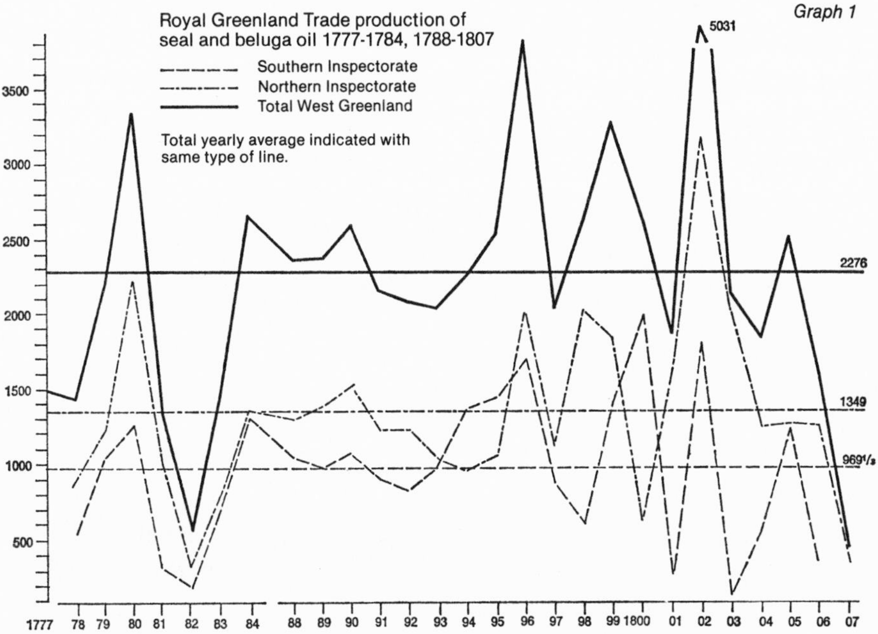

These curves only partially express the fangst results of the preceding year; they represent that part of the fangst produce which was purchased and "exported". The huge dips in 1781 and 1782 are mostly due to shipping delays. The dip in North Greenland in 1797 is presumably due to an epidemic in Disko Bugt in 1796, while the dips in South Greenland in 1797 and 1798 were caused by shipping difficulties. Shipwrecks were at least part of the reason for the dips in 1800 and 1801. 1803 reflected the consequences of the smallpox epidemic of 1800–1801. The dip in 1806 and 1807 was due to erratic and slow shipment because of the war in Europe. The high peaks are mainly due to the arrival of large shipments, sometimes containing the produce of several of the preceding years, as well as the return of ships which had wintered in either Greenland or Norway. Because of these accidental fluctuations the total yearly average are here indicated by straight lines, and the tables are listed in four-year periods.

The annual average has been calculated because the yearly production of oil and export of sealskin was subject to considerable fluctuations independent of the annual take of seals. These fluctuations appear in Graph 1, illustrating oil production from seal and beluga blubber. Diseases, shipwreck and the wintering in Greenland of transport ships for various reasons could give rise to years with a colossal production and others with almost no production. The low figures from 1804 to 1807 are due to the war situation in Europe and the consequent insecurity of shipping. In general we see from the tables as well as the graph that we are here dealing with small absolute figures.

Table 23.

Species of seal	Yearly average of skins exported, 1777–1784, 1788–1800
Harp seal: Blueback	2328
Saddleback	622
Harp seal: Total	2950
Bearded seal	143
Spotted seal	220
"Ordinary skins": Dried	3208
Salted	1254
"Ordinary skins": Total	4462

Both tables reveal a certain growth between 1777–1780 and 1800–1803: for oil production 35% and for sealskins 56%. This may indicate an increase in purchases, and thus in fangst results. But as mentioned previously, there is here no question of exploitation.

A detailed analysis of accounts of exported sealskins shows that the predominant species of seal was that which yielded the so-called "ordinary skins", some preserved by salting, mostly by drying. See Table 23. As the designations of the various species of seal are not quite reliable and do not correspond to later practice, this table must be taken with reservations. "Ordinary skins" must mean those of common seal (phoca vitulina concolor, also called "spotted seal", "harbour seal" or "bay seal", in Westgreenlandic qasigiaq) and ringed seal (phoca hispida, also called "Fiord seal", "jar seal" or "floe rat", in Westgreenlandic natseq). It is closely followed by the harp seal (phoca groenlandica), which as old is called saddleback (Westgreenlandic âtârssuaq) while as young "blue back" (or "beater and bedlamer", in Westgreenlandic agdlagtôq). Other species of seal play a negligable role. Depilated skins, so-called "waterproof skins" (Westgreenlandic erisâq), were very seldom exported, and when they were, it was usually in small quantities, which as a rule were sent back to Greenland for use by whalers.

That the common seal and the ringed seal are represented in such great numbers is presumably due to the fact that it was the special object of netting. If we consider the export of this species of skins alone: i.e., the group "ordinary skins", for the 21 years listed in Table 23 plus one single year, we see a considerable rise, in accordance with the development of seal netting. This is tabulated in Table 24.[4]

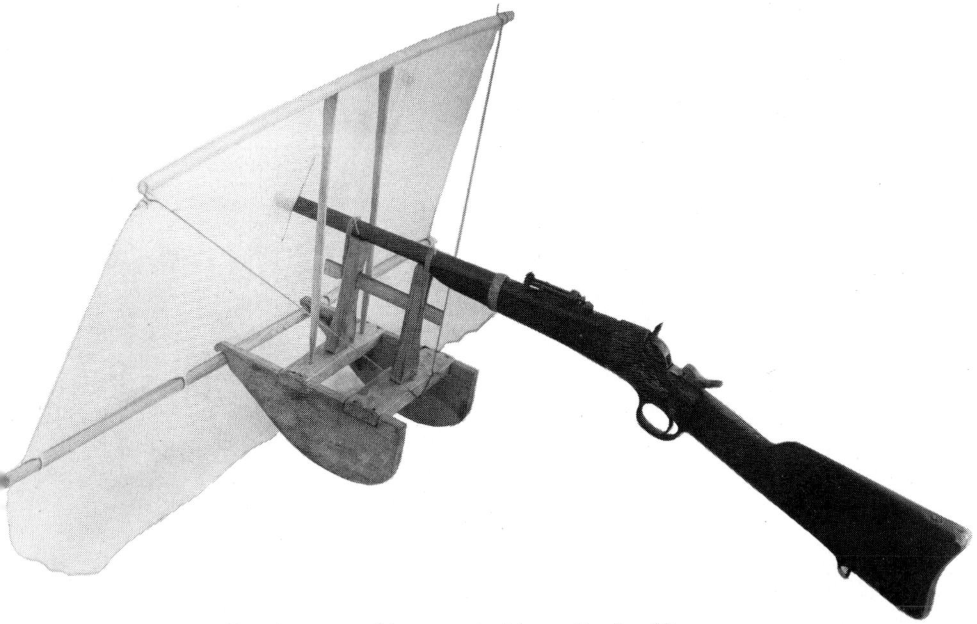

A sled with shooting sail, as it appeared later, and with rest for the rifle.
(Arctic Institute, Charlottenlund, Denmark, Photo Collection no. 2290, Photo M. Porsild, 1910)

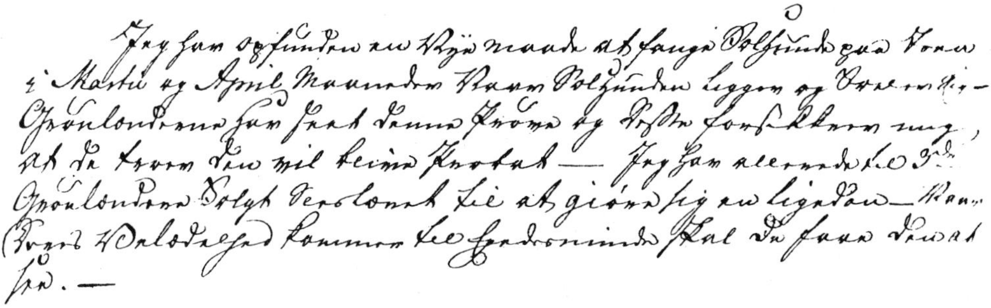

Part of letter from *M.N. Myhlenphort,* the trader, to Inspector *B.J. Schultz,* February 24, 1792. Here he tells about his invention, see page 167, where the lines are quoted in translation. (Half size)

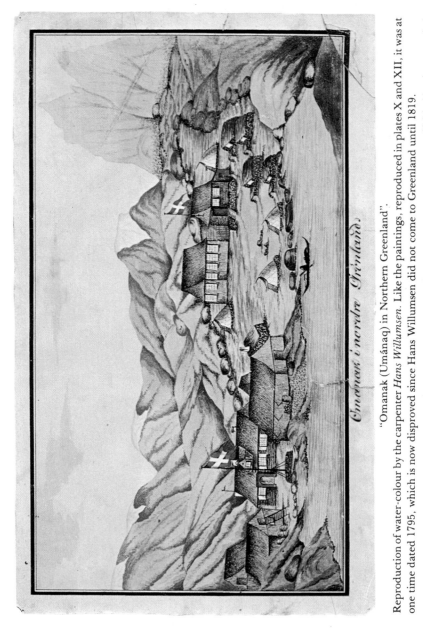

"Omanak (Umánaq) in Northern Greenland".
Reproduction of water-colour by the carpenter *Hans Willumsen*. Like the paintings, reproduced in plates X and XII, it was at one time dated 1795, which is now disproved since Hans Willumsen did not come to Greenland until 1819.

(Original in private possession)

Table 24.

	Total "ordinary skins"	Salted	Dried
1777–1780	5973	4909	1064
1781–1784	2472	1048	1424
1788–1791	3198	612	2586
1792–1795	5666	23	5643
1796–1799	6091	881	5210
1800	3894	224	3670

All these figures say nothing, however, of domestic consumption in Greenland itself: that quantity of sealskin, seal blubber and seal meat which satisfied the needs of the Greenlandic inhabitants and Europeans stationed there. The consumption of skins, both "waterproof skins" and pelts, for trousers for example was hardly as great among Europeans as among Greenlanders, but the former nevertheless did consume a certain quantity of sealskins, blubber and seal meat. The produce of sealing was therefore considerably larger than revealed by our figures.

Graph 1 shows a considerable difference between the two inspectorates in the production of seal and beluga oil; less blubber was usually delivered by the south than by the north. The average annual difference in oil production was close to 380 barrels. Within the 28 years dealt with in the graph, it was only in 1794, 1795 and 1800 that oil production on the basis of blubber from the Southern Inspectorate exceeded that based on the north. In these years as well as in 1802, the curve for the Southern Inspectorate rises above the average curve for the north. This confirms our previously mentioned general impression of the economic predominance of the Northern Inspectorate.

In accordance with the economic theories of the times it was important to increase production. The administration and the inspectors went about this with various means. In each district bounties were given to the fangers who produced the most each year. These bounties gradually came to consist of a certain quantity of coffee and rock candy, as well as highly coveted goods which could not simply be ordered; they belonged to the category of "luxury items", and were thus well suited for prizes. It cannot be seen, however, that this method produced the desired results.

The force of example must have been more powerful.

Netting

We have seen that it was most likely the netting of seals and belugas which was the most important factor in the rise in the production of blubber, and thus of oil and sealskins. In the period under consideration, this fangst method was apparently not wholeheartedly taken up by Greenlandic fangers. This fact has led researchers to declare netting un-Eskimo: an "imported" method.

Development in West Greenland seems to confirm this theory. Before 1763 nothing is heard of the use of seal nets, but only of European proposals to use this method, known from Norway. After 1763 it was apparently difficult to get West Greenlandic fangers to make use of this method.

All indications are that this development started with the initiative of a trader, Johan H. Bruun, in 1763–1764 at Umánaq, apparently entirely based on amateur skills. From the very first colonial period it was common for Europeans stationed in Greenland to procure fresh food for the colony by hunting and fishing; they also sometimes earned a little extra money by fox trapping. If they were fortunate enough to take a seal, the meat became a part of their household diet while the skin and perhaps some of the blubber were sold.

This was the beginning of a development of the colonies away from being pure purchasing centres and towards a growing degree of production. Fangst in West Greenland seemed to have stabilized at its optimal level; no rise in production could be expected. But on such a rise depended the existence of the Trade, and thus the fulfilment of growing demands for supplies. During the time of the General Trading Company, the Management's interest in the participation in production of stationed Europeans grew, at the same time as a formidable campaign was carried out against illicit trade which violated the Company's monopoly rights. Especially for the latter reason, the Management preferred to promote controllable production at the colonies.

For the same reason the Management therefore supported the initiative of Johan Bruun. It must have had at least some success, not among the Greenlanders at Umánaq, but among the colony crew. In subsequent years seal netting was also attempted at certain localities in Disko Bugt. When the Royal Greenland Trade had been established and consolidated, this initiative was continued. In the Order of 1782 seal netting is the subject of special mention (Chapter III, § 3, item 2). Here the encouragement of the colony crew to engage in netting was forcibly emphasized, but it was at the same time laid down that Greenlanders must not be hired by the Europeans to net. In consideration of the generally prevailing idea of forcibly protecting the Greenlandic population, and especially fangst activities, the spread of netting as a fangst method was hereby limited. On the other hand, the existence of the colony crews in Greenland would not be endangered.

To promote netting, the Royal Greenland Trade gave a modest bounty of 6 skillings per seal taken, in addition to the purchase price of blubber and skins. This did promote netting in the Northern Inspectorate, especially in Umánaq District, but the participation of Greenlanders was desired. This caused difficulties throughout the period under consideration.

There were presumably several reasons for these difficulties. As we have seen, this method was, as far as can be determined, not traditionally Eskimo. Initial expenditures were high. If it was really to make a difference, several nets would have to be placed, and they were expensive to acquire. They were also expensive to maintain, for there were always repairs to be made after taking even one seal. The net would be torn to pieces either by the seal trying to get free or by sharks getting a free meal from the dead seal. It was often experienced that nets were completely lost during storms and when the ice broke up. In a subsistance economy it was not possible for a Greenlandic fanger to accumulate sufficient capital to carry on netting. If Greenlandic fangers were to have nets, they would have to borrow, and here the traders exercised a restraint, because they were liable for the debts of Greenlanders, which were already high enough. In addition there was the trouble of maintaining the nets and the unreliability of this method – good weather could better be made use of in other traditional methods which experience showed to be more reliable. So it is easy to understand that Greenlandic fangers were not inclined to take up netting. It was also the prevailing principle that fangers were not to be taken from their occupations.

Nevertheless there were some Greenlanders who did participate in netting, but it was usually because they had no other opportunity of sealing, either because they had no kayak or kayak accessories, or because they were incapable of carrying on fangst by traditional methods. Some of these netted in partnership with the colony crew, so that the crew supplied the nets and the Greenlanders maintained them, naturally receiving a certain share of the proceeds.

At the basis of this practice was a conscious policy. Both Johan Fr. Schwabe and later inspectors saw an advantage in seal netting for Greenlanders who were otherwise unproductive, as well as relief in seasons where traditional fangst methods seemed to fail: i.e., relief from the annual periods of hunger. On the other hand they were obliged to be on their guard against the possible exploitation of the Greenlandic population; but as far as we can see from the source material, they found throughout the years no cause to intervene. Only once was it rumoured that Greenlanders were being exploited, but this was disproven.

These rumours touched one of the pioneers in the spreading of netting: the missionary P.A. Cappelen. Shortly after his arrival at Umánaq in 1783, he began his activities by leading netting experiments. Until he left Greenland in 1792, he was equally active in the mission and in seal netting. In a genuinely rationalistic manner, the material welfare of his congregation was just as important to him as was its spiritual welfare. In spite of personal losses and many vicissitudes, including authority disputes with the various chief traders of the colony, his activity resulted in a continuous growth of seal blubber and sealskin production at Umánaq. He did not succeed, however, in getting the local Greenlandic fangers to take up this method, except in cases of dire necessity. As the location of this colony was unsuitable for netting, due to the instability of the ice, Cappelen enthusiastically advocated moving both the colony and the mission to a more suitable location in the fjord. This resulted in the establishment of a couple of trading posts there and farther out on the Nûgssuaq peninsula (in the hope of also being able to carry on whaling).

It was still, however, just as when Cappelen first came to the colony, almost only Europeans who netted, thus supplying about half of Umánaq's production of seal blubber and sealskin. In 1790 and 1791 the attitude of the Greenlanders to netting seemed to shift. The fangst had been poor for an uncommonly long time, and a newly appointed trader enthusiastic about netting had got more Greenlanders to try this method, seemingly with success. He asserted in a report that their production had been sufficient to keep hunger, want and cold from their doors - that winter. The contribution of the colony crew continued to be the most essential factor, however, at least throughout this period.

A quantitative investigation of production on the basis of netting (netting under ice) shows that Umánaq far exceeded the other colony districts in the Northern Inspectorate. On an average the Greenlanders and stationed Europeans of this district took 140 seals a year per participant, during the 12 years recorded within the period dealt with in this volume. Next in line was Upernavik, with an average of 128 seals a year for seven years. Egedesminde, where netting was carried on rather intensively for 15 years of our period, only attained an average of 63 seals a year per man.

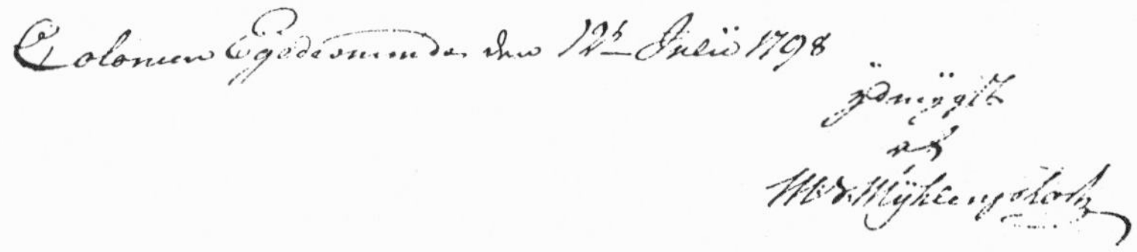

Reduced copy of trader Marcus Nissen Myhlenphort's signature on letter to Inspector Claus Bendeke of 12 June 1798.

Lowest was Kronprinsens Ejland, with 11½ seals per man yearly for 15 years.

At most places netting was carried on by the colony crew, and at the instigation of the colony leadership. At Egedesminde M.N. Myhlenphort, the trader, developed a special practice. Soon after his arrival he had realized the production opportunities inherent in netting.

In 1787, the year after his arrival, Myhlenphort was stationed at Kronprinsens Ejland, where among the crew he met a "mixture": Albrecht Lynge. Lynge had been hired there in 1782 by Inspector Schwabe, who classified him as "incompetent at Greenlandic fangst and married to a daughter of a mixed marriage." He was the son of the well-considered cooper Lars Lynge, sent to Christianshåb in 1750 by the Trading Company.

Albrecht Lynge may have been trained in netting by his father at Christianshåb. His and Myhlenphort's interest in netting seem to have coalesced during Myhlenphort's stay at Kronprinsens Ejland. In any case, these two became so attached to each other that Albrecht Lynge and his family constantly followed Myhlenphort subsequently wherever he was transferred.

At first Albrecht Lynge followed Myhlenphort to Jakobshavn in 1788. It seems that he and Myhlenphort here formed a team of Greenlanders, about four or five, who carried on netting systematically. When Myhlenphort was transferred to Egedesminde in 1791, the entire team followed him. During the 12 years in which Myhlenphort was the leader of this colony, he and Albrecht Lynge built up netting in this district.

But in this district one could only get the other Greenlandic fangers to use netting during certain months of the year. Whenever possible, they resorted to shooting and kayak fangst. When Albrecht Lynge died in 1800, the fangst team seems to have been dissolved; and after the smallpox epidemic netting in general lost ground in Egedesminde District.

The interesting aspect of this development is that this fangst team constantly had Albrecht Lynge as its practical leader, and that its members, according to the source material, lived with him and were, so to speak, members of his family. Their needs were satisfied by the fangst and their shares of the proceeds from sales. Privately, not as a trader, Myhlenphort stood behind the work of this team as its financial guarantor. This is in its own manner the first effective cooperative in Greenland; but it died with its leader and participants. Myhlenphort's direct successors at Egedesminde could not resuscitate it.

Throughout the period dealt with here the administration and inspectors continued eagerly to support the introduction of netting, stimulated by the great increase in production figures from Umánaq. But even there it seems as though in actuality this fangst method was unprofitable for the producer: i.e., the individual fanger. The great expenses for nets, the many repairs and new acquisitions were too great a burden. It was attempted to reduce the price of nets, and Greenlanders went over to making them themselves from imported materials and from old whaling lines. But that did not seem to help. Suggestions were made to organize one or another form of insurance against loss of nets, but they were not realized. Insurance would not be understood by the ordinary Greenlanders.

If the colony leaders continually had their people netting, sometimes in partnership with Greenlanders, this was because this form of fangst did increase the production of their districts, although in some cases only modestly, and because the existence of the stationed Europeans did not have to be assured by the revenue from this fangst. In this manner, it also afforded not inconsiderable employment opportunities, and sources of livelihood for Greenlanders who could not earn their daily bread by any other manner than participating as "partners" in netting. At least at first, Europeans were careful not to pay these Greenlanders, as if they had been hired.

From the Northern Inspectorate the idea of netting wandered south; Myhlenphort especially worked to promote it when he became the Inspector of South Greenland i 1803. Here netting gradually came to be carried on both under the ice and in open water: e.g., in small sounds, where seals often passed.

It was not until well into the period dealt with in this volume that netting began in the Southern Inspectorate; at Julianehåb it only began on an experimental basis in 1805. Everywhere the same difficulties were encountered as in the Northern Inspectorate in changing the attitude of Greenlanders toward this method. At Julianehåb individuals were even known to "assault" the nets, cutting pieces out of them for use elsewhere. Mørch, the trader at Julianehåb, was of the opinion that netting could be useful in his district, but he thought that Umánaq was the best place for netting, and that its production with this method could not be excelled, because the best and most stable conditions for it were to be found there, and nowhere else.

It was also to a predominant extent the colony crew that carried on netting in the Southern Inspectorate, but under a special kind of organization. At both Fiskenæsset and Godthåb, partnerships were formed. Inspector Myhlenphort himself even participated in group netting at Fiskenæsset. It cannot be excluded that Greenlanders, for example the sons of Albrecht Lynge, who after 1803 lived at Godthåb, participated in the partnership there. These organisations were naturally formed to make it financially possible to carry on netting. In 1806, for example, Myhlenphort, representing the Royal Greenland Trade, sold over 199 rigsdalers' worth of nets, tools, net sheds and vessels, stationed at Qilángârssuit and Savssivik near Godthåb, to the partnership at Godthåb.

Netting is not mentioned in the other districts of the Southern Inspectorate. It cannot therefore have spread much in this period. And in any case, it was not taken up by the local Greenlandic fangers. They were in general not interested in changing their fangst methods or in other kinds of fangst. In connection with the fangst of humpback whales, it was, for example, reported from Fiskenæsset that "Two unsuccessful attempts are known to be more than enough for Greenlanders to abandon an undertaking," i.e., to abandon all further attempts.

It is possible that this general attitude should be interpreted as the expression of passive resistance against too great a pressure on Greenlanders to increase their production. The constant exhortation to diligence, carefulness and the increase of production, made by the rationalistically influenced Management through the inspectors and stationed Europeans of the Royal Greenland Trade, was more than the Greenlandic-Eskimo attitude could meet. There are indications that in the prevailing subsistance economy and with the traditional techniques of the fangers, Greenlandic productivity was stretched to its utmost. If production could not be increased by traditional means, untraditional means must be used, that is to say that the Trade itself engaged in production. But it was essential that the traditional Greenlandic occupations were reserved for the Greenlandic population. Only where it was directly necessary did the administration deem it proper to enter into production through its stationed employees.

Down Collecting

This applied also to the collection of eiderdown. As early as 1770, this had been declared a monopoly commodity, but throughout the years it had been difficult to keep the collection of down within proper bounds.[5] It was the experience of the past which made Johan Fr. Schwabe formulate the provisions of the Order of 1782 regarding the collection of down as sharply as possible. In the first place it was necessary to guarantee that eider nests were not ruthlessly exploited, leading to the extinction of this bird; it was also necessary to reserve down collection for the Greenlandic population.

It was hard to enforce the spirit and letter of these provisions. But at first the inspectors were zealous in enforcing this item of the Order. Even the Missionskollegium felt called upon to remind the missionary at Upernavik to see to it that "the eider is preserved" in his district.

The provisions seem to have been evaded - even to a considerable extent. In Disko Bugt, the most important collection of down took place on the islands off Egedesminde. In 1788 a complaint was made that 15 umiaks from other districts "sent by traders, priests, assistants and unmarried sailors," had collected 6 skippunds (960 kilogrammes) of down on the islands of Egedesminde. With cleaned down selling at 20 skillings a pund (500 grammes), this correspond to an income of 400 rigsdalers: a considerable sum which eluded Greenlandic pockets as well as those of the trader at Egedesminde.

This event, as well as quite a few others, led the Inspector of the Northern Inspectorate to issue a detailed circular explicitly stating who was allowed to go on eiderdown expeditions. Only Greenlanders and Europeans married to Greenlanders, if they were part of Greenlandic households, were allowed to collect down; and the down collected by the latter was to be sold. Europeans stationed in Greenland were allowed to lend poor Greenlanders an umiak for an eiderdown expedition, but the collected down was to be paid for at the full scheduled rate. Here we see a clear example of protection against arbitrary exploitation. Greenlandic occupations were to be reserved for the Greenlandic population.

The Inspector also wanted to protect the interests of the Trade. According to his circular, if anyone collected down in another district than the one in which he resided, he was to sell it to the colony in which the down had been collected. In Disko Bugt this meant that Egedesminde was to be the centre of eiderdown "production". The consequence of this was that down collecting in Disko Bugt was mainly reserved for the Greenlanders of Egedesminde, so that the provisions of this circular supported tendencies for the colony districts to be isolated from each other.

Another consequence was that the population of Egedesminde District was unable to exploit fully the many down-gathering grounds of the district. It seems that this led to a general decline in the purchase of down.

This had been predicted by M.N. Myhlenphort, the trader at Jakobshavn, in 1789, when the circular was issued. When he was transferred to Egedesminde in 1791, he went there with the firm intention of promoting the economic potential of this district, so that he enforced its "down monopoly" according to the circular of 1789. At the same time, however, he attempted to get the provisions slackened which reserved down collection for Greenlanders. At about the same time, a new Inspector had taken office, so that Myhlenphort turned directly to the Management in Copenhagen. Since the matter involved a dispensation from the Order of 1782, the Commission had to be consulted. The entire affair seems not to have suited the new inspector, B.J. Schultz; aggrieved that Myhlenphort had bypassed him in going directly to the administration, he informed the trader that it was now permitted, under the supervision of the trader or a reliable assistant, for the stationed Europeans to collect down, but only at Egedesminde. Half of the payment for the down, made according to the purchase schedule, was to be credited to the welfare fund of the Northern Inspectorate, the supervisor was to get one-sixth, and the collection crew the remaining one-third.

Down collection continued to cause difficulties. Cheating could not be stopped. Whether it was the Greenlandic collectors or the assistants and traders who purchased down that delivered sand instead of down is not evident from the circular the inspector felt called upon to issue to "the three northern establishments," by which he must have meant Upernavik, Umânaq, and, located between these two, Prøven.

It must have been the collectors; for later we hear that it was the custom in the Northern Inspectorate to take nests "with straw and whatever else increases the weight," and that the down was wet, which also added to its weight. Nor was it possible to prevent ruthless exploitation. It was reported from Sukkertoppen, for example, that a cooper, a sailor and three Greenlandic women in less than a fortnight collected 5000 eggs and 65 punds of down. It was realized at Egedesminde that Greenlanders from the South District had in 1791 sold their down to the trader at Holsteinsborg; the reason for this must have been that the former trader at Egedesminde had neglected making expeditions to this part of the colony. In any case it caused the relater, the trader Marcus Nissen Myhlenphort, to exclaim: "Marcus swears that this will not be the case next year if God preserves his health and life." He would be sure to get there before the trader from Holsteinsborg. But the "district monopoly" could not be constantly maintained. In 1803, after the smallpox epidemic, and after Myhlenphort had left Egedesminde, Greenlanders from Egedesminde South District again delivered down to the trader at Holsteinsborg, and this time they even brought it to him.[6]

Arrangements could be made in one area or the other, but the Greenlanders did as they pleased. "They are a free people and consider the country theirs; and they just laugh at measures which limit their exploitation of what the country and nature afford." This is the gist of the comments of a trader, speaking about down collecting.

Other Kinds of Fangst and Hunting

Concentration on the most profitable forms of fangst and hunting, as the Trade desired, actually collided - openly and secretly - with the traditional pattern of life in West Greenland. As late as 1792 a trader was still able to present an almost traditional picture of fangst throughout the year at Holsteinsborg: an *almost* traditional picture of the fangst cycle, because at Holsteinsborg it was not quite the traditional forms of fangst which were being promoted. Whaling had assumed the role of the most important occupation. The Spring fangst began in the fjords in April with the fangst of common seals. It lasted to sometime in June, when the angmagssat and the harp seal (âtaq) began to turn up. The harp seals were taken by the proficient fangers in kayaks, while the "poorer providers content themselves with scooping and drying a number of capelins or small herring for winter provisions. Ordinarily at the beginning of July most of the Greenlanders go out to the islands for birds, down and eggs. Some head into the interior hunting reindeer, with which they waste the best of the Summer, to their own detriment and that of the Trade. From this time on they do not do much until the end of September, when they all gather for the Autumn fangst two miles north of the colony, where they spread out over a number of islands and from these shoot seals with their rifles. They never carry on fangst in kayaks in the Autumn. The Autumn fangst is often unsuccessful, due either to the lack of seals or the lack of good rifles; and when the Autumn fangst fails they are exposed to a shortage of food sometimes even in the first months of the Winter. At the end of October or the beginning of November, according to the weather, they move into their winter houses at the colony and then engage in whaling."[7]

It appears from this that at Holsteinsborg the Greenlanders participated in whaling from November or December until April. This description supplements our picture of sealing; there were still no great opportunities for sealing in this district. Angmagssat fangst seems to have been insufficient to assure enough food for the winter. Reindeer hunting intrudes into the pattern.

Not all seem to have gone reindeer hunting at Holsteinsborg: some went bird hunting and down and egg collecting in July and August, while others went into the fjords hunting reindeer, most likely on the great plains towards the south, in the direction of Søndre Strømfjord. This description adds the inevitable remark, which is to be found in almost every mention of reindeer hunting, that on these long trips the Greenlanders "waste the best of the Summer, to their own detriment and that of the Trade."

The Greenlandic fangers seem to have continued to hunt reindeer during their traditional fangst cycle, even though the reindeer population apparently was declining.[8] Complaints came from north and south over the waste of good fangst time which reindeer hunting involved - for the Trade. In order to set a stopper for this hunting and to decrease the Trade's loss on purchases of reindeer hides, Inspector A.M. Lund in 1970 cut the purchase price of reindeer hides in half. This price had previously ranged from 64 to 96 to 128 skillings apiece, depending on quality and size; at the auctions in Copenhagen the Trade would get an average of 64 skillings per hide, and even had trouble getting rid of them.

Fiskenæsset in the Southern Inspectorate complained a lot about reindeer hunting, and the trader there wanted it forbidden, or at least for the Inspector to order that no one was to go hunting in Godthåb District before a certain day. It would have been easy enough to issue such an order, but considerably more difficult, if not impossible, to get it obeyed. "Giving orders which cannot be enforced is seldom beneficial, but often harmful," said Inspector Bendeke in 1795. Raun, the trader, continued, however, in his attempt to have reindeer hunting limited; and even took the liberty of using the inspector's name without the latter's prior knowledge when he forbad the Greenlanders of Fiskenæsset District to go reindeer hunting before they had taken a sufficient quantity of angmagssat. "The prohibition is not obeyed but ridiculed, because the Greenlanders completely realize that I have no coercive means to enforce it," wrote Inspector Bull, in the same spirit as the previous inspector.

However much the two inspectors wanted to see reindeer hunting limited, they did realize the limits of their authority. They had no powers to interfere in the traditions of the fangst cycle. For the Greenlandic families which went reindeer hunting, it was not a question of profit which compelled them, although the hunt did provide them with a necessity of life, but rather the fact that it was an essential part of their life, which they enjoyed.

The need which reindeer hunting satisfied kept people coming all the way from Julianehåb District up to Holsteinsborg. But all things considered, reindeer hunting did not play the role in this period that it had before 1750; now it was more a question of enjoyment, which, of course, was not unimportant, either. The assemblage of people at the Mid-Greenlandic reindeer-hunting grounds was, however, as we have seen, no longer a yearly occurrence, except for those who lived in the vicinity. Perhaps a certain amount of trade – conducted through the Trade or not – replaced it. There was, for example, only a modest supply of reindeer in the Julianehåb area, but there was still a demand for hides and tendon.

The consideration of utility was decisive to the attitude of the Trade and thus of its employees to all forms of fangst and hunting. Whatever did not increase the production of the so-called Greenlandic products was unprofitable in its eyes, and was characterized as misplaced recreation. Therefore there is in the source material hardly any mention of *bird hunting,* which did not contribute to useful production. Down collection, which was undeniably "useful", was not considered as fangst or hunting proper. It is typical that the previous description from Holsteinsborg only just mentions bird hunting as a summer phenomenon out on the islands. In his description of the occupational opportunities of his district in 1788, a trader from Egedesminde does not mention bird hunting at all. What was exclusively devoted to keeping people alive was of no interest, except when it was as fundamental as sealing. In descriptions from other districts during this period, bird hunting is mentioned only occasionally. It is therefore impossible to determine to what extent it was carried on and its significance for the food situation. The periods of famine indicate that it cannot have been very great.

Although silence with respect to bird hunting is characteristic, it is strange that the Holsteinsborg trader did not mention *fox fangst* with a single word. This was considered such a useful occupation that fox hides were purchased and contributed considerable to the revenue of the Trade at the hide auctions in Copenhagen. On the basis of purchases, this fangst can be illustrated with the figures in Table 25. The figures for each year fluctuate considerably as do those for seal oil and hides. The lowest figures are from 1781: 126 hides; the highest from 1797: 1996 hides.

These fluctuations are due to shipping difficulties, ships' wintering in Greenland, shipwrecks and captures in war. In the latter case, the merchandise captured was lost or the capture delayed the shipment for a year or more.

Table 25. White and blue fox hides purchased and exported from Greenland.

	Total	Annual average
1781-1789	6493	721
1790-1798	11619	1291

The figures show a considerably lower average for the first period than for the second. All the figures for each year in the first period, save one, are of three digits; all the figures for each year in the second period, save one, are of four digits. This seems to be a sudden change, with a doubling of fox hide exports from 1789 to 1790; these two years did not, as far as is known, present any difficulties for shipping.

It is, however, unknown whether this doubling of "production": purchase or export, corresponds to a similar increase in the fangst. From 1798 to 1805 the figures show a considerable fall. The average of these seven years is 442, just over a third of the average from 1790 to 1798. This period shows the same fluctuations, due to shipping, as the other periods. The source material does not reveal why exports fell so steeply.

For various reasons these figures do not correspond to the number of foxes taken in Greenland. Some were consumed domestically, some were rejected because they had been taken at the wrong time of the year and the fur was bad, not a few were sold to foreign whalers, and finally, a good deal of hides were sold illicitly by Greenlanders and others to ships' crews, especially the skippers, for coffee, rock candy and distilled spirits. Illicit trade had especially good opportunities in fox hides.

In connection with the development of netting we have seen that from the very first period of colonisation, fox fangst was common as a kind of secondary occupation of the colony crew, and that this was the beginning of the direct participation of the Trade in production. Partly organised in this manner, fox fangst involved a risk of bypassing the monopoly: i.e., of illicit trade. There was, however, no question of interfering with the colony crew in the exercise of their well-earned rights or, as in the case of down collecting, reserving fox fangst for Greenlandic fangers. Illicit trade had to be combatted in other ways.

"Private" fox hide production developed in the Southern Inspectorate in the late 1790's to the point where some members of colony crews trapped young foxes and kept them until they grew up, in order "to sell the foxes alive to any unlicensed person they pleased." The Inspector did not forbid them to raise the young foxes, but they had to be sold to the Trade. In 1798 a circular had been issued which laid down ample fines for bypassing the monopoly. This indicates that some kind of fox farms were gradually being introduced or at least that it was realized that such farms afforded a possibility of increasing production.

Fox fangst was greatest in the Southern Inspectorate, and within this inspectorate still most significant in Frederikshåb District. Frederikshåb's first place was, however, in the period from 1782 to 1808 threatened by both Godthåb and Fiskenæsset Districts. In the period from 1798 to 1805 the average number of fox hides exported annually from these three districts was as shown in Table 26.

Table 26. Average number of fox hides exported annually from three districts of South Greenland, 1798–1805.

		% of total Greenland	% of total South Greenland
Frederikshåb	67	15	17
Fiskenæsset	47	11	12
Godthåb	58	12	15
Total		38	44

The proportion of fox hides from the entire Northern Inspectorate was during the same period only around 13%. But this does not correspond to the actual conditions in fox fangst in North Greenland, for here the Greenlandic fangers had ample access to trade with foreign whalers, bypassing the monopoly.

The Southern Inspectorate was nevertheless predominant in this branch. Here again the Mid-Greenland districts were of greatest importance. There is, however, a distinct decline in exports of fox hides from Frederikshåb during this period as compared with the first years of this colony. Detailed figures from the period from 1781 to 1798 do not exist or are at least very difficult of access. We cannot therefore shed any light on the fluctuations of fox hide production in Frederikshåb during this period, or find the explanation for the rise in total exports from 1789 to 1790.

This rise was, however, followed by a decline both in 1791 and in 1792.

The Management had noticed this and proposed to stimulate "production" by raising the purchase price of fox hides. Perhaps it also imagined it could stop some of the illicit trade in this manner.

It appears from a circular from Inspector A.M. Lund in Godthåb that this proposal was almost to double the purchase price of fox skins. This caused all the traders as well as the inspector to consider whether this was not too great a price to pay to stimulate this form of fangst. It was admitted that fox fangst at Frederikshåb had to be promoted, but it was feared that it would come to be the predominant form of fangst, both because it was more pleasant and, if the price raise were to be implemented, would be just as profitable as sealing. It would then harm sealing, which was otherwise considered the most important form of fangst. In addition it was feared that fox fangst would be intensified to such an extent that it would affect the fox population.

A dangerous threat to the fox population was in the offing in the Southern Inspectorate. The trader at Frederikshåb had ordered poison nuts in 1796. The administration immediately sounded the alarm against fangst using poison; such methods would quickly lead to the extermination of the fox population. Julianehåb was even ordered to confiscate and return the poison which had come to Greenland by mistake.

Fox fangst had apparently declined so noticeably at Frederikshåb that in 1792 the trader found it expedient to offer bounties to women and children for the delivery of four to six foxes which they had taken themselves. It was further attempted to limit the dog population at Fiskenæsset, Frederikshåb and Julianehåb, because it was thought that the barking and wandering around of the dogs was frightening the foxes away.

All this talk of measures to promote production - including raising the purchase prices of fox skins - took place at the same time as the Management was having difficulties selling fox skins in Copenhagen. This seems strange, but there can be only one explanation: that the Management, in spite of poor sales and consequent low prices, still attempted to foster fox fangst, was due to the economic theories of the times. The administration stressed total production and was not interested in the profitability of the various branches of production. This was true of fox fangst as of seal netting. In addition there was the main principle, more social than economic, of promoting the earning potential of Greenlandic fangers. This could only be done by channelling production, so that the administration was against reindeer hunting, for example, as being unprofitable in this connection.

The low figures of purchases and exports of fox skins from Godthåb, Fiskenæsset and Frederikshåb after 1800 show that production was, in fact, not increased. Skins taken out of season, between 1 March and 31 October, seem also to have been still delivered. Greenlanders evidently scraped together whatever they had taken in their traps or shot occasionally while carrying out other forms of fangst.

In 1804, therefore, Inspector M.N. Myhlenphort issued a circular prohibiting the purchase of skins taken out of season or those of young foxes. At the same time, the price of blue fox skins of the best quality was set at 72 skillings, formerly 46 skillings; those of the worst quality were to be bought for 24 skillings. White fox skins seem not to have been especially appreciated; the best ones could now command only 32 skillings, instead of 24 skillings previously. The increase was thus 50% for blue fox skins, and 33% for white fox skins. The Management approved this price increase, but suggested that skins of poorer quality be purchased at a higher price if the fanger insisted, so that not even the poorest skin would "come into unauthorized hands."

Thus there arose a price difference between the two inspectorates; prices were considerably higher in the north. This could give rise to dissatisfaction in the south, not among the Greenlanders, but among Europeans selling fox skins. Inspector Myhlenphort stressed this; he did not think the Greenlandic production of fox skins was so great in the north that the price difference would affect it. This is a verbal confirmation of the assertion that fox fangst was predominantly important in South Greenland.

The moderate price increase in 1804 did bring about an increase in deliveries of fox skins at various localities. At Godthaab deliveries rose steeply, from 49 skins in both 1804 and 1805 to 230 in 1806-1807. The reason was obviously that the Management had given the green light to the sale of coffee, rock candy, etc., as payment for fox skins. "As long as a Greenlander possessed a single fox skin, he would run after provisions, especially coffee and sugar." These were just the items which the Greenlanders had acquired through illicit trade with ships crews. But it was not the Greenlanders who had traded illicitly; it was the skippers. By permitting the licit sale of items in such great demand, the Trade restricted not only illicit trade, but also the killing of foxes out of season: skins taken out of season were purchased, but at very low prices, and they were never paid for with coffee and other "luxury items".

During this period, fox fangst did not develop into an important source of income for the Greenlandic fanger family. The sales of skins could only have represented a welcome extra income. The Greenlandic inhabitants reacted as customers usually do, and took advantage of this relatively easy source of income to acquire the luxury articles they were suddenly allowed. In this case the Trade had, although with much hesitation, to ignore its rationalistic attitude and assume the role of an ordinary merchant meeting the demands of his customers regardless of whether the sale of certain merchandise was to the actual benefit and moral profit of the customers, whether it was "lavish trash" or not. Here we perceive the first tender shoots of the flowers of liberalism.

Of the remaining forms of hunting, we have from this period only material on *bear-hunting*. Naturally it was still carried on occasionally. Although bear skins were a monopoly commodity, a good number of them must have come into "unauthorized" hands, just as quite a few were used by the Greenlanders themselves. We have only figures for the skins sent to Copenhagen; these, listed in Table 27, thus represent only minimal amounts, to partially illustrate the extent of bear fangst.

Table 27. Bear skins sent to Copenhagen.

	Whole skins	Pieces
1781–1789	185	64
1790–1798	138	202
Average per year	18	15

From 1798 to 1805 a total of 130 whole skins and pieces were sent to Copenhagen, for an annual average of 26, 21% lower than the total annual average of the first two periods, but approximately the same as the average from 1781 to 1789. Certain weak fluctuations occurred in the extent of bear-fangst.

As a source of income for the Greenlandic population as a whole, bear-hunting was of no importance; it only represented special income for the individual fanger who was fortunate enough to come upon a bear. It was only in the most outlying districts north and south that the polar bear normally appeared.

Fishing

It was also the Southern Inspectorate which afforded the possibility of more efficient fishing; at least the Management continually insisted that attempts be made. Otherwise, the fishing carried on by the Greenlandic inhabitants was limited to the amount needed for private consumption – especially in hard times, where any kind of food was welcome.

The fishing of species which occurred locally as well as generally in Greenland continued, then, to be carried out all along the coast by the Greenlandic inhabitants. *Angmagssat fangst* provided an important early summer entertainment, in addition to the benefit which accrued from it. From the point of view of food supplies, the Royal Greenland Trade was interested that this fangst should be as great as possible, as expressed in the proposal of the trader at Fiskenæsset to prohibit reindeer hunting until sufficient angmagssats had been fished.

In 1794–1796 an attempt had been made at Godhavn to make angmagssat fishing more efficient, for a larger catch. Herring nets had been used in this attempt, but this had turned out to be too expensive in proportion to the catch.

As early as 1796 the expensive herring net had to be discarded as "rotten". Inspector C. Bendeke thought the use of scoop nets was more efficient: they were cheap to acquire and maintain, and best at this kind of fishing, in which taking the greatest possible catch in the shortest possible time depended on the energy and perseverance of each individual. Herring nets demanded the cooperation of several participants, and experience showed that maintenance difficulties arose. The use of herring nets had had side effects the unfortunate nature of which was pointed out by the inspector. Part of his explanation of these side effects is understandable, taking into consideration the premises and attitudes of the times, but is nevertheless not in accordance with the facts.

Inspector Bendeke thought that the "herring collection" carried out at Godhavn by stationed Europeans with the help of nets had taken place with the best intentions, but that the method employed was incorrect. "The Greenlanders, who saw the Danes collecting herring for them, let it rest at that, without making any effort themselves." He thought this was wrong; it encouraged them to be lazy. "I think indeed we should attempt to make the work of the Greenlanders easier, and help them to harvest its fruits; but we should never do for them the work they themselves can do."

What is wrong with his explanation is that he thought this method encouraged laziness, as if the Greenlanders at Godhavn did not engage in angmagssat fishing for that reason. It is undoubtedly a correct observation that the Greenlanders remained idle when the stationed Europeans took care of the angmagssat supply. There was then no need for them to spend time and energy on this matter; in addition the fishing was being conducted in an untraditional manner which they did not understand

and could not think of using. And it was hardly to be expected that the Greenlanders at Godhavn would adopt this method, any more than they adopted seal netting elsewhere.

Bendeke correctly realized that these netting attempts had in a way taken the bread out of the Greenlanders' mouths, or rather deprived them of the initiative. Therefore he convened a meeting in the winter of 1797-1798 in which he announced that this form of angmagssat fishing would be discontinued, and that the Greenlandic inhabitants themselves would have to take the necessary catch, which he urged them to do, promising to provide preservation possibilities for their catch, perhaps eventually a drying shed. This was the decisive point. In a sense there were no preservation difficulties. It was common all along the coast to preserve angmagssats "in bags of old waterproof skin anoraks and of used kayak hides; but the difficulty usually consists more in getting their herring dried." This point of view was expressed at the same time in other places along the coast. The humid climate was not very suitable for drying fish. Especially in the period from 1780 to 1810 the weather seems to have been very unstable, which explains many strange occurrences in all kinds of fangst and fishing along the coast of West Greenland.[9]

With his remarks about not doing the Greenlanders' work for them while they just looked on, Inspector C. Bendeke had, unknown to him, indicated the danger in the Trade entering too vigorously into production in Greenland. This danger was less in the other kinds of fishing. Neither the salmon, the black halibut nor the halibut was on the whole present in sufficient quantities to afford a surplus after domestic consumption, although a few barrels of salted salmon were sent to Copenhagen during this period. Due to linguistic difficulties we cannot in the source material distinguish between halibut and black halibut, modest quantities of both of which were also delivered salted. As elements of food supply all these species did play a certain role, but not as great as that of angmagssat. Salmon and halibut were also fished by the colony crews. Black halibut apparently played a certain role at Holsteinsborg, but it is uncertain if the reports mean ordinary halibut. It is, however, certain that considerable amounts of black halibut was fished at Jakobshavn; it was important for the food supply in times of need.

The Management persisted in its idea that fishing, especially in the Southern Inspectorate, could be developed into something profitable. This perseverance is due to considerations of efficiency, a cheap food supply, a reserve in periods of famine, the development of occupational opportunities, and production envisaging profit for the Trade. The interest of the Management was therefore focussed on *cod* and *shark fishing*.

The opportunities afforded in 1782 were characterized quite distinctly by Christian Transe, the missionary at Frederikshåb, basing his opinion on a seven-year residence in Greenland. He testified that during his time at Frederikshåb there had not been "any stock of fish; the Greenlanders have in certain seasons one year or another, but not every year, fished halibut and cod for their own use, but only a little: one or two a day. Salmon fishing is of even less importance, only a few small salmon trout that can rarely be caught." Personal attempts by the trader at a pronounced salmon river were unsuccessful, although made at the right season. "Haddock and small halibut can here in late winter be caught in reasonable quantities to help the Greenlander in his household needs." Even the stationed Europeans could catch them for their own needs. "But how Trade employees could carry on this fishing for the benefit of the Royal Trade I do not know, as they are caught in the middle of a fjord about 250 favns deep on a whalebone string which the Greenlander drops through a little hole which he carefully holds open in the ice for this purpose."

Here the missionary had described the situation as it presumably was all along the coast wherever there was fish. In addition he indicated the primitive means used. It is perhaps this latter factor which encouraged the Management to persevere in desiring rationalization attempts; it intended of course to use the most modern fishing techniques of the period, as for example in the angmagssat netting attempts at Godhavn from 1794 to 1796.

Transe mentioned the poor catches of halibut and cod without distinguishing between them. Later, however, he mentioned that the halibut was small, especially "in late winter," i.e., in March and April. He made no further mention of cod. The year following Transe's discouraging account, the Management received from Inspector B. Olrik in Godthåb an extremely optimistic report on fishing opportunities. "The coast from Sydbay at least to Fiskelogen is swarming with cod which is the most suitable for production." This would not make the Management less optimistic.

Their optimism was reinforced the next year by the fact that Sukkertoppen sent 60 barrels of salted cod in 1783 and 64 barrels in 1784; in 1786 the yield sank to 32 barrels. The following year cod fishing failed at this colony, which could only deliver 17 barrels of salted cod. The shipment was again low in 1788, after which there are no further reports of cod from Sukkertoppen. It even appears that the organized fishing at this colony which existed at the beginning of our period had been consigned to oblivion by the close of the period. "Private persons," presumably both Danes and Greenlanders, had in 1803 and 1804 fished, salted and dried cod "in great quantities"; the trader therefore thought fishing could be productive and afford the Trade a source of income, and sent two whole barrels of salted cod to Copenhagen as a sample! Finally successful cod fishing was reported from Sukkertoppen in 1806.

In 1804 Inspector Myhlenphort reported in a circular that "for some years cod has been present in great quantities inshore and in the bays; but so far this rich blessing has only been partially exploited by the inhabitants." Myhlenphort therefore encouraged the chief traders of the various localities to motivate their fangers, in addition to sealing, to fish for cod for drying. "And to give them an inclination for this occupation during the two to three months the cod are inshore," cod liver could be purchased at two rigsdalers per tub, i.e., per 1½ barrel, including overmeasure.

The following year various localities reported relatively good fishing, as we have seen at Sukkertoppen. At Fiskenæsset there were large numbers of cod, but not sufficient crew to cope with the fishing. This does not indicate that the inhabitants to any great extent availed themselves of the opportunity to acquire dried fish and sell liver. Actually, in his circular Myhlenphort had hinted at the reason. Fishing was to be carried on by the fangers *in addition to* sealing, implying that sealing was of course the more important. How much could the individual fanger do in addition to his traditional diversified fangst? We have emphasized previously that there were natural limits to the individual's capabilities. We get the impression that the pressure to increase production which the administration brought to bear on the chief traders, and they in turn on the fangers, was powerless against the limits of the ability and inclination of the fangers to respond. The Greenlanders simply did as they were accustomed.

The Northern Inspectorate also reported cod in quantities which could make fishing profitable. Such reports were not often made, but M.N. Myhlenphort, then the trader at Egedesminde, reported in 1796 that cod fishing had been poor that year, which implies that it had been better previously. In August 1799 cod appeared at Claushavn in extraordinarily large numbers. Fishing them had "given considerable support to their sustenance," i.e., the winter provisions of the local inhabitants. From this catch, Christianshåb and Claushavn together sent six barrels of cod liver to Copenhagen; cod was thus purchased in Disko Bugt earlier than permission was given for the Southern Inspectorate. In 1800 cod fishing failed totally at Claushavn. And later, in 1803, only a few cod were hooked. In 1807 there suddenly appeared cod at Arveprinsens Ejland, where the October weather was unusually mild. Thus conditions varied from one extreme to the other, but were under no circumstances such that regular fishing could be set up and a constant production reached. The reports indicate, too, that the main gain from the occasional cod fishing was the supply of dried fish acquired by the population.

The fishing of *Greenland shark* had been carried on occasionally at Holsteinsborg and farther north. In areas where sled dogs were kept, dried shark meat was used as dog food. In southern areas there was no use for dog food, so that the shark held no interest for Greenlanders there. From the late 1770's, the Trade had been interested in shark liver, which was purchased at Holsteinsborg and in the northern colonies, but never in the southern ones. Inspector A.M. Lund at Godthåb reported in 1790 that the fangers, according to several allegations, "catch no sharks, except what they take by chance, when fishing for cod or halibut, as they cannot acquire the necessary tackle, and lack the necessary vessels."

In the warehouse accounts at the Trade in Copenhagen, shark liver oil figured annually from 1787 on, as illustrated in Table 28. The yearly averages show fluctuations from the large averages of the first period to the great decrease of the following period, again followed by an increase. The warehouse manager seems, however, to have incorrectly assigned 178 barrels, delivered from 1781 to 1789, to the shorter period of 1787-1789, thus making the yearly average for the first (longer) period only 20 barrels, and the difference between the first and second periods considerably less. In any case it was not large quantities which were sent to Copenhagen. This is the only means we have of quantifying fishing for this species; it shows that shark fishing was of little importance in the production of oil, in comparison to sealing and whaling. Shark fishing for the production of shark liver oil was mostly carried on by colony crews, and organised by the local chief trader.

Table 28.

Period	Barrels	Yearly average
1787-1789	178	59
1790-1798	158	18
1798-1805	204	41 (converted)

In Copenhagen the Royal Greenland Trade apparently did not derive the desired quantity of oil from the shark liver. From 1799 on, therefore, it was attempted to render shark liver oil on a local basis. It had evidently been forgotten that this attempt had been made previously.[10] At least in 1777 iron kettles had been sent to Godhavn, Holsteinsborg and Umánaq, and in 1788 Inspector Wille signed a receipt for the shipment of "sperm whale kettles". The intention must have been for him to attempt to render whale blubber in these kettles; but such attempts were probably never made. He personally had no confidence that they could succeed. Nothing is mentioned of the rendering of liver oil after either the shipments of 1777 or those of 1788.

After 1799 liver oil seems to have been rendered in Greenland. In 1801 Mørch, the trader at Julianehåb, made certain attempts, partially with the help of the sun, partly with whatever suitable kettles were available locally. In any case he wanted iron kettles shipped with a capacity of a half barrel. At the same time he unknowingly revealed a factor which may explain why liver oil had not been rendered locally immediately after 1777 and 1788. With local rendering the traders and assistants lost the income which resulted from the overmeasures when seal and whale blubber as well as shark liver were gauged. Mørch was sufficiently idealistic to be willing to lose his income if local rendering of shark liver could be to the advantage of the Trade. As a matter of fact, the traders could hardly suffer great losses when it was limited to this kind of oil production.

The attempts at Julianehåb were apparently not continued; at least Inspector Myhlenphort never mentioned them again, nor did he ever mention similar attempts elsewhere in the south. But in September 1806 he issued a circular, the fifth paragraph of which enjoined the local rendering of all kinds of fish liver. The Management had issued this order on the basis of the successful attempts made by Inspector Motzfeldt in 1805 at Godhavn. Kettles for this purpose did not arrive, however, until 1807; and thereafter it is dubious how much benefit was derived from this local liver oil production. The war situation restricted it for the time being.

Considering the entire period dealt with in this volume and all the species of fish, the impression is that fishing still played a subordinate role as an occupation of the Greenlandic population. Fish was a food supplement, relief in need; fishing was usually done only occasionally. Attempts at regular fishing were only made by the Royal Greenland Trade, and then most often using its own employees, by virtue of a persevering idea that it must be possible to organize efficient fishing, corresponding to that of Norway, in these latitudes.

Animal Husbandry and Gardening

Even less than fishing was animal husbandry an ordinary occupational opportunity for the inhabitants. Except for the keeping of sled dogs, which cannot really be considered animal husbandry, the opportunities for animal husbandry existed, due to climatic conditions, only at a very few places in Greenland.

Traders, assistants, missionaries and others kept chickens, ducks, geese and pigs to satisfy their dietary requirements brought over from Europe. Goats were also kept for their milk. This small-scale breeding gave rise to a number of difficulties, which hardly encouraged large-scale expansion. This was animal husbandry for personal European needs, and no more.

Sheep raising was another matter. Since 1733 quite extensive sheep raising had developed at the various stations of the Moravian Brethren (Ny Herrnhut at Godthåb, Lichtenfels at Fiskenæsset, and Lichtenau south of Julianehåb). The European members of the Moravian congregation did this sheep raising, mostly as a means of assisting their meagre economy. In 1784 the Royal Greenland Trade allowed wool to be considered as a commodity to be purchased; it was paid for at the rate of 5 marks per lispund (8 kg). The Management explained this permission by its wish to promote sheep raising. The wool could be made use of in Copenhagen instead of being used in Greenland for draughtproofing houses!

In subsequent years sheep wool was shipped from Fiskenæsset and Julianehåb. At the latter place it was the missionary. Hans Buch, who kept sheep, in addition to goats and cows. It was not large amounts which were sent to Copenhagen in 1785: 53.5 and 102 kilogrammes, respectively. The source material gives no indication of sheep wool later in the 1780's or in the 1790's. Not until 1804 and 1805 are a couple of figures available: 9.5 kilogrammes from Godthåb and 5.5 kilogrammes from Frederikshåb. This does not indicate any great development of sheep raising in the Southern Inspectorate, rather the contrary. The wool was probably made ample use of locally, especially at the stations of the Moravian congregation, where it is known to have been carded and spun.

In 1782 Buch, the missionary, got three calves from Denmark. He had actually not ordered them, but shortly after his arrival in 1779 only written that he would like to attempt some farming at Julianehåb. As he could not get seed from Norway, he took up sheep and goat raising. The three calves arrived while Buch was on a journey. The trader took them when the ship arrived at the end of September. It was rather late for such a surprise, but he managed to get winter fodder and stalls for them before winter set in for good. By September 1784 these three head of cattle had become six, and one more was expected. The same year the trader was sent three calves by the Royal Greenland Trade. In 1787 the missionary's herd was still seven, but he had supplied meat to the colony each year. That year he had in addition three head of cattle belonging to the Trade, presumably the three sent in 1784. In addition there was one cow, three cow calves from 1786, and two cow calves and one bull calf from 1787, for a total of 16 head of cattle. Cattle raising seemed to be thriving at Julianehåb.

The problem was to get enough hay for winter fodder. Among other difficulties, dissentions arose concerning the places where hay could be harvested; especially, as could be expected, concerning places nearest the colony. These dissentions subsequently raised barriers between the missionary and the Trade. When Buch resigned, the trader took over the cattle belonging to the Trade. It had been maintained for 20 years, but its numbers had been reduced. The three-year-old bull was ill-tempered, dangerous, and apparently not very prolific. The remaining two cows had not given birth to more than one calf in three years. The Trade's cattle was no longer profitable, if it could ever have been expected to be. Mørch wanted to know, however, if new breeders could be shipped out.

This was perhaps the central problem in the entire affair. The maintenance of a herd of cattle, at least at Julianehåb Colony, presupposed the introduction of new breeders from time to time. Otherwise it was not possible to let the herd get so big that a reasonable amount of slaughtering would not threaten its preservation. There was not enough grazing land for a sufficiently large herd.

Deeper in the fjord south of Julianehåb, at Igaliko, the old cathedral city of Garðar, cattle raising seemed, however, to be profitable, or rather, a family could exist partly on the basis of animal husbandry. When Anders Olsen, the trader and founder of Julianehåb, retired in 1780, he intended to settle at some distance from the colony seat and set up a large enough breeding farm to support him, his Greenlandic wife, and those of their children who were still living at home. This plan does not seem to have been realized until 1782. He had at first intended to settle somewhat nearer Julianehåb than Igaliko, but chose this distant place in order not to be in the way of the large-scale cattle raising of Buch, the missionary. The Management had given him permission to move out to a place where he could find suitable grazing land for his sheep. Nothing is mentioned of cows; this can be due to an omission, but can just as well indicate that Anders Olsen did not yet have a herd of cattle. In 1783 he dated a letter "Ittiblik in Igaliko", the tongue of land where the old episcopal residence was located. Itivdleq means portage: a narrow stretch of land over which a kayak and possibly also an umiak is carried.

In 1784 Anders Olsen got the confirmation of the Management of its permission for him to remain where he had built his house; but he was told not to be a burden to the trader or crew of the colony because he was living so far from the colony. Whatever he had ordered for building his house he would have to pay for himself. The first independent farm in Greenland thus did not receive much public support. This sounds even stranger when we remember that this Management as well as previous ones had been enthusiastic about animal husbandry attempts, at times even with Icelanders brought in.

Anders Olsen remained at Igaliko until his death in 1786, and his family continued to live there. His son Johannes Andersen continued animal husbandry; and now there is no doubt that he had cows, and probably also sheep, goats and poultry. This farm seemed to be going to succeed, and this was confirmed by the future, for it is flourishing this very day, and is in the possession of the same family.

Buch the missionary had stated in 1787 that "neither can half-Greenlanders carry on agriculture nor should the Europeans who have been in this country before as colony crew be hired as farm workers." Johannes Andersen, who was a "half-Greenlander", belied these words emphatically. Perhaps they are an expression of the attitude implicit in the disinclination of the Management to give Anders Olsen any kind of support. Later another missionary expressed the diametrically opposite opinion: "But I believe this, that by animal husbandry and other occupations this country could give the idle mixture (half-breed), who in numbers will finally be a burden to the country and harm the Trade, ample support, as we see in the example of the diligent and hard-working farmer Johannes Andersen at the head of Igalikko Fjord." The same description of Johannes Andersen was provided even later by the geologist Karl Ludwig Giesecke, when he visited him.

Johannes Andersen and his descendants were the only ones who carried on animal husbandry as an occupation. Throughout his life he sold meat products, both beef and mutton; but he could only earn his subsistence by supplementary fangst and fishing in the fjord. At that time his situation was unique. As the assistant of the time, Schytte, expressed it in 1805: "Undoubtedly this so-called farmer lives in a beautiful and grassy place, according to the standard of this country, but one must admit that Greenland is and will remain Greenland." By this he meant that there were probably not many places where animal husbandry could be maintained, nor many persons who could imitate him. Under the prevailing circumstances, animal husbandry could not become a common Greenlandic occupation.

Of course Johannes Andersen also had his garden, where he cultivated cabbage, lettuce, spinach, radishes, turnips, and perhaps also potatoes, which were beginning to be common about that time. His family had probably learned gardening from the Moravian Brethren, who set up good gardens at all their stations. Anders Olsen had an old leaning toward the Brethren. It is reported that when he lived at Igaliko, he often went to Lichtenau to participate in the services and meetings of the Moravian congregation, rather than to the mission at Julianehåb. His and his family's garden profited from these trips; it was probably set up with help from Lichtenau.

Gardening was naturally not something which otherwise attracted Greenlanders in general. On the whole it was only stationed Europeans who had gardens, only for their own household use, and these constantly demanded orders of the various types of seeds. Along the entire west coast – perhaps with the exception of Umánaq and Upernavik Districts – there were at the colonies gardens ingeniously set up. In 1788 Muus, the trader at Christianshåb, asked Inspector Wille for permission to build a fence around his garden. The Inspector rejected this request, but suggested that he build a wall of turf around his garden about one and a half metres high, and top it with a low fence. This method was apparently already in use elsewhere, and later became common in Greenland right up to the present.

This garden may have given C.C. Dalager, the trader at Klokkerhuk, the inclination to attempt gardening. In any case, he asked Inspector Wille, who must have had a store of seeds, for some cabbage, chervil, cress, lettuce, turnip and radish seeds. Then as now, these vegetables were common in the small gardens of Greenland.

Gardening thus spread northward, but still only to the advantage of the Europeans. Among those juridically considered as Greenlanders, it was only the half-breeds and their descendants who were interested in gardening and its small crops. As an occupation, gardening could play no role at all.

This does not exhaust the picture of occupational development in West Greenland in the period under consideration. There were other occupations, or rather opportunities for procuring the means of existence, in the society of the time. These were, however, to a greater degree integrated in the function of the established institutions: the Royal Greenland Trade and the Mission, so that they are better considered in the context of the development of these institutions.

The picture just drawn of occupational development also shows how the Trade infiltrated the various occupations, and that this process was a complex of details. In a society as small as that of West Greenland at the end of the eighteenth century, the development of the whole is revealed to us only through random descriptions of situations which have survived. These descriptions do not always bear witness to conflict, but they always tell of small-scale actions and reactions and deal with individuals or small groups. These are seemingly unimportant details, which could be decided with a comment, or remain unmentioned in a generalization.

It turns out, however, that these situations which have survived, often individual testimony limited to a determined area and a single locality, have implications for the past and the future and for the society as a whole.

Together these seeming details illustrate the process of cultural contact in the West Greenlandic mini-society. The same is true of the description of occupations which were more integrated with the institutions.

VIII. Whaling after 1788

Whaling was being carried out "no longer by Greenlanders on their own, as the implements they used were so imperfect that they could kill a whale now and then, but only seldom bring it in. It therefore now always takes place in cooperation with Danes and with the sloops and equipment of the Trade." Thus Jonas Collin summed up the West Greenlandic whaling situation in 1807, after which he mainly dealt with the "pedagogic" aspect of the change in purchase prices of the various whaling products in 1804-1805. His brief summary is not incorrect; but it is strange how it in principle corresponds to Inspector J. Fr. Schwabe's optimistic stock-taking in 1787.

The development from 1784 until shortly after 1788 has been described. After 1788 whaling had indeed become more firmly established, but was by no means subject to a correspondingly uncomplicated operation. Many events and changes, large and small, as well as the reactions to these, open up as many perspectives behind the exterior facade. There were more aspects of whaling, as it developed after 1788, than just the continuation of operations, so that Collin's summary is far too brief and unshaded. Considering the short space at his disposal, his reports could not be sufficiently faceted. He was cut off from perceiving certain aspects of development because he lived in the same period as the events themselves and their background. His reports express how the situation was perceived around 1809; it is therefore interesting to compare his statements with the facts as exposed by the source material.

The Development of Whaling in General

When B.J. Schultz was sent to Greenland in 1790 to take over the leadership of the Northern Inspectorate, he was in his orders specifically enjoined to consider, after having gained the necessary experience, whether the number of whaling stations ought to be reduced. Although the Management had considerable respect for the whaling experiments which Inspector Wille in his period of office had made at places in addition to those established between 1782 and 1787, it – or rather the Commission of 1788 – thought that one nevertheless could "fear, considering the small population of the country, that sealing, the most reliable form of fangst, and that from which the Greenlanders derive their principal sustenance, could suffer or be obstructed when too many of the inhabitants are attracted to and occupied at the whaling stations."

It was not that the Commission was worried that there might be too many whaling stations for the whale population to bear, or that the competition between them would be a hindrance to whaling, as implied above; they were afraid of the undesirable socio-economic consequences of success among the Greenlanders of the reorganized whaling. The fear that the population would migrate to the whaling stations was not unjustified. The possibility of compromising sealing, which was vital, was not to be ignored, since most of the whaling stations were located at poor sealing grounds. But we have also seen that at most of the stations the fangers practiced their traditional fangst cycle, and only participated in whaling in certain seasons. This had given rise to personnel shortages on the watchings. C.C. Dalager at Arveprinsens Ejland had even seen young fangers leave the whaling stations there because fangst conditions otherwise were so poor. They went to Jakobshavn where "the fangst of meat and fish is good." He feared a veritable emigration, so that he would "soon be alone here."

C.C. Dalager was old according to the average duration of life at the time, but it was he, along with his sons, who kept whaling going at Arveprinsens Ejland. As far as can be seen, he made use of all available means to accomplish this. The competition with Ritenbenk, Igdlutsiaq and Jakobshavn was hard in all areas and at times intransigent. It is said of Dalager and his sons that they were extremely headstrong and would disregard any agreement they had made. The diligent and very upright trader Myhlenphort at Jakobshavn preferred, during the short time he served at this post, to have as little to do as possible with C.C. Dalager and his sons. Whaling at Klokkerhuk, the southern tip of Arveprinsens Ejland, literally depended on Dalager. A few years after he died in 1799, this station was closed as an independent whaling station, and dragged on a languishing existence thereafter.

Whaling at Klokkerhuk, as elsewhere, fluctuated considerably during the period under consideration. In 1792 C.C. Dalager thought the whales were migrating west towards "Labrador and James," as he wrote. In 1794 he repeated his conjecture, and thought that whaling operations could be forced over to the Vestis, and this would be the end of whaling along the coast of Greenland. He pointed out what had happened to whaling af Svalbard and Jan Mayen in previous times, and thought it was whaling itself which was driving the whales away. Except for this reason, C.C. Dalager's observations were correct, in so far as present climatic investigations have shown that a rather cold period in the 1780's was followed by a relatively warmer one from around 1790 to around 1810. During this latter period the conditions for whales became poorer, and the whale population presumably decreased.[1]

This is reflected in Graph 2, which records the whaleoil production of the Royal Greenland Trade; the decline in whaleoil production in 1793 reflecting a corresponding decline in the whale harvest of 1792-1793. There are likewise relatively low production figures for eight of the years in the period 1791-1807, all of which are under the average for the entire period from 1777 to 1807. The extraordinarily low production recorded in 1803 and 1807 is due to the smallpox epidemic, shipwrecks, the capture of ships and other obstacles in the way of shipping. In only four of the years from 1791 to 1807 does production exceed the average from 1777 to 1807. There is so far no explanation for the especially high production in 1796; whale blubber did not arrive in Copenhagen that year from previous years' takes.

In the period from 1777 to 1790 whaleoil production in seven, perhaps eight of the years exceeds the average from 1777 to 1807. Nowhere does production decline to such lows as in the following period. Only four, perhaps six, of the years are under the total average. If we compare the averages for each of these two periods, we see that the average from 1777 to 1790 is about 500 barrels higher than the average from 1791 to 1807, revealing a distinct decline in the later period, taken as a whole.

Shipments of baleen to Copenhagen cannot be used to illustrate fluctuations in whaling. There was a relatively large local consumption in Greenland, and a good deal of baleen came from stranded whales, which seldom yielded any blubber of importance. Baleen production was thus subject to a number of contingencies, but it was none the less a positive factor in the proceeds from whaling - until hoop skirts and corsets went out of fashion.

The shipment of baleen was of course subject to the same irregularities as other commodities. Shipwreck, capture, wintering in Greenland, etc., all contributed to making shipping so irregular that one must calculate an average in order to get any grasp of baleen production. Statistics are presented in Table 29. They show a yearly average of 9% more baleen over

Graph 2

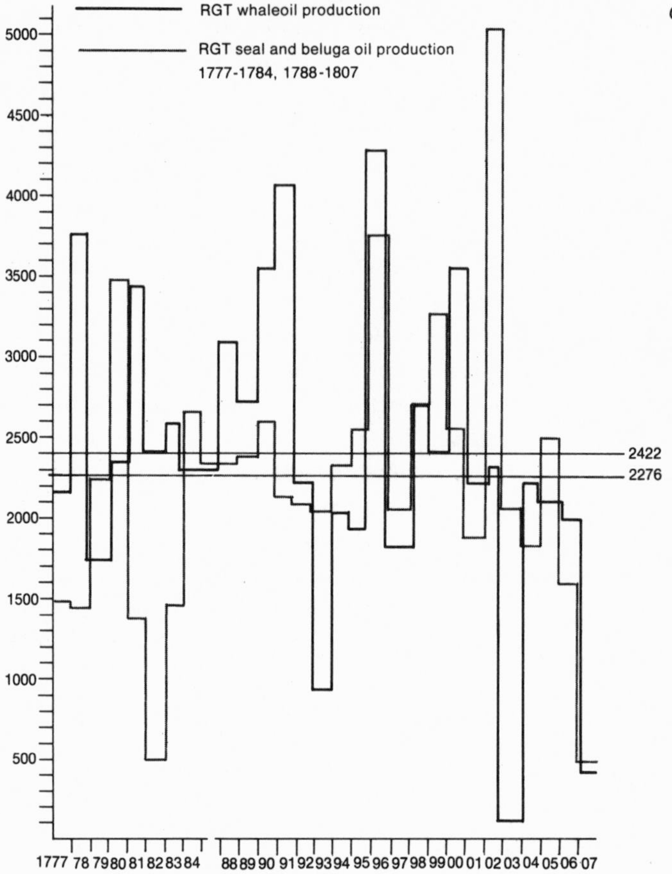

This graph shows fluctuations in the production of whaleoil, as well as that of sealoil and beluga together, on the basis of blubber sent to Copenhagen. The average for each sort is indicated by the straight line. At the same time we see the relationship between the two kinds of production. Most of the whale blubber and somewhat over half the seal and beluga blubber came from the Northern Inspectorate. Thus we also see here the predominance in production of the Northern Inspectorate.

Table 29.

	Baleen over one metre	Baleen under one metre	Total
1777–1790:			
Total	151,435	116,381	267,816
Yearly average	10,816	8,313	19,130
1791–1807:			
Total	200,725	102,393	303,118
Yearly average	11,807	6,023	17,830

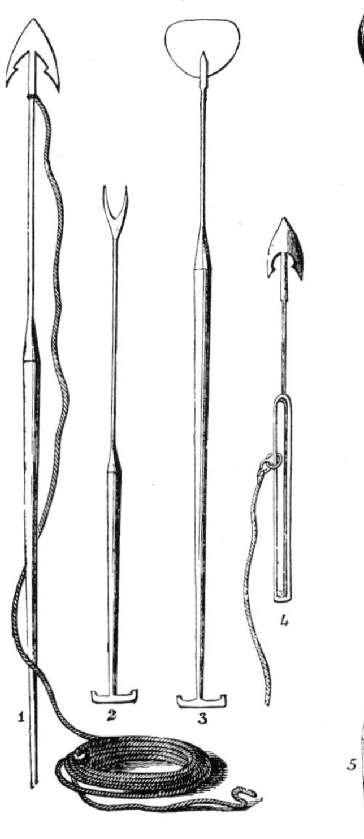

Whaling tools used by English whalers at least up to 1832. 1. hand harpoon, 2. pricker, 3. blubber spade, 4. gun harpoon, 5. lance.

(From Leslie, Jameson and Murray *Narrative of Discovery and Adventure in the Polar Seas and Regions, p. 392)*

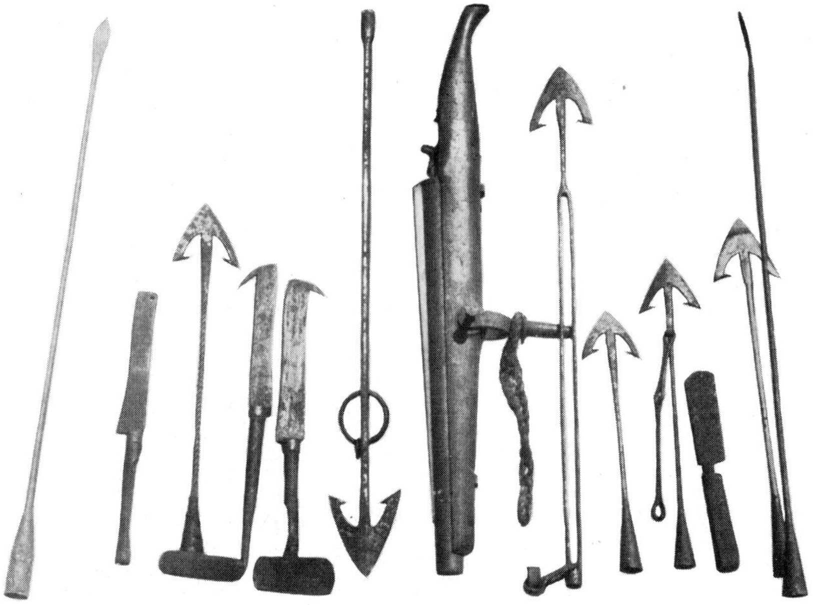

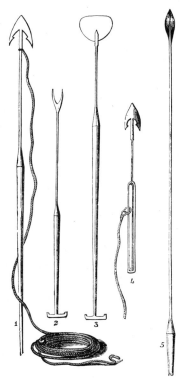

Whaling tools used by Danish whalers in Greenland in 1918. Nos. 1 and 13, counted from the left, are lances; 2, 4, 5 and 11 are blubber knives and spades; 3, 6, 9, 10 and 12 are hand harpoons; 7 is a whaling gun and 8 a gun harpoon similar to no. 4 above.

(Arctic Institute, Charlottenlund, Denmark, Collection of Pictures, 45-475. Photo O. Bendixen, 1918)

The observation post on Godhavns Næs (foreland of Godhavn). The mark of Danish nationality was painted on the door during the Second World War.

(Photo F. Gad, 1957)

The observation post as it looked up to 1939. Its peculiar beehive like form is due to the use of whale jaws as inner support at each corner.

(Date and origin of photo unknown, probably taken before 1918)

one metre in length in the second period than in the first, but about 6% less baleen under one metre in length. Total figures for the two periods show a greater yearly average quantity of baleen shipped in the first period. The reason is probably that not so much shorter baleen was shipped due to local consumption; at auctions in Copenhagen short baleen commanded quite low prices.

The "quality" of the baleen, calculated according to weight, reveals more or less the same picture, presented in Table 30, but on the basis of other figures from slightly different periods.

Table 30.

	Average weight in punds of	
	baleen over one metre	baleen under one metre
1781-1790	3.62	0.63
1791-1798	3.74	0.59

The "quality" of baleen over one metre was evidently somewhat better in the second period than in the first, but that of baleen under one metre was better in the first period; the differences here are insignificant, however. On the whole, "quality" was apparently poorer during the entire period from 1781 to 1798 than previously in the same century, when the average weight of baleen over one metre was 6 punds and that of baleen under one metre 1.8 punds. The average weights from 1781 to 1798 are considerably under these figures. This may indicate that the whales taken towards the end of the century were considerably smaller, on an average, than those previously killed by whalers. Whalers had previously concentrated on large whales, whereas later in the century they also hunted the small species. In addition, earlier in the century more whales were lost because whaling was poorly organized the proportion of large to small whales taken shifted in the course of the century, and thus the average weight of baleen over one metre must also have shifted to a lower figure. One metre continued to be the criterion by which baleen was divided into two categories. The average weight of baleen under one metre may have shifted to a lower figure because more species of whales, including smaller species, were hunted in the later period. Nevertheless, the average weight of baleen under one metre was so low during the period under consideration in comparison with the previous average of 1.8 punds that it indicates a decline.

There was a declining tendency towards 1807 in whaling and in the products it yielded. From 1801 on whale oil production was under the average for the period from 1777 to 1807; the same is true of baleen shipments.[2] But throughout our period whaling was, in addition to sealing, an important occupation, and represented the largest purchases and sales made by the Royal Greenland Trade.

It was still from Holsteinsborg and farther north, including Disko Bugt, that intensive whaling took place. North of Disko Bugt, as south of Holsteinsborg, there was only occasional whaling; here it was most often the qiporqaq (humpback whale) which was taken. It appeared mostly off the coasts of Frederikshåb District. The journals kept by traders and assistants show that this whale rose in importance, but perhaps only for "prestige". The few exact figures available do not bear witness to any great number taken.

We do not know, and perhaps cannot know, to what extent other whales taken south of Holsteinsborg were qiporqaqs. According to the few detailed figures available from 1798 to 1805, very modest shipments of blubber and baleen were made from Godthåb, Fiskenæsset and Sukkertoppen.

A further indication of a decline in the numbers of all species of whales taken is an observation made by Inspector Schultz in 1793 that savssat, whales trapped in holes in the ice, had become rarer in recent years. Such events are also rarely mentioned in the journals. There is a report of a fantastic number of whales locked in the ice at Kronprinsens Ejland from 19 March to 19 April, 1803. This event was reported far and wide, and Greenlanders came from as far as Umánaq District to take part in the fangst. As a rule it was smaller whales that were found trapped in ice holes; in 1803 they were narwhales and belugas.

Nothing is reported of larger whales trapped in such ice holes, but we do read of whaling in ice-filled waters, probably from the edge of more solid ice. Such whaling seems to have been organized, and instead of using harpoons and lines "they were speared to death." There was disagreement as to whether this method always involved loss of the whales. The trader C.C. Dalager thought that such mortally wounded whales did immediately dive under the ice, but that they would later most often be found stranded, so they would nevertheless be of use. The question of "ownership" of stranded whales gave rise to conflict between Greenlandic tradition and the attitude of the "new" organization, and of course also between C.C. Dalager and the neighbouring whaling station.

There were constant attempts to improve whaling in Disko Bugt and at

Holsteinsborg, and make it more efficient. In 1799 the leader of the whaling station at Qerrortussoq near Holsteinsborg ordered telescopes for his Greenlandic whalers, to be used on coast watch. His reason was not only that they could be useful, but also that he could thus prevent illicit trade with English whalers, or at least make it unnecessary for Greenlanders to trade with the English for them. The special "English telescopes or those with red wood" could be purchased for four rigsdalers in Copenhagen; according to the senior assistant they might just as well be sold by the Trade to the Greenlanders, who would otherwise get them directly from "the Englishmen in the North."[3]

This may seem an unimportant detail, but it is precisely such details which reveal how the material culture of Greenland changed by small steps, and how one step could lead to the other. New demands were created by the consolidation of changes. At the same time the necessary exchange between culture areas grew, and mutual dependence increased. These are theoretical truisms, but they must be demonstrated, when possible, in Greenlandic practice. Development there as elsewhere took place slowly but surely.

It was attempted to change the method of whaling itself by trying harpoon cannons, the use of which was learned from English whalers who experimented with them in Disko Bugt in the 1790's. Some experience with them had also been gained in Greenland itself. Before 1764 Niels Egede had suggested using cannons, and in 1767 at Holsteinsborg he experimented with a swivel gun in the bow of a sloop. It was too big and heavy, however, and this experiment did not encourage imitation. Svend Sandgreen, the whaling chief at Godhavn, is also said to have attempted to fire a harpoon with a cannon some time between 1773 and 1783, but this experiment was also unsuccessful. In 1791 Inspector Schultz bought a harpoon cannon and six special harpoons from an English whaler. The English had experimented for several years, reported Inspector Schultz, and had finally arrived at a good result. He intended to use the cannon at Godhavns cape in order to harpoon passing whales from land more quickly than the time it would take to call the crew, launch the sloops and reach the whale, for as a rule the whales usually disappeared by this time. The Management immediately accepted his idea, approved the purchase, and wanted to have the other whaling stations supplied with similar cannons and harpoons; it proved too expensive to manufacture them in Copenhagen. Although Inspector Schultz could not report good results the following year (1792 was a bad whaling year in every way and for everyone, including the English), he still purchased in 1795 a harpoon cannon and six harpoons, again from the English, to be stationed at Kronprinsens Ejland. These experiments must have produced results which fulfilled expectations. Nevertheless, nothing more is heard of harpoon cannons in the remainder of the period.[4]

A special knife was invented, called a "tail knife", presumably to cut the tendons and muscles which enabled a whale to use its tail. The Greenlanders are said to have rejoiced at this invention. It was used at Arveprinsens Ejland in 1807 in the killing of two stranded humpbacks (qiporqaqs). That it was risky business to approach such whales had been proven many times. On his way home from an unsuccessful watching, "harpoonist Sivert Johnsen happened to encounter a sleeping whale, to which he got so near, rowing slowly with two oars, that he harpooned it, but due to such sudden and frightening awakening from its slumber the whale became so raging mad that for almost half an hour, lying in the same place, it threw water into the sky with its tail and flippers and cavorted so frightfully that no one dared to get close enough to place another harpoon. For two hours they fought with it in vain, and then finally the harpoon broke and the whale was lost."[5] A tail knife could probably not have been used on this occasion, but a harpoon cannon would have been helpful.

A weak link was the sloops. They often had to be replaced, and it was quite expensive to have them built and shipped to Greenland: assembled, they occupied a disproportionate amount of space on the relatively small ships. The Management therefore proposed to ship them unassembled and have a stationed carpenter assemble them at Godhavn, but nothing came of it. On the other hand, we do hear of sloops being repaired locally by especially proficient carpenters. Also in this matter the English whalers were of assistance; the inspector occasionally purchased sloops from departing whalers. This was also an advantage for the English, who had trouble transporting them back to England, especially if their ships were fully loaded. The reciprocity of this assistance seems to have extended so far that some English whalers even "deposited" their sloops in Greenland, to avoid transporting them over the Atlantic. Perhaps the "depositees" also had the right to use the sloops while their English owners were away.

By far most of the correspondence to and from the Northern Inspectorate dealt with whaling. This in itself indicates its importance locally as well as for the Royal Greenland Trade. When demand for baleen reached a low, Inspector Myhlenphort suggested using it to manufacture fishing lines and thus created a new export opportunity for whaling. Strangely enough, it was Europeans stationed in South Greenland who had hit upon this idea. Mørch, the trader at Julianehåb, had had some fish lines made from baleen; Inspector Myhlenphort had tested them and observed that they went through the water more easily than lines made out of hemp. It must have been the constantly repeated fishing experiments in South Greenland that led to the "invention" of baleen lines, which Greenlanders had used for centuries. They were apparently not successful with the Management, which otherwise would have joined battle with a stubborn domestic fishing tradition.

The main whaling area was Disko Bugt, and its most important base was Godhavn. Partly because the Inspector of the northern colonies had his seat here and partly because the whaling at Godhavn was the most important in Greenland, this locality was raised to the status of a colony in 1796.

It was also here that the attempts at rendering blubber to whale oil locally were revived. The initiative came, however, from the Management, which in 1788 shipped "some of the sperm whale kettles in stock": i.e., the remaining kettles in which earlier experiments had been made. Attempts were apparently made to render not only blubber, but also whalebone, especially the jawbones. The slightly more than one barrel of which was shipped to Copenhagen in 1792 "was found to be finer and better than usual, and especially useful for burning in lamps." The Management therefore wanted the rendering of whalebone to be made common at the whaling stations. On the other hand, the rendering of blubber seems not to have been especially successful, as exactly the same amount of whale oil was produced as in Copenhagen, and in addition there was so much sediment in the oil that it had to be refined, whereby 25% was lost. If the blubber were rendered early, the attempt could perhaps be successful; the oil thus produced was lighter than that rendered in Copenhagen.

A good deal of time now passed in which nothing was heard of rendering attempts, at least nothing preserved in the sources. A passage in a letter from the Management in 1793 may have led to stopping these experiments. Not until P.H. Motzfeldt became inspector in 1803 do the attempts seem to have been repeated. Now they gave better results; in 1806 the Management observed that space was saved in the ships, the blubber yielded more oil, and the oil was of better quality and commanded higher prices at the auctions. Attempts were made to render not only whale blubber, but all kinds of blubber. Not only boiling was used, but also melting in the heat of the sun. In 1807 the Management sent quite a few iron kettles to the whaling stations. The experiments carried out at Godhavn must not, however, have been reported very far in Greenland, for the trader at Egedesminde wondered what he was to do with an iron kettle he had been sent. Further attempts in Disko Bay were therefore not carried out until the end of the period under consideration.

Prices and Sales

The prices received by the Trade in 1805–1806 for locally rendered whaleoil were considerably higher than the average for other whale and seal oil in that year. The auction price of "white oil" was 2768 skillings per barrel, for so-called "light oil" 2656 skillings per barrel. Auction bids averaged 2496 skillings. All of these prices, however, were under the average of the 1894 auctions, which was 2921 skillings per barrel.[6]

Throughout our period the prices of whale and seal oil fluctuated, not only from year to year, but sometimes also from auction to auction. The highest prices were as a rule paid at the autumn auctions. The market price was revealed somewhat later. Auction prices were as a rule somewhat lower than the market prices, rarely higher. The fluctuations can best be seen in the market prices.

From 1777 to 1781 the market prices of both whale and seal oil were more or less stable, from 1440 skillings to 1632 skillings per barrel. For a short time they rose, then suddenly fell, and stabilized between 1784 and 1786 at between 1536 and 1920 skillings per barrel. In 1787 prices again fell for a short time. For two years from the end of 1788, prices were again at the same level as before 1787. Then from November 1790 for one year there followed a moderate decline. This was followed by a rise, and from November 1792 to around May 1794 there occurred a stable period, but at a slightly lower level. In April 1795 a violent rise occurred; it came suddenly and seemingly unmotivated, and reached a level between 2304 and 2496 skillings per barrel. Market prices remained more or less at that level until November 1799, when they were from 2208 to 2304 skillings per barrel. November 1800 saw the highest prices of the period: from 2880 to 3072 skillings per barrel.

Spot checks of auction prices show more or less the same fluctuations. But a comparison with the level of production of whale and seal oil shows that price fluctuations had very little connection with the supply of oil from the Royal Greenland Trade. To be sure, 1795 saw subnormal production and rapidly rising prices on the market, but the following year the Royal Greenland Trade produced more than double as much oil, and still the market price remained at about the same high level, and even stabilized for a rather long time, in spite of erratic production around the level of the average for the entire period of 1777 to 1807. 1799 and 1800 again witnessed an above-normal oil production, but in spite of this the market prices rose. After 1800 auction bids rose in 1803 and 1804; in 1805 and 1806 prices stabilized at an average of 2496 skillings per barrel - in spite of falling production.

That the Royal Greenland Trade usually sold all its oil in a relatively short time after rendering can also be seen from the fact that it apparently ceased sending "Three Crowns Oil" on the market, at least for some time. This product, which was initiated in 1776, was a mixture of whale, seal and fish oil: usually the re-refined remains of whale and seal oil and the final drops which could be pressed out of the blubber remains. In 1800, however, it reappeared in the accounts; at that time qiporqaq blubber was an ingredient. The price of this product rose, too. In 1776 the Trade received at auctions a price of 12.66 skilling per pot; the average price per pot of other oil was 12.60 skillings. It must have been discovered that the quality of "Three Crowns Oil" was not as good as at first claimed, for in 1800 its price per pot was just over 17 skillings, while that of other oil was over 24 skillings on the average. This changed in 1803; then and later "Three Crowns Oil" commanded a higher price than other oil, perhaps because the supply was not so great.

The market mechanism seems otherwise not to have functioned at the Copenhagen market. It must have been other factors which affected price formation. The oil market outside Denmark can hardly have had any influence. It was seldom that oil was exported from Copenhagen to Hamburg, for example, or Altona; the latter was also within the Kingdom of Denmark. As a rule the Royal Greenland Trade sold all the oil it offered on the market at Copenhagen. At least only small quantities were kept over from one year to the next, except in 1791, 1792 and 1793, in which rather large inventories were carried over from each year to the next. These the Trade attempted to sell through The Fishing & Trade Institution in Altona, along with several other Greenlandic products which were in stock. The prices of all these commodities were very low. In order not to suffer further loss in return transport, the Trade had to sell the oil for bids ranging between 384 and 576 skillings per barrel, when the market prices in Copenhagen at the same time were between 1440 and 1728 skillings per barrel. In subsequent years the Trade usually managed to sell all of one year's production by early in the next year. Its experiences in Altona in 1793 and 1794 did not encourage the Trade to attempt to sell in other markets than Copenhagen.

There were not so many other suppliers of oil to the Danish market than the Royal Greenland Trade. This makes it even stranger that the fluctuations in the Trade's oil production do not seem to have influenced price formation. Demand may well have been on the increase, since the need for oil was rising during the period before 1800 when Denmark was active in trade. There were boom periods for Danish trade during the unstable conditions in France and the war situation after 1792, reflected in the fact that the Trade was paid higher prices for its commodities, including oil. After 1799 there also occurred a kind of inflation in the Danish monetary system because Ernst Schimmelmann's risky transactions in finance politics broke down. These two factors together may have brought about the large price increase around 1800.

The situation for baleen was somewhat different, as appears in Table 31. In formulating the Order of 1782 the sales prices of baleen had been estimated at 6720 skillings per 100 punds. This does not appear directly in the Order itself, but must have been the basis of the conversion sums of the schedule for the various lengths of baleen purchased. This must have been a stipulated price; Table 31 shows that the Trade received more or less the same for baleen in 1790 as in 1745. The demand for and consumption of baleen must certainly have risen between 1745 and 1782.

Table 31. Average baleen prices at auctions in skillings/100 punds.

	Baleen over one metre	Baleen under one metre
1745	4800	2400
1790	4416	2432
1796	2496	1568
1797	2356	1536
1798	2120	1208
1799	1876	1064
1800	1297	768
1802	1352	672
1803	1173	712
1804	1239	488
1805	1294	unsaleable
1806	1344	unsaleable

There is no doubt, however, that the really important price decrease took place from 1796 on. By 1800 baleen prices were approximately half of what they had been in 1796. Now not only the price of, but also the demand for, baleen under one metre declined. From 1805 on this short baleen was unsaleable as was also the lightest of baleen over one metre: three punds' baleen.

The Royal Greenland Trade succeeded, however, almost every year at the auctions in getting rid of the quantity of baleen it had received. This involved accepting prices which sank from auction to auction. The 1806 stock was sold in 1807, in which year only a small quantity of baleen was shipped, which was still listed in the inventory in late December 1808.

This entire elucidation of a limited area: the sale and prices of whaling products, gives an impression of the indirect economic link connecting the mini-societies of West Greenland with Denmark. It also shows how tied the economy of these societies was to a rather narrow market: the Danish market. Only as something distant, almost unreal, could political and economic factors influence the economy of West Greenland, or for that sake the policies conducted in and with these societies, which in the eyes of Europeans of the time were just as distant and unimportant as they were tiny.

"Liberated" European fashion knocked the baleen trade off its feet. The price fall meant that the Management of the Royal Greenland Trade had to lower its purchase price for this commodity.

The Management must at least from 1796 on have noticed the falling tendency in baleen prices at the auctions. It nevertheless took them four years to draw the proper conclusions, by which time, as we have seen, average prices were about half of what they had been in 1796. It took still four more years to implement changes in the purchase rates.

This long reaction time was not the result of the dilatory ways of state bureaucracy, already legendary, or of the stodginess of the Trade's office-holders. If not quite the contrary, it was at least different: it was out of consideration for the Greenlandic inhabitants and production in general that the Management hesitated. The discussions which preceded the decision are also expressions of the by now relatively complicated nature of the price policy which had been laid down. Experiences with price changes, although these were few, urged caution. The development of this economic, trade and production relationship affords a glimpse of how this monopoly enterprise functioned.

In June 1800, when the auction prices of baleen during the previous year had been collated, the Management explained the situation to Inspector Claus Bendeke at Godhavn. The Royal Greenland Trade had in its calculations found that it was earning a small profit on baleen over one metre, but losing considerably on baleen under one metre. The small profit became even smaller when the costs of freight, warehouse rent, cleaning, polishing, weighing, transportation, etc. were considered.

With further price decreases expected, the Management found it "the more necessary to make a change in purchasing."

The Management realized, however, "that lowering the purchase price of baleen, which forms so important a part of the Greenlanders' earnings in whaling, would, if the price were to be proportional to prices here, be felt too sharply." As a kind of compensation, therefore, it had considered raising the purchase price of blubber, but preferably only of seal and beluga blubber. This is what the Management would actually have preferred, in order to encourage this kind of fangst, which yielded more and better oil per barrel of blubber. But this idea was abandoned, again out of consideration for the Greenlandic whalers who would thus get no part of the compensation for the lowering of baleen prices. If the purchase price of blubber was to be raised, it would have to include whale blubber.

"We do not want, however, to make a decision in either matter until we have heard the opinions and suggestions of the Inspector," whether the proposed system and compensation were feasible.

It must to a certain extent have been due to difficult communications over the Atlantic that not until 31 March 1804 was the Management able to propose to the Commission to raise the purchase price of blubber from one rigsdaler to one rigsdaler and twenty-four skillings, an increase of 25%. This raise was to compensate for a decrease in baleen prices of 42% for baleen over 10 fods long, 50% for baleen from five to nine fods and 75% for baleen under five fods.

In 1800 the Management had calculated that the lowered purchase price of baleen would be entirely compensated for by the raised purchase price of blubber. A check must have shown that this would not be so. Since the Management proposed a small raise on all blubber but a somewhat higher average decrease on baleen, the balance must have been even more dubious. The Management then proposed as further compensation a change to the Greenlanders' advantage in the conditions of partnership.

The Greenlanders' Share

There was continuous dissatisfaction in Greenland with the whaling partnership contracts, more precisely with the payment of the share which the Greenlandic whalers were to receive according to provisions. The Management continued to claim half of each whale for the rent of sloops and whaling equipment as well as to cover the costs of possible losses, shipwreck and the repair of various implements. Of the Greenlanders' share, an unspecified amount was paid each year into the welfare fund.

Dissatisfaction with the payment of the Greenlanders' shares arose in Godhavn. Here Inspector J. Wille had made the usual contracts in 1789 specifying 120 rigsdalers per half whale, i.e., half of the blubber and baleen, apparently regardless of the size of the whale. He succeeded in scraping off 20 rigsdalers per half whale, so that the contract specified 100 rigsdalers. He did not justify this in detail to the Management. He notified the senior assistant at Godhavn, however, of an even lower rate, in order to prevent him giving too much credit. But the assistant had let credit get up to about two-thirds of what the Greenlandic whalers were to have when the final payment was made. When the welfare fund contribution was deducted and credit covered, there remained only 58 rigsdalers for the Greenlandic whalers. The consequence was that they became angry and thought they were being cheated. They accused both the inspector and the senior assistant of being thieves who stole whales from the Greenlanders.

They were about to come to blows, but the inspector succeeded in more or less pacifying the spirits of the Greenlanders; still "they mumbled among themselves that they had been cheated." In 1790 the inspector made the same contract with them. As the Greenlandic whalers were the first to harpoon the whales caught they again demanded merchandise on credit before their shares were finally paid. The result was that they again felt cheated at the end of the season, "for what Greenlanders receive in advance they easily forget." Inspector Wille had most likely attempted, in vain, to explain to them what their credit corresponded to in rigsdalers; he could not realize that the angry Greenlanders understood nothing of such evaluation.

The stationed Europeans usually presumed that the function of credit was perceived. This could, however, hardly be expected, considering the long period of bartering, where value was supposed to be compensated for *immediately* by equal value. We have seen that the Greenlanders of Disko Bugt sold their products to foreign whalers, especially Dutchmen, although their produce should have been delivered to the colony trader against credit received. These Greenlanders did not actually intend to cheat the trader, but he took their actions for deliberate fraud. By virtue of the phenomenative reasoning which seems to be characteristic of Eskimos, there was no connection between the previous act of receiving credit and the later sale of fangst produce, which appeared alone in a new phenomenative situation.

This was the situation in the credit incidents at Godhavn in 1789 and 1790. The Greenlandic whalers did not conceive of the value of goods given on credit in terms of rigsdalers, but as repayment for an action. The Trade had taken the blubber and baleen from the first whales, except for a little left over for household use, and given the Greenlanders merchandise for it. That the goods received far exceeded the value of their shares in the first whales, and were considered by the senior assistant as having been given on credit, they neither understood, nor did this interest them. When more whales were taken later, the blubber and baleen delivered to the Trade, and it finally took some time to distribute the Greenlanders' shares to them, they felt cheated, because the value of goods formerly given on credit was deducted from their shares. This credit had nothing to do with the distribution of their shares, according to their view, nor with whales which had been taken later. These were to them individual phenomena. Likewise they considered the distribution of their shares from a phenomenative point of view, and experienced at that moment that they were "paid" very little, so that they felt cheated. They expressed only this latter feeling, and Inspector Wille could, from his premises, only appeal to their awareness of his honesty. They nevertheless insisted - although mumbling - that they had been cheated now, for what did the present situation have to do with the fact that Wille had not cheated them in previous situations?

This is a slightly reduced copy of the first page of the letter from the Greenlanders to the King. The letter was written in Greenlandic, and the copy, here reproduced, is in the archives of the Royal Greenland Trade, with a contemporary Danish translation inserted. The following is an English translation of this Danish translation of the part of the letter written by the whaler Poul Egede. The parts written by the other whalers are almost identical, but not as long. "I shall at length, although I am already growing old, and although I have never seen you, tell you this. This is what it is: that our payment seems to be as small as for one whale; in great cold we suffer much. We would like to take care of our own sealing, but we neglect it much as the only thing we desire is whales; we are hungry, but they will not give us bread. King, is it true that they may not give us anything? Other masters say (incorrect Danish translation; the Greenlandic original reads "The other master says", i.e., the new inspector) that it is. Are you serious, since the others tell (the other tells) us the trader may not give us bread. If it were not for us, you would not get as much blubber as you get. We want as much payment as the Danes, and if we do not get it we will stop whaling. We cannot pay our trader for all the food he has given us; we like Danes like him, since we Greenlanders also give without receiving payment. And I want to tell you this, too: our previous master, Jens Wille, was a good man, but we have not given him any payment for being in the cold and suffering. You, King, are very good; we have heard the other master is not so good. Live much better than the others, and be good to your subjects. (The Greenlandic original says only "Live well until the next", probably ship)"

Poul Egede. – de 6te Martii ... No 9.

taeſsa Okauſinga Okauſianguarkungne tamanut Okauſiugit. Okauſiagut kivaniliarautigit, Okautsit Attauſik Sorlo Okaa piuſarpogut; Ikiſerſuarme nallunernaut autlinek. – Soriſenut piomagaarlutit imanguak pinniartarpogut, Okautsit kiſſeſa pilleraugut. – Pitlerlerſallerpagut tamaitok Tunnuſaniek tunnivongilerſugit. – Konge illomut Okartarpoit Tunnivonnetta Attata Nallegak Okartarpoit Tunnivorbeta; Illomut Okartaravit Okartarpet. Sioradomut ilaugut Tunniuſanek tunnevonita. – Ilaugut pekangiſoutar tama Okauſinik piuſingiſelluarpoit. Kablunat tirſa tamaouta, Akiſanik nanagtunik piſingiſoutat, Suvarſugit. – Neodortok Akiſaruparpoit tunniſenermut Nerkiſanik; Tamatit Kablunat ajungeagit, ſagut Innugit Okorſartuniſſanut Akiangilomut. – Ama Nallegarſuarpoit Jens Dille Ajunginnikok; Tamaitok Akiſarſingelarpoit Akſerſuarme nallunane. – Ablit Konge ajungitotit, alla Nallegak Ajortok tuiſartarparpoit Tuſſernut innuttuarit.

Andreas Egede. –

Ajorſellerangauta tunniſinfartut nallunongilaqut, Tunniſinſellerangautigit kagumeltuto pinniutilerſarpaugut Okauſernut; Tamaitok kivzatit Nallegat Attalarpoit tunnivonta Nerkiſanek; Tamanouta piomaſingelagut Okauſernut. – Ablit Konge ajungitutit, alla Nallegak ajortok tuiſarterparpoit Tuſſernut innuttuarit. –

Christian –

Storlungato okallerpunga Okauſaugut niaxiaiuiſit piuſineq ſarpilleraugit, Ogalunet Akſerſuak nallunernaut, (Tamaitortlo piſerkoſinneta Akſut. – Kablunat kiſſeniekonik ajuſagalluarpoit; Tamaitok Nallegak Tutlivit akſut Akiſaniek tunnivongilatigut. – Ablit Konge ajungitotit, alla Nallegak Ajortok tuiſartarparpoit Tuſſernuk innuttuarit. –

Jens Dille. –

Ukiut Okauſingai ſabbilerkutito, okallerpunga tuiſarama iutliſorniarpaugit Tulliutarinak Piuſiaſaugut ſabbillernutigit. Omartliſut Okauſerit piſarangatigit Sorlo Akauſek piuſarpougut. – Innaittut nalliutluta piſarangauta ajorkomlluarinnak pinniarpuk. Imaxale Kablunat kiſſerneq piuſarelluaronik ajorſagalluarput. – Umiarſuit nauſet piſarelluarpoit Okauſenik ajorput. – Tamaitok akſut Akillerongilait, Nunauſinek Nallegat ajungitut; Nunauſine Nallegat ajornerxaut. – Tamaitok tunnivongilatigut. – Kablunat tunniſinfartut pinniuliartarpougut, Tunniſomangivatta Innuit Okautsit akſut piomaſingilait. – Nalliagtigit nellunartluta tuiſarniarpautigit, Imanguak Okarpogut aikiet Nunauſionut attekauta. –

This interpretation is difficult to explain with European logic, and thus difficult to accept. It is nevertheless supported by two cases. The one event also took place at Godhavn; it was a kind of continuation of the situation in 1789 and 1790. The other event was reported in a short notice from Holsteinsborg.

In 1790 Inspector Wille was recalled to Denmark and B.J. Schultz sent to Greenland as his successor. The year after his arrival, just before the whaling contract was to be made, seven of the Greenlandic whalers delivered a letter to the senior assistant at Godhavn and asked him to forward it to the King. This letter was undated, but was delivered to Inspector Schultz in mid-August 1791.

This letter was actually seven short letters; each whaler, beginning with his own name as a kind of title, expressed dissatisfaction with whaling payment. These seven letters are not identical, but on the whole have the same content, and express an identical mentality. It is characteristic that they mix whaling produce, payment in the form of merchandise, credit, distribution and relief measures (more or less on the basis of credit) in times of need together into one indissoluble whole, without considering the relative values of each phenomenon. This shows that they neither understood nor could have understood the situation.

"When we have taken many whales, we are paid as if for one only," many of them wrote. This must seemingly be interpreted to mean that they conceived of the distribution as an isolated phenomenon which to them did not represent a larger quantity of merchandise than they could expect for one whale, but rather incomprehensibly little. Goods given them on credit and relief measures, which were more or less to be repaid from the coming take of whales, at least some of them took for granted as the same kind of help Greenlanders habitually give needy settlement-mates without expecting anything in return. They directly compared this custom with what they called the refusal to allot them rations in times of need. This shows that they had not at all understood the principle of credit. The two parties to this instance of culture conflict were quite far from each other.

Nor was there apparently any possibility of their approaching each other. Comprehension was further confused by the fact that some of the Greenlanders brought into the picture the distribution of rations during watchings. This distribution was a matter apart, and will be dealt with later as a whole. They also included the fact that the senior assistant at Godhavn had apparently run short of goods wanted by the Greenlanders, including bread, which the letter writers took as his refusal to pay them or help them in a time of distress. This proves that the letter writers at least did not understand the principles on which the Trade was based, and did not realize that it could have trouble with supplies.

"You, King, we have heard, are a good master but that the other one is bad," some of them wrote. The bad other "master" was probably Inspector Schultz, newly arrived, since former Inspector Wille is characterized by one of the whalers as good enough. It was also Schultz who in their opinion had prohibited the allotment of rations to them. The local authority was the real offender. "We are addressing you, because perhaps you will not hear of this from anyone else." "We like you very much, King, and we are writing to you, because you are good." Passages such as these two appear in variations, as justifications for the letter. "They came and demanded that I send it to the big house where they had heard the King lived," wrote Schultz and continued: "It is difficult to part with Greenlanders in a friendly manner when they demand something, without granting it." He sealed the letter in their presence and promised them to send it to Denmark.

Nothing came of it. The letter never reached the King, or rather the Crown Prince. Neither the Management nor the Commission could make heads or tails of its content, and they would have hade enormous difficulties in submitting it to the Crown Prince. This part of the episode is a long story and less important. In brief, the Management could only explain this action as the invention of some malevolent person. The upshot of the affair was that Schultz wrote to the Management: "To be sure the letter I sent last year from the Greenlanders at Godhavn was the result of malicious instigation," of which he had shortly after been assured. "But the Greenlanders have not forgotten the letter they gave me to forward, and they seem to be dissatisfied that they have received no answer." Schultz would "ignore the letter for the present," take the matter into his own hands and attempt to pacify the Greenlanders. If he succeeded, he would be satisfied "and keep quiet." The conflict was insoluble, but it reveals to the present reader how the Greenlandic whalers thought.

The Greenlandic whaler Poul Egede, who was the first of the letterwriters, and who on several occasions acted as a kind of spokesman or leader of the Greenlandic fangers at Godhavn, was most likely the "malicious person" alluded to by Schultz. But the question is whether Schultz really considered him malicious or simply agreed with the Management in order to have this matter, which could hardly be settled at the moment, done with. As far as we can see, Schultz later had a good relationship with Poul Egede, although one characterized by a certain respectful distance.

In other situations in which Poul Egede is portrayed in the sources, he leaves the impression of an independent but not rebellious personality who on various occasions asserted Greenlandic tradition and time-honoured custom.

The time elapsing between whaling and settlement of accounts, as opposed to the immediacy of barter, was one of the problems of getting the Godhavn whalers to understand and accept the credit system. This was dealt with quite differently and firmly by the Holsteinsborgers, which perhaps is due to a tradition from the time of Niels and Jørgen Egede. From these two one could at least expect a deeper understanding and approval of the Greenlandic point of view. Here we have the other case which confirms our interpretation of the Greenlandic reasoning. "The blubber is measured as soon as a whale is flensed, and then the Greenlanders, who are suspicious and afraid of being defrauded, immediately demand distribution and payment," observed Inspector A.M. Lund from Godthåb in his mention of whaling at Holsteinsborg. There was probably no question of the Greenlanders' being "suspicious and afraid" of being cheated, but this was most likely only the way the stationed Europeans perceived the situation. Here evidently a system was found which practiced the "immediacy" of barter. In other words, here the Europeans had cut through the problems of conversion into money values for the closing of accounts, or rather, kept these problems for themselves. This practice was immediately approved by the Greenlandic whalers. Of course there were squabbles about payment at Holsteinsborg, too; but these never developed into large conflicts, probably because the Greenlanders here preserved the traditional "immediacy" of barter between taking a whale and getting paid.

These two payment systems also show that the Management had not yet succeeded in imposing the desired uniformity in whaling, although this was still its objective. In time it did succeed, and was apparently satisfied. This was assisted by an essential change in the purchase schedule in 1804.

In connection with the failure of the baleen trade and the consequent changes in purchase prices, including an increase in the purchase price of blubber to one rigsdaler and twenty-four skillings per barrel, the conditions of partnership whaling were also changed. In the future the share accruing to the Greenlanders was to consist of two-thirds of the blubber and baleen of every whale. The remaining third was to go to the Trade "for the use of equipment and the assistance rendered in whaling by the Danish crew." On the other hand, the Greenlandic participants were now

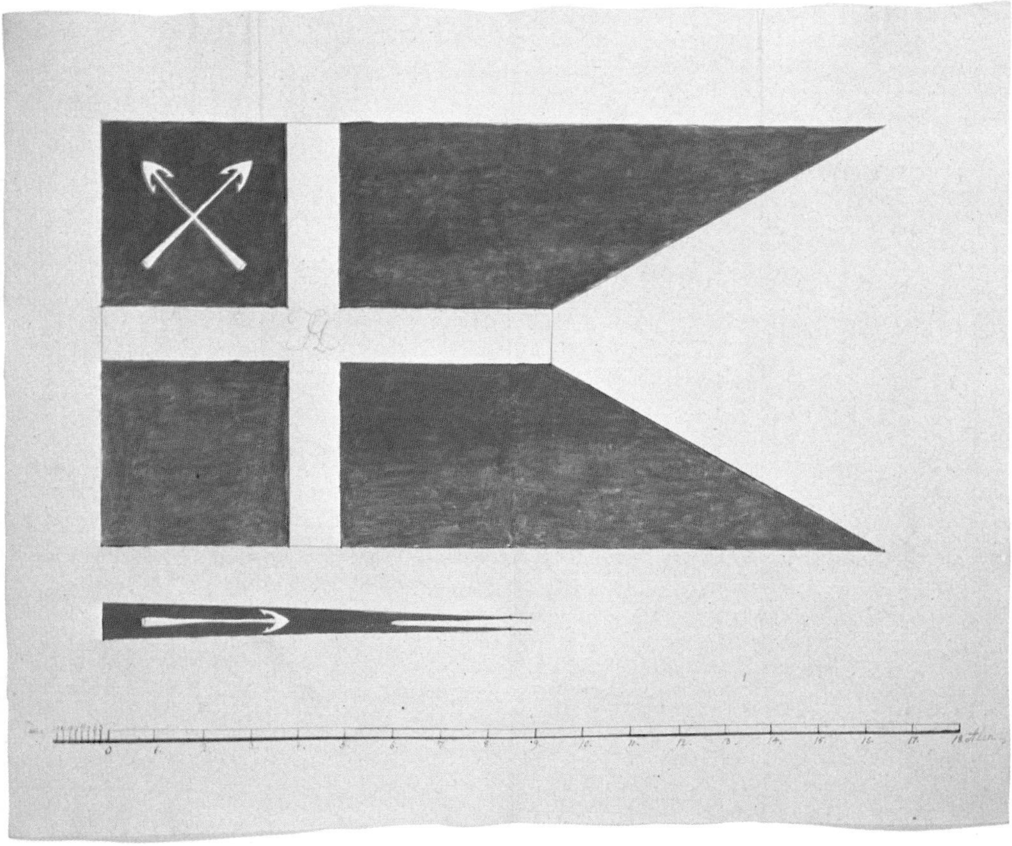

Swallow-tailed flag and pennant of the Royal Greenland Trade, the flag with two crossed harpoons in the upper inner red square, the pennant with only one. The original is a water-colour from which the Royal Danish Admiralty sanctioned the designs May 5th, 1795. The monogram of the Royal Greenland Trade (KGH) can be discerned sketched in the centre of the white cross.

(Reproduction of copy, sent by the Management to the Northern Inspectorate 1795)

Anlaget Arveprindsens Eyland i nordre Grønland

"The whaling station Arveprindsens Eyland in Northern Greenland".

(Reproduced from black and white reproduction of a water-colour made by the carpenter *Hans Willumsen*, cf. plate VI. The original has disappeared)

One of the houses, probably on the left of the above picture, as it stood on Arveprinsens Ejland in 1910.

(Arctic Institute, Charlottenlund, Denmark, Collection of Pictures, no. 693. Photo by District Medical Officer *R.V.G. Bentzen*, August 29. 1902)

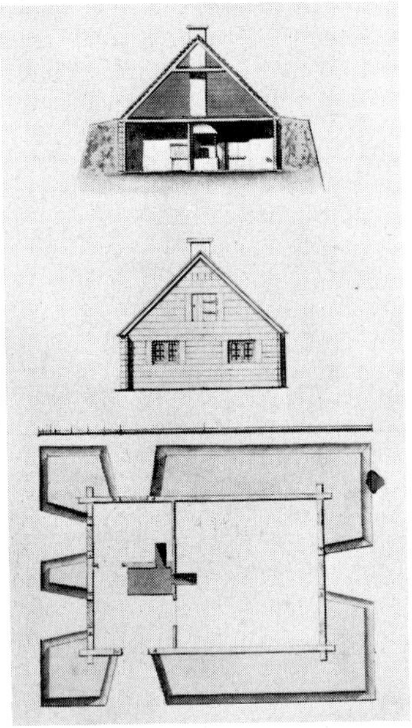

The master-carpenter and architect *A.J. Kirkerup's* designing of "A Whaling Station". The text in the records says: "There have been two houses like this at Arveprinsens Ejland, without the peat walls seen on Kirkerup's drawing." These two houses are visible at the left of the above reproduction.

(Library of the Royal Academy of Fine Arts, Copenhagen, Collection of Architectural Drawings, K.S. 140; much reduced) to be equally responsible for the loss of equipment (the sloops are not mentioned) according to rates to be determined in detail by the inspectors. This system was introduced immediately, and identically in the two inspectorates. It now seems that the stationed crews were of less importance in whaling, probably due to the increased employment of "mixtures" in this occupation. As the participation of Greenlandic whalers in whaling thus increased, it was reasonable to increase their share in the proceeds, although this argument is not directly mentioned in the Management's justification of the change.

With a higher purchase price for all kinds of blubber, the main bone of contention about payment was removed, and the Greenlanders, previously so discontented, appear to have been pacified.

"Danish Provisions"

In 1789 C.C. Dalager, the trader at Arveprinsens Ejland, had asserted to Inspector J. Wille that whaling with stationed crews would not be profitable, at least not in his locality. But neither could it be carried on there with the help of Greenlanders without granting an ample distribution of provisions, as they would otherwise leave the place since it moreover was bad for other kinds of fangst. "An outlay of several barrels of coarse provisions seems, after all, of little importance compared with the total expenditure and the special advantage which His Royal Majesty's Trade gains by these consumed sorts of provisions."

But Dalager himself had been a bit worried about the relatively large consumption in the year 1788–1789. As an explanation, he wrote that it was not only "the Greenlanders living here, who serve at whaling, and have to go to sea every day with our sloops throughout the winter," but also "the families of these Greenlanders down to the smallest child have to be supported." When he set up the whaling station, it had to be manned with Greenlandic whalers from outside, as the settlement had been abandoned by its previous inhabitants because they could not make a living there.

Although for different reasons, similar complaints were heard from Egedesminde the same year about the large consumption of Danish provisions among the Greenlanders engaged in whaling. Here it was apparently more a question of rights. "The Greenlanders, as whalers, consider themselves entitled to distilled spirits, butter, beer, in short all the kinds of provisions granted Danes in this country." If they were denied such provisions, they would "immediately complain that the Greenlandic whalers at

Holsteinsborg, Disko Bugt and the other whaling stations had enough distilled spirits, beer and food."

The question of "spoiling" the Greenlanders from their traditional diet naturally entered into consideration here; in practice, administrative desk philosophy came into conflict with necessity. On one occasion, C.C. Dalager attempted to cut through all the talk with his usual irony: "What they need cannot be denied them if whaling is to be carried on with Greenlanders, who certainly do not grasp, or will not grasp, how to starve themselves and their families to death to be courteous to the Management." If the traders were to be forbidden, as it seems they were, to deliver hulled grain, the only kind of provisions the Greenlanders really liked, one might just as well include peas, wrote Dalager, "which are usually so spoiled that when they are cooked they spread a pestilent stench far and wide." Besides, he had proof that grain was supplied at the other whaling stations. Previously he had asserted that he had never met a Greenlander who preferred to live on Danish provisions rather than on "the natural food he is accustomed to from his mother's breast." He thought that Greenlanders "perhaps often express a desire for our food, but this is only for one kind and for a short time. But when the need arises, and they have nothing else but these partly spoiled Danish provisions to sustain life with, an appreciable change can be seen immediately in them: that they suffer considerably from this manner of life. Wherefore I most humbly can assure you that a Greenlander never wants Danish food as long as he has some of his own left."

Contradicting this were the declarations of the trader Thomsen, who had his experience in the southern colonies of West Greenland, where European provisions played no role except as relief in periods of distress. As the trader at Christianshåb he declared in 1791 that too much provisions were allotted at the whaling stations. According to him it had gone so far that Greenlandic whalers actually had to be bought with European provisions to get them to carry on whaling. Thereby, according to him, they had become so "spoiled that now they have to have not only provisions but distilled spirits, coffee, sugar, tea, etc." Such items were even in stock everywhere for trade for Greenlandic produce. In this he exaggerated, but he did point out the most harmful aspect of whaling, from the point of view of an exclusively Greenlandic diet: it was from a nutritional point of view unfortunate that several whaling stations were located in places where no form of traditional Greenlandic fangst could be carried on. Unknowingly, Thomsen here indicated that the establishment of these whaling stations and their manning with predominantly Greenlandic crews involved a "nutritional culture conflict" situation, as asserted previously.

Conversely, Inspector Jens Wille had indicated that it was difficult to get the Greenlanders on whom whaling depended to perform the whale watchings when the local sealing period began, thereby bringing up the other side of the problems involved in the implementation of industrial whaling in Greenland. He also made light of the question of "spoiling", by stating that at Godhavn there were approximately 200 persons, "men, women and children, who can all eat Danish provisions; and in a whole year they have at the most received 165 rigsdalers and 25 skillings worth, approximately 5 marks' worth" each, roughly corresponding to five-sixths barrels of blubber or just over three large seals. Like C.C. Dalager, he did not believe in the theory of Greenlanders being spoiled from "their national diet". Besides, he had often seen Greenlanders whose wages included a full portion of Danish provisions, exchange "this for seal meat and other Greenlandic food." "Greenlandic women married to traders and assistants enjoyed their national diet on the sly, without their husbands knowing."

The dispensing of "Danish provisions" could not be avoided. It was a necessary evil, a "malum necessarium", as C.C. Dalager formulated it in 1789. Discussions of this problem from the "spoiling" point of view were therefore discontinued, and instead its economic aspects were taken up. These had actually always been a factor in the discussions, as the traders constantly had to apologize for having dispensed provisions for sums which were too large in the opinion of the Management (but compare the remarks of Inspector Wille above). These sums had nevertheless to be approved from one year to the next on the traders' accounts. The Management of the Royal Greenland Trade naturally wanted these expenses reduced to the lowest possible minimum. In the system introduced in 1804, along with the Greenlanders' increased shares in the whales takes and the raised prices for blubber, it was the intention that in the future the shares of Greenlandic whalers would have to cover the provisions they had consumed during the whaling season. This developed into a new problem, which could not be solved immediately.

Whaling Problems after 1804

This time it was the Greenlandic whalers of Holsteinsborg who made difficulties. To be sure, almost the entire population had been "replaced" after the epidemic of 1800-1801. Whaling had thus become operative again relatively quickly, probably under the conditions prevailing in the Northern Inspectorate rather than the local traditions, in which provisions had evidently been dispensed from. It is uncertain whether this dispensing of provisions in the Northern Inspectorate was completely free for the Greenlandic whalers, but it is clear that they did not understand that the expenses of the provisions were at least partially deducted from their whaling shares.

In 1804 the trader at Holsteinsborg must have begun this practice, before mid-May. Toward the end of this month he wrote to Inspector Myhlenphort that "The Greenlanders of Holsteinsborg have revolted because they were to pay for the provisions dispensed to them during the whaling season. But from such an ample take they really should make at least a partial payment on the provisions." He thought that without telling the Greenlanders one could deduct 10 rigsdalers for each whale taken. "This is the custom at all the whaling stations in the Northern Inspectorate." He was well aware that in principle the Greenlandic whalers were to be informed what they were paying, but he thought they had had "prejudices and wrong ideas" drummed into them by "malicious advisers".

Here he was referring to the missionary, and to two of the leading Greenlanders, the half-breed Poul Andersen and his son Elias Poulsen. The missionary, J.C. Büchler, seems on every occasion to have opposed the employees of the Trade and its whaling operations. He was not very active as a missionary, and as a priest was not well-liked by the people. Poul Andersen, in addition to being a whaler, was also a catechist, even a supervisory catechist. The missionary evidently furnished the ammunition which the catechist fired at every opportunity. There is no other explanation in the sources of why Poul Andersen and his son were so aggressive towards the employees of the Trade and its whaling operations. In 1804, when a new trader had come to Holsteinsborg, Elias Poulsen unexpectedly attacked him in the provisions store room. This developed into a disciplinary case, ending with the public reprimand of Elias Poulsen. It was the new missionary, N.G. Wolff, who did the reprimanding. It was probably also with his help that the Holsteinsborg whalers finally approved both participation in liability for the loss of equipment and partial payment for provisions. Whether the Holsteinsborgers actually understood the economic relationships involved must remain unanswered, but they approved the system and this brought tranquillity.

The events at Holsteinsborg led the Management – directly or indirectly – to explain in detail to both inspectors what its actual intention had been in the 1804 reorganization of the payment system. "When the change was approved it was our intention to improve the conditions of the inhabitants in general, make them more industrious at procuring blubber, and give them one more reason not to be wasteful in consuming it." It had therefore been found reasonable to raise prices only on the condition that the Greenlandic whalers became liable for at least part of the loss of equipment. This condition had been found both reasonable and useful, the latter "because the Greenlanders are thereby led to reflect on the value of these things and have an immediate interest in preserving and salvaging them. It was also thought that it could serve as a preparation for introducing some time in the future an equal partnership in whaling, so that the Greenlanders and the Trade would bear equal burdens and receive equal advantages."

Regarding the payment of provisions at Holsteinsborg, the Management stressed that a definitive system must now be laid down; at the same time they made it clear that the demand for payment could be dispensed from: it could be completely abandoned if the whaling had failed or be partially written off if whaling had been bad. The inspector would have to act on his own discretion.

These comments are typical expressions of the special situation of the Royal Greenland Trade as a trading and production enterprise. The Management distinctly deviated from ordinary principles of trade and production, since it had a parallel and corrective concept that an important objective of the Trade was to develop the Greenlandic population, including their economic conditions. This should be compared with our survey of the reform proposal of 1798.

In order to remove one of the hindrances to the implementation of the 1804 whaling system, the Management encouraged cooperation between the two inspectors, so that procedures could be uniform in the North and South, and the Greenlandic whalers could not claim discrimination. Cooperation between the inspectorates had been in operation since the 1790's, and had become closer due to the friendship between Inspectors P.H. Motzfeldt and M.N. Myhlenphort. Now in 1805 this cooperation received a kind of confirmation; it proved to be profitable especially in the coordination of whaling rules and practices. Profitable for all sides and for whaling, for calm prevailed hereafter on the question of payment.

This encouragement of coordination was in addition in accordance with the so often expressed desire for uniformity in every aspect of life along the west coast of Greenland - as far as this could be brought about. It is also an indication that the division of Greenland into the two inspectorates was not exploited according to the principle of divide and rule.

As we have seen, this new system was intended by the Management to reduce the expenses of whaling and promote the production of blubber. It is and must continue to be a question, whether the dispensing of provisions became less of a burden to the operations of the Trade. At least from Egedesminde it was reported in 1805 that other forms of organized production also lay heavy on the provisions account. Netting was now being carried on at Egedesminde with the help of Greenlanders who were not proficient fangers, but who entered into the service of the colony as net tenders; these had to have an allotment of rations, as they naturally could not earn their livelihood by fangst in addition to taking care of the many nets.

The custom of paying a part of the wages of stationed Europeans in provisions thus gradually spread out of this privileged circle to the Greenlanders who served full or part time in the employment of the Trade or the Mission. This was naturally due to the subsistance-economy situation which the tiny societies of West Greenland constantly existed in. The Trade considered it one of its objectives to introduce at least a greater degree of money economy, but at the same time paradoxically felt compelled to maintain and expand a distinct element of subsistance economy. The conversion of values to rigsdalers, marks and skillings was actually only for the benefit of the Trade in keeping accounts.

The now customary difficulties with the reliability and willingness to work of the labour force, especially in flensing and cutting up whales taken, were complained about by whaling chiefs at various stations throughout the 1790's. Instability and laziness were said to characterize both the stationed "sailors" and the Greenlandic whalers. On one single occasion, in 1790, the Greenlanders at Qerrortussoq near Holsteinsborg, succeeded in getting an assistant removed. Judging from the correspondence, he had too openly measured blubber to the advantage of the trader. After 1800, however, all complaints seem to die down, perhaps because those affected had finally accepted conditions as they found them. Attempts to change them in the direction of greater efficiency had presumably proven to be in vain.

Distilled Spirits

When the trader at Umánaq in 1797 had suggested establishing a whaling station on Ubekendte Ejland, under the leadership of one of trader C.C. Dalager's sons and with some Greenlandic whalers from Godhavn Inspector C. Bendeke discouraged this attempt to expand whaling activity. For this reason the proposal was not carried out, but Bendeke's arguments shed a good deal of light on the situation at Godhavn.

C.C. Dalager's son could perhaps be persuaded to go to Ubekendte Ejland as a whaling chief, said Bendeke, but the Greenlanders of Godhavn who had been suggested as harpooners were less suitable. They would cost too much, presumably for provisions and other amenities "to which they are accustomed, and which here can only be excused by necessity and the long recognized excellence of this place for whaling." Such expenses could not be borne by an experimental budget. In addition, the two persons proposed were "the most immoral and intractable of the disreputable Greenlanders of Godhavn," and it would be hard to "satisfy their immodesty". These two were sons of the previously mentioned Poul Egede, who also was no problem-free whaling participant.

Inspector Bendeke's summary characterization of the Greenlandic whalers at Godhavn was sharp and undoubtedly one-sided. But it can hardly be denied that there were tough nails among them. From a European point of view they were actually "demoralized". The question is, how did they get this way?

It has been stressed time after time that the whalers stationed in Greenland in 1776 and subsequently, just as many of the labourers stationed there previously, left much to be desired. Although fewer whaling sailors were sent to Greenland after 1784, and the bad influence of this group was thus reduced considerably, the damage had already been done. The relatively uninhibited consumption of alcohol practiced by this group did not fail to spread to the Greenlanders who were in daily contact with these actually more or less "demoralized" elements.

"Under the highest penalty, the inhabitants must not be got drunk on beer or strong liquor. Distilled spirits especially must not be given to Greenlanders; and under the penalty of 10 rigsdalers' fine or a sufficient amount of corporal punishment, and so forth, never be served to women." Thus stated the Order of 1782 in no uncertain terms. This warning was repeated in a later paragraph. On the other hand it was also clear that "the crew must not be allotted their portions of distilled spirits in casks or pots, but they should enjoy this privilege by the glass, and they should really enjoy it (this means that it should be drunk immediately and not saved for later)." The ration of distilled spirits was considered, as we have seen, as a necessary means of providing heat and energy during ordinary colony work as well as in whaling: on whale watchings, hunting and flensing.

There was thus a conflict between the two ways of looking at spirits: on

There was thus a conflict between the two ways of looking at spirits: on the one hand as a source of necessary calories, and on the other hand as a producer of harmful side effects. Between them hung the "juridical" aspect of the problem, and this is where one line of development of the increase in the consumption of spirits may lie.[7]

There was no doubt that half-breeds employed by the Trade and in whaling were entitled to a ration of distilled spirits, enjoyed by "officers", "inferiors" and stationed crew in quantities according to their rank. Juridically half-breeds were at that time considered as Greenlanders as long as they stayed in Greenland. But there was a distinct difference between the conditions of employment of two groups of half-breeds. Some were whaling assistants, with the alcohol ration of "officers"; others belonged to the "lower ranks". The Order of 1782 did not provide for the alcohol rights of Greenlanders, including half-breeds who were juridically considered as Greenlanders, employed in the service of the Trade.

The traders and whaling chiefs were probably compelled to ignore the prohibitions of the Order against delivering an alcohol ration to half-breeds, when these were otherwise employed under the same conditions as stationed Europeans. Since the allotment of rations was part of the crew's wages, and "real" Greenlanders as well as "mixtures" were eventually employed with a full or partial wage on the same basis, they could not be denied the ration of distilled spirits which formed a part of the customary ration. Since this ration was served by the glass, according to the Order of 1782, this could not be hidden from the Greenlanders who worked with the stationed crew. If the positive effects of alcohol as a "bracer" were emphasized, it would not be fair to discriminate between Greenlanders and Europeans. The general provisions of the Order would have had to be evaded. But there is no doubt that the Greenlanders themselves, as they developed a taste for distilled spirits and their various effects, including intoxication, insisted on their right to be served the raw spirits which were shipped to Greenland for the crews.

In 1805 Inspector M.N. Myhlenphort informed the trader at Holsteinsborg that when he was employed in whaling in the Northern Inspectorate the cutting up of whales and filling of the blubber tubs had at first been done by the stationed crew, but gradually the Greenlanders began to participate. "When one treated Greenlanders in a friendly and reasonable manner, one could get them to do whatever work one asked of them. For this work as well as for flensing they usually were allotted some provisions and one mug of beer or one *sopken* per day." A *sopken* can be nothing other than a glass of distilled spirits of undetermined quantity; the glasses in which spirits were served in Greenland were certainly not small. Even then, this single shot per day did not entail any risk. Since this measure is mentioned in an inspector's report, we can assume that it is the smallest possible measure: it is named as an alternative to a mug of beer. In reality most likely several *sopkens* were served.

In any case this quotation shows that in this respect, too, Greenland was in a "stage of development", and that even the inspectors had to take the categorical prohibitions of the Order of 1782 with a grain of salt. It furthermore shows that the principle of barter still prevailed in the "labour market" in Greenland; that the Greenlanders would do one or another job for food and drink.

Foreign Influence and Competition

It was at Godhavn that local Greenlanders had the easiest access to contact with foreign whalers, who sold gin freely, naturally as payment in a quite illicit trade between Greenlanders and especially English whalers.

After 1777 apparently a growing number of English whalers had gone to the Davis Strait, the waters off the Northern Inspectorate, and into Disko Bugt. Within the period from 1782 to 1808, 1788 seems to have been the peak year of the presence of English whalers in and around Greenland. In that year 100 foreign whaling ships were reported in Greenlandic waters; 90 of them were English. The remaining whalers were Dutch and North German. The Dutch eventually abandoned whaling totally, and the whaling expeditions of the North German Hansa cities were not extensive. The real competition was between Greenlandic whaling from the coast stations and English whaling, mostly from Hull and Leith.

According to the ordinance of 18 March 1776, no foreign ships (meaning any ship which did not belong to or was chartered by the Royal Greenland Trade) was allowed to land on the coasts of Greenland, except in case of shipwreck, lack of fresh water or other matters of urgency. Nevertheless foreign whalers, mostly English and Scots, did land on these coasts, and eventually even openly entered the various natural harbours, including Godhavn. Up to 1788, however, Inspector Schwabe could only remember one real conflict arising between English and Danish-Greenlandic whalers, and that was in 1774. On the contrary, mutual assistance is often reported between them. Competition was apparent, however, as was illicit trade.

The attention of the Inspectors was directed toward the illicit trade which took place contrary to the ordinance of 1776 and in spite of it.

During the 1780's this trade developed into an almost systematic traffic in merchandise which the Danish traders could not supply or which Greenlanders, according to the general schedule, were not allowed to buy. As a rule the Greenlanders paid in home-made articles, such as tobacco pouches of sealskin, at first. Soon the Greenlandic supply seems to have become greater. Narwhal and walrus skins and tusks were exchanged for cans, cups and ... distilled spirits. Eventually the Greenlanders began to sell their clothes, bed skins and fangst equipment. At certain localities furs of various animals were even made to order for English whalers. In 1787 the trader at Egedesminde reported that the English sloops landed to trade with the Greenlanders. They had sold the English fox and seal skins, narwhal tusks, eiderdown and baleen. In quite a few cases the payment was distilled spirits: i.e., gin.

"The unfortunate distilled spirits of the ships lure everything from our Greenlanders, even the furs off their bodies. They impede their fangst and instigate disorder among them." Spirits functioned as a magnet, attracting Greenlanders from far and wide. It was especially the Greenlanders of Godhavn and Kronprinsens Ejland who had acquired a taste for this drink, to such an extent that they had to be given spirits for flensing and coast watches in order to get them to work. Schwabe, who wrote this to the Management, blamed the English for this need for alcohol.

Eventually the English began to land anywhere along the coast not only in order to trade (illicitly) but also to collect eiderdown and carry on whaling, where they could. Complaints were made that they annoyed the Danish-Greenlandic whalers and plundered the islands of down, in addition to buying up Greenlandic produce.

Their many calls at the whaling harbours actually became a burden: they unnecessarily wore out the meagre facilities of the stations. In addition, visitors went on board. The inspector at Godhavn, as well as whaling chiefs elsewhere, had such strong misgivings about the visits of Greenlanders to the English ships, that in 1787 Inspector Wille reported the intolerable conditions to the Management, which he wanted to intervene by emphatically complaining to the shipowners in England.

This could only be accomplished by mobilizing the Foreign Office in Copenhagen, and involving this situation in the tangled web of Danish-Norwegian foreign policy. Probably because of a disinclination to annoy the English government with the less important matters, the Foreign Office dealt quite half-heartedly with the problem of Greenland. The upshot was that the Foreign Office requested the Management itself to take the measure it might deem necessary to assert the rights of the King in and around Greenland.

From 1788 on it was the task of the newly-appointed Commission to deal with this affair, which was a matter of principle. After some discussion it was decided to "arm" the various localities of Disko Bugt, but the weapons shipped were only to be used in cases of "self-defence". When Inspector Wille was informed of this decision and saw the arms shipments, he snorted to the administration and the Committee that it was quite ridiculous to imagine that the small crews of the various localities could defend them against possible English attacks, or that the local authorities could thus effectively assert the rights of the King. He did distribute the weapons, however, and gave instructions how to use and keep them; the latter being more important than the former. Until 1799 they were more or less unused, and in spite of instructions for keeping them they were not maintained properly, so that the firearms were then sold and the remainder sent back to Copenhagen.

Again in 1789 Inspector Wille attempted the path of persuasion with the Greenlanders, but in vain, although in his open letter he depicted the English as the minions of Satan, "whores, thieves, robbers and drunkards." All along Disko Bugt their visits continued, and illicit trade continued undaunted. The English kept intrepidly competing; and now here, now there, made "an awful mess, with the sale of spirits."

There were, however, advantages in the visits of these English whalers. The skippers were interested in narwhal tusks, which were unsaleable in Copenhagen. They were willing to pay rather high prices for even pieces of tusks. They also taught the locals how to fire harpoons with cannons. In 1791 Inspector Schultz bought such a cannon and the special harpoons belonging to it from an English whaler. The Management of the Royal Greenland Trade approved this traffic, and later Schultz bought several other things from the English, even some whaling sloops, as mentioned previously. What is noteworthy here, is that he also paid with fox skins and narwhal tusks, which were absolutely monopoly commodities. On later occasions the Inspectors repeated this method of payment. Another advantage of the English visits was that the Management could get mail to and from Greenland sent more quickly, so quickly indeed that with a little bit of luck the Management could answer a letter in the same year in which it was written.

Nevertheless, the harmful aspects of the English visits predominated. Inspector Schultz therefore soberly reported the situation to the Management, mentioning the insufficient authority the inspectors possessed and the imprecise instructions they were supposed to follow. He submitted in 1791 a long and extensive proposal for changes. Not a few reports of excesses, both violent, sexual and alcoholic, as well as flagrant thefts and similar infringements against the population formed the background of the measures he proposed. The authority of the inspector was being quite ignored by the English whalers.

The Management and the Commission fully realized the seriousness of Schultz' report and proposal. At first it was decided, therefore, to make the office of Inspector more powerful. This was to be done in the way which at the time was thought most effective: the inspector was issued a uniform, which was to give him a certain official stature as a representative of the King, and an armed ship was placed at his disposal. At the same time, the Commission wanted the English informed of the ordinance of 18 March 1776, and that the Management intended to resort to extensive measures in Greenland to counter the foreign violations.

This again led to the mobilization of the Foreign Office, which after negotiations with the English chargé d'affaires in Copenhagen reported that while the English government quite disapproved of the violations by English citizens in Greenland, it could do nothing about them, as they were the acts of private individuals. In each individual case the administrations of the Royal Greenland Trade would have to have recourse to a civil suit in an English court.

Foreign Policy, the Culmination of Conflict and Flag

At the same time the Danish-Norwegian Foreign Office took advantage of this opportunity to put the Royal Greenland Trade in its place within instead of contrary to the general foreign-policy pattern of the realms. The Foreign Office said that the English government had nothing against the announced intensification of measures to assure the "Rights of the King" in Greenland. But in the opinion of the Foreign Office, i.e., A.P. Bernstorff himself, these "measures must only be taken by the Trade, without showing any royal military flag," and it was therefore not advisable to have any ship from the navy make an appearance in or around Greenland. This can only be interpreted as meaning that A.P. Bernstorff, whose opinions were of decisive importance in the government, would not agree to the power of the state backing up and assisting the Royal Greenland Trade in its countermeasures, as the administration attempted to assert the rights of the King, i.e., of the realms, in and around Greenland. A part of the realms was thus deprived of that protection which the state ought to have granted as a matter of course.

This is but one demonstration of how the Danish-Norwegian government from the middle of the 17th century was in general forced, step by step, into a defensive foreign-policy situation. In particular, the Foreign Office's determination of the position of the Royal Greenland Trade in foreign policy was a continuation of the policy conducted from the beginning of the 18th century: to strive for a certain distance between the Danish-Norwegian state and "The Greenland design".

In the present situation the attitude of the Foreign Office was that measures against violations of the rights of the King in Greenland would have to be taken on the initiative of the Trade and with the Trade accepting responsibility for them. The Foreign Office did, however, go so far as to stress to the English chargé d'affaires that in the future English violations would be countered more seriously, and that the government wanted this to be passed on to those concerned in England.

The Foreign Office also informed the Royal Greenland Trade and the Commission that they should not expect approval of a demand for extending the territorial limits off the coast of Greenland. The Management had suggested this as a possible measure to exclude foreigners completely from Disko Bugt, which would be entirely encompassed by such extended territorial limits. There would thus be more distinct rules to be enforced, and the opportunities for conflict would be limited. Taking the attitude that the English would then make counter-demands which would not be compatible with the general interests of the realms, A.P. Bernstorff rejected this suggestion. Navigation provisions to the advantage of Greenland had thus to give way to consideration for the total foreign policy line of the realms.

Meanwhile the most flagrant disregard of the rights of the King in Greenland so far took place. An English whaling ship was reported stranded near Fortune Bay. After an inspection, in which Inspector B.J. Schultz' crew found the ship on the foreshore with most of its superstructure removed, it was declared a prize, made on Danish soil. Thereafter several English whalers appeared at the wreck and began to plunder it. One of these skippers was especially aggressive; he came with a large crew, disregarded all the Danish proclamations of rights to the wreck, and removed from it even what had distinctly been marked as salvaged by the Danish state. He showed no respect for the Danish flag and stole the equipment, beer and even clothes of the Danish crew, which gave rise to a few instances of physical combat. This affair ended with the retreat of the Danish authorities with the four casks the crew succeeded in retaining.

Naturally Inspector B.J. Schultz reported this incident, and enclosed the minutes of the interrogations he had held in 1792, one and a half months after the event. The Management of the Royal Greenland Trade then contacted the Foreign Office directly. The Foreign Office had to admit that the Danish flag had been "insulted" but otherwise dealt half-heartedly with the case. After making inquiries of the Danish ambassador in London, the Foreign Office referred the administration of the Royal Greenland Trade to a civil suit in an English court. The judgment, delivered the following year, was against the Trade. The Foreign Office had hesitated to do anything about the insult to the flag until after the judgment, and then it preferred to "file" the insult.

In the 1792 incident at Fortune Bay the foreshore rights of the Danish crown had been de facto violated. For this reason and because of another wreck, an English ship at Rifkol in Egedesminde District, it was urgent to have an official determination and international proclamation of Danish foreshore rights in Greenland. Inspector Schultz linked this to the assertion of a three-mile limit at sea: a determination of how far territorial waters went.

The Management did not succeed in getting the territorial limits set at three nautical miles, most likely because the Foreign Office still did not want to advocate this claim officially. On the other hand the Management did succeed in getting the Økonomi- & Kommercekollegium to pass a royal decree that foreshore rights in Greenland belonged to the Danish-Norwegian Crown, and that they were assigned to the Management of the Royal Greenland Trade. Thus the authority of the inspector received a much-needed backing, even though he could still not count on military support in case of necessity, nor most likely on support from the Foreign Office.

In order as it were to enforce military assistance, the Commission had in May 1792 applied for permission for the inspectors to fly the swallow-tailed flag and pennant on the ships they used. These symbols apparently had realistic significance in those times. The Admiralitetskollegium had to approve such a request. In accordance with the prevalent foreign-policy line, in harmony with the reserve which the government evidently wanted to show to the Greenland enterprise, and finally as a consequence of the distinct opinion of the Foreign Office in 1791 that no "royal military flag" must be shown in conflicts with foreigners along the coasts of Greenland, the Admiralitetskollegium refused the Royal Greenland Trade permission to fly the swallow-tail flag and pennant.

One passage to royal status was nevertheless kept open. As was the case with the chartered trading companies and royal customs officers, the Royal Greenland Trade could be given permission to fly the swallow-tailed flag and pennant, but of a smaller size than the naval flag, of a deeper red colour, and finally with a distinct marking somewhere or other on the flag. As early as 1776 the Trade's whaling vessels presumably flew the swallow-tailed flag. But the regulations of 1781 provided that this flag was to be of a deeper red colour and sharply distinguishable from the royal naval flag; as a swallow-tail flag it was nevertheless "royal". After other private whalers had received the same permission, it was no longer just the Royal Greenland Trade's whalers that were marked with this swallow-tail flag in Greenland. After much discussion back and forth, it was finally decided that the Royal Greenland Trade would be allowed to fly the swallow-tail flag and pennant, but now with a distinct mark in the centre of the cross. In addition, two crossed white harpoons were to be placed in the upper inside red field. This mark was used, but the initials in the centre of the cross did not last long.

Thus arose the special swallow-tail flag of the Royal Greenland Trade as a shipowners' flag, specially marked with the symbol of whaling, but still royal because of the swallow tail. This harpoon flag was the result of a compromise. The harpoons likewise indicated that whaling was considered the most important activity of the enterprise. It was quite unrealistic that the Southern Inspectorate, where no whaling of importance took place, except at Holsteinsborg, had the same harpoon symbol in its flag. But uniformity was demanded.

The flag issue was decided in 1795. By that time, the "front" had been quiet for a couple of years. Contact and competition seemed to be still peaceful. The Fortune Bay incident in 1792 and its immediate consequences had had a certain calming influence. Relationships between English whalers and officers of the Trade became more relaxed. Mutual assistance took place, but the attitude of the Management towards this was somewhat inconsistent. The one helped was one's competitor, who according to the norms should be opposed. Likewise one ought contemptuously to reject help from one's rival. Illicit English trade continued, along with opportunities for the stationed Europeans to sell for the Trade products which were unsaleable elsewhere. The ambivalent attitude of the Management was in a way a consequence of the foreign policy which the government wanted to conduct towards England, without open clashes, and which was actually conducted, with some difficulty, past 1801 until the total break in 1807. The Management of the Royal

Greenland Trade finally made light of the illicit English trade. Purchase accounts over a long period also seem to show that this illicit trade on the whole never exercised any noticable influence.

The only harmful influence which still came from the English whalers was the consequence of the visits of local Greenlanders to their ships. It was attempted, but in vain, to restrict the opportunities for visits. But only Greenlanders who were employed in whaling or otherwise by the Trade could be prohibited by the inspector from visiting the ships, and this was done, with fines, demotions or discharge as the consequence of violations. But the interest in and need for distilled spirits could not thus be diminished.

Fruitless Projects

English whaling in Davis Stræde was maintained with generally good results, both in catches and economically. This foreign success in the "King's Currents" could not fail to give rise to a certain patriotic indignation among individual Danish and Norwegian subjects of the King. In their outbursts of industrial patriotism they overlooked the fact that quite a few North Frisians hired out on whalers from Altona and Glückstadt; both these cities as well as the North Frisians belonged to the realms. That there were also some North Frisians on whalers from Hamburg and Bremen could only be considered a supplement to this activity. All these whalers had Davis Stræde as their goal. From Bergen and other Western Norwegian ports a special kind of whaling activity took place south of Svalbard. From 1782 to 1808 only one whaling expedition took place from the coast of Norway to Davis Stræde: one of the ships which the Royal Greenland Trade had sold left Kristianssand in 1790. It had most certainly been paid for on the basis of the Notice of 13 October 1784, and strangely enough had an English skipper.

A rather shocking memorandum on whaling in Greenland turned up in 1793 before the astonished eyes of the Commission and The Management. It had only a transitory existence, hardly three weeks. As a whaling project it was of no real interest, as it was just a simple sketch. It came from Matthias Ferslew Dalager, one of the many sons of the often mentioned Greenland trader, C.C. Dalager. From the age of 12, Matthias Dalager had lived in Denmark, in Elsinore, at the expense of his relatives there; he had been educated as an artist.

In 1793 Matthias Dalager was 24 years old, deprived of further support and apparently incapable of earning his living in his art. His father therefore petitioned the Management for support for him, or failing that, employment as an assistant or the like. The support Matthias Dalager was then offered, he rejected as totally insufficient. On the other hand, the Management considered his qualifications too poor for employment in the Trade. They refused to employ him. Matthias evidently got angry and, manifesting a kind of defiance, submitted his "whaling project", whereby he revealed his total lack of economic and organizational understanding.

What was shocking, indeed absolutely incomprehensible, to the Management and the Commission was the argumentation advanced for the project. Matthias Dalager claimed an exceptional position as a Greenlander. This is the first time we see the appearance of a kind of Greenlandic "nationalism". He accused the Management, and later also the Commission, of not wanting to employ him just because he was a Greenlander. Matthias Dalager was a "mixture": his mother was a "real Greenlander". His allegation was, however, due to a misunderstanding, as his three brothers were already employed by the Trade. Nevertheless he repeated his allegation the following year to the Commission on another occasion. His reasoning must therefore have emerged from a feeling, fostered by one or another form of influence. The fact was that his father, born in Denmark, but living in Greenland since he was 19, had ventilated a "national Greenlandic" inferiority complex, in the spirit of which he had presumably raised his sons. This feeling must have been reinforced by the special position given to Matthias in the Danish milieu in which he received his further education, especially because of the special expectations made of him by virtue of his Greenlandic descent as well as his presumed talents as an artist. He became quite conscious of this special position. "Greenlanders are also human beings, with mental powers and sensitivity," reasoned Matthias Dalager in 1793, and continued: "they are just as useful citizens in their sphere as their brethren in other places. The Greenlandic nation should therefore be no more excluded from participation in royal grace than others. Nothing is more natural and reasonable than that the children of the land should eat of the fat of the land." Therefore he was to have permission to conduct whaling in Greenland with no impediment from or duties to the Royal Greenland Trade ; he was, however, willing to pay the King a fee.

The natural outcome of this affair was that the Commission referred Matthias Dalager to the Notice of 13 October 1784, without any discussion of his reasoning. The Commission only stressed that he could not expect special liberties; it did not mention that he was free to return to

Greenland and participate on whaling conditions, most likely because he himself had already rejected this possibility. This was the end of the discussion of this project.

Matthias Dalager's whaling plan was so vague that he himself must soon have realized its impracticability. If he at all attempted to raise the necessary capital, he must have quickly discovered that he could get none. He must have actually only imagined the project functioning. This may indicate that he thought in a Greenlandic (Eskimo) manner. The sources thus show us our first person born and in his decisive childhood years raised in Greenland, who in his 24th year was in a culturally marginal position, where he went "nationally" off the rails.

If this "Greenlandic" whaling project was a wind egg, a later Norwegian project had quite different roots in the world of reality. In 1805 Edvard Christie Heiberg, a former trader in Greenland, published a pamphlet at his own expense.[8] He had resigned in 1804 and was living in Copenhagen.

First of all, Heiberg expressed indignation in his pamphlet that a so rich and reliable whaling harvest eluded Danish-Norwegian whaling activities each year. If English whalers were able to return from Davis Stræde each year with catches of eight to fifteen whales per ship, it must be possible to establish a profitable whaling activity in the Strait beside that of the Royal Greenland Trade. He estimated the average yearly take of the English at eight whales per ship, and from this calculated that twenty ships had in the course of ten years had a combined take of 1600 whales worth 3500 rigsdalers apiece, for a total value, according to his calculations, of 5,600,000 rigsdalers and a net profit of 3,200,000 rigsdalers.

In his opinion the success of the English was due in the first place to an advantageous location for an early trip out, and next to the proficiency of their whalers. Heiberg therefore asserted that Bergen was correspondingly favourably situated, and that proficient Greenlanders could be signed on at Holsteinsborg and other localities in the Northern Inspectorate. He had himself supervised whaling activities at Holsteinsborg and Ritenbenk. He presented several calculations, but fully realized that the memory of former unsuccessful whaling enterprises – and here he must have been thinking of the great project of 1776 – had discouraging effect on private initiative. He claimed, however, that it was now time to consider whaling more optimistically, since the last ten years had not seen one single year with poor whaling. After a number of practical suggestions, he urged the formation of a stock company with 1100 to 1200 shares at 100 rigsdalers apiece. This company would start out small, with three or four ships. Finally in his pamphlet he put himself and his experience at the disposition of a possible future society of investors, just as he placed himself at the head of a collection of promises to invest.

On paper it all sounded quite nice and promising, but seemed calculated to guarantee Heiberg's personal future. He had in the previous year sought employment without success, and in 1805 had actually not much to live on. Heiberg sent his pamphlet to the Økonomi- og Kommercekollegium, asking for support. He petitioned the King to purchase from 100 to 300 shares, and to give him a loan of 5000 to 6000 rigsdalers for three to four years. An inquiry had therefore to be submitted to the Management of the Royal Greenland Trade.

The Management expressed no immediate enthusiasm for Heiberg's proposal, and first of all made a number of corrections in his calculations, so that the project seemed less promising. Then the Management stressed that it was more important to support the whaling which was already being carried on, especially the people who for many years had served meritoriously in it. But it thought that Heiberg had probably made contact with certain wealthy and interested elements. Therefore he should be "made capable of continuing to influence this public by granting him support to live on for some time." It could hardly be expressed more cogently by a state institution that Heiberg actually had no income and was in dire need of support. The Management also proposed holding out to him the prospect of subsidies for the purchase of shares. It could not avoid remarking, however, that although Heiberg had been an enterprising chief of "colony whaling", he was "a mediocre manager and accountant:" i.e., watch out for him in questions of money and accounts and don't trust in him too much!

The Økonomi- og Kommercekollegium must have found this matter sufficiently elucidated and recommended; it applied to the Finanskollegium for the loan to Heiberg. He pressed for a decision, and succeeded in getting 150 rigsdalers in travelling expenses, but when he asked for more and in addition for support for his family while he was away, he was only promised 20 rigsdalers from the poor fund as relief for his wife. The finances of this former trader were so low, that he had to be content with this.

All this took place in 1806. The following year he reported on the result of his trip: 16 of the wealthy merchants of Bergen had in partnership purchased a Dutch ship of 114 kommerce læster (228 registered tons), equipped it for whaling and sent it whaling off Svalbard. Hereafter Heiberg applied for the previously mentioned loan of 5000 to 6000 rigsdalers for the purchase of shares. The Økonomi- og Kommercekollegium was rather positive towards the entire matter, but then Copenhagen was shelled in 1807, and a war situation developed. This set a stopper for this enterprise as well as for so many others which had implications farther than the limits of domestic waters.

It is perhaps characteristic of all overseas activities proceeding from a relatively small country that they develop a relationship over great distances between a narrow domestic milieu and another differently, but equally narrow milieu: in this case the Danish and the Greenlandic milieux. Between them there is a world which gives perspective, but there is also a constant contrast between the two milieux. This left its mark on every single person who was exposed to this contrast: a lurking dissatisfaction with two different kinds of insufficiency - a too slow development toward what is presumably better in the one milieu; and in the other, a painful lack at times of real understanding of the problems of the other milieu. In a period zealous for reforms in the latter milieu, the lack of understanding can cause this zeal to go overboard in both milieux. Heiberg's whaling project was, from this point of view, also the expression of dissatisfaction with insufficiency.

Reform zeal enthused some of the employees of the Trade as well as of the Mission. "I see that Mr. Jansen has hardly set foot in the country before he wants to reform. This worm is not good." Thus reacted Otho Fabricius, adviser to the Missionskollegium, to the proposals of a newly-arrived missionary in his first letter home. These proposals were perhaps the result of the inexperienced missionary's immediate certainty as to how things should be, but they were also the expression of his zeal to go about solving the problems present. The "reform actions" of newly-arrived personnel have been repeated throughout the centuries; they still manifest themselves, undaunted, in the present. In his commentary in 1791, Otto Fabricius expressed both the caution, which in Greenland was felt as an insufficiency, of the leadership in Copenhagen, and the disinclination of this leadership to change existing conditions.

In 1788 the trader C.C. Dalager wrote of the appointment of the Commission the same year: "How desirable would it not be if some experienced and knowing man could give information and suggest the correct means and measures for a happy change from the present state of affairs, and return it to its previous, simple state." By "the present state of affairs" he not only meant the period from 1782 to 1788, but the entire situation in Greenland, especially the condition of whaling, since 1776: i.e., the state monopoly. His secret hope was a return to "the previous, simple state," i.e., the period of the Trading Company from 1750 to 1774. His hidden desire was local freedom for the trader under a little private trading monopoly. As late as 1795 he directed forcible criticism against the great whaling project, and he had not forgotten his fervent distaste for the very existence of the Royal Greenland Trade and Fishery - and his scepticism about its activities.

IX. The Trade

Surplus and Deficit

"A Royal Trade as at present, does not seem quite so advantageous, for as soon as governments in our state as well as in others are to trade, experience has always shown that such things done by the state have inevitably entailed a general loss, although certain individuals have thereby become well-off," commented C.C. Dalager in 1788, thereby expressing a dogma which both before and after him has been uttered so often that it has almost become an accepted truth. This dogma originated in physiocracy, and was still asserted by the spokesmen for economic liberalism. Dalager's words also reflect the fact that this dogma had found fertile soil in an ordinary Greenland trader, far from the centres of economic power and seats of learning.

So far no trading enterprise, neither state, state-supported, nor private, had succeeded in trading in Greenland without loss. Nor was it quite certain that under The Chartered General Trading Company (1749–74) the Greenland Trade had yielded a profit; perhaps it had only balanced.

It was to be the fate of the Royal Greenland Trade to contradict the contention of Dalager and physiocracy. From 1781 to 1789, however, it was not quite economic profit which characterized this institution – on the contrary. It was thought in 1789 that trade and whaling in Greenland had yielded a deficit for the eight years, taken as a whole. This is why a comprehensive programme of rationalization was introduced.

There was a distinct surplus on the books from 1790 and the two subsequent years.[1] 1798 ended with a large loss, greater than the profit recorded for 1790. According to reports, this loss was due to whaling, which failed totally, with only three whales taken in the Northern Inspectorate; and in the Southern, four at Holsteinsborg and two at Qerrortussoq. The Northern Inspectorate usually delivered blubber and baleen from twenty to thirty whales.

The next deficit was in 1801, this time due, still according to the reports, to shipwrecks with loss of both cargoes and ships, as well as to the smallpox epidemic, which had restricted whaling to the greatest extent.

Graph 3

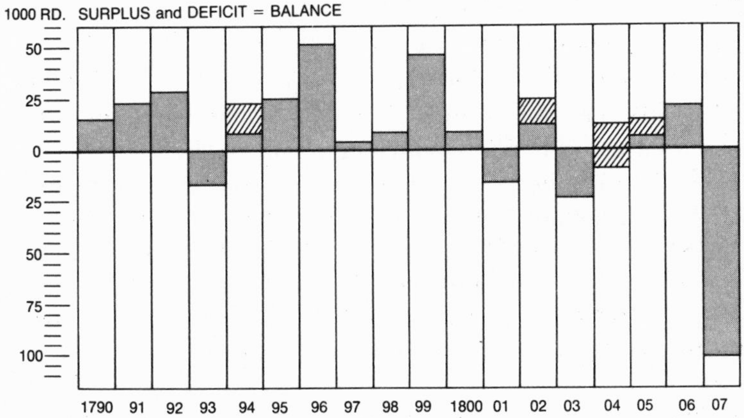

Hatched portions of the columns indicate how much of a year's surplus was used to make up for the deficit of the previous year. It took two years to recuperate the deficit of 1803.

Table 32.

	Income rigsdalers	Expenses rigsdalers	Balance* rigsdalers
1790	145,191	129,655	15,536
1791	136,836	113,256	23,580
1792	138,032	110,601	27,431
1793	89,254	106,629	- 17,375
1794	120,257	96,572	23,685
1795	130,160	106,161	23,999
1796	229,513	177,550	51,963
1797	154,561	150,401	4,160
1798	161,858	152,937	8,921
1799	214,796	168,354	46,442
1800	191,615	182,858	8,757
1801	182,642	198,035	- 15,393
1802	296,419	286,126	10,293
1803	120,352	141,363	- 21,011
1804	162,341	147,726	(14,615)
			- 6,396
1805	171,458	163,070	8,388
1806	205,287	182,751	22,536
1807	72,991	174,680	-101,689

* Sums listed in whole rigsdalers. Deficits were deducted from the surpluses of following years, except in 1804, where the 1803 deficit exceeded the surplus. Thus 1804 appears with a deficit, although the income for that year exceeded the expenses.

1803 again showed a rather large deficit, which it took two whole years to recuperate. Whaling as well as sealing had failed totally in 1803.

For this reason 1805 yielded only a modest revenue, and the profits from 1806 afforded but a transitory joy. The following year the war catastrophe occurred, closing off all channels of shipment of Greenlandic produce, on which the income of the Trade essentially depended.

In figures, as submitted in annual reports to the Commission, revenue and expenditures were as in Table 32. One thing was, however, the balance which appeared in the "Profits and Losses Account", on which payment to the Finanskollegium depended. In Table 33, these two balances are compared, and the distribution of the latter balance is indicated.

The differences between the two balances were presumably due to gains or losses on outstanding debts as well as superseded liabilities and interest payments. We cannot see from the accounts. In deficit years there was naturally no sum for distribution. Surpluses were, on the other hand, distributed with approximately two-thirds going to the Finanskollegium

Table 33.

	Balances		Distribution	
	Reports rigsdalers	"Profits and Losses Account" rigsdalers	Finans-kollegium rigsdalers	Personnel rigsdalers
1790	15,536	15,640	10,426	5,213
1791	23,580	22,794	15,196	7,598
1792	27,431	27,088	18,058	9,029
1793	- 17,375	-18,018	0	0
1794	23,685	6,159	4,106	2,053
1795	23,999	23,590	15,726	7,863
1796	51,963	53,250	25,500	17,750
1797	4,160	3,288	2,192	1,096
1798	8,921	10,814	7,209	3,604
1799	46,442	46,871	31,347	15,623
1800	8,757	9,055	6,519	2,535
1801	- 15,393	-16,216	0	0
1802	10,293	11,889	8,666	3,223
1803	- 21,011	-19,014	0	0
1804	- 6,396	- 5,044	0	0
1805	8,388	9,189	6,616	2,572
1806	22,536	21,053	15,836	5,216
1807	-101,689	-99,933	0	0

Sums listed in whole rigsdalers.

and one-third to the members of the Management and the "officers" of the Trade.

The "distribution" cannot, however, be sufficiently illustrated with these figures alone. The sum paid to the Finanskollegium was to pay interest at 2.5% per annum on the permanent fund, and it more or less corresponded to the annual subsidies given by the state.

The annual state subsidies included the so-called "Navigation Premium", at first 7500 rigsdalers, transferred from contributions of former times to the material maintenance of the Mission. Along with other state subsidies it was in 1791 reduced by 6%: i.e., to 7050 rigsdalers annually. In addition, the state subsidized the wages and office expenses of the inspectors, with 2000 rigsdalers per year up to 1794, 1500 rigsdalers for three years thereafter, and from 1798 on with 1000 rigsdalers annually. The state's share of the Trade's surplus from 1790 to 1807 was 177,297 rigsdalers, but when the navigation premiums and other subsidies were subtracted, the state made a net gain from the Trade of only 22,300 rigsdalers, as illustrated in Table 34. This sum covered only about one-fifth of the 2.5% interest on the 250,000 rigsdaler fund, representing the capital value assigned to the Royal Greenland Trade in 1776, recalculated in the evaluation of 1790.

Table 34.

1790-1807:	Rigsdalers	
State's share of surplus		177,297
Navigation premiums	127,350	
Subsidy for wages and office expenses of inspectors	26,500	
One equipment premium, 1790	1,117	
Total	154,967	-154,967
Net profit for 18 years		22,330

This shows that the state actually made no profit of importance from activities in Greenland, especially if we consider that all the expenses of the Missionskollegium for personnel and supplies, including books for teaching and services, were listed on the accounts of the Missionskollegium itself, and thus paid for by another state institution.

It was furthermore natural that the expenses and receipts of the Royal Greenland Trade in the main were only account entries, set off by other accounts. The same was true of the percentages credited to the Trade's personnel. Just as no wages were paid in money in Greenland, but were settled finally when the person in question returned to Europe, or were paid to his estate, on the basis of wage books; the percentage of the surplus were also credited to the employee's wage book. Receipts in these wage books were set off by expenditures: whatever the employee had purchased on credit from the trader of the district or ordered from Europe. The Royal Greenland Trade in Copenhagen often had to function as a kind of business manager for employees stationed in Greenland by making or receiving payments between the employees and private commission agents in Copenhagen or other persons, such as his family. Thus the Trade administered the economic transactions of private persons as a kind of service organ. In principle this service was maintained up to 1950.

The not very large amounts of cash which the Trade needed, it could draw as a kind of cash credit from Kurantbanken (later Speciebanken). Payments for auction sales of hides and oil were often made by bills of exchange, which were then discounted in the above-mentioned bank, or with bill brokers with whom the Trade had other accounts outstanding, in the form of assurance or purchase and merchandise.

The Royal Greenland Trade was thus a strange mixture of administrative organ, commission agency and trading enterprise. The commissions yielded only labour and expense, and the profits from trading were eaten up by the administration. A surplus from the Trade's activities was therefore only a surplus on paper, not in reality. It was a sublimated patriarchal enterprise worthy of the continued autocracy.

No private trading enterprise would at that time have been able to manage the deficits to which the Trade was at times exposed, especially not those of 1801, 1803 and 1804, without making huge inroads on its capital, and taking so much of it that it would have taken several years to re-establish confidence in the enterprise. At the time neither the accounts of the state itself nor those of state enterprises were published. Confidence in state enterprises thus depended on the limitless confidence everyone had in the state itself. It is therefore typical that the capital behind the Royal Greenland Trade in the form of a state fund remained untouched throughout these years, right up to the state bankruptcy of 1813. It was never even mortgaged.

Examples can be pointed out which illustrate how the Management of the Trade managed to avoid touching its capital fund or even mortgaging it. From 1789 on the Trade had a debt to the Iceland and Finmark Trade Liquidation Commission for certain goods it had taken over. In 1802, when the revenue from trading in Greenland was partly eaten up by the previous year's deficit, the Committee of 1788 had this debt converted into a permanent loan of 50,000 from the Realisation Committee. In the future, only a modest rate of interest was to be paid on the loan, as on the previous debt; but the loan itself was not to be amortized because it was permanent. This transaction did not improve the liquidity of the Trade, but on paper its annual expenses were well compensated for, especially in a year when the previous year's deficit weighed heavily on the debit side.

The deficit of 1807 was quite extraordinary, and had to be covered by a loan. That this extraordinary deficit became ordinary in subsequent years, because of the war situation, is another matter altogether.

The statements of accounts show, not surprisingly, that around 75% of the receipts of the Trade came from the sale of Greenlandic produce: hides, blubber and baleen, processed and refined by the Trade in Copenhagen.[2]

The necessary shipments of merchandise, provisions barrels, materials and equipment weighed heavily on the expense side, constituting an average of 47% of the Trade's expenses. A not inconsiderable amount of these expenses for materials ought actually to have been entered in a maintenance account. Most of these expenses returned as income the following year, however, since merchandise was traded for Greenlandic produce or purchased by the stationed Europeans and debited their wage books. Most of the provisions ought actually to have been listed on the wages account, as they were used for rations furnished as a part of wages.

It is surprising to see from the statements of accounts that expenses for wages were not a very important factor. This is because wages in Greenland were only listed by the amounts outstanding in the wage books. Wages in Copenhagen were of modest proportions: in the nine years from 1790 to 1798, they averaged 6,430 rigsdalers, or 5% of expenditures. Sums outstanding on the wage books in Greenland amounted to 7%.

Our picture of the wages account changes, however, when we follow calculations of total wage expenditures in Greenland. Wages given to stationed employees of the Trade included, in addition to a money wage, the so-called grocery money, "cask money", a percentage of profits, "writing-materials money", possible bounties for animals taken, and finally "maintenance" (excluding firewood, coal and candles). Grocery mony meant a sum allotted according to rank for the purchase of special individual kinds of provisions.

In certain years these wage expenses were calculated seperately in the previously-mentioned reports. Compared with the wage expenses of the corresponding years in Copenhagen, they give a more credible impression of actual wage expenses in proportion to total operating expenses. But this can only be done for the years 1790, 1791, 1792, 1797 and 1798, in which these calculations are listed. Of the total expenditures of these six years, wage expenditures then amount to almost 32%, which is surely closer to the true average. Expenses for merchandise, provisions, etc., should then be reduced correspondingly, but this is impossible for us to calculate.

Included in wages in Greenland was also free residence, if lodgers' quarters can be called a residence. This was a right not deducted from wages. As a rule this residence consisted of one room for each officer, including missionaries. Inferiors and labourers occupied, if they were unmarried, one large room together. If they were married, they had their own house, most of which were built in the Greenlandic manner. Firewood and candles were allotted to each room and were therefore not deducted from wages.

Wage expenditures are thus partially concealed in other entries. Sums are transferred from one account to another, from one entry to another, and partially back again. This entire accounts tangle was due to the subsistance economy which prevailed, and of necessity continued to prevail in Greenland itself. It made a survey of the economy of the Royal Greenland Trade difficult.

A further factor on the expenditures side was transport, which accounted for about 20% of total expenditures. On the other hand, assurance premiums were incredibly low, averaging just over 2% of total expenditures, or about 5% of the estimated value of the shipments. Assurance expenses for the individual ships was presumably included in transport expenses. Special accounts were kept for each individual ship in the ledger.

In Greenland a somewhat different view of transport and assurance expenditures prevailed. In 1792 Inspector A.M. Lund at Godthåb remarked dryly that it appeared from the "Profits and Losses Account" of the various localities that "the greatest expenditure of each locality consists in assurance, freight and the expenditures made in Denmark, where the Inspectors have less opportunity to limit them." These expenditures, according to him, were greater than those of the "necessary provisioning" of the country and "the shipping of goods for the continuation of the Trade." These expenses could not be restricted, as could those for materials and equipment. The latter entry would, however, according to Lund, be of little importance in comparison with all the rest.

This was probably the entries merry-go-round in operation again. It allowed unsuspected opportunities for widely differing interpretations of the accounts, and made the various accounts look different than they were in reality. The statements of accounts of both the individual districts and the Trade as a whole contained at least as many abstractions as entries. This was a reflection, on a much greater scale, of the same abstract accounting difficulties as in barter with the Greenlanders, as previously described in connection with settling accounts of merchandise sold in whales purchased. It was an abstract system, incomprehensible and inexplicable to the layman at the local level, difficult and full of traps for the traders and assistants, who usually had little knowledge of accountancy or reckoning, and who out of scrupulous accuracy made mistakes time after time. To the inspectors the statements of accounts were constant sources of indignation. Nor did the Management itself or the Committee acquire real insight into the yearly balance sheet, or any idea of where savings could be made. It was, however, necessary to rationalize and save after 1790, and expenses had thus to be reduced.

Naturally enough the largest expense listed on the yearly statements was pounced on, and this was the shipments of provisions and merchandise. Seen from a desk in Copenhagen, it had to be possible to make some saving here. But on the other side of the Atlantic it was quite realistic for A.M. Lund to claim that a reduction of these entries would be identical to cutting the life nerve of the Trade. But when he in turn thought that freight and assurance were the reasons for high costs, he was just as mistaken. Shipment was necessary, and it could not be saved on more than on provisions and merchandise. What was necessary was necessary, and it took up the necessary tonnage. It was indeed often complained that there was too little room in the ships. There were few opportunities for saving here; and on the other, much smaller expenditures, it was impossible to make any reductions worthy of mention. Table 33 also shows that in 10 of the 18 years from 1790 to 1807 expenses were under the average for the period, 154,929 rigsdalers. Of these ten years, eight were before 1799, when general price increases took place in Denmark. Only eight of the 18 years exceeded the average, and seven of these were from 1799 on.

Without anyone being aware of it, the entire accounts merry-go-round was a putting into practice of a principle laid down much later (in 1835 and 1925) that the Royal Greenland Trade, the administration and the Mission, should each be self-supporting economically. The evident desire to save must therefore have been the result of rationalism's general principle of thrift, the completely legitimate capitalistic principle that a trading enterprise should yield a profit, and not least, the deep fear of not being able to manage a crisis without the immediate support of the state, which it was the duty of the administration to limit to what was absolutely necessary.

It was obviously economically risky business to trade with and sail to distant and, with the state of technology at the time, dangerous coasts. Such risks demand a relatively large economic margin, which the Royal Greenland Trade never had. On the other hand, these operations could always rely on their state guarantee, but the Management was to be cautious in calling on this guarantee. Budgeting - if any was ever done, for none is revealed by the sources - had to be narrow, and operations demanded thrift bordering on miserliness.

Shipping

Shipping costs were necessary. Shipping was risky, so that the freight costs were expensive. They were also expensive because the Trade, by imposing high freight charges on private merchandise, attempted to rationalize the ships' capacity by limiting the amount of private merchancise so that its place could be taken by necessary shipments. In 1790 the Trade charged 20% of the value of what private persons had ordered shipped. This produced an outcry of indignation among Europeans stationed in Greenland, especially the missionaries. This measure had another objective, too: the Management was afraid that privately ordered goods were all too often being used for unauthorized, illicit trade, of which more later.

It appears that the Management attempted to rationalize shipping too hard. Ships often had to leave behind some of the Greenlandic produce from a district, especially when the fangst there that year had been good. The Management complained that its ships had to sail out with "unproductive" supplies, as if it would have been better for them to sail out half empty.

Shipping was dogged by bad luck and accidents. One of the former whaling ships which was to have been sold, wrecked in a hurricane-like storm in the port of Igdlutsiaq (Arveprinsens Ejland). The same year another ship wrecked in Disko Bugt.

After selling the many whaling vessels which had helped supply Greenland, the Trade was forced to make greater use of chartered ships. In the long run, this seemed too expensive. As early as 1795, Mørch, the trader at Julianehåb, had suggested building a special ship of at least 80 kommerce læster (160 registered tons), arguing that there were specially difficult navigation conditions around Julianehåb and Frederikshåb. The

Storis was mischievous, and transport was often made more expensive when ships had to spend the winter in Greenland, or when the cargo would have to be stored in one or other of the two colonies. After various ships had had to spend the winter, and ships and cargoes had been lost, a ketch was in 1807 stationed at Julianehåb to bring and take the shipments and produce of Julianehåb to and from Frederikshåb, behind the Storis.

Perhaps Mørch's suggestion provided the impulse for the decision in 1796 to purchase nine ships, all of which had previously been chartered in the Greenland traffic. The combined tonnage was 664 kommerce læster (1328 registered tons), and they cost 48,038 rigsdalers. After five of the ships had been improved, they were in 1799 estimated as being worth 51,284 rigsdalers.

Since the accounts of each ship were kept individually, the freight costs had to be listed as an expenditure on the statements of accounts. They therefore showed a rising tendency after 1796, partly because of the war situation, and partly because ships other than those owned by the Trade were chartered: the Trade could not manage without them.

For this reason, and because of several losses among the nine ships purchased in 1796, the Trade acquired seven other larger and smaller ships. But misfortune still dogged the Greenland traffic. In 1799, 1801, 1803 and 1804, shipwrecks were reported, two in 1799 and one in each of the other years. The shipments to Greenland had been lost, so that certain localities there had a shortage of merchandise, which again led to a decline in Greenlandic produce purchased. In certain years ships had to spend the winter in Greenland: in 1802 five were thus trapped in the Northern Inspectorate. Since this meant that Greenlandic produce did not come to Copenhagen, the Royal Greenland Trade had to take out a loan of 30,000 rigsdalers.

It was also difficult getting sufficient crews for the ships. The Danish Navy was manned by taking the most proficient sailors and fishermen. "Most of the seamen are removed from the trafic," the Management complained. These difficulties also applied to skilled craftsmen, so that the need for them at the colony seats could not be satisfied.

As a rule the ships used were not very large, from 15 to 139 kommerce læster (30 to 278 registered tons). This was due to two reasons. Smaller ships were easier to manoeuvre in the dangerous waters, and it was necessary to send a special ship to almost every district. The voyage took a couple of months as a rule, and each district could normally only be visited once a year. Only in Disko Bugt could two districts be supplied with the same ship. For some time Upernavik, when it was considered an annex of Godhavn, was supplied from Godhavn, either with the ship sent there, or with the "jagt" (a sail-carrying sloop) stationed there. It also happened that Julianehåb and Frederikshåb received their supplies with the same ship; or that the ships sent to both places were compelled to unload at either one or the other place, usually Frederikshåb, or spend the winter in Greenland. The shipment to one district was not as a rule so large that a large ship was necessary, but the Greenlandic produce sent to Copenhagen could well demand a larger capacity.

For reasons of economy it was important to keep the fleet as small as possible, thus explaining the Trade's complaints that the holds were occupied by too many private things. From this point of view, these complaints seem justified. The expenses of increasing the tonnage and its operations would be too great for the use the Trade usually had for it.

Shipping took place not only over the Atlantic, but also locally in Greenland: this was done using sloops (also used in whaling). They could take sails. In addition, there were also rowboats, called "Bergens Bisp"s.[3] Umiaks, owned or rented locally by the Trade, were often used.

The districts seldom had large vessels at their disposition. The ketch at Julianehåb has been mentioned. One "jagt" was stationed at Godhavn. A lightly armoured ship, the "Dorothea", was sent to the Inspector in 1792 for use against foreign whalers. It wrecked ignominiously the next year and was not replaced. The Inspector had to manage with the "jagt". Communications between the various districts, and between them and the Inspector, usually took place by means of kayaks.

Thus both local shipping and the Atlantic traffic contributed to delimiting the individual districts and isolating them from one another, as if each represented its own economic unit.

The Districts

After 1776 no further colonies were set up, and thus no more districts. The activity of the Trade was thus not expansive, but rather signified an intensification of operations. The presence of the Royal Greenland Trade in West Greenland contributed to a slow process of integration, which made its activity continually more necessary and indispensable. There was generally a peaceful growth internally, with few external conflicts.

One single district caused special trouble. The conditions at and around Upernavik had from its very beginning in 1771 been difficult to manage. The "expenses" of operations here were out of proportion to the revenue yielded. Among these "expenses" were the desperate conditions

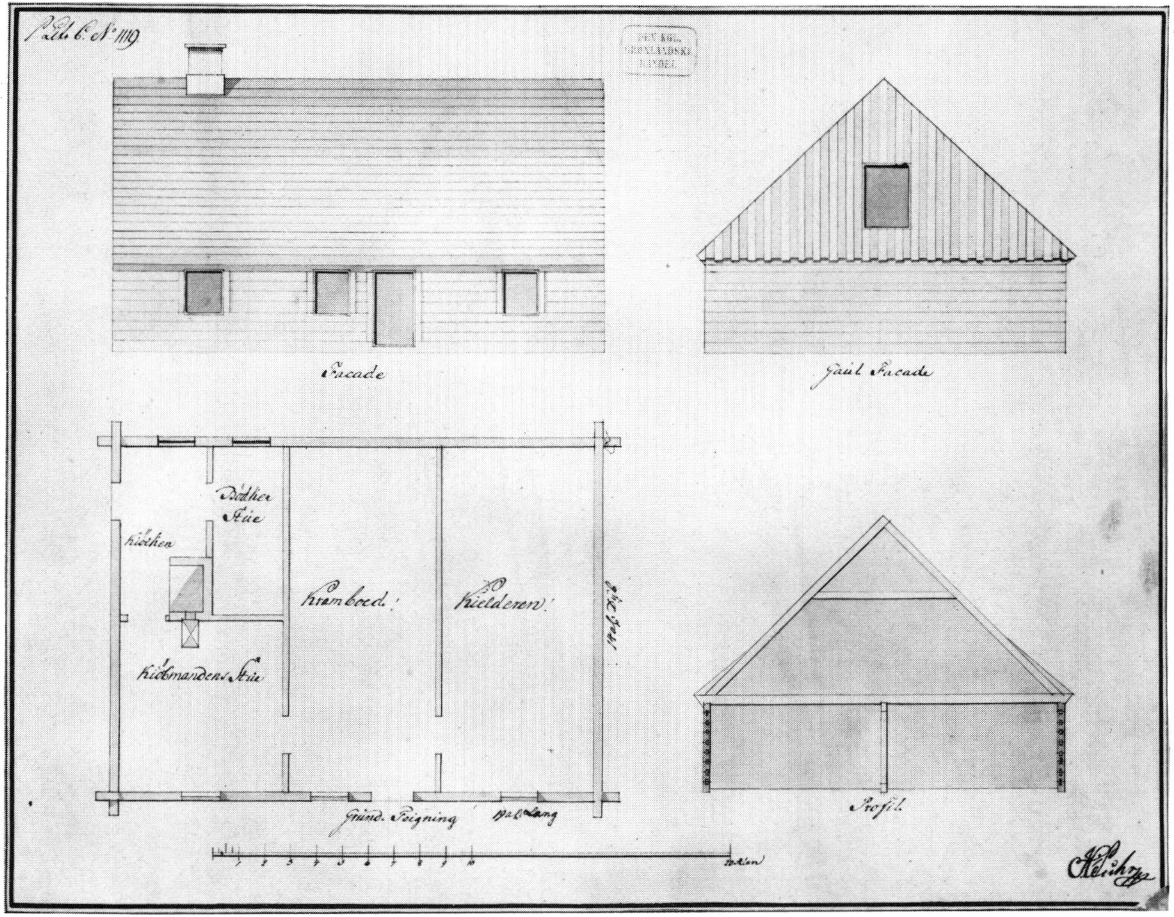

Architectural drawing of "a shop" ("*Krambod*") and "a cooper's room" ("*Bødker Stue*"). The other rooms are: the kitchen ("*Kiøkken*") with the open fireplace, the trader's room ("*Kiøbmandens Stue*") with an iron stove. Two-thirds of the house consists of the shop, with the main door, and the so-called cellar ("*Kielderen*"), which was not in the basement but on the same level as the entire house. It is perhaps this type of house which can be seen in plate XII, the house behind the flagpole with a fence around it. The drawing is signed by the architect *H. Suhr* who also signed the house drawings of 1777 (plate III). The houses were built as designed with local amendments; the design is inverted in Umánaq and a porch has been added.

(Library of the Royal Academy of Fine Arts, Copenhagen, Collection of Architectural Drawings, A 8515 e; much reduced)

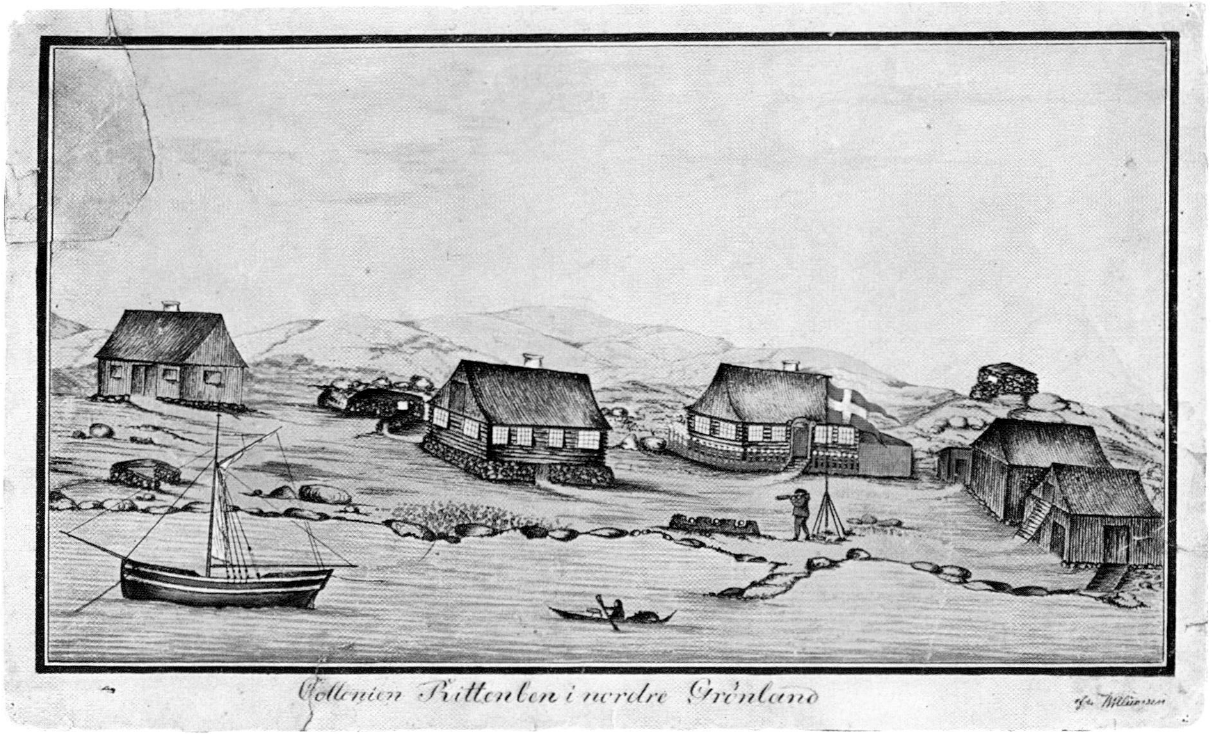

"The Colony Ritenbenk in Northern Greenland"
Water-colour by the carpenter *Hans Willumsen,* wrongly dated 1795 (see plate VI). Some of the buildings may have been there in the 1790s, cf. text to plate XI.

(Original in private possession)

for the local Europeans, who had difficulty dealing with the climate. One trader after the other died. As a rule the reason for death was scurvy with complications. Conditions here exhausted the spirits of the Europeans.

In 1786 things really went bad. On 15 February an assistant died who was to have been replaced the previous autumn, but his replacement could not reach the locality. On 24 February, an elderly pensioned assistant "in troubled thoughts drowned himself." On 15 March the trader was ill in bed, with scurvy and a "stomach ache", but he survived. An assistant was also suffering from this deficiency disease. On 23 March the trader at Umánaq reported that he had received reports of these cases of death and illness, and that the skipper whose ship was spending the winter at Upernavik had also been ill, and that two of his crew were dead. On 6 June the cooper hanged himself in an attack of depression.

It was, however, not only Europeans who did not thrive at Upernavik. "The conditions of the Greenlanders here as well as farther north are as is known very, very poor," reported the new trader in 1788. He must have heard rumours that the Management contemplated closing the colony down. He therefore proposed moving it a good deal farther south. Since some of the inhabitants were immigrants from Umánaq, the trader did not think it would be difficult to get them to move along. Several had already said they were willing. If they would not move, the trader feared that "the entire stretch from Umánaq up here in the north would be left to English and Dutch illicit traders who would soon show up." These considerations must have entered into the discussions of the Management; they are quoted in its representation to the Commission.

The Missionskollegium referred to a report from the missionary R.F. Lassen, who in July 1788 had "given the most frightful description of the famine experienced at this colony, and fully established that a missionary is quite unnecessary here." In his letter the missionary had reported one more case of death due to scurvy: a young assistant recently assigned to Greenland.

The Missionskollegium was obliged to transfer the missionary, also because he had not, as promised, "been furnished the accommodations about which we have corresponded for so long with the Management". There had been a tug-of-war about this from the very establishment of the colony; the expenses of the organization and operation of this colony were to be as small as possible.

The conclusion that a missionary was quite unnecessary here was somewhat drastic. At least it was not a conclusion one could immediately draw from R.F. Lassen's letter. He had only observed that he was in many respects not the right person for the vocation of missionary at Upernavik. It needed quite a different, strong personality, with a considerable mastery of the Greenlandic language. This is quite different from the defeatist attitude of the Missionskollegium; the shocked gentlemen of this body had no one sufficiently qualified to station at this dangerous post with its, to say the least, unacceptable conditions.

In 1790 Upernavik was closed as a colony. But it soon turned out that the hopes of the trader that the former inhabitants of Umânaq would move south, were not fulfilled. The district was, as he had feared, "left to English and Dutch illicit traders." This led the inspector to begin gradually to send ships there, now from Godhavn, and in 1796 the Management finally approved this traffic, which proved to be profitable. It is said that the Greenlandic inhabitants in the district were tired of being cheated by the foreign illicit traders, and wanted to have a permanent trader at Upernavik again. From 1796 on a trusted assistant was stationed there, under control every year from Godhavn. As late as 1799 the administration had not yet decided to reestablish Upernavik as a colony, but had plans of raising the just as undesirable locality of Nûgssuaq to the status of colony, with Upernavik as a kind of trading post. But this also came to nothing, so that Upernavik continued to be trafficked from Godhavn.

In the 1770's the netting of beluga was attempted at a more southern locality called Prøven. In 1800 the assistant at Upernavik set up a netting experiment here, which was approved by the inspector the following year. Some whaling was also carried on from here; at least some baleen and blubber was purchased, perhaps from stranded whales.

Finally in 1805 Upernavik was again made a colony, but in subsequent years it suffered from war conditions and was again closed. Nor could Prøven make it through this period untouched.

This uncertainty in the farthest north also duplicated farther south. It was at least partly due to the conflict which still existed between the Greenlandic settlement tradition and the various expectations of the Royal Greenland Trade. Greenlandic settlement was often determined by changes in the migratory habits of the fangst animals or in their ecological conditions. Thus an installation which seemed promising when planned could turn out to be quite disappointing shortly afterwards.

This is what happened in Egedesminde District, which never yielded the profit that had been hoped for. The colony seat itself was considered "an unproductive place". Although there were good fangst grounds at other places in the district, many Greenlanders moved to the colony seat. A trader thought in 1788 that the fact that the missionary resided here contributed to this; he ought to travel about a good deal more. But he later belied his own words by stressing how impossible it was for him to get around in his district, especially its southern part. How the missionary was then to do it, he did not say.

The trader proposed at the same time, from a trading point of view, that a trading post be established in the south of the district, and mentioned especially Rifkol or Umânaq Island west of the present Agto. Here along the coast the English often landed in the spring, before the Egedesminde trader could reach it. Thus a good deal of produce went to foreigners, including sealskins and fox hides, blubber and baleen, presumably from stranded whales. Many whales were stranded on the coast; especially when the vestis froze up. If the foreigners could be forestalled by establishing a more or less permanent place for buying and selling, this would be to the advantage of both the Trade and the Greenlanders. For the latter it would mean a better supply of necessary items and assistance in times of need. It would also be possible to a greater extent to give them a more short-term credit.

For several years this proposal was discussed back and forth. When M.N. Myhlenphort was to take over the position of trader at Egedesminde in 1791, he laid down as a condition that a trading post would not be set up at Rifkol right away. His reason for this was strange: during the time of former traders, this part of the coast had been visited regularly; and purchases had been made in time and supplies had been brought. It was only during the time of the last two traders that this had not been done. But he would undertake that it would be done during his period in office. So "it cannot be to the advantage of the Trade to set up any establishment at the previously mentioned place, but rather to its disadvantage: for experience has taught us that where Danes live, the Greenlanders become totally corrupted, and it is fortunate if they do not completely degenerate from their native fangst and work."

This was undeniably no positive evaluation of the colonisation effort of the Trade. Inspector B.J. Schultz, who at that time was relatively new in Greenland, must have been of more or less the same opinion, although his attitude toward the establishment of a trading post at Rifkol was opposed to that of Myhlenphort. To the Management he expressed the desire to have built a reasonably good house at the contemplated trading post, because he would like to see the missionary settle away from Egedesminde Colony. "Experience shows that the missionary, if he is what he should be, can do more with the Greenlanders than the trader can with his merchandise."

Then Inspector Schultz referred to missionary P. Cappelen and his netting activity, where the Greenlandic inhabitants could only be persuaded to move to the good fangst grounds by having the missionary move along with them. It was evidently the Inspector's opinion that the missionary's cultural influence on the inhabitants was more important than whether the Trade could acquire more produce. In his letter he regretted that there were so many unbaptized Greenlanders in Egedesminde District, and that blood vendettas were haunting the population. Besides, very few Greenlanders resided permanently at the colony seat. He wanted, however, to let the matter of the trading post wait until he had inspected conditions personally.

The matter had been discussed orally between Inspector Schultz and Myhlenphort. Apparently the latter had unenthusiastically undertaken to improvise a provisional attempt. With hardly concealed satisfaction, Myhlenphort reported that all the families but one had moved away from Rifkol in August. In the same breath he suggested setting up a trading post at another locality: Akúnâq, east of Egedesminde. Here the Greenlanders had their winter houses standing. It was more reasonable, he thought, to establish a provisional trading post where they were than to try to get them to move elsewhere.

In November 1791, Myhlenphort reported, however: "The experiment is now standing on the island of Sautok, about one mile north-west of Rifkol." It consisted of a house built in Greenlandic style, containing stores of provisions, materials, and merchandise, as well as accommodations for an "inferior assistant", two stationed labourers, "and the Greenlanders who are spending this winter at Sautok." He had got three fanger families from the vicinity to settle there. But he did not have high hopes of the success of this attempt: The local fangst opportunities had been declared too poor.

For some years, however, this attempt seemed to develop relatively favourably, so a wooden house was erected. According to Myhlenphort's later testimony, the favourable development was due to the good relations between the first "deputy-assistant and the local population there and in the vicinity. In 1794 or 1795 this deserving man was replaced with another, less successful person; added to this, a number of bad fangst years followed. By 1797 all the Greenlanders had moved away; some to Egedesminde, others to Christianshåb District.

This situation led Myhlenphort to evaluate the entire Rifkol experiment in 1798. In addition to the previously mentioned personnel change and the accidentally simultaneous years of poor fangst, he blamed the development on the missionary. In the middle of the best fangst season, he or the catechist would assemble the fangers of the vicinity and their families at Rifkol to instruct them. In a later letter, intended as a partial explanation of the poor yield of Egedesminde District as a whole, he expressed his opinion thus:

"An orthodox missionary demands of the Greenlanders that they, whenever he thinks it proper, shall leave the most remote places in the district, by dog sled in winter and by umiak or other vessel in the spring, to be baptized, etc., etc. The officers of the Trade, on the contrary, demand that the Greenlanders, during the best seasons of the year, remain at their fangst, and in the summer when they have nothing to do (sic!) visit the missionary or let him visit them. This leads to the Greenlanders finally not knowing whether to follow the missionary's or the officer's requests. The result is this: that the Greenlanders, who consider themselves a free people, move away from the good fangst grounds in order to avoid such circumstances, and it happens quite often that Greenlanders grow indifferent toward their fangst when they are always reading their ABC book." At the time this was written this was not the case, because the missionary, reasonably enough, was willing to compromise. But the previous missionary had been zealous in his vocation, Myhlenphort had to admit. The result of his zeal was the regrettable conflicts mentioned above, with both parties sticking stubbornly to their guns while the third party, the Greenlanders, wisely kept at a distance.

Myhlenphort's opinion of the missionary's influence was evidently opposed to Inspector Schultz' previously quoted tribute to the favourable effect of a missionary. They both must have had the same idea, after all, but only expressed it differently. Schultz presupposed that a missionary "is what he should be." Myhlenphort expressed it more concretely: at the present time, "the missionary in Disko Bugt not only considers the good of the Mission, but also has a view to the advantage of the Trade. He is willing to compromise, and this is also the best for the Mission in Greenland." Ignoring the slightly threatening tone of the final remark, this was an expression of the traditional conflict between trader and missionary. This discussion was futile at the time: The Rifkol experiment had in fact been closed since 1797. The story has been told in such detail here because the development of this attempt can be taken as a typical example of the many, long, detailed and conflicting discussions and solutions of problems which accompanied the establishment of a new trading station, even one of a less important nature. The planners always had to take an important consideration into account: they had to save, and new installations had to be made as cheaply as possible. The traditional fangst cycle and migration, the desires of the Trade and the demands of the Mission clashed constantly. Rifkol was a typical example of all this.

The installation of trading posts in the Southern Inspectorate was somewhat more successful. Purchasing from Julianehåb's South District had long been a problem. From 1778, the establishment of a trading post at Nanortalik was discussed, and it continued to be discussed for almost twenty years.[4] Finally on 15 August 1787 it was actually established, with a "mixture", David Kleist, as its first chief. The following year Johan Chr. Mørch, the trader, reported that 112 casks of seal blubber, over two tubs of shark liver, 1047 sealskins (not including skins for boats and kamik boot soles), 164 fox hides of various kinds, one large bear skin, one small bear skin, and several pieces of bear skin had been purchased. This was a good start.

"Because of a frightfully stormy winter, such fortune was certainly not expected, but the experience of the chief in dealing with Greenlanders and quick tongues, which have had their desired effect, have undoubtedly borne fruit, and give me justified hopes for the future," wrote Mørch in 1798. He thus gave David Kleist most of the honour for the success. Of the "virtue" of these southernmost Greenlanders, Mørch stated that "they stick to the trader so strictly with their produce that the missionary could hardly get three skins for a coat when he was there with me in the spring." The attachment toward authority had been transferred to David Kleist. This is one of the few examples from this period of the development of new *Greenlandic* persons of authority.

Johan Chr. Mørch wanted to follow up at Lichtenau the good fortune of Nanortalik. It was hard to get in to Lichtenau to pick up the blubber which could be purchased in time. A purchasing station nearer the coast would be advantageous, he thought. This resulted in a provisional post at the place which much later was called Sydprøven. Whether or not this attempt was rewarded with the same good fortune as at Nanortalik, the sources do not reveal during the period under consideration.

If there was a district – in addition to Julianehåb – where trading posts were necessary, it was Frederikshåb. Both of these districts covered a relatively long stretch of coast, and expeditions were greatly restricted by storis and stormy weather. What had always been special about Frederikshåb was that only a few Greenlanders had taken up permanent residence at the colony seat itself. It was difficult to visit the most southern areas of the district, simply because expeditions could not reach them in time with the few small coastal vessels of the period. The only coastal vessel possessed by Frederikshåb was one single rowboat.

It therefore turned out to be a laborious affair when it was finally decided - again after many long discussions - to set up a southern trading post on Putugoq Island at Arsuk Fjord. This was not accomplished until 1805. The problem was to transport from the colony seat to the site of the future trading post materials for the house which was to be built. This took place in umiaks, and transports had to be arranged in succession. An epidemic at the colony seat prevented a shipment from leaving there in the early summer, but finally in late September the future local manager Johan Berglund left with merchandise, his family and movable property. He was a deserving carpenter and foreman, married to a Greenlander. Of course he had not taken along enough construction material, so that neither his residence nor the blubber house could be completed. He spent the winter in a Greenlandic peat house, where the rain poured through the roof. This was the more unfortunate, as the weather most of the autumn was "constant rain and storm." "I have therefore great difficulty in salvaging the merchandise of the Trade as well as my own provisions," he wrote in his diary. Not much produce was purchased, because very little fangst took place. In subsequent years the advantages of this installation seemed difficult to discern.

This entire installation activity, of which these trading posts are examples, was due to the settlement policy which the Royal Greenland Trade attempted to impose. It was opposed, as we have seen, to the most fervent wishes of the Mission. But in a period in which the Mission was considerably weakened administratively, as we shall see later, there was correspondingly less possibility of conflict between the Mission and the Trade. On the issue of dispersal from overpopulated localities, we have seen that open conflict resulted with the Moravian Brethren. Perhaps the provisional establishment of Sydprøven should be seen in the context of Johan Chr. Mørch's previous criticism of the concentration of population at Lichtenau, only six kilometres north-east of Sydprøven, but considerably more isolated. Here too the Moravian Brethren had refused to disperse their members. This they continued to do, and this may be the reason why Sydprøven was no immediate success.

The principle of the Trade's settlement policy was that the Greenlandic fangers should live dispersed, when this was good for the fangst, and not concentrate in the colony seats. If this principle were to be follwed, the Trade would have to divide the districts into smaller units, with the consequent establishment of trading posts.

This consequence was actually a compromise between the difficulties of making expeditions and centralization by districts. The Greenlandic inhabitants were in a threefold dilemma, hovering between their relation to the Mission, their need for the Trade in several respects, and their traditional interests, material and spiritual.

Illicit Trade

The installation of trading posts was also partly determined by the desire to stop illicit trading, or at least to forestall this so-called illegal trade. The struggle against "these disorders" was likewise dictated by the attempts of the Royal Greenland Trade to consolidate its position on the west coast of Greenland. The more forcibly demands for operational savings were made, the more scrupulous the Management was about illicit trade. Even the tiniest trifle could involve extreme retaliation.

When in 1781 a skipper asked for clemency in not prosecuting him for illicit trade, the Management thought that on the one hand compassion was justified, but "on the other hand illicit trade is an evil aspect of the Greenland trade which deserves the greatest attention. It is an evil which creeps up slowly in many diverse ways and, unnoticed, devours the Trade. Seldom or never will such good evidence be available that the criminal will be able to find nothing in excuse;" and recommended against clemency in deference to the preventive example of full punishment. As far as we know clemency was nevertheless extended in this case of illicit trade.

The Management itself admitted that it seldom had real evidence that illicit trade had taken place. It was perhaps therefore, too, that they took this abuse so seriously.

"National" illicit trade apparently took two forms. The more serious was that organized by skippers and crews of ships. They would surreptitiously purchase various produce from Greenlanders as well as stationed Europeans and transport it across the Atlantic without entering it on the bill of lading. These goods were presumably sold when calling at Norwegian ports on the return voyage. It was really astonishingly often that skippers found it necessary to call at one or another Norwegian port on their way back to Denmark. It was only once revealed that a skipper, with the connivance of a night watchman, had unloaded illicitly purchased produce at the Trade's dock in Copenhagen.

The other form of illicit trade was less important, but it led to zealous watchfulness on the part of the inspectors and trading officers. This was the petty barter which took place on a private basis between Greenlanders and Europeans stationed in Greenland. The Europeans usually bartered for certain services, fresh provisions, skins for clothes and boots, down and other necessities which could be acquired in Greenland. When such cases were discovered and prosecuted with a zeal bordering on pettiness, they more led to local friction between the superior officers of the Trade and the other Europeans than they restricted this traffic or even promoted the interests of the Trade.

At times, especially when the opportunity offered as, for example, when taking inventory of an estate, veritable searches were conducted of the effects of stationed Europeans in order to find, if possible, "unauthorized goods". If anything suspicious was found, the apparatus would be put into action. Olrik, the trader at Sukkertoppen, found "unauthorized goods" in the possession of the colony crew as the result of such a raid. This he reported to the Inspector, who imposed substantial fines on the offenders. On the same occasion the trader had inquired whether he was even authorized to conduct such searches. In other words, he had felt it an encumbrance to function as a kind of policeman in this matter. The Inspector confirmed, however, his authorization to conduct searches "of the European crew or of Greenlanders who are of the same class, when you have reason to suspect that they have carried on illegal trade with Greenlanders," but added "that you are not authorized to conduct inquisitorial searches of Greenlandic women for Greenlandic products, whether they are in the service of a European or of their countrymen."

This inspectorial interpretation is in several respects illustrative of the transitional situation of the West Greenlandic society at the time. In the first place, it established that a group of Greenlanders had been formed "of the same class' as "the European crew". By this Inspector Myhlenphort meant that these Greenlanders, employed by the Trade, were subject to the regulations of the Order of 1782. They were thus to acquire whatever they needed of monopoly produce either through fangst or by buying it from the trader.

In the second place, Inspector Myhlenphort thus ranked these Greenlanders juridically on an equal footing with stationed Europeans - in this respect. In other respects the Order - as previously mentioned - gave these Greenlanders, usually half-breeds, a special position, although they were on the whole juridically considered as Greenlanders while in Greenland.

In the third place, Myhlenphort clearly maintained the right of the ordinary Greenlander to the monopoly produce he possessed before selling it, which from a European point of view was a matter of course. The ordinary Greenlander was also free to barter for products which he could not acquire through fangst. It was therefore unwarranted to search or confiscate monopoly products in the possession of a Greenlander, even if this Greenlander was a servant of someone who was not allowed to have them in his possession.

This again, in the fourth place, testifies to the legal balance it was necessary to keep under such circumstances. There was no limit to how much monopoly produce a Greenlandic servant might possess. This was an unplugable loophole for anyone who wanted to take advantage of it. The arm of the law could not interfere until such produce was used for "unauthorized trade", to acquire merchandise one was otherwise not allowed to obtain; this was mostly carried on with ships' crews, both those of the Trade and foreigners. In this case it was only Europeans and those of the same class who could be held responsible, ignoring the case of foreigners.

Illicit trading was a violation of the decree of 18 March 1776. It was not the bartering Greenlander, who violated the decree, but rather the European, whether stationed in Greenland, a member of a ship's crew, or a foreigner, who *purchased* monopoly produce from the local inhabitants. There was no authority for retaliation against the Greenlandic party to illicit trade.

This was in accordance with the attitude of the inspectors to the visits of local Greenlanders to foreign ships. There was consistency in the general rule that Danish laws and provisions did not apply to Greenlanders.[5] Although the Greenlanders were considered subjects of His Danish-Norwegian Majesty, the West Greenland society was not automatically subject to the laws of the realms, but only to the constitution under the autocratic King. As we shall see later, this principle was maintained out of consideration for the special nature of the Greenlandic society and culture within the realms.

There was no question of "unauthorized trade" when the Trade through its representatives in Greenland sold monopoly produce to foreign skippers, although it might appear to the Greenlanders that the Trade personnel was here doing something they were not allowed to do. We must remember that the ordinary Greenlander identified the Trade with the stationed Europeans; the abstraction of the Royal Greenland Trade as an institution was quite vague, if it at all existed in the consciousness of the Greenlanders of the time. The Management, as well as the inspectors and traders, seem to have realized this. In any case, the relation of the Trade to the problem of illicit trade became somewhat ambivalent as it gradually became the custom to sell produce which in Copenhagen was considered more or less unsellable to the skippers of foreign whalers in return for articles much needed locally by the Trade, and which were thus acquired cheaper. This factor, along with the gradually more relaxed relationships with the English, led the Management, toward the end of the period we are dealing with here, deliberately to make light of foreign "illicit trade". The situation was thus eased considerably.

Inspector Schwabe had already made clear that the best countermeasure to foreign illicit trade was to sell the Greenlanders the goods they wanted more cheaply than they could get them from the English, and preferably also in better quality. This suggestion resulted in a slowly expanding selection of merchandise, including more "useless" things. But distilled spirits were still quite out of the question; this drink, along with coffee gradually became the most demanded item from foreign ships. Coffee was also in demand in another way, which will be dealt with later.

The Management attempted, in vain, to take measures to combat illicit trade, which continued, seemingly undaunted. In 1806, Inspector P.H. Motzfeldt at Godhavn regretted that all his efforts and those of others had not borne fruit, when the Management again complained that illicit trade "has increased quite considerably in recent times." He was well aware that "a number of sealskins, as previously, have been sold by the Greenlanders to unauthorized persons, partly in order to get coffee and designed English stoneware, and partly because our prices, not proportionally but for some sorts, are so low that Greenlanders have told me right out that they would not sell their skins to the Trade for that price. I knew that, but that this is likewise the case with either blubber or other products is quite contrary to my hopes and expectations."

In other words, Motzfeldt made use of the comments of the Management on the rise in illicit trade to complain to the same Management that purchase prices for sealskins were too low and not sufficiently differentiated. This was according to him an important reason for the existence of illicit trade. His remarks were thus more an element in the discussion of changes in purchase prices than an exposition of ways to prevent illicit trade. Finally he pointed out to the Management that it was by no means profitable to make more drastic searches in ships, in which the previously loaded cargo had to be unloaded in order to make a more thorough check, perhaps to no avail. All in all Motzfeldt's letter gives the impression of a very diplomatic admonition to stop all this talk of illicit trade.

Those responsible in Greenland did all that the Management could reasonably demand of them to restrict illicit trade in their localities. This appears from the previously mentioned example of the missionary being unable to get a few skins at Nanortalik, from Motzfeldt's letter just quoted, and from various other examples in letters and diaries. "I put out four nets today, which I had to do to catch, if possible, one seal to feed my small puppies, for it is not possible for the assistant or anyone else to get any from the Greenlanders, as they do not dare sell it to us for fear of the trader." This was written by the assistant at Umánaq in 1801; his trader must have been on the watch for illicit trade down to the last detail. This is just one example among many others.

The prohibition against foreigners and private persons acquiring monopoly produce was being turned in Greenlandic consciousness into a prohibition against their selling it to such persons. This was probably supported by the practice of the various traders. Although this can by no means be proven, it would seem that the authority of the trader had grown to such an extent over the decades that the local inhabitants felt in one way or another dependent on him and actually subject to his discretion. When illicit trade was discovered, the Greenlander concerned was in one way or another made to feel guilty, although there was no authorization for this in the provisions. This is also related to the previously mentioned "district ties" of the Greenlandic population: that traders considered it illoyal to purchase produce from Greenlanders who belonged to another district.

It can be added that here again we are probably dealing with an identification of the trader with the Royal Greenland Trade and vice versa. Greenlanders' ideas of the difference between employees of the Mission and those of the Trade, as well as the difference between both of these and foreigners, were probably quite vague. It is an open question whether the ordinary Greenlander was fully aware of these differences. In his phenomenative mentality they probably appeared as parallel, equal phenomena in function. Their individual functions had nothing to do with one another in the Greenlandic consciousness. To distinguish between who violated an abstract prohibition of which they had only a vague perception, and to whom this prohibition did not apply, was quite outside their train of thought. They only saw that the authority, the trader, became angry, and it was advisable to avoid this.

These sound like undocumented insinuations; they should not be considered as such, but rather as attempts to penetrate behind the historical sources and through special instances find a possible explanation of these more general relationships.

One thing is certain, however: dependence on the trader increased, as well as on the merchandise shipped to Greenland – as far as the Greenlanders could see – on his orders and quite according to his whim.

"As long as you have only poor merchandise to sell us, we will trade with those who give us good merchandise," said a prominent fanger at Hunde Ejland in 1783. By "those" he meant the Dutch and English. The trader had discovered this illicit trade and made use of the opportunity to admonish the Management that the only way to stop it was to ship proper merchandise. This trader had seen the quality and attractive appearance of the foreign merchandise: tin boxes with gilded edges, mirrors, baskets, scissors and scarves; but he had expressed his displeasure with this trade. One of the other fangers then said, "When you give us just as good merchandise, then we will only trade with you."

This is another example of the local trader being held responsible for the quality of merchandise and its being shipped. The Greenlander considered himself free to chose, and we must emphasize that the trader was apparently of the same opinion. Since the previously mentioned examples of a possible change in Greenlandic consciousness date from late in this period, there is some indication that the shift took place during the period, and possibly also that there was a difference in attitude between Greenlanders of the whaling districts and those who lived more isolated from contact with foreigners. One thing is certain, however: the demand for good merchandise was not new. In the competition with the Dutch, and later the English, this was the constantly repeated request of the employees of the Trade in Greenland.

Supplies

Supplies fell into two categories: the so-called *provisions,* including *groceries;* and *sales merchandise,* including *materials. Provisions* were generally reserved for stationed Europeans, as part of their wages, or for the Greenlanders who were employed by the Trade or the Mission. This category also included relief provisions for the Greenlandic inhabitants in periods of famine. The so-called "Greenlander provisions", which at the beginning of our period were shipped especially for this purpose, were, as we have seen, abandoned from 1804 on. *Groceries* were the special types of provisions, such as spices, preserved things, coffee, tea, wine and distilled spirits, etc., which the stationed Europeans had the right to purchase, to a certain limited extent, on account: i.e., have debited their wage books.

Sales merchandise included the types of merchandise which were used in barter with the Greenlandic inhabitants. We have already seen that the General Schedule of 1783 divided this merchandise into three groups according to their degree of necessity or usefulness, but that this division was abandoned from 1796 on. We shall therefore in the following ignore this division as the strangely clumsy system it was even in its time.

Materials actually formed a category in themselves; shipments of materials were to satisfy the needs of the colony districts in connection with the production carried on by the colony crew, modest new installations and the maintenance of existing installations and boats. They were also to satisfy the needs of the Greenlandic inhabitants for wood, hardware and tools.

All these articles were ordered by the trader according to quite definite rules, taking the consumption of the previous year into consideration. The small capacity of the ships used often led to priority being given to certain quantities or certain types of commodities when shipment was made from Copenhagen. The result of this was that at times a district could be out of entire categories of goods ordered, or be supplied with smaller quantities than desired. The quality of the goods shipped did not always correspond to what was ordered. The final decision on what to ship and how much of it rested with the Royal Greenland Trade in Copenhagen, which, extensively considering the ever-present attempts to save, had a close eye to what could be purchased in the largest quantities at the lowest prices. Certain mercantilistic methods were still practiced: the Trade attempted as far as possible to buy Danish, Norwegian, Icelandic or Faroese products, and when necessary also things from the duchies Slesvig and Holstein which played their part in the economy of the monarchy.

The elevation of spirits through the enjoyment of material goods, however, modest as they might seem, was actually necessary for the emotional welfare of the Europeans in Greenland. When this elevation was prevented, they quickly approached the limits of their endurance. What was even worse for many was that their best intentions in their work were restricted by incomprehensible tight-fistedness and lack of understanding in Copenhagen. Complaints about all kinds of supplies were the order of the day, considering that in this period, shipments were sent but once a year.

Protests were made about supplies from here and there, from traders, inspectors and missionaries. Towards merchandise of mediocre quality the inhabitants reacted, as we have seen, in their own way. The Greenlanders of Julianehåb reacted to a poor quality of tobacco according to the testimony of the trader Mørch: "Tobacco is quite an important item in Greenland; the thoughts of the simple Greenlander reach no further than to the person who directly sells him the tobacco; this person becomes, if he is not fortunate enough to be able to convince him of his innocence with his own mouth, despised, and the Trade loses in more than one respect."

Supplies of provisions were absolutely necessary; the Europeans could not manage without them. This appears from a complaint of the trader C.C. Dalager about some more or less spoiled beef which in 1794 had been shipped to Klokkerhuk. He had heard that "when the ships were to be sent no meat could be got anywhere for supplying this country, but finally this rejected meat was got from Sweden. When it came to the Greenland Trade, more than ten loads were rejected and thrown in the harbour, but people were hired to smell at some of it. The worst was thrown away and what had less smell was accepted and sent to this country. It follows that even if I had known that this beef had been spoiled, it could not have been returned, as I had no other. However disgusting it may be, its smell has been diminished by fresh water, and it has so far been eaten by my people and the others. So the little which will perhaps be left over at the end of the trade year will only be a little and perhaps a sample for the public."

The salt meat shipped was not quite that bad every year, and even that year at Klokkerhuk there were no deaths from meat poisoning. Although we can count on a good deal of exaggeration in the account of C.C. Dalager, there remains enough truth to illustrate how bad supplies of provisions could be. And it was impossible to get replacement for the supplies which had to be returned or thrown away. It was not a perfect enjoyment to eat the Trade's provisions.

The savings attempts of the Trade and its apparently miserly attitude toward supplies was partly determined by the warehouse capacity available in Greenland. When in 1787 Inspector Wille ordered the traders of the Northern Inspectorate to order supplies of all types of provisions for two years, as the practice, not always carried out, had been; C.C. Dalager at Klokkerhuk ordered three years' supply of baked bread and two years' supplies of all other types of provisions. The Commission reacted by saying that such huge orders from all the colonies would "have the result that more or larger buildings will be necessary in the colonies."

Due to this - and various complaints that the ships were poorly supplied and often had to draw supplies from the colonies - the Commission decided in 1790 that it should be "an unalterable rule for the future that the northern colonies, with the exception of Umánaq, shall upon the departure of the ships in autumn always be supplied with provisions for one and one-half years, determined by the ration schedule and the estimated population at each colony, taking in addition consideration of the support of the Greenlanders as in the previous year. The southern colonies and Umánaq shall have provisions for two years."

In the case of an acute shortage at one locality, other places would have to help. This was a practice which developed out of necessity. As such situations could arise during the course of the year, it was not possible to replace what one place had given to another until the following year, for which it had already been ordered by virtue of the prevailing rules.

If we take a look at what kind of provisions were shipped, we do not get the impression of a specially sumptuous menu. Salt pork, of which some was presumably also smoked in Greenland, salt beef, salted butter (with a shorter durability than hoped for), hardtack, ship's biscuits, yellow and green peas, barley groats, malt and hops for brewing beer. Of *groceries* there were coffee, tea, sugar, various spices, corn spirits, better quality spirits, cognac and various sorts of wine.

The list of sales merchandise is rather boring, but it gives a good impression of what was in demand in Greenland in this period, especially by the Greenlandic inhabitants, to whom these items were traded for Greenlandic produce.

There was a rather large selection of drapery goods: "Silesian linen" (sheeting), fine and coarse flax linen, blue-and-white-checkered and red-and-white-checkered cloth, cloth with printed designs, felt, kersey, ordinary calico, ticking duck, and white and coloured homespun. Of clothing articles there were scarves; Jutlandic, Icelandic and Faroese stockings and sweaters; wristlets; two sizes of gloves (woollen); and hats. Then there was yarn, buttons, sewing thread, sewing needles, and thimbles.

It sounds strange, but both prepared and unprepared lambskins were for sale, as were woollen horse blankets of various sizes.

Hardware included various tools, nails, bolts, knives, ulo-blades, various kitchen utensils of iron and copper, faience and some pottery, and cutlery and ladles of various sizes. It also included toys, beads, mirrors, tin boxes, wooden chests, etc.

Of the assortment of *materials* we can mention boards in various thicknesses and lengths, lumber, laths, and spruce poles; oar wood; "wainscot" (knotless logs of oak); pitch and tar.

Weapons and accessories still included sword blades for bird darts, but now also as permanent items rifles and shotguns with fine and coarse powder, bars of lead for founding bullets, and various calibres of shot, and furthermore especially harpoons and lines. Fish nets and seal nets, as well as strings to repair them with or make new nets, could be ordered. Fish hooks, shark hooks and fishing lines. Ropes of various kinds.

Salt, both coarse and fine, was consumed in the European households as well as for the preservation of local produce and the re-salting of provisions. Boats and yawls were shipped; at one time the construction of a small boat wharf was contemplated, or sending a carpenter who was proficient in boat-making.

For office use especially, paper, ink powder, sealing wax and so forth were shipped. It is strange to see wallpaper on the list. It was used in various ways, in addition to its proper use. It is often found used as a cover for diaries or bound copies of internal letters.

The sale of wallpaper to Greenlanders was of special importance. "You, Sir," wrote the trader M.N. Myhlenphort in 1790 to Inspector Wille, "know Greenlanders as well as I. You know they want something to please the eye, and if they cannot get it from the Trade, they will seek it from foreign ships, or even the ships of our own fatherland, when they come into harbour." It had become the custom to paper earthen huts inside with wallpaper: a dubious change of tradition. Myhlenphort saw in this an opportunity to acquire more hides, if the price of wallpaper was not too high.

Presumably Myhlenphort had no evil intention in this, taking into account his general respect for the Greenlandic way of life. He only soberly observed the need which Greenlanders evidently had for wallpaper, and saw the advantage of the Trade in acquiring that many more skins. The desire of the Greenlanders to paper their walls at least partly with colourful wallpaper was so great that they attempted to satisfy it by also trading with foreigners; wallpaper was thus an article of illicit trade, which it was important to combat, on the same level as English faience, showy tin boxes and other unaccustomed items from the outside world.

The great selection of fabrics and articles of clothing represented an increase over previous periods, but it was by no means a new custom for Greenlanders to use woven fabrics for their clothing. Lars Dalager had noticed it at Godthåb as early as the 1750's. Since then the demand had risen and the need for European clothes become natural, especially at places where there were insufficient opportunities for acquiring sealskin, the traditional material. Now it was a disaster if the trader at a whaling station ran out of trousering. "There is not a single length of blue Copenhagen kersey here, and as the Greenlanders mostly demand and use it for trousers, etc., this variety is very necessary," wrote the senior assistant at Kronprinsens Ejland in 1788 in ordering an emergency supply of at least 50 alens from Godhavn.

The demand for sales merchandise was thus on the rise. One of the relatively common kitchen utensils of the time, the copper kettle, was used to a great extent by both the Greenlanders and the Europeans. But there were difficulties with maintenance and repair. The trader at Jakobshavn pointed out the large number of copper pots and ladles sent to Copenhagen every year for tinning or other repairs. The number was so large that it must be profitable to employ an expert in the Northern Inspectorate, a tinker. "The tin plating in a copper vessel lasts only ¼ year in Greenland, so for ¾ of a year or often longer we have to eat food from untinned pots, which a filthy cook makes even more harmful to our health by not cleaning them immediately after they have been used." A tinker would also "be able to satisfy a great need of the Greenlanders. Every Greenlandic family, however poor, wants a copper kettle for water as well as to cook in." The so-called rich Greenlanders throw them away as soon as they have been damaged the least." Savings could be made here.

This bears testimony to an expansion and differentiation of the Greenlanders' demand for imported goods, and also to how difficult it was to adapt a maintenance tradition to new consumer goods. Similar maintenance problems were encountered with firearms, as we have seen.[6]

Firearms had to be sent to Copenhagen for repair. This often took one year or even two from the time the weapon was delivered by its owner for repair; sometimes the price of repair was more than what a brand new gun cost. An investigation at the gunsmith's in Copenhagen of a certain repair firm showed that many of the firearms had been so mistreated that it required an enormous amount of work just to make them more or less serviceable.

Baade, the trader at Egedesminde, in forwarding the complaints of the Greenlanders about the quality of firearms and locks (hammers were worn out after being used five or six times) emphasized that rifle fangst was "the most fashionable" there. In his answer, Schwabe remarked that "the Greenlanders often misuse their rifles: bend, break and beat them," which the trader must have been aware of.

Nevertheless gun repairs do seem to have been made in Greenland itself. Irgens, the trader at Christianshåb, reported in 1784 that the smith at Claushavn had assured him that he only did smith's work in connection with mining, and continued: "This is rather untrue, as I have seen that he surreptitiously repairs flintlocks for the Greenlanders, and takes payment for it in hides." Gun repair was thus the object of a kind of illicit trade; the smith was not allowed to receive payment in monopoly produce. This traffic did not set a precedent, however, and most repairs still had to be done in Copenhagen.

As we have seen, Greenlandic fangers were enormously quality conscious when purchasing their indispensable firearms. This choosiness applied to other items, such as kersey, where it was not only a question of quality, but also of colour. Blue was absolutely the preferred colour. This was an expression of consumer conservatism; they preferred what they had become accustomed to.

One example of such consumer conservatism seemed odd to European eyes, and was also uneconomical. At Christianshåb a new trousering was introduced: blue Icelandic kersey, which cost only 34 skillings per alen, as opposed 63 skillings for the former foreign kersey. The Greenlanders of Christianshåb nevertheless preferred the more expensive material, although they were of the same quality. The Icelandic kersey was perhaps slightly coarser, but would certainly wear just as long. No, these Greenlanders preferred to stick to what they were used to.

Consumer consciousness also had as a result that Greenlanders preferred to acquire foreign goods. "The stoneware made in Kastrup which we have received will probably be impossible to sell, as the price is too high and in addition the English bring a prettier, finer and better kind here which they sell for a trifle." "The Greenlanders are sensible enough to see that the English merchandise is more beautiful, of better quality and cheaper than ours; I often hear that my merchandise is poor, and I cannot contradict them as I myself and every Dane in this country well knows that the calico, printed cloth, flannel, "Silesian" linen, scarves, etc. which are now here is what the shopkeepers could not sell in Copenhagen and was pushed off on Greenland."

This salvo was fired in 1789 by a senior assistant at Godhavn, and it hit the Management. Perhaps it was one of the reasons why the same assistant was not promoted and left the Trade and Greenland a few years later. What he said about the quality of the Trade's merchandise was too harsh and too sharp. The Trade did not buy goods which otherwise could not be sold, and the fabrics it shipped to Greenland were not of poor quality. That earthenware was more expensive than what the English provided was commonly known, but there was nothing wrong with the quality of Danish faience. It was expensive to produce in Denmark, considerably more so than in England.

Under constant economic difficulties, the Management of the Royal Greenland Trade attempted to satisfy the growing demand for consumer goods in Greenland. The risks of shrinkage, leakage and damage in transport made it difficult to keep up a supply service. The Trade found new merchancise at lower prices but of the same, at times perhaps better quality. Even in items which offended the rationalistic mentality as "the trash of sumptuousness," the Trade attempted to satisfy the demand. Thus it appears that a new kind of beads, both large and small, for the well-known head embroidery was shipped in 1795.

"Luxury Goods"

The previously mentioned assistant at Godhavn was transferred to Christianshåb/Claushavn, where he was to supervise whaling at Isefjords Station. His activity there was perhaps a further reason why he was not promoted and was sent back soon. "It is unpleasant to hear that trade could only be expected to be good if you had distilled spirits, coffee and sugar to sell," wrote Inspector B.J. Schultz to him in 1792. "I know that the Greenlanders both are acquainted with these goods and are foolish enough to demand them," but the fact remained that employees of the Trade were not allowed to sell them. The assistant must be able to purchase some skins, thought Schultz, in exchange for other, useful and permitted goods.

Apart from this unquestionable reprimand to the assistant, this letter testified quite clearly that it had become a general desire among the Greenlanders of Disko Bugt to purchase these items. The local population at Claushavn and other places had presumably acquired a taste for them through illicit trade with foreign and Danish ships, or as gifts or a kind of payment for services rendered or Greenlandic food.

It appears that the inhabitants of Claushavn were especially demanding in this respect. In 1796 the trader at Christianshåb reported: "The Greenlander Ole at Claushavn, who not only is the best whaler there but also the best kayak fanger, has requested me to order for him for next year four punds of coffee beans, four punds of rock candy sugar and two punds of tea." The trader had pointed out to him that according to the "wishes of the big shots back home," such goods could not be ordered for ordinary Greenlanders, because they would get accustomed to such things, which they would not be able to get later without sacrificing what they needed to stay alive.

Ole not only exhibited an unimpressed outspokenness by even making this request, but also a sense of his own worth which was just as natural. He knew quite well that these items were forbidden, and he understood and approved the principle involved, but he thought it proper to enforce it only with poor fangers. On the contrary, "he thought that such things should not be denied the good fangers who can well stand the expense, and that these things would all the more cheer them up when they come home from their fangst tired and frozen. He especially thought them important for himself in whaling." The trader had not put his requests on his order to the Trade, but without mentioning it he actually hoped that they would be shipped. The Trade did not even bother to answer this question.

Ole did not get his coffee, sugar or tea on this occasion; but fortunately it is reported that his thirst for coffee was officially quenched in 1798. "I gave the Greenlander Ole at Claushavn, whom all agree in praising for his rare industriousness and his excellent kindness to his countrymen, four punds of coffee and two punds of sugar, which he received with appreciable signs of satisfaction," confessed Inspector Bendeke to the Management. Ole was so well off that none of the trader's usual goods could be given him as a token of appreciation. He would "not have appreciated anything which he could otherwise have bought, but coffee cannot be bought, and this drink is as irresistibly attractive to Greenlanders as it is to many Europeans."

These few testimonials as to the penetration of this life-giving elixir into West Greenlandic society show us the same gradual process as with spirits. The sources also indicate that just as with spirits, the whaling districts of the Northern Inspectorate were the furthest advanced. Holsteinsborg seems to have kept up, too. As late as 1804 Inspector Myhlenphort of South Greenland still thought that traders should not order coffee and rock candy for Greenlanders. "As soon as some Greenlanders get into the habit of ordering coffee and sugar on commission, the mass of Greenlanders will soon present the same demand, for one has just as much right to do it as another." It appears that even by 1805 Greenlanders at Frederikshåb and Julianehåb had not yet acquired a taste for such items. Southernmost Greenland was thus late on the "path to perdition".

By this time the Management itself had already knocked a hole in the bulwark against coffee. The previously mentioned "reward" given by Inspector Bendeke to Ole at Claushavn in 1796 actually came to set a precedent. It appears from various reports from Inspector Bull in Godthåb that rewards of one pund of coffee and sugar were commonly offered in the colonies of his inspectorate. The Management was compelled to yield to this practice in 1802, both in the north and in the south. "As the inspectors often have cause to reward special diligence shown by the crew in money credited to the account of the person in question, we wonder whether the encouragement intended by such gifts would not be better attained if the person in question were given things he could immediately use and which otherwise cannot be acquired from the Trade: for example a quantity of coffee or sugar, which items can be presumed to be common articles in Greenland." It this suggestion were approved, the Management would see to it that suitable quantities were shipped for the purpose.

It is noteworthy that the Management here explicitly uses the word "crew" not distinguishing between Greenlanders and Europeans. The letter is addressed to the Northern Inspectorate and there naturally meant the whaling crew. It appears from the quotation that rewards should be given to those who could otherwise not purchase or order coffee or sugar, which must mean the local Greenlandic crew.

Such a system of rewards was instituted both in the north and in the south: for a provisional period of three years. The administration stipulated three small prizes to be awarded every year to the three Greenlandic fangers who delivered the most produce to the Trade at each colony. It hereby intended to encourage "diligence, activity and the spirit of acquisitiveness." The first prize was to consist of four punds of coffee and two punds of sugar, the second prize of two punds of coffee and one pund of sugar, and the third prize of one pund of coffee and one-half pund of sugar. If several fangers delivered the same quantity, lots were to be drawn.

"It is also possible that Greenlanders at places where coffee and sugar have not become welcome items, would rather have their rewards paid in useful merchandise, which in this case should not be denied them, but they must make their own free choice." This was actually the final remnant of the bulwark against "the destructive appearance of coffee." By use of a means the effects of which were actually considered demoralizing, the Trade attempted to foster work morale in Greenland. Here we have in a nutshell the ambivalent attitude of the Royal Greenland Trade.

Of course this and the illicit trade which had been going on in coffee, tea and rock candy led to a growing demand for the open sale of these "luxury items". At Qerrortussoq in Holsteinsborg District the Greenlandic whalers suggested in the Spring of 1800 "that they be shipped coffee and sugar so that especially during the whale watchings, when they often have to leave their homes at one, two, or three in the morning in the most penetrating cold, they might have something to enjoy." The senior assistant there took the liberty, well aware that it was out of the ordinary, of ordering these items for sale "so much the more as the Greenlanders from quite distant times have been accustomed to this drink, which for these persons has far from the harmful effect imagined." He also thought that the sale of this merchandise would cut off illicit trade, and perhaps even increase purchase of fox hides and so forth.

The previous year a former senior assistant at Qerrortussoq had submitted a defence for selling tea. He had ordered 24 punds of tea to sell to Greenlanders, "as the water at Umânârssugssuaq is, as has been reported, quite poor, or rather, stagnant, rotten, and therefore almost quite undrinkable." This had been the main reason why it had not been possible to get this place inhabited in the winter. By promising that immigrants would be shipped tea to purchase, and that tea would be distributed free to whalers on coast watch in season, he had got this locality inhabited and whaling operations started. Nor could this trader see that tea could be harmful to either the Trade or the Greenlanders, since it was not "a drink which either goes to the head of the Greenlanders or in any other way weakens or refines them in their usual hard way of life."

Inspector Myhlenphort adopted the ideas of the senior assistant and in 1805 proposed that coffee, tea, bread and groats be sold as payment for fox hides and good sealskins. This was done the following year, thus definitively penetrating the bulwark against these "luxury goods", which continued to be more and more commonly used by Greenlanders.

It was somewhat different with distilled spirits, as we have seen. But even this stimulant had gained a footing more or less openly. In 1806 Inspector Myhlenphort observed with a certain amount of resignation: "There are individual occasions on which it is necessary to give a male Greenlander a dram but I know of no cases where it is necessary to serve females any of the same." This statement is from a circular issued in 1803. To continue, he enjoined "the trading chiefs not only themselves, but also by holding their subordinates under close observation, to limit as far as possible the distribution of all provisions to Greenlanders, as well as to keep them from enjoying strong and intoxicating drink; for the misuse of both of these will undeniably result in the spoiling of the nation and finally in loss to the Royal Greenland Trade." It was quite possible, he wrote in introduction, "with respect to spirituous drinks, not only to limit, but also to remove their abuse."

Not only at the whaling stations of the Northern Inspectorate and at Holsteinsborg in the south had distilled spirits gained a certain footing. Rønning, the missionary at Holsteinsborg and Sukkertoppen, complained in 1796 that ships' crews bartered for used depilated waterproof seal skins clothes, which they were in great need of on their return voyage, paying for them with distilled spirits. Of this Greenlanders in general spoke quite little until they became intoxicated, he wrote. Considering this, Myhlenphorts's circular seems even more resigned in tone.

Inspector Motzfeldt at Godhavn could not avoid the fact that spirits, taken in moderation in certain circumstances, which he did not list in detail, must be considered beneficial; but abuse was harmful. In a long circular in 1807, he attempted to "regulate" their "beneficial use". Spirits were in general only to be taken in connection with work. On holidays only the crew were to have spirits, but not until after divine services. The kayak man who brought the mail could have a glass on arrival and one when he left.

The eighth point in Inspector Motzfeldt's circular is of special interest: "Just as no one should take spirits except as a refreshment, everyone, Dane or Greenlander, who is offered a dram or a glass of spirits should drink it up and swallow it immediately, unless it disagrees with him, so that they do not, as can be and has been the case, collect these drams or mouthfuls until they fill a bottle and then either drink it all at once themselves, or sell it to others who likewise abuse this drink which in such large quantities deprives people of their reason, by means of which disturbances and disorder are produced."

This sounds like a revival of the provisions of the Order of 1782, paragraph 4 of Chapter Four and paragraph 7 of Chapter Five, with amendments brought about by twenty-five years of practice, and with the interesting addition and revelation of the practice of "saving up" which had also developed. It was most likely not possible to stop this "saving up". Right up to the end of the 1930's Greenlanders who on New Year's Eve were served a glass of spirits, were to drink up and say "qujanaq" ("thank you"), which was supposed to be impossible with the spirits in one's mouth.

A proposal submitted in 1808 to Inspector Motzfeldt by the trader of Upernavik seems quite astonishing and unrealistic: he suggested abolishing the serving of spirits by the glass to the colony crew – the ration to which they were entitled – and replacing it with a ration of coffee and sugar. The colony crew here had seconded this idea, quite simply because they were usually stationed out in the district most of the year where they did not get their spirits ration since it had to be served them by the glass. They could however, quite easily take a coffee ration out with them. We do not know whether this practice was introduced. As with so much else, nothing may have come of this initiative because of the war situation, and abolition was not introduced in Upernavik.

It was not only spirits which had as a result that "a number of Greenlanders, women as well as men, at various times, especially either while beer is being brewed or immediately afterwards, have been excessively drunk; even yesterday, on such a solemn and important feast as Good Friday, I saw a number of Greenlanders who were shamefully and unchristianly scandalized by instructed Christians, who ought to serve as an example, but who in a worse than bestial manner filled them to excess and drunkenness."

In a circular issued at the same time to the Greenlanders of Godhavn working in whaling, he threatened "the loss of beer rights" if they abused this right by getting others drunk. This local brew, which was both rather thin and insufficiently fermented, was enough to produce a state similar to inebriation, probably more a psychogenic wish-fulfilment than actually created by its percentage of alcohol. Nothing much is reported of the harmful effects of this home brew. In places it was actually healthier than the drinking water which could be procured, such as that at Umânârssugssuaq which had to be made potable as tea.

Prices and Price Changes

There was a lively demand for "luxury goods'" probably created by the seasonal abundance of Greenlandic produce which existed in between periods of famine, poor fangst and other unpredictable unfortunate conditions. The habit of trading fangst produce for "things", whether one needed them or not, was several decades old.[7]

It was consumer goods in themselves that Greenlanders wanted to possess. The Greenlandic consumer was not so interested in the price unless it changed so noticeably that the usual relation between the quantity of produce sold and the quantity of merchandise desired shifted considerably. The trading Greenlander reacted when he received unusually little of the desired merchandise in return for the quantity of produce delivered. This was a directly concrete relationship, but prices and price changes were abstract phenomena. Here again, the immediate, the phenomenative, was what counted.

This was clearly shown at Upernavik in 1780 and 1781, when the inhabitants actually struck by refusing to deliver their produce to the trader, because they were offered in return smaller quantities of tobacco than previously. The tobacco prices had gone up, but the Greenlanders could only see that they were offered smaller quantities.[8]

It was also habit which caused Greenlanders at Christianshåb, as we have seen, to prefer in 1785 the blue kersey which had previously been shipped instead of Icelandic kersey, although the latter was cheaper. In 1787 Baade, the trader at Egedesminde, reported to Inspector Wille that the blue-and-white-chequered cloth that had been shipped the year before was narrower than previously, so that it took six alens instead of five to make a "skirt" – which must mean a cloth anorak. "The Greenlanders are grumbling about this and think the trader is cheating them; for in their opinion a skirt of one kind of cloth should always cost the same; they are not concerned with the number of alens." This was an incorrect interpretation, for it was precisely the number of alens, the quantity, they were reacting against. He succeeded in getting the price of the 84 alens he had on stock reduced, so that consumers could now get 5½ alens for the same price as 5 previously. These are trifles, but the trifles of everyday life, which reveal the changes in everyday life in West Greenland.

Sticking to the accustomed was assisted by the price policy which the Trade in principle practiced. Perhaps it in turn was influenced by knowledge of the attitude of Greenlandic consumers. There was to be as little price movement as possible: a kind of balance between the prices of the produce purchased and the merchandise sold was to prevail. In this manner the operations of the Trade would be most stable and calm – and easy to grasp. Necessary and useful merchandise was to have more or less stable prices in order to maintain the level of purchases of Greenlandic produce. Production could be raised and stimulated through careful raising of the purchase prices of Greenlandic produce, through rewards, or by decreasing or keeping low the prices of goods for which there was a special demand among the Greenlanders. Then the prices of "luxury goods" had to be raised to recompensate.

But the Trade could even feel compelled to lower the prices of these "luxurious goods". From 1796 on, as we have seen, the classifications introduced in 1782 were abolished, although there were still goods which were not for sale to Greenlanders, still in order not to "spoil them". In competition with the English, and in order to prevent illicit trade, the Trade felt compelled to reduce the margin of profit on certain merchandise. After 1796 the markup on "luxurious goods" was 46%. In 1802 the markup on china and stoneware was reduced to 12% "in order by a lower price to prevent these goods being brought into the Establishments by the English whalers." On the same occasion all English tin wares were omitted from the general schedule, which seems inconsistent considering the objective of the price decrease on china and stoneware.

Special conditions prevailed with respect to merchandise such as gunpowder, lead and tobacco.

Gunpowder was purchased and sold by the Trade in two varieties, called fine and coarse powder. Until 1794 the Trade's purchase price for these two varieties had been 20¼ and 18¼ skillings per pund, respectively, and in the general schedule they had been listed at a sales price of 24 and 20 skillings. In 1795 the Trade had to pay a considerably higher price: $40^{4}/_{5}$ and $38^{22}/_{25}$ skillings per pund, more than double the previous price, due of course to the European war situation.

The Trade did not think the Greenlandic fangers could stand such a steep price increase. It therefore decided to maintain the previous sales price of gunpowder: 24 and 20 skillings per pund, respectively. It thereby expected to lose a total of 531 rigsdalers on this item of merchandise alone, which, like lead, was considered something "which as necessary goods should not be made difficult for the inhabitants to get."

In this and the following trading years, prices fluctuated as shown in Table 35. The Trade maintained its low sales price for these two varieties of gunpowder up until 1800. Although the Trade's purchase price fluctuated, its loss increased each year, because there was still a growing use of firearms. In 1800 another price increase was observed, and no decrease could be predicted in the near future. The Trade therefore no longer felt it could continue to lose money on this item of merchandise, so that another system was resorted to. Both varieties were sold at the same price, which did not make up for the loss, but decreased it considerably.

Table 35.

		Skillings per pund	
		Fine powder	Coarse powder
1796	Purchase price	40.8	38.88
	Sales price	24	20
1797	Purchase price	40.8	39
	Sales price	24	20
1798	Purchase price	35.04	32.75
	Sales price	24	20
1799	Purchase price	35.04	31.5
	Sales price	24	20
1800	Purchase price	40.8	38.4
	Sales price	32	32

The Management figured on a loss in 1799 of 8.8 skillings per pund on the average, and in 1800 and 1801 of 6.8 skillings per pund. In 1800 it was proposed to make a distinction between Greenlanders and Europeans, so that the Europeans would pay the Trade's purchase price for the gunpowder they used, while the Greenlanders would enjoy the low price of 32 skillings. It was left to the inspectors to take this measure. The Management did not think it could servey its consequences, but feared abuses and peculation.

It appears throughout the correspondence during the years on this matter that the administration's constant leitmotif was that the Greenlandic fangers were not to be restricted in using firearms for fangst. Sales prices for this item of merchandise were thus set partially because of social reasons, although it was also to the advantage of the Trade that fangst be restricted as little as possible.

This principle naturally also applied to lead for bullets, so that the Trade here also attempted to keep European price fluctuations from influencing its prices. It wanted to make it possible for the Greenlandic fanger always to acquire lead without insurmountable economic difficulties.

In order to promote trading in skins, the prices of such quite unnecessary goods as wallpaper and plaster impressions were lowered at Christianshåb when skins were delivered in payment. In this case they were sold at a loss to the Trade: the smallest plaster impressions for the same price as a skin: 6 skillings. Lead had a normal price of eight skillings per pund, but it could be lowered to six skillings per pund if one sealskin was delivered per pund. But the sale of lead was not to be made dependent on skins being delivered.

This example from 1792 shows how the prices of the various goods were manipulated in consideration of the above-mentioned principle, and in order to promote the purchase of skins. The main provision of the Order of 1782 still applied, however: that the trader was to see to it that Greenlanders did not deprive themselves of the products they needed to stay alive.

"This day was a sad one: I have just sold the last inch of tobacco, and 15 or 1600 voracious noses are shouting for their daily feed, but how do you get blood out of a turnip?" lamented Johan Chr. Mørch, the trader at Julianehåb, in February 1802. A few days later he wrote: "They will buy nothing but tobacco; the word is on everyone's lips." He got six kayaks to leave Julianehåb by promising them four punds of tobacco each. In mid-March they returned with 176 punds of Dutch tobacco from Frederikshåb, "and were paid with 24 punds of tobacco worth 7 rigsdalers 48 skillings, and 6 double-barbed dart heads worth 1 rigsdaler."

When in 1799 the Management of the Royal Greenland Trade was compelled to raise the price of tobacco to 36 skillings per pund, it was "worried that this sudden increase of an item which has become an indispensable necessity to the natives could result in an unpleasant shock for them, especially as we well understand that it is no easy matter to make the real reason for this price increase understandable to them." It was therefore left to the inspector to determine whether the price of tobacco should be lowered to 32 skillings per pund for Greenlandic purchasers, and only for them. "It would in any case be good, however, if the Greenlanders could possibly be informed of the favour shown them and be prepared to be resigned if further unfavourable conditions make further rises necessary."

The Management perhaps remembered the consumer strike at Upernavik; it was also caused by a rise in the price of tobacco. On the occasion just mentioned the prices of other kinds of tobacco were raised in accordance with the purchase prices of the Trade; it was only Dutch tobacco in rolls of various sizes which was thought to be of interest to the Greenlanders.

These two accounts show in no uncertain manner how important tobacco had become as a stimulant. It had become a necessity. How this took place has been described earlier.[9] Tobacco in small quantities was still the most utilized medium of exchange. It was therefore almost a disaster if the Dutch tobacco shipped was of poor quality: it could damage considerably the trader or assistant who had delivered poor tobacco for the good produce or services of the Greenlanders. It was perhaps also the realization of this which lay behind the statement of the Management in connection with the price raise of 1799. It was obviously a relief for the Management that the market price of Dutch tobacco later fell so that the Trade's sales price of 32 skillings per pund covered its purchase price.

Procuring various kinds of merchandise and setting sales prices caused the Management and the Commission a lot of trouble. As we have seen, it was often the traders and assistants who at first had to account to their Greenlanders; at times they could be exposed to more or less violent reactions from Greenlanders who thought they had been wronged. It was in any case the stationed employees of the Trade who had to ward off the blows not only of the Greenlanders, but also of dissatisfied persons in their own ranks and those of the Mission. It could even be a question of direct economic loss when merchandise was poor, or the inhabitants would not barter their produce for it because, due to rises in the general schedule which they did not understand, they suddenly and inexplicably received lesser quantities than normally.

By the price policy conducted by the Trade – which became more and more complicated from one category of merchandise to other, as consumption rose and became differentiated; by continuing to keep more and more prices in the general schedule far under the Trade's purchase prices, as more and more goods were considered "necessary"; by attempting to promote production through price and sales policies; by all of these means the Royal Greenland Trade isolated the economy of Greenland more and more from that of the world at large.

It is hardly probable that the members of the Management or the Commission ever gave a thought to the broader aspects of this policy; they were only interested in its more limited aspects. But there were more factors than they were aware of. There was an interplay between isolation and monopoly. The former could only be enforced through the latter, and the latter was supported by the former. Only through the monopoly could the Greenlandic population be economically and thus also socially protected. Therefore the monopoly had to be profitable, as far as possible, in order to be maintained. This was the objective towards which its leadership had to strive, and for which each employee had to work.

Step by step the liberalistic mentality which had inspired the Commission of 1788 in its first period was abandoned. This was probably not done consciously. In the acts and directives of the Management there was concealed no desire to frustrate the Commission. It seems rather that one provision led to the next one until a net had been woven from which it was not so simple to break out. There was thus a slow movement towards the principle that the Royal Greenland Trade should be self-supporting, but this principle was by no means conscious.

Trading Methods

Trading activities in Greenland had very little in common with what is generally understood as *trade*. This is true not only of price formation, in which the trader was bound to the general schedule: in some cases he could disregard it, but did this reluctantly, as he himself had to bear the risk. But neither did the other activities of the traders and assistants have much in common with trade. "A trader in Greenland can only be considered a country pedlar who himself must travel and wander about to collect from the Greenlanders what they will sell him," wrote C.C. Dalager in 1782, to inform the Management of conditions they apparently did not have the slightest idea of. The other functions of the traders and assistants, such as supervising production, keeping accounts, supervising the maintenance and repair of various buildings, administrating the district, etc., have been mentioned; nothing of this really had anything to do with trade.

In his letter C.C. Dalager continued his informative remarks by describing the processing of blubber and its purchase using the new blubber measures. On purchasing itself his opinion was that "I have so far had to give the Greenlanders credit. They borrow every day, but the time of payment falls only at a certain time of the year. They are unstable people who move around: their situation and occupations demand this of them. I have trusted them, but before you are informed they can have moved far from the place where they lived, and perhaps never return. Others die, and what they owe is totally lost. A Greenlander never leaves anything by which a trader could be paid."

Credit has been mentioned several times. There were many conditions which made this credit necessary. It was so common that no trader could refuse to give it. Production and therefore purchases actually depended entirely on credit, which gave rise to a number of bookkeeping difficulties, and was actually never really understood by the Greenlandic population.

Credit was and remained a nightmare for the traders, but they could not avoid it. In 1799 Inspector Bendeke attempted to limit credit "which is always greatest at the whaling stations." When he had come to Godhavn two years previously he had numerous annoyances because in 1797 the Greenlandic whalers had been given so much credit that it "ate up most of each one's profits." He then gave the assistant orders only to give credit for the most necessary things. Those who wanted more credit and were "insistent" were referred to the inspector, which gave him many "annoyances; but I finally had the satisfaction, at the distribution and payment of 1798, at which I myself was present, of seeing the Greenlanders delighted and admitting that it was good that they had not borrowed too much." He hoped to restrict credit by having talks with the trading officers of the inspectorate; in this hope he was disappointed. Credit could not be avoided, as the fanger economy was organized.

There are indications that accounts of such credit were not really kept.[10] According to the Order of 1782 the traders were to keep a proper journal of what each individual had sold; but it is not certain whether what each individual was given in return was always written down.

We can see that in 1805 Inspector Myhlenphort introduced the use of an authorized "Greenlander Debt Book" so that "all the Greenlanders of the locality can have their proper accounts at the Trade; it is therefore your duty to keep this account book in such a manner that it can always be seen how much a Greenlander owes or has coming." This must also be true of the later so-called "Credit Lists", the arrangement and objectives of which were not explained to the ordinary Greenlander. If they had been, he would not have understood them.

Myhlenphort himself had certain experiences of the unpleasant aspects of credit from his own period as a trader at Egedesminde. He even refused in 1800 to be transferred from there immediately, because he could not collect all the debts owed him in a short time and during a bad period for purchases. Traders had often had bitter opinions of credit during the laborious and protracted audits, the results of which were often that they themselves were made answerable for uncollectable debts. Some kind of system had to be created for these messy conditions. Bookkeeping corresponding to that ordered by Myhlenphort was probably introduced at the same time in the Northern Inspectorate.

It is curious to find a circular on this kind of bookkeeping as late as 1805. The Order of 1782 had actually already prescribed the keeping of a journal of what Greenlandic produce was purchased and what merchandise was given in return. At the time loud criticism was voiced against this journal, but they were actually kept at some places. When the trade officers took them around with them on their expeditions in the districts, they could not help getting "somewhat disfigured", "as the Greenlanders often demand back what they have sold, shortly after trading, and return the sales merchandise, or they want to exchange this for something else." Trading demanded patience and an extensive spirit of service; the "customers" did not actually behave much differently from what customers have always done everywhere.

Now Myhlenphort introduced an authorized "Greenlander Debt Book", to serve the trader as documentation in audits or when a new trader took over because the old one was transferred or in some other way left his job in his district.

This entire tenacious system of credit was partly dependent on barter. Purchases from Greenlanders could only take place at certain times, but the Greenlanders would need sales merchandise before this. In order to be able to supply produce, fangers would have to have the necessary fangst equipment: e.g., powder, lead, wood, dart-heads, etc. Credit was therefore a necessity. It was considered that in order to help the trader recuperate his losses, he at least had an overmeasure on blubber purchases: he got 50% more than he paid for, or one-and-a-half barrels for a barrel. But this overmeasure had to cover the large shrinkage of blubber from the time it was measured to when it was finally put into casks for shipment to Denmark.

The trader C.C. Dalager gave a quite detailed description of blubber purchasing in 1782 for the information of the Management. "Blubber is a fluid matter which continually shrinks under processing. It often has to be transferred from one container to another and from one vessel to another before it reaches the blubber house, where it is cut up into small pieces and put into casks. These are often old and cannot be as perfectly leak-proof as they should be. They are of random sizes, and even when they are of one calibre, one is obviously larger than the other. Blubber is always received from the Greenlanders in large, whole pieces. It cannot be purchased in any other form. In the cold season it is also hard and frozen, which creates many empty spaces in the measure, or tub. When it is cut up to put in the casks, it shrinks to almost half of what had been measured loose. It is forcibly pressed with forks into the casks, and when they have stood, they must often be filled again. When purchases take place in the warm season, this causes more of the blubber to melt. When it first begins to run and cannot immediately be casked, it can shrink in a few days to very little. Or nothing. Looking at the places where it is transported and processed, one can see how it decreases and how the labourers who are casking the blubber drip with oil!"

According to this it appears that at the most the overmeasure could cover shrinkage, but not the trader's credit losses. Dalager continued his exposition by asserting the necessity of credit and the poor opportunities available to the trader for collecting what was owing him. On the other hand, credit could not be avoided so long as there was no medium of exchange. Even though tobacco, coffee, and sugar, as we have seen, functioned as a kind of currency, they could not be used as such for larger transactions.

Trading was and remained difficult. In 1791 the trader at Christianshåb reported a typical example of how difficult it could be. In November and December he had gone twice to Claushavn, but was only able to purchase very little blubber. The last time he was there a fanger had eleven blue and white fox skins, which the trader wanted to buy from him. The fanger demanded a rifle for his skins, which had a purchase value of 3 rigsdalers 80 skillings, whereas the cheapest rifle available then cost eight rigsdalers. The trader then offered him the rifle if he would also deliver four tubs of blubber in the Spring, but the fanger would give no more than his fox hides for the rifle. "Finally to get the fox skins I told him, 'Give me your fox skins now, and I will write the Master at Disko and ask whether I am allowed to pay you a rifle for them.' This fanger was not born yesterday; he answered, 'I won't give you my fox skins now, but if you will write to the Master at Disko that I must be paid a rifle for them, then you and no one else will have them; and so you won't think I am cheating you, I will bring you my skins myself to keep." With this the trader had to be content and go home. In late December the fanger came and delivered the eleven fox skins for safekeeping; if he were not given a rifle for them, he was to have his skins again. After corresponding with the Inspector, the trader was in this special case allowed to pay the fanger with a eight rigsdaler rifle, "because he has brought in so many skins at one time."

The traders were allowed to raise the price of 32 skillings per blue fox skin of the first quality to 48 skillings, if large quantities were purchased together: twenty to thirty skins at once. This is contrary to all the principles of trade, according to which the unit price falls when larger quantities are offered. The reason for this seemingly reverse method was that the Management wanted to increase the production of fox skins, and thus used price raises for larger quantities as a means of stimulation.

Barter was especially difficult when it involved small items; example of this can be seen time after time. Thus in 1793 the trader at Umânaq began to doubt whether yarn should be sold by weight or in skeins. In any case it would be impossible to supply the Greenlandic purchasers with yarn except in the latter form. "For they do not usually buy thread when they buy merchandise for which they need it; they have to be given as much as they need to sew what they have bought with." The trader would either have to throw the necessary thread into the bargain at his own expense or dock the quantity of something else sold at the same time. He and presumably his predecessor in office had made use of the former practice. "It is impossible to explain to Greenlanders that such small things, the value of which can sometimes amount to that of one skin, either have to be paid for, or deducted from other goods, and it is useless to sell them more than what they need on one occasion."

The trader at Umânaq mentioned other merchandise, including articles of absolute necessity, which he had to provide free, such as flintstones, sewing needles, smoking pipes and toys. "If you do not want them to hate you, you have to give it to them in the end," for they thought that "such things cost the trading chief nothing." He had reckoned all this up and seen that it was certainly not to his economic advantage.

This was actually the result of the system of throwing something into the bargain which had developed because when purchasing Greenlandic produce it was not always possible to pay its full value in merchandise, so that such small items were used as "filling".[11] Now it had gone so far that the Greenlandic customer thought it his right to get such things free. The Management had decided – not only for Umânaq as the trader thought –

that the various traders would recuperate such expenses in the overmeasure on blubber.

The inspector answered this trader that it was evidently a misunderstanding if he thought that the overmeasure was intended as an advantage which the trader could appropriate undiminished. The idea was that the trader was to be responsible for small items thrown into the bargain or other free merchandise. This had already been decided in 1786, especially for Umánaq and Upernavik. The system of throwing something into the bargain could not be stopped until barter was discontinued. It gave rise to continual difficulties, especially when one of the parties involved was a scrupulous assistant. If he was not scrupulous, he risked getting in trouble when his trader discovered it.

The overmeasure for blubber purchases also gave rise to much discontent. The missionary Rudolph Heide at Holsteinsborg has described the measuring of blubber there; his description is a valuable supplement to C.C. Dalager's description of shrinkage. "The officers have seen fit to measure the whale blubber from the Greenlanders thus: with a blubber fork they stuff the blubber into the tub, then they jump up into the tub and tramp on it, and then put a cone 2½ kvarters on top. However simple the Greenlanders may be, they can easily see they are being cheated. They say they are being robbed. And this is no lie, as they get nothing for the cone on top. These are adjusted tubs; I believe they are here so that the Greenlanders shall not be cheated when the blubber is measured."

This and other examples, taken from letters sent from Greenland in the same year, caused the Commission to send a somewhat harsh letter to the Management. The Commission stated openly that it suspected the traders of "taking impermissible advantages when purchasing blubber from the Greenlanders, as if the overmeasure were a gift to them." The Commission intended to insist that the inspectors see to it that the Greenlanders were not wronged; in addition the Board of Managers was ordered to organize an effective control of the overmeasure by measuring the blubber sent from each district.

The overmeasure was and remained a thorn in the flesh of those who purchased produce. Although the missionary Heide was undoubtedly ignorant of the fact that frozen blubber was to be measured with heaping measures, a 2½ kvarters (about 40 cm.) cone on the tub (1½ barrel for one barrel) was more than enough, especially when the blubber had been well tramped into the tub, but this could not be done if the blubber was frozen stiff. The colony crew at Umánaq, who sold blubber from seal netting, were also not stimulated to produce more blubber by the fact that the overmeasure was of no benefit to them. They were even responsible for filling up the blubber barrels before shipment. For the same reason the local Greenlanders presumably did not feel actuated to produce more when they actually had to deliver more than twice the blubber for which they were paid at the rate of one rigsdaler per barrel.

"I cannot avoid mentioning that during the past trading year the Greenlanders have made unusual complaints about being cheated in trading. Whether their complaints are justified or not I cannot say, as I since last year have never been present when the trader dealt with the Greenlanders," wrote an assistant at Sukkertoppen. To be sure, he himself had been demoted from the post of trader at Holsteinsborg because of drunkenness and neglect, and in 1806, the year in which he wrote this, he was definitively discharged. But this does not mean that what he wrote was false. The trader at Sukkertoppen at the time was an irascible gentleman, but otherwise maintained honest relations with the inhabitants. Undoubtedly the overmeasure was a perpetual bone of contention, but with the present organization of the Trade it was indispensable.

At times, although quite rarely, a certain cunning was practiced by Greenlanders. According to the purchases schedule in the Order of 1782, a whole bear skin was worth 1 rigsdaler 32 skillings, and parts of bear skins were paid for proportionately. Bear hunters must have noticed that they actually received a higher total price if they divided their skins into pieces. It was not so simple a matter for the traders and assistants to determine the proportional price. It is, however, possible that those who sold bearskins first took from them what they themselves needed and then sold the rest, so that there was no conscious dividing, but that the sale of pieces was simply more frequent that the delivery of whole skins. However this may be, the traders on the average gave rather too much than too little for the pieces, in order to be able to buy the skins at all.

This may be one of the very few examples indicating that the fangers had the impression that the Greenland trade was actually a sellers' market. Only in a few cases does it seem that they took advantage of this. When the fanger at Claushavn got an eight rigsdaler rifle for his fox skins instead of less than half that price, it was the individual fanger against the trader. The practice of cutting up bearskins seems to have developed among an entire group, perhaps as a trading trick. The administration countered this practice by raising the price for whole, large, well-processed bearskins from one to three rigsdalers. Pieces of bearskin were to be paid for proportionally, presumably on the basis of one rigsdaler per skin.

Naturally the traders were interested in buying as much as possible of the various kind of produce. By virtue of a per cent system, calculated on average purchases over a period, they derived some economic advantage from an increase in purchases. Calculations of the average limited the amount of this extra income, however. An increase of purchases did not produce results until the average figure was recalculated.

It was in order to assure this percentage that the traders asserted the "ties" of the inhabitants to a certain district, to the trader of which the population were to deliver their monopoly produce. To increase purchases they also attempted to raise production, as has been described. A further measure was to increase the number of producers in a district. This could best be accomplished in the outlying areas.

After Nanortalik (in Julianehåb South District) was established in 1797, 14 fangers came from the East Coast the following year. The trader Johan Chr. Mørch saw this "as a good omen, as such quick effects promised further consequences." They had, however, one or another infection, and some of them died. "These Easteners, who have left some of their tents, could not be prevented from returning but we all attempted to persuade them to return to us and to tell the other Easterners how good it is here. Small rewards were distributed to them in the spring by Kleist and me – at my expense," wrote trader Mørch. This must be an example of an "active mercantilistic" demographic policy. An immigration of fangers from southernmost East Greenland would bring Nanortalik industrious "producers" and this increase purchases. There was enough room in the south for this increment to settle dispersed, so there was no question of a concentration of population. This would in any case be opposed by Mørch, considering his attitude toward this problem.

These various examples of trading methods can only with reservations be accepted as generally valid. Where the source claims tradition and previous practice, the reservation must be made that this is but one opinion of tradition and practice. A strong spirit of individualism was everywhere noticeable in West Greenland. What seemingly was true of one place was not immediately applicable to another place. The degree of geographic dispersal, the changing district chiefs, assistants stationed at one place only to be transferred after a few years, the changing inspectors (with an average of six years in office) and missionaries: all these factors contributed to variations in the general picture. The only constant factor could have been the population, but even this constancy was doubtful because of settlement traditions. The needs of the population changed, imperceptibly from day to day but noticeably over the long run. Obvious differences prevailed between districts and between the south and the north, but these were differences of detail, not in the general pattern.

The provisions of the Order were to create a certain uniformity in the functions of the Trade, and thus also in relations between the Trade and the inhabitants. In the course of time, however, these provisions had to be adapted to local conditions and the local way of life, and thus adjusted according to changes in practice and local needs. Thus the uniformity and similarity of conditions along the coast was broken. It is therefore impossible to determine to what extent the letter and spirit of the provisions of the Order were enforced. There are numerous examples in which circumstances made it impossible to enforce both letter and spirit at once. The harshness of life interfered with well-meant regulations.

On the whole our impression of the first twenty-five years under the Order of 1782 is that its spirit had an effect as close to its intention as possible. This was especially due to the influence of the inspectors. Five of the nine who served during these twenty-five years are characterized by really excellent performances and a tolerant discharge of their duties.

Many of the traders can also be characterized as proficient and honest, dominated by a pronounced understanding of the needs of the inhabitants. But even the best of them was subject to the system. They were first and foremost employees of the Trade, and they were clearly expected to be traders, although C.C. Dalager quite soon pointed out that the possibilities of real trade were so-so. The trader could really be considered as an itinerant hawker. It should be emphasized that in one respect both the letter and the spirit of the Order of 1782 were followed: the sources do not reveal one single case during these twenty-five years of traders having purchased so much of the produce of Greenlandic inhabitants that they were not left with enough to stay alive. (Later the Trade was unjustly criticized for having had a harmful effect in this respect.) As with a sigh a trader wrote in 1796: "The other fangst of the Greenlanders (the somewhat more successful whaling had been mentioned first) was this winter as it usually is: neither good nor bad; they had enough to stay alive, but little or nothing to sell." Not a word of his having attempted to purchase anything, whereas letters usually mention at least one single hide or a half tub of blubber. He hoped that the fangst would improve later in the year, but was disappointed.

"Domestic Trade"

Self-sufficiency in products necessary for subsistence was of course of primary importance to Greenlanders, but due to circumstances this self-sufficiency was usually only a short-term affair. It is not usual to hear what C.C. Dalager, the trader at Klokkerhuk, had to say in 1792:

"In spite of the careless economy of the Greenlanders, they are nevertheless so provident here, as they know that an evil and deficient winter is always coming, that they put aside a quantity of blubber for the winter in leather bags sewn for that purpose." These are the famous blubber bags, the content of which could be dangerous to health in the southern regions, including even Disko Bugt; if they had hung too long, eating this blubber could result in serious food poising, ending fatally.

"Likewise they also keep some baleen," continued C.C. Dalager, "for their own use as well as for trading with their countrymen to get the things they might need and which they cannot get from the Trade: things actually necessary for their existence as Greenlanders - all kinds of tools, kayaks, umiaks and many other things which it would be too protracted to list. Of these the Greenlanders most often have to buy hides they need for tents, umiaks and kayaks. All such trade takes place by means of baleen, as long as they have it. It is quite dear and highly esteemed among them for its usefulness and as a currency they cannot do without for their necessities."

Here Dalager not only described a quite natural form of domestic trade, but also revealed that baleen was used as the means of payment. The need for baleen was great in Disko Bugt and farther south down to the tip of Greenland, so it is no wonder it was in demand. He also established the fact that there were several necessities which the Greenlandic fangers could not everywhere procure for themselves.

Trade between Greenlanders, mentioned previously, seems to have been restricted to some degree by the decrease in long trips and as well as by the incipient ties of Greenlanders to one district. But supplies of Greenlandic produce in short supply locally were still necessary. The Trade sometimes had to help the Greenlanders procure these necessities.

Baleen seems to have "sold itself", but it was probably not the universal currency represented by Dalager, but rather functioned as a commodity to be exchanged with others. Other things seem also to have been traded between Greenlanders, even over longer distances: e.g., beluga and narwhal tendon and walrus and narwhal tusks. The Management wrote that it "has heard that in the Northern Inspectorate a large quantity of a kind of thread is made out of beluga tendon, and that this thread is not obtainable in the southern colonies and is avidly sought after there. Perhaps beluga teeth could also be used here for some kind of small turning." Inspector Schultz, to whom this inquiry had been addressed, answered: "It is true that there is a good deal of tendon here in the North, but only at certain places, and all the Greenlanders need it. Besides, it is a commodity which the Greenlanders barter to the Southerners, so the Trade cannot expect much from it."

Inspector Schultz seems here to have imagined that the Management was thinking that tendon could become a merchandise which could be sold for profit, and established immediately that there was not much the Trade could do in this respect. But nowhere in the Management's letter is there the least indication that the Trade was thinking of making a profit on this kind of domestic trade. It was evident that it wanted to help the southern Greenlanders get their thread of beluga and narwhal tendon.

The Greenlanders themselves could manage such trade and supply services through barter, explained Inspector Schultz. When the Management realized this, there was no longer any reason for it to want samples sent and to propose operating as a go-between. The teeth, samples of which were sent, as well as hareskins, were totally useless for any purpose; the latter could not be coloured black and were therefore useless to hatters. It appears from this that the Management had imagined that through this action new sources of income could be created for Greenlanders.

There was a great shortage of walrus and narwhal tusks and whale ribs in the south. These materials were indispensible for the manufacture of fangst equipment, from kayak knives to kayaks themselves. In 1792 Johan Chr. Mørch, the local trader, called attention to this need at Frederikshåb and gave a detailed description of what these materials were used for. He ordered narwhal and walrus tusks from Copenhagen! He wanted to be well-supplied with materials because he was constantly asked by local Greenlanders to procure them.

The Management got Mørch his materials, but at the same time ventilated the idea that Greenlandic fangst equipment could be manufactured from other materials: for example iron and brass, perhaps tinplated! Mørch actually considered this suggestion, but rejected it, because metal equipment would be too heavy, whereupon the Management also abandoned the idea.

There was also a need for tooth materials in the south. There are innumerable letters between the inspectorates in which other colonies order such materials. The Southern Inspectorate continually wanted walrus and narwhal tusks and whalebone. Baleen seemed to find its own way into the South. The Northern Inspectorate needed finished and unfinished soapstone.

One of the mountain climbers who had been sent out in 1778 to investigate coal deposits with an eye to mining was in 1782 transferred to Godthåb to look at soapstone deposits and see if a sufficient amount could be quarried to make a profitable production of construction stone. The results were negative. In 1784 the mountain climber died. The pieces he had quarried were presumably made use of in some other way.

In any case, in 1792 the Northern Inspectorate sent out an appeal for help, which was forwarded by the Management to the Inspector of the Southern Inspectorate. The Management was prepared to arrange the shipment of finished soapstone lamps to the Northern Inspectorate, and wanted about thirty sent as soon as possible. If that many were not ready, the Management wanted raw materials, and would have the lamps made in Copenhagen! This probably never took place, but the need for soapstone lamps did not decrease.

The Greenlandic whalers of Holsteinsborg District even sent a written request to the inspector to send them soapstone lamps and pots. It was thus a strange order which Inspector Schultz sent in 1796 to Inspector Bendeke at Godthåb: "If it is possible to supply this inspectorate with some soapstone lamps and kettles, it is very important. The former are needed at many places. The latter I would like to have for my own use."

The lack of soapstone in sufficiently large chunks to be able to make pots was so great in the Northern Inspectorate that the need of copper kettles and copper cooking vessels is easy to understand. In other words, things had gone so far in the Northern Inspectorate that soapstone pots had gone out of use. Inspector Schultz did not even think of procuring soapstone pots or material for them so that local Greenlanders could hang these traditional vessels over their soapstone lamps. There is no explanation of what use he himself had planned for them, since he ordered them.

South of Godthåb there must also have been a need for soapstone lamps. In 1800 Inspector Bull reported that Julianehåb could receive "a small shipment of soapstone lamps" every year from Godthåb "to sell to the Greenlanders of Julianehåb in order, if possible, to prevent them emigrating to the North for these necessities." The soapstone deposits in Godthåb Fjord seem to have been a kind of soapstone mine for all of Greenland. Strangely enough, nothing is heard in this context of the deposits in Frederikshåb District; they were well enough known at the time and were closer to Julianehåb.[12]

There was another peculiarity in this letter from Inspector Bull. In addition to soapstone he also mentioned reindeer antlers, which he said Julianehåb District needed. This indicates a considerable decline in reindeer hunting in that district.

There thus appeared in the years from 1782 to 1808 a distinct need in certain parts of Greenland for various domestic products which had formerly been the object of barter between Greenlanders of the West coast, and to acquire which long trips had previously been made. The need for the Trade to act as an intermediary presumably also reflects the district ties which had gradually developed. Conversely if the Trade acted as a go-between, there was then no reason to move from one's own area to acquire these needed domestic materials.

Domestic trade also included local trade in fresh Greenlandic produce, game birds, hares, various species of fish, etc., as well as "big game" such as reindeer meat and other meat products from various kinds of fangst. As long as there was no medium of exchange in the form of money, these goods were bartered in small portions for all kinds of easily divided consumer goods, especially stimulants such as coffee and tobacco, but also hardtack and ship's biscuits.

Whether such items were also traded among Greenlanders is not revealed by the sources. But it is known that Greenlanders who received part of their wages as rations often sold the provisions they were allotted in unprocessed form for necessities they could not acquire themselves because they either were not competent in or did not have time or energy left over for fangst.

Europeans stationed in Greenland most often bought fresh provisions which were a necessary supplement to their diet, paying in various kinds of merchandise, or even supplied a Greenlandic fanger with powder, lead, shot, or nets, and then received some of his fangst produce as a kind of payment. It was, to be sure, quite forbidden to actually hire Greenlanders to carry on fangst, but the method just mentioned, a kind of camouflaged hiring, is known to have been common.

By 1783 the "prices" of fresh provisions at Godhavn had evidently become inflated; the inspector had to stop the "price spiral". The crew were forbidden to give more than "at the most 2 ship's biscuits without butter for a grouse, and a proportional payment for other refreshments (but never butter)." If this prohibition were violated, the offender's rations would be reduced. "For if anyone has so much provisions in the form of rations that he can give Greenlanders ship's biscuits with a thick layer of butter, then his rations are too ample." Thrift was just as important for the individual as for the public. Sumptuousness was immoral.

The lack of domestic materials could result in extra shipments, in order to be able to supply what was necessary for the consumption of the population: in other words a growth in the service function of the Trade. In the Northern Inspectorate there was a noticeable lack of driftwood and thus of "timber for kayak rings and paddles as well as umiak bows and sled posts, etc." Inspector Johan Fr. Schwabe therefore requested the trader C.C. Dalager, then at Jakobshavn, to send samples of these various articles to Copenhagen so that the Trade could supply the districts of the Inspectorate with the most suitable materials for each item. Later various kinds of woods were actually shipped for these purposes. We have seen that "wainscot" (knotless oak) was shipped for use by Greenlanders, and that they preferred to have pliable wood for kayak rings rather than use old barrel staves.

The Management attempted to procure driftwood from the Southern Inspectorate in 1787, but the assistant at Godthåb, who had been asked to collect it, reported that it was so difficult to procure suitable driftwood at Godthåb that the fangers of the district purchased what they needed from the Trade. "Driftwood does fall around here, but it is quite unsuitable for such purposes," he wrote.

It was actually only suitable as fuel, and even here it was not sufficient. The fuel problem was beginning to be serious. Beechwood was taking up too much room in the ships. Coal had also to be sent to most of the districts, both for the local smiths and for heating. In 1793 a warning was issued of a coming fuel shortage at Julianehåb. "Firewood at Julianehåb, which must be collected fourteen mils away by sea and carried about ½ mil over land to the shore, is, according to the unanimous statements of the missionary and others, now so depleted that what remains cannot supply the colony for more than two to three years." It was thought best to avoid this ruthless exploitation in order to have a reserve in case the ship failed to come.

In 1802 the trader, Johan Chr. Mørch, wrote of the fuel situation at Julianehåb, this time about heather and scrub. These were "continually decreasing due to excessive use, as the new growth is not one-tenth of what is taken each year." He complained especially about the missionary, who used heather and scrub as fuel instead of his fuel ration, which he sent back to the Trade, putting the money in his pocket. This resulted in a reprimand being given to the missionary and a prohibition against cutting without the permission of the Trade. This prohibition could of course not apply to the local inhabitants: the Greenlanders everywhere used heather and scrub for fuel, especially in the summer. In winter, the blubber burning in the many lamps was used for heating.

Minerals

The century-long uninhibited inroad made by the Greenlanders on the heather and scrub growth was naturally increased by the need for fuel which the Europeans had all year around. What was still left of it reasonably near the colony seats was, as we have seen, insufficient. Beechwood had to be shipped, and has had to be shipped right up to the present time. Especially due to the small amount of room in the ships, the administration wanted to make use of domestic sources of fuel to as great an extent as possible, but with a sensible consideration for the conservation of resources. Peat cutting was therefore continued, but its quality was on the decline, and resources dwindled precariously.

Attention had previously been called to coal deposits.[13] There was such a great interest in finding new coal deposits that people began to see coal everywhere and were deceived by false rumours of deposits. In 1796 Inspector Bull reminded Heiberg, the trader at Holsteinsborg, of a promise he had made to Bull's predecessor. Heiberg had promised to investigate "the coal reported by the Greenlander Felix in Isortok Fjord." Two years later the assistant wrote in his diary that it had been impossible to get Felix or anyone else to join a reconnaissance trip to Isortoq Fjord. "Everyone had an excuse why he would not come, but they were unanimous in confessing that they had never seen the mineral which was now to be investigated seriously, but that everything they had said or reported about it had been told them by Northerners." So the entire story was a canard.

The canard had perhaps originated, as so many of this type of migratory bird, by whalers from the north speaking of coal deposits at Godhavn or Umånaq, and that the leadership was interested in mining this coal. Felix and others could then have imagined that they must also have some at their whaling station: this was Greenland, with mountains here as well as there. It was possible that there really was coal, this they can have intimated, expressing themselves vaguely, and their words can have been taken for more than they were worth. The canard can thus be due more to a typical European misunderstanding of the Greenlandic manner of expression, and it is because of this interpretation that the story has been told.

There was really substance in the coal deposits which had been investigated on Disko Island and at Umånaq. The prospecting which had been begun by experts in the late 1770's was continued by the Trade on its own. Although it was thought almost impossible to transport the coal mined at Skansen on Disko Island, Inspector Johan Fr. Schwabe started systematic mining in 1782. A former foreman at the coal mine at Umánaq was put to work mining at Skansen with eight to ten labourers. This was the beginning of this mining venture, which was, however, only capable of more or less satisfying Godhavn's demand for coal. In 1791 some coal mining was attempted at Marraq, somewhat nearer Godhavn, but here the shipping conditions were just as hopeless as at Skansen.

Coal mining at Umánaq was also mostly of local interest. The quality of the coal was only so-so; a missionary reported that he had received his fuel ration of Greenland coal, of which over 12% was useless powder. The rest yielded only moderate warmth, and was insufficient, as his supply was exhausted by April, three months too early.

At various times coal was mined at different places on the north side of the Nûgssuaq Peninsula. Around 1806 mining took place at Kûk, about 80 kilometres directly south-west of the colony seat. This yielded somewhat more than the district itself required, but under no circumstances was there ever any question of coal mining, either at Umánaq or on Disko Island, being able to supply more than a fraction of the demand of the entire West Coast. This mining of coal in the basalt areas of Disko Bugt should be seen in connection with the previously mentioned attempts at rendering blubber to oil at the whaling stations.

Other coal deposits along the coasts of Disko Bugt were known of at the time, but they all had impossible shipping conditions at the time. There were no natural harbours or places to land ships, and the giant icebergs as well as the many small ones made navigation risky. It was quite difficult to transport the coal which in a very simple manner was mined by hand a way up the hill: the chunks of coal rolled down as far as they could towards the shore, and then had to be taken the final distance by hand or on sleds.

The knowledge of these coal deposits was due to local experience, which had its roots far back in the century. Even the Dutch knew of them. The coal at Skansen was quite inflammable. It was said that it could be lit with a match. The local Greenlanders had quite early called this place *Aumarûtigssat,* which means "the glowing material", *aumaroq* being the North West Greenlandic dialect word for *ember* or *glowing coal.*

This experience of useful minerals in the ground of West Greenland continued to be an incitement to find more, and other types than coal. The Order of 1782 directly enjoined "the officers of the Trade to make efforts to find samples of whatever fine sorts of clay or minerals, etc. can be found there," and to send them to Copenhagen with a report on the details of the find: place, quantity and mining opportunities. It must also have been this instruction in the Order which underlay Inspector Bull's pressure for an investigation of the non-existent coal deposits at Holsteinsborg.

Dreams of mineral deposits in Greenland were still alive. There were still schemers who wanted the official blue stamp on the prospecting they contemplated. In spite of the amateurish nature of the prospecting carried on locally, it was more promising of results than the phantasms of the schemers.

The report of Eulner the surgeon in 1795 was therefore disappointing. When hired he had been instructed, in addition to his demanding position as the only medically trained person in the Northern Inspectorate, to make geological, i.e., mineralogical investigations wherever he went. "Among all the curiosities I have seen here so far, except for coal I have not yet found anything useful. I have found only mica, pyrite ore, crystals and such trifles." It had been impossible for him to collect a sufficient amount to send samples, "since everyone saves them carefully, either in order to have the honour of bringing them in himself, or else with ideas of personal enrichment. People who have never seen real ore declare all that glitters as silver or gold, and that may be why so much is heard of the rare minerals of Greenland." Something of value might be found farther inland, but the prospecting would be expensive and demand a special man to carry it out "who had nothing else to do." "It is also possible that the result would correspond to several previous hopes based on reports from Greenlanders, and no one would find it to his advantage, except for curiosity-sellers." The "coal deposits" at Holsteinsborg were apparently not unique.

At Julianehåb the assistant, Edvard Christie Heiberg, found something he took for copper ore. This took place around 1792. It was later attempted to find the site again, but this was not done until 1796: it was on the Island of Qeqertarssuaq in Igaliko Fjord. Johannes Andersen, the son of the former trader at Julianehåb, Anders Olsen, had a rather large collection of unusual minerals which his father had collected during the years. Johannes Andersen went to Qeqertarssuaq but found nothing resembling the sample of copper he took along; nor did he find anything resembling it in his father's collection. Less than a month later, however, Mørch, the present trader, reported that he had been there and found the copper ore in a vertical cliff over the surface of the water in a vein of feldspar fifteen to twenty centimetres wide. The ore was quite difficult to cut out, since the slope was so steep. "With a chisel and equipment as well as two half-barrels of hopes of good luck," Mørch went to work, but after four hours of exhausting work he obtained only some small samples of the ore and some of the feldspar it was encapsulated in.

Not until four years later did Mørch return to this copper deposit, where he observed that two veins seemed quite rich, and he intended to send samples to the administration. This was all that resulted from this "sensation" during the period from 1782 to 1808.

Offhand it seems quite peculiar that Mørch allowed four whole years to elapse before again taking samples of copper ore from Qeqartarssuaq. He simply had not had the time, and the site was located out of his expedition route.

This he said directly in 1798 in reacting to a circular from the Management, which had already requested the trading officers all along the coast to do as some had already done and find noteworthy specimens to send back to Copenhagen. Now the Management wanted to establish a collection of minerals and one of shells. Mørch expressed his opinion of this circular unreservedly: "Generally speaking the trading officers who come to this country are unskilled in mineralogy and conchology; may providence keep those who have some from studying them." "He who properly fulfills his important duties has - according to the importance of the establishment - very little time for extra excursions, and thus - it could at least be desired - this has been a reason why little or nothing has been done of what is recommended by Chapter Two of the circular." At the same time he asked for some literature on the sciences in question to be shipped, so that he could study them in his free time, as well as some samples of various ores. He also wanted to be told something about the use of a magnet in prospecting for minerals. He thought he could remember "having seen such wandering miners with their magnetised seekers." The Management replied gently that Mørch must have misunderstood the circular. What it desired was not scientific investigation, but only to attract attention to mineral deposits. It sent him a textbook of mineralogy, but told him that the use of magnets belonged to the world of superstition or fraud.[14]

The Management's circular must have had some stimulating influence. Mørch himself even renewed his investigation of copper ore in 1800, as we have seen. That year Schade, the assistant at Umánaq and Ubekendte Ejland, wrote in his diary that he and his trader had travelled to a settlement he calls "Sermisukken", but which must have been Sermiarssuit diagonally south of the colony seat on Nûgssuaq Peninsula. Here they saw the local Greenlanders with "a kind of red wood which was petrified." The Greenlanders said that there was more farther up a glacial stream. They "found several pieces: some large and small pieces which the ice stream had brought down. It shows that once there must have been woods on the land which is now covered with ice: the pieces of wood we found seemed to be from rather large trees." This must be the first report of botanic fossils in Greenland.

The reports given by Greenlanders of strange occurrences in nature were not always hot air, as the hoax about the coal deposits at Holsteinsborg. For a long time the inhabitants of the southern part of Frederikshåb District had known of a strange white, clouded mineral, found in the fjord east of Arsuk. They used it in a more or less powdered form to make their snuff last longer.

As a result of the general encouragement to send natural curiosities to the Management, samples of this mineral were most likely sent to Copenhagen. In 1795 it was mentioned for the first time in a European country at a meeting of the Natural History Society in Copenhagen. In 1799 it was investigated in detail by the Portuguese mineralogist d'Andrada e Silva, who called it cryolite: i.e., "ice stone". In 1804 both the trader and the missionary of Frederikshåb sent to Copenhagen "some stones from a mountain called Karusuktout, which lies in a bay called Amaksivik in Arsut Fjord." Although we have not been able to identify these localities, there is hardly any doubt that the stones which were sent to Copenhagen as samples were cryolite.

Ludvig Manthey, the Professor of Chemistry at the University of Copenhagen, became interested in the mineral samples sent from Greenland. In 1804 he gave an opinion on some clumps of ore he had investigated. These clumps do not seem to have been cryolite, but lead ore and what were presumably the samples of copper ore sent from Igaliko Fjord.

It was most likely the same Professor Manthey who called the attention of the Management to the fact that the Austrian-Prussian mineralogist Karl Ludwig Giesecke had returned to Copenhagen in September 1804 after a stay in Sweden. The Management followed up this matter and requested Giesecke to make a mineralogical expedition to Greenland. Giesecke replied on 1 March 1805, but not until July, when it was too late for the expedition to begin, did the Management get a royal decree that the voyage could take place. So Giesecke did not leave until the following year.[15]

On 19 April 1806 his ship left Copenhagen; it arrived at Frederikshåb on 31 May. He immediately began excursions in the vicinity of Frederikshåb, but when the ship was to sail farther south he decided to go with it to Julianehåb. In his diary he wrote what he saw of geological interest and gave a running survey of the geological formations and the main features of the geological structure. At certain places he wrote short notes on the flora.

It seems peculiar that on his first trip along the coast, from Frederikshåb to Julianehåb and a way up the East Coast and back to Godthåb where he spent the winter, he did not write a single word about cryolite. On his trip back to Godthåb, which he took in a small vessel, he must have gone to Ivigtut, seen cryolite and taken a rather large piece of it with him. At least there was a piece of cryolite in the large collection of minerals he tried to send to Copenhagen in 1807. Unfortunately the ship transporting it was stopped by the English, and Giesecke's mineral collection was sold at auction. The sample of cryolite which apparently was a part of the collection was evaluated at £ 5000 in 1812. Later Giesecke succeeded in getting most of his collection back.

The administration had guaranteed Giesecke a free stay in Greenland and free transportation all along the coast. The latter was relatively easy to arrange, but the former ought to have taken place by accounts through the inspectors. It was actually at the expense of the inspectors that Giesecke stayed in Greenland from 1806 until as late as 1813, due to the war situation. If he had not been an extraordinarily tactful and pleasant person, his stay would have been another burden for the inspectors in addition to the numerous difficulties they experienced during the war.[16]

Giesecke understood extraordinarily well how to make himself inconspicuous. It is said that even before his departure he had learned to speak and write some Danish. He naturally wrote his diary in German, but from Greenland he wrote several letters in Danish. His Danish must have been so excellent by 1807, that Inspector Motzfeldt could use this foreigner as his deputy. When Giesecke took the brig "Hvide Bjørn" from Godhavn to Upernavik in 1807, Inspector Motzfeldt gave him, if not a power of attorney to act in his name, at least various circulars and letters to take along, as well as a covering letter which stated "Both the Management and I will be much obliged to you for attending and directing this matter."

The matter mentioned was contained in an order to the assistant who was to inspect Upernavik for the Inspector. It must have been felt by this assistant as a repudiation that Giesecke was especially empowered to direct this matter, which consisted in assembling the local Greenlanders "in order to investigate with the greatest solemnity a) whether anyone has any complaints against Danes or Greenlanders, and if so, what they are; b) who have deserved" rewards. A little farther down the order to the assistant states: "If the Honourable Mr. Giesecke would as promised have the kindness to attend this assembly with the Greenlanders, then he is to be considered quite the same as if I myself were present, and whatever he says or does or arranges on this occasion is to be observed by everyone just as if it had been said or done or arranged by me myself." The assembly was held on 26 July, a Sunday, practically enough, and Giesecke played his part with much tact and understanding. That he was able to do this must indicate that his Danish was excellent. Nothing is mentioned of his having learned Greenlandic. There was no one present who could speak decent German, much less understand this language.

The reason why Motzfeldt allowed Giesecke to represent him must have been the fact that this Prussian honorific had been sent in the service of the Royal Greenland Trade, by royal decree, and since he was already in the service of the King, it must be allowed to make use of him. This could have been a burden for Giesecke himself; but by virtue of his humaneness the result was the opposite. He had good friends among both Europeans and Greenlanders. It was typical of him that on his trip from Godhavn in 1808 he explicitly remarked in a letter that the north wind saw to it that the women rowing the umiaks carrying him and his baggage did not have to work too hard. He was full of praise for his Greenlandic escorts. "I can find no faults with any of them: they are all helpful, and I also hope they are all satisfied with me."

There have been throughout the centuries few travellers to Greenland of whom so much positive and enthusiastic comment has been heard and read as of Giesecke. His stay and travels in the small world of Greenland were a breath of life from the great world outside. In addition these travels contributed to a greater knowledge of Greenlandic nature. They also form a prelude to that spirit of internationalism which on the whole has characterized scientific investigation in Greenland.

Giesecke's travels from 1807 to 1813 resulted in a somewhat greater and perhaps somewhat more systematic knowledge of the mineral deposits of Greenland. Compared to the dispersed information available previously, this was a large step forward, but it did not have any immediate significance for the exploitation of mineral deposits. The objective of the Management in sending Giesecke to Greenland had far from been attained, and it must have felt disappointed. Then and for quite some time it was only the coal deposits which were mined, mostly for local consumption.

The Greenlandic Labour Force

For this local coal mining local labour was used. Assistants in the service of the Trade took the main responsibility, while either stationed European craftsmen or intelligent Greenlanders served as foremen. The working crews in the coal deposits probably consisted mostly of colony crew, but Greenlanders seem also to have taken part.

In 1806 Inspector Motzfeldt thought that the rule should continue to be that the assistant supervised the mining and kept "the important and necessary things, e.g., distilled spirits and gunpowder in safekeeping." But if this were not possible because of illness "I have nothing against entrusting the powder, spirits and the like to that member of the crew in whom you have the most confidence, whether he was born in Greenland or Europe, and in this case there is no doubt that this man, on the recommendation of the trader, will receive a suitable reward."

The following year this decision was applied at Umánaq. Neither the assistant nor the otherwise suitable member of the colony crew could take on the exhausting work of climbing around the coal mine. They had both got hernias. The trader therefore asked for permission to hire the Greenlander Matz for this job, "for which no one here is more suitable." "During my time as foreman he also worked in the coal mine, and went on expeditions." During that time Matz had received a full portion of rations, except beer, and two marks a week; the trader suggested the same payment for him now, and this was granted. He was in this job for a total of twenty weeks, and received 6 rigsdalers 64 skillings, corresponding to an annual wage of 17 rigsdalers 64 skillings, plus rations. This was hardly a princely wage.

Matz' job in the mine is one example among many of how Greenlandic labour came gradually to be used and to be indispensable, in areas other than whaling. We have previously told of relations between the European leadership, including local leaders, and Greenlandic whalers; they were not frictionless. The conflicts which arose in this area contributed to the characterizations of the Greenlanders made by the Europeans.

The Greenlanders of Upernavik were especially given a broadside, both before it was closed as an independent colony and after ships were again sent there. "About three to four mil around the colony there live many Greenlanders," wrote the trader, who judging by other factors was not very bright. He continued: "- most of whom are the most incompetent and laziest people." Instead of looking for good fangst grounds, they concentrated around the fjords, "and with the most indifferent patience in the world they starve frightfully, only waiting for the arrival of spring. Most severe hunger is quite common almost every winter." He did, however, see some explanation in the condition of the colony in 1787, when its leaders had died for several years in a row. Due to these unfortunate circumstances their deputies, in order to relieve the situation, had given too much credit too often and supplied the local Greenlanders with Danish provisions, so that they had become accustomed to begging.

Even the otherwise so gentle and understanding Inspector Wille spoke in 1788 of "the indolence of the Greenlanders of Upernavik." On the whole this was one of the reasons for closing this colony. And as we have seen, when a trading post was again established at Upernavik in 1796, the bad reputation of the local Greenlanders continued. They were "stubborn and spoiled", and wanted European provisions for their produce even at times when there should have been an abundance of Greenlandic food.

Much depended on the behavior of the European colony crew, and especially of the traders and assistants. C.C. Dalager, who among many coarse words could produce some quite pertinent remarks, wrote in his journal in 1790 under 27 August: "the kind of people, of whatever rank they may be, who are to deal with this nation, will never win the least respect from them if they affect a somber, proud and retired manner, which does not impress the Greenlanders in the least; and such a person will never be able to accomplish anything good or useful for the Trade in such things (and this includes most things) where the assistance of the Greenlanders is necessary. They will always be quite immovable and indifferent, and do not tolerate a surly, even less a commanding tone of voice."

The difficulty was to combine the Greenlandic way of life with the European concept of duty, keeping agreements and constant work. It was enormously difficult for the Europeans to understand the Greenlandic mentality at all, much less to understand the Greenlandic attitude, bound as the Europeans were to the rationalistic concepts of the period – and by their meagre education, which had definitely not equipped them for working in Greenland. The colony crew, from labourers to skilled craftsmen, were often themselves in conflict with the moral attitude of the times in the widest sense. They were absolutely subject to the authority of their superiors, and further to that of the distant Management. This authority they automatically transferred to their own relations to the Greenlanders, as if the latter were subject to them.

The Greenlanders had only just begun to consider the local authorities, to whom the colony crew were subject, as authorities. The colony crew, and for that matter also assistants and traders, were in a way in a tight fix between the Greenlanders on the one hand and the local authorities on the other. This led almost unavoidably to an aggressive attitude.

The local authorities, including both the inspectors and the missionaries, represented, along with individual traders and assistants, the level of education of Denmark-Norway. But neither did they really realize that Greenlanders reacted differently from people they were used to associating with in Denmark and Norway. They were, of course, just as tied to their own milieu.

Various customary mechanisms went into action in the Europeans' relations to the Greenlanders, such as the manner in which they addressed them, the "educational" methods they used, and especially their judgement of the Greenlander's work in areas to which they themselves were accustomed. Such mechanisms also functioned in the personal association which of course also took place. In the mind of the individual European the actions and reactions of the individual Greenlander were generalized to apply to all Greenlanders.

This entire interpretation can of course likewise be called a generalization. For at that time there were of course both Greenlanders and Europeans who distinguished themselves by a positive attitude to the functions of society both on the individual as well as on a more general level. Among the best of the Europeans there was a distinct desire to penetrate behind the Greenlandic exterior. The language was for them a path which led behind the invisible wall.

Therefore those who had less command of the Greenlandic language constantly appealed to those who had more. "For those who have a mastery of the language of the country, I think it must be eminently easy to manoeuvre the Greenlanders as they wish, if they only take them in the right way," wrote Inspector C. Bendeke in 1799 to the assistant at Upernavik. He did not define in detail which way was the right way, but he did detail what the assistant ought not do.

Proficiency in the Greenlandic language caused everything to go more smoothly, to the astonishment of a senior assistant. In 1800 he took over the leadership of the whaling station at Qerrortussoq with much fear and worry, because the former chiefs, especially his immediate predecessor, had in vain attempted, using an interpreter, to get things to run smoothly, but the local Greenlandic whalers had become more and more refractory. Although this was rather an exaggeration, it was at least the impression he had of the situation. His fear and worry proved quite unjustified: everything turned out quite well for him, "perhaps because fate has been favourable to me and given me a slight proficiency in the language," sufficient for him to be able to straighten things out in person with the Greenlandic whalers. "According to assurances from local people," he succeeded "with reasonable pliability and mild persuasion in getting these people to abandon their previous torpidity and unwillingness to lend a hand," when it was necessary. To his own astonishment and satisfaction, he saw that he was awakening the desire to be useful "in these people, who are not yet so completely depraved or inured in vices, but more flexible" and easier to get to do something, if the Moravian missionaries had not made it "the duty of religion: to be against everything which is not of this sect."

This was perhaps an exaggeration of the influence of the Moravian Brethren. As far as can be seen, the leaders of the Brethren had not succeeded in making themselves authorities as far north as Holsteinsborg District. Perhaps this senior assistant had certain experiences from his former service in more southern latitudes. Many promising young talents were suddenly torn away in Greenland throughout the years. This promising senior assistant resigned the next year, but perished in the total wreck of the "Diskofjord" in 1801. It must have been the smallpox epidemic that got the better of him and caused him to resign.

The most pressing problem involved in the use of Greenlandic labour, especially at work which was not traditional for Greenlanders, was reliability, or getting them to keep an agreement, or "contract". It often happened, more often than related in the accounts, that Greenlanders hired for a job quit before their agreement had run out. The few examples committed to writing indicate that this phenomenon occurred more often than it was mentioned. Soraerneq, as this is called in Greenlandic, could have various causes, more or less incomprehensible to the one who had hired the person involved. For example, a Greenlander was hired by a whaling commander as a carpenter, but went his way for unknown reasons before his time of service had expired, and even, to the unqualified astonishment of the commander, without collecting his pay.

A Greenlander working as a cook was given provisions for six weeks, from which he was to make food for the colony crew, including the leading chief assistant. But on the third day he came and said he had no more provisions to make food from. The chief assistant, who was himself quite untidy, thought the cook had "wasted" the provisions on his countrymen, so that according to the chief assistant he had shown his lack of desire to work for the Trade. The assistant must have scolded him severely, after which he quit his job. The assistant reported that this cook "without any special reason has left the service of the Trade": soraerneq. It is quite clear what mistakes were made in this matter by the assistant; he did not at all understand that the abuse he gave him was enough of a reason for him to quit his job. The humourous aspect of this situation was that after this, the senior assistant was without a cook. How he and his crew got their food made after this is not reported.

A single reprimand could cause a Greenlander to quit his job. This has been experienced not once, but many times, right up to the present. It was - and still is - an enormous insult to be addressed harshly. The Greenlander could not answer back and rehabilitate himself, for at the time this could only be done by a song duel, and this could not be arranged with a European.

But even when a Greenlander on a job was scolded by a half-breed superior, he reacted in the same manner. The half-breed, Carl Dorf, the whaling assistant at Ritenbenk, gave in March 1799 "the national cook Jonas Danielsen", likewise a half-breed, "a well-deserved reprimand", after which the cook left his job. Over the summer Jonas Danielsen earned a wretched living for himself and his family, after which he was re-hired in October, but now as a carpenter, because he knew how to repair small vessels. This surely suited him better than being a cook. Besides, a new trader had come to Ritenbenk.

Although Jonas Danielsen regretted that he quit his job, he does not seem to have directly apologized, as another half-breed did, at Holsteinsborg. This half-breed left his job "in spite, because he could not tolerate mild truths and reprimands." A year later he asked for "and received forgiveness," and was re-hired at his previous wages. He remained in the service of the Trade until he was pensioned in 1840.

The soraerneq of two Greenlanders at Ritenbenk "without valid reason" led Inspector B.J. Schultz to order that they were not to be re-hired, but that the trader should rather "hire Greenlanders by the day according to need" until he could get a European, perhaps a member of the crew of the ship at harbour. The instability of Greenlandic labour was such a problem that even the Inspector suggested taking on casual labour, at least in an emergency. Then the trader would at least know where he stood.

It seems that around 1800, Europeans to an ever greater extent hired Greenlanders as casual labour or got them to lend a hand as a makeshift or when optional work was to be done and the crew was insufficient because some of them were away on special business, such as expeditions, coastal watches for whales, or the like. The work done by such casual labour was as a rule of secondary importance and was only done when it did not interfere with the fangst. It seems generally to have been difficult to get Greenlanders to take occasional jobs, even when paid, which were not connected with the fangst, such as mail trips or similar one-time jobs. If they themselves had some interest in or advantage from the work, then there was no trouble. It was for example easy enough for Mørch, the trader at Julianehåb, to get six kayaks to go for tobacco supplies, as everyone there was hungry for his daily dose. Individuals were willing enough to function as escorts or guides on trips or rowers in umiaks and the like, if the trip coincided with their own travel plans.

When netting was attempted at the various localities, the European crew available was not sufficient, least of all for the extensive use of nets. It therefore quickly became the practice to hire Greenlanders as net tenders; but the Europeans always saw to it that Greenlanders were hired who were more or less incompetant at kayak fangst.[17]

It was as a rule important to unload and reload the Atlantic ships as quickly as possible, so they could leave for Copenhagen while weather conditions were still more or less calm. As neither the ships' crews nor the colony crews were sufficiently large to do this quickly, the trader was often compelled to hire Greenlanders to help, but this could only be done with the permission of the inspector. That permission was necessary was due to the injunction of the Order not to take Greenlanders away from what was most important: their fangst.

It was thus based on an interpretation of the provisions of the Order that Falck, the trader at Frederikshåb, hired Greenlandic labour in April 1800 without getting the necessary permission. In this case he hired female labourers. When he departed on his spring expedition south, he left the leadership of the colony to his housekeeper and the colony work to the Greenlandic girls, "who have been told to stir the oil every day in the blubber house, which runs from the mass of loose blubber lying on the floor, and also from Michel's casks." Michel was the cooper, presumably a European. This is the first example so far of women doing work not traditionally Greenlandic. It appears from trader Falck's diary that this practice was not uncommon for him, but it was otherwise not ordinary. His remark can also be interpreted as a demonstration of how understaffed Frederikshåb was.

The sources are generally silent on children's work. This silence was, however, broken in 1791 and 1792 by the missionary at Godhavn, who in reports to the Missionskollegium those years complained that "the instruction of youth in the teachings of God was much impeded by the fact that before they are confirmed they are constantly put on whale watching." The reaction of the Management to this complaint is not known. But at a time when child labour in all occupations was a matter of course in Europe, the Management could not have been expected to set a precedent in child welfare and directly forbid the employment of children. In Greenland, as well as in Europe and the rest of the world, children's work was a factor in their training. The somewhat older children participated in the daily work, contributing according to their strength, capacity and degree of training, just as right up to the present older children on e.g. Danish farms have had their special tasks.

It seems that the optional hiring of Greenlanders as casual labourers took place at the trader's expense, or, if especially approved by the inspector, was listed as an expense on the accounts of the colony. It became more and more common during the period under consideration for this approval to be given. This was the beginning of the development of the group of Greenlandic women and men who were not capable of carrying on traditional Greenlandic occupations, or who had no special skills or training. Later this group was designated by a special word: *lâjat,* a word borrowed into the West Greenlandic language from the Danish *lejet:* hired. It was presumably first used around 1925.

Acute understaffing made the use of casual Greenlandic labour necessary, but this form of employment could not satisfy the need for staff at the colonies and whaling stations when the staff shortage was of a more permanent nature. A slow growth therefore took place in the number of Greenlanders employed more permanently in the service of the Trade, sometimes for the rest of their lives.

Table 17 shows that between 1780 and 1785 a great increase took place in the number of Greenlanders employed; this increase was greatest in the Northern Inspectorate, and within this Inspectorate greatest at Godhavn. This is connected with the change in whaling. The same table shows that the other districts in the north kept well abreast, although on the whole Godhavn presented the largest numbers of Greenlandic employees. Between 1805 and 1810 the two inspectorates had about the same number of Greenlandic employees, with a slightly larger number in the north.

This could be indicative of a conscious employment policy, which also appears in the written sources. In 1789 the former Inspector Johan Fr. Schwabe summed up the employment policy which the Trade in his opinion ought to follow. It was naturally kept in accordance with the Order of 1782, Schwabe's own work.

Schwabe thought it a matter of course that the European craftsmen and whaling sailors stationed in Greenland should be as proficient as possible. "National" labourers and sailors should only be chosen among the sons of Europeans: i.e., "mixtures" who were not trained in Greenlandic occupations. But "they should never be hired unless they are so proficient that they can perform their duties." Hiring "mixtures" should not result in the administration's having to hire further Europeans anyway, and thus increase the number of crew specified for one locality. The Trade should also insure that these "national" employees saw to it that their children were trained as "good Greenlanders"; i.e., for all kinds of fangst.

"I must furthermore remind you that but little is saved by employing nationals in the service of the Trade." They were to be paid with the same portion of rations as the Europeans, and their families had to be assisted, too, "as other colony crew" with blubber for their lamps. Transportation over the Atlantic was saved, the lower wages in money was a saving; "and these people are put to a useful activity," i.e., several good harpooners could be acquired for whaling, of which he names six "mixtures" in a row for their special proficiency. The "little" spared was nevertheless something.

Along with the growing problem of getting European labour, this saving was one of the motives for the Trade to promote the employment of Greenlanders.[18] This was not done, however, without much discussion and a good deal of worries. The possibilities of further savings were held out.

The employment of Greenlanders took place mainly in whaling. Inspector B.J. Schultz at Godhavn had stressed in 1791 that if more Greenlanders were to be employed in whaling, their conditions would have to be improved. This could be done by giving them part of the Greenlandic share of the whaling production, which they would not get if they were employed exclusively under the same conditions as Europeans. This would thus not be an increased expense for the Trade, but rather a nice saving. Furthermore, the Trade would be able to save on their rations if "it could be brought about that they, at least partially, could be supported on the food of their own country, thus saving Danish provisions." The Management referred specifically to C.C. Dalager's statement "that Greenlanders always prefer the food of their own country." It was only a question of procuring such food; this had at least to be possible at certain places and in certain seasons. The Management quite well realized that this was a problem, especially at Godhavn.

Naturally the Management had its misgivings about hiring more Greenlanders, and for two reasons. In the first place, it pointed out the usual reason! the fear of "unstability", and cited several examples. Perhaps, it thought, improved conditions would cause this abuse to change. In the second place, as opposed to B.J. Schultz, the Trade thought that

Greenlandic employees would not be reluctant to go in debt to the Trade. But that would be up to the bookkeeper, i.e., the trader or whaling chief involved. The Management only wanted to point out this danger to the inspector, or in other words stress that he should have no illusions about credit. A similar statement was sent by the Management to the Southern Inspectorate. 1792 can therefore be laid down as the year in which the Management of the Royal Greenland Trade went over to a new employment policy, compelled, as we have seen, by very realistic reasons.

This shift in employment policy was also based on certain relatively favourable results, so that the tendency to employ more Greenlanders was continued. The favourable results had been achieved in the 1780's, and after 1792 the tendency was increased in both north and south. Table 17 shows this clearly.

It appears from letters and wage books that the wages of Greenlandic employees of the Trade, in addition to a half or full portion of rations, rose from six or seven rigsdalers per year at first up to ten or fifteen, or even seventeen rigsdalers. This latter sum was, however, what the Greenlander Matz earned on a yearly basis in the twenty weeks he worked in the coal mine at Umánaq. Likewise the Greenlander Michel Michelssen Grætze was employed as a kind of part-time harpooner at the whaling station at Godhavn in 1787. He received a full portion of rations and 15 rigsdalers a year "on the condition that in the six summer months he was to be given leave from his service at the Trade to carry out his own kayak fangst." Here there seems to have been some doubt whether he was to get his rations in his six months on leave, as it was stated that of what he took by fangst during these months he was to sell what he himself did not need to the Trade.

This situation does not seem to be elucidated, but it shows how the inspectors were attempting to combine the injunction of the Order with the actual employment of proficient kayak fangers in whaling. This was a dilemma, since proficiency in both fields was usually united in the same persons.

When a Greenlander was hired as a craftsman at one of the colonies, there sometimes appeared a consequence which the Trade had not calculated on. It was the custom for a craftsman to provide his own tools. But an ordinary Greenlander was unable to do this, as appears from the case of a "mixture", the son of an ordinary labourer at Ritenbenk. The trader purchased a set of carpenter's tools from a carpenter leaving the colony, and listed it as equipment on the accounts of the colony, but on loan to the "mixture", who was hired as a "mediocre carpenter". The Management also raised his wages and promised him an annual reward if he proved proficient in this craft.

This dextrous half-breed was hired as a craftsman, but at a wage which only with the help of the yearly reward could exceed 10 rigsdalers per annum. It was different with Henrich Kleist, a "mixture" hired as a cooper at Fiskenæsset in the Southern Inspectorate. He had been taught his craft by his brother David Kleist, the first local manager at Nanortalik. He had been tested by the European cooper at Julianehåb and found worthy of his craft: i.e., he was recognized as a trained cooper and was hired with full rations and a wage "to be determined by the inspector." The Management added, however, "We will only point out that 30 rigsdalers seems, in comparison to the conditions of European coopers, to be the highest wage which should be given to a national craftsman. In the present case you should probably begin with somewhat less, so that when you are assured of his proficiency you can encourage him with raises." He was therefore hired at 16 rigsdalers and full rations. There were no raises, for he died in 1799.

The consequences of giving rations to Greenlanders as a part of their wages were not quite as had been expected. The Management had also indicated its scepticism, and Inspector Wille had expressed his misgivings about the rations. He feared that even giving a half portion to a single harpooner of outstanding ability would result in the other whalers refusing to go out without receiving the same. It worked out this time because the harpooner in question was also the only catechist at the locality. Wille experienced, however, that this catechist was, because of his rations, in danger of being "mistreated by his Greenlandic brothers," "when our friends the English treated the Greenlanders to too much spirits."

The allotting of rations did degenerate to some extent. In 1797 Inspector Bendeke granted a fanger a whole portion of rations to get him to settle at Igdlutsiaq, but he was reprimanded for this by the Management. When M.N. Myhlenphort was the trader at Egedesminde he expressed his misgivings at the decision of the Management that the portion of rations could be converted into money. He was only worried about this in the case of Greenlandic colony crew and sailors, who would, he thought, use all their money up quickly and then go hungry.

The case of allotted rations paralleled that of imported food in general: consumption was on the increase. This is why in 1804 the Management proposed conversion, to take place in connection with the issuance of credit notes as a kind of money. The credit note system will be dealt with later under reform policies. The war situation from 1807 to 1814 brought about a provisional halt in reforms. On account of rationing during the war, the Greenlandic employees of the Trade were, to a greater or lesser extent, deprived of their rations. Although these could be converted into "money" this was not worth much, because "money" lost its value as a medium of exchange.

The wages of Greenlanders more or less steadily employed by the Trade generally improved during the period under consideration; in comparison to previous periods they were much higher. This had an unfortunate result for the Mission. During the reduction of 1792 the Missionskollegium had to cut down on wages, and a number of catechists had to be deprived of their rations. Rudolph Lassen, the missionary at Jakobshavn, declared that he neither would nor could take this step, "as I avow to my superiors that the result would have been that all the catechists receiving rations would immediately have left the service of the Mission." The Missionskollegium would have to try to spread the burden somewhat equitably. This did not improve the current situation.

In 1798 the missionary at Umánaq wrote that "Last year two catechists rebelled and said straight out that they did not respect their wages, and that they would be satisfied at being released from their positions." To be sure, their resignation did not take effect. It was also motivated by the fact that they wanted to have permission to settle where it was otherwise more advantageous economically for them to live: where they could carry on fangst and sell fangst produce. The advantages of employment by the Trade over that of the Mission had gradually become far too conspicuous.

There were therefore quite a few catechists who had one foot in each camp. Thus the catechist Jonas at Godhavn was also quite industrious at whaling, and died in service in 1786. His successor as catechist, Benjamin, became renowned as the one "who by his example had taught the Greenlanders at Godhavn to throw a harpoon in the European manner."

In a way these catechists were following in the footsteps of Niels Egede and serving both masters. This was also true of most of the sons of the former trader J.C. Hammond.

The wage problems came to a head with one of these sons. In 1784, shortly before he became 19, he was employed by the Trade at an annual wage of 8 rigsdalers plus full rations. By 1790 his wage had risen to 14 rigsdalers. At the same time he had attracted extremely favourable attention in netting. In 1799 Rosenstand, the trader, said of him: "Whatever work this man is set to of what can be expected of the best Danes, he never refuses and performs his tasks easily." It was not necessary to supervise him. In short he was and had for some time been an inexplicably stable and dutiful member of the colony crew. Even Randulf, Rosenstand's predecessor, had praised him and evaluated him as equal to the European crew, and even better than most of them.

In 1793 Randulf recommended him for the full wages of a European, 30 rigsdalers, and the rations pertinent thereto, among other reasons because Jonas Hammond worked for the Trade all summer and had thus no opportunity to carry on fangst for his own needs; he and his family, which included many children, had to live on his rations.

The Management replied to this recommendation with a decision of principle on the issue of wages. "With respect to the main principle we agree with Randulf that all of equal proficiency should receive the same wages. But we also consider that a Danish member of a colony crew who receives 30 rigsdalers cannot be said to be better off than a national with 16 to 20 rigsdalers. The former often has an absent family to support, to which he must give some of his earnings; he is bound to stay in the country a certain number of years, and after this time he naturally wants to be reunited with his friends, so that he must try to save up something to start with when he returns home. The latter has, or at least should have, fewer and less expensive needs than the European; he is in the midst of his family, whose support cannot be much of a burden to him, if the natural advantages of the country are made proper use of; and he is not bound to any set time, but can leave his employment on an impulse, when he desires, often thus putting the Trade into an awkward position. If he on the contrary wishes to remain at his post and behaves well in it, he will not be chased away by the Trade, and is thus free of worries about his future old age." The Management was willing, however, to give this particular Greenlander a raise of 6 rigsdalers per year, which Inspector Schultz, considering the consequences among other Greenlandic members of the colony crew, converted into an annual reward of 5 rigsdalers, to be applied for every year.

This particular passage of the Management's letter has been quoted in its entirety, because it is presumably the first time a statement of principle was made on the concept of "Greenlandic wages". This concept had assumed a definite form by 1794 and was taken for granted by the Management. It did make a dispensation from the principle by granting a personal raise, which the Inspector did not approve and converted into a reward. The arguments used for maintaining a difference between the wages of Europeans and those of native Greenlanders were actually untenable. It had been proven that it was burdensome for Jonas Hammond to procure Greenlandic food, and that he had the same difficulty in supporting his family as Europeans did. Besides, a European received the same money wages whether he had the family mentioned by the Management or not. Even this early we see the argument used that the European was suffering deprivation, for which he must be compensated. Actually the Management as early as the late 18th century was using "the lower Greenlandic level of prices" in its calculations. The development of this case contributed to a great degree to maintain Greenlanders' wages at a lower level than those of Europeans. The nice introductory words about equal wages for equal work and equal usefulness to the Trade were wafted away by a rationalistic zeal for saving, camouflaged with moral arguments.

Jonas Hammond's superior, the trader Randulf, did not abandon this case. He brought it up again in 1798, as Jonas Hammond was seriously considering quitting his job. The next trader persuaded him to stay, but did not dare apply again for a raise which had been refused so categorically a second time. The fact was that Jonas Hammond had got into debt to the Trade because he could not manage on his wages.

However this may have been settled, it appears from his wage book that not until 1811 were his wages raised to 24 rigsdalers. This did not satisfy him; in 1814 he left the Trade and went over to the Mission as a catechist, in which position he died five years later.

Jonas Hammond was, as we have seen, a "mixture". The Management had many anxieties about this group. Juridically they were considered as Greenlanders when they were in Greenland, but in many cases they were not raised as ordinary Greenlandic boys - and it was actually only boys who gave the Trade trouble.

It was not possible, as foreseen in the Order of 1782, to channel "mixtures" into the Greenlandic occupations. Often, however, they reacted in the same way as "real Greenlanders" when they were hired by the Trade. Because in one way or another they were in a marginal position socially and culturally, they seldom settled down. Soraerneq was just as prevalent in this group as with full-blooded Greenlanders: i.e., they reacted as Greenlanders in acute situations.

Finally the Management could only see one way to solve the complex of problems surrounding half-breeds, especially boys. It considered and discussed in detail their raising and education. This then developed into a schooling issue, which involved the Missionskollegium. It also formed a part of the reform programme the rudiments of which occupied the planners of the Trade up to 1808.

X. The Mission, Science, and Other Aspects of Culture

The Mission

Schooling – if the instruction of children that took place in West Greenland in the 18th century can even be called schooling – was the monopoly of the missions and was narrowly limited to the objective of the missions: the conversion of the population to Christianity. This was true of both the Royal Mission and the Moravian Brethren. Instruction therefore included reading religious texts, learning the catechism, hymns and certain prayers by heart, and some elements of writing. The Moravian Brethren, who stressed personal revival more in their mission, concentrated less on the acquisition of religious knowledge and the skills connected with this acquisition. In no respect did these schools take secular objectives into account, although the ability to read and write was naturally used in secular situations.

By means of the daily instruction, as far as possible, of both children and adults; devotions morning and evening with the constant repetition of the more important articles of faith interspersed with learning the catechism; and divine services on Sundays and holidays, Christianity had steadily spread in the districts of the Royal Mission. In the areas of the Moravian Brethren, on the other hand, it seems to have found a certain equilibrium.[1] These tendencies are illustrated in Table 36.

However unreliable these figures may be, they at least serve to illustrate external conditions to some extent. They reveal distinctly that there was in 1789 a great difference in the degree of connection with the mission between areas situated near Godthåb, the first mission station, and those farther removed. There was likewise a considerably higher proportion of baptized persons in the south of West Greenland than in the north. In the Northern Inspectorate it was again the site first established which had the highest proportion of baptized persons: Christianshåb with Claushavn. This seems to indicate a certain "local tradition", created by the Mission.

Ignoring Julianehåb with its undetermined number of unbaptized persons, the percentage of unbaptized persons was greatest in Egedesminde

Table 36.

	Male			Female			Total		
1789	Total	Unbap.		Total	Unbap.		Total	Unbap.	
N.I.			%			%			%
Umánaq	75	42	56	98	44	45	173	86	50
Ritenbenk	150	83	55	167	93	56	317	176	56
Godhavn	65	34	52	74	35	47	139	69	50
Arveprinsens Ejl.	40	28	70	50	21	42	90	49	54
Jakobshavn	105	51	49	128	52	41	233	103	44
Christianshåb	113	40	35	167	51	31	280	91	33
Egedesminde	141	100	71	157	116	74	298	216	72
Kronprinsens Ejl.	19	10	53	28	15	54	47	25	53
TOTAL	708	388	55	869	427	49	1577	815	52
S.I.									
Holsteinsborg	153	11	7	204	27	13	357	38	11
Sukkertoppen	109	4	4	140	0	0	249	4	2
Godthåb	192	0	0	273	0	0	465	0	0
Fiskenæsset	141	1	1	201	0	0	342	1	0
Frederikshåb	270	172	64	423	241	57	693	413	60
Julianehåb							1443	930	64
TOTAL	865	188	22	1241	268	22	3549	1386	39
GRAND TOTAL ...							5126	2201	43

and Frederikshåb districts, with 72 and 60 per cent, respectively. Characteristic of both these districts was that the population lived rather dispersed and moved around a lot. In both districts Trade employees complained of difficult communications within the districts, which the missionaries also noticed, as they were entirely dependent for their transportation on the local secular leadership. At both colony seats the local Greenlandic population was small. It was rare that Greenlanders came for services to the colony seats, and long stays there for instruction or preparation for baptism could create food problems.

Table 36 shows that only in Godthåb District, including the Moravian Brethren at Ny Herrnhut and members of the congregation at a few other localities in the district, were all the inhabitants baptized. At Fiskenæsset the Moravian congregation at Lichtenfels contributed considerably to the large proportion of baptized persons. The one unbaptized person there is almost negligible.

According to this table, 39% of the Greenlandic population of the Southern Inspectorate was unbaptized, and 52% of the Greenlanders in the North. This tells us no more than that these percentages on an average had not joined the Christian congregations. There is no question of being able to say that such and such a per cent were Christians and lived as such, while the other percentage opposed Christianity and kept the faith of their fathers. These figures can only show us the size of membership of the Christian organization, but not the success of the missions in reality.

Within our period from 1782 to 1808, we can choose certain years to illustrate the growth of this membership in the Northern Inspectorate. This is illustrated in Table 37. According to these figures, a considerable adherence to the Royal Mission seems to have taken place between 1789 and 1800. The year 1800 has been deliberately chosen, because the census was taken before the smallpox epidemic of 1800–1801. This could have brought about either a relatively large adherence or a rather great decline in the number of baptized persons, thus unreasonably upsetting the balance. But the table shows that the decline in percentages of unbaptized persons took place before 1800, and a comparison with the figures for 1807 (1808) indicates that adherence was relatively constant throughout this period. This indicates a quiet growth in the results of the Mission.

Table 37.

Unbaptized Persons/Total Pop.	1789		1800		1807	
		%		%		%
Umánaq	86/173	50	83/441	19	62/432	14
Ritenbenk	176/317	56	30/311	10	11/363	3
Godhavn	69/139	47	22/196	11	31/254	12
Arveprinsens Ejl.	49/ 90	54				
Jakobshavn	103/233	44	34/271	13	3/250	1
Christianshåb	91/280	33	18/358	5	7/282	2
Egedesminde	216/298	72	93/335	28	39/266	15
Kronprinsens Ejl.	25/ 47	53	19/153	12	3/162	2
TOTAL	815/1577	52	299/2065	14	156/2009	8

Egedesminde still had the largest proportion of unbaptized persons, closely followed by Umánaq. By chance the civil registry lists of Christianshåb/Claushavn give separate figures for these two places for 1801 and from 1804 to 1807. These figures are reproduced in Table 38. The total population at Claushavn was relatively constant, as was also the number of unbaptized persons. The population of Christianshåb seems to have been more unstable, with immigration and emigration. The table indicates that the unbaptized Greenlanders actually seem to have moved out between 1804 and 1807.

Table 38.

Unbaptized Persons/Total Pop.	1801		1804		1807	
		%		%		%
Christianshåb	30/ 72	42	36/106	34	5/ 58	9
Claushavn	2/230	1	2/217	1	2/224	1

In 1808 the number of unbaptized persons at both places was listed as 0.

Claushavn and Christianshåb are relatively close to each other. A missionary had been resident at Claushavn for many years. The life of the congregation thus had a more stable framework there, which may explain the low proportion of unbaptized persons.

These figures also show that unbaptized Greenlanders were disinclined to settle permanently in such a closely welded settlement of Christians. The congregation at Claushavn was rather exclusive. This was not so strange, since association between baptized and unbaptized persons, not to mention cohabitation, was, if not a mortal sin, at least the object of the greatest disapproval of the missionary and congregation.

The baptized Greenlanders were actually isolated from the unbaptized ones. A rather widespread typhoid epidemic reached Jakobshavn in the autumn of 1785, where the baptized Greenlanders were afflicted. Not until the following year were the unbaptized ones, who lived a short distance from the colony seat, also attacked. They were not infected until their help was painfully necessary for the food supply of the population of the colony seat. This bears added witness to the isolation which it was attempted to maintain, more or less successfully.

The isolation of Greenlanders belonging to the Moravian congregations not only from unbaptized Greenlanders, but also from those belonging to the Royal Mission, was a long held and often expressed desire. It is suspicious that this isolation was felt to be necessary to the communal life characteristic of these congregations; but in the last analysis the background was what some call church discipline.

The organization and practice of church discipline in the Moravian congregations rested partly on a burning desire to assist each other spiritually in common, and partly on a fear of defection or misconduct on the part of members of the congregations. The fear of misconduct was expressed directly in the correspondence concerning dispersal, which as we have seen caused the Moravian Brethren much anxiety. The constant effect of being together and the organization of life by means of a division into choirs were means of keeping a rather close watch on each individual member and enforcing church discipline. Upon dispersal both Ny Herrnhut and the other Moravian localities experienced a degree of dissolution of the choir system: the division itself into choirs was maintained but the distribution of members to certain choir houses was totally abandoned.

There is no doubt that the communal life of the Moravian congregations, as well as the less aggressive solidarity of the congregations of the Royal Mission, was of paramount importance for the spread of Christianity among the West Greenland population. There were gradually created certain new, stable traditions, which for a long time existed parallel with the traditional Eskimo forms of common activity. The latter were not completely superseded during the period under consideration: there are several examples of "song-rallies" and other similar get-togethers.

That the sense of community was highly effective can only be a possible interpretation; it cannot be proven how this factor functioned. There is, on the other hand, abundant documentation that Eskimo beliefs and customs were still going strong, and not only among unbaptized Greenlanders. There occurred during this period a number of murders: one in one of the most prominent half-breed homes, the others in purely Greenlandic environments, all of which were motivated by old Eskimo beliefs which were naturally characterized by the European authorities as superstitions and attributed to the lack of education.

But even this does not really tell us how deeply Christian morals, not to speak of Christian beliefs, were integrated into the daily lives of West Greenlanders. In the minds of many, the two ideologies must have functioned side by side, with a preponderance first on the one, then on the other side.

This would correspond well with what else has been said of the Eskimo mentality. Two or more mutually incompatible factors can function together in this mentality, although to a European they would exclude each other. That conflicts of a specific nature could arise on this basis is obvious. Eskimo explanations and ways of dealing with inexplicable or antisocial phenomena could quite well have their raison d'être alongside the Christian-European ideology. It was the Christian attitude which was exclusive, not the West Greenlandic-Eskimo mentality. The function of the moment was decisive to this mentality, and thus also the reaction of those involved.

Christian morality seems to have coalesced with the West Greenlandic mentality to just as slight a degree as it was decisive for the actions and reactions of many Europeans. Superstitious beliefs haunted the minds of many of the Europeans stationed in Greenland, alongside the orthodox

Christian beliefs; especially in the realm of sexual morality the Europeans deviated considerably from Christian ideals. This appears in no uncertain manner from the entire problem of paternity cases. In this connection some paternity cases occurred among the Christian Greenlanders, who were strictly confined to the practice of monogamy; and some catechists working for the Mission sinned against the sixth commandment.

The Danish variety of European culture, including morals and social values, was integrated step for step into the tiny societies of West Greenland, but these steps were extremely slow. This was not accomplished without conflicts, both of a deeper nature, which at times surfaced to the level of consciousness to be preserved in the sources, and more superficial external conflicts, revealed in the actions and reactions of individuals and groups. As with all individuals living in a society, cultural conflicts could give rise to a divided mind, an inner spiritual conflict which in some cases would remain silent but in others take on external expression.

Conflicts appeared on several fronts: toward Eskimo tradition and its living representatives, the unbaptized Greenlanders; towards the Christian-European views and the moral demands they made on the individual, as well as towards the Europeans stationed in Greenland, who represented these views. Finally, many a baptized Greenlander got into the same kinds of conflicts as many a European in Greenland, as appears from paternity cases between Greenlanders.

In the ordinary Greenlandic way of looking at things there was an identity of idea, function and individual. An idea was perceived quite indistinctly, but it revealed itself on the spot and immediately in the concrete function, which was closely associated with the individual acting. Likewise in the Eskimo mentality functions were isolated phenomena. It apparently did not bother the ordinary Christian Greenlander that the great majority of Europeans in Greenland had an enormously loose relationship to European morals, which the missionaries fought for almost with their life's blood, and in any case were constantly preaching about.

These opposite phenomena could well exist side by side and function with equal right. This must have involved an infinite or at least for a time a growing uncertainty in the individual. Presumably without reflecting, the individual found support in the common activities performed, whether traditionally Eskimo or Christian, material or spiritual. When the function of a common activity faded away, when it stopped "functioning", the activity disappeared from social life or was demoted to rudimentary entertainment or pure child's play. This is a well-known development in other societies.

West Greenlandic society changed slowly. During the last quarter of the 18th century the Trade developed as a continually more important factor. The more it interfered in the material life of Greenland, as depicted and documented above, the more necessary was its presence in Greenland, even as a pure supply factor. The more the functions of the mission and the church were integrated into the life of West Greenland, the more these institutions came to function as spiritual supply factors.

There is no doubt that this was all the same to the ordinary Greenlander, just as to him the spiritual and the material were inseparable. The missionary could also to a considerable extent attend to the material aspects of life as well as the spiritual ones, as, for example, Cappelen with his active contribution to netting at Umánaq. This way of looking at things was incidentally not very far from the rationalists.

It must be emphasized that this "survey" of culture conflict is a construction, but it is based on material previously documented here and elsewhere. Sometimes such a fictitious development can be made to seem probable by an event which forms a contrast. A movement which apparently came into being suddenly in the northern part of Sukkertoppen District can be interpreted as such a contrast. This was the so-called Habakuk movement.

The Habakuk Movement

In order to place this peculiar movement, sometimes called "fanatical", in a probable relationship to the general development in West Greenland, it is necessary to some extent to look back at what is related of previous conditions at Sukkertoppen.[2]

From the mid-1770's on a relatively mild emigration took place from the colony of Old Sukkertoppen (Kangâmiut). This created a looser association between the various settlements in the northern part of the district and the colony seat. The southern part had always been far from the colony. From 1775 on the chief trader eagerly advocated setting up whaling activities in the district, which resulted in moving the colony seat farther south in 1781. The centre of gravity of the district was thus pulled out of the area which so far derived advantages from its proximity: the presence of the Trade and the Mission. As it was rather difficult, especially in the Winter and Spring, to travel from New Sukkertoppen to, for example, Kangerdlugssuatsiaq (Evigheds Fjord) and the other settlements of the north, contact with them became rare and occasional. On the other hand it was no easy matter for those living in the north to go south for trading and unifying church festivities.[3]

The missionary at Old Sukkertoppen, Bertel Laersen, had in 1773 complained of difficulties in getting catechists for those who emigrated. The residents of Evigheds Fjord had none. There is no doubt that the methods of this missionary approached those of the Moravian Brethren, just as the Moravian hymn book was in extensive use here. Bertel Laersen's preaching was certainly to a great extent based on revival. A prerequisite for revival is "inspiring" prayer meetings. His congregation was not, however, organized as that of Ny Herrnhut; it was not a concentrated settlement. Thus the common revival meetings could not be held as frequently or with the same effect as those of the Moravians.

Nor is there any doubt that these common assemblies were important to the Greenlanders of the district. Bertel Laersen revealed this himself in a report written in 1770, in which he said that the local Greenlanders assembled when he held the daily devotions for the Danish colony crew, in order to be ready to get a seat in the "chapel", when it was their turn. Many had to leave, if they had not secured a seat in time; others stayed away because they thought that all the seats would be occupied before they could get there. In the summer tent the situation was just as hopeless. There was, then, among the Greenlanders an unsatisfied need for these common "inspiring" meetings. Their dissatisfaction must have grown even greater when the population was dispersed and the "catechist supply" became insufficient. From 1775 on, when the trader began to work on plans of moving south, there prevailed a spirit of exodus which flared up from time to time. After the move was finally made, Bertel Laersen died. Due to the precariousness of the new colony, the post of missionary was actually vacant for two whole years. Bertel Laersen's sons, including the quite experienced, capable and sensible Frederik Berthelsen, together with the two or three other cathechists, managed as well as they could. But since there were certain ecclesiastical functions which these catechists could not perform, the service function of the church was partially halted for two whole years.

Whaling at New Sukkertoppen was, as previously described, no great success. From the very beginning this initiative came into conflict with the local Greenlanders, who had no intention of allowing themselves to be disturbed in their fangst cycle by the uncertainties of whaling, or to risk life and limb by going out onto the capricious open waters, which in whaling was necessary on the watchings. Since the entire attention of the trader was focussed on whaling, other aspects of the economy of the district suffered: i.e., purchases of Greenlandic produce were small, and conversely, the supplying of the Greenlanders with necessities was poor. The sources mention a large amount of credit, and partly for this reason, the trader was discharged in 1783. The post was vacant for a whole year, after which there followed a succession of four traders, of quite varying quality, until 1794; the post was also unoccupied from 1788 to 1791. A couple of these traders were discharged for disorder in their accounts or bad conduct. The continuity in the leadership of the district had been broken. Nor were relations between the Greenlandic inhabitants and the Trade improved by the fact that from 1782 on, Bendt Olrik, whose view of the Greenlanders was not very flattering, was the Inspector in the South.

During this period of instability the new missionary, Niels Hveyssel, arrived at Sukkertoppen in 1784. From the very beginning he was exposed to several unpleasant circumstances, all of such a nature that they discouraged especially this man, who seems to have had a mild temperament. There were his miserable accommodation at the newly-established colony seat, the arrogance of Inspector Olrik, and especially the language difficulties which he experienced, as did the most newly-arrived missionaries. To a great extent he was forced to rely on the catechist Frederik Berthelsen, which kept the latter from leaving the missionary to make himself useful elsewhere.

Niels Hveyssel was a Danish theology graduate, and naturally influenced by the rationalism then prevalent, far from the Moravian revival emotionalism. He must have thought it his duty to extirpate whatever of this weed flourished in his congregation. In 1770 Bertel Laersen had counted the congregation as numbering "over two hundred souls." In 1789 it was counted at 249, and 4 unbaptized persons were listed. The same year Hveyssel himself lists the figure at 298 and explicitly declares that there are no longer any unbaptized persons. He also mentions that he himself has baptized several Greenlanders. Between 1784 and 1789 he encountered the problems of polygyny, where he got into formal conflict. After baptizing a man, should he marry him to both his former wives, or only to one of them, and in this case which one? The Missionskollegium resolved that he could tolerate a catechumen with two wives keeping both of them after baptism, but that the church could not confirm this state by a marriage which would sanctify polygamy. As a transitional form, two wives could be tolerated (more than two seem not to have existed).

Underlying Hveyssel's inquiry in 1785 must have been a desire on the part of the newly-baptized polygamists for a regular marriage. This cannot be clearly documented, but it can be taken as a sign that ceremonies held in common played a role for the Greenlanders of Sukkertoppen. This was also shown in the institution of confirmation.

When confirmation was introduced, there were several baptized adults who wanted to be confirmed. It was ecclesiastically meaningless, but was taken as a festivity and as a special "ticket" entitling one to participate in another ecclesiastical ceremony held in common: communion.

In 1787 Hveyssel had several controversies brought about by the extremely loose-living trader, who had continued undaunted the way of life he had practiced at the other places where he had been stationed. Inspector Olrik protected him, but he was sent back to Denmark the following year.

These are of course only coincidences, but in a Lilliput society as the many small West Greenlandic societies were, where the behaviour of the individual was rumoured and discussed and generalizing conclusions drawn from it, individual events could not help being compared. In that very same year, 1787-1788, the Habakuk movement started, with the same sexual offence as that in which the trader excelled, but with the difference that he was single. The Greenlander Habakuk was married, and it was his wife who started what was to be a relatively short-lived movement: organized, but only loosely and casually.

According to the contemporary sources, this is what happened: One summer, while reindeer hunting, Habakuk "led immoral life with his servant woman." In the opinion of Niels Hveyssel, Habakuk's wife, Maria Magdalene, discovered this affair but pretended to Habakuk and his "servant woman" that she had found out about it from a couple who had long since died, but who had come to her one night and told her all about Habakuk's affair. Perhaps subconsciously in order to cover herself and make her tale more credible, she said that the deceased couple had told her some things about several other persons. When she had started, one word must have led to another, and she worked herself into an ecstasy. In any case she advertised these conversations with the divine messengers, the content of which, according to Hveyssel, consisted of the faults and mistakes committed by a number of other people. This then developed into a kind of belief that dead people did not go directly to heaven, but to a kind of transitional stage. God had sent the dead couple back from this transitional stage, so that Maria Magdalene could make known the faults of her companions.

Niels Hveyssel could not go to Evigheds Fjord, but he castigated Maria

Magdalene, Habakuk and "the servant woman" in a letter. Judging by his mention of this "disorder" in his report and his countermeasure, he did not take this matter very seriously.

The ecstasies of Maria Magdalene seem to have been contagious. Around the Christmas of 1788 another Greenlander at the settlement in Evigheds Fjord heard "The sound of songs and instruments in the air, and called out to his countrymen, who almost all claimed to hear the same, and even more, to see a large host of souls of the dead hovering in the air not far from the ground. They claimed to hear the souls of the dead singing hymns and the loud ringing of a bell, and this still continues incessantly."

At other places in the district, even at the colony seat, Greenlanders claimed to hear the same. "Of the Danes none has heard it, except for me, who have once heard something muffled," Hveyssel wrote. Apparently a kind of psychosis was spreading which ignited these emotional temperaments during the course of the winter. This is not uncommon during the dark period in Greenland, when there is something bewildering about the snow-covered landscape under the millions of twinkling stars set in a dark blue sky; this mood is even stronger in the white moonlight.

Maria Magdalene apparently continued at the settlement in Evigheds Fjord to tell her settlement-mates of her conversations with the deceased, and thus whipped up a sentiment among the inhabitants there. In any case after the Christmas event she must have embroidered on what she said she had heard from the dead, adding more fundamental messages to the previous information. It was thus not until later that she actually functioned as a prophet. "Doomsday was near," "God was infuriated at the infidelity of those who had contradicted her two years previously, at the godlessness of the Greenlanders, which mostly consisted in the fact that they had neglected the good Moravian customs which the late Mr. Larsen had introduced among them." She repeated and elaborated her concept of the transitory condition of dead souls "in the air or a special heaven with the large bell they could hear. But not until doomsday arrives will the faithful possess salvation." "Angels have not been on earth except for the Angel Gabriel to announce the birth of Christ." God had sent a number of dead souls, whom they themselves had been able to hear along with the ringing of the large bell, so they would better believe what she said.

On the basis of this source material, one-sided to be sure, it can be observed that Maria Magdalene's "gospel" did not involve any return to traditional Eskimo beliefs. On the contrary, it appears from Niels Hveyssel's reports that it was – as far as he could see – a return to certain Moravian common activities which the late Bertel Laersen was supposed to have introduced. In Hveyssel's formulation there is no doubt that Maria Magdalene directly refers to "the good Moravian customs" to which she wants to return. Further along in his report, Hveyssel elaborates on this by claiming that these customs "are still so fixed in their minds," and that the catechists, in spite of his prohibitions, continued to use Moravian hymn books, "of which the Greenlanders have many, some from former times, and some acquired recently from the Moravians." Among the Moravian customs, he names "Kissing during songs and the divine service, singing kneeling around the graves of the deceased, etc." It would have been kind of him to reveal what "etc." meant. Hveyssel shows his honesty in explicitly writing that he had inspected these Moravian hymn books, but found nothing in them which contradicted the "true teaching of the Christian faith."

Nevertheless, he sent some hymn books to the Missionskollegium for examination and a clear pronouncement on their permissibility. Hveyssel thought they should be prohibited for fear of the influence they could wield unknown to him. "The Greenlanders object, on the other hand, that I give them none of our hymn books; and though I tell them I have none and can get none, they are not content with this answer, but ask me why I will forbid them to use the books they can get, if I will not give them any myself." Hveyssel had to give up before such unmistakable logic.

The "phychosis" must have spread violently, for Niels Hveyssel took a drastic countermeasure which seems to have been unwise in just this context. "Since autumn of last year I have not admitted any Greenlander to Holy Communion; I have told them the reason why, and that I will not give them communion until they change their minds." Thus he excluded them from one of the common activities which this congregation particularly appreciated. At the same time he himself revealed that not until May 1789 had he been able to go to Evigheds Fjord, due to ice conditions. He had previously written to the local inhabitants and admonished them; but either his letters had not been read, or they had been burned. Neither his letters nor his trip in person had produced results. For over a year the missionary had not held divine services at this settlement or the other settlements in the north of Sukkertoppen District.

When we consider the previous vacancy in the post of missionary from 1782 to 1784, the few times between 1784 and 1788 that the missionary appeared in the north of the district, his refusal to admit his parishioners to communion, and furthermore that he could not give them hymn books, but still forbad them to use the hymn book they were accustomed to using unchallenged, one can hardly blame the members of this otherwise not difficult congregation for searching for the spirit of solidarity which they could not find in the mission. Not realizing this, Niels Hveyssel had made matters worse, contrary to his intentions.

It is most probable that the Greenlandic inhabitants realized the antagonism between the missionary and the Trade in this District, or rather, they could hardly have failed to realize it. During the time of Bertel Laersen at Old Sukkertoppen (Kangâmiut), the clash of interests was so obvious that when the Greenlanders were dispersed, Bertel Laersen felt quite superfluous as the missionary at the colony seat. The trader at the time, who was the most eager to move the colony south and start whaling, attempted through the Management of the Royal Greenland Trade to keep the Greenlanders away from the colony seat and divine services during church festivities. The Trade frowned on this crowding together of Greenlanders at the mission during the best fangst season.

At New Sukkertoppen, after 1781, the fangers of the district, as we have seen, felt some antagonism towards the Trade, toward its employees, who were so quickly transferred, and to the local leadership, because of the demands it made on them in connection with the hopeless whaling project. Finally, the Trade employees permitted themselves the sexual liberties which the missionary constantly chastised both Greenlanders and Europeans for. But the Trade employees took little or no consideration of the admonitions of the missionary. Therefore he was in the eyes of the Greenlanders incapable of functioning, just as he did not seem to function appropriately as a missionary.

Purchases of Greenlandic produce were for many years small at Sukkertoppen, which in turn meant that the local inhabitants were not as well supplied as they presumably wished. In accordance with local Greenlandic reactions there and elsewhere at all times, even the present, the local representative was most likely held responsible for what was lacking. So the Trade also did not "function" sufficiently.

It is probable that all these factors prevalent from 1776 to 1788–89 accumulated and made spirits tense with an indeterminate dissatisfaction or feeling of having been let down. There was thus fertile ground for the spread of some kind of psychosis. From this point of view, Maria Magdalene's conversations with the dead and resurrection of the common festivities which had been missed were only the spark which ignited what was already inflammable. Maria Magdalene and apparently also Habakuk intensified their activity.

It is actually unjust that this acute religious movement has taken the name of Habakuk, for it was his wife Maria Magdalene who actually started it and played the role of prophet. Habakuk participated actively in the movement. Whether by virtue of the inertia of development, whether consciously or unplanned, Maria Magdalene was recognized as the leader of the "congregation" along with Habakuk, and a kind of organization developed. This was expresses in measures taken against those who did not believe in her statements and in the judicial powers she assumed. Contemporary sources tell us no more about the organization.

Reactions against "infidels" were actually quite refined. Hveyssel reported them in 1789: "When the Greenlanders come to me, or I to them, and begin to speak of their errors, they give me no answer, but either leave immediately or begin to sing hymns in order not to hear me. It is quite impossible for me to achieve anything with warning, admonition and persuasion." The same was told by other contemporaries. There is no doubt that in the Greenlanders' eyes, Hveyssel was the losing party in a song duel: he did not have the laughter on his side. Only the form by which he lost had nothing to do with Eskimo tradition.

Quite untraditional, on the other hand, was the judicial authority which Maria Magdalene is said to have assumed. "She is carrying her malice and recklessness so far that she sentences whomever she wishes to exile, thrashing, or even to death; and her sentences are executed without hesitation by the Greenlanders." "The Greenlanders are so captivated by her pretended revelations that she needs only to say one word to get them to kill and practice the most outrageous violence, even on their own kin and closest relatives." Two women were killed because Maria Magdalene accused them of witchcraft. This is actually the only evidence of anything traditionally Eskimo in the movement. But it was not peculiar to this movement: all along the coast women as well as men were occasionally accused of witchcraft and necromancy.

Rumours of the executions in Evigheds Fjord were spread far and wide. A. Ginge, the missionary at Godthåb, wrote: "It is dangerous to visit, live, or associate with these confused people, as they do not spare the lives of those who are not faithful to their confused beliefs; they tied a stone around the neck of a girl and pushed her into the sea; two other people were persecuted for so long that they of their own volition jumped from high cliffs into the sea and drowned."

The Habakuk movement apparently reached its peak in 1789. Niels Hveyssel wrote to Inspector A.M. Lund in late August that Maria Magdalene was in many respects harming the Trade, "as she not only with her unreasonable talk keeps the Greenlanders who are with her from their fangst, but is even attracting the other crowd, those who previously were the real Greenlanders of the district as well as those who have come here this summer from both Holsteinsborg and Godthåb, so that almost all of them this coming winter will be concentrated at one place in Evigheds Fjord fourteen to fifteen mils from the colony seat."

In Sukkertoppen District itself the movement in 1789 captured almost all the Greenlanders. Another prophet even made his appearance. Later tradition tells that Elias, as he was called, came to Evigheds Fjord from the more southerly Agpamiut, and that he claimed that all those baptized were baptized in the blood of Tornarsuk. Niels Hveyssel also mentioned him, but in a considerably more tolerant manner than he dealt with Maria Magdalene. He apparently considered him a rather harmless disciple.

What was worse was that the catechists of Sukkertoppen District proved to have little resistance to the "gospel of Maria Magdalene, of the six catechists mentioned in the district, only Frederik Berthelsen was completely on the side of the missionary. Even he had almost "been blinded, when he in the spring accompanied me to Ikkamiut, where he thought he heard the melody of a hymn." But he had persevered in the true faith.

His brother Joseph was evidently quite bewitched by Maria Magdalene, although he admitted her absurdity to Niels Hveyssel. He presumably stayed with the two prophets in Evigheds Fjord. Two of the catechists apparently had some belief in this couple, but withdrew from dealings with them because of their "absurdities" and "inhumanity". Hveyssel described one of them as having "had his eyes opened, although for fear of his countrymen he dares not contradict her as harshly as he did before."

A fifth catechist, Isaak, previously considered as "one of the smartest and most diligent," moved to the settlement of Maria Magdalene and Habakuk "and let himself be deceived by her, so that he vehemently defends her cause." He was led to believe that he was Christ, while she called her own husband Jesus, "and says he is like the great God."

The sixth catechist had always been considered rather poor in his vocation. He had gone head over heels into the Habakuk movement, and was as a catechist, in the words of Hveyssel, "now so much worse that he not only himself has laid hands on his decrepit old mother, because the woman accused her of witchcraft, but has even persuaded his countrymen likewise to hit her. Yes, in spite of my warnings he forced her with his bad treatment to pass away, if he himself did not actually push her into the sea. He, along with several other Greenlanders, has actually done away with and cast into the sea another woman who had recently come there from Holsteinsborg, on the orders of Maria Magdalene." These may be the two women Hveyssel mentions in another letter, mentioned previously.

It is more than suggested that the movement started in 1787 as the result of an emotional reaction on the part of Maria Magdalene due to jealousy because her husband, Habakuk, had while reindeer hunting "led an immoral life with his servant woman." In 1789 Hveyssel wrote, "An unmarried woman has recently given birth to a child, of which the husband of Maria Magdalene, Habakuk, is the presumptive father. It has since become known that he stays with several women, married as well as unmarried." If Maria Magdalene thought that by her prophecies and conversations with the spirits she would gain more grip on her husband, she was obviously mistaken; but now the snowball was rolling and the role of prophetess must have suited her well. Habakuk did not take a co-wife until 1790.

It must be this knowledge of Habakuk's continued extramarital escapades and his final polygamous condition that caused the adoption of polygamy to be attributed to the movement. But there is nothing in any of the contemporary reports which indicates that this was the case. In the Mission congregation polygamy was only tolerated, as we have seen, if it existed previous to baptism. Polygamists in Sukkertoppen District may, however, have found a kind of security for their state by joining the movement. Freer relationships seem to have prevailed in this "congregation".

According to Hveyssel, the excesses of Habakuk "had so much influence that various Greenlanders who previously would not listen to me when I told them of her impostures, now speak of them themselves with contempt; other circumstances have also helped open the eyes of some. I hope that this will soon be common." We can only guess what these other circumstances were.

In August 1789 the trader of Sukkertoppen wrote the Management of the Royal Greenland Trade that blubber purchases had been more or less good only because a whale carcass had been found about 50 kilometres north of the colony seat, but without baleen. "Other trade with the Greenlanders has been mediocre; the reason is that they much neglect their fangst." Then he mentioned the Habakuk movement and its "madness", which he called its prophecies, continuing, "The Greenlanders now spend most of their time singing and listening to the supposedly wise woman who pretends to be their prophetess; the efforts of the missionary to straighten out these errant Greenlanders have so far been in vain; the catechists are with the exception of two, just as crazy as the others."

The trader could well characterize Niels Hveyssel's efforts as in vain. On the other hand, the missionary could reproach the trader because neither he nor any other employees of the Trade had given him the least help. Hveyssel had attempted to get support from Inspector Olrik, but he evidently did not want to get involved in mission matters, and besides he was about to be sent back to Denmark, so he did not want to have to account for more than absolutely necessary. His successor in 1789, Andreas Molbech Lund, was no advocate of using secular methods to combat a spiritual movement. Hveyssel had in his distress requested that "this Greenlandic woman and the most prominent of her followers be chastised with force; I myself am both too weak and have too little authority for this." He wanted to stay within the limits of the "Danish Law of King Christian V", but thought that by virtue of this code the trader or assistant could be ordered to chastise her, or at least render him some assistance.

Inspector Lund replied that he thought it best to act with leniency, "as time, if nothing else, will show the poor errants that the prophecies of the hag have been false. To convert her and her followers by force or in a Mexican manner, I would never dare to order." He had quite misunderstood the missionary, who would never dream of "converting errants by force or in a Mexican manner." But he did want them punished to set an example. He received no help here, however. In such an extraordinary case it was the duty of the inspector to submit the matter to the Management first.

But neither from the Management of the Royal Greenland Trade, from the Missionskollegium, nor from the central government did Niels Hveyssel get any support. Not until 1790 did Otho Fabricius deal with this matter, as one among many others, in a long report. Here he predicted that the Habakuk movement might spread to other districts in the winter of 1789–1790, unless the affair takes "a certain turn to disgrace its starter in front of her countrymen. In my opinion the only means which can be used is to get this prophetess out of the way, in the best possible manner. And her crimes must be great enough to make such a decision. It is only a question of how to get rid of this woman." He did not think it would help to move her away; rather, this could spread her teachings to other districts. There is no doubt that Fabricius contemplated having her killed: his words "make such a decision" mean "put such an end to her." He does not specify what means he considered – perhaps through the courts. These are like strains from a time long past, when the church called on "the secular sword" in spiritual cases, the solution or liquidation of which demanded physical force.[4]

Tâterât rock in Evigheds Fjord. (Photo F. Gad, 1942)

The tomb of Habakuk, near Igdlut in Evigheds Fjord.
(Arctic Institute, Charlottenlund, Denmark. Picture Collection no. 45.562. Photo O. Bendixen, 1918)

Otho Fabricius

(Photograph of illustration, probably in Fürst and Hansen: *Crania Groenlandica,* cf. *Meddelelser om Grønland,* vol. 60, plate XXXVIII, fig. 79. Reproduced from negative in Picture Collection of the Arctic Institute, Charlottenlund, Denmark)

Peter Hanning Motzfeldt as Inspector in the uniform authorized 1801.

(Reproduction after negative in Picture Collection of the Arctic Institute, Charlottenlund, Denmark. The original is a water-colour miniature, now in the local museum at Godthåb, Greenland)

The Missionskollegium had, however, before Fabricius sent his report, submitted the situation to Danske Kancelli, which resulted in a good deal of procrastination. The Danske Kancelli seems only to have functioned as a go-between for letters and inquiries according to customary procedures. An indirect and direct correspondence between the Missionskollegium and the Board of Managers of the Royal Greenland Trade thus continued well into 1791. By that time the Habakuk movement in Greenland had subsided - for a time.

In 1790 Niels Hveyssel had bitterly commented on the lack of help, but at the same time he had reported that "the fanaticism which arose last year among the Greenlanders has now mostly subsided, so that some of the fanatics, principally Elias, have voluntarily confessed to the imposture, shown serious contrition and promised to improve. The others are so deprived of supporters that their fanaticism is of no importance, as all the Greenlanders have promised and assured that they never more will allow themselves to be deceived by them." Habakuk and Maria Magdalene had been abandoned by all except the brothers of Habakuk. "Her husband's violent treatment of the Greenlanders was actually what first opened their eyes and deprived him of their support."

Hveyssel still wanted Habakuk and "the hag" to be properly punished. Habakuk had taken a co-wife "in the heathen manner", as we have seen. The missionary could not get him to send her away, so that he declared Habakuk a heathen and refused to have anything else to do with him or his family in the future. They were to be isolated and could only get out of their isolation by humiliating themselves. This actually took place in 1794, when Habakuk and his wife reported for confirmation to the missionary at Holsteinsborg, to which Sukkertoppen District now belonged. The fact that this missionary had arrived only half a year before may have played some role.[5]

The main reason why the great crowd in Evigheds Fjord dissolved and the supporters of the movement renounced it was, according to Niels Hveyssel, because Habakuk had treated them violently. He does not say what this violent treatment consisted of, nor do other contemporary sources satisfy us on this account. It most likely does not mean the execution of Maria Magdalene's sentences, since the treatment is explicitly ascribed to Habakuk. He must in some way have acted tyrannically toward the other male inhabitants of the settlement. Their reaction in 1790 can hardly be due to Habakuk's sexual excesses.

Oral tradition, written down much later, can perhaps afford some basis for an interpretation. According to this tradition, Habakuk went so

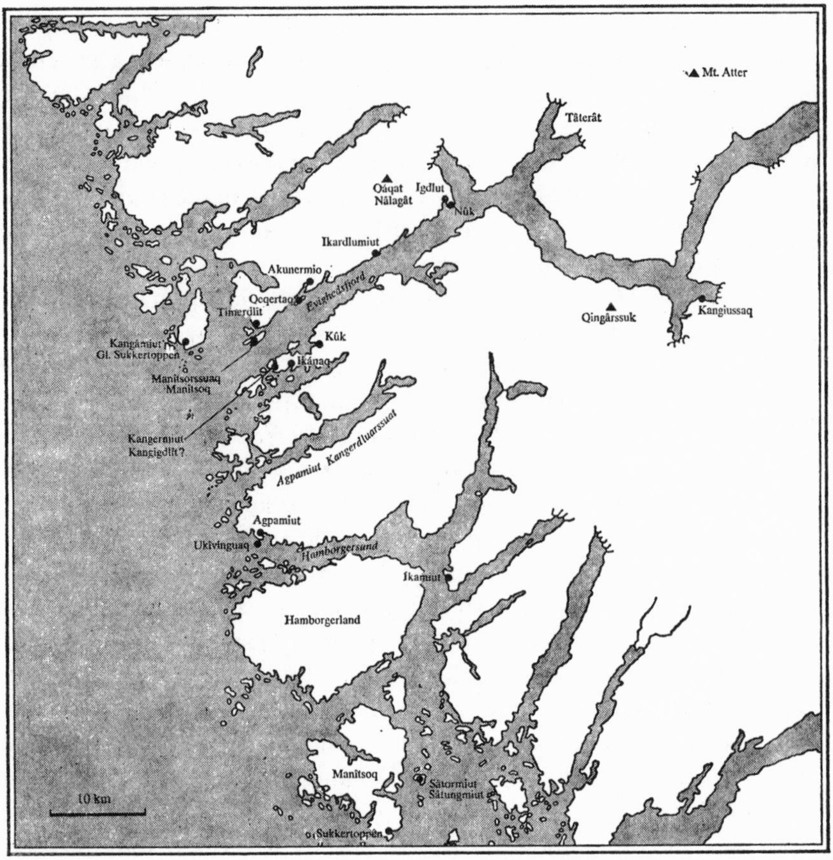

Sketch map of the northern part of Sukkertoppen District, including *Evigheds Fjord.* The various settlements are indicated by black dots, some mountain tops are indicated by black triangles, and areas of glacial edges by scalloped lines. On the north shore of the Evigheds Fjord, just opposite the contemporary settlement *Nûk,* is *Igdlut,* the settlement of Habakuk and his family. Some of the locations marked in and outside Evigheds Fjord are former Eskimo sites. Contemporary with Igdlut were *Kangâmiut* (Old Sukkertoppen), *Agpamiut, Îkamiut* and *Sukkertoppen. Kangigdlît* (Kangermiut), in the southern part of the mouth of the fjord, and perhaps Timerdlît, north of the mouth, were inhabited in the 1780's. On Manîtsoq (Manîtsorssuaq) Habakuk's descendents lived for a time. *Ukîvínguaq,* southwest of Agpamiut, was in 1788–1789 abandoned by Habakuk's supporters, and never reinhabited. Two names at one place indicate uncertainty about the name. (Sketch map drawn by A. Gaarn Bak, 1976.)

far as to forbid the fangers who had moved there to carry on their fangst. It is suggested that when the fangers whom he did order to carry on fangst returned with their take, he demanded that they give it to him. One of the reports amplifies this formulation to a fixed compulsory delivery of all fangst produce. But finally all the inhabitants, it says, became "so involved in all Habakuk was doing that they no longer carried on but lived on their winter reserves."[6]

This, compared with the other descriptions we have, may afford one possibility of interpretation. The need for common rituals was satisfied by the movement, but only partially. The movement took the place of the mission. Habakuk "functioned" as the other side of the Europeans' activities, as the Trade, but only unilaterally, as a "purchaser". Greenlanders were accustomed to deliver blubber and so forth to the trader, and this delivery was not connected to being supplied with merchandise, as we have seen: in the mentality of the time these were – as far as can be understood at present – two separate functions. Habakuk only "functioned" as a "purchaser". This could not continue in the long run if the supplies of merchandise were lacking. Nor could the need of common rituals be completely satisfied, as certain essential elements were lacking, such as baptism, communion and divine services.

None of the leaders of the movement, who had assumed an authority unheard of so far, could "function" in the long run. The doomsday prophecies of Maria Magdalene did not agree with reality, and her "revelations" could simply not continue. Supplies of ammunition were presumably depleted, partly because gunpowder was wasted on salutes, as mentioned in later reports. The assembled supporters were materially destitute by sometime in the spring, just as their need for common rituals had not been satisfied. Then they deserted: rebelled against the authority which was intolerable in the long run.

Ten years later at Kangeq in Godthåb District, there took place another rebellion against an authority. An ailing mother forbad her son to carry on his fangst. This led to the son rebelling against the maternal authority and finally murdering her. This reaction to a demand which was preposterous and impossible to fulfill, was drastic. A similar reaction could have been expected to the demands of Habakuk. But his authority, along with that of Maria Magdalene, was presumably already weakened, perhaps mainly by the fact that Frederik Berthelsen, who was quite well-liked, had not been deceived.

The reaction was not drastic, on the contrary. By July of 1790, Inspector Lund was able to report that the two prophets in Evigheds Fjord now "no longer are to them the important beings they have been; on the contrary, they now serve to amuse them, they compete in ridiculing them and find delight in telling disgraceful things about them both and calling them names."

This is surely as truthful a report as could be imagined. The reaction is typical. Habakuk and Maria Magdalene were in the eyes of the inhabitants similar to one who has lost in a song duel. This is on the whole the only really Eskimo aspect which can be documented in the entire history of this movement. Habakuk and Maria Magdalene had failed, just as the Trade and the Mission had failed previously. The Greenlanders returned to their settlements and apparently resigned themselves to what in their eyes failed least.

As related and interpreted, mostly on the basis of contemporary sources, the elements of which together form the history of the Habakuk movement confirm as a contrast what is postulated in the above survey of culture contact.

Greenlanders reacted, although not vehemently, to Habakuk's sexual excesses, which quite revealingly are amplified by the later tradition. This gives us a modest hint that Christian morals, as manifested on the surface, were beginning to make an impression on Greenlandic consciousness, likewise on the surface.

Bertel Laersen's form of mission and organisation of parish life had created a complex of traditions to which the adult generation was accustomed, and which had become necessary for the well-being of the Greenlanders. The Habakuk movement was based on random pieces of the gospel of the Christian church, sprinkled with Moravian elements, especially its common rituals and the testimony of those awakened. No obvious, unambiguous Eskimo beliefs can be found connected with the message of this movement. This must mean that the Christian religion, more or less deeply understood, but in any case with diverse elements, had taken root in Greenlandic consciousness. This does not exclude the possible continued existence of Eskimo beliefs in the form of superstitions, but conversations with deceased persons are not exclusively of Eskimo origin. Superstitious beliefs of general and specifically Greenlandic character were common in West Greenland, as we shall see.

The herd mentality: the fact that almost all were bitten by the movement and joined it, is a general human phenomenon, but due to the rather narrow confines of the society which the settlements in a district like Sukkertoppen constituted, the act of joining what the others were doing had a greater reciprocal effect. This perhaps also helps to explain why on the whole, the mission succeeded relatively quickly. A former example of the power of the community exemplified in the desire to be baptized as soon as possible had been mentioned in connection with the congregation at Ny Herrnhut.[7]

The Repercussions of the Habakuk Movement

It may sound brutal when the distress which prevailed in Sukkertoppen District in the winter of 1790-1791 is given as one of the reasons why the Habakuk movement subsided - for the time being.

This was perhaps one reason why - considering that Frederik Berthelsen would continue to be present at Sukkertoppen - Niels Hveyssel was recalled to Denmark and Sukkertoppen mission was placed under the jurisdiction of the mission at Holsteinsborg during the reduction of mission activities in 1791-1792. To be sure, Hveyssel's term of office had expired, but from 1791 on he would have had the opportunity for calm in his vocation after many difficult years. "I am especially afraid that when the congregation is without a shepherd, it will again return to its former heathenism," wrote Frederik Berthelsen in Greenlandic to P.R. Heide, the missionary at Holsteinsborg. "Its former heathenism" is Fabricius' translation of a complex expression which can just as well mean "their former bad ignorance" or "their former ignorant badness," and thus refer to the Habakuk movement. If this assumption is correct, Frederik Berthelsen was pointing out a previously mentioned possible reason for the rise of the movement: that the Mission had failed the Greenlanders. Now it was to fail them again, and therefore Berthelsen asked Heide to come to the district as soon as possible.

Heide had continually kept abreast of what was happening in these years in Sukkertoppen District during the crisis of the mission. He was on his guard against Habakuk and his sympathizers. There were Greenlanders from his own district that had joined the movement in 1789. He was anxious about what could happen now. He therefore thought it necessary in 1793 to "make an example of the well-known fanatic Habakuk." Although the supporters of the prophet were limited to her closest family, P.R. Heide shared Frederik Berthelsen's fear of what could develop. He wanted this couple to be publicly mocked, or preferably exiled to a place south of Julianehåb far from baptized Greenlanders: exile and isolation as punishment.

In 1791 Inspector Lund had had a pillory erected at Sukkertoppen; this may be what kept Habakuk and his family from approaching the colony seat - he remained secluded in Evigheds Fjord as long as Heide was the missionary, and it was not until the new missionary arrived that he in 1794 presented himself and his wife for confirmation. This can in any case be interpreted as an expression of the Eskimo concept of the close connection between person and action. Whether he was actually confirmed we do not know, but as long as they were both alive nothing more was heard of the Habakuk movement.

From 1792 on - and all the way up to 1902 - Sukkertoppen District did not have its own missionary. As early as 1795 the Missionskollegium dared to move Frederik Berthelsen to Godthåb, but he returned to his native district two years later, and remained until 1814. In 1795 and later on the congregation at Sukkertoppen must have been considered so reliable that no relapse into the Habakuk movement or anything similar was to be feared.

But such a relapse did occur. In May 1803 Frederik Berthelsen wrote to J.C. Büchler, the missionary at Holsteinsborg, "that a new fanaticism had broken out in this district around a certain Daniel, a son of the deceased Habakuk." In July the missionary was at Sukkertoppen, but most likely only for a short time, as he explicitly wrote that both in writing and orally he had ordered Frederik Berthelsen to "restrict by gentle persuasion the fanaticism which had broken out and hinder its further spread, by constant instruction and catechisation, performed by himself and the other catechists," after which J.C. Büchler seems to have withdrawn from this affair.

This missionary had been sent to Holsteinsborg and Sukkertoppen in 1800. He had experienced the smallpox epidemic of 1800-1801, which exterminated almost the entire population of Holsteinsborg, while sparing the Greenlanders of Sukkertoppen District. It appears that the resettlement of Holsteinsborg in 1803 drained Sukkertoppen of some of its inhabitants, although a larger number of immigrants replaced the many who left. The population of Sukkertoppen District from 1800 to 1805, according to civil registry lists, is listed in Table 39. The decline in 1805 may have had a special reason, one connected with the mission: the contemplated transfer of Frederik Berthelsen to Holsteinsborg. The decline in 1803 was certainly due to emigration to Holsteinsborg, but this in its turn may have been due to the fact that the Habakuk movement began to be active again, and that some of the inhabitants of Sukkertoppen District fled from it. There are no reports, however, to confirm this.

The reactivation of this movement must have had more or less the same reasons as previously. J.C. Büchler was not a missionary to leave Hol-

Table 39.

Population of Sukkertoppen District 1800-1805	
1800	323
1802	330
1803	282
1804	301
1805	277

steinsborg without special and very important reasons, i.e., he was not effective as a missionary in such a large area, not to speak of the care of the souls entrusted to him. Sukkertoppen was by and large left to Frederik Berthelsen, who was not ordained as a priest. In August 1804 another missionary, who had just come to Holsteinsborg, related that "The Greenlanders have not taken communion for 1½ years, and there are a number of children baptized at home, whose baptisms have not been confirmed." He had to postpone his trip to Sukkertoppen until the spring of 1805, quite simply because in the autumn there were no Greenlanders at the colony seat.

Sukkertoppen District had thus not been served by a missionary for one and a half years, since the summer of 1803, when Büchler had been at the colony seat, probably for a rather short time, and at a time when there were relatively few Greenlanders there. This district had, then, been poorly served by this priest for more than two years, during which time the Habakuk movement was coming to life again.

The winter of 1802-1803 was abnormally hard, and thus brought periods of hunger to the inhabitants. The Trade had presumably just as much difficulty in rendering assistance in the northern part of the district as in the south. The Trade thus failed the Greenlanders just as the mission did - but to a lesser degree. People from Evigheds Fjord came to the colony seat once to trade in 1803, the very day when Frederik Berthelsen left to stay with them. The same took place once in 1804.

The movement did not spread this time as it had previously done. "This fanaticism will have but little influence on the sensible Greenlander, but such craziness will the more easily find acceptance among the unenlightened and ignorant of the nation," wrote M.N. Myhlenphort on 19 May 1803 to the trader at Sukkertoppen. "If this fanaticism can by any means be expected to be eradicated, I surely believe that this must be done by a man for whom the Greenlanders have respect and confidence," he continued, and then named Frederik Berthelsen as the one who could presumably best fulfill this task. The trader was to take the matter in his own hands and explain to Frederik Berthelsen "how important it is for his countrymen" that the movement be quelled, as if Frederik Berthelsen himself did not realize this. At this early stage of development, Myhlenphort did not at all mention the missionary: he must have had no confidence at all in his activities in the service of the mission.

The movement now could not get a grip on the inhabitants, for the simple reason that many of them had moved north out of the district, perhaps to avoid the influence of Daniel. The activity of Frederik Berthelsen was this time decisive in nipping the movement in the bud. His position among the inhabitants was considerably more important than it was in 1789. From 1797 on he had in fact functioned as the priest of the district, if not officially, at least to the extent permitted by his status as catechist. As a teacher, a curer of souls, and a kind of director of the congregation, he was in constant contact with the inhabitants of the district. He also conducted devotions for the Europeans. In short, he functioned to a great extent as the European missionaries did, and did what was most important: he attempted as far as possible to satisfy the needs which existed.

After a few years farther north, Frederik Berthelsen returned to the colony. The Habakuk movement had faded away, but it had apparently spread to the north. A woman living at Holsteinsborg is said to have claimed that she was divinely inspired, and that "the spirit of God" spoke through her. She also thought she could predict the day of her death. "Nevertheless she speaks as one who has lost her wits, for example of cutting Edel's hair off and breaking her legs, etc. She has so frightened my girl that she has left me." This was written by an ordinary member of the colony crew: his "girl": i.e., his kivfaq ("servant woman") was named Edel. He must have thought this woman was mentally retarded, but her conduct was quite similar to that of Maria Magdalene. Nothing is reported of her further conduct, however, and there was most likely no question of an actual movement.

"Superstition" and Old Customs

Belief in conversations with the dead, divine messages and the sound of a divine bell were components of the ritual of the Habakuk movement. But these are not elements of mythical or mystical beliefs from the previous Eskimo ideology. Accusations of witchcraft were, on the other hand; but as we have seen these were not peculiar to this movement, but took place along the entire west coast of Greenland. Nor had many decades passed since Europeans had experienced similar phenomena on their home territory. Many a European stationed in Greenland at the end of the 18th century must have had more or less concealed beliefs of the same nature in supernatural forces which could reveal themselves. Even Niels Hveyssel, the missionary, was about to fall for the divine bell.

Of course elements of the Eskimo ideology continued to survive among baptized as well as unbaptized Greenlanders. They cannot be documented completely, but cases turn up in the sources which allow us to conclude that several elements of West Greenlandic Eskimo tradition had survived into the period under consideration.

Superstitious beliefs must, for example, have been the reasons why Greenlanders sometimes refused to settle at a location which was known to be a good fangst site. It might have been because someone had died there, or because a fanger carrying out kayak fangst from that locality had been killed by an enraged hooded seal. The souls of the fangst animals might have been insulted in one way or another, so it was most advisable to keep away from that place. When a whale carcass was found at Prøven in Upernavik District, it was said that no Greenlander, either from Upernavik or from Prøven, would go there to salvage blubber and perhaps baleen, partly because they were afraid of bad weather, partly because their umiaks could not load enough, partly for fear of illness (one man had died after the carcass had been discovered), "but mostly because of their damned superstition and laziness."

The manager of the trading post was here giving vent to his vexation at the profit missed by the colony, and also to his prejudices against the local Greenlanders. What kind of superstition was involved here is not known: the one death may have been considered as revenge on the part of the whale. Shortly afterwards, several families left, equipped with flensing knives. It really appears that the superstitious element was one of many excuses used to keep the Trade away from the blubber profit the Greenlanders themselves could take. There were probably no mystical beliefs involved in connection with this carcass.

Right up to the present time – of course with more or less conviction of correctness – mountain wanderers, qivîtut, have haunted, mostly in February and March. There is one documented example from Ritenbenk in 1787, and another from Frederikshåb in 1799. Concerning the murder at Kangeq in 1799, which has been mentioned above, Inspector Bull wrote that the "convicted" murderer "Peter has become invisible this winter; it is presumed that he died in his kayak." The uncommon expression "has become invisible" can indicate that there were rumours that Peter had "gone to the mountains" to achieve forcible and final revenge, as his previous attempts at revenge had failed. Bull himself hesitated to believe these rumours and added in the same breath a more plausible and realistic explanation of Peter's disappearance.[8]

"The great eclipse of the moon which occurred this morning caused the Greenlanders who were hired to transport Rasmussen such a fright that they left their dogs and sleds and in the sweat of fear hurried into their houses, from which they did not return until it began to dawn," noted Johannes Winding, the assistant at Ritenbenk, in his journal in March 1801, when assistant N.J. Rasmussen was to go to Godhavn. The old custom that men must not be outdoors during an eclipse of the moon was still operative in the 19th century. It was no wonder that they sweated the cold sweat of fear: they could risk being eaten up by the falling moon. But of this the assistant apparently knew nothing: so little prepared were the Europeans stationed in Greenland.

Other natural phenomena could awaken "strange feelings in the Greenlanders," such as a thunderstorm at Godthåb in February 1808. Distant thunder at Arveprinsens Ejland in October 1807 does not seem to have produced any reaction in the inhabitants at the colony seat; but this may not have been the case nearer the thunder.

From Umánaq in 1797 we hear of ritual infanticide in connection with illness, and also of infants who were killed if their mother died in childbirth. The local trader was afraid that this would take place if a woman at a trading post did not get medical help soon for a painful tumour in her breast which prevented her from nursing her child.

An old mourning custom may have been observed at Jakobshavn in November 1807. A fanger had been drowned in his kayak. A missionary named Bram, who had hurried to his rescue, attempted in vain to resuscitate him. "It was deathly quiet in the house as long as I was occupied with the dead man, because the bereaved widow and her family still had hopes that I could save him; but hardly had I stepped into the corridor before hope disappeared along with me, and all present began to wail, a sound which penetrated me with a fearful shudder and awoke previously unknown painful feelings in my soul." It is known in our time that when the news of someone's death is reported, the survivors give extremely violent and sudden expression to their sorrow.

Expression of greater joy were the constantly recurring Greenlandic ball games. It was not with undivided glee that Trade employees observed Greenlanders gathering to play ball. "Today the Greenlanders are beginning to gather for their unfortunate ball games, where in stead of going on fangst they would rather starve than neglect the game," wrote an assistant in Umânaq District in 1803. To a certain extent one can understand the annoyance of this assistant: quite a large number of people could gather on such an occasion. In 1808 another assistant, at Upernavik, reported, but with considerably more tolerance, that one Saturday in March, 24 dogsleds had come with the inhabitants of Tassiussaq, north east of the colony seat, to play against the Greenlanders of the colony seat. "For this game is the greatest amusement of the Greenlanders!!" The Greenlanders of the colony seat won, "a great shame for the northerners, who had gathered in the hope of taking the ball away." The "ball" was not a ball as we understand it, but a stuffed old sealskin or the like. The victors either took the ball away or kicked it in the water on their side.

Other traditional amusements were kept up; some were enjoyed indoors, others out in the open. The customary song contests seem also to have been maintained, partly as "judicial decisions", and partly as pure competitions. In 1799 Motzfeldt wrote of the Greenlanders' "public games or dressing down, which consist in them in turn, with jokes and songs, poking fun at each other's faults," but he ignored the fact that such song contests did not absolutely have to be held for "judicial decisions". Song contests were also held, for example, in which the inhabitants of different settlements would "deride" each other.

At least one "song contest" should be thus interpreted: it was reported by the newly-arrived Inspector M.N. Myhlenphort in 1787. In May of that year a large number of Greenlanders gathered at Igdlutsiaq in Ritenbenk District, coming from Jakobshavn, Claushavn and Klokkerhuk, as well as from the Ritenbenk colony seat. The latter presumably came to "support" the inhabitants of Igdlutsiaq. When those from outside the district left, Myhlenphort counted five umiaks full of women and 97 men in kayaks. "It was a beautiful sight to see all these kayaks floating on the water," he wrote. The idea of the "song contest" was that the inhabitants of Ritenbenk and Igdlutsiaq had taken no whales, seals or beluga that winter, "with more or the same." After the contest, there was a quick meal. "For it is a unanimous and invariable custom of theirs that when such song contests are finished none of those from other settlements must remain, even if a storm is blowing." They were accompanied to the shore with songs and the beating of drums. Participating in this get-together were baptized as well as unbaptized Greenlanders, as far as we can see.

Another example from this period of an apparently periodically resurrected song-contest tradition appears in the diary of an assistant written in 1800. Shortly after New Year there arrived at Claushavn a number of people from settlements in the eastern part of Egedesminde, as well as some from Syd-Ost Bugten. Some of the inhabitants of Claushavn went with the newcomers north to the coast of Jakobshavn Ice Fjord to await the arrival of inhabitants of Jakobshavn as their opponents in the contest. When the latter refused to cross the fjord, those who had come from the south resolutely crossed around the fjord (a daring exploit through masses of ice) "to hold their amusement." They returned the following day. The next year, now in February, a number of inhabitants of Jakobshavn came to the south coast of the fjord "in order to hold a baliârneq there, in accordance with their still prevalent customs, or practice the so-called contest songs." The next day they returned.[9]

The participation of baptized Greenlanders in such "heathen" customs was not appreciated by Otho Fabricius, as expressed in a general critique of the missionary at Holsteinsborg in 1791. Among other things, he ironically criticized the custom which the missionary had introduced of confirming Greenlanders baptized as adults, and continued by complaining of another custom "which even less should be tolerated, that the baptized Greenlanders participate with the heathens in their songs and dances. This custom has spread to other areas: a national catechist from another colony has complained to me about it this year and requested me to submit to the Missionskollegium" that it be prevented. "But this is not so easy to quell as it dates from former times, and one of the former missionaries at this colony publicly defended the song contests of the heathens twenty years ago."

This was a reference to Henric Christopher Glahn, who had analyzed the various song customs of the Greenlanders in a long treatise and attempted to classify the songs into permissible and impermissible. Belonging to the first group were the songs which constituted the main content of the song contests. According to him these were useful and "almost the only thing which keeps this free nation more or less within the limits of honour and decency." He could therefore see no reason to forbid baptized Greenlanders to participate in them. Otho Fabricius apparently did not share Glahn's opinions on this matter, perhaps due to a more deeply rationalistic mentality, inimical to sumptuousness and amusement.

The Central Administration and the Mission

Not that the situation of the Mission in the 1790's was apt to develop any sense of humour or tolerance which might lie concealed behind the seriously heavy exterior of Fabricius.

In 1789 Poul Egede died, and a new Greenland expert was to be appointed to the Missionskollegium. It had been the intention that Henric Christopher Glahn, the son-in-law of Poul Egede and formerly the missionary at Holsteinsborg, would succeed him as the advisor of the Missionskollegium. But although he had been appointed titular professor in Greenlandic in 1779, he had not been able to function as the direct assistant of Poul Egede, for example in teaching the students at the Seminarium Groenlandicum, because he occupied posts far from Copenhagen. Instead of him Otho Fabricius functioned as Poul Egede's assistant.

In the last years of his life, Poul Egede began a revision of his translation of the Bible into Greenlandic. Evidently he did not want to make use of Otho Fabricius in this endeavour, not even for proof-reading the sheets which were already in type. It appears, on the contrary, that Glahn helped Egede here, which was quite reasonable.

When Poul Egede died on 6 June 1789, Fabricius wanted a confirmation of his own position, and a decision made as to Egede's successor. This took place with indecorous haste on 8 June. Fabricius evidently wanted to forestall Glahn. This is actually not an attractive aspect of Otho Fabricius, but it can be excused to some extent, because he was so busy. He knew that not very much had been changed in the Bible translation, and not at all in accordance with what he himself thought best from a linguistic point of view. And now the printers were exerting pressure, because they did not want to be idle.

"The orthography of the deceased is quite different from mine because, as he himself continually said, he had not been used to stick to grammatical rules," wrote Fabricius. Fabricius, on the contrary, had continually made an effort to do this, and he found his translation and spelling of Greenlandic more in accordance with the language of writings which the Greenlanders had best understood so far. In addition, Poul Egede had used the Danish words for "sin" and "holy", where good Greenlandic terms had long ago been introduced. This latter fact bears witness to how deep the message of the church had penetrated into the Greenlandic consciousness. Poul Egede's translation was, all in all, out of date.

There were also other and just as important things which Fabricius wanted to see changed. The most important thing was that he made this a kind of condition for his possibly being able to completely take the place of Poul Egede. It cannot be seen that the Missionskollegium took up this matter right away, but rumours reached H.C. Glahn at his vicarage on the Danish island of Falster.

With a son-in-law's veneration for "the deceased bishop", he protested against the changes proposed by Fabricius: they would signify the ruin of all that Poul Egede had worked for. Glahn reminded the Missionskollegium of "the intentions the Missionskollegium had at the time for him, and how he had been chosen to occupy the post which is now vacant upon the death of the deceased Bishop Egede," and which he did not intend to apply for, least of all now. At the same time he characterized Fabricius as unworthy to unbuckle the shoes of Poul Egede. This letter is just as unpleasant as that of Fabricius, but in another way. In any case, it was an expression of the uncritical maintenance of a tradition which life in practice had abandoned.

This chain of events has been related because it explains the conflict between Glahn and Fabricius, and reveals something of the "power struggle" in the central administration, which took place even in the usually quite silent pavilions of the Missionskollegium.

The words "power struggle" are deliberately enclosed in quotation marks, because it was not really a struggle for power, but rather a clash of policies. This was a constant conflict, forced on the Mission by external economic, social and financial circumstances. If one wished to join this conflict and wage it for a certain objective, one had to have influence. Fabricius had a definite intention: that of using the mission to make the Greenlander a moral individual, inspired and strengthened as a Christian, and on a Greenlandic foundation, especially through the cultivation of the language. This was to take place *in Greenland,* and thus - in so far as he thought in a socio-economic matter at all - under local conditions. On this point he was in accordance with the Order of 1782, and thus with the principles according to which the Trade was to be managed in Greenland.

This was also the only agreement between the two institutions. Disagreements arose on matters of practice. To carry through one's principles, one had to have influence; this Fabricius acquired when he was finally appointed the Greenland expert of the Missionskollegium. He asserted to the utmost that the Mission was the most important factor in Greenland; the Trade was only to be considered as a supporting factor, and should therefore function as one and not counteract the mission, generally or locally.

It was therefore a frightful blow against Fabricius' principles that the government put a spoke in his wheel. Due to a momentary crisis the government found it necessary to reduce the expenses of the state. On 14 January 1791 the Finanskollegium got a royal decree providing for "a reduction of 6% per annum of several of the funds on the civil budget," thus reducing both the subsidy granted to the Royal Greenland Trade and the 1500 rigsdalers which the mission received from the royal treasury.

This naturally caused consternation in the Missionskollegium, which already had deficits each year on its Greenland account. The Missionskollegium had already pressed the Finanskollegium for replies to its requests for additional grants for missionaries' supplies. Now it was not only deprived of any hope of having these grants approved, but had to look forward to a further reduction. The Missionskollegium actually appears to have been at wits' end.

On 30 April the Finanskollegium sent another letter with a more detailed set of rules for what the Royal Greenland Trade was to provide the Mission with in the future. This was based on a representation to the king and subsequent decree, so the rules would be very hard to have changed, even more so cancelled. The Missionskollegium had to swallow this very bitter pill.

According to this royal decision, the Mission was to continue to get an annual subsidy of 2263 rigsdalers from the Royal Greenland Trade, which thus had to shoulder the burden of the six per cent reduction. But in quite a different manner the Mission was nevertheless affected by the reduction of this subsidy. It was to be limited to the four so-called "old" colonies: Godthåb, Holsteinsborg, Jakobshavn and Christianshåb. At each of these places one missionary and one European catechist could be appointed, with free board, light and fuel (and presumably also accommodations, although this is not explicitly mentioned), free transportation to and from Greenland, and up to a certain amount of freight transported free. At these and the other colonies the Royal Greenland Trade was to undertake to maintain all existing buildings used by the Mission, and to build new buildings. The supply and maintenance of equipment was to apply only to four "old" colonies, where one labourer was also to be paid by the Trade to work for the Mission. In these districts the Trade would pay the Mission's expenses for trips around the district, but in all the other districts, all these expenses were to be paid for by the mission on account. Out of the so-called navigation premium of 7500 rigsdalers (now minus 6%), however, the Trade was to grant 300 rigsdalers to each of the other colonies, and 150 to each trading post or smaller place, where a missionary or catechist was "kept". Expenses incurred by the Trade at each locality in connection with the mission were, however, to be deducted from these sums. Deficits in these accounts were to be compensated for by the Mission. Missionaries or catechists who travelled from or left colonies other than the four "old" ones were to have free transportation, but would have to pay for their meals on board and for the freight charges on their baggage, but at a reduced price.

It was finally decided "with respect to the deficit of the Mission, nothing has been granted for this from His Majesty's treasury, but such reductions will have to be made that the Mission, with the income it now has, can balance its accounts." This was quite simply impossible. Such a reduction would be almost tantamount with the abandoning of the Mission. Not even the congregations which had long ago been established could be served. The Missionskollegium gave up completely in the face of this problem, which it was actually impossible to solve satisfactorily – from the Mission's point of view. The memorandum of the Finanskollegium was sent to Otho Fabricius with a request that he give the Missionskollegium "accurate and detailed information how this can best be implemented, especially adding information on the locations of the other colonies with respect to the above-mentioned four, from which the other districts will have to be served hereafter."

Otho Fabricius at once recognized that it would be impossible to practice such a system. One cannot help wondering how the Finanskollegium, which must have had some knowledge of geographical conditions in Greenland through the Commission, could dictate so hopeless a system. It is also strange that the Missionskollegium did not know better when it forwarded this order to Fabricius. It is possible that the Finanskollegium wanted to be equally fair to both Inspectorates, for two of the colonies in either Inspectorate are called "old" colonies.

This choice of districts did not indicate much expertise. Godthåb and Christianshåb were the oldest colonies, but now they were actually the least populated districts. Jakobshavn was chosen, but why Jakobshavn instead of Frederikshåb, or why not Frederikshåb instead of Holsteinsborg, which was younger? This was decidedly a desk decision. What was worse was that in a way the Finanskollegium forced the mission to keep a missionary and a catechist at the four colonies, if this order could not be adjusted. If no missionary and/or catechist were kept there, the Trade was only to reimburse the mission for "the amount of such an absent officer's ration of provisions, etc. but not coal," and apparently not his remaining wages in money, either. This provision was to be retroactive from 1 July 1787, but as every colony had had a missionary, and most places a catechist also, this provision was not applicable for the time being.

Otho Fabricius must have been partly ignorant of what had passed between the Finanskollegium and the Missionskollegium during the Spring. It took him almost a fortnight from 8 July, possibly to blow off steam, at least to send a worthy reply to the order he had received.

Fabricius stated right away that the Missionskollegium's letter of 8 June

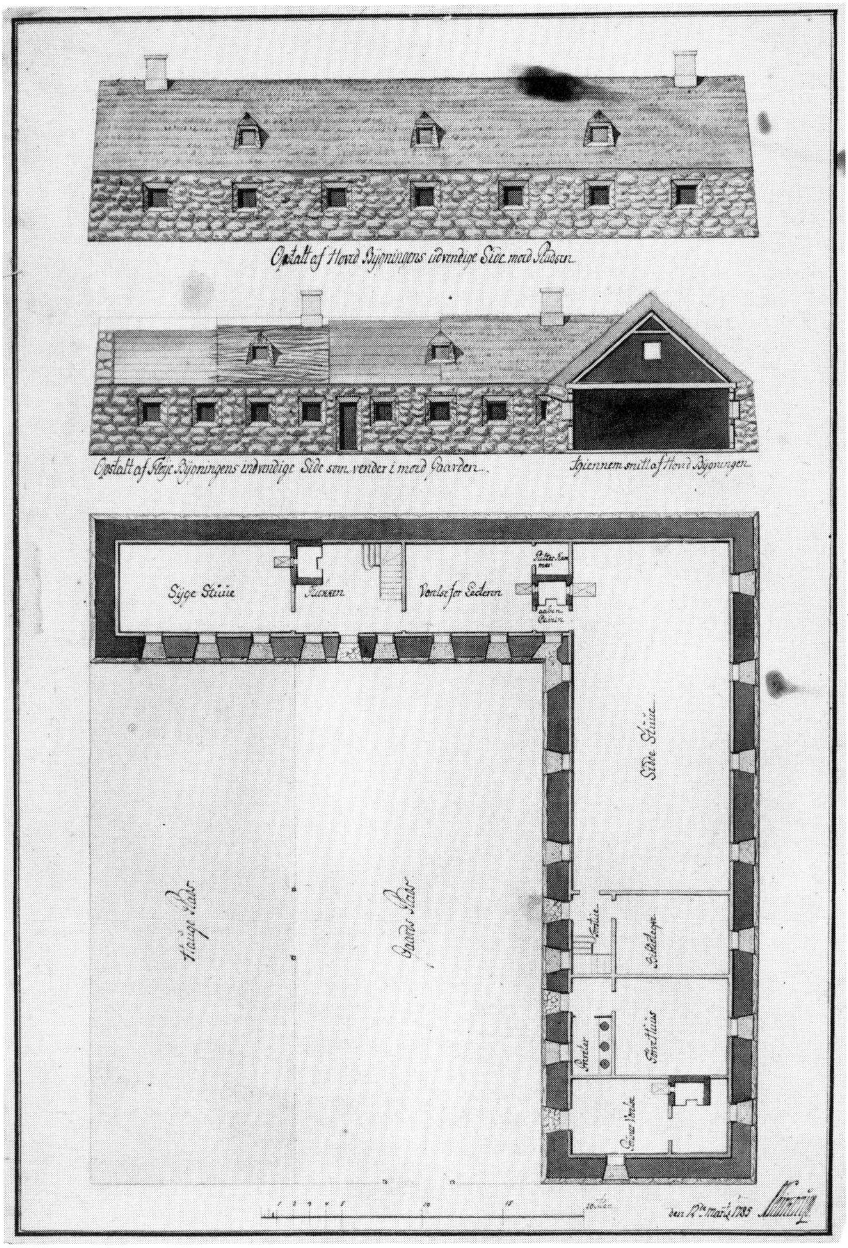

Master carpenter and architect *A.J. Kirkerup's* design of the Moravian Brethren's house at Lichtenau, dated March 12, 1785.

(Royal Academy of Fine Arts. Collection of Architectural Drawings, K.S. 141. Much reduced)

"The Ascension". Oil-painting on a veneered table top, probably painted by *Matthias Ferslew Dalager* 1792, original (73 × 104 cm) in Jakobshavn Church.

(Photo by Hans Petersen, Statens Museum for Kunst (the National Gallery), Copenhagen) had caused him "great anxiety and furthermore, embarrassment." He first called attention to the many baptized Greenlanders, for whom an affiliation with the Evangelical Lutheran Church and belief was natural. If they were not under constant influence from the church, they would feel abandoned. He did not directly use the Habakuk movement as an example, but it may have been in his thoughts when he stated that if the Mission let the Greenlanders down, there would be defections. These would especially occur, Fabricius feared, among those "who were not yet sufficiently strengthened" and would "make them half heathens." "May God take pity and in His mercy take care of these poor people, who are to be pitied in more than one respect." First they had accustomed themselves to various vices "of which they were previously ignorant," mostly through the bad example of the depraved colony crews. Now they were to "lack the necessary education to stop them on the path of vice." "With a passion becoming one who has loved and still loves the souls once entrusted to me, I therefore urgently beg the Royal Missionskollegium to attempt all possible means to continue the mission with missionaries at the same places as hitherto, before it incurs such a responsibility as the implementation of this decision will in my opinion involve."

Could the promotion of religion be the only activity which could not get support in these times, Fabricius asked. Were the royal finances really in such a poor state that not even the mission's deficit could be covered? People are willing enough to contribute to collections to build churches, for the poor and the unemployed, to support the liberation of the peasants, and to various societies and other objectives "the intended use of which is of unequally less importance and duration than that of the mission, which aims at the honour of God and the prosperity of many souls for all eternity." He recommended the Missionskollegium to have a collection taken up in churches.

If the Missionskollegium should feel that this proposal was unfeasible, Fabricius for his part would have to "directly confess my inability to satisfy its demand" for a complete plan of how to implement the royal decree. "For I consider it quite impossible for 4 missionaries to administer what 10 missionaries have hitherto been unable to." He then informed the Missionskollegium in brief of the conditions of the Mission in Greenland at the time: facts which this body should already have realized.

Fabricius pointed out the inappropriateness of the royal choice of mission stations which were to be central, and asked whether the Misskonskollegium was absolutely bound to maintain them. If it could be done, he would rather see Frederikshåb, Holsteinsborg, Jakobshavn and Godhavn as the central mission stations. And with this he thought that he had expressed his opinion of what could be done in the existing situation. He had not gone into details, because he in advance considered the entire proposal too insufficient to be implemented.

With this contribution Otho Fabricius had distinctly refused to cooperate with the Missionskollegium and in addition indirectly reproached the leaders of present and former times for not having publicized sufficiently the development of the mission in Greenland, in other words for not having long since stirred up a public feeling favourable to the work and position of the mission. Fabricius must then have attributed considerable importance to such a public expression of opinion in the Danish society under the autocracy. In his reply he not only struck out at the Missionskollegium, but through this body at the Royal Greenland Trade, the Commission, the Finanskollegium and finally, the government. That was bold.

During the following month the changes proposed by Fabricius were discussed. But the Missionskollegium did not agree to the substance of his letter of 20 June. This led Fabricius to attempt once again to get the Missionskollegium to obtain a change in the royal decree and not just remain passive and blindly obey. "I dare to repeat my urgent and humble request that the Missionskollegium see to it that the frightful storm is repelled which is approaching poor Greenland; for I do not think that the implementation of this plan can be defended before God." The reduction would not be a blessing, nor would it produce the expected savings for the Mission, he wrote. More catechists would have to be hired and they would surely be expensive. In addition the distant travels of the missionaries would be a burden on the budget. The Missionskollegium resolved laconically to let this request remain "in abeyance for the time being."

With this letter Fabricius had put himself out of action. The Missionskollegium had to take the matter in its own hands, but it did to some extent follow the advice of its advisor - Fabricius - on the location of the missionaries.

Fabricius' reaction, as well as that of the Missionskollegium, must be seen against the background of growing attacks in Denmark/Norway on the state church as an institution, and in general on the teachings and function of the church. The 1790's were the decade of deism and anticlericalism in these realms, perhaps most vehemently expressed in Copenhagen under the prevailing freedom of the press. The reduction of the Mission in Greenland must have been perceived by Fabricius and the Missionskollegium as an expression of the mentality of the time. That the reduction was dictated by the secular authorities only intensified the bitter feelings which every ecclesiastical person must have harboured. The officers of the Royal Greenland Trade both in Greenland and in Copenhagen had for years been opponents of the Mission. Now they were apparently fishing in troubled waters, and in the last analysis it was perhaps they who were now attempting to smash the Mission definitively. The Missionskollegium would have to insist on its rights. But precisely because the reduction was dictated by the government, this subordinate body would have to deal with caution. Its members were up against a wall with their opponents surrounding them, and there was an eerie feeling that someone was about to crawl over the wall and attack them from above.

Before the final decision, however, a confrontation of a rather bitter nature took place, which showed that the Missionskollegium, when sufficiently provoked, could fight for its rights. The confrontation also revealed the front lines between the Royal Greenland Trade and the Mission.

In 1790 the Missionskollegium had, as we have seen, complained to the Commission of the Royal Greenland Trade about various conditions in Greenland, especially the burdens placed on the missionaries in the form of demands for the payment of freight charges and percentage fees for the provisions they ordered for their personal use in addition to the provisions furnished by the Trade, which were most often inedible. The Missionskollegium had amassed its big artillery: "since His Royal Majesty founded the Trade in Greenland to help the Mission, it can by no means be in consonance with His most gracious will that the Mission is pressed on all sides by the Trade," not to mention "the improper way many trading officers deal with the officers of the mission." The conditions afforded the missionaries were so intolerable that many of them had threatened to leave Greenland before the expiry of their period of service. The Missionskollegium received no answer to this letter, although it pressed for an answer four times in the following period.

In one of these reminders the Missionskollegium mentioned in addition a complaint which had already been made about the annual deficiencies in the treasury of the Greenland Mission. By February 1791 no decision had as yet been made on a representation submitted in August 1785! The Missionskollegium had then asked for "some kind of support" for the mission in Greenland. Now instead, as an answer to all the requests and reminders which had been submitted, the Missionskollegium received the communication from the Danske Kancelli and from the Finanskollegium, the royal decree of 30 April.

No wonder the deputies of the Missionskollegium were dumbfounded; their actions had achieved a result which was diametrically opposite to what they had intended. One of these actions had even taken place before Fabricius took office. On this basis one can better understand why the Missionskollegium could not adopt Fabricius' proposals and had to qualify them in advance as hopeless.

During the summer and part of the autumn a rather unpleasant correspondence took place between the Management of the Royal Greenland Trade and the Missionskollegium. Each of these two parties naturally wanted to unload as much of the reduction on the other as possible. But here the Missionskollegium was on firm ground: the letter of 30 April from the Finanskollegium.

During the autumn the Missionskollegium finally found a basis on which it could more or less stand. At least it thought it could invent a system so that its accounts would balance. Income was estimated at 3480 rigsdalers and expenses at 3467 rigsdalers, which should even yield a modest surplus. This calculation proved to be quite inadequate, but the proposal on which it was based nevertheless remained as the final standpoint of the Missionskollegium. On 22 December the Missionskollegium sent its proposal to royal representation.

As the representation of the Missionskollegium contained certain interpretations of the letter of 30 April of the Finanskollegium regarding the economic duties of the Trade toward the Mission, including the refunding of provisions and fuel rations as well as accommodations in the four "old" colonies, transportation, and a prohibition against employing catechists in the service of the Trade, the Danske Kancelli sent the proposal to the Management of the Royal Greenland Trade for its comments. The reply of the Management was quite acrid, considering the circumstances; it insisted on its right to refund as little as possible and to charge for as much as possible. The Management actually had its own hard-pressed economy to think of. It admitted that it must be unpleasant for the Mission when a catechist went over to the service of the Trade. Only one example of this was known, but the Management was willing to serve the Mission by refusing to hire catechists who had been discharged. The Mission in its turn would have to refuse to hire employees of the Trade.

On this point the hands of the Trade were not as clean as the Management implied. It was often possible to tempt a catechist to leave the Mission with the higher wages and better rations which the Trade was able to offer. But this was a problem which will be dealt with later.

The Management took advantage of the opportunity to lash out at the

Mission. It was not a matter of indifference to the Trade, it said, where missions were established, "as it is a generally recognized truth that Greenlanders concentrate around the places where the missionary stays." It stressed the importance of establishing missions where there were good fangst opportunities. For economic and food reasons, especially considering the general periods of famine, the Management wanted negotiations to be held between itself and the Mission before a missionary was sent to stay at a locality, and before essential changes were made in the Mission.

The Missionskollegium took all this as improper interference in its rights. In addition, the concluding comments of the Management, about the concentration of Greenlanders where the missionary resided, were contrary to the instruction which the Missionskollegium had issued on 4 April 1791 to all its missionaries, the first paragraph of which said: "It must be observed with the greatest care that baptized Greenlanders are not dispersed over too many places, but that they, as far as possible, remain near each other, so that a smaller number of catechists will be needed, and education can best be promoted." Here was the germ of a permanent clash of interests between the Trade and the Mission, on all levels, both central and local. The Management could not have been unaware of this paragraph in the instruction, but it must also have based its comments on years of experience of local controversies concerning dispersal. On the other hand one can not blame the Missionskollegium for not wanting immediately to disavow the instructions it had just issued.

When the comments of the Management were submitted to the Missionskollegium, it did not take long to reach a final decision, and notified the Danske Kancelli that it was "determined, without engaging in further negotiations with the above-mentioned Management, to effect the changes and reductions in this mission," which were deemed necessary, and which the Missionskollegium felt authorized to do. It also referred to the Royal Order of 10 December 1714, the basis for the entire activity of the Missionskollegium.

On 2 March 1792 the Missionskollegium notified the Management of the Royal Greenland Trade of the decision it had made. This was later committed to an instruction to the missionaries in Greenland. In the future there were to be five missionaries stationed in Greenland: at Julianehåb; Frederikshåb with Godthåb; Holsteinsborg with Sukkertoppen and Egedesminde; Claushavn with Christianshåb, Godhavn and Jakobshavn; and finally Umánaq, which like Julianehåb was to have its own missionary because of the relative isolation of these two districts. At first glance it appears strange that Ritenbenk and Arveprinsens Ejland (Klokkerhuk) are not mentioned, but they had always been under the jurisdiction of the missionary at Jakobshavn, so there was no change in the status of these two places. Other unmentioned places remained under the mission from which they had previously been served. There were naturally no changes in the missions of the Moravian Brethren, which were still outside the jurisdiction of the Missionskollegium.

In that same year, 1792, five missionaries left Greenland. Two of them had especially distinguished themselves, Hveyssel and Cappelen. A third missionary, Andreas Ginge, had been active in special areas: "health service" and natural science.

The system and division laid down in 1792 did not last long. In subsequent years it was changed according to what proved to be most feasible, especially considering the difficult nature of communications. The Missionskollegium continually had to attempt to restrict the number of its missionaries to five, for four of which the Royal Greenland Trade granted subsidies. The Trade kept strictly to the size of the subsidy to be granted, and to the limitations of the privileges of the missionaries. Feelings between the two institutions were not the best.

The Mission in Greenland still felt pushed aside both locally and generally, and it still considered the Trade as the responsible party. This caused the Mission to entrench itself behind its prerogatives, thus to some extent excluding itself from influence over events, which was all the more inappropriate as its personnel stationed in Greenland had been cut in half. Conversely, the dominance of the Trade grew. This dominance had already been gradually increased since the 1770's, partly by virtue of the economic development and the more direct and material function of the Trade in Greenland, and partly, and especially, because the number of its employees stationed in Greenland and in general far exceeded that of the Mission. This difference was intensified by the reduction in 1792 of the personnel stationed by the Mission.

This reduction may, however, have involved a strengthening of the Mission on a quite different front. The mission was forced to a much greater extent than previously to depend on the catechists, the majority of whom had been born and had grown up in Greenland and were in close contact with the population, such as Frederik Berthelsen at Sukkertoppen. This is perhaps part of the explanation why in the years following the reduction the Mission did not experience a decline in the numbers of baptized Greenlanders, but rather continued to receive growing adherence from Greenlanders. The Mission and thus the ecclesiastical "service" became the Greenlanders' own to a much greater extent than the Trade.

Local Reactions to the Reduction

For the time being relations between the Mission and the Trade were poor. This was not only due to clashes of interest on the central level, but was also expressed in Greenland itself, where an Inspector such as Bendt Olrik had not helped iron things out, but rather the contrary. As we have seen, he had been recalled from Greenland, especially at the instigation of the Mission: this was one of the few instances in which the Missionskollegium had interfered in the affairs of the Trade, and it had been right to do so. In 1792 the Missionskollegium had, on the contrary, flatly rejected the right of the Trade to exercise any influence on the stationing of missionaries; the Trade thought it should draw the proper conclusions.

This took place almost immediately with letters to the two inspectors in which the Management expressed its annoyance at not having been asked in advance whether the changes in the mission suited the Trade. The inspectors were therefore requested to report "whether it must not be feared that this sudden reduction of teachers of religion could arouse a harmful sensation among such an unenlightened people as the Greenlanders; and in general what effect or influence you think this will have on the interests of the Trade in general, as well as with respect to individual places in particular." By this the Management must have meant the places where missionaries were not to be stationed.

To this the Management added a request to the inspectors, which would not improve the climate between the Trade and the Mission if the latter ever learned of it. The Management mentioned the "considerable contribution" which the Trade paid every year for the "support" of the Mission, and asked the inspectors to check, on their tours around, "whether this contribution is being spent as properly provided or not." This meant a kind of espionage, or at least a quite improper form of control by the one institution over the other.

Andreas M. Lund, the Inspector of South Greenland, realized this immediately, and reacted with an inquiry to the Management about the legal status of the missionaries. He himself thought that in consideration of their office they were under the jurisdiction of an ecclesiastical authority, and that the inspector, as a secular authority, could not interfere in the conduct of their duties. He did, however, send a list of catechists for the information of the Management.

In a later letter, Inspector Lund characterized the Mission reduction as "so strange that no one with the least local knowledge of this country could imagine it taking place without making Christians into fanatics and heathens." The missionary who was to serve Holsteinsborg, Egedesminde and Sukkertoppen together, including the settlements and trading posts, had to undertake a task "of which he is almost as incapable as the man in the moon, if he is to discharge his current duties." He feared that the Habakuk movement at Sukkertoppen would rise again; to the commendation of the missionary, it had been defeated. If it rose again, much evil would take place. Besides, "some of the Greenlanders of the colony of Sukkertoppen have begun to threaten that if they are going to lose Mr. Hveyssel and get no missionary in his place, they will leave the place and go over to the evangelical brethren, or move to a place where there is a missionary." One can perceive the admonitory voice of Frederik Berthelsen behind these words, for immediately thereafter Inspector Lund reported that the catechists born in Greenland, with the exception of a few, would follow. Frederik Berthelsen was one of the exceptions.

Børge Johan Schultz, Inspector of the Northern Inspectorate, had only been in office for two years and was more cautious in his reply to the letter of the Management and its summons to control the proper use of the subsidy. He actually avoided this embarrassing issue by simply suggesting that the Management take over the Mission and thus get around the Missionskollegium completely: it was the Trade which through its contribution paid four of the missionaries and the catechists, while the Missionskollegium "only" paid the salaries of the rest. One cannot exclude the possibility that the Inspector himself realized the impossibility of such a reorganisation because of the provisions of the "Danish Law of Christian V" and the legal status of the clergy. His suggestion therefore gives the impression of a retreat.

Inspector Schultz pointed out, however, something much more central. He first directed his criticism against the activities of the missionaries up to that time: a critique which was like an echo of others' somewhat scathing mention of these activities. Then he specified – in other words, to be sure – the interpretation of the situation made above. The Trade was making splendid progress according to Schultz, but just as it was getting a footing, "one foot seems to me to be beginning to slink away unnoticed, leaving the entire weight resting on the other one." The missionaries had not made a sufficient contribution in the past, nor trained a sufficient number of catechists. Nevertheless the welfare of the Trade was closely bound up with that of the Mission. "Mediocrity in the progress of the Mission will fetter the rise of the Trade." He could not more distinctly tell the Management that the Trade would have to render vigorous assistance. But he camouflaged his opinion to a great degree with many words of praise for the Trade as well as the suggestion to take over the Mission.

On his path through these flowery expressions he managed to reveal the reactions of the Greenlanders. This could give the Management something to think about in connection with its cool relationship with the Mission. "Some families whom Myhlenphort had persuaded to settle this winter for netting around the many good netting grounds of the colony, left Egedesminde when they heard the missionary was leaving them. Jens Wille, one of the best-natured and most well-informed Greenlanders at Godhavn, asked me if the great master was angry at the Greenlanders, since he now only wanted them to catch seals. The expression he used was really even more harsh. Two other Greenlanders here, who have recently been baptized, told me 'we would rather not be baptized than know the little we know, but have no more.' This is how it is translated: the idea is clear enough." No one could reassure the Greenlanders satisfactorily. One "would have to be an almighty being to remove the consequences of the change."

"The effect of this on the Trade is proportional to its influence on the Greenlanders." If they were dissatisfied, they would wander about from place to place "for enlightenment; if they get the idea that this Christianity which is here spoken of is a fraud, and that these masters are only interested in their products; if the Greenlanders lose their respect for those of the Danes whom they call masters, which respect has so far been supported by the instruction given by the mission; if the baptized Greenlanders slide back into heathendom, then they will be worse than they have ever been, and the consequences for the Trade in the future will be seen."

He feared "an unfortunate consequence of this unwise plan." But it was already implemented. The only possible means of straightening out the situation would be to train good catechists; "for a national catechist has more influence on the Greenlanders than a ten times better informed missionary." But a prerequisite for acquiring catechists was "giving them tolerable conditions." "I have attempted to pay equal attention to the needs of the Trade and the poverty of the Mission; and I have attempted to take care not to make a mistake in speaking of a mistake made." Here Inspector Schultz must have meant that the Trade should be careful of putting the entire burden on the Mission, for it was allotted quite limited economic means. Immediately after this followed his proposal that the Trade undertake the entire economic burden of the Mission. Without it being expressed directly, this proposal quite well suited the general desire for uniformity and centralization which was characteristic of the autocracy, but which was, as we have seen, impracticable.

Both inspectors pointed out the mutual dependence of the Mission and the Trade, in different words, to be sure. Schultz' report was the most profound and far-sighted, but both reports gave the Management food for thought. It is not improbable that these statements had an influence on the attitude of the Trade toward the Mission and missionaries in the following decade. The attitude of the Missionskollegium did not change, however; its members had apparently crept into their shells.

The Missionaries and their Training

The fortunes of the mission in the future depended, judging for reactions in Greenland, on the quality of the catechists. The demands made on the missionaries were impossible to fulfill. In the future, there were only to be five of them in Greenland. Under the conditions prevailing in 1791 og 1792, it was difficult to procure them.

Missionaries were trained for Greenland at the so-called Seminarium Groenlandicum in Copenhagen. Here the practice had gradually been adopted of accepting students of theology before they had their degrees. Several candidates applied, but mostly in order to reap the economic benefits of the scholarships granted. As early as 1787 Fabricius had complained about the Greenland seminarists, as they were called. They absented themselves from lectures, making excuses that they had an examination coming up soon, which was continually postponed, that they were ill, or that they had various urgent tasks, such as acting as pallbearers, which they had to attend to in order to stay alive.[10]

Even just getting candidates ready to replace the remaining five missionaries was difficult and involved wasted efforts in the form of writing around and wasted time. In 1788 two candidates did go to Greenland, but three had to be recommended for exclusion. Two years later two applicants left the ranks before they were even accepted. In 1794 three students, or "seminarists", had to be seriously warned by the Missionskollegium that if they did not pull themselves together soon and take their theology degrees, they would lose their scholarships. At the same time, in late January, the Missionskollegium accepted a candidate who had originally been intended for the mission in Finmarken; Fabricius was now asked to give him an intensive course in the elements of the Greenlandic language. Not much was accomplished before he left for Julianehåb. This fundamental ignorance of the language impeded him during his entire period as a missionary. In 1796 one of the previously mentioned three students warned in 1794 succeeded in taking his degree. He went to Greenland and functioned well as a missionary, but he especially distinguished himself in promoting vaccination.

About three years passed before there was another student taking courses from Otho Fabricius. This student functioned from 1802 to 1813 as a proficient missionary, confronted with many difficult problems. In 1803 the applicant situation looked desperate, probably because of the unstable conditions in Europe. The University regretfully notified the Missionskollegium that no one had answered the notice posted by the department of theology advertising the Seminarium Groenlandicum. Finally in late August a student of theology applied. He was sent to Greenland in 1804 to replace the quite unprepared and extremely incapable missionary who had been sent to Holsteinsborg and Sukkertoppen in 1800.

On the whole the impression is that training as a Greenland missionary was not in great demand. It hardly had an encouraging effect when students heard of the conditions prevailing in Greenland and the opportunities for missionaries there. The spirit had to a great extent gone out of the Greenland Mission.

This was repeatedly expressed by Otho Fabricius. In 1802 he referred to his reports submitted in the summer of 1791. In the meanwhile Upernavik had been partly reestablished as a trading post, and Umánaq had been put under the jurisdiction of the missionary at Jakobshavn/Claushavn. Upernavik was to be served occasionally from Godhavn. Fabricius hoped the Missionskollegium would see that it was necessary for Upernavik and Umánaq to have their own missionaries. In general the number of missionaries should be raised to the previous number "For what I objected from the beginning of the reduction, and have since several times thought it my duty to call attention to, I still find justified by the far too sad experience that in its present state the Greenland Mission is but half of what it could and should be." Still, the number of baptized persons in Greenland was increasingly steadily.

Fabricius' most important task was to instruct his students. This led him to continue to study the Greenlandic language and revise the orthography and translations of the books used by the Mission in Greenland. In 1774 he had been entrusted with the task of compiling a new dictionary.[11] This work was apparently under constant revision, which must have been carried on at the same time as the other linguistic work he had begun. His instruction necessitated a grammar, but the number of those who had one was quite small. Poul Egede's grammar from 1760 was in Fabricius' opinion out of date. Therefore he resorted to the methods of previous times in his Greenlandic lessons, and his students were forced laboriously to copy his new grammar.

This grammar as well as his dictionary were to incorporate the new and improved orthography which Fabricius formulated and had used in other books, which were published during his period as the adviser of the Missionskollegium. Poul Egede's grammar and dictionary had been printed in such large editions, however, that the Missionskollegium could not see its way to providing means for publishing the manuscripts of Fabricius' dictionary and grammar. His changes in both orthography and grammar were so radical that he got into open conflict with Henric Christopher Glahn, Egede's son-in-law.

This conflict revolved especially around the revised translation of the New Testament, which had been entrusted to Fabricius. In 1794 it had progressed so far that the manuscript had been sent to the printer. Only the foreword was lacking. Fabricius had promised Glahn to "remember the late Bishop Egede in a foreword in an honourable manner." Now he wanted the Missionskollegium to decide whether the previous foreword should be retained or a new one written. The previous foreword was "addressed by the late Bishop Egede to the Greenlanders in Greenlandic, Danish and Latin, and contains much that is not in accordance with this latest edition." Actually this revised edition of the New Testament was more a new translation than it was a revision, and was furthermore couched in the new orthography. It was published the same year, with a new foreword, in which Fabricius kept his word.

In 1791, the year of the reduction of the mission, Fabricius' grammar was printed. The stocks of both this and the New Testament were lost in the Copenhagen fire of 1795. The archives of the Missionskollegium were stored in Vajsenhus, which was a prey to the flames. The diaries of many missionaries and many original manuscripts from the hand of Hans Egede were lost on that occasion. A new printing of Fabricius' revised version of the New Testament was not made until 1799. The grammar did not appear until 1801. And finally, the new dictionary was published in 1804.

Fabricius justified the wage he was paid for teaching the Greenland "seminarists", who were conspicuous by their absence, by all the other work he undertook with the Greenlandic language, and the books he published. His revision of the Greenlandic hymn book was also printed. As we have seen in connection with the Habakuk movement, the Royal Mission in Greenland was in great need of hymn books. Former editions had long since been out of print. The Moravian Brethren had their own hymn book. By 1788, when the Habakuk movement reached its peak, Fabricius had got so far with his revision that by summer only six sheets remained to be printed. It was completed the same year, but could not be shipped to Greenland until the following year. A large part of this edition presumably arrived in Greenland, but some of it was most likely lost along with other books in the Vajsenhus depository in the fire of 1795. By 1801 the Missionskollegium had to pay for a new edition.

In the hymnbook of the Royal Mission various prayers and short texts were included. A substitute for Pontoppidan's catechism, called his "Explanations", as adapted by Hans Egede, was also worked on. As early as 1785 Cappelen, a missionary, had called attention to the unsuitability of the "Explanations", especially in the northern missions. A more concise catechism, with "a short excerpt of Christian moral teaching", written by a language expert, "who could determine which truths actually needed to be developed most" was necessary. The reason for this was, according to Cappelen that "there is hardly any certain or stable congregation at any colony" because of the constant arrivals and departures at each place. In order to minimize confusion it was necessary to have something stable to stick to. In addition, he put his finger on an essential linguistic problem which is still of importance. "Lucidity demands, because of the nature of the language, the most free and natural translation, which again demands the same insights of the translator as of the original writer himself." By 1787 so much progress had been made that the new, more "convenient" textbook was on its way.

All these editions were published with the improved orthography which Fabricius had introduced. This also created confusion, because the large and continually growing number of Greenlanders who could read were used to the old spelling. But there were also other problems: "I also wish that in the general textbook which had been shipped - the new explanation of the catechism - the spelling had not been taken so much from the ordinary pronunciation of the Greenlanders and mixtures living in the colony seats, which is rather different from that of the Greenlanders here in the north. But it is not so much for listeners as for readers that this spelling will at first create some difficulty. As for me, I know of no better rule for the orthography of the Greenlandic language than the ordinary pronunciation of genuine Greenlanders." The new orthography did not take enough consideration of the pronunciation, which in Cappelen's opinion ought to form the basis of an orthography, and unambiguously. He was here advocating a quite modern principle.

Although relatively much printed matter was sent to Greenland for use in divine services and education, no uniformity was achieved. Various hand-written material circulated and were also used in teaching. This is due to the fact that instruction was actually a constant repetition of phrases learned by heart. When those "taught" had once learned a certain wording, and this had been written down or printed in a certain form, it was almost impossible for them to learn the same phrase by heart in another form. So formalistic were the demands of the time on "knowledge" that the correct literal version was always demanded. This led H.P. Jansen, the missionary at Umánaq, to use two sets of "Explanation", a hand-written one for the older Greenlanders, and a new printed one for the younger ones, in the hope that in time, the older Greenlanders might be able to absorb the printed version.

We have only had a glimpse of the difficulties encountered by the missionaries in their calling, and only one aspect of them. The reduction in the number of missionaries continued to be the most important restraint on those who remained. In 1804, for example, Bram, the missionary at Jakobshavn, sent a short description of the difficulties posed by the weather, wind and ice. When he would finally succeed in arriving at some place where Greenlanders were said to be, these would be on fangst trips or would have moved, and only a few would remain. For various reasons long periods of time could elapse between ecclesiastical rituals for which a priest was necessary - sometimes they could be put off for years under especially unfortunate circumstances.

Restricted by the language and thwarted by all kinds of external difficulties, most of the missionaries did the work they had undertaken to do. Only one missionary can be characterized as completely incompetent and even in many respects harmful. On the other hand no enthusiasm can be detected for their calling among the 16 others who filled mission posts from 1792 to 1808. Their working conditions did not quite have an inspiring influence. Most of them religiously served their term of office: ten years for those who were married, six years for single missionaries.

During all their years in Greenland they moved around to the main localities of their district, or they went on trips when this was possible, or they were transferred with the shortest notice after just a few years' stay at one or another colony. Their accommodations were often in a lamentable state. Their wages in money were hardly bountiful. That part of their wages which was paid in kind, their rations, was insufficient for their needs. The raw materials from which their food was to be made were not always of sufficiently high quality; they were sometimes unfit for human consumption. There were few consolations. Their reports are full of complaints about one thing and another; they constantly call attention to deficiencies and difficulties. Their problems were often felt to be heavier than necessary; their correspondence presents an unmistakable picture of restricted conditions.

The Finances of the Missionskollegium

The primary reason for all this misery was the hopeless financial condition of the Greenland Mission. A survey of the accounts of the Missionskollegium from 1772 on shows that a deficit was calculated on every year. Between 1782 and 1808, it fluctuated between 21 and 5800 rigsdalers. It was only under special circumstances that the deficit was as low as the 21 rigsdalers in 1784. It was usually a four-digit figure. In 1791 expenses had been calculated at 3457 rigsdalers and a small surplus had been predicted, but the accounts showed a deficit of 1556 rigsdalers. Strangely enough, the accounts were not at all submitted for one year (1800-1801), presumably because of accounts lacking from Greenland due to shipping difficulties. The accounts for 1801-1802 exist only in a kind of draft. Only one year, 1798-1799 was there no deficit; the balance sheet amounted to 4610 rigsdalers 4 marks and 12 skillings. The highest balance registered was in 1806-1807, with the net sum of 9423 rigsdalers 5 marks. The deficit this year totalled 437 rigsdalers 1 mark 8 skillings.

The revenue of the Missionskollegium came from various sources. There was of course first and foremost the subsidy from the Royal Greenland Trade, i.e., from the state, and in addition an annual subsidy of 500 rigsdalers from the royal treasury, from 1791-1792 reduced by 6% to 470 rigsdalers. A large amount of the revenue came from interest on trust funds and mortgages on property in Copenhagen. Some trust funds were limited to special purposes: two were intended for paying the salaries of catechists in Greenland, one was appointed for church and school buildings. The capital of the Greenland Mission was in 1790 evaluated at 19.142 rigsdalers 3 marks $8^1/_6$ skillings. This capital yielded in that year an interest of 717 rigsdalers 5 marks, corresponding to 3.75 per cent per annum. Total income that year was estimated at 3480 rigsdalers 5 marks. Expenditures were calculated to be at least 5560 rigsdalers, which would produce a deficit of at least 2080 rigsdalers. The final balance showed a deficit of 2524 on a balance of just under 6595 rigsdalers. The deficit was thus 21% greater than had been estimated. It is incomprehensible that the Missionskollegium could calculate on a small surplus, even though the wages in money of five missionaries were deducted. The money wages of the missionaries amounted to 209 rigsdalers per annum according to the budget of 1790.

According to the Royal Ordinance of 8 February 1737, the deficit of the Greenland Mission was to be paid by the treasury of the Finmark Mission. This continued throughout the years up to 1802. One of the members of the Missionskollegium, the president of the Danske Kancelli, Frederik Moltke, proposed to the Missionskollegium in March 1802 that the Finmark Mission be taken from its jurisdiction and placed under the Norwegian Department of Danske Kancelli. This implied that the landed property and capital assigned to the Missionskollegium, the income from which maintained economically the Mission in Finmark, Nordlandene, and the administration of three parishes in Trondheim diocese, would be removed and transferred to Danske Kancelli, which in turn would delegate the administration of the revenue to the local authorities in Norway.

Another member, Bishop Nikolaj Edinger Balle, had nothing against this proposal, provided that the missions in Greenland and the East Indies would not lose the funds assigned to the Missionskollegium for their administration. This he expressed in more common language, "that when the proposal is implemented it be provided that the Greenland and East Indian missions suffer no injury." He considered it a matter of course that these two missions should be capable of honouring the commitments the Missionskollegium had made on behalf of them.

Bishop Balle thus expressed as distinctly as possible, without saying it outright, that the revenues of the Finmark Mission were necessary to cover the deficits of the two other missions. Measures would have to be taken to cover these deficits in some other way.

The proposal of Frederik Moltke was not based on any depreciation of the two poorer missions, but on his experiences in his former position in Norway, from which he realized that the Finmark Mission itself had a great need for these large revenues. The construction and maintenance of churches, the operation of schools, and the wages of several priests and teachers demanded greater means. In other words the two missions were millstones around the neck of the other one. The system aimed at by Frederik Moltke was actually fair.

The proposal became a quite wordy representation to the King, which was resolved on 7 May 1802. The decree transferred the Finmark mission to Danske Kancelli, but the Greenland and East Indian missions were to continue "to enjoy the support and contribution which may be found necessary for their maintenance, and for which the Missionskollegium is to apply to Danske Kancelli to arrange for payment." The change was to begin on 1 July the same year.

According to this the deficit of the Greenland Mission were apparently to be covered by Danske Kancelli, which would in this matter negotiate with the Finanskollegium and Rentekammer. In 1802 a conflict developed between Christian D. Reventlow and Christian Colbiørnsen on the one hand and Frederik Moltke on the other, which resulted in the latter being removed from the post of President of Danske Kancelli in 1803. With this the decision to cover the deficits of the Greenland and East Indian missions was presumably forgotten.

It appears from a 1809 memorandum on an entirely different matter that the Missionskollegium had had to resort to other means, which were not quite tenable juridically or correct administratively. One of the trust funds in the Greenland fund of the Missionskollegium, the Karen Ørsted Fund, had since it had been assessed in 1790 grown to 6450 rigsdalers by 1808.[12] The capital, originally 2250 rigsdalers, and interest were at the time it was established in 1775-1776 determined to be used for the construction of church buildings and school houses. But since the Missionskollegium had since 1802 not received from Danske Kancelli compensation for the deficit of the Greenland Mission, as provided for by the decree of 7 May 1802, the otherwise meritorious and honest secretary of the Missionskollegium, Jacob Gude, had taken the liberty of drawing on the account of the Ørsted Fund to cover some of the deficit, "for where else should we get it?" The finances of the Missionskollegium were constantly in bad shape throughout the period under consideration.

The capital of the Missionskollegium, put aside for the Greenland Mission, should have been expected to decrease from 1790 to 1802. Some of this capital, likewise coming from funds such as the Karen Ørsted Fund, was invested in royal bonds. Nothing happened to them - for the moment. On the other hand some of the capital of both the Greenland and the East Indian missions was invested in mortgages on property in Copenhagen. A provisional account of the loss suffered by the Missionskollegium in the Copenhagen fire of 1795 listed the not inconsiderable sum of 45,500 rigsdalers; "as far as I can calculate at present, for from the house members on the bonds I cannot judge whether one or the other building could be on a side of the street or place spared by the fire," wrote Jacob Gude.

It does not appear from the sources how this developed, but the statements of account in 1802 clearly show that at least financially the Missionskollegium suffered no effects from the fire. The fire aroused emotions in Greenland, in fact condolences came in from various quarters. Contributions had already been collected in Greenland for rebuilding Christiansborg castle, which had burned down in 1794. Perhaps it is only due to the somewhat exaggerated style of the time that many letters to the Management of the Royal Greenland Trade and to the Missionskollegium give the impression of great sorrow over the disaster. Fires were relatively rare in Greenland, astonishingly enough, but people there fully realized what a catastrophe it would be if the quite inflammable wooden buildings of the colony seats caught on fire.

On the night between 5 og 6 June 1806 the blubber house at Jakobshavn burned down in five hours. In this fire, 30 casks (60 barrels) of whale and seal blubber as well as shark liver, plus all the stored equipment and materials "were completely consumed by the fire." It was not known how the fire had started; perhaps it was lit by children playing. All the houses of the colony had just been tarred, so it was "due to the blessing and protection of God that these houses, which would have been easy to ignite, were not also prey to the fire." Not only was the loss of blubber and materials regrettable, but what was worse was that the Trade was now in the middle of the fangst season and winter was approaching with no place to store what would be purchased. "The fear and anxiety I now experience will constantly disturb my peace of mind in this country," wrote the trader.

This fire led Inspector P.H. Motzfeldt to issue the first fire circular in Greenland, on 5 September 1807. Its provisions were mostly of a preventive nature: even shooting on New Year's Eve was forbidden. If a fire did start, the trading chief would have to act according to his own discretion. No fire corps or even general rules in case of fire would be set up, nor could they be.

Church Buildings

The fear of fire breaking out in the warehouses and residences of the colony seats, built as they were of wood and regularly tarred, was absolutely justified. But even stronger must have been the fear of fire in the few monumental buildings which were spread out along the coast, including the stately buildings of the Moravian Brethren at Ny Herrnhut near Godthåb and the few churches in Jakobshavn, Holsteinsborg, Godthåb and Frederikshåb. Disasters could occur when these churches were crammed with people, as for example for celebrations, especially during the dark season.

In 1803 the missionary Bram figured out that the annual consumption of candles in the Jakobshavn church amounted to three lispund (3 × 8 Danish punds or about 12 kilogrammes), "for since the divine service during the long dark season is made more solemn by the amount of candles which must be burned in the chandeliers, chairs and around in the church, the Greenlanders especially in this season often wish to assist." Just when the danger of fire was greatest because of the many candles, the church was full of people. The many candles gave the service a special festiveness.

At the same time Bram described the structural state of the church building at Jakobshavn. This stately edifice had been built mostly on the basis of funds derived from blubber contributions made by the Greenlanders of Jakobshavn; it was consecrated in 1782.[13] The maintenance of the church was actually a responsibility of the Trade according to the general provisions concerning buildings entrusted to the use of the Mission, but it does not appear that the Trade had taken this obligation very seriously, at least not as far as the church at Jakobshavn was concerned. This church was also in a special class, just as that of Holsteinsborg, because the construction of these two buildings was financed by means collected from the Greenlanders of the two districts. In any case, twenty years after its consecration Jakobshavn's church was in dire need of repair. It needed tarring, and the roof leaked so that at least on the south side it had to be covered with canvas. Bram fully realized the lean state of the Missions's finances, so he made an arrangement with Inspector P.H. Motzfeldt. The North Greenland welfare fund advanced the missionary the necessary capital for repairing the church. How much the Trade thought it could contribute must then have depended on correspondence between the Trade and the Missionskollegium. For his part, Bram collected blubber from the Greenlanders of the district as their contribution to the maintenance of the church; this principle had also been made use of when the church had been built: that the Greenlanders themselves were to make a contribution.

It appeared that at Godthåb, too, the Trade did not take its obligation to maintain the Mission's buildings very seriously. In 1788 Ginge, the missionary, complained that he found the church building, in which his residence was also located, still in bad condition. He had complained about this two years previously. It was so bad "that I cannot live there without risking my own health as well as that of my wife and children, so I am forced either to go to a Greenlandic house, or rent a room from other Europeans here." Either this building would have to be thoroughly renovated, or a new one constructed; the old building was in such a poor state that he did not think the first alternative would be sufficient.

Fifteen years later the situation did not seem brighter. The missionary had "before it was used as a storehouse for merchandise salvaged from the frigate which wrecked near the colony, used it continuously for divine services," but now it had "been so much more disfigured that it cannot be repaired without a complete renovation," which, however, would not be very expensive. We cannot see whether it was restored before 1808.

From this description in 1803 of the Godthåb church building, it appears that these relatively spacious buildings were in cases of emergency used for other purposes than those for which they had been intended. It was actually a sacrilege to use a church as a storeroom. But what could be done when the situation was urgent? Such sacrilegious use was also made of the not very impressive church at Frederikshåb.

The trader at Frederikshåb was so to speak in constant need of storage space. If not every year, at least frequently, Frederikshåb had to store either Greenlandic produce from or European merchandise destined for Julianehåb; ice conditions together with the slowness of shipment over the Atlantic meant that the ship destined for Julianehåb often could not get there. Sometimes filled blubber barrels were brought from Julianehåb in the summer and autumn and left outdoors at Frederikshåb. "I see no way of getting storage space for the considerable shipment from Julianehåb Colony; the provisions room is chock full and the attic over the warehouse likewise. All the merchandise and goods sent on order are in the church, and still half of the shipment has hardly been unloaded," wrote the trader at Frederikshåb in 1807. He had previously complained over lack of space for a load of 200 casks of blubber from Julianehåb, remarking that it was impossible to get extra crew at the colony seat. "No Greenlanders live here, so there are none to hire."

The use of the church as a warehouse led the missionary at Frederikshåb to write in his diary the same year: "I really have much reason to complain that each year the church is made into a warehouse for lack of other space for the materials of the colony. At present half of the church is quite filled up with barrels and casks. I am sure that trader Astrup is as unsatisfied with this as I am, but tells himself that necessity knows no law." The Missionskollegium forwarded the missionary's complaints to the Royal Greenland Trade, which admitted that it had several times previously been necessary to use the church for lack of other storage space for Julianehåb's cargo. This correspondence took place as late as 1810. The administration had contemplated building more storage room at Frederikshåb, but the war of 1807–1814 impeded the progress of this matter.

The church at Frederikshåb was not very well constructed. Otho Fabricius had had it built in 1772–1773. As early as 1782 it had had some scanty repairs, the materials for which had been shipped in insufficient quantities. The building "which from its very beginning was deficient," was after these repairs so poor that it had to be repaired again every year. In 1782 all the load-bearing construction had to be replaced.[14]

During the entire period under consideration here, only a very few Greenlanders lived at the colony seat itself, where the church was located, i.e., it was only used by the baptized Greenlanders of the district on special occasions. It was considered a rare exception in 1807 that in late March, nine umiaks came with over 200 persons to go to church on Holy Thursday, and on Easter towards evening three more umiaks full of people arrived, perhaps somewhat disappointed that they had arrived too late for Easter services. Perhaps the church was used for Easter. A fortnight later the trader reported a lack of storage space for barrels.

The chapel at Claushavn seems also to have been used "as the domicile of various things belonging to the Trade." "Services were only conducted a few times a year" in this chapel. This was used by the inspector as a justification for not "spending more than absolutely necessary" to repair and supply it with church equipment. The missionary and the inspector had agreed that "the chapel had sufficient space for the congregation," and that "a little altar, a kneeler, a pulpit and the necessary benches" should be procured, but it would be unreasonable to have an altarpiece installed and the room painted, and not in accordance with demands for thrift.

That was in 1798. In the early 1790's the Greenlanders at Claushavn were dissatisfied with this chapel. It was not very far from Claushavn to Jakobshavn, where the inhabitants had built an attractive and spacious church. Around 1792 the Greenlanders at Claushavn wanted to contribute blubber and hides to build a church like that at Jakobshavn, but not as large. This gave rise to a protracted discussion of the pros and cons. By 1796 quite a bit had been collected, and the next year yielded more. By 1797 a total of 67.5 barrels of various kinds of blubber and 154 sealskins of different types had been sent to the Royal Greenland Trade, but at the same time the Management reported that it was sceptical as to the further fortunes of the collection.

Although a little more was contributed, there was not enough to build a new church, even a little one. The conclusion of this long story is that some of this amount was used to repair the chapel, although the missionary thought the Trade should pay for this and for new equipment, since the chapel was mostly used to store its goods. Funds to supplement the amount collected by the Greenlanders were not available from the Missionskollegium, in spite of interest drawn by the Karen Ørsted Fund, and the Trade would not make a contribution. The Greenlanders at Claushavn seemed to tire of all this talk, however, and thought they were getting nothing for the produce they had collected. In 1798 they mostly wanted to have their sum paid out in the form of tangible merchandise. And thus it was, while the Trade paid for the repairs and scanty equipment mentioned above. The congregation had not decreased in size, but it still had to be content with its little chapel. The administration had had it painted and it "was found spacious enough for the entire congregation, so that the intended church at the same place was dropped." By 1799 this affair was terminated.

During this affair the Trade had distinctly revealed its dislike of collections of blubber and hides for purposes which did not directly serve its own interests. Such collections were to be considered as unseasonable interferences with the monopoly rights of the Trade, even though the produce was sold through the Trade itself, to whom it only gave a lot of trouble and whose expenses in this connection were not covered. Besides, there could be no question of contributing more to the mission than what the Royal Greenland Trade was obliged to do.

The Trade therefore seized an opportunity when it found out about the funds of the Missionskollegium earmarked for building churches in Greenland. This happened when the missionary at Julianehåb, R. Knudsen, expressed, each year from 1803 to 1805 and even three times in 1805, the burning desire of his congregation for a church building. The number of baptized persons at this southern colony was 948 in 1800, and about 300 of these must have belonged to the Moravian congregation at Lichtenau. The Royal Mission had no church nor even a large room at the colony seat. The divine services must have been lacking a good deal in festivity.

R. Knudsen knew of the Karen Ørsted Fund and its provisions. In 1806 the Missionskollegium was compelled to notify him that the mission treasury had been so lean that the interest on this fund had had to be used to pay for "the support of the missionaries and catechists, without whom churches would be of no use."

Meanwhile, the Management of the Royal Greenland Trade had got wind of this fund, probably through Johan Chr. Mørch, the trader at Julianehåb, who found out from Knudsen. In 1807 the Management collected copies of all documents concerning the Karen Ørsted Fund and sent them to the Commission for the Royal Greenland Trade requesting the Commission to see to it that the fund be used for a church building at

Julianehåb, "which needs it most of all the colonies." On the basis of this request the matter was referred back to the Missionskollegium. It was because of this desire for a church at Julianehåb that Mission Secretary Jacob Gude was in 1809 compelled to confess what he had done with the interest from the Ørsted Fund as he had already notified the missionary at Julianehåb three years previously. But even this way the colony did not get the church it so badly needed. There was naturally no question of directly using the capital of the Ørsted Fund; and finally, no more was done in this matter because of the war.

On the whole divine services at colony seats which did not have a church were not very festive. As a rule they had to be conducted in the chapel provided for this purpose, which was, as in the time of Hans Egede, the residence of the missionary. These rooms were soon filled, so the doors had to remain open so that those outside could get some idea of what was being said.

Perhaps one of the reasons for the spread of the Habakuk movement was that the conditions at Sukkertoppen were so poor for divine services. Hveyssel, the missionary, complained about these conditions in 1787. He had to hold the Danish-language services in the trader's room and take care every Saturday to "compliment him for it," if not, the trader would remind him of it. The Greenlandic-language service he had to transfer to one of the Greenlanders' houses, where he not only had to "complement" the man of the house, but also its women. "In addition to this there are many inconveniences in performing divine services in a Greenlandic house; it happened one time that something fell down from the roof into the Communion wine, which I had to skim off after the consecration, before I could begin to administer it." The consecrated wine was actually desecrated by this, and useless for another consecration, and could he do this, he wondered. Although the Missionskollegium attempted, they did not succeed in getting Sukkertoppen a church building. He therefore notified the Missionskollegium that he performed the Danish service every other Sunday and the Greenlandic on the other Sundays; when he did not perform the Greenlandic service, Frederik Berthelsen gave a sermon in Greenlandic. That was in 1788, when the Habakuk movement reached its peak, and the Greenlandic congregation was only getting half service from its missionary. Their dissatisfaction was not unjustified.

At the same time the conditions at Egedesminde were no better. The morning and evening devotions which had been ordered, as well as adult instruction, took place in 1786 in the catechist's room, "with how much devotion this takes place I will avoid mentioning, but it takes place as well as it can with the screaming of children, seal flensing, etc." Neither did Egedesminde get its own church for the time being, nor even a real chapel.

Divine Services

Many services had to take place out of doors, weather permitting – at settlements often with the missionary's trunk or a simple wooden box as a kind of altar. We get the impression that services were well attended, but this cannot be illustrated with any figures, either of the number of services held in each district, or of the number assisting and going to communion. We must be content with the remarks which are scattered at random in diaries and letters. We have, for example, seen that in 1807 over 200 people assembled at Frederikshåb to celebrate Easter.

As time went on, church festivals came to play an important role. Remaining in Frederikshåb District, the Greenlanders of the vicinity celebrated Christmas in 1805 at the relatively recently established trading post of Arsuk, to which they brought their own catechist. Greenlanders did not assemble exclusively for the divine services, but also because these were the occasion of festive get-togethers. It was, for example, difficult, because of the proximity of Christmas, for Mørch to get umiak rowers to bring provisions out to some of the men who were hunting, without giving them ample extra payment.

The crowding together of Greenlanders at Easter was a thorn in the flesh of the Trade. This festivity seems even then to have had a special "social" significance. Partly "because Easter was approaching, when the Greenlanders, besides going to services, will not for anything fail to turn up in their new clothes, acquired for the feast," the trader could not get a couple of whales flensed at Holsteinsborg in 1799, unless he declared them carcasses and thus open to free flensing.

Divine services had a special atmosphere, which impressed new arrivals. 24 June 1804 was a windy, rainy Sunday in Frederikshåb. The missionary was not at home, but the catechist conducted services for the Greenlanders of the colony. "I went, and although I understood nothing of it, it was a real joy to see the order and devotion that exist in their devotional practices. They sing excellently, and far more correctly than I have ever heard in our village churches in Norway." The assistant who wrote these words in his diary, had shortly arrived from his native area via Copenhagen.

Seen in a wider context one gets the impression that divine services at the time satisfied a need for festivities in common. An obvious interpretation - which can not in any way be documented - is that the trips to the place where services were held and the togetherness before, during, and after them took the place of the song contests which were still heard of in the Northern Inspectorate, but which seem to have died out completely in the south.

Greenlandic church singing was explicitly stressed in the above quotation. It is uncertain whether it was unisonant or polyphonic at that time. One thing is certain, that only the Moravian services were accompanied by musical instruments. Outside their divine services, the use of musical instruments in church was beginning to gain footing. Thus Meyer, the missionary at Frederikshåb, received in 1790 two transverse flutes, which his two catechist pupils were to play. In 1805 Hjorth, the trader at Holsteinsborg, reported that the Greenlanders of the colony had requested him to get "a little organ or positive organ" for the church. Inspector Myhlenphort understood that this wish was due to the presence of a Greenlander from Lichtenfels, who had settled at Holsteinsborg when that colony was reorganized after the smallpox epidemic. This Greenlander "can play almost all the hymns in the hymnbook; I have heard him myself in Lichtenfels' church, and I therefore believe he can perform the duties of an organist - in Greenland," wrote the inspector, but added that the trader would have to realize in advance that such an instrument would cost between 150 and 200 rigsdalers. Perhaps the Management of the Royal Greenland Trade could be persuaded to donate a little organ "in the expectation of the good behaviour of the Greenlanders in the future."

Even this small matter was stopped by the war. Inspector Myhlenphort promised for his part to investigate it as far as he could. The schoolmasterly finger he pointed at the Greenlanders in his letter was typical of the attitude of most of the officers in Greenland at that time. But it was also an indication that they were aware of their educational obligations, although the final objective also involved the welfare of the Trade.

The use of musical instruments thus spread slowly from the Moravian congregations to others. This period most likely witnessed the first stages of this development. It was in Frederikshåb District, which had much contact with Godthåb District, that flutes were ordered. And it was from the Moravian congregation at Lichtenfels near Fiskenæsset that the organ-playing Greenlander came to Holsteinsborg.

The newly arrived assistant at Frederikshåb in 1804 had noticed the order and devotion with which the Greenlanders participated in the divine service. From 1783 on the ritual of the service was more fixed, as Poul

Egede had composed a ritual "adapted to the concepts of the nation and the nature of the country." This must mean that it could also be used out of doors and under very primitive conditions. It was naturally based on the Danish-Norwegian ritual of the state church, and the influence of the Moravian Brethren could be traced only in certain external features.

Around 1800, then, the boundaries between the two missions began to be more flexible. The repopulation of Holsteinsborg after the smallpox epidemic and other demographic movements facilitated a spread of customs from one district to another, in spite of the meagre movement from the Moravian congregations.

Catechists

Ecclesiastical life apparently did not stagnate, in spite of the reduction in 1791 of the number of missionaries and the consequent drastic expansion of the jurisdiction of those who remained. The number of baptized persons rose smoothly; the reasons for this cannot be discovered, but in addition to the influence of the baptized Greenlanders on the unbaptized, assisted by the need to be a part of the community, the quiet activities of the catechists must have been of significance. This must be especially due to the fact that most of them were "natives", and could speak a language everyone could understand. The angákut, who had previously helped and supported the people in an undependable existence, were now out of the picture at most places. In their place came the catechists, but only when they were personalities.

Only in the outlying districts were there still angákut; they thus existed right up to 1807 in Upernavik District, which after being reestablished as a kind of trading post under Godhavn had not been better supplied with mission service. A refined means was used to combat them. When the Trade established a reward system for the three best fangers at each colony to promote production, it was specifically emphasized for Upernavik District that men who posed as or recently had posed as angákut would be excluded from these rewards. Strangely enough, nothing is heard of angákut in Julianehåb District; this may be because they were ignored in the sources. There were so many heathens, especially in the southern part of the district, that there must also have been angákut here.[15]

The christianization of Julianehåb seems to have taken place rather quickly. At least the Missionskollegium claimed in 1806 that the entire colony, which in 1800 had still had "some 100 heathens, had been properly instructed in the Christian religion and by baptism incorporated into the

Christian church, without one single one leaving the religion again, which often happens; they have all been faithful to it, and grace it with good conduct." As this witness is contained in the Missionskollegium's recommendation for a recently returned missionary, it should perhaps be treated with some reservation, even though the signature on the recommendation is that of the Missionskollegium itself. To what extent those Greenlanders were included who had joined the Moravian congregation at Lichtenau is not known. At least neither the missionary nor the Missionskollegium could take credit for them.

The contribution of this missionary should not, however, be disparaged, especially as there is no reason to depreciate it. His predecessor complained often, however, that it was impossible to get around in the district, so that he did not know the exact number of baptized persons. He had four or five catechists to help him - not many for such a large area with such a dispersed population.

It appears distinctly from the activity of the Missionskollegium in 1791-1792 that it thought it could manage the situation in the future by depending on the catechists. One result of this was that the Management about that time requested the inspectors to send it lists of the catechists, mostly in order to control the Missionskollegium.

According to the lists sent by the inspectors there were 35 national catechists, i.e., catechists born in Greenland, in 1793. The South Greenland lists failed to include at least three catechists at Holsteinsborg, however. The year before the lists were compiled there must have been 38 national catechists, plus one European one, who was stationed at Umánaq. In 1796 this European went over to the Trade. From this year on the offices of catechists were exclusively filled with native Greenlanders.

Of the 37 Greenlandic catechists mentioned by Otho Fabricius in his list in 1791, 12 were "mixtures", among them the most prominent and meritorious of the catechists. In his 1791 list Fabricius gives the various catechists short testimonials. The one European at Umánaq was only characterized as "moderately suitable", but then, he left his post a few years later; later, however, he also functioned in his locality as a teacher as well as a Trade assistant.

One of the "mixtures" was qualified by Fabricius as "one of the most capable," but he added that "previously he was very dissolute, but is now said to have improved." This was not true. In 1793 he was the highest paid of the national catechists: 50 rigsdalers in money and a full portion of ordinary provisions. It appears that in addition he improved his economic situation by at the same time being a catechist and the leader of whaling operations at a station in Egedesminde District. His conduct was too colourful for the Missionskollegium, and in 1797 he was discharged. By this time his whaling position had long since ceased, and his attempt to become an assistant for the Trade in 1798 was unsuccessful.

Next in line was Frederik Berthelsen, previously mentioned in connection with the Habakuk movement in Sukkertoppen District. He received 35 rigsdalers in money plus six rigsdalers expense money for official trips and a half portion of rations. Fabricius listed him as "competent", which must have been a very high evaluation, as he was the only one of all the catechists, who received it.

Of the "mixtures", three were "good", two "rather good", two "serviceable", one "acceptable", and one was listed as a beginner. The catechists who were supposed to be of pure Greenlandic descent also received marks. Eight were "good", five "rather good", seven "acceptable", one "mediocre" and two were classified as beginners, including one of the sons of Frederik Berthelsen. Joseph Berthelsen, the elder brother of Frederik Berthelsen, was considered a "mixture", but was lumped with two catechists of the latter group because all three had defected to the Habakuk movement. By 1791, however, Joseph Berthelsen had moved to Holsteinsborg, which Fabricius could not know, and he remained here until his death during the smallpox epidemic of 1800-1801. One of the other defectors seems to have been rehired at Sukkertoppen, but the other one disappeared from the lists.

A survey of these evaluations had been made to give an impression of what resources Fabricius thought the mission had to depend on in the future. Of the 37 catechists he mentions there were only 12 who in his opinion were fully worthy of the confidence of the mission. Seen from another point of view, only one was declared "mediocre": i.e., useless. Fabricius' evaluations do not, of course, mean that the catechists actually functioned that way in Greenland. This is seen most distinctly in the personal activities of Joseph Berthelsen at Holsteinsborg, where he did considerable good work for the mission. It can also be seen in the blind assistant catechist Bartimæus in Julianehåb District, who was much appreciated locally and functioned excellently. Fabricius had evaluated him as "good in insight and conduct" but had some doubts as to his suitability because of his blindness.

A more summary characteristic was given by Inspector A.M. Lund at Godthåb when he sent in his list of catechists. He put his finger on a tender spot in the existence of these catechists: perhaps the real reason why some of them had become catechists at all. "From what I know of these people, most of them are very poor providers or no providers at all, and must therefore grovel for their countrymen, whom they mostly need. On the other hand, a few of them are good enough, and can do more for their countrymen than others who either do not understand much of their language or will not bother to go to them." This final remark was a dig at the missionary at Godthåb, who had left the previous year.

The less competent catechists were evidently a burden on some missionaries of the more impatient type. In 1796 the missionary in Disko Bugt wrote of the lack of education among Greenlanders; by publishing more "useful" books in Greenlandic "much more would be gained than through the many ignorant and mediocre catechists, who must of necessity be retained, and by means of which the Trade also, which attracts all attention, would undoubtedly increase and spread more."

The missionary in Disko Bugt here painted the general picture which we have already seen in detail. But he did not appreciate that the catechists, even the least competent of them, were Greenlanders. This had, however, been stressed by Inspector Lund, in his manner. When this missionary spoke in 1796 of the ignorant and mediocre catechists, he revealed without realizing it a deficiency in the entire activity of the mission, which had not succeeded in training catechists properly. Perhaps this was due to the usual lack of financial means.

After 1782, and partly influenced by the Order of the same year, the Missionskollegium encouraged the missionaries to choose boys born of mixed marriages and persuade them to become catechists. This means in fact that the missionaries were encouraged to continue and possibly intensify the training of catechists in individual districts by the individual missionaries. This practice persisted throughout the period in consideration, but some attempts to improve the training were made.

The meritorious European catechist Jacob Rachlew, who in general was quite interested in the schooling of children in Greenland, suggested in 1784 the establishment of a seminary for national catechists at Julianehåb. But since he died the same year, this plan petered out.

Under the impression of the reduction of 1791, the Missionskollegium, in its General Order of the same year, resorted to the same practice for the training of catechists. The custom then developed, when the occasion permitted, of actually keeping some intelligent "mission boys". Otho Fabricius was not happy about this kind of catechist training. In 1797 the case of a specially unfortunately developed example of such mission boys led him to fire the following salvo to the Missionskollegium: "I have also long feared that little advantage would be acquired from these so-called pupils, and I also did not neglect to warn of this in good time some years ago; I preferred to let them practice earning their living in a Greenlandic manner rather than finally being a burden to themselves and the treasury." If the Trade wanted, it should rather employ them, "for there are already enough scandalous catechists."

Fabricius' dislike of the kind of training extended so far that he even advised in 1798 against accepting as "pupils" the sons of the competent catechist Jakob Berthelsen. This catechist had even requested that at least one of them be sent to Copenhagen to learn proper Danish. But Fabricius could see no sensible reason for this, nor where the expenses would come from. The Missionskollegium resolved, however, that their father could take them as "mission boys", and granted him one rigsdaler per annum for each. There is no confirmation in the sources that he actually did this, but it appears from Otho Fabricius' report in 1798 that the Missionskollegium had stopped granting money for "mission boys", and that this institution itself had ceased. On the other hand, new persons were hired as catechists, however they had been made suitable for service.

On various occasions during the 1790's and into the 19th century the necessity of a proper catechist training was insisted on, and this was more and more linked to improve schooling for children in general. But this alone was not enough: the economic conditions of catechists had also to be improved. Because of the meagre wages, varying from three to 35 rigsdalers per annum, usually without rations (the catechist who earned 50 rigsdalers was a unique exception), it was difficult for a catechist with a family to get along. Therefore it was hard to get anyone to become a catechist, and even harder to keep those who had been hired. In addition the Trade, if it did not directly lure them away, at least exercised an attractive influence with both higher wages and whole, part or periodic rations. The dominance of the Trade in the life of the colonies undoubtedly also exercised its influence.

Inspector Lund's opinion that the national catechists had to "grovel for their countrymen" cannot be correct. Most of them were prophets respected in their own country. The blind Bartimæus in Julianehåb District was actually accepted in the house of a fanger. This relationship existed for several years without economic difficulties for Bartimæus, who even had wages owing to him when he died in 1803.

Most of the catechists were notoriously poor fangers or could not even row a kayak, but they could well do some fishing from land and hunting on land, if they were not physically handicapped. They had often become catechists because they for various reasons could not join the host of ordinary fangers, but this was on the whole accepted because they did fulfill a function which satisfied a need. Absolutely not all the catechists were poor fangers. At Godhavn, for example, a catechist was the best whaling harpooner in the 1780's, but he was not more respected as a catechist for this reason. The "devotion" observed in the catechist's service at Frederikshåb in 1804 must have also applied to the catechist himself as leader and preacher.

Inspector Lund meant what others had said and written previously, that the catechists, by virtue of their postulated dependence on their associates, would lack the necessary authority to instruct and chastise them. This is quite a logical conclusion from the European consciousness and experience of the background of an authority to chastise. It might well apply to many a Danish or Norwegian parish priest who was not a good farmer, for example. Lund and others did not realize that the kind of authority they were thinking of did not exist in Greenlandic society, and that castigation as an "educational" means was seldom if ever used by catechists. This means was actually still quite foreign to the Greenlandic mentality.

Social distinctions among Greenlanders, the development of which has previously been implied, had not yet left profound traces on their society, and did not really do so until the twentieth century. Boundaries between the few "layers" were fluid, mostly becuse the conditions of material existence did not permit any sharp divisions. In the field of the Mission this could be expressed by a layman functioning as a "teacher of Christianity" when there was no catechist available. The prerequisite was apparently that the inhabitants at this place really had a deep desire to belong to the congregation.

At a settlement in Ritenbenk District in 1793, for example, an ordinary fanger by the name of Gabriel "read for six catechumens and brought them so far that through baptism they could incorporated into the congregation." No one had ordered him to give these instructions; they must have been the result of a local desire. It seems quite touching that a year later the Missionskollegium asked the missionary in Disko Bugt to declare, on behalf of that body, that "although the joy this righteous man must feel at having brought these previously ignorant persons to the true knowledge of God must far exceed whatever humans could give him, we nevertheless feel that we should honour him among Greenlanders with (the silver medal enclosed), which you will be pleased to confer on him at a suitable occasion in the presence of his assembled countrymen."[16]

The ceremony took place shortly after the arrival of the ship carrying this message in August 1794. The medal in question was quite large and had but one connection with the church and the mission: on its reverse side, over an extremely classical picture, were the words "Pietas augusta" (sublime piety). This picture with its heading and the glossy portrait of Christian VII on the face of this shiny medal must have had a strange effect on its recipient, as well as on the assembled Greenlanders, when it was awarded to Gabriel and presumably hung on his anorak. What could he do with it? Amulets and amulet bands were forbidden! A medal had never before been seen hanging on the chest of a person in Greenland. Could he barter it for something?

This was feared by Inspector Schultz at Godhavn. He even made this the subject of a circular to all the trading chiefs in the inspectorate, telling them to "attempt to prevent any of the Danes in this country, or the people sailing on the colony ships, buying this medal from Gabriel"; any purchaser would have to give it back without compensation. We do not know whether Gabriel kept his medal, or what happened to it.

"Unenlightened" fangers and more or less knowledgeable catechists were then, together with the few remaining missionaries, to satisfy the lively need for instruction in "the true knowledge of God." Gabriel was an exception. Where there was no suitable layman, a catechist was needed, and it was seldom that the local missionary could procure him. In 1798, for example, the missionary at Julianehåb complained of this. He revealed at the same time that groups of Greenlanders reacted to the missionary in precisely the same way as they reacted to the trader or his assistant when there was a shortage of something. "For it seldom occurs to them to distinguish between impossibility and unwillingness, and most of them never ask whether the priest is really making an effort to fulfill their request or whether he is indifferent to it." They held the missionary directly responsible for the fact that they did not have and could not get a catechist; that was his function, and if he could not get them a catechist, he was not functioning satisfactorily.

What was even worse was that the missionary also thought that those Greenlanders (in Julianehåb District) who once in vain had requested a catechist to be stationed with them, seldom repeated their desire during the time of that missionary. They would give up on him, because at least in that respect he was not functioning in the context of their narrow little world.

This emphasized the painful need to train catechists which was expressed all along the west coast of Greenland in the 1790's. In 1793 Inspector Schultz expressed it to the Management of the Royal Greenland

Trade: "The idea of increasing the number of good catechists should be a permanent principle, as they if anything promote the intention of the mission." Then he elaborated on their miserable wages. In a previous letter he had emphasized the progress of the mission as favourable to the trade and the assurance of order in the country. And now he said of the economic conditions of the catechists: "If the Management does not lend a hand here, all the assuidity and trouble taken by the inspectors and missionaries will be useless."

This led the Management of the Royal Greenland Trade to change its attitude to the catechists, and thus to the Mission, to the extent that it requested the inspectors to submit their "detailed report on whether you consider that the Trade ought, as cheaply as possible as with a reasonable hope of benefit, to undertake to improve the conditions of the national catechists with respect to rations." The Management did not, however, fail to point out that as "the Trade already bears so considerable a share of the economic burdens of the mission, it must naturally have misgivings about increasing these." The Management seems to have ignored the fact that it received a considerable subsidy from the state for the sole purpose of helping the Mission. In any case, this memorandum did indicate some change in attitude.

At that time, 1794, only a modest number of catechists received rations; only one of them seems to have received a whole portion, and he was discharged, as we have seen. A few received half portions. The great majority, who needed it most, received not a crumb.

The Management must have considered the opinions of the inspectors on this matter important. In March 1794 it had already communicated with the Missionskollegium on the question of rations for the catechists, but it failed to mention that it had previously used all available means to prevent the catechists from getting rations. At practically any cost the Management wanted to keep imported food out of Greenlanders' pots in order not to "spoil" the population to live on European food.

All the greater was the surprise of the Missionskollegium at the about-face of the Management; its surprise was even great at the amenable tone in which the change of attitude was expressed. The Missionskollegium inhaled the mild breezes: "we are glad to have learned from the memorandum of the 26th ult. from the Royal Management that it is now working with us for a common goal: the welfare of the Mission, at least by telling us what a sensible and honourable man in Greenland (Inspector Schultz) has proposed." There is hidden irony in this introduction. But in the further text the Missionskollegium regretted that it already was short of funds and therefore could not cover the cost of full rations for all catechists. The high prices and freight rates of the Trade, it said, had been "the main reasons which have compelled us to reduce the number of missionaries and limit the wages of the catechists." With many circumlocutions and mildly ironic expressions the Missionskollegium was now observing that the Trade itself now evidently felt the loss occasioned by the reduction of the Mission, for the promotion of which the Trade itself had been established.

No more rations resulted from these efforts; the provisions of the Order sent by the Missionskollegium to the missionaries in 1792 continued to be followed. This Order divided the Missions temporarily into main missions and annexes. Each missionary was responsible for supplying the main mission as well as the annexes with "the necessary number of catechists, of which the most capable, preferably a mixture if there is no European, is to be entrusted with the supervision and management of the others and ordered to submit to the missionary every year a proper account of all that is undertaken." Each missionary was to give these catechist foremen, as they were called, their necessary instructions.

The catechist foremen were not ordained as priests, and had therefore only the following tasks: they were to baptize children, visit and console the sick, "supervise the education of youth", exercise a kind of control of the other catechists, and in addition supervise the "customary catechisations of the Greenlanders." The baptism of adults and all actual religious ceremonies were reserved for the missionary alone, as an ordained priest. The wages of the missionaries were increased because of their increased work and larger jurisdiction, but nothing was said about the wages of catechists, nor even general guidelines.

Up to 1808 the number of catechist foreman positions was with time fixed at five. Their wages were set at from 25 to 35 rigsdalers plus half rations. The other catechists fluctuated between three and fifteen rigsdalers per annum without rations. It was no wonder that it was still hard to get suitable persons as catechists, and that they left their vocation for employment in the Trade, some with regret.

Some catechists had occasional extra jobs at the colony seat. One catechist at Godthåb worked for a time as a smith; at another colony the catechist was "skilful at forging and carpentry;" but neither forging nor carpentry gave any real extra income. Catechist service was always of primary importance and kept these craftsmen from profiting fully from these other opportunities for earning money.

The Trade employees apparently made use of the catechists for all kinds of jobs, often because they had learned some Danish. This presumably got out of hand in Disko Bugt. Therefore - and perhaps also because Inspector Schultz wanted to support the catechists in their true vocation, and thus also the Mission - he issued a circular in 1793 dealing with this matter. He warned "each of the trading officers to refrain from employing the catechists in any kind of work or business for the Trade, by means of which they neglect what they are paid and kept for; and especially not to use them for express mail in the winter, which is precisely the time they can best accomplish something in their posts." It had thus become an extensive practice to send the catechist off with the express mail: his ordinary job was not considered by the employees of the Trade as important as the interests of the Trade. It just consisted of devotions and instruction.

But the catechists had to get food for themselves and their families. Those who could carry on fangst took time off to do it during the day. This was at least the case at Frederikshåb and Godthåb around 1798. "Instruction never deprives the catechists of an opportunity to carry on fangst, when the weather is good; since in my time it has been and still is a custom among them all in this case to make up in the evening for what they have neglected during the day," reported the missionary. This later developed into a general right: the so-called hunting day once a week.

If the catechist was carrying on fangst during the day, instructions had to wait until evening, which must have delighted both children and adults. At all localities catechists were responsible for keeping school. Where a missionary was present, he also took part in the instruction of children. Where there was neither a catechist nor a missionary, the so-called "teaching mothers" were hired. This was an old practice, intensified with time and the slowly growing proportion of literate Greenlanders. In 1793, 15 of these teaching mothers were employed in South Greenland, but it cannot be seen that there were any in the Northern Inspectorate. Their wages were exceptionally poor: only one received the princely sum of one rigsdaler per annum; the other 14 received three punds of tobacco or its corresponding value; 4 marks 8 skillings, or three quarters of a rigsdaler: a fourth of what the most poorly paid catechist received. Naturally teaching mothers received no rations.

Other Problems of the Mission

Conditions were extremely restrictive for all the Greenlandic staff. The authority of the catechist as the representative of the mission, and thus of the church, was limited. They had no opportunity to counter local deviations from the moral rules which the church demanded be observed wherever it was present. Some catechists even had difficulty observing these rules themselves. The conflicts of cultures were here irreparable and long lasting. And at this time the missionary was in more than one respect a distant authority to the small, scattered local societies.

The struggle against the many violations of the sixth commandment was characterized by many drastic decisions on the part of the missionaries. They attempted various forms of church discipline: e.g., excommunication, as was also attempted by the missionary in connection with the Habakuk movement in Sukkertoppen District. The strict rules about getting married were a serious hindrance to a more tolerable development of the moral situation. The reduction of the Mission made a great problem of the marriage of young Greenlanders in time and in the right place.

Neither the catechists nor the catechist foremen could conduct wedding ceremonies; the arrival of the missionary had to be awaited. When he did come, he had a number of ministrations to take care of. In the passages of the Order of 1792 dealing with the powers of the catechists, nothing was said about funerals, strangely enough. It must be assumed that the missionary in one way or another could delegate some of his powers in this context to the catechists, perhaps allowing them to bless the grave. During the great epidemics at Egedesminde and Holsteinsborg, it was totally impossible for the missionary to assist at all the many burials.

Newborn infants, whom the catechists were authorized to baptize, were to be brought to the missionary, when he came, for his blessing, which the catechist was not authorized to give. But there was no question of the catechists being able to conduct weddings. Therefore the missionary at Holsteinsborg/Sukkertoppen proposed in 1799 that the catechist foremen be allowed to perform a "kind of betrothal, etc.," whatever "etc." may mean. Fabricius was favourable to this proposal and recommended it, although not whole-heartedly. But the Missionskollegium rejected it flatly because the institution of betrothal had been abolished in Denmark/Norway. Fabricius had remarked that the missionary in question had already allowed such betrothals, and that the same took place at "certain other colonies." The Missionskollegium preferred then to let this institution function secretly.

This may have led the missionary at Julianehåb in 1805 to express his desire to "see betrothals introduced in Greenland," because marriage was "so beneficial for the reproduction of the people," and pregnant women would thus acquire a provider to raise their child. Betrothals probably still took place. No decision came from the Missionskollegium this time because of the war. The struggle against "loose morals" continued.

Other Aspects of Culture

The activities of missionaries and traders in West Greenland in this period do not seem to have left much room in the sources for the so often celebrated "smiling Greenland." The picture presented is grey and disconsolate, full of problems large and small. Pale images of festivities do appear at times from the closely written pages. Scattered throughout the previous account are events such as song contests and old forms of entertainment, and we have seen that many customs actually prohibited by the Mission continued secretly, some as children's games. Both baptized and unbaptized Greenlanders took part in these forbidden pleasures.

New customs were formed. Divine services, especially on church festivals, must also be considered as a substitute for previous festivities. A curious mixture of secular and "church" festivities took place at Arveprinsens Ejland in the last part of the period of the old trader C.C. Dalager. When the missionary came to this whaling station in October 1797 everyone, Europeans and Greenlanders, took communion. Afterwards "the trader turned my room into a dance hall for the Greenlanders." He "himself called the Greenlanders into my room, without warning me in advance, to dance and make merry to the music, of a kind, of the fiddler Jacob Dalager. The trader was present as a spectator. Two of the Danish crew came in just to see the dancing, but they were immediately chased away by the chief." The indignant assistant who wrote this in his journal "naturally preferred peace" after having taken communion and was actually quite outraged that by this dance music the trader literally induced the Greenlanders to "be indifferent to religion, from which depravity and vice can well result."

There are at least three peculiar aspects of this short narration. One is that C.C. Dalager evidently wanted to restrict the dancing party of the Greenlanders. This may have been an expression of the same despotic temperament which led him to confiscate the assistant's room without notice to hold the festivities in. It may also be that he did not want to give any of the local crew an opportunity to start one or another form of "disorder". They were hard nails, especially when they had had too much to drink. Perhaps, then, C.C. Dalager, the wiser for deplorable experiences, wanted especially to protect the Greenlandic women.

The other strange thing is that the assistant became indignant. He thereby revealed that he had not understod the Greenlandic reaction to having gone to communion. But especially this part of the narration affords us a welcome glimpse of a Greenlandic reaction to a church event. When going to communion the Greenlandic communicant presumably, according to good Lutheran custom and the wording of the ritual, confessed in his heart the total sum of his sinfulness - whatever that might have been. This confession and contrition, according to the Greenlandic mentality, obliterated all his less respectable acts. On this point the Lutheran mentality agreed with the Greenlandic. So there was every good reason to celebrate.

The third and most noteworthy aspect of the narration is that it mentions dancing to a violin. This is - as far as can be seen - one of the first times this is mentioned. But it is mentioned as something common, and the dancing party was arranged as a matter of course. This follows from the fact that C.C. Dalager took over the newly arrived assistant's room for this purpose. The fiddle was evidently no delight to the ears of the poor assistant. He was a legal graduate, the son of a priest from central Norway, and the younger brother of the previously mentioned missionary P.A. von Cappelen, the netting pioneer. His ears were probably accustomed to something better.

What kind of dancing was done to the accompanying and hopefully suitable violin? This was not reported. It cannot have been a form of traditional Greenlandic dancing, as it was not accompanied by any sounding instrument. It must have been a kind of dancing in which the two "uninvited" members of the crew could have participated, because they obviously did not come just to "see the dancing." At that time the so-called Pols dances - a kind of old fashioned leaping dance - were common among both peasants and townfolk in Denmark and Norway, and for that matter in Sweden, too. These dances were accompanied by a fiddle and/or clarinet. It is not improbable that in the late 18th century these folk dances gained a footing in West Greenland, but that not much is said about this in the sources.

In connection with King Christian VII's birthday on 29 January 1804, the usual "king's rations" were distributed at Umánarssuk near Holsteinsborg, and the inhabitants were allowed "to make merry with dancing here in the Danish house this evening." Here, too, it is not mentioned what kind of dancing was done, but it was in general a dancing party with the approval of the local chief. This was also quite common on feast days.

At these two places dancing parties are mentioned, most likely with European dances, as something rather customary. The dances done may of course have been learned from English and Scots whalers, but there is no proof that such dances can have been introduced as early as the end of the 18th century. These dances are, however, designated by West Greenlandic terms: *sisamât,* which as we have seen indicate a quadrille, and *arfineqpingasut,* which means eight, a multiple of four, also indicating a quadrille. The form of both words points to the 18th century, but the terms themselves do not seem to have been known at the time.

Fabricius translated the verb "(he) dances" into *tapárpok,* which also means "jumps; makes merry". This points to a jumping dance. This word still means "dances", but now seems to be less common than *qitigpoq*. This latter word, written as ketikpok, at the end of the 18th century meant "lives freely; is brazen in his conduct; is irresponsible; seeks worldly enjoyment." From this one can draw a suitable conclusion as to the development of attitudes toward dancing. In any case, the trading assistant found dancing unsuitable to the occasion in 1797.

Of other recent factors in the cultural life of Greenland, we have already mentioned books for Christian instruction and church use, which were generally distributed. Even at that time, the need for reading material seems to have been great. The missionary Bram suggested in 1803 that the Royal Greenland Trade ought to "ship Greenlandic books as merchandise to every establishment; for in the first place if Greenlanders, who so deeply desire books, could get as many as they wanted for a reasonable price from the Trade," this would not only satisfy a great demand, but also promote "the introduction of money" by "promoting industry," The Greenlanders would produce and sell more, he thought, if they could also buy books. Books they themselves purchased would surely be better treated than those they now received more or less free. Before these books were worn to shreds, they had quickly been spotted by fingers greasy with blubber and the sputtering of oil lamps. The same was true of the few and poor schoolbooks of the children. "The Greenlanders would not treat their books as carelessly as they now do, in spite of the fact that whenever I arrive at a locality, I demand to see the children's books and give them a well-deserved rebuke if they have dirtied or torn them," continued Bram, like a finicky schoolmaster demanding the impossible of his children.

Each of the catechists had a modest stock of books, according to his economic circumstances. Those among them who knew Danish had Bibles, hymnbooks and some other devout writings in Danish for their own edification and information. Some of these Danish-speaking catechists were made use of by the Missionskollegium: i.e., Otho Fabricius, in revising church writings and making new translations.

Books seem still to have been sent to the various mission localities. Thus most of the colony seats were supplied with a copy of Poul Egede's "Information" in 1788-1789. As late as 1968 the first bound fascicles of *Floræ Danicæ Iconum* 1761-1787 were kept in Godthåb, shipped there in connection with the collection of plants in Greenland for a kind of Herbarium Groenlandicum in Copenhagen. In this connection were also shipped five works of Carl von Linné, including *Genera Plantarum,* 1764, and *Systema Naturae,* 1767. All in all it appears that at least at Godthåb and Julianehåb there then existed a rather general stock of books, considering the circumstances.

The general impression of the cultural level of the Europeans stationed in Greenland is not very inspiring. As a rule they were a bunch of roughnecks, naturally with the exception of the missionaries. The standard of the inspectors fluctuated, but most of them had had some academic finishing and showed a deep interest in intellectual activities. Among the assistants and traders some can be singled out because they had had a good middle-class upbringing in their native country or because they had had one or another form of education. Some of them were graduates in law. Others were quite well-read, for example, the trader C.C. Dalager. From his remarks in various letters and "certificates" it appears that he must have read Adam Smith's *The Wealth of Nations* quite soon after the Danish translation was published in 1779. He must have had a relatively large library, in comparison with other Europeans. In 1797 Inspector B.J. Schultz encouraged him "to set up a reading and circulating library," most likely on the basis of the books he himself owned. B.J. Schultz himself lent his own books to others, including so topical a work as "Rigsdaler-Sedlens Hændelser" (The Adventures of a Rigsdaler Note), which was published from 1787 to 1789, continuing to 1793, and which he most certainly took with him to Greenland. The trader M.N. Myhlenphort borrowed it and returned it in 1791, by which time the instalments had been through many hands. It was "dangerous" reading for royal civil servants at the time.

These hints of literature circulating among the Europeans are the only indications of the first attempts to establish a book and library service in Greenland. The need to read was great - also among the Europeans. Inspector Schultz' attempt to get C.C. Dalager to lead a lending library was unsuccessful. Inspector P.H. Motzfeldt was the first to get such a reading society established, in 1804, but it was limited to the Northern Inspectorate. The Southern Inspectorate seems to have managed with private libraries and these of the Mission. Remains of collections of books exist at

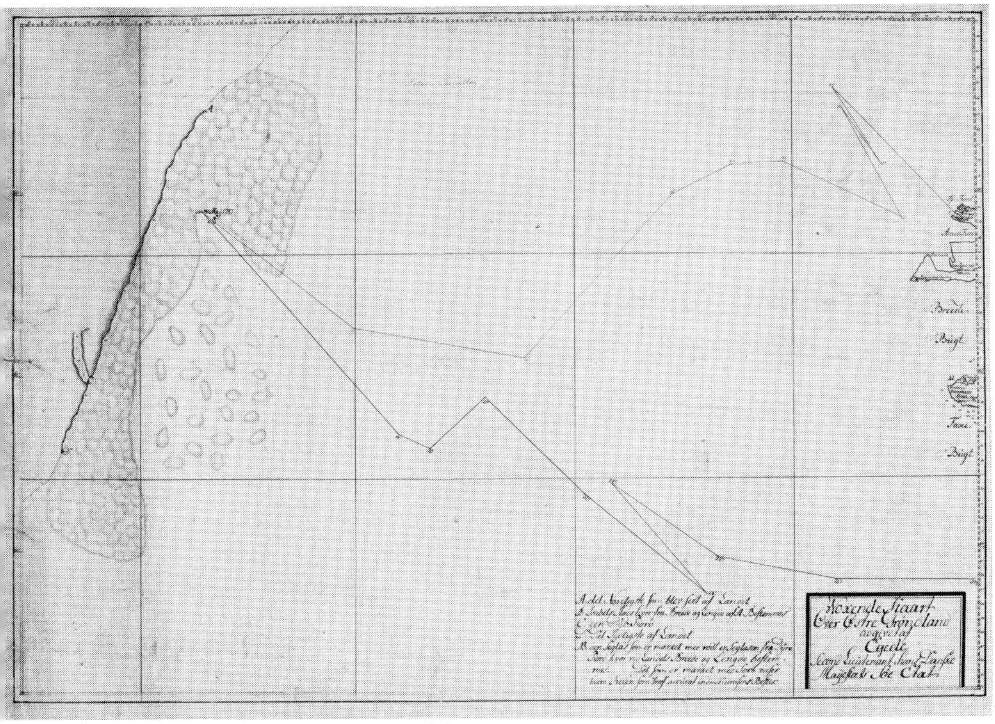

Chr. Thestrup Egede's Mercator chart of the sailings May 8-27, 1787 from Iceland to East Greenland, and the return course towards Copenhagen. The original measures 56 × 38 cm.

(Rigsarkivet, Copenhagen. Collection of Maps 225V)

Christian Thestrup Egede as captain in the Royal Danish Navy.

(Royal Library, Copenhagen. Collectionof Maps and Pictures)

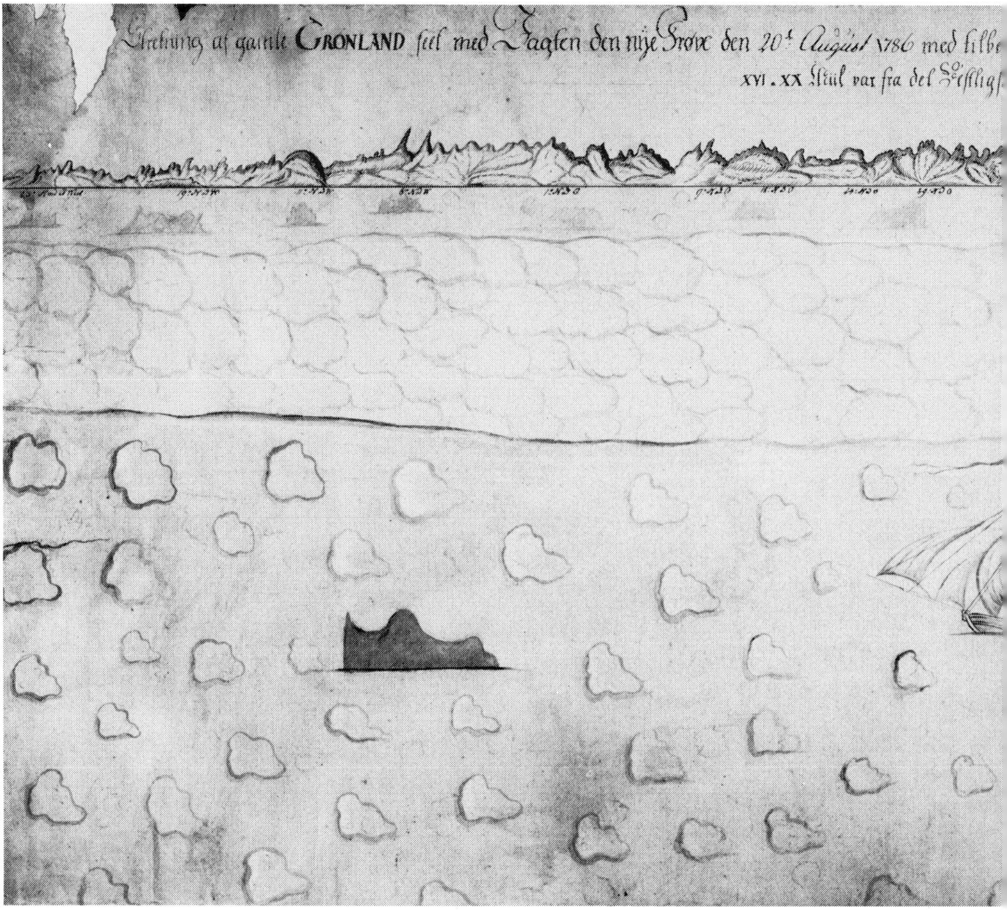

View, dated August 20, 1786, made by Chr. Th. Egede of the stretch of the east coast of Greenland, probably from Ikerssuaq (39°30′ W. Long.) to Qulusuk (37° W. Long.), including the mouth of Sermilik Fjord, shown in a sort of bird's-eye view centered a little to the right of the middle of the drawing. This fjord was for a long time named after Egede and Rothe. Four days later he draws a similar view from a slightly different position. (Original measuring 116 × 49.5 cm in the Rigsarkiv, Copenhagen. Collection of Maps 225 I)

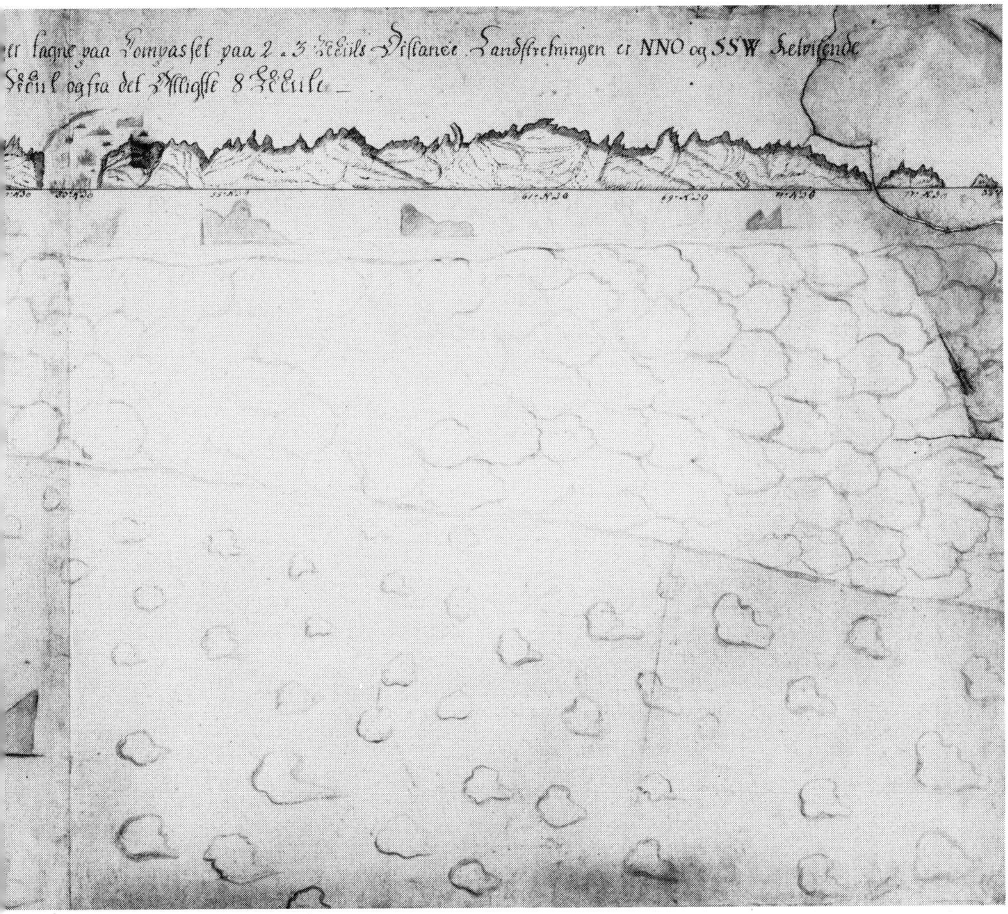

These costal views, the Mercator's chart (plate XVII) and the drawing plate XIX were engraved on copper plates, in a totally distorted version, by J.G. Friederich, and printed in Chr. Th. Egede's book on the expedition: *A Narrative of a Journey to Discover East Greenland, made in the years 1786 and 1787,* Copenhagen 1789 (translated title).

(The light coloured original measures 120 × 48 cm; Rigsarkivet, Copenhagen. Collection of Maps 225 II)

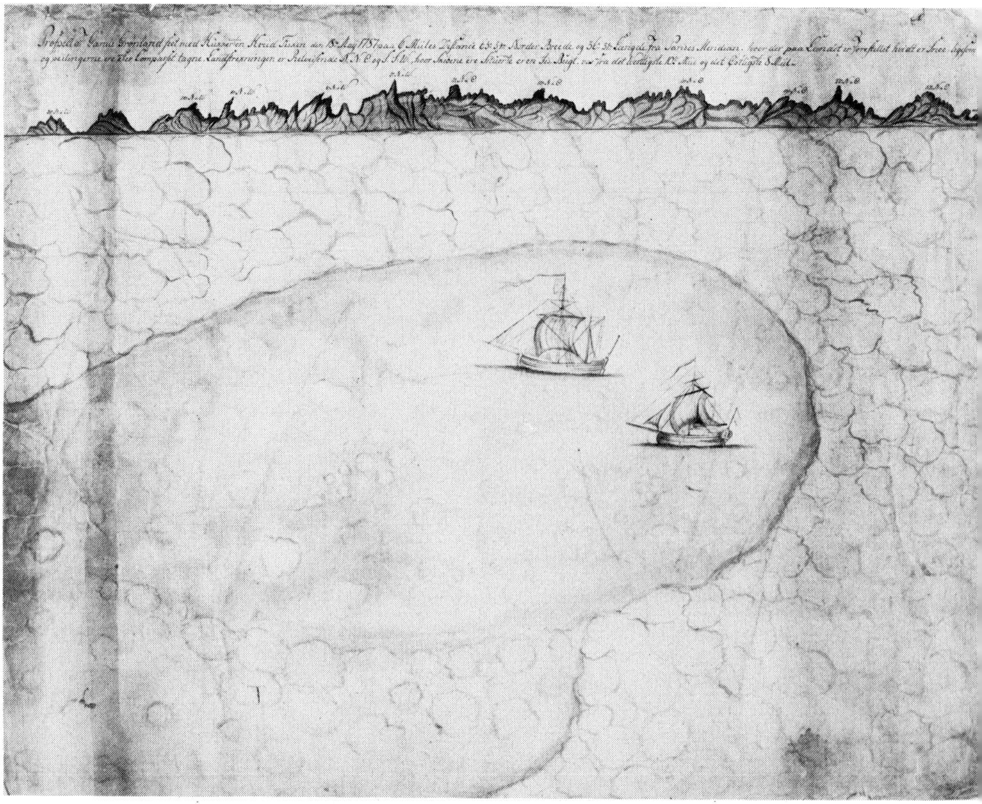

Coastal view by Chr. Th. Egede, May 18, 1787, from a position corresponding to that shown on the Mercator's chart plate XVII. His ship was apparently about 70 km from Leifs Ø.

(Size of original: 66 × 51 cm. Rigsarkivet, Copenhagen. Collection of Maps 225 III)

Naval Lieutenant *C.A. Rothe,* 1801.

(Royal Library, Copenhagen. Collection of Maps and Pictures)

Holsteinsborg, Sukkertoppen, Frederikshåb and Julianehåb, as well as the larger collection at Godthåb. The reading society of the Northern Inspectorate was financed by subscription payments from its members. At first this amounted to three rigsdalers per annum. In 1805 Motzfeldt paid 55 rigsdalers to the "correspondent", i.e., the office manager of the Royal Greenland Trade, for which sum he was presumably to purchase books for the reading society. How many books the society could get for this amount, we cannot say. The first volume of P.A. Heiberg's "Rigsdaler-Sedlens Hændelser" cost one rigsdaler, and the following instalments four skillings apiece. The prices of books had probably risen somewhat by 1805, so about 40 books must have been purchased for the approximately 18 members of the society. What is more important than these calculations is the fact that the reading society was viable and for many years served to maintain contact with the intellectual life of Denmark.

Books printed in Greenlandic were limited to religious literature: i.e., the Bible, the hymnbook, the catechism and the like. "Secular" works were at that time not printed in Greenlandic. Several items were translated, however, mostly "useful things" such as a treatise on how to resuscitate drowned persons. For a modest fee the catechist at Godhavn translated this useful little publication in the years before 1806, and it circulated in various copies and was sent to the different localities. This led the Management to ship ten copies of "Mangor's information on the best ways of saving the lives of asphyxiated persons, to be distributed as inventory to the colonies" of the Northern Inspectorate. The Southern Inspectorate presumably received a similar shipment at the same time. Besides this there were copies of the first aid for illness which the surgeon Eulner had written before the epidemic at Egedesminde in 1800.

In the same manner a selection of the moralistic tales and conversations written by W.F. Koren, the trader at Egedesminde from 1803 to 1807, most likely circulated in a more or less oil-stained condition. In connection with the modest reforms undertaken and the realization acquired of the cultural and educational obligations of the Trade, its management encouraged the inspectors to have works on various subjects written in Greenland, originally the idea of Inspector C. Bendeke in 1799. In 1803 Inspector P.H. Motzfeldt made this the object of a circular. He wanted to form "a collection of approximately written tales for Greenlanders, adapted to their understanding, and describing their domestic life, their work and entertainment and principally their virtues and vices, etc." Koren was one of the few who undertook this assignment; during the course of time mentioned he delivered two collections of "conversations and tales". His model was the current collections of moralistic anecdotes of the times, but the subjects were all taken from the life of West Greenland. They dealt with subjects such as buying and selling, money, credit, fangst bounties, diligence, thrift, etc., all with a "good" and a "bad" person conversing. Some of them are purely instructive: e.g., about the sun and the moon; others served the interests of the mission; and still others consist of moral philosophy: "Can you tell me how I can be happy?" etc.

It was intended to have the previously mentioned Danish-speaking catechist at Godhavn translate Koren's "conversations and tales", but he died in 1805. It was, however, most likely Koren's manuscripts which were used by trading assistant Rasmus Jensen Brandt, and some of which were translated by him to Greenlandic, especially expert in the language as he was one of the very few employees of the Trade who learned West Greenlandic. Along with his translation of the novel "Hanna von Ostheim", they circulated from around 1810 in copies and copies of copies, until they were published in 1839 by the missionary Peter Kragh. It is not definitely known whether copies of other works were circulated in Greenlandic. The literature mentions later that it was common for the Greenlandic population to supply itself with reading matter in this way.

The publication and printing of books and pamphlets in Greenlandic for the use of congregations took place in Copenhagen for the Royal Mission, and for the German-speaking Moravian Brethren as a rule in Barby, a Moravian centre in Germany. The art of printing suddenly appeared in Godthåb, or rather in Ny Herrnhut, for a short visit. In 1790 the Moravian missionary Jesper Brodersen arrived - from Tønder in what was then Slesvig - with a simple hand-operated press and a small letter case. In 1793 he used this apparatus to print a little liturgical book for the Moravian congregation. The text was not complete, but it was used until 1801, when a new complete and authorized version of the liturgy was shipped to Greenland. Hereafter it seems that this hand press was unused. Jesper Brodersen, who must have been the only one with patience enough to use it, had to leave Greenland due to illness in 1794. His little book - the first one printed in Greenland - was one swallow which did not announce the near approach of summer.

Oral narration still played an immense role. Traditional legends were maintained, and accounts from the recent past could form a part of this tradition.

Science

Both Europeans and Greenlanders thus had interests which transcended the material and religious aspects of every-day life. The rationalistic Zeitgeist was actually quite well suited to the society of West Greenland in the late 18th century. Its cultivation of usefulness was surely the reason why some of the missionaries found time to cultivate other fields than the narrowly limited ones of the mission. When the missionary A. Ginge functioned as a sort of physician in his district of Godthåb around 1790, it was more the Christian demand to help one's fellow man in need that motivated him. This was probably also true of the active participation of missionaries and catechists in the vaccination campaign in 1804 and subsequent years. If the catechists at certain localities received a limited training in lancing boils and bloodletting, this was if anything because the catechists were considered the brightest of the Greenlanders. But "what do the Greenlanders care of the paths of the stars, or whether the one or the other is called Venus, Mercury, Jupiter, or something else?" wondered Inspector A.M. Lund in 1793, with a clear reference to Ginge. It was no worldly use talking to Greenlanders about such things; the missionary who took time to do so must not be worth his wages. This prosaic inspector frowned on the astronomic observations which Ginge made systematically in the period after 1782. In that year he was granted the enormous sum of fifty rigsdalers for an observatory at Godthåb. By 1785 his observations included a number of determinations of Godthåb's location, as well as of the compass conditions of certain channels. He calculated the compass deviation at Godthåb each year to see "its increase and decrease", and observed the deviation quite accurately. He also observed the movements and changing positions of certain planets, including Jupiter and its moons. From 1784 to 1787 he made systematic observations of Godthåb's weather. He thus produced tables of barometric pressure, temperature, air humidity, compass deviation, wind velocity and precipitation for some of the years, and finally a table of "the Appearance of the Air and Meteora". The dates of these latter observations reveal that he must have stayed rather permanently at Godthåb, if his observations were made there.

There were also others who sent in meteorological observations throughout the years, not to mention the materials which could be collected from the daily remarks of skippers in ships' logbooks. Even such an inactive missionary as J.C. Büchler at Holsteinsborg sent in temperatures, but only during his first year, not later.

Scientific observations in the broadest sense of the word were made sporadically on the basis of the general appeal to do so contained in the Order of 1782. Mineralogical investigations, culminating in the sending of K.L. Giesecke to Greenland, have already been mentioned.

An entirely different field of science, botany, had been cultivated since the Greenland years of Poul Egede, but not intensively. As was the case with all other scientific investigations in Arctic areas in these times, botanical investigations were only done occasionally. From the hand of Poul Egede there still exists the first Greenlandic herbarium. On the basis of the plant identifications contained in it, the professor of botany at Copenhagen University, Dr. Christen Friis Rottbøl wrote the first Danish treatise on Arctic plants in 1770. Not much seems to have been done in botany in subsequent years, except that some time after 1787 the perhaps still extant fascicles of Floræ Danicæ Iconum must have been shipped to Greenland, as we have seen. In 1801 the dynamic professor of botany Erik Nissen Viborg urged the Management of the Royal Greenland Trade to have plants collected in Greenland. He wanted "seeds of Greenlandic plants, living specimens in soil of osier and all species of bushes, dried and, as well as can be, conserved plants for herbaria." It was evidently his intention to continue and add to Poul Egede's herbarium. "There is reason to assume that unknown species are discovered around on the mountains." The intention was good enough, but it produced no results both because of the war and because this not very popular professor resigned as the professor of botany. Not until after the war was the collection of botanical specimens resumed.

Characteristic of explorations of Greenland was that they were few, sporadic, and without really energetic efforts, either financial or personnel-wise. Denmark/Norway of the time lacked several of the prerequisites for a deeper and more systematic series of exploration campaigns. But one object of research had not been totally forgotten during the difficulties of daily life. Where had the Norse Østerbygd been, and what about the Greenlanders who came from the East every year to the southern localities of Julianehåb District?

Assistant Aron Arctander's identification of Norse place names with localities in Julianehåb's fjord complex was first published in 1793. The previous year they had been the object of better scientific substantiation. It was the postal officer Heinrich von Eggers who in 1792, relying on Arctander's notes, proved the probability that Østerbygd had been located in Julianehåb District.[17]

Previous to this, two expeditions had been made to the East Coast. In 1793 Anders Olsen repeated his tour de force, going by umiak to the East Coast and back again. This was to a great extent inspired by the interest of the Trade in finally determining to what extent the southern tip of Greenland should and could be incorporated under the Trade. There had to be opportunities for purchasing Greenlandic produce, since people constantly came from the East to trade. Anders Olsen had himself proposed this reconnaissance trip in his report in 1781, in connection with the discussion on establishing a southern trading post in the district. His daring trip failed to produce the desired result, and the southern trading post was not established until 1797, at Nanortalik.[18]

The second expedition, this time from outside Greenland to its East Coast, was inspired by Jon Erichsen, then deputy in the Rentekammer and member of the Management of the Royal Greenland Trade.[19] He was, however, in different connections persona ingrata, which led to his suicide 1787. It was perhaps too the reason why Bishop Poul Egede and Lieutenant Commander Poul Løvenørn took the initiative and in 1785 appealed to the Crown Prince. Then the necessary expenses were granted by the Ad Usos Publicos Fund.

As a basis for his expedition Løvenørn had got an old map of the East Coast of Greenland, dated 1761 and drawn by the whaling commander Volquard Bohn (or Boon) from Boldixum on Før. After having drawn this map, Bohn had been in the sound which was later sailed by William Scoresby Jr., from which it has received the name Scoresby Sound. Løvenørn's expedition took place in 1786. It consisted of two ships, one commanded by Løvenørn, the other by Christian Thestrup Egede, the son of Poul Egede. Løvenørn did not succeed the first year in penetrating the drift ice off Angmagssalik, although he attempted two times with his point of departure in Reykjavik. According to plans he was to return to Copenhagen, whereas the other ship was to make attempts in both 1786 and the following year. It attempted a total of five times to reach the coast, but only once in 1786 did it succeed in getting so close that some drawings could be made of views of stretches south of Angmagssalik. In 1787 the coast was again approached, but the ship had to return home with no success.

The 53-year-old whaling commander Volquart Bohn had apparently whetted his appetite; in 1788 he proposed a new expedition to the East Coast to discover Østerbygd, but this idea found no response in the higher ranks. The desire to find Østerbygd and the hope of finding it were still alive, however, as we have seen, but were coupled with the desire of the Trade to derive some benefit from the southernmost part of Greenland. Thus the Trade in itself was not much interested in attempts to reach the coast from the east through the Storis. Some time after Von Eggers had published his opinion of the true location of Østerbygd, and at the same time as the final plans were made for the establishment of Nanortalik, the diaries of Peder Olsen Walløe were rescued from oblivion.[20] It was, however, mostly his description of Tunugdliarfik Fjord and Igaliko sandstone which were of interest, in connection with the encouragement of mineralogical surveys in Julianehåb District.

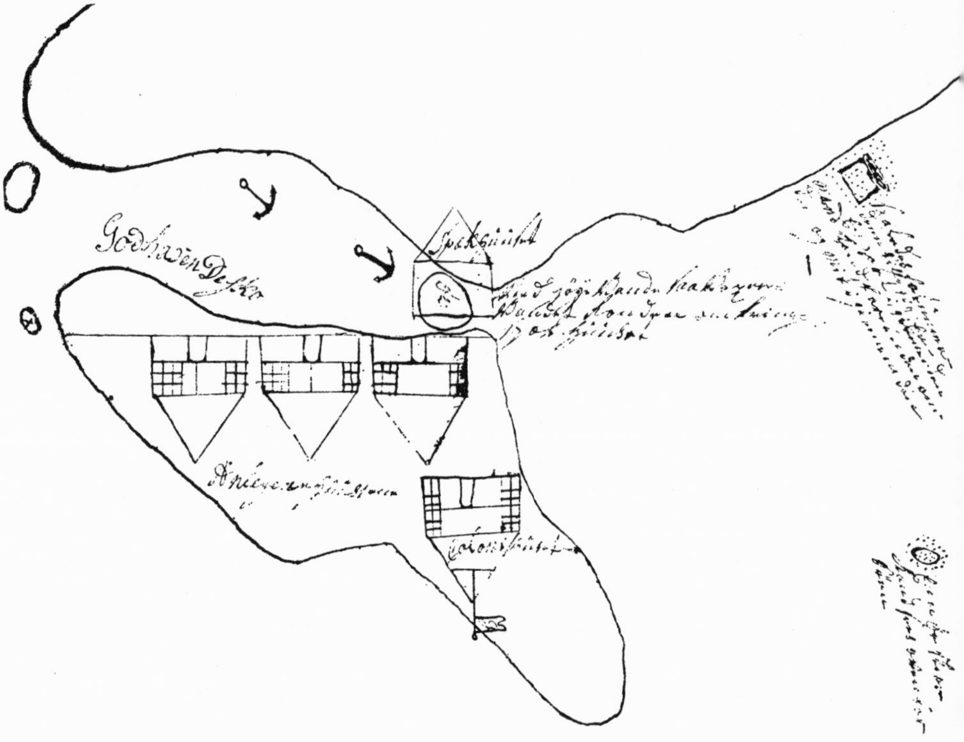

Godhavn. Excerpt from J.A. Geraae's map sketch 1781. The entire sketch measures 255 cm by 93 cm. This excerpt measures 29 cm by 25 cm. The inscriptions are, from left to right (here translated): "Godhavn Disko", "Houses built etc.", "The Colony building", "At high tide the water surrounds the blubber house". The circle between the two coasts is marked "Øe", i.e., "Island", upon which the "blubber house" is placed in a very "primitive" manner. Utmost to the right, off the coastline, there is a square with an elipse over it and many dots and the text (translated): "Thus appears this column i.e., a solitary rock. There is a gate in it. One can pass between it and the coast and straight through it." (Søkortarkivet, Copenhagen, A/18-23A, 1:2,21.)

There were several more or less flimsy projects for expeditions of geographical discovery. There was somewhat more traffic in Greenlandic waters than previously, and somewhat more daring to venture out into these capricious currents. A name suddenly makes its appearance in the sources: a name which was later to be especially distinguished - Ross. Whether this is the renowned English rear-admiral John Ross cannot be said with certainty. In any case an English or Scots Captain Ross, commanding the whaling ship *Cathrine* was at Godhavn in July 1806 along with two other whalers. Davis Strait and the southern part of Baffin Bay along the West Coast of Greenland gradually became well-known to English whalers in these decades.

These whaling skippers did not sail haphazardly, although the personal knowledge possessed by each individual of the waters sailed was the most essential guideline. They did have charts probably mostly of Dutch origin, and it can be assumed that the skippers themselves constantly corrected their charts according to their own experiences. At that time there were no official charts of Greenlandic waters.

Neither these charts nor maps of the coasts were satisfactory: they were quite lacking in detail, to say the least. A quite primitive map of the coasts of Disko Bugt showing the more important localities was drawn by Jens Andersen Geraae, the assistant and later the trader at Ritenbenk; it naturally had Ritenbenk as a kind of centre. It is dated 17 April 1781, the same year that this colony was moved to the northwest coast of Arveprinsens Ejland. He supplied his map with small sketches of the more important colony buildings, and added comments, often quite funny ones, to each locality.

There was quite a different style to the map which the Norwegian Olav Olavsen delivered to the Management of the Royal Greenland Trade in 1783. It is described as an "ordinary map of the now known part of the western coasts of Greenland," collected "from many special maps." The General Board of Directors of the various northern Trades granted him 100 rigsdalers, which he was not paid until 1784. Later he received an additional 50 rigsdalers for a corresponding map which he delivered to the Rentekammer. It is explicitly stated that he had not yet engraved it on copper plates. Nor was it later published, so it was of no use to his contemporaries.

XI. Thwarted Reforms

The Spirit of the Leadership

During the 18th century and quite a ways into the 19th, scientific investigations did not deal with social conditions. Huge comprehensive social systems could well be thought out by socially interested philosophers, and the 18th century had many of these. But just because they philosophized about the state of society, in their opinion more or less unsatisfactory, their relationship to reality was somewhat tenuous.

Economy was a new, likewise philosophical science; it had hardly yet become a real science, or was at least not recognized as such. Because it was still more or less philosophical, it still dealt mostly with systems, with ideas and ideal situations, just as the social critical writers did. But by virtue of "reason", the economic thinkers took their basic material from the world of experience, especially bad experiences, and thus came to take positions on current issues.

The practical elaboration of the ideas of social philosophers and economic thinkers was in the hands of social practitioners: administrators and politicians. These two categories cannot be sharply distinguished from each other. Whether reforms took place or the status quo was maintained depended not only on them but also on whether the acquiescence of the symbol of state power could be obtained. In Denmark/Norway this was the autocratic monarch, represented in the period under consideration by Crown Prince Frederik, later King Frederik VI.

Characteristic of the Danish-Norwegian monarchy from 1784 on was that it included a number of administrators and politicians eager for reforms who were able to win enough acquiescence from the Crown Prince and thus the power of the state for a comprehensive reform programme to see the light of day.

These men were inspired by the rationalistic spirit of the times, as has often been stressed in this work. Committed to the traditional layering of society in estates, these civil servants were nevertheless tolerant and had a deep respect for the individual and his innate worth, regardless of estate or condition. They were sensible, but still feeling. Many, perhaps most, were rooted in open religion but unaffected and moderate in its expression; they did not submit uncritically to the prevalent religious organisation. They were liberal but had a distinct and honest desire for orderly conditions for and in the best interest of the citizens of the state. They were unswervingly but not uncritically loyal to the prevailing form of state. They desired healthy growth and welfare for the individual and the eradication of "the barrier between 'uncivilized' and 'civilized' people".

These terms were used by Christian Ditlev Reventlow, and refer to the Danish common people. They are not the expression of pride of intellect or class, but on the contrary, of a desire to spread the good and orderly way of life of civilization to as many people as possible. This could best be done through schools, so that Reventlow was greatly interested in the severely needed improvement of them and of teachers' training, primarily in Denmark/Norway. Enlightenment was the factor he as well as many others put their trust in to develop better conditions for society and its citizens.

This great interest which Reventlow had in the improvement of the school system spread to the civil servants surrounding him and from them further outward. The establishment of schools and the spread of enlightenment were one of the leitmotifs of the last decades of the 18th century. As a member of the Commission of 1788, Reventlow must also have been interested in an improved school system for Greenland, just as his idea of eradicating the barrier between "civilized" and "uncivilized" people must also have included the inhabitants of Greenland. It must then be reasonable to see Reventlow as the actual prime mover of the reform proposals for Greenland which made their appearance during the 1790's.

Education Problems

It does not appear, however, that Reventlow himself directly initiated the discussions which took place on Greenlandic schools and teachers' training. As seen above, it was especially Inspector B.J. Schultz who raised the issue of the poor conditions and deficient training of the catechists. In 1795 he went further and stressed that a better training of the catechists would not only increase their potential for working to the benefit of their countrymen, but would also have favourable consequences for Greenlandic society as a whole. Better grounded teachers would lead to better education and greater enlightenment. These are thoughts and ideas which to an astonishing extent agree with those which Christian Ditlev

Reventlow championed in the Great School Commission of 1789 and which he and his brother Johan Ludvig Reventlow carried out in practice on their own estates. Schultz wrote: "The enlightenment of the Greenlanders and their conversion to morality and diligence should take place through education."

This was amplified for the Missionskollegium in 1796 by the Management of the Royal Greenland Trade. Education should be given by "national teachers, since these have so many advantages and much fewer difficulties to overcome, if they otherwise have some degree of enlightenment and unite a good will with an honest intention." The education of catechists at the time was poor and their economic conditions likewise. In somewhat equivocal expressions the Management offered to participate in a discussion of the economic problems involved in implementing Inspector B.J. Schultz' idea of a veritable training institute for Greenlandic teachers, just as Johan Ludvig Reventlow had had a state teachers' training institute set up on his estate Brahetrolleborg on the Danish island of Funen in 1794.

The offer of the Management to discuss the economic problems involved in financing such a teachers' training institute was, certainly under the influence of the general activity in Denmark in the area of schools and teachers' training, and especially Reventlow's opinions toward them, a continuation of the change of attitude toward the Mission and its pressed economic situation which the Management had cautiously begun in 1793.

This change must have seemed so astonishing to the Missionskollegium that it did not even bother to answer the inquiry of the Management regarding the teachers' training institute. The Missionskollegium could supposedly not at all embark on the discussion of plans which it could not see the slightest possibility of realizing. In consideration of the previous letter from the Management in 1793 on the wages of the catechists, the Missionskollegium may have felt this renewed interest as an improper interference in its own special jurisdiction. However this may be, the Management reported to Inspector Schultz that his proposal had been communicated to the Missionskollegium in vain.

Thus this reform proposal fell to the ground. In the same year, 1796, B.J. Schultz left Godhavn and Greenland for good. Greenland and especially its catechists thus lost a potential champion of better education and enlightenment. Others took his place, but on other premisses. The Management did not lose interest in the question of education, but shelved the issue – for the time being.

The Renewal of the Commission

Improved instruction in the schools and intensified enlightenment activities in Greenland had been dealt with in 1788 by Carl Pontoppidan - on the assumption that the monopoly would be disbanded. His report was submitted to the Commission of 1788 in its first year of existence. The Commission had been appointed to work out a winding up of the monopoly, but in its final resolution this objective was abandoned for the time being. Pontoppidan's sketch of comprehensive development measures, including some to improve the general level of culture, was not adopted. The Commission was only to supervise and control the Royal Greenland Trade.

The Commission's mandate was for ten years, and this actually expired in 1798, although the Royal Decree setting it up was not assented to until 1790. By the Royal Decree of May 1798 it was now decided that the Commission was to continue the supervision of the Royal Greenland Trade. The Finanskollegium was to function as a superior authority.

At the same time it was decided that at the end of each year the Board of Managers were to submit reports on the state and results of their Trades during the previous year. As far as Greenland in particular was concerned, a detailed annual report was to be submitted on each individual district, including its economic condition, population, demographic movements, opportunities for new occupations, purchases and sales of produce and merchandise, and finally "whether any arrangements might be suggested to improve their (i.e., the Greenlanders') condition".

When the Management of the Royal Greenland Trade passed this order on to the inspectors, it did so with an eloquent interpretation. The inspectors were told themselves to collect and send each year "everything which can shed some light on the state of the country in general and the points listed here in particular, as well as to arrange by circular that all the officers of the Trade make efforts to investigate this, so that the contributions expected of them may be as detailed and interesting as possible."

By using the word "interesting" the Management limited the size and content of such reports considerably. Reporters were thus to limit themselves to communicating items which were of interest or could arouse interest. Perhaps the Management wanted to avoid too long-winded reports which would demand a good deal of editorial work before the formulation of the final annual report. But the Management did have to have some information from Greenland. Its very order to the inspectors revealed that it lacked sufficient knowledge on conditions at the various places. It was not itself capable of giving a distinct picture of the state of the country, in general or in particular, but hoped, modestly, that local reports could shed "some light" on this. It is almost a symbol of continuity that these annual reports to the government have been faithfully submitted each year, from 1798 to the present.

The decision to renew the mandate of the Commission in 1798 entailed certain regrettable consequences. Christian Ditlev Reventlow left the Commission. He had become member of the Konseil in 1797 with the title of Minister, but continued as the leader of the Rentekammer and a member of the Finanskollegium. In this manner he preserved a certain contact with Greenlandic affairs, which nevertheless had to give precedence to matters which were more important for him and his entire activity. H.E. Schimmelmann also left, but this was in a way less regrettable. He was still the leader of the Finanskollegium, the body with jurisdiction over the Commission and the Royal Greenland Trade.

Shortly after New Year of 1791, Johan Fr. Schwabe seems to have left the Commission to definitely take charge of the office of lagmand (judge) in the Opland District of Norway to which he had been appointed in 1788. From 1798 on the members of the Commission were limited to the now quite elderly former prefect L.A. Thodal; Jacob Edvard Colbiørnsen; Carl Pontoppidan; the executive co-managers of the Royal Greenland Trade: Hartvig Marcus Frisch, Fr. Martini and Hans Leganger Wexelsen (appointed third co-manager in 1790 and member of the Commission in 1793); and finally Professor Christian U.D. von Eggers. No new members were appointed to replace those who had resigned.

Two years after the renewal of the Commission the ten-year period of the Royal Greenland Trade expired. The Finanskollegium therefore asked in relatively good time for the Commission's recommendation on the future organisation of the Trade, and this request was naturally passed on immediately to the Management of the Royal Greenland Trade. The Management replied at the last possible moment: the last day of the year. The entire matter was actually only a formality. No one contemplated changing the "arrangement" on such short notice, among other reasons because of the "feeler" which the Commission had put out dealing with thorough reforms, and which will be dealt with later in detail.

The Management nevertheless maintained in many words that it would be dangerous to abolish the monopoly. The Commission sent these many words on unchanged to the Finanskollegium. In a covering letter it summarized that the conclusion of its recommendation must be "that monopoly trade still seems to be the most suitable for Greenland, in consideration of the nature of the country itself as well as of its relationship to the other states of His Majesty the King; and that with respect to the Greenlanders no monopoly is to be preferred to that conducted on behalf of His Majesty himself."

In its recommendation the Trade had expressed a certain insecurity with respect to trade conditions in the near future, after the expected "pacification of Europe." The "treaties of peace" were not signed until 1801-1802, and lasted, as we know, only to 1803-1805. Neither the Commission nor the Management of the Royal Greenland Trade dared in 1799 have any opinion whether it would be dangerous to continue the existing organization of the Trade out of consideration for the burden on the Royal treasury in the future. They had thus in advance insured themselves against all possibilities. As we have seen, they had good reason to attempt to cover themselves. Trade conditions after 1799 were not bright. Factors which could not have been predicted further muddied the risky waters. Under such conditions no change in the conditions of the Trade could be contemplated. By Royal Decree of 17 December 1800, on the basis of this recommendation, the previous system was continued from 1 January 1800 "until further notice".

"Law and Order"

The fluctuating trading conditions which prevailed after 1799 were also decisive as to whether the Commission and the Management could realize desired reforms and thus create a better basis for abolishing the monopoly; this was still the final goal of the liberalistic members of the Commission and the government.

Among them was Carl Pontoppidan. In his recommendation of 10 July 1788 he had stressed the impossibility of demonopolizing trade with Greenland without first developing the Greenlandic population for a period of six to ten years so that a money economy, saving, and the acquisition of property and estate could prevail among them. In addition it would have to become settled, and "law and authority" would have to become established.

Ten years had now passed. How much progress had been made towards the attainment of these prerequisites? Apparently not so much that it was found advisable to abolish the monopoly. Demonopolization would thus still have to wait.

It was not as if Carl Pontoppidan had not exercised pressure. When several cases of homicide were reported from Frederikshåb in 1787, which evidently had not caused any social reaction, Carl Pontoppidan felt called upon as early as 1788 to suggest the introduction of penal provisions in Greenland for "premeditated murder and homicide"; he was afraid of the reactions of "the Omnipotent".

Nothing resulted from this for the time being. When the Commission in 1798 discussed the question of reducing the fine for paternity, as suggested in 1796, the idea of penal provisions for "murder and other grave crimes committed by Greenlanders" was again aired. There is a direct connection between this discussion and the "culture drive" which the Commission attempted the same year. It was also directly connected to the letter of 5 May 1798 of the Finanskollegium, which as we have seen notified the Commission of the Royal decree renewing it and at the same time demanded yearly reports, including arrangements "suggested to improve the condition" of the Greenlanders.

As early as 21 May, eight days before the Management of the Royal Greenland Trade was notified of the renewal of the Commission's mandate and the annual reports, the Commission took up the question of fundamental reforms. We cannot avoid the impression that the Commission had a kind of bad conscience that nothing at all had been done to follow up the guidelines laid down by Pontoppidan. Perhaps even a direct initiative on the part of Pontoppidan was involved, as in his repetition of the idea of penal provisions for murder and serious crimes, but we have no proof of this.

But with a direct reference to the Royal Decree of 2 May 1798 and a partial quote of the applicable passage the Commission stated that it had been ordered to consider "whether any arrangement" could be suggested which would create better conditions for the Greenlandic population. The most important "such arrangement", the Commission thought, "must be how the Greenlanders can gradually be brought under the beneficial coercion of civil laws, which by securing their lives and property from passionate revenge and the arbitrary treatment of the stronger, and by expanding and correcting their concepts of property and property rights, alone can help them farther along on the path of culture."

The Commission could not imagine that the Greenlandic inhabitants "could be more happy and their morals be higher in their original state of nature." This would contradict all experience. The Commission thus did not believe in the postulate of "the happy savage". Murder – and this points to Pontoppidan as having taken the initiative – was committed because of superstition. Theft did not occur among Greenlanders alone,

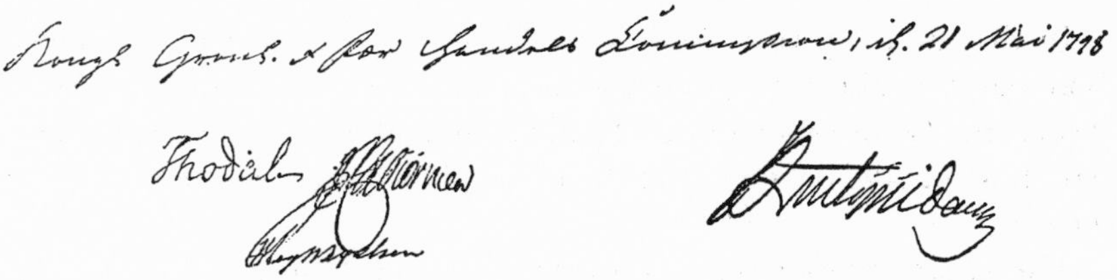

Signatures on the reform memorandum of 21 May 1798.

which was only due to the fact that "they have no idea of property rights, and because one seldom has anything which can tempt the greed of another." This seems at first glance a rather backward argument for introducing the concept of property rights, but this impression fades to some extent when one reads further. The Commission linked the concept of property rights to savings, which in its missive are called "providence". "Greenlanders work only for the moment. Nothing is saved for future shortages. Their lives and those of their families depend on the coincidence of good or bad fishing." This statement was based on the then common, unsubtle view of the Greenlandic economy. Europeans did not ask why the Greenlander did not save, or whether he could do so.

"By being more closely united in a civil society, misdeeds must become more seldom by means of suitable penal laws. Enterprise is brought about by enlightenment, which would result in the improvement of their domestic life." On the basis of this a recommendation was requested from the Management. But as the Commission presupposed that the Management would get statements from the inspectors in Greenland, it listed the main questions it wanted elucidated.

These main points were: 1) "which laws the Greenlanders in their present state mainly need and could accept," 2) "which coercive measures are the same, according to the character, mentality and customs of the nation," 3) "how the judicial and executive power could be organized in the present state of the country." To this last point the Commission added some comments: in its opinion executive power "as belonging to the competence of the authorities" must be a function of the inspector or the senior "colony officer" present, if the inspector cannot come. Judicial power "should if possible be organised so that one or more of the most sensible and moral Greenlanders and those most respected by their countrymen participate in it," as a kind of lay judge. For it was not the idea of the Commission that the inspectors or colony officers should participate in judicial power: at least nothing distinctly saying so is in the Commission's letter.

In the unhappy year 1798, as General and First Consul Napoleon Bonaparte was beginning to remodel southern Europe with his military power, the Commission of the Royal Greenland and Faroese Trade prepared to remodel the society of West Greenland, but with more peaceful means.

The argumentation and phraseology of the Commission's memorandum are clearly based on the common rhetoric of the times, taken from formulations of human rights and socially critical philosophy. In the Commission's covering letter the following year, accompanying the Trade's recommendation of continuing the monopoly, the fear of disintegration of the Danish-Norwegian united monarchy was latently expressed. It was there stressed that the monopoly had to be considered as the most suitable form "considering the nature of the country itself as well as its relationship to the other states of His Majesty the King," although this last word is not adequate in this context. "States" must mean "countries of the King," since Greenland could not be considered as a state, and neither could the Faroese Islands, Iceland, Slesvig or Holstein - at that time.

Just at this time, between 1797 and 1801, the former interdependence between "states" was in the full process of dissolution as a consequence of the Napoleonic advance. Everywhere Bonaparte came he introduced reforms on the French republican pattern. The comparison with this near European danger signal above was therefore not without justification; there were really cogent reasons for the Crown to gather its countries around itself and bind them more closely to the whole. An opportunity to do this was afforded by economic and social reforms in the sociological and philosophical spirit which at that time seemed to be gaining ground - in the most literal sense of this phrase.

Reaction to the Reform Drive

No more than the Commission did the Management of the Royal Greenland Trade feel capable of taking a more definite position on the reform proposals which the Commission had sketched. These proposals were therefore combined with the request to send contributions for the annual report so that it must have seemed to the authorities in Greenland as though the Management wanted general descriptions of each district and statements of what arrangements could be made "to introduce among the Greenlanders the order of a civil society, based on civil and criminal laws," as Inspector Claus Bendeke expressed it in Godhavn, to where he had been transferred one year after being sent to Greenland in 1795 as the Inspector of the Southern Inspectorate.

Claus Bendeke was rather new in Greenland, as was his colleague Niels Rosing Bull, sent to Godthåb in 1796. Their immediate reactions to the reform proposals were rather subdued. Bendeke regretted that he did not have a minute to spare in which to write a report immediately: "even if I could use several days, or even weeks, just to consider this equally difficult and important matter, I would have both to forget my talents, which are quite feeble for this work, and possess the blindest self-confidence, if I immediately dared to submit such an immature embryo to such an enlightened body." He wanted to postpone the matter until the next year.

Niels Rosing Bull evidently did not dare to make any suggestions at all. As far as we can see he submitted no recommendation on these issues. On the other hand he did immediately issue a circular to the officers of the Trade the same year, telling them to send their "reflections" concerning "1. What laws the Greenlanders in their present state need and can accept. 2. What coercive measures should be added to the same according to the character, mentality and customs of the nation. 3. How the judicial and executive power could be organized in the present state of the country." As appears from the wording, this was a concentrate of the Commission's memorandum of 21 May.

In his circular, Bull added the collection of material for the annual reports. In subsequent years rather comprehensive descriptions of the districts were submitted to both the Northern and the Southern Inspectorates, and they were presumably all forwarded to the Management. Unfortunately but few of them have been preserved. Besides that of Inspector Bendeke, dated 20 July 1799, there exist at present only five recommendations, descriptions or opinions: three from the Southern Inspectorate and two from the Northern.

For want of more, these six opinions must be taken as representative of the views possessed by Trade officers of conditions in Greenland, and the opportuneness and possibility of introducing "the order of a civil society," to use the words of Bendeke.

These opinions seem to have come to Copenhagen in small batches, as they are dated in Greenland from 1799 to 1800. Shipping from Greenland was during those years pursued by a number of unfortunate wrecks, so it was more likely in 1801 or 1802 that they came into the hands of the Commission. The Royal Greenland Trade does not seem to have made any summaries of the recommendations it received from Greenland.

One of these, that of the trader Johan Chr. Mørch, is dated "Julianehåb, 10 February 1800." It takes the form of a little book, called "A Mite for the Fortune of Greenland," a title which even at the time must have seemed too pretentiously "modest", bordering on the comical. Its content is, however, far from comical or pretentious.

Like the five others he reported as briefly as possible on conditions as he saw them, and made certain proposals for reforms in accordance with the Commission's memorandum. Except for one of the recommendations there was unanimity that there was no distinct need to introduce actual civil laws for the West Greenlandic inhabitants. There are of course nuances of difference among the five points of view, ranging from one's total lack of proposals in this field to another's mention, in spite of reservations, of certain areas where order based on law could be created. The only recommendation which in a big way advocated comprehensive legislation, even including a kind of adscription, was the one which was different from the other five. This was the one written by the now aging trader Hans Raun at Fiskenæsset, who formerly, in 1776–1777, had ventilated a "stillborn" proposal of a "penal code".[1]

The rather confused recommendation of Hans Raun is so obviously affected by his personal difficulties that it can now be disregarded. This was probably also its fate at the time, due to its incoherence and at times its extreme nature, but it is among those which have been preserved.

The general impression of the other five was probably the same at the time as the student gets of them now. There is no doubt that the writers are interested in the welfare of the West Greenlandic inhabitants and in the best possible development for them. But they did not fail to keep an eye on what could also be beneficial to the Trade. It must be mostly for this reason that some of them make positive suggestions, for these were desired by the management, the Commission, and presumably also the government.

In the five recommendations, the writers examined mutual relations among West Greenlanders and the relations of the individual to the whole. It is quite clear that this could only be done in broad outline and with the qualifications possessed by each one, determined by the length of time he had spent in Greenland and the experiences he had gained locally. Finally, the recommendations were also evidently based on discussions which took place before they were written.

If we disregard the interesting descriptions of districts which some of these recommendations contain, our general impression of them can actually be expressed by a resumé of Inspector Bendeke's recommendation of 20 July 1799, not sent until 20 September of that year. It reveals in places the unmistakable, though no direct, influence of the ideas expressed by the trader Myhlenphort and the senior assistant Motzfeldt in theirs. Bendeke himself was aware of the incompleteness of his recommendation and called it therefore only "ideas in reply" to the questions asked.

In his introduction, Bendeke refers to "history". All peoples, he thought, originally lived "in the greatest degree of freedom," and "hunting and fishing were their only sources of livelihood and only enjoyment." As hunters they were nomadic, without the concept of property, "from which follows the greatest equality, and as the principal reason for strife, property, was unknown, they had no laws and seemed not to need them either."

In his transition to what follows Bendeke is missing one link in his logical chain of premises. He may have thought, but he did not write, that some peoples developed a settled way of life with agriculture, property rights and a number of laws and rules based on these, as well as a religion. Such peoples, he then says, seem to have forced their social order and religion on other, less developed, peoples, as a rule with bloody violence. The subjugated peoples were first enslaved, and their way of life slowly changed. Not until the economic basis had changed were "arrangements" and laws necessary, and this necessity was realized by the subjugated peoples.

"If we now consider the Greenlanders in their present state," Bendeke continued, "we find that they lead a nomadic life and that hunting on land and especially at sea is their only livelihood; and even that due to the nature of the country and its climate, there is no prospect of any other. That they enjoy the freedom associated with their state of nature, and that they consider and recognize themselves as the only owners and masters of the country; that they do have a concept of property and contracts, but that these concepts are extremely vague; that the law of retaliation is the only one they recognize and that it is practiced by each according to his ability, but that they otherwise recognize no form of coercive law. If therefore we were to bring forth a Greenlander, who according to Danish law was even guilty of capital crimes, in order, after a legal judgment, to inflict on him even a slight corporal punishment, we could be certain of thereby arousing all his countrymen present, who would immediately support and defend him." He referred to experiences gained by both himself and Inspector B.J. Schultz in this respect.

Bendeke philosophized further, and feared that the spirit of harmony between the Europeans stationed in Greenland and its native inhabitants, which was to the benefit of both, would be destroyed if it was attempted "to interfere with their freedom and against their will press on them laws and arrangements the necessity of which they do not at all realize or feel." He then mentioned that slight punishments applied to the Greenlanders employed by the Trade were actually quite ineffective, and sometimes and in certain situations directly harmful, and continued "There is hardly any reasonable cause to believe that Greenlanders are more free of human shortcomings than other people. The accusation that Greenlanders steal whatever they can get their hands on from the Danes seems rather harsh to me. At times they do steal things to eat and drink," but if they really were so thievish, there would be far more thefts here, where "so many things cannot be kept under lock and key. Theft even occurs among the Greenlanders themselves."

Murder and homicide did take place, said Bendeke, but as a rule these were executions of witches and thus based on superstition. "If we look at common folk in our fatherland, we will surely find that witches and their crafts are still in rather high esteem, and that a good old smith's wife or another equally respectable matron is extorting most of our villages," after which he mentions that 25 to 30 years ago, people in Bayern "burned a witch with all the formalities of justice." The execution of witches was declining in Greenland, he thought, and since they "are a consequence of ignorance and superstition, enlightenment must be the most certain and perhaps the only means of eradicating it."

"As laws can hardly be introduced in Greenland with force," because the government perhaps lacked the means of enforcing them, and because it would contradict the principles of the present government, "and as there is hardly sufficient reason to believe that the Greenlanders would submit voluntarily to even the most lenient laws, in my opinion there is no other means left to promote this matter than persuasion; by teaching the Greenlanders to feel and realize the necessity and benefit of law."

"By correcting the Greenlanders' concepts of property, or rather by giving them some concept of it, by helping them to acquire and to keep and enjoy what they have acquired, by encouraging industriousness," this could be developed, and also by means of the bounty system which had already been introduced. Then he unfolds a rose picture of how competition between Greenlanders would promote the understanding of the usefulness of ownership.

"The correction of their concept of property" could also be promoted by replacing barter with another form of trade. He described in brief the Eskimo number system, in which it was difficult to reach large numbers, and maintained that "the Greenlanders have, however, no real concept of such a large quantity." He revealed that "One rigsdaler is in Greenlandic called napartarsoak: i.e., a large tub, and 24 skilling are called nappartanguaq: i.e., a little tub, because a large tub of blubber is worth one rigsdaler and ¼ tub 24 skillings. Some other values are designed by hides and baleen". As a consequence their concepts of the values of things were poor, as was also their calculation of values in their media of exchange. For this and many other reasons they would immediately purchase merchandise for the total value of their produce sold on any other occasion. They seldom left "credit deposited with the Trade, but rather prefer to take immediately what can be got all at once." As a rule no Greenlander ever had a skilling to spend a short time after selling his produce or receiving his share of whaling proceeds, and would have to buy on credit what he needed to carry on fangst. Because no one had anything to pay with, there was no trade between Greenlanders either.

"I could list further examples of the deficiency and harmfulness of barter, but I believe the above are sufficient. I therefore consider its abolition and the introduction of money as the first and most important step which can be taken to improve the conditions of the Greenlanders". He stressed the difficulties of introducing money as a medium of exchange partly because the Greenlanders were so poor at arithmetic, and partly because confidence in money would have to be built up. On this point he would have to rely on the catechists and missionaries.

This led him to the educational system; he stressed that it was absolutely necessary that it be improved, but such improvement would involve many difficulties. A short-cut could perhaps be taken by giving literate Greenlanders some light reading, as they "are quite eager to hear adventures and tales," to which he later, quite revealingly, added that if a literate Greenlander "could then amuse himself and a group of Greenlanders by reading tales to them, it might be that for the first time he would feel joy at having learned to read". In such narratives "their domestic life, their work and amusements, their virtues and vices should be depicted." It is this idea of reading material for Greenlanders which was implemented in more or less the same wording as here quoted.

It is astonishing to see that most of these recommendations are unanimous in stressing that the Greenlanders were a "free people." By "free" they all meant, as Bendeke formulated it, "that they enjoy the freedom associated with their state of nature," and as a consequence did not recognize or would not accept any form of coercive law. It would be difficult if not impossible to introduce laws which would interfere with this freedom.

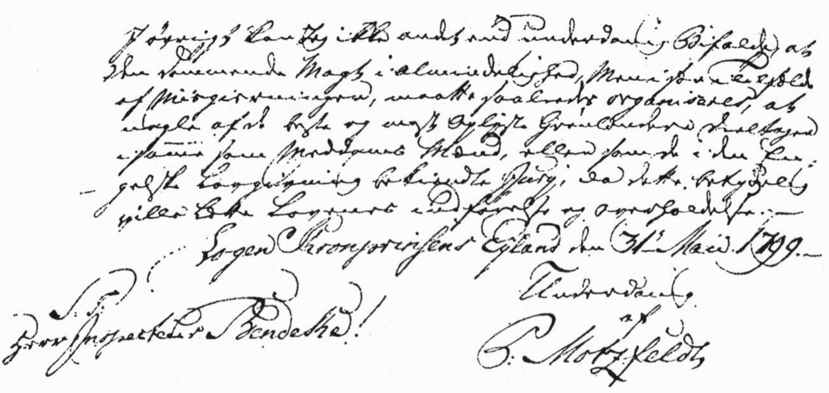

The final lines of P.H. Motzfeldt's recommendation of 31 May 1799. They read: "In addition I can but humbly approve that the judicial power in general, and especially in the case of misdeeds, be organized so that some of the best and most enlightened Greenlanders participate in it as lay assessors, or as the jury known from English legislation, as this would considerably facilitate the introduction and observation of the laws."

Johan Christian Mørch, the trader at Julianehåb, even doubted in his "A Mite for the Fortune of Greenland" whether the autocratic king was entitled to force even the slightest measure of legal regulations on the Greenlanders.

The trader Falck at Frederikshåb went even further in his recommendation, as he did not know in which areas there was any need for legislation. He thought it would be directly harmful to change the prevailing conditions or make rules which could not be expected to be followed. Experience showed, in his opinion, that both the Trade and the Greenlanders were best served by letting the Greenlanders continue being Greenlanders and not interfering at all to change their culture. This point of view stemmed, however, from rather poor relationships with the missionary, with his own colleagues, and with the Greenlanders subordinate to him, especially "mixtures". He was later accused of having cheated in measuring blubber purchased from Greenlanders, but this affair did not result in any determination of his guilt. His entire conduct in Greenland indicates, however, that by his opinion of the reform drive he meant that the Greenlanders could best be kept under his thumb if they were allowed to act as they had been traditionally accustomed to. But it was not for this reason that he was asked for his opinion.

Myhlenphort at Egedesminde stated briefly and to the point that laws should not be introduced as long as the inhabitants were so unenlightened that they had no ideas of what law actually was, and of what use it could be. There existed a certain order in the West Greenlandic society: a number of unwritten conventions which were generally observed, associated by tradition with the various occupations. New laws would hardly be observed, and the traditional conventions were sufficient. If laws were introduced, this must not be done precipitously, but be preceded by enlightenment and more enlightenment.

P.H. Motzfeldt at Kronprinsens Ejland emphasizes more or less the same, but in greater detail: that laws should not be imposed from above, but grow out of a natural need. Reforms, including legislation, should not be pressed down on the heads of the people. Motzfeldt elaborated more on criminality, which he did not think really existed in Greenland. He distinguishes sharply between relations between Greenlanders and Europeans on the one hand, and relations between Greenlanders alone on the other. For the latter he finds the prevalent customs and conventions quite sufficient for the maintenance of a reasonable degree of order because they "agree closely with the laws of nature and equity." He disregards here misdeeds committed out of superstition, which he naturally finds harmful. Only in a very few special circumstances did he think that certain legal provisions would be useful: e.g., to deal with wrecks and the salvaging of wreckage, where pure anarchy existed at the time, which was also unfortunate in connection with the rights of foreign nations.

Motzfeldt also dealt with the production of suitable secular and instructive reading material, the prerequisite for which, he thought, was improved schooling. He considered it a further prerequisite that there be provided for "the establishment of an institute of learning or school in this country where suitable children of the country itself could be educated and made capable of being the teachers of their countrymen."

It is typical of all the recommendations which have been preserved that their authors expressed themselves with an astonishing amount of independence, without other consideration of the authoritarian regime than the decorum demanded of a civil servant. Some of them were even bold enough to doubt that the king was at all entitled to legislate in Greenland. Their free speech did not at all harm them, which could perhaps have been expected, rather the contrary. Both Myhlenphort and Motzfeldt later became inspectors, and Johan Christian Mørch continued to be highly esteemed. It was other circumstances which injured Gert Falck. None of them seems to have had the slightest impression that they could not write what they sincerely meant. This speaks well of the atmosphere in the bureaucracy, although freedom of the press was being limited at precisely the same time. Internal freedom of expression was apparently not interfered with.

The Consequences

Seen from the point of view of the Management, the Commission and the government, these recommendations must have represented one big disappointment. The disappointment of the Management must have been the least, but that of the Commission and the government must have been all the greater. The Commission, and especially Carl Pontoppidan, had in its memorandum of 1798 given a broader interpretation of the order in the Royal Decree of 2 May 1798. Behind this was the Finanskollegium, i.e., Schimmelmann and Reventlow. It was their desires for liberalization which inspired the decree and the Committee, and which were now disappointed. This was just one of many disappointments experienced by liberalists in these years.

We can only guess as to the degree of disappointment. The sources are totally silent about the "reform drive". Even Carl Pontoppidan seems to have kept quiet about it. Neither the Commission, the Finanskollegium, the Rentekammer or the government (Statsråd) discussed these matters in subsequent years.

It appears, however, from what happened subsequently that the Commission and the Management of the Royal Greenland Trade did not just intend to continue to administer in the traditional manner. Some of the suggestions made in the various recommendations were taken up and attempts were made to put them into practice. But there resulted only a few reforms, and they were impeded by external conditions. The uncertain times from 1800 past the end of the period dealt with here exercised their influence. The lack of stability which especially the Royal Greenland Trade experienced, and which gave rise to fluctuating revenue and general deficits, did not encourage large-scale reformistic adventures.

It therefore bears witness to the good will inspiring the Commission as well as the Management and the inspectors that those reform proposals were nevertheless adopted which seemed to be totally or partially feasible without too much economic risk.

One of the desires of the Commission was to see the Greenlanders' "concepts of property and property rights" corrected. It was another matter to fulfill this desire. Bendeke saw an opportunity to do this in certain respects and at the same time to insure the Trade against local exploitation. In 1801 he issued a circular to the trading chiefs of the Northern Inspectorate in which he in the first place asked for a proper inventory to be taken at each locality in order to determine what belonged to the Trade and what was privately owned. This already implied a demonstration of the concept of property rights.

The second point in the circular was even more so. The inspector specified that in the future title would have to be produced to prove that one owned a half-timbered house, and that one had had permission to use stationed European craftsmen to build or help build it. One would also have to document that one had had permission to use the imported materials in the house, or that they had been purchased from the Trade. The same provisions were to apply to small boats, either imported or purchased in Greenland; in the latter case the seller would have to be named.

It appeared on this occasion that quite a few privately-owned half-timbered houses had existed for a long time but that it was almost impossible to prove ownership of them. In this case the inspector could grant title to own the houses after an appraisement.

In subsequent years a number of such titles were issued, but only to houses, not to the land on which they stood. There was no question of issuing regular deeds to land and houses, and as a consequence there was no possibility of mortgaging property - apart from the fact that its value could never be great enough to mortgage. Thus Greenland was at this early stage different from other societies governed by law in this economic area. Among those who received property titles were several "mixtures", so that these titles came to function as a correction of the Greenlanders' "concepts of property and property rights," but of only one side of them.

As we have seen, it was Inspector Bendeke who started this practice, but it was continued by his successor Peter Hanning Motzfeldt. It must have played a role in the detailed implementation of the reforms desired that Bendeke, after leaving Greenland for good, stayed in Copenhagen from August 1801 to some time in 1804, and that Motzfeldt spent the winter of 1803-1804 there. This may have helped to get the proposals which they had advocated in their recommendations adopted: first and foremost the introduction of "money" as a medium of exchange and the improvement of education.

Credit Notes

In July 1801 the acting Inspector P.H. Motzfeldt at Godhavn introduced a kind of currency there "after speaking with Mr. Inspector Bendeke". This seems to have occurred quite spontaneously, but the conversation with Inspector Bendeke must have taken place before he left Godhavn on 7 June 1801. Upon issuing this currency Motzfeldt listed a number of reasons for doing so, but in a letter to the Management he related that he "was primarily moved to do so" by a definite occasion. When he was distributing the whaling proceeds from 1800–1801, he found that "the Greenlanders had been given an enormous amount of credit." A certain Greenlandic harpooner still owed 11 rigsdalers, although he received over 67 rigsdalers as his share of the whaling proceeds: he had purchased over 78 rigsdalers worth of merchandise on credit. The whalers pleaded "that they did not know or could not calculate the value of the merchandise they had received," i.e., that they actually had no idea how much they had bought on credit. The other aspect of his reasoning were the same as Bendeke had brought out on the practice of barter in general. Now Motzfeldt would take advantage of the opportunity "to give the Greenlanders more distinct concepts of the value and use of money and thus lead them to more thrift and a better economy." It was a rather modest start, as he issued credit notes in the quantities and denominations listed in Table 40. They were entrusted to the trader at Godhavn to be paid to "the Greenlanders after having received the necessary produce" for whatever "credit they might have with the Trade, and then as they demand, be exchanged for merchandise which must then be accurately listed in the manual", i.e., the cashbook which the trader or assistant kept of the debts and credits of the fangers. The notes were only valid for payment at Godhavn "between the trader and Greenlanders and between Greenlanders." It would be proclaimed that none of the stationed Europeans would receive either merchandise or cash for any notes they might come into the possession of. Motzfeldt thus saw to it that no exploitation of the local Greenlanders could take place on the part of the Europeans, and that no illicit trade could be conducted with the help of these credit notes which Motzfeldt had issued on an experimental basis.

Table 40.

	10 × 10 rigsdalers	=	100 rigsdalers		
	20 × 5 »	=	100 »		
	50 × 1 »	=	50 »		
	40 × 48 skillings	=	20 »		
	40 × 24 »	=	10 »		
	24 × 12 »	=	3 »		
	48 × 6 »	=	3 »		
TOTAL:	232 credit notes worth		286 rigsdalers		

This 286 rigsdalers was a rather large sum when one considers that Peter Hanning Motzfeldt was personally responsible for it. He not only had to have confidence in the Greenlanders who received them, but also in the trader and his assistants, and even all the other Europeans stationed at Godhavn. He also ran the risk that the notes could get outside the colony seat and cause difficulties. At the time they were issued, or at least one and a half months thereafter, the system seems to have functioned to Motzfeldt's satisfaction and reassurance. He felt that his reasons for issuing the notes were confirmed "by the satisfaction with which the Greenlanders received this money after having purchased their necessities, and the care with which they have kept it since then."

"But although I feel convinced of the utility of the introduction of this or real money both for the Trade and for the Greenlanders," he felt insecure towards the Management. It is further testimony to the spontaneity of this action that by these words he distinctly showed that the initiative was entirely his own.

Motzfeldt's insecurity was soon to be wafted away, however. The following year the Management approved his experiment and allowed him to expand it. Inspector Motzfeldt immediately had 131 rigsdalers' worth of notes of similar denominations issued, valid in Kronprinsens Ejland. At about the same time he notified the Management: "I can with equal truth and satisfaction assure you that the introduction of money has had the best influence on the economy of the Greenlanders and on their concepts of value." It had often occurred during the course of the year that a Greenlander who wanted to buy one thing or another pulled his credit note back because he thought the merchandise was too expensive. In 1802 there were several Greenlanders who still had credit notes left which they had been paid the previous year. He himself used his credit notes as payment for the game birds he bought - to the satisfaction of the hunters.

Thus we see introduced a kind of money as a medium of exchange, cautiously and only where the need seemed to be greatest: at whaling stations, in the Northern Inspectorate. The Europeans stationed here had also some need of a means of exchange, but they were not allowed to use Motzfeldt's "money". In 1803 the missionary Henrik Schou at Egedesminde/Godhavn asked Jakob Gude, the secretary of the Missionskollegium, to send a round sum, say 50 rigsdalers, to Greenland. It was obvious that money was not generally current in Greenland, "but still occasions can arise where it both can well be used and cannot well be dispensed with". The missionary did not here reveal, however, what "occasions" he meant. We must assume that he was thinking of occasional payments to other

Europeans. Nothing is mentioned of "real money" circulating among the Greenlanders. They could not have used it to purchase anything at the Trade, which did not accept it - officially. What no one suspected at the time can only accidentally be revealed later. Paper is perishable - in Greenland too. It is said that Motzfeldt's credit notes were actually destroyed after being handed in. Coins could be used as ornaments, medals or amulets: an old custom in Europe with coins of precious metal. It is true that the 18th century scrap heaps in West Greenland relatively seldom contain coins, but they could nevertheless have sneaked into Greenland before 1804.

The idea behind this single reform experiment had, as we have seen, been hinted at by Carl Pontoppidan as early as 1788, but he did not participate in its experimental formulation. It had been supported by several of the recommendations sent from Greenland in 1799-1800. The details were those of P.H. Motzfeldt, perhaps inspired by Inspector Claus Bendeke. The seemingly positive implementation of this idea in the Northern Inspectorate, and the evident satisfaction of the Greenlandic fangers with the system, tempted the Trade to go further.

This further step was taken by the Management in 1803, but in a manner which did not accord with the original intention of the credit notes, as they gradually came to be called. The Management issued a certain number of numbered certificates with a printed value and the signature of the Management. The strange thing was, however, that these credit notes were only to be used by "Europeans" and only at Julianehåb: at no other places in the Southern Inspectorate, nor in the North. This issue of credit notes can only have been intended as a means to facilitate the local purchases and sales of the Europeans stationed at Julianehåb and services rendered by one to the other, not in dealings with the Greenlandic inhabitants. They are thus outside the reform movement in the proper sense of the word.

The Management did not intend to stop at this seeming digression. In 1804 it contemplated a comprehensive emission of credit notes, now valid for all the districts of West Greenland, "to be used for paying the inhabitants in Greenland when they would rather accept them than merchandise." They were to circulate for five years. The Royal decree permitting the circulation of these credit notes was, however, slow in coming, so they had to be postponed until the following year. Inspector Motzfeldt received permission temporarily and on "his own authorisation" to supply the districts of his inspectorate with as many credit notes of his own manufacture as were deemed necessary for a year. It appears from the Manage-

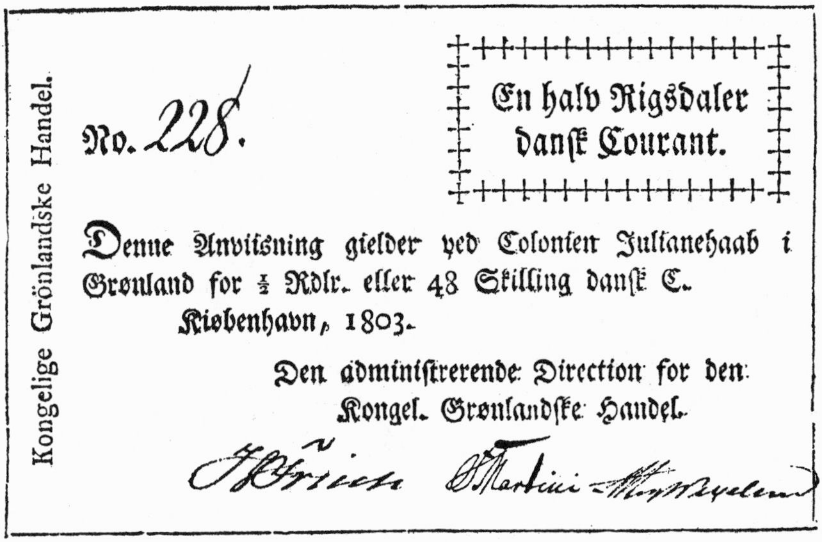
Kongelige Grönlandske Handel.

No. 228.

En halv Rigsdaler dansk Courant.

Denne Anviisning gielder ved Colonien Julianehaab i Grønland for ½ Rdlr. eller 48 Skilling dansk C.

Kiøbenhavn, 1803.

Den administrerende Direction for den Kongel. Grønlandske Handel.

A credit note issued in 1803, valid at Julianehåb. The text, from left to right, and top to bottom:
Royal Greenland Trade
No. 228
One half rigsdaler Danish currency
This certificate is valid at the Colony of Julianehåb in Greenland for ½ rigsdaler or 48 skillings Danish currency.
Copenhagen, 1803
The Board of Managers of the Royal Greenland Trade
(three signatures)
¾ size. The Royal Collection of Coins and Medals, The National Museum, Copenhagen.

ment's letter to Motzfeldt that in 1804 credit notes were not shipped to the Southern Inspectorate, either. Some of the sum of 10,000 rigsdalers provided for by the permission could be sent to the Southern Inspectorate "if they should express the desire to receive them." This presumably did not take place, as appears indirectly from the following.

Inspector Motzfeldt had asked whether Greenlandic recipients of credit notes could use them in times of need to purchase European provisions. The Management would neither approve nor disapprove this, but stated that it had previously been the custom to provide free support in especially difficult times. But now that the introduction of credit notes made it possible for the Greenlanders to save up some of what they earned, it would be a natural consequence of the new system that these provisions be paid for with the notes. It is evident that the Management clearly

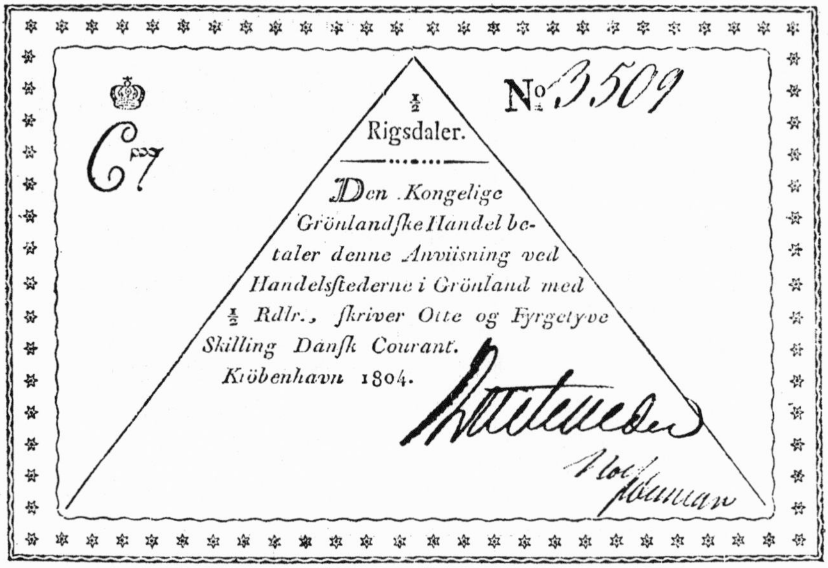

One-half rigsdaler credit note of the 1804–1805 series. The text, from left to right, and top to bottom:
C7 (monogram of King Christian VII)
No. 3509
½ rigsdaler
The Royal Greenland Trade will pay (to the bearer of) this certificate at its trading posts in Greenland ½ rigsdaler, forty-eight skillings Danish currency.
Signed by Carl Pontoppidan and countersigned by assistant Duncan.
¾ size. The Royal Collection of Coins and Medals, The National Museum, Copenhagen.

realized that this would be an attack on the time-honoured rights of the Greenlanders. It was therefore left entirely to the judgment of the inspector, whether this should take place, and when. The Management took additional advantage of the occasion to stress that "the intention of introducing money should not be to give the inhabitants access to Danish provisions or foreign food, but to give the natural produce and foodstuffs of the country a previously unknown value, which could lead all to make thrifty use thereof and some to acquire more than they need with the prospect of advantageously bringing them to others."

In plain language, the Management hoped that a kind of retail trade in Greenlandic produce, including food, would develop. This is a consequence of the introduction of money which had not been suggested previously. Actual retail trade failed to develop, but there did later develop a fluctuating but relatively stable pricing of Greenlandic foodstuffs.

In 1805 the issue of credit notes contemplated in 1804 arrived at the districts in West Greenland. Twelve thousand rigsdalers' worth of notes had been issued, as listed in Table 41. Every single one of these credit notes was signed personally by Carl Pontoppidan and trading assistant Duncan.

Table 41.

	800 × 5	rigsdalers	=	4000 rigsdalers
	2000 × 1	»	=	2000 »
	4000 × ½	»	=	2000 »
	8000 × ¼	»	=	2000 »
	8000 × 12	skillings	=	1000 »
	16000 × 6	»	=	1000 »
TOTAL:	38800 credit notes worth			12000 rigsdalers

It appears from correspondence with Greenland and internal correspondence between the inspectors and traders that the Management had sent not only these credit notes, but also some copper change, probably with values from ¼ to 5 skillings, as the coins of the time in Denmark/Norway. Thus began a practice which seems to have continued right up to the present.

The credit notes were not based on any value, so they were not money in the proper sense of the word. They were only valid for trade and other purposes in Greenland, and the value printed on them only indicated what the Royal Greenland Trade issued and redeemed them for. The value in a single credit note was thus the value of the quantity of produce its owner had sold for it, or more abstractly, the value of the services he had performed for it.

Such a system, it must be admitted, can only be maintained and function within a closed area which has no direct dealings with other areas. The credit note system was based on the monopoly and the isolation of the small coastal societies of West Greenland from direct contact with the outside world. In the whaling regions at certain other localities, this isolation from the outside world was not, as we have seen, quite so absolute. Therefore the credit note system was further restricted to a closed circuit by the fact that the Royal Greenland Trade from the very beginning refused to redeem with Danish bills or coins of legal tender credit notes presented to the Trade outside Greenland, or in Greenland by unauthorized bearers: i.e., foreigners or persons not entitled to be in Greenland. The small coins of legal tender which were shipped were so few that they played no economic role either for the Trade or for the state.

There is a peculiarity of this credit note system which was probably not noticed at the time. This closed system would in the long run impede a possible later liberalization and normalization, because it reacted on the entire monopoly organisation and supported it, so that it became more closed in almost all fields of exchange.

The credit note system had been consciously planned as a means and an opportunity for a certain amount of saving among the Greenlanders. Although a savings bank was suggested by one trader, none was established. Credit notes were not real money, but only certificates which could not draw interest. Nor did the Management imagine that any saving would be of such a long-term nature that the recipients of the credit notes would only save those which were left over as a small surplus, when their accounts were settled, from good fangst times to the more needy seasons of the year. True long-term savings were not expected, although it must vaguely have appeared desirable to the originators of the system. Now the most important thing was to get the system to function.

Of this first issue of actual credit notes, the Management sent less than one-fourth plus 50 rigsdalers in copper coins to the Northern Inspectorate. Presumably a smaller portion of notes plus some coins were sent to the south. One month after he had received the new credit notes, Inspector Motzfeldt put them into circulation in the Northern Inspectorate. The trader at Godhavn received 54% of the holding in August. This shows that Motzfeldt thought it most important to circulate the new notes and coins at Godhavn, where the residents were already accustomed to such notes by four years of practice. The system was thus not introduced immediately in all the districts of the north.

Motzfeldt's idea was probably that this system should be slowly and cautiously introduced, on an experimental basis as it were, in the districts which had not participated in the previous trials. Inspector M.N. Myhlenphort of the Southern Inspectorate acted in the same manner. In July 1805 he notified the trader at Holsteinsborg that in 1804 he had requested the Management to send him "some coins of the type introduced and in use in trade with Greenlanders in the Northern Inspectorate." This was a misunderstanding of Myhlenphort's: the credit notes used in the Northern Inspectorate from 1801 to 1804 were home-made. It appears from the same letter that Myhlenphort wanted the credit note system tested at Holsteinsborg before being introduced in other places in the south. Holsteinsborg was again a whaling station, where the final distribution of whaling proceeds created difficulties, and where credit notes and coins could exercise an especially favourable influence. This showed in addition that whaling was still specially favoured by the inspectorates and the Management, and that their attention, worries, and difficulties were focussed there.

As late as November 1806, Inspector Myhlenphort had not extended the experiment with credit notes to other districts of the south. In a letter written in early November, he notified Inspector Motzfeldt that money was still in circulation only at Holsteinsborg, and for trade "with the Europeans at the colony of Julianehåb". The latter obviously refers to the special certificates issued in 1803. "But I expect to have this splendid arrangement introduced soon over the entire Southern Inspectorate". He also expected in this context discussions on accountancy, as Motzfeldt had encountered in the north. They had produced good results there, and would most likely do the same among the trading officers in South Greenland, thought Myhlenphort.

The new method of payment thus quickly gained ground at all the colonies in West Greenland, and all indications were that it would facilitate dealings between the Greenlandic inhabitants and the Trade. This favourable development was then stopped, at was much else, by the long war of 1807-1814, which disrupted all normal contact with Copenhagen. But that is another story. This reform produced good results, at least in its first years.

The introduction of credit notes and coins into Greenland by the Trade was actually the only real result of the "reform movement" of 1798 for Greenland. That it could be carried out was perhaps due to the fact that the inspectors, the Management of the Royal Greenland Trade and the Commission agreed on this measure, and that the Trade alone implemented it in Greenland. Finally, its success was also due to the fact that the notes were used at places where the Greenlanders as well felt them as an aid.

Education Again

Among the many wishes expressed by the recommendations sent from Greenland, most of them contained one essential one, which even a united Commission and Management alone could not fulfill. A fundamental reform of the school system and teachers' training could only be carried out in collaboration with the Missionskollegium. Here the

Management and the inspectors encountered insurmountable difficulties, mostly based on the Missionskollegium's lack of economic resources. Of course the Trade could arrange certain minor things itself, such as shipping to Greenland some instructive pamphlets on practical matters. As we have seen, the Management, partly at the instigation of Motzfeldt, encouraged trading officers and other persons in Greenland to write instructive stories. This was done by W.F. Koren, but death stopped the translation of his "Tales and Conversations", and the war thwarted the intentions of the Royal Greenland Trade in the field of enlightenment.

Schools, the education of half-breed children and teachers' training were matters to be dealt with by the Trade and the Mission together. Schools and teachers' training at least were under the jurisdiction of the Mission, but the initiative for a reform would have to come from the Royal Greenland Trade and the Commission. The Missionskollegium seemed at the time incapable of doing anything positive to improve the education situation.

The Management therefore dealt with this matter in 1803, possibly in order to achieve the implementation of another of the proposals which had been made in 1799–1800. The Management trod this path into the jurisdiction of the Missionskollegium quite cautiously: it invited the Missionskollegium to "open a school in which primarily the children of mixed marriages, who are destined to enter the service of the Mission or the Trade, can receive instruction and practice in the Danish language." The Management based this request on the provisions of the Order of 1782: Chapter II, paragraph 7 and Chapter IV, paragraph 6 of which had listed certain rules for the training of "mixture boys" and Greenlanders who were incompetent at fangst. The Management wanted to clear the road for proper craftsman training in Greenland. When Greenlanders had previously been trained as craftsmen, communication problems had arisen between "master" and "apprentice". The Management therefore thought that instruction in Danish at an early stage would be a good help. But this demanded another kind of schooling, just as craftsman training itself could improve if schooling improved. The Management does not say directly, but we have already seen that, for example, arithmetic was not taught in Greenlandic schools: only reading, and at certain places writing – all in Greenlandic.

The Management probably did not realize that its request for Danish instruction touched a central point in the fundamental attitude of the Missionskollegium, or rather of its adviser Otho Fabricius, to the entire question of schooling. As early as 1790 Otho Fabricius had opposed teaching catechist apprentices Danish, and for that matter incomprehensibly to his own times as well as ours, had stopped the training of catechists and half-breed children. Now he reacted similarly to the proposal of the Royal Greenland Trade. He completely disregarded the fact that nothing at all had been done to even approach compliance with the provisions contained in the Order of 1782. His reaction led the Missionskollegium not even to answer this request of the Management of the Royal Greenland Trade.

The following year, the Management took the matter in its own hands; it sent a more detailed proposal to the Commission on 31 March 1804. In its arguments for this proposal, the Management referred explicitly to the "reform memorandum of 21 May 1798, writing that centuries would pass "before the inhabitants of Greenland will be able to be made participants in a civil organisation on an equal footing with the other subjects of the Danish King. But it was the intention of the present arrangement to prepare for this and also make it possible to carry on proper trade".

By placing the lines quoted among arguments for a school reform, the Management took a position in line with tendencies prevailing in discussions in Denmark of schools and schooling. Schools were not only to give instruction in support of the church and religion, but they had a broader purpose in the development of youth into good, useful and morally stable citizens.

The Management boldly criticized the schooling given by the Mission. But the Mission had neither the economic nor the staff resources to improve and effectivise its schooling. The Management therefore proposed that the missionaries should concentrate on the training of catechists, so that there could be more of them. The congregations would then be turned over to them. The horizons of the catechists should be widened by proper instruction in Danish, thus leading to greater enlightenment. "If the Greenlandic nation is not continually to be excluded from access to the knowledge of older cultivated nations which is useful to them, we know of no other means" than a thorough knowledge of the Danish language. "Access through their own language will be difficult or will never be opened to them." An opportunity was seen of channeling the energy revealed by half-breed children, as it was feared that this energy could develop into "disorders". Administratively the Management desired, as it now above all was proposing the secularization of the educational system, that the inspectors be given the supervision of the entire educational apparatus in their districts.

The Commission sent the Management's proposal to the Missionskollegium, where it was sent to Otho Fabricius for his comment. There is no doubt that he regarded this proposal of the Management as one move among many others being made at the time against the church and the dominant creed in Denmark-Norway. In addition he considered it an improper interference by outside forces in the jurisdiction of the Missionskollegium, and especially as an attempt on the part of the Trade to take from the Mission direction of the development of Greenlanders. He actually reduced this entire action of the Management to an absurdity, and struck out against the idea of eventually instituting a "civil government" which would give Greenland's "inhabitants access to the same advantages as others" within the realms of the King. Instruction in Danish he declared quite useless, and even insinuated that the Management intended to wipe out the proposal to give the inspectors the direction of the Greenlandic educational system. This was the Mission's territory, and should not be subordinated to the Royal Greenland Trade. "The Mission was the first consideration, and the Trade was only created for the Mission". The principles laid down at the beginning of the 18th century should be maintained. Fabricius totally disregarded the actual development which had taken place since 1776 and the impossible situation of the Mission since 1791-1792. Because of this and his arch-reactionary views, the proposal he himself made was quite deficient and without perspective as well as totally unfeasible; the reality of Greenland was quite different from what Fabricius could see from Copenhagen.

The Missionskollegium answered the Commission in accordance with Fabricius' report, but without his sharp comments. Although the Missionskollegium was notorious for the slow pace of its bureaucratic procedures, it was still quite extraordinary that almost two years passed before its report was submitted to the Commission. In this report it asked the Commission to cooperate in getting full support given to the Mission again, instead of making plans for reforms within the Mission's jurisdiction.

The Commission was quite willing to discuss this point, but wanted at the same time to proceed with the proposal of the Management and attempt to have a school established in each of the two inspectorates. "The sooner the better, effective means" must be taken "to advance the culture of the Greenlandic race". Or expressed in terms used in the present Greenland debate: The Commission wanted to advance the modernization and normalization of Greenlandic society - at that early stage.

This time the Missionskollegium delivered its reply considerably faster. It undoubtedly felt it had its back to the wall, and proposed negotiations on a school project. By this time the members of the Commission had become impatient and decided to send their school proposition to the Finanskollegium without further negotiation with the Missionskollegium.

The Commission's plan was noteworthy because it proposed the establishment of a combined school system: schools with the ordinary subjects taught to Danish children, and a vocational school proper. The ordinary subjects were in the opinion of the Commission religion; Danish; grammar; writing; arithmetic; a kind of hygiene including nutrition; zoology, botany and some mineralogy; and mechanical physics. The vocational school was to include training in Greenlandic skills, so that its pupils could earn their living; as well as instruction in cooperage, forging, and house and ship's carpentry, but only for those pupils who requested these subjects. The proposal was submitted in April 1806. There is no sign of whether it was approved or not. The war situation in 1807 and subsequent years interrupted any wide-range initiative in this as well as other fields.

There is no doubt that the slowness of the Missionskollegium and Fabricius' narrow views retarded considerably the implementation of these comprehensive school plans. In Greenland the way was paved for their favourable development. The missionary E.S. Bram had orally and in writing discussed with Inspector P.H. Motzfeldt plans for improving the school system, but only by establishing a teachers' institute for catechists.

In 1807 Bram sent his final proposal to both the Missionskollegium and the Trade management. The main content of his argumentation was that the enlightenment of a nation and its "industry and prosperity" are promoted by the improvement of the school system and the reading of useful books. In this he ranged himself alongside the Management and the Committee. On instruction in Danish and other secondary school subjects he opposed Fabricius and the Missionskollegium. Incidentally, in spite of Fabricius several missionaries had given private lessons in Danish throughout the years.

Bram's proposal was the best thought-out and most realistic of the propositions which made their appearance in this period. But its fate was the same as that of the Commission's proposal: it was shelved by the way. Just at the threshold of the war, however, Inspector M.N. Myhlenphort was about to start "higher education" in Godthåb, but when reports of the war arrived in 1808, this local initiative had to be abandoned.

It seems strange that in the context of this entire issue of schooling and education, the training of Greenlanders in Denmark was never suggested. From occasional remarks scattered in letters we can see that individual "mixture boys" were sometimes sent to Denmark for one or another kind of education or vocational training. One trained craftsman returned to Greenland and was employed by the Trade. At the age of 12, Matthias Ferslew Dalager was sent to distant relatives in Helsingør, where he went to school. He was later educated as an artist, and attempted for a short period to return to his native island. Another boy was sent by his father with an English whaler to get an education; he seems to have completely disappeared from the Greenland scene. In general it is noteworthy that a very slight number of Greenlanders went to Denmark or Norway during this period.

The Penal Code

Whether it was the gods who punished Greenland and Denmark/Norway will be left to the judgment of the reader. At the time, at least, there were Danes who considered the war events in 1801 and from 1807 on as the retaliation of higher powers against a far too materialistic race. Rationalism was on its last legs, although reason and utility continued for some time to be fundamental maxims.

The thoughts and ideas of rationalism could quite well rise above the sticky clay of every day life; but reason and experience held them back when they became too volatile. In the context of Greenland, this was true of ideas of introducing an actual penal code, a so-called coercive code. This was mentioned in the Commission's "reform memorandum" of 21 May 1798: "By being more closely united in a civil society, misdeeds must become more seldom by means of suitable penal laws". Later, attention was called to the question of how judicial power should be organized. Almost unanimously, trading officers in Greenland had warned against the introduction of a penal code proper: coercive provisions would in general not have a beneficial influence on the population, they had said. Experience also showed, they thought, that there was no need for judicial authority, at least not for permanent courts.

Nowhere, however, is the prevailing juridical situation summarized: there is no contemporary description of it. We have an impression, however, of what it was like. There were in general four types of relations to be considered in Greenland: 1) Relations between Greenlanders and Europeans stationed in Greenland; 2) relations between Greenlanders and other foreigners; 3) relations between Europeans stationed in Greenland; and 4) relations between Greenlanders. A special case, peculiar to Greenland, was a fifth set of relations: those between half-breeds and all the others.

The conditions of "mixtures" have been dealt with previously in other respects. Generally they were considered Greenlanders when they were in Greenland, but they did have a special position, as they were free to leave Greenland if they could pay their fare or otherwise had the opportunity to do so. When in Denmark or other possessions of the Danish-Norwegian king, they were considered Danish citizens, as far as that concept was at all relevant at that time. Their juridical status as Greenlanders in Greenland meant that when employed by the Trade they could not be dealt with according to the Danish Law of King Christian V, but only according to the provisions of the Order of 1782 concerning Trade personnel. Several paragraphs of the Order contained exceptions from the rules for "mixtures", precisely because they were juridically considered as Greenlanders. It was beginning to get complicated to know where you stood in Greenland.

This was due to the fact that the Order of 1782 and the Danish Law of King Christian V only applied in Greenland to Europeans stationed there, not to Greenlanders or to relations between these two groups. In cases of relations between Europeans and Greenlanders the Order provided rules, but only for the conduct of the Europeans towards the Greenlanders, not - except in special cases - for the conduct of the Greenlanders towards the Trade and Europeans. It was assumed that the general rule not to employ Greenlanders in the service of the Trade would be maintained and observed. Only when Greenlanders put their heads into the lion's mouth could it close its jaws on them if they made trouble.

This shows that the Danes did not wish to interfere in relations between Greenlanders, and felt compelled to do so only in specific cases. It is a practical expression of the fundamental principle that the Greenlanders were a "free people", who formed a society without laws: without a coercive code, as several of the recommendations sent from Greenland in 1799 and 1800 expressed it. In cases where Europeans had attempted to interfere in relations between Greenlanders, their interference had proven ineffectual. Only in areas where Danish rules had been assimilated into the lives of Greenlanders, such as marriage regulations, could Danes interfere juridically. But even in this special area an adjustment to the special conditions prevailing in Greenland was necessary, as we have seen.

The ordinary Greenlander could actually do as he pleased. Thus the inspector could not prevent an ordinary Greenlander from going where he pleased, or visiting foreign whaling vessels; he could not even prevent him from making a long trip on board such a whaler. Relations between the Greenlander and such foreign mariners were unrestricted by any rules. The Royal Greenland Trade and the government could only attempt to restrict them by tackling the matter from a different quarter: i.e., by the ordinance of 18 March 1776, as repeated in the Order of 1782. It was the foreign ships and their captains, not the Greenlanders, who violated the rules when they allowed anything to take place contrary to the letter or spirit of these provisions.

The question that Greenlandic society had no coercive code was not quite true. There was a certain amount of coercion in the many traditional rules of various kinds, including tabu regulations and rules for distributing the proceeds of the fangst. The fundamental difference between Greenlandic and European society was in the form of retaliation against a person violating the rules, or "conventions", as they were then called. West Greenlandic and Eskimo legal concepts in general did not imply punishment as a sanction exercised by society against the violation of a rule, or "a crime". When a person was murdered, the one who was closest to him was obliged to kill the murderer in revenge. But in this there was not and could not be any element of prevention against killing another person. Prevention, distinctly expressed by European law, was quite unknown in Greenland and in the Eskimo world in general. It was quite another matter that as far as possible individuals acted in accordance with the prevalent customs for each situation, because this was the safest and most reasonable course of action.

The recommendations sent from Greenland emphasized that there was actually no need for a penal code; Greenlanders did not commit serious crimes against each other. This was proven by experience, the respondents thought, and when we attempt to ascertain the correctness of this assertion by thorough study we find that really serious misdeeds, even from a European point of view, did not occur.

The cases of theft which are related were usually due to need and hunger. One single case of serious theft occurred at Upernavik: a Greenlander appropriated various articles of merchandise by breaking into the "warehouse" of the Trade, which was a peat building. Otherwise we hear only of petty pilfering.

It was correct, as claimed by both C. Bendeke and P.H. Motzfeldt, that homicide only occurred because of superstition, and that the only means to prevent it was enlightenment. Only one case was reported where murder seems to have taken place for the sake of gain, but the murderers pleaded that witchcraft was involved. On several occasions, comtemplated murders of *ilisîtsoqs* were averted in time by convincing the intended murderers that it would be unreasonable to commit this act. The authorities even declined to interfere and punish a murder undoubtedly committed out of superstition in a half-breed family in 1805, although the case was brought to the highest authorities and was decided by royal decree.

In this case and in a couple of previous ones the authorities, i.e., first and foremost the inspectors, had interfered, more or less compelled by the circumstances or inspired by moral indignation. But in all these cases the inspectors acted cautiously and with full realization of their lack of authority to interfere at all in cases of this nature. The murder committed in 1805, which has just been mentioned, was, however, a borderline case. The murderer was a "real Greenlander", the widow of the trader C.C. Dalager, and her victim was her own son by this marriage: a "mixture" employed in whaling and thus by the Trade. The authority of the inspector to take evidence could entitle him to interfere in this case, but it was clearly against the will of Inspector Motzfeldt that the case was dealt with so high up in the administrative apparatus. Motzfeldt assumed no judicial authority in this case, nor did other inspectors in other cases.

In one single case of homicide Inspector Bull at Godthåb did take the liberty of pronouncing a kind of judgment, but this did not create any precedence.

The Commission considered judicial authority in Greenland and in its reform memorandum" of 21 May 1798 it sketched how judicial power might be organized in Greenland, in case a penal code was introduced. Motzfeldt, who actually did not support the introduction of a penal code, did, however, come out for the Commission's sketch for the organization of judicial authority as a kind of lay court. He thought it was a good idea "that some of the best and most enlightened Greenlanders participate in it as lay assessors, or as the jury known from English legislation, as this would considerably facilitate the introduction and observation of the laws." Mørch the trader thought it would be impossible to let the inspector act as judge, because at the more distant places cases could not wait until he could get there. He wanted to have several courts of law set up, on the other hand. In each district "secular" cases should be decided by the trader, his assistant and a couple of "Greenlandic elders", while in marriage and murder cases the priest would join this court.

Since no penal code was now proclaimed, or even individual penal regulations for cases which could arise between Greenlanders, and the idea of any such had evidently been shelved completely, there could be no question of establishing courts of law in West Greenland. The West Greenlandic inhabitants had to continue living with their traditions and the legal concepts they had lived with so far, and this they apparently did without any substantial conflicts. The Greenlanders did not come under "the beneficial coercion of civil law". Their small societies were still juridically incapable of "enjoying the same rights as the other inhabitants of the realms." Laws and rules had to develop in the course of time, as Motzfeldt desired. In the same manner one or another form of judicial authority could develop.

There was already a tendency to involve the inspector in certain cases of a criminal nature. The borderline case in 1805 has been dealt with above. But also in local conflicts which in other places would be called cases of civil law, since the middle of the 18th century the traders, and later the inspectors were beginning to be involved, functioning as a kind of referees. Motzfeldt among others attempted to support this tendency by developing a practice.

Around New Year of 1808 a number of Greenlandic fangers at Umánaq administered corporal punishment to a poor person who had passed himself off as an ilisîtsoq. Motzfeldt disapproved of this act of the Greenlanders taking the "law" in their own hands, because it was the duty of the colony chief to maintain law and order. He was compelled, however, because he found out about the case so late, to resign himself to the punishment suffered at the hands of the fangers. He added, however, the very eloquent remark: "Moreover I wish that the Greenlanders would allow themselves to be persuaded in similar and all other cases, in which they are or feel offended by anyone, be it one of their countrymen or a Dane, to make a proper complaint to the nearest trading officer to be forwarded to the inspector for his decision and punishment, which wish of mine I hereby instruct you to proclaim to the Greenlanders through the catechist Jacob Hammond".

Here Inspector Motzfeldt assumed an authority to which he had no right, beyond the order in his instructions to supervise the maintenance of law and order in the inspectorate *on the basis of the Order of 1782;* but this order conferred on him no authority over relations between Greenlanders. The tendency of this remark was clear.

The view of the inspector as judge and chief of police in the same person was already beginning to gain a footing. On the same occasion, Bram, the missionary, had distinctly informed the local fangers that they ought not to have taken the punishment of this ilisîtsoq in their own hands, but should have taken the matter to the inspector: "for in the first place the Inspector alone has been appointed by God and the King as judge in this country for such cases and others; and he is also the one who best and most impartially can judge the size of the offence and the degree of punishment." Consciously or not Bram was here saying too much. His statement, made before that of the inspector, shows that this attitude was held by others than just Motzfeldt.

There is no proof that these two in all respects well-meaning and well-thinking officers ever discussed the question of judges and legal proceedings in West Greenland with each other, or in a larger group of employees of the Trade and the Mission. This idea from 1798 must have been in the air, as it were, among the Europeans stationed in Greenland. All indications are that the Greenlandic inhabitants felt no need of a judicial authority; there is at least no evidence, direct or indirect, that they did. Only in cases of an insoluble conflict which in one way or another was connected with the Trade or whaling, did they refer to the inspector as a kind of deciding authority, whose competence in other fields was also known to the Greenlanders. In "criminal" cases the reverse seems to have been true; there are examples of Greenlanders openly opposing interference in such cases.

This was by and large all that resulted from the "reform drive" of 1798; or perhaps rather, all that did not result from it. Good will had been present, and for that matter still was. But it was obvious that the Finanskollegium and the Commission had fielded their reform ideas too soon. This appears not only from the various replies from Greenland, but also from the fact that the Management, although it did not directly say so, nevertheless seemed relieved to be spared the direct interference of the government, acting through several royal officers, in Greenlandic affairs.

The Management of the Royal Greenland Trade was confirmed in its opinion that the policies conducted so far, including the trading monopoly and the closing of Greenland, were the right ones - for the time being. But this did not mean that those concerned were to refrain from effecting reforms which had possibilities of development in the society of West Greenland.

Prelude to Stagnation

In dealing with the various aspects of development of West Greenlandic society, we have continually followed events up to 1808, and in some cases further. It appears that in the years after 1800 there were more than enough aspects of daily life which officers in Greenland and the Management in Copenhagen had to decide on or take direct action to save the inhabitants from. In addition there were special problems to which the

Royal Greenland Trade itself was exposed, such as shipwreck, supply failures, price increases, and the lack of merchandise essential for Greenlandic fangst. Disasters such as the frightful smallpox epidemic, especially in Egedesminde and Holsteinsborg, greatly thwarted the general development towards more favourable living conditions for the Greenlandic inhabitants. It did, however, accelerate the development of vaccination in Greenland; but that, too, had to be organized.

There were limits to what the Trade was able to manage. When the government therefore found space in a Royal decree to award the Management and its employees stationed in Greenland great recognition for its efforts so far in Greenland, it is not strange that with a certain pride the Management had this forwarded to Greenland so that every one "who by a stay of some length in the country has worked for its benefit and that of the Trade," could "by learning of His Majesty's most gracious favour be encouraged to continue to earn it to the best of his ability". This must also have removed the last remains of anxiety from those who had freely and boldly expressed themselves in reply to the "reform movement" of 1798.

The Management's letter informing of the Royal recognition contained an interesting reminder. The inspectors were to take advantage of the occasion to 'impress on some of the officers that their duties are not limited to the Trade alone, but that the inhabitants of the country to which the Trade owes its existence also have reasonable reciprocal demands on the Trade and its officers; and that the latter, being more enlightened, should even in their private lives set the former a good example, be of service to them by word and deed in their occupations, attempt to correct their concepts, which are especially quite false with respect to economy, and on the whole with gentleness and wisdom attempt to lead them towards improvement".

This "reminder" was the result of an extremely pessimistic letter to the Management from Johan Christian Mørch, the trader at Julianehåb, which to some extent must have been affected by his disappointment at not having been appointed inspector. For that post the Management and Commission had preferred M.N. Myhlenphort. Nevertheless, his description, in all its brevity, of his revisit to Frederikshåb after an absence of eight years, is shocking, although Mørch himself adds that "it is not totally untrue - forsooth". The inhabitants were "spoiled" by European provisions. "No fowl, fish, or anything similar could be bought except with bread, hulled grain or pork", or even with hardtack, but only "when buttered". Distilled spirits were so common that even women rowers on hay expeditions received a bottle as rations for the journey. Those who connived at this and practiced this abuse were quite indifferent, or felt compelled by necessity.

Perhaps this description was intended as an accusation against Gert Falck, the trader at Frederikshåb, without mentioning him by name. He had just been discharged and had left Greenland the same summer of 1802, accused of failing to fulfill the duties of his office and cheating when purchasing Greenlandic produce. Nothing resulted from this case, but Mørch's lamentation led the Management, in its letter to the inspectors, to certain comments.

"It is not within the power of the Trade to remedy most of this, and the most substantial help should be expected from the teachers of religion." The Management did not comment on the nature of this assistance or the opportunities of the missionaries to render any assistance at all. But between this passage and the following one, we sense the opinion of the Management: no real help can be expected from that quarter. The Management then again stressed the need for better schooling and a more thorough teachers' training, and in addition enlightenment and more enlightenment. This the Trade and its officers would have to undertake.

This, as well as the comments of the Management on the royal recognition, was actually a return to the Order of 1782 and its "educational" provisions. Nevertheless it seems that it was not until now at the end of the 1790's that the Management became aware of the cultural obligations of the Trade. Just as the Trade, through whaling, by its continuously greater infiltration into the daily life of West Greenland, and by the undesired reduction of the activities and influence of the mission, acquired a considerable predominance in everyday life, thus the responsibility of the Trade grew for the development which was the fate of the Greenlandic population.

It was thus disastrous in so many respects that contacts between West Greenland and the rest of the realms was so brutally cut off by the events of 1807.

Indeed a portent had come of what could happen. The English fleet under Sir Hyde Parker and Lord Nelson passed Helsingør 21 March 1801 and headed for Copenhagen. Why it appeared and what happened is another story which cannot be told here. Nelson attacked the Danish fleet in the front of the harbour of Copenhagen on 2 April. It was so early that reports reached West Greenland the same summer. It was as if the residents of Godthåb had a foreboding that something might have happened. Apprehension spread of what the ship seen to be entering on 17 July could bring. It proved to be the ship sent to Godthåb that year from Copenhagen. With it arrived not only welcome supplies, but also news of the war; nothing was learned, however, of the extent to which the war had developed or whether it was already over.

The Northern Inspectorate received the news from the south, and Motzfeldt immediately ordered general rationing of all provisions and ammunition, as well as a general inventory of stocks of merchandise and materials. In the south Inspector Bull only gave general orders to save. As three supply ships arrived at Godhavn in the beginning of September, Inspector Motzfeldt was able to call off rationing in his area. He must evidently have been finally notified that the war had not developed into more than what had already been reported. But this was bad enough: it gave rise to a bitter feeling and continued fear in Greenland, even among the Greenlandic inhabitants.

Moreover, shipping was haunted by a number of unfortunate circumstances. Seven ships which had left Copenhagen in 1800 had not returned by April 1801. An embargo was placed on all Danish ships on the seas; but in June those which had been taken in to English ports were released. Six ships were then sent to Greenland, including three to Godhavn and the Northern Inspectorate. The following year five ships failed to show up. In 1803 one ship wrecked and the next year another one. All this contributed to the economic loss suffered by the Trade at this time, also because no profitable products arrived. Although the war itself was over, the situation did not actually improve. Greenland had even to suffer the ravages of a smallpox epidemic. From 1803 to 1807 it appeared that the Trade would have opportunities to recuperate what it had lost. To be sure, there was war in Europe and the seas were unsafe. But dangers seemed to pass south of the twin realms. Dealings between English whalers and the localities of North Greenland had apparently returned to normal.

The Northern Inspectorate as well as the Southern spent the winter of 1807-1808 without the slightest suspicion of what had happened in Denmark in September of 1807 - the shelling of Copenhagen - and that a state of open war now prevailed between Denmark-Norway and England.

In Copenhagen the situation triggered a number of difficulties for the Management and the Commission. They both had trouble making themselves heard in the general confusion. But finally certain steps were taken. It was important to get supplies through in 1808 to unsuspecting Greenland. With one of the small ships from Norway which the Trade succeeded in dispatching, news of the situation reached Sukkertoppen on 21 April 1808. From here it was spread north and south.

Reactions in Greenland were a mixture of fear and resentment: the latter at the misfortune which had befallen the realms, the former of what the future would bear, how the future, both near and distant, could be weathered, and finally of what could be expected from the English in the sea off West Greenland.

Whatever would happen, both the Management and the Commission in Copenhagen realized that perhaps for a long time now it could only be a matter of just pulling through. All in Greenland were immediately prepared for the same. All plans for reforms and innovations were shelved.

Many decades would pass before they would be taken off the shelf again.

Notes and References

II. THE ORDER OF 1782

1. Concerning this correspondence, see vol. II, pp. 422 ff.
2. The title *in extenso* is (translated) "Orders to which especially the Traders or those who manage either the Trade or the Whaling Stations in Greenland, as well as generally Everyone who are employed by the Trade, shall conform, and according to which they shall conduct themselves". The content has not been published in English. It appears in Danish in *Diplomatarium Groenlandicum,* MoG LV,3 as no. 291, pp. 264 ff.
3. This fifteenth chapter seems superimposed, and is in fact a supplement, adapted from the regulations provided in August 1781 for the whalers who had to winter in Greenland. It is published in full in Danish in *Diplomatarium Groenlandicum,* MoG LV,3 as no. 290, which is the Royal Order (with the same content) of July 1781.
4. The development of the "Mixture" problems are dealt with in vol. II, pp. 310, 353, 355 ff. and 370.
5. See vol. II, pp. 358 ff.
6. See vol. II, pp. 294 and 296.
7. See vol. II, pp. 411 ff.

III. THE ROYAL GREENLAND TRADE AND WHALING

1. These figures are taken from the Royal Greenland Trade's accounts, concerning goods in return and materials in 1775 and following years. There is a gap in the series for 1785-87.
2. See vol. II, p. 407. The antecedents of the payment problems are dealt with in vol. II, pp. 405 ff. At Kronprinsens Ejland Adam Thorning, the whaling assistant, caught four whales. One was sold to Egedesminde, two were received at the whaling station at Kronprinsens Ejland as hire for sloops and whaling equipment, and the whole of the fourth was sold by the Greenlanders to the whaling station as payment for merchandise to the amount of 300 rigsdaler. There had thus been an equal sharing.
3. "Taasinge Slot" ("The Palace of Taasinge", the latter being a small island immediately south of the larger island of Funen in Denmark. The ship was far from being a floating palace). This ship was used not only in whaling, but also for local transport. In 1787 it sailed to Greenland for the last time, probably returning to Copenhagen in 1788. Three years later it was sold for 995 rigsdaler.
4. For statistics on the production of train-oil see Chapter VIII, p. 206.
5. See vol. II, p. 286.
6. See vol. II, pp. 293, 300, 308, 392, 409 and 412.
7. See vol. II, pp. 411 ff.

IV. THE COMMISSION OF 1788

1. Carl Pontoppidan was born in 1748, son of Erik Pontoppidan, Bishop of Bergen (mentioned in vol. II). In 1766-74 he was employed as a trader in the Icelandic Trade, for the last year as an inspecting senior trader, domiciled in Copenhagen. In 1781 he was appointed executive manager of the Icelandic Trade when this was connected with the other "Northern Trades", see vol. II, p. 425.

IV. THE COMMISSION OF 1788

2. The Royal Decree of February 13th 1772, which reorganized the Royal Administration after the Struensee period. However, its provisions were gradually put aside by Ove Høegh-Guldberg.
3. It does not stand clearly to reason why L.A. Thodal became a member of the Commission. However he was a remarkable figure. The son of a middle-class Norwegian, he was probably born in 1718. We know nothing about his education, but he appeared as the prime mover in a Danish-Norwegian boundary commission in 1762-66. He was later employed in the local administration in Bergen, and from there became prefect (Stiftsbefalingsmand) for Iceland and the Faroes in 1770. In 1785 he came to Copenhagen and became assistant secretary at the Rentekammer in the Office for Iceland, the Faroes and Greenland, which was almost a sinecure. He never graduated in law as used to be required of other senior civil servants. The only reason why, at about the age of seventy, he became a member of the Commission of 1788 seems to have been his involvement in the Rentekammer with "North Atlantic affairs", and his membership of the Iceland Trade Liquidation Commission. It does not appear in the records of the Commission of 1788 that he expressed any opinions.
4. See vol. II, pp. 416 ff.
5. See vol. II, pp. 390 ff. and 422.
6. In 1784 the Royal Greenland Trade had hired out four ships to another government institution for trading in the Virgin Islands. One of these was damaged in the Channel, and for several years there was a tug-of-war as to how much this institution should pay towards the expenses caused by the damage. In 1790 it was still not settled.

V. DEMOGRAPHY

1. The following remarks refer to all the statistical material in this volume. All censuses, calculations, summaries and tabulations from the eighteenth century are inaccurate, yet - in my view - they are not without any value. The figures must be defective, due to several sources of error, from the primitive counting methods to the summaries, and are therefore used here with the utmost caution. Compared with later, more reliable statistics, these earlier ones may reveal tendencies, which have been in force over a longer period.

   The figures used are from various sources, published and unpublished. It is useless in this English edition to refer to them in detail; they are always commented on in Danish, and the unpublished ones can only be seen in the Danish archives. Among the sources are many local Greenlandic census papers. Sometimes it is possible to follow a single district for a couple of years, in the period under consideration, and thus draw comparisons with contemporary and later summaries. This has been done and appears sometimes in the text. Some of the sources are so-called designation-lists which the missionaries were obliged to present every year to the Missionskollegium dealing with different statistics on their respective congregations, and thus counting only the baptized. Sometimes the secular statistics make a distinction between baptized and unbaptized, especially the earliest ones. But for details the interested reader must be referred to the Danish edition of this volume.

   The number of Europeans employed by the Trade can be counted from the muster rolls (from 1721 onwards the colonies were organized as a ship with the names of "officers" and "crew" put down in muster rolls). As time went on the Greenlanders employed by the Trade were listed there too. The same can be seen from the "wage-books"; these were account-books containing every employee's wage-account balanced with the amount of his yearly personal buyings. At this time there was one wage-book for each colony. They are kept in the archives, and the collection is almost complete.

Some of the summaries are printed in special contemporary publications. Others are kept in the archives with the annual reports from the Trade to the Commission, some only exist as copies. It has been possible to correct the contemporary published statistics by means of the unprinted original census.

All this is mentioned here to show that there are quite a lot of sources, from which details are pieced together for the statistical summaries and tables in this book.

2. It may be appropriate to call attention to the fact that official statistics (The summaries from the Greenland Administration, 1942 seq., and other Danish official statistical publications) show another total figure (6.046) for the year 1805. Hence several others, including international studies, have used this figure. It is wrong because of three errors in the source used. This source is a summary made by the contemporary assistant secretary in the Rentekammer Jonas Collin, who published a short survey of the state of West Greenland 1809 with statistical tables. The Table I here is based on the same source, but corrected by means of the original census of 1805. It is a matter of a discrepancy between the figure for Umânaq in the original local census, 392, and that given by Collin, 348. It seems more reasonable to follow the original census. The second is more serious. Collin has a figure, 483, for Christianshåb which seems quite improbable. The local census 1805 has 282, which fits quite well into the series of figures concerning the population of that district; the original censuses of 1793-1808 are still kept in the archives. They show the population of Christianshåb steadily decreasing. The third is a simple arithmetical error. The figure 5.888, is thus the most probable. On Jonas Collin, see below Chapter VI, note 1.
3. Ritenbenk's population in 1789 was 317 to which 90 from Arveprinsens Ejland should be added because this abolished whaling station from 1801 onwards was a part of Ritenbenk District. How many went to Jakobshavn in 1801 we do not know, and likewise how many chose other places.
4. See vol. II, pp. 257 and 417; six unbaptized are not included in the figures for 1777.
5. The figures for 1782 and 1783 are calculated on the basis of contemporary sources. Those of the Moravian Brethrens' congregation are compared with the table in Heinz Israel *Kulturwandel grönländischer Eskimo im 18. Jahrhundert*, Berlin 1969, p. 179. The figures in this table have been cautiously compared with the other figures because the dates of counting are different.
6. See vol. II, pp. 342 and 369.
7. See vol. II, index entry: "population".
8. See vol. II, p. 404 ff.
9. For the development of concentration versus dispersal, see vol. II, pp. 340-44.

VI. SOCIAL CONDITIONS

1. Jonas Collin has been mentioned before in this volume (note 2 to chapter V) and shall be mentioned several times later. Born in 1776 into a family of well-off commoners in Copenhagen, he graduated in law 1795. Two years later he got an appointment in the Rentekammer, and henceforth he worked his way up in the Finanskollegium, in which from 1816 to 1850 he was a deputy, and from 1831 to 1840 in the Rentekammer as well. As such he was a member of several commissions of the most varied kind.

The public life drew heavily on his working power which seemed inexhaustible. In his long life - he died 1861 - he proved to be among the most prominent, most noble-minded, diligent and efficient civil servants, always loyal to the Danish autocratic king. He was not uncritical of the Crown, but never opposed it officially, preferring the positive attitude. His profitable influence can be traced in the whole economic and cultural life of Danish society in the period 1800-60. He dedicated his efforts especially to carrying the economy of Denmark through the hard times in the years after 1814, and to agricultural development in particular. Apparently from his start as a civil servant he was *inter alia* occupied by Icelandic, Faroese and Greenlandic affairs, and even more so after the death of L.A. Thodal in 1808 (see chapter IV, note 3). Since that time he was constantly interested in the affairs of these islands. In addition to this he twice held the post of director of the Royal Theatre in Copenhagen, and it was by his arrangement that most of the works of the Danish neoclassicistic sculptor Bertel Thorvaldsen were gathered in Copenhagen to a special museum, still existing. Perhaps Jonas Collin is best known outside Denmark for the unselfish and paternal support he offered the Danish poet and writer of fairy-tales, Hans Christian Andersen.

2. Chr. Vibe: *Arctic Animals in Relation to Climatic Fluctuations,* MoG. 170,5, Copenhagen 1967. See vol. II, index entry: "famine".
3. Inspector A.M. Lund was about to leave Greenland for good.
4. See vol. II, p. 369 ff.
5. The Commission sanctioned the proposal, and at the same time expected a similar provision to be issued by the Southern Inspectorate "in due course". This probably means, when a similar welfare-fund was established there.
6. "The Welfare Fund for Needy Greenlanders in Southern Greenland" appears for the first time in the ledger of the Royal Greenland Trade in 1803, with a balance of 1,203 rigsdalers and 2 skillings. It is not revealed from where this income derived. This remained untouched in 1804. In 1809 the fund had a deposit of 1,411 rigsdalers and 40 skillings, and it kept that balance up to 1813.
7. Chr. J. Møller, the trader, had been in Greenland from 1791. He had been chief trader at Christianshåb/Claushavn, and the production had grown considerably in his times. He knew the main conditions of life and trade in Disko Bugt, but had no experience, besides that which he gained during his stay at Godhavn and Christianshåb. His Statement may have as its background the situation after the epidemics, when so many fangers had died. "Professionalism" may have developed locally for a short time.
8. See vol. II, p. 423.
9. See vol. II, pp. 87, 220, 253, 365 ff. and 388.

VII. OCCUPATIONAL DEVELOPMENT

1. See vol. II, p. 120 ff.
2. "Silesian linen" is not "linen from Silesia", but the term for a fine, thin sort of bleached linen for sheeting and shirtmaking.
3. The Greenlandic printer and editor *Lars Møller* (1842-1926) told that it was as late as in 1883 when he learned of the shooting sail, used on the kayak. If this had also been the use of it in the time just after its supposed "invention", Myhlenphort should have spread the knowledge in Southern Greenland when, in 1803, he became the Inspector there. Lars Møller then would have known of it before 1883. So Myhlenphort did

not bring the use of this sail on kayaks with him. Consequently the use must have developed in Disko Bugt during the years between 1803 and 1883. Lars Møller var born and brought up as a fanger in Godthåb.

About Myhlenphort's "invention" of the shooting sail there is still one possibility. He may not have actually invented it, but "improved" it. It is conceivable that a shooting sail made of bleached sealskin may have been in use, and Myhlenphort then may have proposed to use bleached linen to save more sealskin for the Trade; the zeal to save to the utmost dominated every trader. This must however remain a hypothesis. It seems to me the crucial point, that we have no evidence of any form of shooting sail or the little "shooting sled" before the date of the invention, which Myhlenphort claimed.

4. The alternating proportion between salted and dried skins is due to changes in the methods of conservation. In a letter to Inspector B.J. Schultz the Management complained that sealskins were difficult to sell for the time being. Some of the produce was sent to Altona for possible sale, but there the Greenlandic washing and drying methods were not acceptable to the customers. The Management therefore wanted salted skins shipped from Greenland. This immediately caused a rise in the figures of salted skins shipped 1796; but this was followed by a considerable decline until 1800. The reasons for this decline we may only guess; perhaps the salted skins were not shipped to Altona, but sold at the auctions in Copenhagen, but the customers there were not interested in getting salted skins - and so it was then not necessary to salt them in Greenland. From 1801 until 1808 there is no specification in the records. Thus it was not customary to salt the skins; only when salt was shipped to Greenland in sufficient quantities might this be done. That means that salt was not requisitioned from Greenland every year, or that the quantities shipped were used for other purposes. It was difficult to transport the salt in the relatively small ships, where it occupied much space, and the shrinkage was considerable both during the transport and the storage in Greenland.
5. See vol. II, pp. 392-94.
6. Perhaps these were immigrants from the south after the smallpox epidemic, and felt more attached to the trader at Holsteinsborg; but it is not explicitly mentioned.
7. This is a description, as the year 1792 shows, of the population which had lived at Holsteinsborg for many years, and thus before the smallpox epidemic had its decimating effect and a "new" population, with possibly different traditions of fangst, filled the empty places.
8. See Chr. Vibe, MoG. 170,5, p. 166.
9. See ibid. passim, esp. p. 98.
10. See vol. II, pp. 391 and 412.

VIII. WHALING AFTER 1788

1. It is not evident what Dalager means with "Labrador and James". The latter points to the southern part of Hudson Bay. Apparently his remarks derive from studying a map, sitting in his armchair (if he had one) and using guess-work. His remarks about the Vestis have more sense.
2. The average of the entire period 1777-1807 is 18,480 baleen. The average for 1801-07 is blurred by the facts that several cargoes of 1792-1802 arrived together with the cargoes of 1803. The cargoes from 1798-1800 cannot be differentiated from one another. Leaving this out of consideration, the average for 1801-07 is estimated

to be 18,240, but should be reduced. As a rough estimate this would be between 17,000 and 17,500. The decline is not great but certainly obvious.

3. Remembering the smallpox epidemic which few years later ravaged and almost devastated the district, this report renders a special perspective.
4. The mounting of the cannon on the foreland of Godhavn may have brought about the tradition on which it was fired to alarm the crew to take to the sloops, because a whale had been observed from the observation post (see plate VIII). Perhaps the cannon was later used for this purpose, but it seems unlikely. It is impossible that the peculiar building, the so-called "Whale-observation-post", was erected on this promontory east of the entrance to the harbour of Godhavn.
5. That it must have been a knife for cutting the tail of a whale appears from a letter which the senior assistant, Fleisher, at Arveprinsens Ejland wrote on January 4th to Inspector P.H. Motzfeldt: "On one of the qiporqaqs which were lost on October 20th 1806 the above mentioned Jens Dalager (son of C.C. Dalager) used the tail knife highly effectively, so that all the Greenlanders shouted with joy over this god invention; according to Dalager's report he hew the whale somewhat too high towards the back of it, and thus the tendons in the part of flesh and blubber were not completely cut; the fish, however, remained quiet for a while, unable to move its tail". This clearly shows the use for which this knife was intended.

   A tailknife, perhaps of another sort, was used by the British whalers in the beginning of the nineteenth century. William Scoresby jn. in *My Father,* London 1851 (Caedmon Reprints, Whitby 1978), p. 192, describes the tailknife and its use in this way: "This instrument, designed for making perforations in the tail and fins of the captured whale, when preparing to be towed to the ship, constitutes a portion of the furniture of every whaleboat, and consists of a nearly three-feet straight sharp-pointed blade, with a wooden handle of like measure. It resembles the blade of a cutlass, out of which weapon, indeed, this kind of knife is frequently constructed." A knife of such shape might have been of use both in perforation and cutting, so it might be the same implement as the Danish one, mentioned above.
6. The prices are converted into skillings, making allowance for comparison with the tables in Friis and Glamann *Prices and Wages in Denmark 1660–1800,* I, pp. 297–314. For figures from before 1782, see *History of Greenland,* vol. II, esp. p. 390.
7. This only deals with a possible development, an interpretation of its course. It cannot be substantiated by documents in general, only the actual situation can be documented.
8. Translated, the full title of this pamphlet is *The Whaling in Davis Strait, with some Reports, Calculations, Information, Proposals and Remarks, by Edward Christie Heiberg, former trader and chief of the Whaling of the Royal Greenland Trade: Printed at the Author's own expense, by Sebastian Popp, Copenhagen, 1805.*

IX. THE TRADE

1. There is no real closing of the accounts in the ledgers of the Trade, but a so-called balance. This seems to apply to the state between the creditors and debtors of the Trade, but not income and expenses connected with the Trade itself. The capital account only covers the 250,000 rigsdaler, which remained until 1813. The cash book is closed every year by a "general balance", which is less than transparent for one without an auditor's patience and trained eyes. From 1790 onwards the Management of the Royal Greenland Trade were to present annual reports to the Commission. These

reports contain surveys of the most important revenues and expenses in which a surplus or a deficit appeared. Usually this "result" differed from that in the annual "general balance" per December 31st, which was enclosed in the annual report. Enclosed too was a "Profit and Losses Account" from which the real surplusses or deficits could be learned. This account had an explanatory text, but these texts do not exist any more. Most of the annual reports we only have in copies. It may be that the "explanation" is the same as the text, which in the cash book's "general balance" is placed under the heading "Distribution of the Surplus", which in this work can be seen on Table 33. Table 32 thus shows the total income and expenses, year by year, placed against each other, and the yearly surplus or deficit shown as simple subtractions. It can be seen that a deficit is deducted from the next year's income, the deficit thus included in the next year's expenses. In Table 33 this "calculated" surplus or deficit is shown along with the same on the "Profit and Losses Account". And in the two last columns the distribution is shown, two thirds to the Finanskollegium and one third to the higher ranking officers of the Greenland Trade.

2. It was almost a tradition that the trade on Greenland had its facilities in Copenhagen, more exactly the nearby Christianshavn. Already in the times of Peter Klauman (about 1700, see vol. II, pp. 5 and 7) there was a train-oil refinery there. Since that time buildings and other facilities were sold and sold again to the different traders and companies. 1790 the Royal Greenland Trade bought the harbour, called Trangraven (The Train-Oil Grave) and its surroundings.
3. Several times small rowboats are called "Bergens Bisp" or only a "Bisp", which actually means "a Bishop (of Bergen)". This was probably a rowboat, bigger than a skiff, but not as big as a yawl or a sloop. Several experts, domestic and foreign, have been consulted, but no one knew of the type. Its peculiar name may derive from its equally high stem and stern, and its shortness. It looked like a bishop's mitre. This is, however, simply a supposition.
4. See vol. II, p. 416.
5. Greenlanders employed by the Trade, or, as Myhlenphort expressed it, "in the same class" as the European employees, were the only ones whom the Inspector could forbid to visit the ships. In cases of infringement of such prohibition he could arbitrarily fine the person, disrate or dismiss him, for the rest of the whaling season or indefinitely.
6. See vol. II, p. 410 ff.
7. For examples of how the Dutch trade formed habits and developed demands, see vol. II, pp. 120 ff. and 132.
8. "Consumers' strike" 1781 at Upernavik, see vol. II, p. 411 ff.
9. See vol. II, index entry: "Tobacco".
10. See vol. II, p. 306 ff.
11. About the development of "making-weight", see vol. II, pp. 132, 297 ff. and 230.
12. See vol. II, pp. 291 and 370.
13. See vol. II, index entry: "Coal".
14. The Management was not right in referring the magnetic method to the world of superstition or fraud. At any rate in Sweden a so-called "mine-compass" was in use from 1640 onwards. This consisted of a suspended magnetic needle, by which the richest lodes were found in the iron mines. (*Communication from the Greenland Geological Investigations, Copenhagen*). The same may have been the fact in English and other European mines.

15. The story of Giesecke's expedition is told in a concentrated style. It seems appropriate to state here, that, considering Giesecke was an internationally known person, the development of his appointment and expedition is much more complex, and this can be learned from the Danish edition of this volume III, p. 554-56.
16. The missionary at Jakobshavn, Eskild Sønnichsen Bram, characterized Giesecke as follows, translated from a letter of February 1st 1808 to Inspector P.H. Motzfeldt: "I do not know what to admire most in this superb man, - either his plain, straightforward, and therefore most charming nature, which is partly a noble fruit, a lucky effect of a long and reflective intercourse with many and different classes of men, - his merits as a scientist for which he is highly honoured, but which he never stresses, only mentions incidentally, - or the inner ardour which, powerful in itself without the command of Nature, has induced him to brave the coldness, the mountains, the drift-ice, etc." And he continues "With anxious impatience I wish to have the honour and pleasure, at least for some days, to benefit from the stimulating and interesting company of Your Honour (the Inspector) and the Bergrath (Giesecke)."
17. It is mentioned above, p. 176 ff. and 180 f., that hiring Greenlanders as net tenders was usually and cautiously avoided. That must have been confined to the Northern Inspectorate. A.M. Lund, the Inspector in the south, described in 1793 the development of seal netting in his Inspectorate, and stated clearly (concerning Fiskenæsset) "a total of six (men is needed) when the netting is to be carried on, and if it is expanded, it will be necessary to hire Greenlanders otherwise unfit for the kayak". The custom must have slipped into the Northern Inspectorate as well. In 1801 the assistant at Umânaq complained that he got a net tender as late as September, because all were occupied as net tenders for "other net-users".
18. See above, p. 148, about the lack of stationed professionals and the training of Greenlanders in different crafts.

X. THE MISSION, SCIENCE AND OTHER ASPECTS OF CULTURE

1. It has not been investigated why and how Christianity spread among the Greenland population in this period. Studies in sociology in Angmagssalik (East Greenland) indicate that the source material is too flimsy and one-sided.
2. It is difficult to fathom the real progress of the Habakuk Movement, and thus how it really developed. From a scholarly point of view it seems rather untenable to use oral traditions, handed down locally and later written down. On the other hand the contemporary sources are insubstantial. They have been either partly destroyed or otherwise lost. Only some letters from the missionary Hveyssel and single reports and remarks in letters from other missionaries and secular persons remain. A variety of interpretations is possible, some of which may be different from what here has been told. It has been considered best to keep clear of excessive interpretations; on the other hand the development has here been described in some detail, as far as the contemporary sources have allowed. This has been considered necessary, partly because the development - as far as I know - has not been described properly elsewhere and in international handbooks of the history of religion. The treatment of it has been too summary and based on misunderstandings or misinterpretation, and partly because it has not been told in the context in which the movement ought to be placed. Nevertheless the account here inevitably involves an interpretation, especially as an attempt is made to put it in historical perspective. Dr. Staffan Söderberg, Lund (Sweden), in his dissertation *Profetens roll i religionsmötet* (The role of the prophet in the

religious contact situation) with a summary in English, Lund 1974, discusses the Habakuk Movement as his chief-subject, along with other "prophets" in West Greenland. He has partly used my account. His little book includes a list of literature, both domestic and foreign, about the movement. Some of the later local traditions are given, but only in Danish.

3. See the map, p. 336, and vol. II, pp. 332 and 416.
4. It is surprising that Fabricius, as late as in June, sent his report in which he considers the Habakuk Movement and possible counter measures. He must have been aware of the fact that it was too late that year to despatch any orders from Copenhagen, because the ships of the year had left.
5. P.R. Heide, the missionary at Holsteinsborg, left Greenland for good in 1793 and was replaced by N.C. Rønning. Later (1795) Otho Fabricius commented on Habakuk and his wife being "confirmandi". He was opposed to the confirmation of "old people" (which Heide had practiced). Perhaps Fabricius did not know, or had forgotten, that the missionary at Sukkertoppen, N. Hveyssel, had excommunicated the Habakuk couple from the congregation. When the notorious couple insinuated themselves as "confirmandi", they expressed the wish to be members of the congregation again, or considered there was a chance to get out of the isolation, in which they undoubtedly found themselves. We do not know if the two were confirmed. Habakuk's tomb does not lie on a churchyard.
6. Some of these traditions are written down, but not printed. The unprinted include an account, written in Greenlandic and told by the senior catechist Iver Berthelsen in the 1850s. He was a grandson of the senior catechist Frederik Berthelsen, several times mentioned in the text. I have used this account here and indirectly previously. The printed ones are, as mentioned above (note 1), only in Danish, retold by H.J. Rink and Knud Rasmussen. One of these traditions is quoted here at the conclusion of the paragraph. It shows a clear rationalization *post festum*. The inhabitants quite logically had to live on their fangst. But it is not told how plentiful the winter reserves actually were, considering that the procedure, as mentioned above, had been "rationalized". The truth seems to be, that the fangers resigned from the fangst, because Habakuk forced them to hand their fangst to him. He himself had assumed the responsibility for the providing of the inhabitants with what they needed. Surely, it must be the famine which drove the fanger (told below) to revolt against the "forced requisition" of his fangst. This also corresponds with the contemporary reports, that Habakuk's rough treatment of his companies compelled them to quit the movement.
7. See vol. II, p. 327.
8. A quasi-parallel to this is told in a report from the missionary at Frederikshåb in the same year: "The catechist Ananias has drowned in his kayak or has taken the so-called hermit-course". On this Otho Fabricius comments: "Whether the catechist Ananias has drowned or taken the hermit-course, I suggest that his wife shall not be prevented from getting permission to marry again, as the hermits usually do not return, but stay high up in the mountains, as long as they are alive."
9. For "song contests", see Inge Kleivan: *Song Duels in West Greenland,* "Folk" XIII, Copenhagen 1971, p. 9 ff. What the term *baliârneq* means is not quite clear. In the letter here quoted in translation the term is written in Danish as "Balliaring". In the translation here it is altered into the form of a Greenlandic verbal noun, because the meaning and the etymology of the word is doubtful, and the linguists disagree, their proposals not being cogent. In a rather long note I have (in Danish) contributed my

humble mite, being in no way a scholar in linguistics, and conclude that the term may be Greenlandic and mean (the verbal form) "to seek a flat foreland", where song contests and other amusements usually were practised. F. Gad: *Fire Detailkomplekser i Grønlands Historie 1782–1808,* Copenhagen 1974, pp. 269–72, note 49.

10. See vol. II, index entry: "Seminarium Groenlandicum".
11. See vol. II, pp. 319 and 396.
12. See vol. II, p. 429.
13. See vol. II, p. 348.
14. See vol. II, p. 348.
15. It was clearly expressed by Inspector P.H. Motzfeldt 1807, "that these persons ... are considering impostors and instigators of several calamities among their simple countrymen". Thus it was not directly to help the Mission, but for the matter of "good order", that the Trade made this provision.
16. This silver medal was the so-called *Indfødsretsmedaille,* which was instituted on the occasion of the law of 1775. This law provided for individuals who were or could become Danish citizens, and thus could be appointed civil servants or officers in army and navy. It may seem a strange idea to award Gabriel this medal, but in fact it was not. The Missionskollegium had no money for an award "in cash", and this medal was usually awarded to civilians (Danes) who had served Danish society well.
17. See vol. II, p. 401.
18. See vol. II, p. 400.
19. See vol. II, p. 401.
20. See vol. II, p. 281.

XI. THWARTED REFORMS

1. See vol. II,p. 419. It is necessary to state here, that the title of Raun's proposal has been mistranslated; it has been called a "police order", in Danish of that time "Politie-Anordning". "Politie" in the eighteenth century sense has nothing to do with "police", but means "good social order". Raun's "Politie-Anordning" thus was a "set of regulations, with some penalties appending", forming, as it is translated this time, a sort of "penal code".

Notes on the Source Material

In general the reader should refer to the same note in volume II, pp. 430 ff. But for the period 1782-1808 there are some differences.

THE UNPRINTED SOURCES

There are fewer archives for this period, but then more comprehensive. The unpublished documents, originals and copies, records, ledgers, etc., are to be found in the Rigsarkiv (the Danish Main Record Office) in Copenhagen. The Royal Library (Det kongelige Bibliotek) in the same city, in its collections of manuscripts has some copies, reports and accounts, tales and traditions e.g. all in more or less private collections, but accessible. The Rigsarkiv keeps most of the source material, such as all the archives of the different departments of the central administrations, that of the Foreign Office too. There the archives of the institutions under the central administration also are to be found, such as the Missionskollegium, the Royal Greenland Trade Commission for 1788-1816, and the Royal Greenland Trade (and Whaling). For the time being the local archives of the Northern Inspectorate (covering 1781-1955) are in Copenhagen. It supplies the central archives in the Rigsarkiv. Sometimes we have two or three times the same documents vice versa (in originals and copies). The scholar often wonders how much work in these times was done by handcopying; but he often looks upon it with gratitude, because the one collection sometimes covers single gaps in the other. In the same way the collections in the Royal Library may serve. The archives of the Southern Inspectorate unfortunately have disappeared, with the Royal Greenland Trade's ship *Hans Hedtoft* which sank in January 1959 on its maiden voyage, returning to Copenhagen. For many reasons that was one of the most sad disasters in the modern history of Greenland. In our context here it is particularly unfortunate, because several unica were destroyed by that. The local archives kept the Inspector's local correspondence which seldom in copies, most often in abstracts, were communicated to the Royal Greenland Trade in Copenhagen, being kept in the Rigsarkiv. Now we only have the archives of the Northern Inspectorate with its originals and copies, fortunately containing letters from and to the Inspector of the Southern.

Other archives, The Archives of the Navy, Søkortarkivet (The Danish State's Hydrographic Department, started by Poul Løvenørn, which is mentioned in this volume) and some others keep specialities only, but have of course been consulted for those. The Moravian Brethren keep their archives in the Archiv der Evangelischen Brüder-Unität, Herrnhut in Oberlausitz, East Germany. These represent narrow localities, in fact only three (in this period). It has been "consulted" indirectly by means of the book by Heinz Israel, mentioned below.

The Library of The Royal Academy of Fine Arts and the Royal Library, both in Copenhagen, keep collections of drawings and pictures, as well as the Arctic Institute in Gentofte, Denmark. It will appear from the text of the plates, that I have picked up from these collections what served my aim.

All documentary material is written in Danish, except of course that of the Moravian Brethren, which is in German. It is therefore necessary to repeat what is expressed both in volume I and II. "In the Danish original every statement and all quotations are referred to the sources and their location. - The student who wants to study the documents and the special literature must have a good knowledge of the Danish language, and it is therefore rational to refer him to the Danish edition".

Tracing other information, concerning relations between foreign whalers and the Greenlanders or the Greenland authorities e.g., I have consulted British archives, but found nothing of interest in this context.

THE PRINTED SOURCES

The quotation from volume I and II above may be repeated about the printed sources. Some of the literature can be repeated too from volume II.

The selection of documents for 1492-1814 made by Dr. Louis Bobé covers the period of the present volume, but the documents printed are very few. Besides no collections of sources are printed.

Accounts of the period 1782-1808, as mentioned in the preface, never appeared before, either in Denmark or in other countries. None of the existing shorter surveys is based upon deeper studies of the period. With this qualification the reader may be referred to *Greenland, vol. III,* 1928-29, the survey of the history of the Trade and the colonization of Greenland until 1870, by Dr. Bobé, the condensed history of the Mission, by the Rev. H. Ostermann. It must be revealed that Dr. Bobé's survey, as far as the period under consideration in this volume is concerned, is unsatisfying and defective. Ostermann's account is more accurate, but disfigured in some way by his animosity against the Trade in general, and the Moravian Brethren in particular. Years ago I have written two surveys to the *Handbook of the North American Indians,* but they are not yet brought to the press. The reader cannot be referred to any other surveys on this subject.

The contemporary literature is scarce in Danish, and as far as I know there is nothing in other languages. The few Danish books are referred to in the notes (with translation of the Danish title of the book or pamphlet in question - as far as this title is mentioned).

Newer literature concerning problems of the period in question is as well scarce. One may have expected that the history of whaling in the waters off Greenland might have been represented by several works in Danish or foreign languages. But none has dealt with it in such a way, that it could shed some more light on the whaling, e.g. in its relations to Greenlanders, or similar subjects.

Consequently I only, and finally, refer to the following works in other languages than Danish, and otherwise refer to the Danish edition for those in Danish:

A. Friis and Kr. Glamann, *A History of Prices and Wages in Denmark 1660–1800,* I, Copenhagen 1951.

Karl Ludwig Giesecke's Mineralogisches Reisejournal über Grönland 1806–1813, 2te vollständige Ausgabe (ed. O.B. Bøggild) mit Einleitung und biographische Mitteilungen von K.J.V. Steenstrup, MoG XXXV, Copenhagen 1910.

Heinz Israel, *Kulturwandel grönländischer Eskimo im 18. Jahrhundert,* Abhandlungen und Berichte des staatlichen Museums für Völkerkunde, Dresden, Band 29, Berlin 1969.

Inge Kleivan, *Song Duels in Westgreenland – Joking Relationship and Avoidance,* FOLK (the periodical of the Ethnographical Department of the National Museum in Copenhagen), vol. XIII, 1971.

John Leslie, Robert Jameson and Hugh Murray, *Narrative of Discovery and Adventure in the Polar Seas and Regions ... and an Account of the Whale Fishery,* Edinburgh 1832.

Knud Olsendow, *Printing in Greenland,* Copenhagen 1959.

P. Scavenius Jensen, *Den grønlandske kajak og dens redskaber* (The Greenland Kayak and its Equipment), Copenhagen 1975; notable on account of its list of literature on the subject.

Staffan Söderberg, *Profetens roll i religionsmötet. Iakttagelser från religionsmötets Väst-grönland.* Studentlitteratur, Lund (Sweden) 1974, with summary in English: *The Prophet in the Encounter of Christian Mission and Traditional Religion in West Greenland.*

Chr. Vibe, *Arctic Animals in Relation to Climatic Fluctuations,* MoG. 170,5, Copenhagen 1967.

MoG, here and in the Notes and References, means *Meddelelser om Grønland,* (Reports and papers on Greenland), Copenhagen 1878 seqq.

Glossary

Alen. The ancient Danish measures for length were *tomme* (= inch, but 2.615 cm. compared to the English inch of 2.54 cm.), *fod* (= foot, but 31.38535 cm. compared to the English foot of 30.48 cm.) and *alen* (68.77 cm., thus not the same as the English yard of 91.44 cm.).

Bay. As used in Greenlandic geographical names, this is not an English word, but Dutch, and is thus pronounced as the English word "by", e.g. Fortune Bay (fortoone by). It means however the same as the English "bay". The Danish word is "bugt", pronounced approximately (bogd), e.g., Disko Bugt (= Disko Bay).

Cabinet. The King's private office.

Cabinet Order. A Royal Order issued by the King himself, often written by his private secretary, who could thus obtain considerable influence and sometimes actual political power, as happened in 1770–72, and afterwards again 1781–84 (but not in the same arrogant way). From 1784 such Royal Orders were extremely rare. Usually they passed through the Statsråd (Konseil).

Colony, lodge, station, trading post and settlement. It has been difficult to fix a terminology concerning the different sorts of settlement. Some short definitions may be appropriate. "Colony" means the central station in a district, with a trader as its chief, helped by one or two assistants, some craftsmen and the "crew". "Lodge" (loge) is a station which is not the centre of a district, but governed by a trader or a senior assistant. "Station" or "Whaling Station" explains itself. A trader might be the head of it, but most often it was a senior assistant. "Trading Post" (udsted) was a place in a district where a foreman or a reliable craftsman was stationed to manage the trade in the environment, being responsible to the chief trader of the district. "Settlement", used as a term (boplads) was a site where a small group of Greenlanders lived, having no special trade facilities.

Danske Kancelli. Organized as a *kollegium,* the central administration department concerned with the affairs of the interior and justice, both in Denmark and Norway, with its adjacent islands, thus Greenland too, but not the duchies Slesvig and Holstein (see *Tyske Kancelli,* vol. II, p. 435).

Deputy. Member of a board of a *kollegium.*

Fanger (English pl. *fangers*). One who is occupied with whaling, sealing, hunting mammals and birds at sea and on land, fishing and trapping. In the Eskimo language *piniartoq,* i.e., one who endeavours to get something.

Fangst. This Danish word is used in this volume, because the English language has no equivalent term. The word strictly means "what you get by whaling, sealing and fishing, the game you get from hunting, before it is refined in one way or another". It also means "the act of whaling, sealing, fishing and hunting", and is sometimes used here in this sense.

Finanskollegium. The central administration department which governed the finances of the realms. The president of this kollegium was *statsminister* (of finances) and as such a prominent member of the *Statsråd.* The board of deputies to the Finanskollegium in fact governed finance policy, and thus administered the tax system, official salaries, the bank system (see *Kurantbanken*), and nearly all appropriations.

The Foreign Office. A department under the *Tyske Kancelli.* It developed very much into an independent *kollegium* in the period in question, during most of which it was headed by Count Andreas Peter Bernstorff. In 1797 his eldest son followed him as Foreign Minister, and a little later a younger son was appointed director of the Department of Foreign Affairs.

Kammerraad. Impossible to translate. Originally it was the title of members of the *Rentekammer kollegium* (therefore the first part of the compound); later (in this period already) it was an empty title which only served to distinguish the holder as an official reward.

Kollegium. The Danish central administration was from 1660 to 1849/50 organized in *kollegia,* every "branch" being directed by a board of *deputies,* all appointed by the autocratic king. Among the deputies one was called First Secretary, *Præses* or President. The head of one *kollegium* could be deputy of the board of another, e.g. the head of the Rentekammer was a deputy in the Finanskollegium. Most heads of the *kollegia* were *Statsministers* (in this period) and members of the Statsraad. This does not include the inferior *kollegia,* e.g. the Missionskollegium.

Kommerce læst. A Danish "bulk-weight", corresponding to 2.600 kilogrammes. When measuring a ship's capacity it is equal to 2.56 English tons dead weight.

Konseil, Conseil, Geheimeconseil, Geheimestatsråd, Statsråd, cf. vol. II, p. 433, and Statsråd below.

Kurantbanken. Established 1736 in Copenhagen as a private institution, but with the right to issue banknotes which were legal currency, hence the term *courant-banque.* It was the only bank in the eighteenth-century kingdom of Denmark and Norway (there was another in the duchy of Holstein). The Danish government, that is to say the Finanskollegium, was the real head of the board of the Kurantbank's directors. The Minister of Finances actually directed the monetary policy and the major operations of the Kurantbank. In 1797 a disastrous inflation started, and the bank was reconstructed as the Speciebank. The inflation continued, grew during the war of 1807-14, resulting in the so-called bankruptcy of 1813, which in reality was a reconstruction of the monetary system.

Mil. The Danish road-measure, 1 *mil* = 12,000 alen. It is equal to 7,533 kilometres, while the English statute mile is 1,609 kilometres. The Danish *mil* is a little longer than 1 geographical mile, which is 7,408 kilometres.

Missionskollegium. Established 1714, and organized as a *kollegium* with three or five members, in close connection with Danske Kancelli. It was concerned with the Royal Missions in Tranquebar (India), the Virgin Islands, the Gold Coast (now Ghana), Finmarken (Norway) and Greenland. It also had the administration of the *Vajsenhus* (the Royal Orphanage), where it had its seat and its archives. The Vajsenhus was destroyed by fire in 1795, whereby most of the archives were lost.

Officers. The higher servants of the Trade were "officers", because from the start the colonies were organized like ships with officers and crew. The crew, i.e., the main workers, the "men", were often called *matroser* (sailors). The traders, senior assistants and assistants were the officers. The missionary was ranked as an officer.

Pot, barrel, cask and tub. Like other societies contemporary Denmark had several cubic measures, depending on what had to be measured. The measures concerning fish produce and train-oil seem the most suitable to use here. The Norwegian measures were, furthermore, different from the Danish; it is impossible to decide in every situation whether the Danish or the Norwegian measures are meant. The Trade had its headquarters at this period in Copenhagen. Consequently the Danish cubic measures may have been used as a rule. Thus *1 pot* is approximately 0.966 litre. *1 barrel* (translation of *tønde,* i.e., (here) train-oil barrel) is fixed at 120 pots, i.e. approximately 116 litres or 25.5 Imperial gallons. *1 cask* (translation for *fad,* which contained *2 tønder*) is fixed at 240 pots, i.e. 232 litres or 51 Imperial gallons, or a little less than a hogshead. *Tub* (translation for Danish *balje*) is not a measure in itself, but a means of measuring. Tubs of different sizes could be used. In Greenland the blubber was measured in tubs which contained 1⅓, later 1½ barrel (blubber barrel = 120 pots + 40 pots, later + 60 pots). Tubs containing half or quarter of full capacity were verified in the Southern Inspectorate. Other cubic measures are explained in the text.

Reindeer. As in vol. II, attention is drawn to the fact that up to 1953 all the Greenland reindeer were wild, and they were not the same type as the caribou. Hence our use of the term *reindeer.*

Rentekammer. A central administration department, established in about 1540, dealing with the State's finances and auditing official accounts. It was reorganized as a *kollegium* with another name, but from 1680 it was again called the Rentekammer, still having the same functions. In 1771-73 it was combined with the General Customs Administration under the Finanskollegium, but later was established once again with its old name, besides several other branches of the financial administration, after 1784 under the Finanskollegium and with restricted functions.

Rigsdaler, mark and *skilling* are in this volume always written in full. They were, up to 1874, the Danish monetary system: 1 rigsdaler = 6 mark = 96 skilling. The value of the mintings changed, so it is difficult to fix the market value. (Reference: FRIIS and GLAMANN: *The History of Prices and Wages in Denmark 1660–1800).*

Specksioneer derives from the Dutch term *specksnyder,* or the Danish *spæksnider,* both literally meaning "blubber-cutter". It may be the Dutch word, pronounced in an English manner. In Dutch and British whaling this person was the officer in charge of the fishing apparatus and flensing operations, and a principal harpooner as well. In the Danish-Greenlandic whaling the specksioneer was not an officer, but ranked between the officers and the crew, a sort of midshipman. At each whaling station there was at least one, often two or three specksioneers, in charge of the same tasks as their Dutch and British counterparts.

Stationed. As in the previous volume this English word is here used terminologically. E.g. *a stationed carpenter* would be a carpenter born and educated in Denmark or elsewhere outside Greenland, and sent to a post in Greenland. He might stay there, but would always have the right or the opportunity to return after a certain period.

Statsminister, minister. Up to 1849 the title held by the members of the *Statsråd,* most often the heads of the board of deputies in the different major *kollegia.*

Statsråd. New name of the Konseil, when it was reorganized 1784. It was the king's council, consisting of the Crown Prince (King Christian VII being increasingly insane), the heads of the boards of the most important *kollegia,* some special appointees, but always a rather narrow confidential circle.

Storis. The tremendous quantities of field-ice which flow southwards along the East coast of Greenland from the Polar Basin round Kap Farvel and then northwards, usually as far as Frederikshåb, barring access to the coast sometimes as far north as Godthåb. Some way north in the Davis Strait it bends westward and then, more or less combined with the Vestis (see below), spreading or melting, again southwestwards. It consist of polar field-ice, sometimes packed together and piled up in fantastic formations, and icebergs calved from East Greenland glaciers.

Vestis (West-Ice). Field-ice from Baffin Bay, Melville Bay and the straits between Greenland and Ellesmere Land. The quantities are less than the Storis, and it is not quite so compact. The field-ice goes southwards accompanied by huge icebergs from the glaciers in Northwest Greenland, especially those from Jakobshavn Isfjord. The Vestis flows more or less in a westerly direction, sometimes getting very close to Disko Island and Egedesminde District, but seldom as far south as Holsteinsborg. It drifts southwards with the current and absorbs the remainders of the Storis further to the southwest.

Økonomi- & Kommercekollegium. The central administrative department which dealt with the economic life of Denmark (agriculture, trade, industry etc., but not the finances and bank operations). It also had some relation to foreign policy as it administered the Danish consulates in foreign harbours, and was thus in cooperation with the Foreign Office, e.g. in case of treaties of trade and commerce.

Index of names

Index of places

Subject index

List of Illustrations and Graphs

Contents